The Bedford Glossary of
Critical and Literary Terms

The Bedford Glossary of Critical and Literary Terms

Second Edition

Ross Murfin
Southern Methodist University

Supryia M. Ray

Bedford/St. Martin's   Boston   ◆   New York

For Bedford/St. Martin's

Executive Editor: Stephen A. Scipione
Production Editor: Diane Schadoff
Production Supervisor: Jennifer Wetzel
Marketing Manager: Jenna Bookin-Barry
Text Design: Maureen Murray
Copy Editor: Carla H. Breidenbach
Indexer: Maro Riofrancos
Cover Design: Donna Lee Dennison
Composition: Pine Tree Composition, Inc.
Printing and Binding: Haddon Craftsmen, Inc., an R. R. Donnelley & Sons
    Company

President: Joan E. Feinberg
Editorial Director: Denise B. Wydra
Editor in Chief: Karen H. Henry
Director of Marketing: Karen R. Melton
Director of Editing, Design, and Production: Marcia Cohen
Managing Editor: Erica T. Appel

Library of Congress Control Number: 2002112261

Manufactured in the United States of America.

8   7   6   5   4   3
f   e   d   c   b   a

For information, write: Bedford/St. Martin's, 75 Arlington Street,
Boston, MA 02116   (617-399-4000)

ISBN: 0-312-25910-7

Published and distributed outside North America by:

PALGRAVE MACMILLAN
Houndmills, Basingstoke, Hampshire RG21 2XS and London
Companies and representatives throughout the world.

ISBN: 1-4039-0505-3

A catalogue record for this book is available from the British
Library.

Acknowledgments and copyrights appear at the back of the book on pages 502–
506, which constitute an extension of the copyright page.

Contents

Preface

The Bedford Glossary of Critical and Literary Terms grows out of our work on the Bedford/St. Martin's *Case Studies in Contemporary Criticism* series, which presents classic literary works reprinted together with editorial material and critical essays designed to introduce college students to current literary theories, concepts, and terms. The success of this series and of our collaboration encouraged us to undertake this admittedly formidable project.

Although we have admired and learned from other available glossaries, we also concluded that they are not fully attuned to current developments in literary studies or to the needs of today's students. Accordingly, we set out to produce a glossary that would not only redefine old terms in a concise and accessible manner but also comprehensibly introduce the newest critical theories, approaches, and terminology. In the process, we sought to incorporate a wide variety of examples reflecting the diversity of the arts and the world itself. Furthermore, we saw the glossary as an opportunity to help students understand how "literariness" figures in their lives, not only in the classroom and in the books they read but also in all the "texts" that shape their experiences, including those of popular culture.

Notable Features of This Glossary

It defines more than 800 important terms. To establish the boundaries of the territory we would cover, we began by sifting through existing glossaries and identifying more than 500 traditional, indispensable terms, such as *irony, metaphor, romance, form,* and *narrative.* We then sought to define and describe these terms in a manner that readers would find clear and current, taking into account their changing inflections in modern critical discourse. (For example, we refer to deconstructive theorist Paul de Man's view of irony as a figure of speech and suggest that the gender-reversal scene in Neil Jordan's film *The Crying Game* is an example of anagnorisis as currently understood.) We also reworked the discussions of critical terms that had previously appeared in the *Case Studies* series. Writing and rewriting, building on the suggestions of reviewers, we continued to add and define terms. Some of these additions were traditional terms, but most were new terms and concepts (for instance, *domesticity, jouissance, hypertext, orientalism,* and *phallocentric*). The result was a glossary containing more than 700 entries. The second edition is even more comprehensive, defining more than 800 terms.

Its examples are drawn from both literature and popular culture. As we drafted our definitions, we searched for illustrative examples not only in canonical literature but also in contemporary literature, older literary works that have often been overlooked, and popular culture. We included hundreds of examples from major figures commonly cited in literary glossaries: Homer, Shakespeare, Swift, Dickinson, Joyce, and other classic writers. But we also looked to the work of numerous other writers who reflect the rich variety of literature. Accordingly, we reference previously marginalized writers such as Olaudah Equiano and Aphra Behn, as well as culturally diverse contemporary authors such as Isabel Allende, Toni Morrison, Amy Tan, and Salman Rushdie.

Most distinctively, we have included examples from "nonliterary" forms and genres, including architecture, movies, music, television shows, newspaper columns, political speeches, and comic books. In our glossary, students will see literary strategies and devices at work in episodes of *Seinfeld, Far Side* cartoons, and political propaganda posters. Such pop culture examples acknowledge the recent theoretical blurring of the boundaries between "high" and "low" culture. They also invite those students who find literary studies formidable yet pride themselves on their familiarity with popular culture to discover that traditional literary concepts pervade all of our arts — and our lives. Similes and flashbacks are as common in the texts students know best as they are in literary works more traditionally defined.

It is designed to be a straightforward and handy reference. We aimed to produce a glossary that would be accessible and enjoyable. Accordingly, we endeavored to keep our definitions succinct and our examples lively. Entries are arranged alphabetically, from *absence* to *zeugma.* Cross-referenced terms appear in boldface within definitions, signaling that the boldfaced term has been defined separately in another entry. (For a more detailed explanation of technical matters — the use of boldface and italics, the meaning of the phrases *See* and *See also,* and how we handle dates and foreign language titles — turn to the section entitled "A Note on References and Cross-References," p. xiii.) We have included an index of examples at the back of the book, in the event that a reader wants to see if and how the glossary makes use of a particular work.

New to This Edition

A new edition offers an invaluable opportunity to update and improve a book. There is nothing like the passage of time and a jury of peers — instructors and students who class-test a book and discover gaps and shortcomings — to alert authors to the need for revisions. A nationwide survey of instructors who assigned the first edition of the *Bedford Glossary* led us to make the following changes to the second edition.

Over 70 new terms are defined. Literary glossaries are almost infinitely expandable. No matter how comprehensive, every glossary omits some terms that are important or likely to become important. In the second edition of the *Bedford Glossary,* we have added definitions of many traditional terms, topics, and genres, such as *anachrony, folklore,* and *prolepsis.* In particular, we have tried to increase our attention both to classical rhetorical terms, such as *anaphora* and *paralipsis,* and to mass-market genre writing, such as *detective fiction* and *fantasy fiction.* We have also defined a number of contemporary critical terms that are often overlooked — such as *epistémé* and *heteroglossia* — and ventured introductions to emerging fields of critical study such as *disability studies* and *ecocriticism.*

Many more diverse and contemporary examples have been added. To appeal to today's students, we have increased the number of examples drawn from contemporary and world literature and from popular culture. Such examples range from Barbara Kingsolver's novel *The Poisonwood Bible,* Stephen King's cyberfiction, J. K. Rowling's *Harry Potter* series, and Rigoberta Menchú's autobiography to zen koans, proverbs from countries around the world, African American and Native American folk tales, and even urban legends.

Visual examples have been included. We have also — with a rhetorical nod to *Star Trek,* one of the world's most recognizable pop-culture franchises — boldly gone where no literary glossary has gone before by including visual examples that illustrate some of the principles discussed in the entries. For instance, we use a strip from Garry Trudeau's *Doonesbury* to show that allusions can be visual as well as verbal, and we include a *New Yorker* cover as an example of intertextuality. We often hear that images are displacing texts in the cognitive realm of students; with our visual examples, we try to suggest that text and image can be equally "literary."

Acknowledgments

Our initial thanks go to the colleagues and reviewers who helped shape the first edition of the glossary: Tom Arp, Sylvan Barnet, Susan Belasco, Shari Benstock, Patrick Brantlinger, William Cain, Russ Castronovo, the late Pascal Covici, Michael Demson, Vincenzo DeNardo, Paul Fry, Tom Goodman, David Hausman, Tracy Helenbrook, Paul Holdengräber, Carolyn Jeter, Steven Mailloux, J. Hillis Miller, Scott Moss, Audrey

Murfin, Jennifer Negrin, Margot Norris, Sylvia O'Sullivan, Brigitte Peucker, Philip Rollinson, John Paul Russo, Brook Thomas, Benjiman Webb, and Bonnie Wheeler.

Our second round of thanks is to those who reviewed the first edition in order to help us prepare the second. These people include Mark Addison Amos, Southern Illinois University at Carbondale; Susan Blake, Lafayette College; Christine Brandel, Bowling Green State University; Richard Braverman, Columbia University; James Brock, Florida Gulf Coast University; William Crenshaw, Erskine College; Susan Cruea, Bowling Green State University; Amie Doughty, Lake Superior State University; Natalie Grinnell, Wofford College; Julie Haught, Bowling Green State University; Michael Hennessey, Southwest Texas State University; Martin Hipsky, Ohio Wesleyan University; Carol Kessler, Pennsylvania State University in Delaware County; Jeanette McVicker, SUNY at Fredonia; Fran Michel, Willamette University; Barry Milligan, Wright State University; W. Jason Nelson, Bowling Green State University; Arthur Robinson, Diablo Valley College; Jack Ryan, Gettysburg College; Julie Shaffer, University of Wisconsin at Oshkosh; Jason Steed, University of Nevada; Rebecca Steinitz, Ohio Wesleyan University; Zabelle Stodola, University of Arkansas at Little Rock; Brad Sullivan, Florida Gulf Coast University; Lee Upton, Lafayette College; Stephen Warner, SUNY at Fredonia; and Rebecca Wood, University of California at Santa Barbara.

Where the preparation of the second edition is concerned, our major debt of gratitude is to Carolyn Jeter, who researched dozens of terms and produced working drafts of many new definitions. We are also indebted to Michael Demson and Steven Barney for their assistance in defining numerous rhetorical terms not included in the first edition; Rosemary Garland Thomson and H. Lewis Ulmann for help in defining *disability studies* and *ecocriticism,* respectively; Noelle Bowles, John Paul Riquelme, and Brian Buchwitz for their work on our definition of *fantasy fiction;* and John Paul Riquelme for his work on our definition of *postcolonial literature and postcolonial theory.* In addition, we wish to thank Rob Hampton for providing examples of *cliché* and *confessional poetry;* Dennis Foster for improving our definition of *epistémé;* John Chun for providing our example of *foot;* Jacques Lezra for providing our example of the term *overdetermined;* Richard Bozorth for critiquing our definition of *queer theory;* and Sarah Scofield for her assistance in researching a wide variety of points.

Thanks also go to the editorial staff at Bedford/St. Martin's: former president Charles H. Christensen, who signed the project; current president Joan E. Feinberg, who continues to believe in it; and executive editor Steve Scipione, for managing the development of both editions. We remain grateful to Pam Ozaroff for her work developing the first edition. We also thank those on the production end of the process: Marcia Cohen, Elizabeth Schaaf, and especially Diane Schadoff, the second edition's freelance editor, who skillfully steered the book through an accelerated production schedule. We appreciate the efficient permissions-clearing work done by

Sandy Schechter and the editorial assistance of Emily Goodall and Anne Noyes.

Finally, and most importantly, we would like to thank our spouses, Pam Murfin and Todd Nystul, who have spent hundreds of hours surfing the Net to find dates and verify details, served as the sounding board for many of our ideas, and patiently and graciously allowed countless evenings, weekends, and even vacations to become occasions for what we have come to refer to as "glossarizing."

A Note on References and Cross-References

A glossary is a reference book that, in addition to referring to authors and works exemplifying literary concepts, inevitably refers to itself via cross-references. We wish to provide interested readers with a more detailed explanation of our cross-referencing system — and then say a few things about the way we reference literary examples, particularly with regard to foreign language titles and the dates we have provided in connection with *all* titles.

1. Our Use of *See* and *See Also*

Where we have felt that the understanding of a specific term is particularly important to understanding the definition at issue, we have emphasized the importance of looking up that other term by using *see* or *see also*. *See* signals the most crucial terms to look up; we have used it infrequently. For instance, the term *Apollonian* can hardly be understood without reference to the term *Dionysian*, nor can *tenor* be understood without its counterpart, *vehicle*. *See also* signals the added usefulness, though not the dire necessity, of looking up a particular term.

We use *see* in three other contexts as well: to direct readers from a less common term to its most common synonym; to direct readers from a less common spelling of a term to its more common spelling; and to direct readers to another entry in which the term being looked up is actually (or more fully) defined. An example of the first type of cross-reference is the term *paranomasia*. *Paranomasia* is synonymous with *pun*, but the latter is more commonly used, and so the concept is defined there; readers looking up *paranomasia* will find a cross-reference that says "See **pun**." In the second case, a reader looking up *katharsis* will find a cross-reference that says "See **catharsis.**" In the third, a reader looking up the term *absence* will find a brief definition followed by a cross-reference that says "See **presence and absence.**"

2. Our Use of Boldface

We have defined more than 800 terms in this glossary, and whenever one of these terms is used in the definition of another, we have typically boldfaced that term — whether or not we are using *see* or *see also* to encourage you to look it up. (We say "typically" because we have generally avoided bolding words that are commonly understood — words like *fiction* and *play* — even though we define them.) Thus, if you look up **metaphor,** you will see a number of terms printed in boldface type within that definition, including **figure of speech, simile, tenor,** and **vehicle.**

The use of boldface type simply alerts you that we have separately defined the boldfaced term so that you can look it up if you so choose. Sometimes when boldfaced words are juxtaposed, they refer the reader to a single term and entry (e.g., **long measure**). At other times, each word is its own term and is defined separately (e.g., **anapestic hexameter** refers the reader to our separate definitions of **anapest** and **hexameter**).

Usually we have boldfaced only the first appearance of the term so as to avoid visual clutter; occasionally, however, we have chosen to boldface some later usage of a term where that action seemed more helpful and therefore appropriate. Note that we have typically boldfaced terms in whatever form they first appear. Hence you may see **new historicist** but discover that the term we actually define is **the new historicism.**

3. Our Use of *Italics*

Occasionally, italics is used as part of our cross-referencing system. Specifically, we have italicized, rather than boldfaced, the first appearance of a term that has its own entry elsewhere if that entry is followed by a *see* that would merely refer you back to the term you initially looked up. For instance, if you are reading the definition of **Marxist criticism,** you will come upon the italicized terms *base* and *superstructure*. If you were to look up the latter two terms, you would find boldfaced entries for them, but those entries would send you back to the definition of Marxist criticism via the phrase "See **Marxist criticism.**" We want to let you know that italicized terms are important enough that they may have their own entries, but we don't want to send you on a wild goose chase that leads you back to where you started. We also, of course, want our cross-referencing system to permit you to come upon these terms boldfaced within other definitions (*base* and *superstructure* appear as **base** and **superstructure** within the definition of **gaps**), in which case you will look the terms up and be told to "See **Marxist criticism.**"

Usually, however, italics is used for one of five other purposes. The most common, as you may have guessed, is to refer to titles of novels, other long works, or plays. The second most common use of this typeface can be spotted throughout the preceding paragraphs, where we use it in connection with terms that are being used as such — that is, as terms. In essence, if you see the phrase "the term" in front of a term — or if you could insert that phrase without disturbing the flow of the sentence — that term will be italicized (unless it has already been bolded). For instance, witness our italicization of *Apollonian, Dionysian, tenor,* and *vehicle* in the second paragraph of this essay. Note that, in the same paragraph, *see* and *see also* have also been italicized because they have been used as terms in this context. (Of course, *see* and *see also* are not italicized in the glossary proper because there they are used to signal a cross-reference, not as terms in and of themselves.)

We have also occasionally italicized terms *purely* for emphasis, as in this very sentence. Additionally, we have italicized important terms (such as *die Klassik* and *Rococo*) that have been separately defined in older glossaries but that we have glossed in our definition of some other term that, in our view, is more essential for modern readers to understand. Finally, we have sometimes used italics to highlight a series of some sort, particularly types or classifications. For instance, under **accent** we discuss *word accent, rhetorical accent,* and *metrical accent.*

4. Our Use of Dates

In referring to examples of the literary terms and concepts we define, we have attempted to provide what no other major glossary does — a date for each and every example, whether from traditional or popular culture sources. Note, however, that although we have tried to provide the best dates possible, this glossary is not intended to be a scholarly sourcebook for dates. By "best," we mean that we have tried to provide the date that would be most helpful to our readers. Usually that is the work's original publication date — but not always. Some works were written and became known long before the advent of movable type (Geoffrey Chaucer's *The Canterbury Tales,* for instance). Other works were written early but not published until late in an author's lifetime. (Thomas Hardy, for instance, didn't publish many of the poems he wrote in his twenties until he was in his fifties and had ended his novelistic career.) In such cases, the date of composition, not the date of publication, best places the poem in biographical and historical contexts.

There are other reasons why we have sometimes chosen not to pair a given title with its initial publication date: for instance, when we are quoting the better-known, later version of a work such as D. H. Lawrence's poem "Love on the Farm" or when it makes the most sense to pair a title that has been translated into English (say, Fyodor Dostoyevsky's *Notes from the Underground*) with an original language publication date. The point is that the glossary is by no means a consistent bibliographic tool; we have made subjective judgments to further our aim of defining terms via telling historical examples.

5. Our Use of Foreign Language Titles

As our reference to the dating of *Notes from the Underground* suggests, we have not always cited original foreign language titles along with their English translations. (For practical reasons, we have *never* included original foreign language titles when the work in question was not written in a language using the Roman alphabet.) Whether the original title, the English language title, or both titles appear depends upon what we felt constituted relevant information within the context of a given definition. Hence you will see the French philosopher Michel Foucault's work *The History of Sexuality* listed using both its original French title, *L'histoire de la sexualité*, and the aforementioned English translation. Just keep in mind that, as with dates, the glossary should not be used as a bibliographic reference. We have not made a comprehensive effort to search out all original foreign language titles; we have merely included them in certain cases where the reader might find the information useful.

For ease of reference, we have alphabetized foreign language titles in the index according to the first letter of the first word, even if that word is an article like *une* or *la* that translates as "a" or "the." Thus, while you will find *The History of Sexuality* alphabetized under *H* rather than *T*, the corresponding foreign language title, *L'histoire de la sexualité*, appears under *L*, not *H*.

The Bedford Glossary of Critical and Literary Terms

Glossary of Critical and Literary Terms

A

absence: The idea, advanced by French theorist Jacques Derrida, that authors are not present in **texts** and that meaning arises in the absence of any authority guaranteeing the correctness of any one interpretation.

See **presence and absence** for a more complete discussion of the concepts of presence and absence.

abstract: The opposite of *concrete*. Abstract terms and statements describe ideas or **denote** general qualities of persons or things; concrete terms or statements refer specifically to particular persons or things. For example, the statement "Vivian hates Carly" is concrete; the statement "Hate is an ineradicable component of human nature" is abstract.

Literary critics have extended the term *concrete* to refer to any passage that is rich in detail (especially in language that appeals to the five senses) and that creates a clear **image** for the reader, whether through literal or **figurative language.** Passages written in a general manner or lacking vivid detail or specific experience are called abstract.

FURTHER EXAMPLES: Robert Burns's most famous poetic statement, "O, my Luve's like a red, red rose / That's newly sprung in June" (1796), is a concrete poetic statement. W. H. Auden's statement on love in "Heavy Date" (1940) is abstract:

> I believed for years that
> Love was the conjunction
> Of two oppositions;
> > That was all untrue. . . .

Absurd, the (absurd, literature or theater of the): A phrase referring to twentieth-century works that depict the absurdity of the modern human condition, often with implicit reference to humanity's loss or lack of religious, philosophical, or cultural roots. Such works depict the individual as essentially isolated and alone, even when surrounded by other people and things. Although **drama** has been the medium of choice for Absurdist writers, the term may be applied to any work of literature that stresses an **existential** outlook, that is, one depicting the lonely, confused, and often anguished individual in an utterly bewildering universe.

Because writers associated with this movement believe that the only way to represent the absurdity of the modern condition is to write in an absurd manner, the literature of the Absurd is as bizarre in **style** as it is in subject matter. **Conventions** governing everything from **plot** to **dialogue** are routinely flouted, as is the notion that a work of literature should be unified and coherent. The resulting **scenes,** actions, and dialogue are usually disconnected, repetitive, and intentionally nonsensical. Such works might be comic were it not for their obviously and grotesquely tragic dimensions.

The **genre** has its roots in such literary movements as **surrealism** and **expressionism** and owes a great debt to the works of Franz Kafka. It developed in France during the 1940s in the novels and philosophical writings of Jean-Paul Sartre and Albert Camus. The theater of the Absurd emerged around 1950 with Eugène Ionesco's *La cantatrice chauve* (*The Bald Soprano*) (1954), in which, not surprisingly, there is no soprano, let alone a bald one. Equally influential was Samuel Beckett's play *Waiting for Godot* (1954), in which two tramps wait in vain for someone who may not even exist — and with whom they are not even sure they have an appointment.

Several novels written during the 1950s and 1960s in Great Britain and the United States contained Absurdist elements, but most Absurdist works have been written as plays. Harold Pinter was primarily responsible for developing British Absurdist theater; Edward Albee is America's leading Absurdist playwright.

FURTHER EXAMPLES: Jean Genet's *Le balcon* (*The Balcony*) (1957), Edward Albee's *The Sandbox* (1959), and Harold Pinter's *The Homecoming* (1965). Joseph Heller's *Catch-22* (1961) is at once a popular novel and an Absurdist work.

accent: The **stress,** or emphasis, placed on a syllable (the symbols ´ and ˘ are used for stressed and unstressed syllables, respectively). Three main types of accent exist. *Word accent* refers to the stress (or lack thereof) placed on syllables of words as they are pronounced in ordinary speech. *Rhetorical accent,* by contrast, refers to the stress placed on syllables or words according to their location or importance in a sentence (and may thus be different from word accent). A third type of accent, *metrical accent,* refers to the stress placed on syllables in accordance with the poetic **meter;** when the metrical pattern of a poem "forces" a syllable to be stressed that would not be stressed in ordinary speech, the accent is said to be **wrenched.** In **versification,** accent refers specifically to the meter itself, the more or less regular pattern of stressed and unstressed syllables. Some poets and critics, however, differentiate between *accent* and *stress,* reserving the term *stress* for metrical emphasis and *accent* for the emphasis used in everyday **discourse** (word accent).

Other common usages of *accent* refer to distinctive regional speech patterns and intonations (for example, a Brooklyn or Texas accent) and to emphasis placed upon an idea or **theme** in a work.

EXAMPLES: Accent in the following sentence is different depending on whether word accent, rhetorical accent, or metrical accent is used. Using word accent, you'd probably say it like this:

"I'll do the grocery shopping *later,* Pam." [word accent]

However, if you wanted to stress the fact that you, and not someone else, were going to do the shopping, you'd probably say the sentence more like this:

"*I'll* do the grocery shopping later, Pam." [rhetorical accent]

If you were using this sentence as a line in a poem written in **iambic pentameter,** a meter in which every line contains a regular pattern of five alternating unstressed and stressed syllables, the accents would look like this:

"I'll dó thĕ grócĕry shóppĭng látĕr, Pám." [metrical accent]

In the following poem, "'Faith' is a fine invention" (c. 1860), Emily Dickinson has indicated a rhetorical and metrical accent on the word *see* and placed a rhetorical accent on the entire word *Microscopes.* Note that the last syllable of the last line (*cy*) carries a metrical accent made evident, in part, by the stress placed on *see* two lines earlier.

> "Faith" is a fine invention
> When Gentlemen can *see* —
> But *Microscopes* are prudent
> In an Emergency.

accentual-syllabic verse: Verse in which the number of syllables and the number of **stressed** and unstressed syllables are relatively consistent from line to line. Accentual-syllabic verse is the **meter** of choice for poets writing in English.

acrostic: A **text** is which certain letters are placed so that they spell out words, phrases, or other significant sequences when read horizontally, vertically, or according to some other specific sequence. Acrostics may be composed using **verse** or **prose** or simply as freestanding puzzles for entertainment or education. Ancient Greek and Roman acrostics — imitated by **medieval** monks — were likely intended as games or memory-enabling devices. Some ancient acrostics, such as those found in Egypt and Ethiopia, were thought to have magical or spiritual meaning.

There are several different types of acrostics, all of which are defined in terms of the positioning of the letters forming meaningful sequences. The *true acrostic* is the most basic one, in which the first letter of each line (or paragraph or sentence or other unit) forms part of a word (or words) when read "down," that is, vertically. When the middle letters have meaning when read vertically, the acrostic is referred to as a *mesostich;* when the last letters do so, it is a *telestich.* When both the first and last letters are used in this way, the text is a *double acrostic.* A still more complicated form is the *cross acrostic,* in which the text is arranged so that the initial letter of the first line or other unit, the second letter of the second, the third letter of the third, and so forth, spell a word. *Abecedarian acrostics* follow an alphabetical pattern, such that the first letter of each line or other unit begins with the letters of the alphabet, in order.

Today, acrostics are often found in newspapers, magazines, and puzzle publications. They are also used as an educational tool to teach the alphabet or creative writing and are still viewed as helpful mnemonic devices.

EXAMPLES: The following Roman acrostic (c. A.D. 500), written in Latin and discovered on an Egyptian papyrus, is an *all-round acrostic* that has been interpreted by some to mean "the sower Arepo holds the wheels carefully":

$$S \ A \ T \ O \ R$$
$$A \ R \ E \ P \ O$$
$$T \ E \ N \ E \ T$$
$$O \ P \ E \ R \ A$$
$$R \ O \ T \ A \ S$$

Edgar Allan Poe's poem "Elizabeth" (1829) is a true acrostic; when read "down," the initial letters of the poem's lines spell out the name "Elizabeth Rebecca." David Mark Hummon's book for children entitled *Animal Acrostics* (1999) includes "vertical" descriptions of animals as well as instructions to help children write acrostics. Abecedarian acrostics can be found in a number of psalms and in the Dead Sea Scrolls, as well as in Geoffrey Chaucer's "An ABC" (c. 1360s).

Recent examples of abecedarian acrostics include Steven Schnur's *Spring: An Alphabet Acrostic* (1999), as well as his similar publications about fall and summer. *The New York Times Acrostic Puzzles* is an ongoing series of volumes written by Thomas Middleton. The common crossword puzzle contains acrostic arrangements, though it is not itself a true acrostic.

act: A major division of the action of a **play** or **drama.** Acts are generally subdivided into **scenes.** Acts and scenes were developed by ancient Roman dramatists, who normally divided their plays into five acts. William Shakespeare followed this Roman tradition; later, playwrights such as Henrik Ibsen and Anton Chekhov wrote plays in four acts. Modern plays typically consist of two or three acts, but some playwrights have dispensed with acts altogether in favor of serial scenes or episodes.

aesthetic distance (distance, psychic[al] distance, dramatic illusion): A separation between the audience and a work of art that is necessary for the audience to recognize and appreciate the work as an **aesthetic** object rather than as reality. The term has also been used to refer to the relatively **objective** perspective writers may maintain toward their work. Such objectivity (or aesthetic distance), some critics argue, allows the writer to relate the **story** and present its **characters** without recourse to personal, judgmental commentary. Distance, however, does not imply complete detachment. In fact, it allows the writer (and audience) to view the work "free" from overly personal identifications and thus to render (and experience) its contents fully and freely.

Recently, critic Hans Robert Jauss has used *aesthetic distance* in a new way. In the context of **reception theory** (a type of **reader-response criticism**), the term refers to the difference between how a work was viewed when it was originally published and how that same work is viewed today.

See also **aesthetics.**

Aestheticism (Aesthetic Movement): A movement that developed in Europe in the second half of the nineteenth century that insisted on the separation of art from morality or, to put this another way, that insisted that art need not be moral to have value. *L'art pour l'art* (**"art for art's sake"**) was the rallying cry for writers who valued art for its inherent **aesthetic** quality rather than for its **didactic** potential.

The literary influences on the movement included Théophile Gautier, who wrote in his preface to *Mademoiselle de Maupin* (1835) that art has no utilitarian value; Edgar Allan Poe, who developed a theory of the supremacy of the "poem *per se*" in an essay entitled "The Poetic Principle" (1850); and the English **Pre-Raphaelites,** whose poems (like Pre-Raphaelite paintings) showed an extraordinary appreciation for color, shape, and beauty in and of itself. Charles Baudelaire, Gustave Flaubert, J. K. Huysmans, and Stéphane Mallarmé, French writers who were early leaders of the Aesthetic Movement, promoted the idea that art is the supreme human endeavor. In England, the work of painters and illustrators such as Aubrey Beardsley, Max Beerbohm, and James McNeill Whistler complemented the writings of Algernon Swinburne, Walter Pater, and, especially, Oscar Wilde, who insisted perhaps more than anyone else on the prerogative of the artist to ignore moral questions. The **Parnassians,** a group of French and English poets who strove to write **objective** poetry that exalted **form** and minimized the author's **presence** and preferences, also played a significant, if lesser known, role in Aestheticism.

FURTHER EXAMPLE: Oscar Wilde's *The Decay of Lying* (1889) expresses some of the attitudes of Aestheticism through a **character** named Cyril, who at one point remarks:

Art never expresses anything but itself. It has an independent life, just as Thought has, and develops purely on its own lines. It is not necessarily realistic in an age of realism, nor spiritual in an age of faith. So far from being the creation of its own time, it is usually in direct opposition to it, and the only history that it preserves for us is the history of its own progress.

aesthetics: The study of beauty in nature and the arts. Two divisions, or approaches, to aesthetics exist: (1) the philosophical approach, which poses questions relating to the nature or definition of beauty; and (2) the psychological approach, which examines the perception, origins, and effects of beauty. Aesthetics is relevant to literary criticism insofar as it considers the relationship between beauty and other values, such as truth. The study of aesthetics also involves inquiry into the nature of artistic creation and audience appreciation.

In the late nineteenth century, an extreme philosophy of aesthetics emerged that came to be called **Aestheticism.** Adherents of Aestheticism valued literature for its beauty (for its inherent or affective qualities) rather than for any practical or moral considerations. They maintained that art is completely separate from morality and does not need to take moral or practical issues into consideration at all, hence their slogan **"art for art's sake."**

The eighteenth-century German philosopher Immanuel Kant used the term *aesthetics* in another sense, one that has prompted a response from late-twentieth-century critics. When Kant spoke of the aesthetic, he referred to the effort to relate the material to the spiritual. Aesthetic objects, according to Kant, combine the two realms insofar as they simultaneously entail tangibility and sanctity. This idea that the aesthetic is somehow a locus of universal or even divine truth—a realm where words are somehow not just arbitrary **signifiers** but rather revelatory **signs** with some special status—has been debunked recently, both by **deconstructors** like Paul de Man and **Marxist critics** like Terry Eagleton. In *Aesthetic Ideology* (1988) and *The Ideology of the Aesthetic* (1990), de Man and Eagleton, respectively, have argued that the **privileging** of aesthetic language and the belief that it has some kind of transcendental significance are but manifestations of the prevailing Western **ideology** and, to use Eagleton's paraphrase of de Man's argument, "pernicious mystifications."

affective fallacy: First used by William K. Wimsatt and Monroe C. Beardsley to refer to what they regarded as the erroneous practice of interpreting **texts** according to the psychological responses of readers. "The Affective Fallacy," they wrote in a 1946 essay later republished in *The Verbal Icon* (1954), "is a confusion between the poem and its *results* (what it *is* and what it *does*). . . . It begins by trying to derive the standards of criticism from the psychological effects of a poem and ends in impressionism and relativism." The affective fallacy, like the **intentional fallacy** (confusing the meaning of a work with the author's expressly intended meaning), was one of the main tenets of the **New Criticism,** a type of **formalism.** The affective fallacy has recently been contested by **reader-response critics,** who have deliberately dedicated their efforts to describing the way individual readers and **interpretive communities** go about making sense of texts.

See also **authorial intention.**

affective stylistics: A phrase coined by **reader-response critic** Stanley Fish in an essay entitled "Literature in the Reader: Affective Stylistics" (1970) to refer to the impact that the **structure** of a given **text** has on the minds of individual readers as they read and, more generally, to a personal and private process of reading that Fish once believed everyone employs. In setting forth his **theory** of affective stylistics, Fish significantly developed the ideas of reader-response critic Louise M. Rosenblatt and **hermeneutical** theorist E. D. Hirsch. He suggested that meaning is an "event" that takes place in the mind of an individual reader during the act of reading and was concerned with how meaning changes over time as the reader progresses through the work. Fish argued that reading is a temporal process in which each succeeding word, sentence, **stanza,** paragraph, and so forth provides additional information that readers must incorporate into their understanding of the work. At each step, readers reevaluate their interpretations, forming new expectations and perhaps rejecting old ones, recognizing past mistakes and making new ones.

Fish substantially modified his reader-response theory in the latter half of the 1970s, beginning with an essay entitled "Interpreting the Variorum" (1976), where he shifted his focus away from the individual reader. He asserted that multiple and diverse reading groups (which he called **interpretive communities**) exist within any large reading population and that members of a particular interpretive community tend to share the same "reading strategies." (American college students reading novels as class assignments comprise an interpretive community; their reading strategies are more likely to include **symbol**-hunting than are the reading strategies of teenage romance novel readers.) Within a given community, Fish argued, interpretations tend to be more alike or "stable," whereas the interpretations generally arrived at by *different* reading communities (employing different reading strategies) may differ sharply. In making this shift, Fish did not wholly scrap his earlier work; rather, he came to view affective stylistics as one of several possible reading strategies.

Age of Johnson (in English literature): The last of three literary eras within the **Neoclassical Period** in English literature, an age generally said to range from the middle of the eighteenth century until 1798, the year in which poets William Wordsworth and Samuel Taylor Coleridge published the first edition of *Lyrical Ballads,* a volume believed by many to mark the beginning of the **Romantic Period** in English literature.

Called the Age of Johnson because of the powerful influence exerted by poet, critic, and fiction writer Samuel Johnson (1709–84) over writers such as Edmund Burke, Oliver Goldsmith, Edward Gibbon, and James Boswell, this epoch is also called the *Age of Sensibility*, although the latter term brings the works of different writers to mind. The term *Age of Johnson* invokes works such as Burke's *A Philosophical Inquiry into the Origins of Our Ideas on the Sublime and the Beautiful* (1757), Goldsmith's *The Vicar of Wakefield* (1766), Gibbon's *The Decline and Fall of the Roman Empire* (1787), Boswell's *Life of Samuel Johnson* (1791), and, of course, Johnson's own works, from his essays in *The Rambler* (1750–52) to his *Dictionary of the English Language* (1755) to his fictional work *Rasselas* (1759).

When referred to as the Age of Sensibility, however, this same chronological era suggests a different set of writers — ones who placed a premium not on the neoclassical **aesthetics** and Enlightenment values of Johnson's circle but rather on the anti**classical** (or antineoclassical) features of old **ballads** and visionary or **bardic poetry.** De-emphasizing the qualities of intellect, reason, balance, and order characteristic of **neoclassicism,** they began to embrace new forms of literary expression and developed an interest in subjects eschewed by the neoclassicists, such as **medieval** history and **folk** literature. These authors, mainly poets, included William Collins, William Cowper, Thomas Gray, and Christopher Smart. Laurence Sterne's *Tristram Shandy* (1759) and Henry Mackenzie's *The Man of Feeling* (1771) are considered **classic** prose fiction examples of the Age of Sensibility.

Whereas critics often view the Age of Johnson as the final stage of English neoclassicism, the Age of Sensibility is seen as anticipating the Romantic Period in English literature, with its emphasis on individualism, **imagination,** and the language of common people.

See also **neoclassicism, romanticism.**

Age of Sensibility (in English literature): See **Age of Johnson (in English literature).**

Agrarians: Broadly used, authors prone to exalting **pastoral** virtues and the countryside. However, the term is used more specifically to **denote** a group of American writers (most of whom were associated with Vanderbilt University) who published a magazine of poetry and criticism entitled *The Fugitive* between the years 1922 and 1925. This group, which included such critics as Cleanth Brooks, Donald Davidson, Merrill Moore, John Crowe Ransom, Allen Tate, and Robert Penn Warren, opposed the ways of the Old South while simultaneously promoting agrarian regionalism. In the 1930s, the Agrarians were also active in promoting an agricultural base rather than an industrial one for the American economy.

The Agrarians influenced the development of the modern Southern novel, as exemplified by William Faulkner, and **the New Criticism,** a type of **formalism** practiced in the 1940s and 1950s by writers such as Ransom and Warren (both of whom had been associated with the Agrarians).

Alexandrine: A **verse** form consisting of six **iambic feet** (iambic **hexameter**). First used widely in Old French **romances** of the twelfth and thirteenth centuries to commemorate the adventures of Alexander the Great, it was resurrected in the **Renaissance** by the English poet Edmund Spenser. An Alexandrine appears as the ninth and final line of each **Spenserian stanza** (following eight lines of **iambic pentameter**).

EXAMPLES: The second of the following lines by Spenser, which is the ninth and last of a Spenserian stanza appearing in *The Faerie Queene* (1590, 1596), is an Alexandrine:

> A loathly, wrinckled hag, ill-favoured, old,
> Whose secret filth good manners biddeth not be told.

The second line of the following **couplet** exemplifies what Alexander Pope, in his "An Essay on Criticism" (1711), calls "needless Alexandrine":

> A needless Alexandrine ends the song,
> That, like a wounded snake, drags its slow length along.

allegory: The presentation of an **abstract** idea through more **concrete** means. The typical allegory is a **narrative**—whether in prose, verse, or drama—that has at least two levels of meaning. The first is the surface-level story line, which can be summed up by stating who did what to whom and when. Although allegories have coherent **plots,** their authors expect readers to recognize the existence of a second and deeper level of meaning, which may be moral, political, philosophical, or religious. To that end, allegories are often thinly veiled; sometimes **characters** even bear the names of the qualities or ideas the author wishes to represent. (**Personification** is a device common to many allegories.) Allegories need not be entire narratives, however, and narratives may contain allegorical elements or figures. Many critics consider the allegory to be an extended **metaphor** and, conversely, consider metaphors—which involve saying one thing but meaning another—to be "verbal allegories."

Allegories generally fall into two major categories: (1) the *political and historical allegory*; and (2) the *allegory of abstract themes*. In the first type, the figures, **settings,** or actions correspond directly and specifically to historical personages, places, and events (Napoleon's defeat at Waterloo, for instance). In the second type, the characters stand for ideas or abstract qualities. (In an allegory warning against laziness, the main character might encounter figures such as Sloth and Perseverance.)

Allegory continues to be used as a narrative device today, although its popularity peaked in the **Middle Ages,** when the **dream vision** was a prevalent form. Types of allegory common in other historical periods include the **fable,** *exemplum,* **beast fable,** and **parable.**

EXAMPLES: John Bunyan's *Pilgrim's Progress* (1678), an allegory of abstract themes, is the most famous English allegory. On the surface, it tells the story of a man named Christian who journeys from one city to another, but on a deeper level, the problems he encounters represent obstacles that a good Christian must overcome to live a godly life. Christian encounters such blatantly allegorical figures as Mr. Worldly Wiseman and places such as Vanity Fair and the Slough of Despair. In Garry Trudeau's comic strip *Doonesbury*, a modern example of a political and historical allegory, Mr. Butts is an allegorical figure representing the tobacco industry. The graphic novelist Neil Gaiman introduces an allegorical dimension to his *Sandman* series (1991–97) by giving the major recurring characters names such as Dream, Desire, and Destiny.

alliteration: The repetition of sounds in a sequence of words. Alliteration generally refers to repeated consonant sounds (often initial consonant sounds or those at the beginning of **stressed** syllables) but has also been used by some critics to refer to repeated vowel sounds. When *s* is the repeated sound, the result is said to be **sibilant**. Alliteration was especially important in **Old English** verse, establishing the **rhythm** and **structure** of the poetic line. Since then, its role has been less critical and essential, although poets to this day use alliteration to create powerful musical effects and to highlight and emphasize key words, concepts, and relationships.

Densely alliterative utterances (such as "Peter Piper picked a peck of pickled peppers" or "She sells seashells by the seashore") are sometimes difficult to pronounce and are referred to as "tongue twisters."

EXAMPLES: Note the alliterative repetition of *s, b, d,* and — most obviously — *f* in the last three lines of Wallace Stevens's poem "Of Mere Being" (1955):

> The palm stands on the edge of space.
> The wind moves slowly in the branches.
> The bird's fire-fangled feathers dangle down.

S appears as a sibilant alliterative sound in this passage from Kate Chopin's *The Awakening* (1899):

> The voice of the sea is seductive; never ceasing, whispering, clamoring, murmuring, inviting the soul to wander for a spell in abysses of solitude; to lose itself in mazes of inward contemplation. The voice of the sea speaks to the soul. The touch of the sea is sensuous, enfolding the body in its soft, close embrace.

The following passage from Michael Byers's short story "Blue River, Blue Sun" from the collection *The Coast of Good Intentions* (1998) is packed with *s* and *p* sounds and also contains a **simile** in the first sentence:

> The plastic water vials shifted in his pack like tiny men shifting in sleep, and when he dipped to fill a sample his old knees popped and pinged. Away across the grasses he could see his students advancing one slow step at a time.

Sheryl Crow's rowdy pop song "All I Wanna Do [Is Have Some Fun]" (1993) is heavily alliterative. Of the twenty-eight words in the song's opening two lines, for example, eleven (among them "beer," "bar," "early," "Billy," "peel," "labels," "Bud," and "bottle") alliteratively repeat the letters *b* and *l*.

allusion: An indirect reference to a person, event, statement, or **theme** found in literature, the other arts, history, **myths,** religion, or popular culture. An author's use of this device tends to presuppose that readers in general will possess the knowledge to recognize the allusion, but sometimes allusions are used that only a choice few can understand. Because of the **connotations** they carry, allusions are used to enrich meaning or broaden the impact of a statement.

EXAMPLES: At the end of Margaret Mitchell's popular novel *Gone With the Wind* (1936) (and in the movie version), Rhett Butler decides to leave his wife, Scarlett. When she asks him how she'll live without him, he replies, "Frankly, my dear, I don't give a damn." Someone who says "Frankly, my dear . . ." is probably making an allusion to this famous statement.

When, in T. S. Eliot's *The Waste Land* (1922), a voice says

> I remember
> Those are pearls that were his eyes

many readers will recognize the allusion to William Shakespeare's *The Tempest* (c. 1611). But when, in Eliot's "Gerontion" (1920), the speaker says

> I was neither at the hot gates
> Nor fought in the warm rain

only readers of Greek would know that "hot gates" is an allusion to the fifth-century B.C. Battle of Thermopylae (literally, "hot gates") between the Greeks and the Persians.

Allusions to ancient events and literary **classics** may be found even in popular culture. Hot Gates is the name of a porn actress opposed by the superhero Batman in Frank Miller's graphic novel *Batman: The Dark Knight Returns* (1986). The Eagles' song "Get Over It" (1994) alludes to William Shakespeare's *Henry VI, Part 2* (c. 1594) by quoting "Old Billy's" famous line "Let's kill all the lawyers" verbatim.

In the *Doonesbury* comic strip shown here, Garry Trudeau visually alludes to Charles M. Schulz's *Peanuts* with an image of Trudeau's lovable hippie, Zonker Harris, who is dressed like Schulz's Charlie Brown and looks addled atop Snoopy's **iconic** doghouse.

ambiguity: The result of something being stated in such a way that its meaning cannot be definitely determined. Some of the major causes of ambiguity are the use of pronouns without the proper referents, the use of words that have multiple meanings, unusual **syntax,** and inordinate brevity.

Although ambiguity is often considered a flaw, especially in speech, it is a virtue in literary works whose authors seek to create multiple meanings or levels of meaning or to leave meaning indeterminate. Indeed, the richness and complexity of literature to a great extent depend on ambiguity, thanks to which a single word or phrase can suggest or **connote** a number of different things. In short, where **denotative** precision is required or desirable, ambiguity is a fault, but where *plurisignation,* or multiple meanings, are called for, ambiguity is highly desirable. William Empson identifies and describes seven types of ambiguity in his aptly named *Seven Types of Ambiguity* (1930).

EXAMPLES: The following lines of poetry contain verbal ambiguities:

> When the hounds of spring are on winter's traces . . .
> — Algernon Charles Swinburne,
> *Atalanta in Calydon* (1865)

Does the word "traces" mean "last vestiges" or "remnants" (that is, the traces of winter's last snowfall), or does it mean "tracks" (as in animal footprints being followed by "the hounds of spring")? Or, alternatively, did the poet have in mind the reins and harnesses used to drive an animal (sometimes referred to as "traces" in preautomobile days)?

> Piping songs of pleasant glee
> On a cloud I saw a child. . . .
> — William Blake, "Introduction"
> to *Songs of Innocence* (1789)

Who is piping: the speaker or the child? And who is on the cloud?

> The Soul that rises with us, our life's Star,
> Hath had elsewhere its setting. . . .
> — William Wordsworth, "Ode:
> Intimations of Immortality" (1807)

Does "setting" mean "going down" or "place, locale"?

> The pears are not seen
> As the observer wills.
> —Wallace Stevens,
> "Study of Two Pears" (1938)

What point is Stevens trying to make? That the observer does not want to see the pears and so does not see them? Or that the observer wants the pears to be seen in a certain way, but they have not been depicted in that way by the painter of the "Study"?

Sometimes ambiguity is of a more general nature. Whether the ghosts of Emily Brontë's *Wuthering Heights* (1847) and Henry James's *The Turn of the Screw* (1898) are supernatural beings or hallucinations is left ambiguous. General ambiguity, of course, depends upon an accumulation of verbal ambiguities, as may be seen in the passage from *The Turn of the Screw* in which the death of the boy Miles is related by his governess, also the story's **narrator**. The governess, who suspects her little charge of having referred to the existence of the evil ghost of Peter Quint, asks Miles a question:

> "Whom do you mean by 'he'?"
> "Peter Quint — you devil!" His face gave again, round the room, its convulsed supplication. "*Where?*"

Is Miles's exclamatory statement an answer to the governess's question (in which case he is calling his governess a "devil"), or is it an address to the ghost of Quint (in which case he is calling Quint a "devil")? And why is Miles asking "*Where?*" The governess's narrative continues:

> They are in my ears still, his supreme surrender of the name and his tribute to my devotion. "What does he matter now, my own? — what will he *ever* matter? *I* have you," I launched at the beast, "but he has lost you for ever!" Then for the demonstration of my work, "There, *there!*" I said to Miles.
> But he had already jerked straight round, stared, glared again, and seen but the quiet day. With the stroke of the loss I was so proud of he uttered the cry of a creature hurled over an abyss, and the grasp with which I recovered him might have been that of catching him in his fall. I caught him, yes, I held him — it may be imagined with what a passion; but at the end of a minute I began to feel what it truly was that I held. We were alone with the quiet day, and his little heart, dispossessed, had stopped.

Has the governess frightened Miles to death? Murdered him in some more direct way? Is the child the victim of a successful but fatal exorcism? James chose to leave the answer to these and many other questions ambiguous, thereby initiating a century of critical controversy.

amphibrach: See **foot.**

amphimacer: See **foot.**

amplification: A **rhetorical figure** involving a dramatic ordering of words, often emphasizing some sort of expansion or progression, whether conceptual, valuative, poetic, or even with regard to word length. Among those who have criticized this once common form of verbal flourish is Alexander Pope, who in *Peri Bathous [On Bathos]: Of the Art of Sinking* *in Poetry* (1728) derides amplification, calling it "the spinning wheel" of **bathos.**

EXAMPLES: In the following lines from Geoffrey Chaucer's *Troilus and Criseyde* (c. 1383), the narrator uses **metaphor,** then **synecdoche,** and then **personification** to amplify his subject, finally attempting to bring his increasingly poetic description to **climactic** culmination with the simple, literal term "sunne":

> The daye's honour, and the heven's ye,°   *eye*
> The nyghte's foo° — all this clepe° I the sunne.   *foe, call*

A more recent example of amplification is also an instance of **asyndeton:** "It's a bird, it's a plane, it's *Superman!*"

anachronism: Something that is not placed in its proper historical time period. When this "error" occurs, an author places an event, person, or thing during a time when it could not have existed.

EXAMPLES: The clock that strikes in William Shakespeare's *Julius Caesar* (1598), for no such clocks existed in the Rome of Caesar's time. The film *A Knight's Tale* (2001), described by critic David Ansen in *Newsweek* as "wildly anachronistic," includes a scene in which the crowd at a jousting tournament set in **medieval** England not only sings along to "We Will Rock You" (1977), a heavy metal song by Queen, but also does "the wave."

anachrony: The literary technique of presenting material out of chronological order; alternatively, the achronological presentation of events. Anachronous **narratives** are characterized by **plots** in which events are recounted in an order different from their chronological sequence. **Narratologist** Mieke Bal has therefore described anachrony as "chronological deviation."

There are three major types of anachrony: (1) **analepsis,** the insertion of **scenes** that have occurred in the past; (2) **prolepsis,** the insertion of scenes that preview future events or developments; and (3) **ellipsis,** a chronological **gap** indicating that material has been omitted. Analepsis, the most common form of which is **flashback,** usually occurs near the beginning of a work and often recounts an event that occurred before the opening scene. Prolepsis, which includes **flashforward** and other techniques of hinting at future development, is commonly used in television and films to create feelings of anticipation, curiosity, and suspense. Sometimes prolepsis takes the form of a **figure of speech** that hints at an eventual outcome. Ellipsis is a form of chronological deviation that enables an author to skip over long or short chronological periods rather than directing the reader or audience backward or forward in time. Some authors use ellipses to invite the reader to "fill in the gap," whereas others use this technique to achieve brevity. **Reader-response critic** Gérard Genette refers to an analepsis that fills in the gap left by an ellipsis as a *completing analepsis.*

Genette has also used the terms *internal analepsis* and *internal prolepsis* to refer to the achronological presentation of events that take place *within* the work's time line. By contrast, he uses the terms *external analepsis* and *external prolepsis* to refer to the anachronous presentation of events occurring *outside* the work's chronological boundaries, that is, before the beginning or after the ending of the time period covered by the **story** proper. Genette uses the terms *repeating analepsis* and *repeating prolepsis,* respectively, to refer to internal analepsis and internal prolepsis that flash back or forward to events that have been previously presented or that will be presented later.

Both analepsis and prolepsis have been described by Genette in terms of "distance" and "span," with distance referring to the interval from the moment at which the story is interrupted to the interrupting past or future event, and span referring to the time elapsed during that event.

EXAMPLES: Thornton Wilder's play *Our Town* (1938) contains an analeptic flashback to the twelfth birthday of Emily Webb, the play's main **character.** "The File on the Mayfair Witches," a lengthy analeptic section of Anne Rice's novel *The Witching Hour* (1990), provides readers with relevant historical background. Perhaps the most famous example of proleptic anachrony is found in William Shakespeare's *Hamlet* (1602), in which the wounded **protagonist** says, **figuratively,** "Horatio, I am dead." The film *Terminator 2: Judgment Day* (1991) contains a similar, more recent example: the heroine's statement to the disbelieving doctors at a mental institution that "You're already dead. . . . This whole place, everything you see, is gone."

The cartoon from Gary Larson's *The Far Side Gallery of 2001 Off-the-Wall Calendar* on page 16 mixes analepsis with prolepsis, quickly propelling the reader forward from the present, in which a man shoots a werewolf, to the future point at which he will be "ripped to shreds" and then back to a moment "earlier in the day" when he first saw the tie sported by the attacking werewolf.

Examples of external prolepsis occur in the TV series *The Simpsons,* which has occasionally revealed what certain family members will look and be like twenty years in the future. Movies about psychics regularly use internal prolepsis to flashforward to what their prescient protagonists subconsciously know. For instance, in *The Gift* (2000), the character played by Cate Blanchett is troubled by proleptic glimpses of the muddy feet of a school principal's fiancée — and of herself being clubbed with a flashlight.

The phrase "FOUR YEARS LATER," which fills the screen near the end of the movie *Cast Away* (2000), is an example of elliptic anachrony, indicating the omission of the intervening four years, which are presumably irrelevant to the movie.

Examples of anachrony that fall outside the three main types include television episodes (e.g., *Seinfeld,* Episode 164, "The Betrayal") and movies (e.g., *Memento* [2001]) that present scenes in reverse chronological order.

See also **analepsis, prolepsis.**

THE FAR SIDE® By GARY LARSON

Moments before he was ripped to shreds, Edgar vaguely recalled having seen that same obnoxious tie earlier in the day.

Anacreontic poetry: Verse named for the sixth-century B.C. Greek poet Anacreon. Usually written in **tetrameter** lines consisting of a **pyrrhic foot,** two **trochees,** and a **spondee,** Anacreontic poetry treats the **themes** of eroticism, love, women, and bacchanalian pleasures. Thomas Moore, Irish author of the *Odes of Anacreon* (1800), is noted for having written Anacreontic poetry.

anacrusis: One or more extra un**stressed** syllables at the beginning of a **verse** that are not counted as part of the **meter.**

EXAMPLE: Samuel Taylor Coleridge's "The Rime of the Ancient Mariner" (1798) is written primarily in four-line **stanzas** that alternate **tetrameter** and **trimeter** lines. The first tetrameter line of the following stanza exhibits anacrusis; the "and" at the beginning of the line is an extra, unstressed syllable not counted as part of the meter:

> And the bay was white with silent light,
> Till rising from the same,
> Full many shapes, that shadows were,
> In crimson colors came.

anagnorisis: A term used by Aristotle in his *Poetics* (c. 330 B.C.) to refer to the moment in a **drama** when the **protagonist** "discovers" something that either leads to or explains a reversal of fortune — that is, the protagonist gains some crucial knowledge that he or she did not have. In a **tragedy,** the revelation is usually closely associated with the protagonist's downfall, whereas in a **comedy** it usually signals his or her success.

EXAMPLES: Sophocles' *Oedipus Rex* (c. 430 B.C.) presents a well-known example of anagnorisis. Oedipus vows to find and bring to justice the murderer of King Laius; in the course of his search, he discovers that he himself killed Laius. This revelation portends a reversal of fortune for Oedipus, who ultimately blinds and banishes himself as punishment for having, however unwittingly, killed his father and married his mother. The term *anagnorisis* might also be loosely applied to the most famous scene in Neil Jordan's film *The Crying Game* (1992), in which the protagonist's relationship with another **character** is drastically altered by a startling revelation. The protagonist becomes involved with a person who he believes is an attractive female, but whom he subsequently discovers to be a male.

A more recent example of anagnorisis occurs in the movie *The Sixth Sense* (1999), in which Malcolm Crowe, the character played by Bruce Willis, discovers that he is dead.

analepsis: The evocation in a **narrative** of scenes or events that took place at an earlier point in the **story.** One of the three major types of **anachrony,** analepsis is commonly equated with **flashback,** but **reader-response critics** Gérard Genette and Gerald Prince have recently argued that it is in fact a broader term (much as its opposite, **prolepsis,** is a broader term than **flashforward**). For instance, analepsis may involve an **image** or **figure of speech** that harks back to something encountered earlier. Sometimes a retrospective thought or meditation disrupts the chronological flow of material being recounted. Occasionally, analepsis even involves a subconscious memory or vision of the past that suddenly manifests itself in the consciousness or dreams of the **narrator** or of a main **character** whose mental processes are recounted by the narrative — for instance, via **free indirect discourse.**

EXAMPLES: The italicized clause in the following sentence: "Carolyn was surprised when she read the exam questions because, although *she had spent the entire weekend studying,* she couldn't answer a single one." In her novel *Interview with the Vampire* (1976), Anne Rice repeatedly uses flashback as the narrator-**protagonist** Louis tells a young reporter how he became a vampire.

In Memoriam A. H. H. (1850), the **elegy** Alfred, Lord Tennyson wrote following the death of his friend Arthur Henry Hallam, contains numerous examples of analepsis more broadly defined, including powerful recollective experiences ("The dead man touched me from the past") triggered by sights and sounds ("Thy voice is on the rolling air") and various **mystical** experiences and **dream visions,** some of which recall Hallam in aspects and situations more **surreal** then real ("The man we loved was there on deck, / But thrice as large as man").

See also **anachrony, prolepsis.**

anapest: A metrical **foot** in **poetry** that consists of two unstressed syllables followed by a **stressed** syllable ˘˘´.

EXAMPLES: contradict, interfere, in the buff, "are you mad?"

The following lines from Algernon Charles Swinburne's "Hymn to Proserpine" (1866) are anapestic:

> Will ye bridle the deep sea with reins, will you chasten the high sea
>   with rods?
> Will ye take her to chain her with chains, who is older than all of you
>   Gods?

Edgar Allan Poe's poem "Annabel Lee" (1849) contains many anapestic lines, such as:

> For the moon never beams, without bringing me dreams
>   Of the beautiful ANNABEL LEE;
> And the stars never rise, but I see the bright eyes
>   Of the beautiful ANNABEL LEE.

"Helter Skelter," a famous and controversial song from the Beatles' *White Album* (1968), is predominantly anapestic.

anaphora: A **rhetorical figure** involving the exact repetition of words or phrases at the beginning of successive lines or sentences. Anaphora is a type of **parallelism.**

EXAMPLES: The following **stanza** from Geoffrey Chaucer's *Troilus and Criseyde* (c. 1353):

> Swich fin° hath, lo, this Troilus for love;   *Such ending*
> Swich fin hath al his great worthinesse;
> Swich fin hath his estaat real° above;   *royal*
> Swich fin his lust, swich fin hath his nobleness;
> Swich fin hath false worlde's brotelnesse:°   *brittleness*
> And thus bigan his loving of Criseyde,
> As I have told, and in this wise he deide.

Martin Luther King employed anaphora in his famous "I Have a Dream" speech (1963), in which several successive sentences begin with the phrase "I have a dream that..."

anastrophe: See **hyperbaton.**

anecdote: A brief account of some interesting, often entertaining and often humorous incident. Lacking the complexity of the **short story,** an anecdote simply relates a particular episode or event that makes a single point. Since an anecdote is supposed to be true, the incident described and the point made by the anecdote are typically more important than *how* the anecdote is told — that is, the artistry or style involved in the telling. Anecdotes frequently relate an incident in a particular person's life that reveals a character trait.

EXAMPLES: The story about George Washington and the cherry tree is an anecdote. It reveals Washington's honesty and the importance of telling the truth. When his father asked him who chopped down the cherry tree, Washington supposedly replied "I cannot tell a lie" and told the truth, even though he expected to be punished for his actions.

In Joseph Conrad's *Lord Jim* (1900), a pathetic guano exporter named Chester tells Marlow, the novel's **narrator,** a story about Holy-Terror Robinson, who was once shipwrecked on an island with six other men but found alone some time later, "kneeling on the kelp, naked as the day he was born, and chanting some psalm tune or other." To clarify what he is implying, Chester "put[s] his lips to Marlow's ear. 'Cannibal?'" he asks suggestively. This darkly humorous anecdote suggests that morality and civilized behavior may break down when at odds with the survival instinct.

At the beginning of many episodes of his **classic** television show, comedian Jerry Seinfeld appears on stage in a comedy club, telling anecdotes that are subsequently dramatized. It is, therefore, difficult to tell whether the comedian's stand-up routine distills "real-life" incidents and situations — or whether his show elaborates dramatically on humorous stories.

Anglo-Saxon Period (in English Literature): See **Old English Period (in English literature).**

antagonist: The **character** pitted against the **protagonist** — the main character — of a work. An evil or cruel antagonist is a *villain;* however, the antagonist is not necessarily a villain.

EXAMPLES: Creon is the antagonist in Sophocles' *Antigone* (c. 441 B.C.). Heathcliff, in some ways the young **hero** of the first half of Emily Brontë's *Wuthering Heights* (1847), is the antagonist throughout most of the novel's second half. Darth Vader is the antagonist and villain of the original *Star Wars* trilogy (1977, 1980, 1983). Examples of antagonists who are not remotely villainous — who simply hinder or block the protagonist — may be found in short stories like Frank O'Connor's "My Oedipus Complex" (1963), in which the antagonist is the **narrator's** father, whose return from war interferes with the boy's exclusive relationship with his mother, and Amy Tan's "Two Kinds" (1989), in which the antagonist is the narrator's mother, whose goals for her daughter conflict with what Jing-mei wants for herself.

anticlimax: A **rhetorical** lapse, usually sudden, that involves a descent from a higher to a lower emotional point — from an event, statement, subject matter, or **tone** with greater drama, significance, or authorial power to one with less impact or importance. Anticlimax typically results in the disappointment or even reversal of expectations.

An anticlimactic effect may be achieved over the span of several pages or even several chapters. Anticlimax may be used intentionally, usually for comic effect, or it may be unintended, the result of authorial ineptitude. When such an unintentional descent from the lofty to the trivial or even ridiculous occurs while the writer is trying to achieve **the sublime,** the effect is known as **bathos** rather than anticlimax.

EXAMPLES: The following sentence from a Knight Ridder News Service dispatch (1995) offers an example of rhetorical anticlimax: "The crime bill passed by the Senate would reinstate the Federal death penalty for certain violent crimes: assassinating the President; hijacking an airliner; and murdering a government poultry inspector."

William Shakespeare makes frequent use of anticlimax in *Cymbeline* (c. 1610), continually frustrating the audience's expectations. The audience expects tragedy, but something trivial occurs instead. For instance, having taken a sleeping draught, Imogen awakes next to the dead body of someone she believes to be her husband. She laments his death, just as Juliet lamented Romeo's death when she awoke next to his dead body; unlike Juliet, however, the distraught Imogen doesn't take her own life. Instead, she becomes the servant of a Roman conqueror, the first person who passes by.

The last ten chapters of Mark Twain's *Adventures of Huckleberry Finn* (1884) — chapters in which Huck arrives at Aunt Sally Phelps's place, is joined by Tom Sawyer, and goes along with Tom's ridiculously and needlessly elaborate plans to rescue the runaway slave Jim — are often said to be anticlimactic.

In the following passage from Isabel Allende's *The House of the Spirits* (1982), Clara's anticlimactic response to her husband's angry tirade reduces his fury to a pathetic and ineffectual effort to control her:

> He shouted like a madman, pacing up and down the living room and slamming his fist against the furniture, arguing that if Clara intended to follow in her mother's footsteps she was going to come face to face with a real man, who would pull her pants down and give her a good spanking so she'd get it out of her damned head to go around haranguing people, and that he categorically forbade her to go to prayer meetings or any other kind and that he wasn't some ninny whose wife could go around making a fool of him. Clara let him scream his head

off and bang on the furniture until he was exhausted. Then, inattentive as ever, she asked him if he knew how to wiggle his ears.

antihero: A **protagonist** in a modern work who does not exhibit the qualities of the traditional **hero.** Instead of being a grand and/or admirable figure — brave, honest, and magnanimous, for example — an antihero is all too ordinary and may even be petty or downright dishonest.

EXAMPLES: Willy Loman, the salesman in Arthur Miller's *Death of a Salesman* (1948); Jim Stark, the **character** played by James Dean in the movie *Rebel Without a Cause* (1955); Alex, the sociopathic protagonist of Anthony Burgess's *A Clockwork Orange* (1962), played by Malcolm McDowell in Stanley Kubrick's film adaptation; and Ben Sanderson, the alcoholic character played by Nicholas Cage in the movie *Leaving Las Vegas* (1995). The brutal, sardonic character of the Comedian in Alan Moore's graphic novel *Watchmen* (1986) could be considered an antihero.

antimasque: An interlude frequently featuring **grotesque** or bawdy humor that is interspersed between the more serious elements of the **masque.** Whereas the masque was performed by amateur members of the nobility or even royalty, the antimasque generally used the lower class of professional dancers and actors. The invention and development of the antimasque are attributed to Ben Jonson, a seventeenth-century English poet and playwright generally considered one of the greatest writers of masques.

antinovel: A type of contemporary **fiction** that attempts to present the reader with experience itself, unfiltered by **metaphor** or other vehicles of authorial interpretation. Antinovelists attempt to depict reality without recourse to a moral frame of reference; they avoid the kind of subjective **narrative** evaluation that tends to creep into more traditional fiction, including so-called **realistic** and **naturalistic** narratives. Antinovelists deliberately violate and flout established novelistic **conventions** and norms. Confusion is an intended result of the narrative experiments they perform, experiments that typically involve fragmentation and dislocation and that require the reader to assemble and make sense of disparate pieces of information.

EXAMPLES: Alain Robbe-Grillet's *Le voyeur* (*The Voyeur*) (1955); John Hawkes's *The Blood Oranges* (1971).

antistrophe: (1) The second **stanza** of the **classical** Greek choral **ode.** It followed the **strophe,** which was sung while the **chorus** walked from right to left; singing the antistrophe, the chorus moved back from left to right before beginning the **epode.** (2) The second stanza in a **Pindaric ode.**

antithesis: A **rhetorical figure** in which two ideas are directly opposed. For a statement to be truly antithetical, the opposing ideas must be presented in a grammatically parallel way, thus creating a perfect rhetorical balance.

EXAMPLES: The following line from Adrienne Rich's "Toward the Solstice" (1977) is antithetical:

I long and dread to close.

This passage from John Lyly's *Euphues* (1579) relies heavily on antithesis:

> So likewise in the disposition of the mind, either virtue is overshadowed with some vice or vice overcast with some virtue: Alexander valiant in war, yet given to wine; Tully eloquent in his glozes [flattering or fine speeches], yet vainglorious; Solomon wise, yet too too wanton; David holy, but yet an homicide; none more witty than Euphues, yet at the first none more wicked.

The opening lines of Charles Dickens's *A Tale of Two Cities* (1859) likewise employ antithesis:

> It was the best of times, it was the worst of times, it was the age of wisdom, it was the age of foolishness, it was the epoch of belief, it was the epoch of incredulity, it was the season of Light, it was the season of Darkness, it was the spring of hope, it was the winter of despair, we had everything before us, we had nothing before us, we were all going direct to Heaven, we were all going direct the other way. . . .

Even former president Ronald Reagan's speeches made frequent use of antithesis. In a speech given to the British House of Commons on June 8, 1982, Reagan contrasted totalitarianism and freedom, two ideas that are themselves antithetical, asking:

> Who would voluntarily choose not to have a right to vote, decide to purchase government propaganda handouts instead of independent newspapers, prefer government to worker-controlled unions, opt for land to be owned by the state instead of those who till it, want government repression of religious liberty, a single political party instead of a free choice, a rigid cultural orthodoxy instead of democratic tolerance and diversity?

antithetical criticism: A method of literary **criticism** proposed and practiced by critic Harold Bloom in his revisionist phase that involves reading poems as *mis*readings (by the poet) of earlier poems written by powerful and influential precursors. Thus, a critic practicing antithetical criticism might see Percy Bysshe Shelley's *Prometheus Unbound* (1820) as a strong misreading of John Milton's epic *Paradise Lost* (1667).

Antithetical criticism is grounded in a **theory** of literary **influence** that Bloom set forth in *The Anxiety of Influence* (1973) and developed in *A Map of Misreading* (1975); in these and several subsequent books, Bloom suggests that the writing of all poets involves the rewriting of earlier poets and that this rewriting always and inevitably involves some form of misreading or "misprision." Bloom also believes that all readers misinterpret works, since they read them "defensively" — that is, with an eye to preserving their own autonomy and creativity. With this in mind, Bloom recognizes that the readings of antithetical critics (including his own readings) are necessarily misreadings as well. He justifies antithetical criticism, however, by arguing that its strong misreadings culminate in interesting interpretations widely divergent from what the poet may have thought he was saying, as well as from the "weak misreadings" produced by critics taking other critical approaches who purport to ascertain and reveal what a poem really means. Bloom predicts that the inherent difference of antithetical readings from other kinds of readings will secure a place for them along with all the other strong misreadings throughout history.

See also **anxiety of influence.**

antonomasia: A **rhetorical figure** involving the regular substitution of an **epithet** for a proper name.

EXAMPLE: John Milton's frequent substitution of "The Great Adversary" for "Satan" in *Paradise Lost* (1667).

anxiety of influence: Contemporary critic Harold Bloom, who is now best known for his controversial book *The Western Canon* (1994), developed a brand of "revisionist" or **antithetical criticism** in the 1970s that challenged conventional conceptions of **influence.** In *The Anxiety of Influence* (1973), Bloom significantly developed ideas set forth by Walter Jackson Bate in his book *The Burden of the Past and the English Poet* (1970). Whereas Bate had argued that poets inevitably feel that their precursors may have already accomplished all that *can* be accomplished, Bloom discusses the way in which poets deal with this fear, or "anxiety." He suggests that the writing of all poets involves the rewriting of earlier poets, and that this rewriting always and inevitably involves some form of "misprision," a kind of misreading that allows the later writer's creativity to emerge. Bloom acknowledges the long-standing view that any given poet (particularly since Milton) is in fact influenced by a "precursor" poet or poets, but he further contends that the "belated" poet (or *ephebe*) fears that the precursor poet has overshadowed him, encroaching upon his territory and thereby negating his creativity. Bloom relies heavily on Sigmund Freud's theory of the **Oedipus complex** to explain the anxiety of the belated poet, who jealously regards the precursor poet as a competitor even as he admires that earlier poet's work. The belated poet, or son, respects and learns from the **patriarchal** precursor poet, or father, but also envies and resents his predecessor's precedence and preeminence. In an effort to preserve a sense of autonomy and individual creativity, the belated poet reads the precursor poet's works "defensively," subverting them through one or more of several processes or, as Bloom would put it, in accordance with one or more of several "revisionary ratios." (The ephebe, for instance, may write a poem that appears to correct or complete a poem by a precursor; he may also write a poem that appears to have influenced an earlier poem by a precursor — a poem that, in fact, influenced his own poem.) Bloom's distortive processes, or revisionary ratios, are modeled on Freudian defense mechanisms. In composing his own works, the belated poet cannot help but incorporate elements of the precursor's work — many of which are themselves distortions of *his* great precursor's work — even as he ardently seeks to establish his originality.

Since Bloom believes that everyone employs revisionary ratios in reading, he also argues that *all* reading can be considered misreading of sorts; any interpretation inevitably involves some misinterpretation. He thus ultimately asserts that no one can understand a "poem-in-itself."

See also **antithetical criticism.**

aphorism (*sententia*): A concise, pointed, **epigrammatic** statement that purports to reveal a truth or principle. Aphorisms can be attributed to a specific person. Once a statement is so generally known that authorship is lost, it is called a *proverb* rather than an aphorism. A statement that gives behavioral advice rather than simply revealing a truth or principle is called a *maxim*.

EXAMPLES: Aphorisms include "A rose by any other name would smell as sweet" (William Shakespeare), "No man is an island unto himself" (John Donne), "No man is a hero to his valet" (La Rochefoucauld), "Beauty is truth, truth beauty" (John Keats), "Death is the mother of beauty" (Wallace Stevens), "Character is like a tree, and reputation is like its shadow. The shadow is what we think of; the tree is the real thing" (Abraham Lincoln), "Mistrust first impulses; they are always good" (Charles Talleyrand), "All you need is love" (the Beatles), and "Life is like a box of chocolates — you never know what you're going to get" (*Forrest Gump*, 1994).

Proverbs include "Still waters run deep," "A rolling stone gathers no moss," "There are many paths to the top of the mountain, but the view is always the same" (Chinese), "A sandal is not a shoe; a cap is not a turban" (Afghan), "The witness of a rat is another rat" (Ethiopian), "It takes a whole village to raise a child" (Yoruba of Nigeria), and "An ember burns where it falls" (Turkish).

"A stitch in time saves nine" is a maxim, as are "The early bird gets the worm" and "The lawyer who represents himself has a fool for a client."

Apocalypse, apocalyptic literature: *Apocalypse* is an alternative name for the book of Revelation, the last book of the New Testament of the Bible, which through complex and detailed **symbolism** depicts a catastrophic end to the world. The term also refers to the violent end of the world and subsequent Day of Judgment prophesied in the book of Revelation and Christian theology more generally.

The term *apocalyptic* stems from the word *Apocalypse,* which is in turn derived from the Greek word *apokaluptein,* meaning "to uncover." Literature is called apocalyptic when it purports to uncover, reveal, or prophesy the future. A number of Christian and Jewish writers produced apocalyptic religious works during the period 200 B.C.–A.D. 150. In general, these works as well as subsequent apocalyptic **texts** involve visions of unbridled doom and destruction—predictions of an imminent, often fiery and terrible end to the world.

Recently, some critics have used *apocalyptic* even more generally to refer to visionary or revelatory literature; thus, William Blake's prophecies (*The Book of Thel* [1789], *The Four Zoas* [c.1800]), John Keats's "Hyperion" poems (1818–19), Percy Bysshe Shelley's *Prometheus Unbound* (1820), and William Butler Yeats's *A Vision* (1925) have all been called apocalyptic. Mary Shelley's novel *The Last Man* (1826), certain stories by Edgar Allan Poe ("Ligea" [1838], "The Fall of the House of Usher" [1839]), James Thomson's poem "The City of Dreadful Night" (1874), and H. G. Wells's *The War of the Worlds* (1898), are also commonly cited as nineteenth-century examples of apocalyptic literature. Twentieth-century apocalyptic novels include Nevil Shute's *On the Beach* (1935) and Walker Percy's *Love in the Ruins* (1971). Mark Waid and Alex Ross's graphic novel *Kingdom Come* (1998) builds to an apocalyptic **climax.** Other recent examples of apocalyptic literature include Tim LaHaye and Jerry B. Jenkins's *Left Behind* series of novels (1995–).

In giving his 1979 retrospective film about the Vietnam War the title *Apocalypse Now,* director Francis Ford Coppola used the term *apocalypse* somewhat loosely, since an *apocalyptic retrospective* is something of a contradiction in terms and, as noted **deconstructor** J. Hillis Miller has pointed out, "apocalypse" is "never now."

apocryphal: See **canon.**

Apollonian: An adjective describing writing that exhibits a serene and orderly quality, derived from Apollo (the Greek god of music and light and the **symbol** of reason and culture). In *The Birth of Tragedy* (1872), Friedrich Nietzsche uses *Apollonian* in conjunction with the term **Dionysian** (signifying impulsiveness and irrationality) to refer to the delicate balance struck by the two sides of Greek **tragedy.** Apollonian writing or qualities are often called **classical,** whereas **romantic** writing draws on the more passionate Dionysian tradition.

See **Dionysian.**

apologue: See **fable.**

aporia: A term borrowed from logic for use in literary criticism, most frequently in **deconstruction,** to indicate an interpretative dilemma or impasse involving some **textual** contradiction that renders — or seems to render — meaning *undecidable.* Deconstructors often speak of the aporic "juncture" or "moment" as the point at which the reader lacks the justification to choose or cannot choose between two meanings.

Aporia can also be used more generally to refer to any indecision or doubt expressed by the speaker of a work, whether actual or voiced with **ironic** intent.

aposiopesis: A **rhetorical figure** involving individual sentences left suggestively incomplete or otherwise involving a dramatic breaking off of **discourse,** often suggesting that a speaker has been rendered speechless by a flood of emotions. In written texts, aposiopesis is usually indicated by ellipses (. . .) or a – (—).

EXAMPLES: A famous speech by Demogorgon in Percy Bysshe Shelley's *Prometheus Unbound* (1820) employs aposiopesis:

> If the abysm
> Could vomit forth its secrets. . . . But a voice
> Is wanting, the deep truth is imageless.

The following line from Thomas Hardy's "The Temporary the All" (1898) also uses aposiopesis: "Thus I . . . but lo, me!"

Novelist Henry James, who employs this device regularly, generally follows each aposiopesis with the same three-word sentence: "She hung fire," a nineteenth-century colloquialism meaning that a person is overcome by strong feelings. Poet T. S. Eliot uses aposiopesis in "The Hollow Men" (1925):

> For Thine is
> Life is
> For Thine is the
>
> *This is the way the world ends*
> *This is the way the world ends*
> *This is the way the world ends*
> *Not with a bang but a whimper.*

Aposiopesis is also used in soap operas, whose characters regularly become overwhelmed with anger or affection, sadness or passion, and say things like "I am so mad at you that I . . . that I could just . . . *Oh!*"

apostrophe: A **figure of speech** in which the speaker directly and often emotionally addresses a person who is dead or otherwise not physically present, an imaginary person or entity, something inhuman, or a place or concept (usually an **abstract** idea or ideal). The speaker addresses the object of the apostrophe as if this object were present and capable of understanding and responding.

Apostrophe is distinguished from the **invocation,** which refers to an explicit request for aid in writing made to some supernatural entity.

EXAMPLES: George Gordon, Lord Byron, apostrophizes the sea in the following line, taken from the fourth **canto** of his long poem, *Childe Harold's Pilgrimage* (1818): "Roll on, thou deep and dark blue ocean, roll!"

Thomas Hardy addresses "Love" in his cynical poem "I Said to Love" (1901):

> I said to Love,
> "It is not now as in old days
> When men adored thee and thy ways

All else above;
Named thee the Boy, the Bright, the One
Who spread a heaven beneath the sun."
  I said to Love.

  I said to him,
"We now know more of thee than then;
We were but weak in judgment when,
    With hearts abrim,
We clamoured thee that thou woulds't please
Inflict on us thy agonies,"
  I said to him.

The sixteenth-century French poet Louise Labé addresses her absent lover in this excerpt from *Les délices et les épreuves du corps* (*The Delights and Trials of the Body*):

Baise m'encor, rebaise-moi et baise:
Donne m'en un de tes plus savoureux,
Donne m'en un de tes plus amoureux:
Je t'en rendrai quatre plus chauds que braise.

[Kiss me again, kiss me once more and kiss:
Give me one of your most savory,
Give me one of your most amorous:
I will give you four that are hotter than embers.]

applied criticism: See **practical criticism.**

appropriation: The tendency of readers to interpret **texts** according to their own cultural presuppositions, regardless of those of the author — and even if the author wrote the work from a different cultural or **ideological** perspective.

approximate rhyme: See **half-rhyme.**

Arcadia: A real, geographical region of Greece that was popularized and idealized in literature first by the Greek poet Theocritus, later by the Roman poet Virgil, who turned it into the ideal **pastoral** environment, a place where singing shepherds and shepherdesses peacefully watch over their flocks. **Renaissance** poets such as Edmund Spenser and Sir Philip Sidney wrote poems with Arcadian **settings** and **themes.** (Sidney entitled his great prose **romance** *Arcadia* [1590], thereby alluding to *L'Arcadia*, an early-sixteenth-century Italian work by Sannazzaro that mixed poetry with prose passages.) Today, the word *Arcadia* still suggests this supposed Golden Age, when the virtues of simplicity and harmony reigned supreme in an unchanged and unchanging land. Tom Stoppard, however, has recently used the word **ironically** as the title of his play *Arcadia* (1993).

archaism: A word, expression, or phrase that has become obsolete. Archaisms are sometimes used intentionally to evoke **images,** sensations, and attitudes associated with the past.

EXAMPLES: "Bloomers" for undergarments, "ice box" for refrigerator, "perpendicular railway" for elevator, "alienist" for psychologist. One can also loosely refer to an attitude as archaic. For example, the idea that a girl should not allow herself to be kissed on a first date could be considered archaic.

archetypal criticism: A type of literary **criticism** that emerged in the 1930s that focuses on those patterns in a particular literary work that commonly recur in other literary works. Archetypal criticism owes its origin chiefly to the work of the analytical psychologist Carl Jung, who argued that humanity has a **collective unconscious** that manifests itself in dreams, **myths,** and literature through **archetypes:** persistent **images, figures,** and **story** patterns shared by people across diverse cultures. Archetypal criticism was also influenced by the studies of a group of Cambridge University anthropologists who found that certain **myths** and rituals recurred in a wide variety of cultures.

Critics taking an archetypal approach to literature seek to identify archetypes within both specific works and literature in general. Some argue that the presence of certain recurrent images, story lines, **character** types, and so forth is ipso facto evidence of their status as memories in the collective unconscious; others refer to persistent elements and patterns in literature (and other forms of **representation**) as archetypes without reference to Jung's theory of the collective unconscious.

Heavily influenced by Maud Bodkins's *Archetypal Patterns in Poetry* (1934), archetypal criticism subsequently developed until the 1950s and 1960s, when it emerged as a dominant critical practice. The influential critic Northrop Frye further explored and refined archetypal criticism in *The Anatomy of Criticism* (1957). Incorporating into archetypal criticism a typological interpretation of the Bible and the visionary poet William Blake's concept of **imagination,** Frye challenged the **conventional** terrain of literary criticism and **theory.** He proposed the existence of four *mythoi* (types of **plots**), which formed the basis of the four major **genres,** each of which has archetypal associations with one of the four seasons: **comedy** (spring), **romance** (summer), **tragedy** (fall), and **satire** (winter). Individual works may, of course, contain other archetypes. Frye viewed the vast corpus of literary works as a "self-contained literary universe," one created by the human imagination to quell fears and fulfill wishes by reducing nature in all its threatening vastness and incomprehensibility to a set of basic, manageable (archetypal) forms.

EXAMPLE: A "Fryed" reading of Alfred, Lord Tennyson's "The Lady of Shalott" (1832) would view it as a tragedy whose overall archetypicality is therefore autumnal but that contains other archetypal images as well; for example, the river, the virgin bower/tower, the unrequited lover, and the **phallic** male.

See also **archetype.**

archetype: Generally, the original model from which something is developed or made; in literary criticism, those **images,** figures, **character** types, **settings,** and **story** patterns that, according to the Swiss analytical psychologist Carl Jung, are universally shared by people across cultures. Archetypes, according to Jung, are embedded deep in humanity's **collective unconscious** and involve "racial memories" of situations, events, and relations that have been part of human experience from the beginning. They not only manifest themselves in the subconscious material of dreams but are also persistently expressed in the more consciously constructed material of **myths** and literature. Jung postulates that when an author recounts a **narrative** based on such unconscious memories, the reader's mind is subconsciously stirred, producing a singularly powerful psychological effect because the memories evoke primordial feelings, concerns, and responses that cannot logically be explained.

Literary critics who follow Jung's theory seek to identify archetypes within both specific works and literature in general. Referred to as **archetypal, Jungian,** or (even more commonly) **myth critics,** they look for and analyze certain recurrent images, character types, and story lines under the assumption that their persistence in literature indicates their presence in the memories of the collective unconscious. Some practitioners of archetypal criticism use the term *archetype* in a more limited fashion to refer to recurrent elements and patterns in literature and other **representational** forms and **discourses,** but without reference to Jung's theory of the collective unconscious. Preeminent among archetypal or myth critics was Northrop Frye, whose interest was in images and **symbols** so prevalent in literature as to provide a common thread through the diverse literary experiences of individuals.

EXAMPLES: The snake is an archetypal image (or figure), as is the trickster. The Flood is an archetypal image persistently expressed in the myths and literatures of most of the world's cultures, even as the Savior is an archetypal personage. Like Easter, the Hindu observance of Mahashivarati celebrates deliverance from death. The day commemorates the sacrifice of the god Shiva, who drank a poison that otherwise would have polluted the oceans and threatened the future of life as we know it.

argument: An introductory prose statement to a long poetic work that summarizes its **plot** or its main meaning.

EXAMPLE: Each of the books of Milton's *Paradise Lost* (1667) is prefaced by an argument.

arsis: In Greek **poetry,** the unstressed syllable in a **foot** of **verse** (as opposed to the **thesis,** or **stressed** syllable). In later Latin usage, however, the terms became reversed, with *arsis* referring to the stressed syllable and *thesis* referring to the unstressed syllable. Modern **prosody** (the study of **versification**) tends to follow the Latin use of the terms. According to this latter (Latin) usage, the arsis of the word *arsis* is the first syllable.

See also **accent.**

art for art's sake: See **Aestheticism, aesthetics.**

aside: A **convention** in **drama** whereby a **character** onstage addresses the audience to reveal some inner thought or feeling that is presumed inaudible to any other characters onstage who might be in earshot. It is as if a character delivering an aside has momentarily stepped outside of the world of the play and into the world of the audience in order to provide it with illuminating information.

EXAMPLE: In William Shakespeare's *As You Like It* (c. 1600), Touchstone, a clown, while being married to "a country wench" named Audrey by Sir Oliver Martext, the bumbling vicar of a country village, is advised by a character named Jaques to "Get to a church, and have a good priest [marry you] that can tell you what marriage is . . .":

> TOUCHSTONE: [Aside] I am not in the mind, but I were better to be married of [Martext] than of another. For he is not like to marry me well, and not being well married, it will be a good excuse for me hereafter to leave my wife.
> JAQUES: Go thou with me, and let me counsel thee.
> TOUCHSTONE: Come, sweet Audrey. We must be married or we live in bawdry.

assonance: The repetition of identical or similar vowel sounds, usually in **stressed** syllables, followed by different consonant sounds in proximate words. Assonance is different from **perfect rhyme** in that rhyming words also repeat the final consonant sounds.

EXAMPLES: *Fate* and *cave* show assonance; *fate* and *late* show perfect rhyme. In the opening stanza of D. H. Lawrence's "Love on the Farm" (1928), *large, dark,* and *are; hands, at,* and *Grasping; those* and *golden; window, in, its,* and *wind; weaves* and *evening;* and the *ing* suffixes are all assonant. Only *light* and *delight* rhyme:

> What large, dark hands are those at the window
> Grasping in the golden light
> Which weaves its way through the evening wind
> At my heart's delight?

See also **consonance, half-rhyme.**

asyndeton: A **rhetorical figure** involving the deliberate omission of conjunctions to create a concise, terse, and often memorable statement.

EXAMPLES: Julius Caesar's famous three-word Latin sentence — first recorded in his history of *The Gallic Wars* (c. 58–50 B.C.) but subsequently repeated in countless translations (for instance, by the **character** Falstaff in Shakespeare's *Henry IV, Part 1* (c. 1597) — "*Veni, Vidi, Vici*" ("I came, I saw, I conquered"). A more recent example of asyndeton is also an instance of **amplification:** "It's a bird, it's a plane, it's *Superman!*"

atmosphere: The general feeling created in the reader or audience by a work at a given point. *Atmosphere* is sometimes used as a synonym for **mood,** although *mood* has also been equated with **tone,** from which *atmosphere* is distinguished. Unlike *atmosphere,* which refers to the feeling experienced by reader or audience, *tone* refers to the attitude of an author toward reader or audience, subject matter, or even himself or herself.

aubade: A **lyric** or song delivered at dawn, generally involving lovers who must part or, occasionally, one lover who asks the other to wake up. The aubade is related to the Provençal *alba,* a lyric form that also involves lovers parting at dawn. The German equivalent of the aubade is the *Tagelied.*

EXAMPLE: William Shakespeare's "Hark, hark, the lark," from *Cymbeline* (c. 1610):

> Hark, hark, the lark at heaven's gate sings,
>   And Phoebus 'gins arise,
> His steeds to water at those springs
>   On chaliced flowers that lies;
> And winking Mary-buds begin
>   To ope their golden eyes;
> With every thing that pretty is,
>   My lady sweet, arise;
>   Arise, arise!

Augustan Age (in English literature): Once commonly used to refer to the literary age of Virgil, Horace, and Ovid (all of whom wrote during the reign of the ancient Roman Emperor Augustus, 27 B.C.–A.D. 14), a term primarily used by twentieth-century scholars to refer to the second of three literary eras within the **Neoclassical Period** in English literature. Writers most commonly associated with the Augustan Age, which is generally said to span the first half of the eighteenth century, include Joseph Addison, Alexander Pope, and Jonathan Swift. These English "Augustans" modelled themselves after their **classical** precursors, emphasizing the importance to society of order, balance, propriety, civility, and **wit.**

See **neoclassicism.**

authorial intention: Defined narrowly, an author's intention in writing a work, as expressed in letters, diaries, interviews, and conversations. Defined more broadly, "intentionality" involves unexpressed motivations, designs, and purposes, some of which may have remained unconscious. The debate over whether critics should try to discern an author's intentions (conscious or otherwise) is an old one.

William K. Wimsatt and Monroe C. Beardsley, early pioneers of **the New Criticism,** coined the term **intentional fallacy** to refer to what they viewed as the wrongheaded practice of basing interpretation on a writer's expressed or implied intentions.

autobiographical criticism: See **personal criticism.**

autobiographics: See **autobiography, feminist criticism.**

autobiography: A **narrative** account typically written by an individual that purports to depict his or her life and character. Unlike diaries and journals, which are kept for the author's private use, autobiographies are written expressly for a public audience. Autobiographies are distinguished from **memoirs** (also produced for public consumption), whose authors render an account of the people and events they have known and experienced without providing the detailed reflection and introspection characteristic of most autobiographies. Some fiction writers draw so heavily on their own experiences that their works, though not autobiographies in the strict sense of the term, are correctly perceived and described as being autobiographical in nature or even as thinly disguised autobiographies.

Recently, some **feminist** literary scholars and critics have argued that traditional **biography** is a **gendered,** "masculinist" **genre,** one whose established **conventions** call for a life-**plot** that turns on action, triumph through **conflict,** intellectual self-discovery, and often public renown. The body, reproduction, children, and intimate interpersonal relationships are generally well in the background and often absent. Arguing that the lived experiences of women and men differ — women's lives, for instance, are often characterized by interruption and deferral — certain feminists have developed a theory of self-**representation** that Leigh Gilmore has termed *autobiographics.*

EXAMPLES: St. Augustine's *Confessions,* written in the fourth century A.D., is the earliest fully developed example of the genre. Benjamin Franklin's *Autobiography* (1790) is a famous Early American example. Trappist monk Thomas Merton's *The Seven Storey Mountain* (1948) is a modern spiritual **classic.** Vocalist and actress Ethel Waters wrote two autobiographies: *His Eye Is on the Sparrow* (1951) and *To Me It's Wonderful* (1972). More contemporary examples of autobiography include poet Maya Angelou's *I Know Why the Caged Bird Sings* (1969), wildlife conservationist Kuki Gallman's *I Dreamed of Africa* (1991), Mel White's *Stranger at the Gate: To Be Gay and Christian in America* (1994), and physicist and intellectual Paul Feyerabend's *Killing Time* (1995).

Not all autobiographies are written directly or entirely by their subjects. Literary commentator and collaborator Digby Diehl has cowritten autobiographies of figures ranging from former CIA agent Duane Clarridge (*A Spy for All Seasons* [1997]) to actress Esther Williams (*The Million Dollar Mermaid* [1999]) to singer Natalie Cole (*Angel on My Shoulder* [2000]). In 1982, Elisabeth Burgos-Debray interviewed Rigoberta Menchú, a 23-year-old Quiché Indian activist from Guatemala, and then transcribed and edited Menchú's oral **narration** of her harrowing life story into a **monologue.** The result is Menchú's autobiography, *Me llamo Rigoberta Menchú y asi me nació la concienca* (*I, Rigoberta Menchú*) (1983).

Terry McMillan's *How Stella Got Her Groove Back* (1996), a novel about a middle-aged woman who meets a much younger man in Jamaica and falls passionately in love, is an example of fiction that is autobiographical in nature.

avant-garde: See **modernism.**

B

ballad: A **poem** that recounts a **story** — generally some dramatic episode — and that has been composed to be sung. Although *traditional ballads* (also called *popular* or *folk ballads*) may address "noble" subjects (for instance, tragic love), they are normally sung by common people and thus employ simple language. The traditional ballad was at its height in sixteenth- and seventeenth-century Britain. Francis J. Child's *English and Scottish Popular Ballads* (1882–98) remains the standard compilation of traditional ballads in English.

Popular or folk ballads are called "traditional" ballads because they are passed down orally from one generation to the next. This oral transmission results in ongoing and continuous modifications to the ballad, which accounts for, among other things, the many variations a ballad is likely to undergo over time and across geographical space. The tradition of oral transmission from generation to generation also results in the fact that a popular or folk ballad is common property, its authorship long forgotten.

Traditional ballads typically exhibit the following features: (1) simple **stanzas,** many of which take the form of the **ballad stanza;** (2) abrupt transitions between stanzas due to weak verses that have been dropped from the ballad at some point; (3) **refrains,** which often include a nonsense line that probably resulted from a mistake or misunderstanding in oral transmission; (4) stock descriptive phrases, often incorporated to make it easier for the singer to remember the words of the ballad; (5) **incremental repetition,** the restatement of a phrase or line with a variation that adds additional information or meaning; (6) **dialogue** used to create **character** and advance the story line; and (7) impersonal language that does not belie the singer's personal feelings or judgments about the ballad's content. Despite the "objectivity" of the singer's language, however, ballads typically veil a great deal of emotion.

Other types of ballads besides the traditional ballad include the *broadside ballad,* the *literary ballad,* and the various contemporary works we currently refer to as ballads. The broadside ballad was a poem about some current event or person that was printed on a broadside (a large sheet of writing material) sold by sixteenth-century English street vendors. A literary ballad is a poem written in deliberate **imitation** of the traditional **folk** ballad. (Nineteenth-century poets such as William Wordsworth, Samuel Taylor Coleridge, and Thomas Hardy wrote literary ballads in an attempt to reground poetry in the language and emotions of common people.) Since the 1960s, *ballad* has been used loosely to refer to **folk songs, lyrics** associated with social protest movements, and slow love songs.

FURTHER EXAMPLES: Well-known traditional ballads include "Bonny Barbara Allen" and "The Demon Lover"; more recent examples include

"Alouette," "Camptown Races," and "Michael, Row the Boat Ashore."
Two of the most well-known literary ballads are Samuel Taylor Coleridge's "The Rime of the Ancient Mariner" (1798) and John Keats's "La
belle dame sans merci" (1820). Arlo Guthrie's "Alice's Restaurant"
(1967) is an example of a late-1960s protest song containing traditional
ballad elements. Several of Bruce Springsteen's songs (such as "Born in the
U.S.A." [1984]) exhibit ballad characteristics, as do John Mellencamp's
"Jack and Diane" (1982) and Billy Joel's "Downeaster Alexa" (1989). The
term *ballad* has been applied more loosely to "slow-dance" love songs such
as the following: The Eagles' "Desperado" (1973), Diana Ross and Lionel
Richie's "Endless Love" (1981), Chris De Burgh's "Lady in Red" (1986),
Whitney Houston's "I Will Always Love You" (1992), Boyz II Men's "I'll
Make Love to You" (1994), Selena's "I Could Fall in Love with You"
(1996), and Celine Dion's "My Heart Will Go On," featured in the movie
Titanic (1997).

ballade: A **verse** form that originated in **medieval** France consisting of
three long **stanzas** (typically eight lines in length) and a concluding four-
line *envoi* (usually addressed to a patron or other important person). The
ballade was especially popular in the fourteenth century; however, its most
famous practitioner was the fifteenth-century poet François Villon. The
nineteenth-century English **Pre-Raphaelite** poet Dante Gabriel Rossetti
loosely translated some of these ballades, his most famous translation
being of Villon's "Ballade des dames du temps jadis" (1489).

ballad stanza: A four-line **stanza** used in the traditional (or popular or
folk) **ballad.** The ballad stanza is usually characterized by an *abcb* **rhyme
scheme**, although the rhyme may be approximate (**half-rhyme**) rather than
perfect rhyme. The first and third lines typically have four **accent**ed syllables while the second and fourth lines have three.
    EXAMPLES: Scottish poet Robert Burns's "Ye Flowery Banks" (1792) is
written in ballad stanzas:

> Ye flowery banks o' bonnie Dunes,
>   How can ye blume sae fair?
> How can ye chant, ye little birds,
>   And I sae fu'° o' care?   *full*

Samuel Taylor Coleridge and William Wordsworth experimented with
ballad forms and traditions in their breakthrough volume, *Lyrical Ballads*
(1798). "The Rime of the Ancient Mariner," by Coleridge, was published
in that volume and is composed mainly of traditional, four-line ballad
stanzas:

> All in a hot and copper sky,
> The bloody Sun, at noon,
> Right up above the mast did stand,
> No bigger than the moon.

Frequently, however, Coleridge modifies the ballad stanza by adding extra lines and rhymes, as he does in his famous description of the sea snakes:

> Within the shadow of the ship
> I watched their rich attire:
> Blue, glossy green, and velvet black,
> They coiled and swam; and every track
> Was a flash of golden fire.

bard: A term originally used to **denote** early Celtic poets who composed poems glorifying warriors and heroes, now sometimes used to refer to William Shakespeare (the Bard), to any individual poet, or to poets (or the poet) in general.

bardic poetry: Declamatory or proclamatory **verse,** often honoring or celebrating a great person, group of people, or place. Walt Whitman is sometimes referred to as a bardic poet; Carl Sandburg's "Chicago" (1916) has been called a bardic poem.

baroque: From the Portuguese *barocco* for "rough pearl," a term originally used by art historians to malign a style in architecture and art that flourished throughout Europe from about 1600 to 1750 (after the **Renaissance** but before the *Rococo* period). The term is now used in a more neutral manner to refer to a style characterized by a certain ornate and elaborate flamboyance that threatens to overshadow Renaissance elements of the work. Baroque works inject more picturesque, unusual, "wild," or even **grotesque** elements into the order and balance of Renaissance **aesthetics** to create formal tension and a kind of counterpoint between disquiet and composure. Energy, movement, and the heavy use of the diagonal are characteristic features. After its original application to art and architecture, *baroque* came to be applied to musical works, such as the preludes and fugues of Johann Sebastian Bach.

As a literary term, *baroque* is less common, but it has been used to refer to a period of seventeenth-century post-Renaissance literature as well as to any writing characterized by a consciously elaborate, ornate, and dramatic style. **Conceits** are generally considered baroque, as is much of the writing of the **metaphysical poets.** Most critics regard the work of poets such as Giambattista Marino, Luis de Góngora, and Richard Crashaw (all of whom wrote elaborate, ornate, even fantastic conceits) as baroque. Some would argue that the most elaborately Latinate, **allusive, imaginative,** and **metaphorical** passages of John Milton's *Paradise Lost* (1667) qualify as examples of baroque literary style.

FURTHER EXAMPLES: Baroque qualities abound in Richard Crashaw's poem "The Weeper" (1646), in which the following lines are addressed by a speaker to Mary Magdalene (who washed Christ's feet with her tears and her hair):

> When some new bright guest
> Takes up among the Stars a Roome,
> And Heav'n will make a feast
> Angells with Chrystall Vyalls come,
> And draw from these full eyes of thine,
> Their master's Water; their owne wine.

base: See **Marxist criticism.**

bathos: Descent into mundane or sentimental language by a writer who is striving for the noble and elevated. Bathos is a stylistic **anticlimax,** the unintended (and therefore ridiculous) result of an unsuccessful attempt to achieve **pathos** or **the sublime.** Alexander Pope gave prominence to the term in an essay entitled "Peri Bathous [On Bathos]: Of the Art of Sinking in Poetry" (1728), in which he mocked much of the poetry of his time.

EXAMPLES: Pope's generally lofty, philosophical poem entitled "An Essay on Man" (1733) itself sinks into bathos in the following lines, each pair of which is also a **closed couplet:**

> The lamb thy riot dooms to bleed today,
> Had he thy reason, would he skip and play?
> Pleased to the last, he crops his flowery food,
> And licks the hand just raised to shed his blood. . . .

More modern examples of bathos may be found in Robert James Waller's novel *The Bridges of Madison County* (1992); in the following passage, an itinerant photographer named Robert Kincaid — visiting Iowa to photograph covered bridges — attempts to corral his errant attraction to Francesca Johnson, a lonely Italian American married to a farmer who has taken his children to a state fair for the weekend:

> The old ways struggling against all that is learned, struggling against the propriety drummed in by centuries of culture, the hard rules of civilized man. He tried to think of something else, photography or the road or covered bridges. Anything but how she looked just now.
>
> But he failed and wondered again how it would feel to touch her skin, to put his belly against hers. The questions eternal, and always the same. The goddamned old ways, fighting toward the surface. He pounded them back, pushed them down, lit a Camel, and breathed deeply.

Also bathetic is the following anonymous poem, entitled "The Handwriting on the Wall." Widely circulated on the Internet as a "forward," it tells of a "weary mother" who, upon being told by her "8-year-old" that his younger brother "T.J." has written in crayon on the wall, begins to "rant and rave" at the younger child "about the expensive wallpaper and how she had saved." Then

> She headed for the den to confirm her fears.
> When she saw the wall, her eyes flooded with tears.

The message she read pierced her soul with a dart.
It said, "I love Mommy," surrounded by a heart.

Well, the wallpaper remained, just as she found it,
With an empty picture frame hung to surround it.
A reminder to her, and indeed to all,
Take time to read the handwriting on the wall.

beast fable: A **story** in which the principal **characters** are animals, the beast fable is commonly characterized as a type of **allegory**.

EXAMPLES: The story of the tortoise and the hare (the moral of which may be summed up: "Slow and steady wins the race"); the story of the little red hen, whose animal friends don't want to help her plant, water, or harvest the grain but who *do* want to help her eat her bread. Geoffrey Chaucer's "The Nun's Priest's Tale," one of the *Canterbury Tales* (c. 1387), is a kind of beast fable warning against the sin of pride. In it, a rooster named Chauntecleer is nearly the victim of a fox who challenges him to prove that he can sing as well as his father. When Chauntecleer stretches his neck to sing, the fox nearly grabs it.

Aesop, Jean de La Fontaine, and Joel Chandler Harris are other well-known beast fabulists.

Beat writers (Beat Generation): A group of American poets and novelists who were active and influential in the late 1950s, Beat writers rejected the prevailing social mores. Feeling oppressed by the dominant culture, they held and publicly advocated anti-intellectual, antipolitical, and, in general, antiestablishment views. *Beat* not only referred to feelings of oppression ("beaten down") but also to a desired, "beatific" state of vision or of ecstasy. Beat writers tended to express their alternative values through the form of their writing, which, compared to more conventional modern works, has a very loose structure and uses a great deal of slang.

Beat Generation (like the term *beatnik*, which refers to a member of that generation) applies to those who came of age just after World War II and who revolted against the dominant political and social culture of that complacent and materialistic era by acting in various ways (riding motorcycles, smoking marijuana) that defied the staid and crew-cut **conventions** of the times. The Beat movement of the 1950s had considerable influence on the 1960s' and 1970s' idea of counterculture. During this later era, the **connotations** of *Beat* expanded to include not only oppression and ecstasy but also the rebellious rhythms of rock 'n' roll (The Beatles).

EXAMPLES: Jack Kerouac's *On the Road* (1957) is the best-known novel produced by a Beat writer. The following lines are taken from "Howl" (1956) by Allen Ginsberg, a Beat poet:

I saw the best minds of my generation destroyed by madness,
    starving hysterical naked,
dragging themselves through the negro streets at dawn looking for
    an angry fix,

angelheaded hipsters burning for the ancient heavenly connection
to the starry dynamo in the machinery of night. . . .

The character played by James Dean in *Rebel Without a Cause* (1955)
typifies the feeling of oppression experienced by the members of the Beat
Generation.

More recently, "poetry slams" — readings and recitations of aggressive
personal poetry on college campuses and in urban coffeehouses and bars —
have signaled a revival of Beat poetry. Henry Rollins, former lead vocalist
for the punk rock band Black Flag, has figured significantly in this revival.

bildungsroman (*Bildungsroman*): A **novel** that recounts the development (psychological and sometimes spiritual) of an individual from childhood to maturity, to the point at which the **protagonist** recognizes his or
her place and role in the world. Also called an *apprenticeship novel* or
novel of formation (after the **etymological** meaning of *bildungsroman*),
such a work is often **autobiographical** but need not be. The **genre** was
heavily influenced by Johann Wolfgang von Goethe's *Wilhelm Meister's
Apprenticeship* (1796), which is also said to be an example of *Erziehungsroman,* the novel of upbringing or education.

Bildungsroman may be used synonymously with *Erziehungsroman,* but
it is properly a more general term, encompassing *Erziehungsroman* as well
as other similar types of novels. A special type of bildungsroman, the ***Künstlerroman*** ("novel of the artist"), explores the artist's development from
childhood to the recognition of his or her artistic potential.

EXAMPLES: Charles Dickens's *Great Expectations* (1861), Somerset
Maugham's *Of Human Bondage* (1915), Zora Neale Hurston's *Their Eyes
Were Watching God* (1937), Ralph Ellison's *Invisible Man* (1947), and
Chaim Potok's *My Name Is Asher Lev* (1972).

binary oppositions: A concept borrowed from **linguistics** by **poststructuralist** theorist Jacques Derrida, a philosopher of language who coined the
term **deconstruction,** to suggest that people in Western culture tend to
think and express their thoughts in terms of contrary pairs. Something is
white but not black, masculine and therefore not feminine, a cause rather
than an effect. Other common and mutually exclusive pairs include begin-
ning/end, conscious/unconscious, and **presence/absence.** Derrida suggests
that these dichotomies are not simply oppositions but also valuative hierarchies, containing one term that Western culture views as positive or superior and another considered negative or inferior, even if only slightly so.

Derrida has deconstructed a number of these binary oppositions, including two — speech/writing and **signifier/signified** — that he believes to be
central to linguistics in particular and Western culture in general. He doesn't
seek to reverse these oppositions, however, because doing so would simply
perpetuate the same forms that he seeks to deconstruct. He instead aims to
erase the boundary between binary oppositions — and to do so in such a
way that the hierarchy implied by the oppositions is thrown into question.

Traditionally, criticism has involved choosing between opposed and contradictory meanings and arguing that literary works support one meaning rather than the other. Derrida and other deconstructors have argued that **texts** contain opposed strands of **discourse,** providing no basis for choosing one reading over another. They may therefore support readings involving *both* reason and passion, life and death, hope and despair.

French **feminist critics** have adapted the ideas of Derrida and other deconstructors in their critique of Western language and culture. They have not only argued that language is structured in accordance with binary oppositions such as male / female, reason / emotion, and active / passive, but that qualities such as reason and activity are associated with masculinity, whereas emotion and passivity are aligned with femininity. Furthermore, they have asserted that (**patriarchal**) Western culture values those qualities associated with masculinity over those associated with femininity; reason, for instance, is valued more highly than emotion. French feminist critics have thus concluded that language is both hierarchically structured and **phallocentric,** or masculine-centered.

biography: A written account of the life of a particular person from birth to death that attempts not only to elucidate the facts about that person's life and actions but also to draw a coherent picture of a self, personality, or character. Biographies should be distinguished from **autobiographies** (in which individuals depict their own lives and natures) and **memoirs** (in which individuals render an account of things, people, and events they have experienced without focusing as directly on themselves).

As a **genre,** biography has changed over the centuries. Ancient Greek and Roman biographers, with some exceptions, were more interested in depicting an individual's character than in chronicling the straightforward facts of his life. Writers of **medieval** biography, which was mainly *hagiography* (the recounting of saints' lives), seem to have been less concerned with detailing the events of a life or even depicting an actual person than with presenting an exemplary model of human piety. Whether it took a saint or a ruler as its subject, medieval biography often relied on **legend** and was intended to make a moral point rather than to represent and examine a human life.

Not surprisingly, the **Renaissance** ushered in a new focus on the individual, and it became far less common for biographers to turn their subjects into illustrations or theses, examples, or exaggerated human types. Seventeenth-century England witnessed not only the birth of the detailed secular biography but also the birth of *biography* as a term. The poet John Dryden, who first used it in 1683, defined *biography* as "the history of particular men's lives."

The complexity and popularity of biography as a literary genre, however, increased most markedly during the eighteenth century in England. Samuel Johnson wrote fifty-two biographical studies, including lives of the poets Milton, Dryden, and Pope. James Boswell made Johnson the subject of his 1791 *Life of Samuel Johnson*, still thought by many to be the greatest biography of all time. By using concrete details and examples to flesh out a character and his ways of thinking and feeling, Boswell helped establish the authenticity of biography. He also helped establish the essential freedom of the biographer to search out and examine anything that might facilitate or deepen the reader's understanding of the subject. This freedom was temporarily curtailed during the subsequent **Victorian Period,** when the view of biography as a revealing and critical endeavor had to contend with the implicit notion that biography should not shake the public's faith in its great men and women. Consequently, the authorized "life and letters" biographies typical of this period cared more for appearances and politesse than for truth.

Biography of all types remains a very popular genre today. Serious modern biographies (not the "kiss-and-tell" or tabloid-style "unauthorized" type, such as those by Kitty Kelley on Frank Sinatra, Jackie Onassis, and Nancy Reagan) are usually grounded in research and are dispassionate in **tone.** Their authors generally accept the proposition that one can present an accurate view of an individual's life and character only after examining the facts with a critical and neutral eye. This is not to say that modern biographies are devoid of interpretive speculation. Some twentieth-century biographers influenced by Freudian (or post-Freudian) **psychoanalytic** theory have attempted to psychoanalyze their subjects and hypothesize about such things as unconscious motivations and inner thoughts.

Celebrated twentieth-century biographies include Catherine Drinker Bowen's *Yankee from Olympus* (1944) (detailing the life of the renowned Supreme Court Justice Oliver Wendell Holmes), Irving Stone's *The Agony and the Ecstasy* (1961) (a biography of Michelangelo), and Fawn Brodie's *Thomas Jefferson, An Intimate History* (1974). Noted twentieth-century literary biographies include Walter Jackson Bate's *John Keats* (1979), Shari Benstock's *No Gifts from Chance* (1994) (a biography of Edith Wharton), and Carlos Baker's *Emerson Among the Eccentrics* (1996). Elisabeth Roudinesco's *Jacques Lacan: Esquisse d'une vie, histoire d'une système de pensée* (*Jacques Lacan: Outline of a Life, History of a System of Thought*) (1993) details the life and thought of Jacques Lacan, a French psychoanalytic theorist who has profoundly influenced contemporary literary criticism.

Recent, best-selling biographies of political figures include David McCullough's *Truman* (1992) and *John Adams* (2001), Doris Kearns Goodwin's *No Ordinary Time* (1994) (a biography of Franklin and Eleanor Roosevelt), and Anthony Sampson's *Mandela: The Authorized Biography* (2000). Other noted contemporary biographies include Matthew Stephens's *Hannah Snell: The Secret Life of a Female Marine, 1723–1792* (1997) (Snell was also the subject of a highly popular biography titled *The Female Soldier, or the Surprising Life of and Adventures of Hannah Snell,* published two-and-a-half centuries earlier, in 1750, by Robert Walker), Sylvia Nasar's *A Beautiful Mind* (1998) (a biography of schizophrenic mathematician and Nobel Laureate John Forbes Nash, made into an Oscar-winning film in 2001), and Dava Sobel's *Galileo's Daughter* (1999).

black humor: A dark, disturbing, and often morbid or **grotesque** mode of **comedy** found in certain modern **texts,** especially **antinovels** and **Absurdist** works. Such humor often concerns death, suffering, or other anxiety-inducing subjects. Black humor usually goes hand in hand with a pessimistic worldview or **tone;** it manages to express a sense of hopelessness in a wry, sardonic way that is grimly humorous.

EXAMPLES: Joseph Heller's *Catch-22* (1961), Thomas Pynchon's *V* (1963), and John Kennedy Toole's novel *A Confederacy of Dunces* (1980) contain a great deal of black humor. *Little Shop of Horrors*, originally a Roger Corman film that was made into a long-running musical and then remade as a movie (1986), contains many instances of black humor. Other contemporary films utilizing black humor include *Eating Raoul* (1982) and *Fargo* (1996). The writer and illustrator Edward Gorey consistently incorporates black humor into children's books; in *The Gashlycrumb Tinies* (1962), Gorey presents each letter of the alphabet via the name of a child who met an untimely death: "A is for Amy, who fell down the stairs. B is for Basil, assaulted by bears. . . ."

blanks: See **gaps.**

blank verse: Broadly defined, any unrhymed **verse** but usually referring to unrhymed **iambic pentameter.** Most critics agree that blank verse, as it is commonly defined, first appeared in English when the Earl of Surrey used it in his translation (c. 1540) of books 2 and 4 of Virgil's *The Aeneid*. It appeared for the first time in drama in Thomas Sackville and Thomas Norton's *Gorboduc* (originally performed in 1561). Over the centuries, blank verse has become the most common English verse form, especially for extended poems, as it is considered the closest form to natural patterns of English speech. Christopher Marlowe, William Shakespeare, and especially John Milton (particularly in his **epic** *Paradise Lost* [1667]) are generally credited with establishing blank verse as the preferred English verse form.

FURTHER EXAMPLES: The following passage is from Elizabeth Barrett Browning's "verse novel" *Aurora Leigh* (1857), an extended poem of some eleven thousand lines:

> . . . But poets should
> Exert a double vision; should have eyes
> To see near things as comprehensively
> As if afar they took their point of sight,
> And distant things as intimately deep
> As if they touched them. Let us strive for this.
> I do distrust the poet who discerns
> No character or glory in his times. . . .

The opening lines of Robert Frost's poem "Birches" (1916) are written in blank verse:

> When I see birches bend to left and right
> Across the lines of straighter darker trees,
> I like to think some boy's been swinging them.
> But swinging doesn't bend them down to stay
> As ice-storms do. . . .

blues: A term initially used to refer to slow, melancholy **lyrics** composed and sung by black slaves in the American South. Directly descended from what African American poet Imamu Amiri Baraka (LeRoi Jones) has called the "shouts and hollers" of "Negro . . . work songs" that originated in West Africa, early blues songs were typically sung a cappella in a minor key and were composed of short three-line **stanzas,** frequently repeated, in which the first and second lines were identical. Subsequently, blues recounted the struggles of emancipated former slaves living in a primarily white American culture and therefore continued to express feelings of despair, hopelessness, grief, and oppression. Blues lyrics, which are a branch of **folk** literature, usually deal with **themes** of nature, dying, and loss of love and should not be confused with the more uplifting songs known as Negro spirituals. The following is an example of an early blues stanza:

> Gwine lay my head right on de railroad track,
> Gwine lay my head right on de railroad track,
> 'Cause my baby, she won't take me back.

The blues gradually evolved to become a form of entertainment, one that continued to advance an intensely personal account of the African American experience but that changed considerably in style with the addition of musical accompaniment and the infusion of developing elements of popular American music. Singers included Ida Cox (1896–1967), Sara Martin (1884–1955), Bessie Smith (1894–1937), and Gertrude "Ma" Rainey (1886–1939), who pioneered what is sometimes referred to as "classic blues." The following excerpt from the song "Put It Right Here or Keep It Out There" (1923) is an example of a **classic** blues song written by Porter Grainger and sung by Bessie Smith:

> I've had a man for fifteen years, give him his room and board;
> Once he was like a Cadillac, now he's like an old, worn-out Ford;
> He never brought me a lousy dime and put it in my hand;
> So there'll be some changes from now on, according to my plan:
> He's got to get it, bring it, and put it right here,
> Or else he's goin' to keep it out there;
> If he must steal it, beg it, or borrow it somewhere,
> Long as he gets it, I don't care. . . .

During the **Harlem Renaissance,** a literary and cultural movement that began in the 1920s, novelists, poets, musicians, and dance bands began to celebrate and improvise this form of artistic expression. Over time, the term *blues* came to refer not just to lyrics or songs recounting the African American experience but also to works by other American authors and musicians exploring the trials and tribulations of growing up outside the confines of established American culture.

FURTHER EXAMPLES: Works by Harlem Renaissance novelists such as Jean Toomer (*Cane* [1923]) and George Schuyler (*Black No More* [1930]), as well as the poetry, fiction, and drama of Langston Hughes. Jazz dance bands and orchestras inspired by the movement included those of Duke Ellington, Chick Webb, Luis Russell, and Louis Armstrong.

Examples of contemporary blues literature include Toni Morrison's novels *Song of Solomon* (1977) and *Jazz* (1992), as well as Sheldon Epps's dramatic musical revue *Blues in the Night* (1982). The Robert Cray Band's albums *Bad Influence* (1983) and *False Accusations* (1985) are viewed as inheriting a black blues tradition that has, more recently, spilled over into other **racial** and ethnic tributaries. Notable examples of the blues most widely defined include "Reservation Blues" (1995) by Jim Boyd (a Colville Confederate Tribe member) in collaboration with Sherman Alexie (a Spokane Indian) as well as white blues guitarist Stevie Ray Vaughan's posthumous album *Blues at Sunrise* (2000).

bombast: Inflated, extravagant, often ranting language, particularly common in **Elizabethan** literary works and political speeches.

EXAMPLE: These lines from Christopher Marlowe's *Tamburlaine the Great* (1587), spoken by Tamburlaine himself:

> The host of Xerxes, which by fame is said
> To drink the mighty Parthian Araris,
> Was but a handful to that we will have.
> Our quivering lances, shaking in the air,
> And bullets, like Jove's dreadful thunderbolts,
> Enroll'd in flames and fiery smoldering mists,
> Shall threat the gods more than Cyclopian wars;
> And, with our sun-bright armor as we march,
> We'll chase the stars from Heaven and dim their eyes
> That stand and muse at our admired arms.

A more recent example of bombast, rife with absurdly **mixed metaphors,** can be found in an 1870 Nebraska newspaper editorial discussing legislative turmoil: "The apple of discord is now fairly in our midst, and if not nipped in the bud it will burst forth in a conflagration which will deluge society in an earthquake of bloody apprehension."

Breton lay: See *lai.*

bucolic (poetry): From the Greek for "cowherd," a term that has traditionally been used to refer to **pastoral** writings. Bucolic poetry typically concerns itself with the pastoral subjects of shepherds and their country ways and values. The plural (*bucolics*) was originally used to refer to the entire corpus of traditional pastoral works by writers such as Theocritus and Virgil. Today, *bucolic* and *bucolics* are used more loosely to refer to works with rural or rustic **settings** or **styles.**

burlesque: A type of **comedy** in which distortion and exaggeration are employed to evoke ridicule, either through the trivialization of some lofty subject or through the glorification of a lowly or commonplace one. Humor thus results from the disparity between subject and **style.** Some critics distinguish between *high* and *low* burlesque, the former referring to works with an inappropriately heightened style for an inconsequential subject and the latter to works in which a lofty subject is degraded by an inappropriately base style.

Burlesque works may be written purely to entertain, but writers more commonly employ burlesque as an instrument of **satire.** Since burlesque frequently imitates another work or some aspect of that work in a mocking way, it is often used to deride specific (and often identifiable) works or their authors, certain subject matters, or even entire **genres.**

Burlesque is sometimes confused with **parody** and **travesty.** The three terms are not synonymous, although varying critical usage of these terms has contributed to the confusion surrounding them. Burlesque is generally thought to encompass both parody and travesty; in this view, parody is a type of high burlesque (as are the **mock epic** and **mock heroic**) and travesty a type of low burlesque.

Recently, the term *burlesque* has been extended to refer to a variety of popular stage entertainments ranging from vaudeville shows to stripteases to boisterous skits and songs.

EXAMPLES: Miguel de Cervantes's *Don Quixote* (1605, 1614) is an example of high burlesque; Monty Python's *Life of Brian* (1979), which makes a travesty of the New Testament story of Jesus, is an example of low burlesque.

See also **parody, travesty.**

C

cacophony: A mixture of harsh, unpleasant, or discordant sounds. Although this term is usually applied to poetry, it can refer to any type of writing and can be either unintentional or purposely used for artistic effect. Cacophony is the opposite of **euphony.**

EXAMPLES: In his long poem *The Bridge* (1930), Hart Crane writes cacophonously to convey the chaotic energy, the sinister unworldliness, of the modern industrial world:

> The nasal whine of power whips a new universe . . .
> Where spouting pillars spoor the evening sky,
> Under the looming stacks of the gigantic power house
> Stars prick the eyes with sharp ammoniac proverbs,
> New verities, new inklings in the velvet hummed
> Of dynamos, where hearing's leash is strummed . . .
> Power's script, — wound, bobbin-bound, refined —
> Is stopped to the slap of belts on booming spools, spurred
> Into the bulging bouillon, harnessed jelly of the stars.

Contemporary pop culture examples of cacophony may be found in Lou Reed's grinding *Metal Machine Music* (1975), in music associated with the industrial rock movement, and in many songs recorded by the rock group Nine Inch Nails.

See also **dissonance.**

caesura (cesura): A pause in a line of **poetry.** The caesura is dictated not by **meter** but by natural speaking **rhythm.** Sometimes it coincides with the poet's punctuation, but occasionally it occurs where some pause in speech is inevitable. In **scansion,** the caesura is indicated by the symbol ‖.

EXAMPLE: In the following lines from William Butler Yeats's "The Lake Isle of Innisfree" (1893), the caesura in the first line coincides with Yeats's punctuation, whereas the second is indicated solely by natural rhythms of speech:

> I will arise and go now, ‖ for always night and day
> I hear lake water lapping ‖ with low sounds by the shore. . . .

canon: A term used since the fourth century to refer to those books of the Bible that the Christian church accepts as being Holy Scripture — that is, divinely inspired. Books outside the canon (noncanonical books) are referred to as *apocryphal. Canon* has also been used to refer to the *Saint's Canon,* the group of people officially recognized by the Catholic Church as saints. More recently, it has been employed to refer to the body of works generally attributed by scholars to a particular author (for example, the Shakespearean canon is currently believed to consist of thirty-seven plays that scholars feel can be definitively attributed to him). Works sometimes attributed to an author, but whose authorship is disputed or otherwise uncertain, are called apocryphal. *Canon* may also refer more generally to those literary works that are **privileged,** or given special status, by a culture. Works we tend to think of as **classics** or as "Great Books" — **texts** that are repeatedly reprinted in anthologies of literature — may be said to constitute the canon.

Contemporary **Marxist, feminist,** minority, and **postcolonial** critics have argued that, for political reasons, many excellent works never enter the canon. Canonized works, they claim, are those that reflect — and respect — the culture's dominant **ideology** or perform some socially acceptable or even necessary form of "cultural work." Attempts have been made to broaden or redefine the canon by discovering valuable texts, or versions of texts, that were repressed or ignored for political reasons. These have been published both in traditional and in nontraditional anthologies. The most outspoken critics of the canon, especially certain critics practicing **cultural criticism,** have called into question the whole concept of canon or "canonicity." These critics, who do not privilege any form of expression, treat cartoons, comics, and soap operas with the same cogency and respect they accord novels, poems, and plays.

canto: A division of a long **poem.**
EXAMPLES: Dante Alighieri's *The Divine Comedy* (1321), Edmund Spenser's *The Faerie Queene* (1590, 1596), and George Gordon, Lord Byron's *Childe Harold's Pilgrimage* (1812–18) are divided into cantos.

caricature: From the Italian for "to load," an exaggeration or other distortion of an individual's prominent features or characteristics to the point of making that individual appear ridiculous. Caricatures exaggerate distinctive or idiosyncratic characteristics, such as a large nose or a habit of apologizing frequently. The term *caricature* is applied more often to graphic representations than to literary ones, where the term **burlesque** (or sometimes **satire** or **parody**) is usually used.
EXAMPLES: Garry Trudeau has caricatured many political figures in his comic strip *Doonesbury*. He represented former vice president Dan Quayle as a feather and former president George H. W. Bush as being invisible, for instance.

The **Victorian** novelist Charles Dickens is famous for depicting characters with features so pronounced or even extreme as to border on caricature. An example would be Fagin in *Oliver Twist* (1837), "whose villanous-looking and repulsive face was obscured by a quantity of matted red hair." The following passage from Anthony Trollope's novel *The Warden* (1855) describes a fictitious novel (*The Almshouse*) by a fictitious author (Mr. Popular Sentiment), parodying Dickens's tendency to create caricatures rather than three-dimensional **characters:**

The demon of *The Almshouse* was the clerical owner of this comfortable abode. He was a man well stricken in years but still strong to do evil; he was one who looked cruelly out of a hot, passionate, bloodshot eye, who had a huge red nose with a carbuncle, thick lips, and a great double flabby chin which swelled out into solid substance, like a turkey cock's comb, when sudden anger inspired him; he had a hot, furrowed, low brow from which a few grizzled hairs were not yet rubbed off by the friction of his handkerchief; he wore a loose unstarched white handkerchief, black loose ill-made clothes, and huge loose shoes adapted to many corns and various bunions; his husky voice told tales of much daily port wine, and his language was not so decorous as became a clergyman.

carnival: In popular parlance, a festival or a traveling amusement show (with rides, clowns, games, etc.). More specifically, the term also refers to the extravagant (perhaps even excessive) celebrations held in the Christian world before Lent (Mardi Gras, the "Fat Tuesday" that precedes Ash Wednesday, when Lent begins). As a literary term, however, *carnival* is associated with Soviet critic Mikhail Bakhtin and with **dialogic criticism,** a method of literary criticism based on Bakhtin's theories.

In the book *Rabelais and His World* (1940), Bakhtin used the term *carnival* to refer not only to such festivities as Mardi Gras — celebrations during which commoners (and the more privileged classes) were temporarily free to transgress all kinds of written and unwritten social and ecclesiastical laws — but also to "low" or popular culture, such as fairs and spontaneous **folk dramas** (including puppet shows).

The **discourse** of carnival, as Bakhtin understood it, is infused by the down-to-earth priorities and values held by the underprivileged or plebeian "second world" of commoners, or **folk.** Because that world was necessarily concerned with basic issues of survival, with the sustenance and reproduction of life, the language of carnival is substantially concerned with the body, with eating, with sex, and with death, its **images** infused with an "obvious sensuous character" and a "strong element of play." In carnivalesque discourse, as well as in actual practice, matters of the body are treated with a kind of profound humor — neither simply funny as we might say about a situation comedy, nor serious as we expect a high drama to be, but something in between. This doubleness produces an ambivalent or **grotesque** quality to carnivalesque discourse that allows it to contrast starkly with the official discourse, the language of power and propriety. As Bakhtin wrote, "carnival celebrated temporary liberation from the prevailing truth and from the established order; it marked the suspension of all hierarchical rank, privileges, norms, and prohibitions. Carnival was the true feast of time, the feast of becoming, change, and renewal. It was hostile to all that was immortalized and completed."

Dialogic critics have followed and expanded upon Bakhtin's concept of carnival. Michael Bristol, for instance, has argued that the scene in which

William Shakespeare's famous gravedigger reminisces about a fool named Yorick (whose skull he has plucked from the site of Ophelia's grave) is a carnivalesque moment in *Hamlet* (1602), a play whose official discourse concerns the usurpation of power and its tragic consequences. Bristol also suggests that King Claudius functions as a carnivalesque Lord of Misrule in *Hamlet* and gives as an example Claudius's statement that he has "taken to wife" his murdered brother's wife, the Queen, "with mirth in funeral, and with dirge in marriage."

Caroline Age (in English literature): An age spanning the reign of Charles I (1625–49) and often classified as the fourth of five literary eras within the **Renaissance Period** in English literature. The Caroline Age derives its name from *Carolus* (the Latin source of the name Charles) and succeeds the **Jacobean Age,** named for James I (*Jacobus* is the Latin source of the name James). Some Caroline authors, for example Robert Burton, author of *Anatomy of Melancholy* (1621–51), began to write during the preceding Jacobean Age, and others, such as John Milton, did their greatest work in later eras — namely, the **Commonwealth Age** (sometimes called the **Puritan Interregnum**) and the **Restoration Age.** Writers whose careers are most closely associated with the Caroline Age include the great Renaissance prose writer Sir Thomas Browne and the so-called **Cavalier poets:** Thomas Carew, Robert Herrick, Richard Lovelace, and Sir John Suckling. The use of the word *Cavalier* to describe these poets and their **courtly love lyrics** refers to the loyalty of these poets to the cause of the Cavaliers, who supported Charles I against his Puritan, parliamentary opposition (the Roundheads) when civil war broke out. In their famous **satirical** history of England entitled *1066 and All That* (1931), Walter Carruthers Sellar and Robert Julian Yeatman described this war as the "utterly memorable Struggle between the Cavaliers (Wrong but Romantic) and the Roundheads (Right but Repulsive)."

See also **Renaissance.**

carpe diem: Latin for "seize the day," a phrase referring to the age-old literary **theme** (particularly prevalent in **lyric** poetry) that we should enjoy the moment before it is gone, before youth passes away.

EXAMPLES: *Carpe diem* is the theme of the movie *Dead Poets Society* (1989). The schoolmaster urges his students to "seize the day" — to live for the moment and for themselves, enjoying life. Robert Herrick's "To the Virgins, to Make Much of Time" (1648) ("Gather ye rosebuds while ye may / Old Time is still a-flying . . .") is a more classic example, as is sixteenth-century French poet Pierre de Ronsard's **ode** to Cassandre (c. 1552), the last **stanza** of which follows:

> Donc, si vous me croyez, mignonne,
> Tandis que votre âge fleuronne
> En sa plus verte nouveauté,

Cueillez, cueillez votre jeunesse:
Comme à cette fleur la vieillesse
Fera ternir votre beauté.

[So, if you believe me, darling,
While your age is blossoming
In its green freshness,
Gather, gather your youth
While it flowers, for old age
Will tarnish your beauty.]

catachresis: From the Greek for "misuse," a term referring to the incorrect or strained use of a word. Catachresis often involves a mixed or "illogical" **metaphor.** The phrase *tooth of a comb* is a strict example of catachresis since combs do not really have teeth. The meaning of the word *dry* is strained when we refer to a town in which liquor cannot be purchased as "dry." A classic literary example, involving a mixed and illogical metaphor, occurs in John Milton's "Lycidas" (1638):

Blind mouths! that scarce themselves know how to hold
A sheep-hook. . . .

catalexis (truncation): Omission of one or two un**stressed** syllables in the last **foot** of a line of **verse.**

EXAMPLE: The **trochaic octameter** lines of Edgar Allan Poe's "The Raven" (1849) are sometimes lacking the last un**accented** syllable, as in the second line below:

While Ĭ nóddĕd, néarlў náppĭng, súddĕnlў thĕre cáme ă táppĭng,
Ás ŏf sóme ŏne géntlў ráppĭng, ráppĭng ăt mў chámbĕr dóor —
Ónlў thĭs ănd nóthĭng móre.

See also **feminine ending.**

catastrophe: The culmination of a play's **falling action,** which in turn follows the **climax** or the **crisis** of a drama. Catastrophe is one of five structural elements associated with **Freytag's Pyramid,** a model developed by Gustav Freytag for analyzing five-act plays and **tragedies** in particular. The term *catastrophe* may be applied to the concluding action of any play but is usually reserved for tragedies. (The term ***dénouement*** is typically used for nontragic dramas; the culmination of a novelistic **plot** is generally referred to as its **resolution.**) The catastrophe often involves the death of the **hero,** but some other tragic outcome may occur instead.

EXAMPLE: In William Shakespeare's tragedy *Macbeth* (1606), the catastrophe occurs in the penultimate scene in which Macbeth dies during a sword fight with Macduff.

See also **Freytag's Pyramid.**

catharsis (katharsis): The emotional effect a **tragic drama** has on its audience. Aristotle introduced this term (which can mean either "purgation" or "purification" in Greek) into literary criticism in *The Poetics* (c. 330 B.C.). He sought to explain the feelings of exaltation or relief (rather than despondency) that playgoers commonly experience during and after the **catastrophe** (which invariably **foregrounds** suffering, defeat, and even death). Aristotle argued that while viewing such a work, the audience experiences a purging or cleansing of emotions (specifically fear and pity), which in turn produces the resulting, beneficial sensation of relief or exaltation. The final line of John Milton's long poem *Samson Agonistes* (1671) provides a fine, poetic description of the carthartic state: "Calm of mind, all passions spent."

Since Aristotle's comments regarding catharsis are **ambiguous** (in part due to the multiple significations of the word in Greek and the brevity of his remarks), two schools of thought exist regarding the nature of catharsis and, more specifically, how it is effected. Some argue that emotions are purged or cleansed though a vicarious identification by the audience with the tragic **hero** and his or her downfall. (A few critics who maintain this line of argument have gone so far as to suggest that viewers learn to avoid the actions that produce the pity and fear they feel; they "learn by example," one might say.) Others claim that viewers (or readers) are so caught up in emotions of fear and pity for the hero that they forget their own problems and emotional conflicts. Presumably, the expenditure of emotion on the hero engenders the beneficial feelings associated with the cathartic experience.

Cavalier poets: Lyricists associated with the reign of Charles I of England (1625–49). The term *Cavalier* refers to supporters of the king against Parliament. Cavalier courtiers wrote graceful, polished, **witty,** even brazen **lyrics** exalting love, women, and gallant actions. These poets are also sometimes called **Caroline** poets (*Caroline* is an adjective derived from the Latin for Charles) or Sons of Ben (because they were influenced by the dedicated and polished poetic style of their predecessor Ben Jonson).

EXAMPLES: Thomas Carew, Richard Lovelace, and Sir John Suckling are well-known Cavalier lyricists. Even though he was a country parson rather than an urbane courtier, Robert Herrick is also frequently classed with the Cavalier poets because many of his lyrics treat **themes** of love and gallantry in the Cavalier manner.

Celtic Renaissance (Irish Literary Renaissance, Irish Revival, or Celtic Revival): A movement of the late nineteenth and early twentieth centuries intended to promulgate an indigenous Celtic, especially Irish, cultural tradition and history to counter centuries of English domination. Writers of the Celtic Renaissance sought to construct an independent and nationalistic Irish literature based on Irish traditions, **themes,** and subject matter, such as those preserved in Celtic **legend.** The Celtic Renaissance paralleled a movement to preserve and promote the use of Gaelic, the Irish language. Although many of those who helped bring about the Celtic Renaissance approved of and encouraged the Gaelic revival, they nonetheless wrote about Irish subject matter in English.

Leaders of the Celtic Renaissance included writers such as William Butler Yeats, Lady Gregory, A. E. (George W. Russell), J. M. Synge, and Sean O'Casey. Even James Joyce, who sometimes ridiculed nationalistic excesses, is viewed as a writer of the Irish Renaissance, because his English-language writings are devoted to Irish subjects and themes. The impetus for the movement is generally traced back to Standish O'Grady's *History of Ireland: Heroic Period* (1878).

One of the goals of the Celtic Renaissance was to establish Irish institutions to rival those of England. The Irish Literary Theatre, the Abbey Theatre (home of the Irish National Theatre Society), and literary societies such as the Irish National Literary Society were founded during this period.

EXAMPLE: *The Playboy of the Western World* (1907), by J. M. Synge, who is generally considered the most talented playwright associated with the Celtic Renaissance movement.

center (decenter): An idea, event, or image that, once identified or posited, gives apparent structure to a **text** — be it a relatively short utterance, a literary work, or an entire social **discourse** — thereby limiting its possible meaning or meanings. For example, the creation of Eve from Adam's rib has served as a "centering" idea, event, and image in Western culture. Jacques Derrida, the theorist most closely associated with **deconstruction,** relates the term *center* to beliefs regarding beginnings and endings, by which he means the origins and purposes assumed to govern the components of a text.

Practitioners of deconstruction (as well as many **new historicists** and other **poststructuralist** critics) aim to *decenter* the text, that is, to undermine the defining character of the text's presumed center and its concomitant structure. By drawing attention to the divergent meanings that arise from the diverse associations and **connotations** of **signifiers** within the text, they challenge the assumption that its "meaning" is either determinate or determinable.

Similarly, poststructuralist **psychoanalytic critics** have deconstructed the subject, or self, suggesting that — not unlike the text as understood by deconstructors — it is without the defining center and structure typically posited by traditional theories regarding personality and character. Psychoanalytic theorist Jacques Lacan contends that the concepts of the subject, self, **ego,** and "I" are merely constructs, fictions of coherence that hide the inconsistency, contradictoriness, and indeterminacy of being.

cesura: See **caesura.**

character, the character, characterization: In its most general literary sense, a character is a figure in a literary work. That figure need not be human, although most characters are. Characters may be nonhuman animals or even nonliving entities, provided that the author characterizes them by giving them the attributes of a human individual. *Character* also carries the nonliterary **connotation** of personality and even of morality (or lack thereof) — hence, we speak of persons of good, bad, and "shady" character.

Occasionally literary critics use the phrase *the character* in a highly specialized way to refer to a literary **genre** that developed in seventeenth- and eighteenth-century England and France. The character, based on the late-fourth- and early-third-century B.C. Greek philosopher Theophrastus' *Characters,* is a genre in which a character *type*, rather than a truly individual character, is sketched in a brief work written in prose or verse. The particular virtue or vice of the character type being described (such as the braggart soldier or the pedant) is briefly delineated. Modern versions of the character are generally called *character sketches.*

The term *characterization* refers to the various means by which an author describes and develops the characters in a literary work. In discussing depth and complexity of characterization, E. M. Forster makes a distinction between **flat and round characters** that is still in use today. He argues that flat characters are types or **caricatures** defined by a single idea or quality, whereas round characters have the three-dimensional complexity of real people. Characters may also be divided into *static* and *dynamic* characters. Static characters do not change significantly over the course of a work no matter what action takes place, whereas dynamic characters change (whether for better or worse) in response to circumstance and experience.

Characterization is inextricably intertwined with **plot.** In order for a work to be believable, the reader must find the characters convincing; in order to find the characters convincing, the reader must be able to visualize them. Authors must therefore make their characters "come alive" by describing not only such things as physical attributes, actions, conversations, and their effect on other characters but also such things as thoughts and emotions. The author may employ direct characterization, explicitly presenting or commenting on the characters, or indirect characterization, setting forth characters through representations of their actions, statements, thoughts, and feelings. In the first case, the author is *telling* the reader about the character; in the second case, the author is *showing* the reader what the character is like. In order to make their plots believable and cause readers to identify with (or oppose) the characters in their works, authors must describe their characters convincingly and provide compelling **motivation** for their actions and beliefs.

chiasmus: A **rhetorical figure** in which certain words, sounds, concepts, or **syntactic** structures are reversed or repeated in reverse order. The term *chiasmus* is derived from the x-shaped Greek letter *chi;* the implication is that the two parts of a chiastic whole mirror each other as do the parts of the letter *x*.

EXAMPLES: William Shakespeare's *Macbeth* (1606) contains the obviously chiastic line, "Fair is foul and foul is fair." James Joyce used chiasmus in "The Dead" (1907) when he wrote, "His soul swooned slowly as he heard the snow falling faintly through the universe and faintly falling. . . ." ("Falling faintly" and "faintly falling" mirror reach other in a perfect chiastic design.)

Not all chiasmus is this precise, however. Samuel Taylor Coleridge, for example, wrote that "Flowers are lovely, love is flowerlike." His famous poem "Kubla Khan" (1816) begins with what some would call a *sonic* chiasmus (chiasmus effected by sound): "In Xanadu did Kubla Khan . . ." The opera *Narcissus* (1888), by Samuel Butler and Henry Festing Jones, contains some examples of chiasmus strictly defined ("For life is death, and death is life"), but other passages are merely chiastic in nature ("He that is born begins to die, / And he that dies to live"). President John F. Kennedy's speeches were often chiastic; two of his most famous statements — "Ask not what your country can do for you; ask what you can do for your country" and "Let us never negotiate out of fear but let us never fear to negotiate" — both display chiastic structure.

Chiastic structure may also create or heighten **paradox.** The **protagonist** in Carrie Fisher's *Postcards from the Edge* (1987) tells her diary that "I was into pain reduction and mind expansion, but what I've ended up with is pain expansion and mind reduction. Everything hurts now, and nothing makes sense." Likewise, in Amy Tan's novel *The Joy Luck Club* (1989), a **character** named Lena gorges herself to the point of sickness on strawberry ice cream and wonders "why it [is] that eating something good could make me feel so terrible, while vomiting something terrible could make me feel so good."

A pattern of syntactic reversal such as the following also constitutes a kind of chiasmus: "Into the rain ran the cat; the dog followed into the darkness." In this sentence, the syntactic pattern is prepositional phrase, verb, subject, subject, verb, prepositional phrase. Alexander Pope used this type of chiasmus in his "An Essay on Criticism" (1711), a long poem in which he stated that art "works without show and without pomp presides." Here the syntactic pattern of the quoted line is verb ("works"), prepositional phrase ("without show"), prepositional phrase ("without pomp"), and verb ("presides").

Chicago School: Originally a group of literary critics associated with the University of Chicago; other critics who have followed in their footsteps have also been referred to as Chicago School critics or, more simply, as Chicago Critics. In 1952, the original group of Chicago Critics collectively published a landmark book entitled *Critics and Criticism,* which outlined their thinking about both **practical criticism** (a type of literary criticism) and the general history of **criticism.**

Chicago School critics typically examine works on an individual basis (as do practical critics and **objective critics**). They view the **text** in terms of its **form,** or shaping principle, and the way in which that form is articulated in the work's **structure.** They also, however, consider the relationship between individual works and broadly defined categories of works, or **genres.** Because they combine a historical interest in schools of criticism and literary genres with a practical or objective focus on the internal structure and relations of elements within individual works, the Chicago School critics are sometimes said to be *Neo-Aristotelian* critics. The approach of the Chicago critics has also been called **formalist** insofar as it involves analyzing works on an individual basis; it is important to note, however, that the Chicago critics' interest in historical matters is decidedly not formalist. Influential Chicago critics include such figures as R. S. Crane, Elder Olson, and Wayne Booth.

chivalric romance: See **medieval romance.**

choriambus: See **foot.**

chorus: In Greek **drama,** a group of people who sang and danced, commenting on the action of the **play.** A chorus was also used to chant **odes.** The chorus has its origins in an ancient Greek religious event and was later used in Greek **tragedies** and Roman plays. The use of such choruses generally declined with the continuing development of the drama. By **Elizabethan** times, the chorus, when used, often comprised a single **character** delivering a **prologue** and **epilogue** and occasionally making other explanatory remarks, such as act-by-act introductions and notes on offstage happenings. Modern critics have adopted the term *choral character* or *chorus character* to refer to a character in a work who comments on characters and events, thereby providing the audience with an additional perspective. Although choral characters are occasionally used today, few modern or contemporary plays use actual choruses.

Chorus is, of course, a musical as well as a literary term. As a musical term, *chorus* has two meanings. It can refer to a group of singers who sing pieces composed in at least four parts (soprano, alto, tenor, bass), and it can also refer to the **refrain** in a piece of choral music, such as an anthem. In operas and musicals, choruses often perform the "classical" function of setting the scene and commenting on the action.

EXAMPLES: Plays by the ancient Greek dramatists Sophocles and Aeschylus typically contain choruses with an active role. Algernon Charles Swinburne's *Atalanta in Calydon* (1865), a late Victorian **closet drama** deeply influenced by Greek tragedy, has a chorus, as does *For the Time Being* (1944), a modern Christmas oratorio by W. H. Auden. T. S. Eliot's *Murder in the Cathedral* (1935) is an example of a modern play with a chorus. Woody Allen's film *Mighty Aphrodite* (1995) is one of the few contemporary works to include a chorus. The Fool in William Shakespeare's *King Lear* (1606) is often cited as an example of a choral character.

In *1876* (1976), Gore Vidal uses the term *Greek chorus* **metaphorically** to contrast grand old man and Democratic presidential candidate Samuel

Tilden with his supporters as they await the result of the 1876 election. Tilden was the first of two presidential candidates to lose the presidency while winning the popular vote: "In a room just off the main ballroom, Tilden seated himself comfortably near the ticker-tape machine. Hewitt sat on one side of him; Green on the other. The rest of us served as Greek chorus to the grand single Aeschylean protagonist."

chronicle play: A **play** that purports to be based on and to recount historical events. Chronicle plays were at their height in late-sixteenth-century England, particularly after the defeat of the Spanish Armada during the reign of Elizabeth I. The **Elizabethan** chronicle plays, sometimes called **history plays,** were based on the *Chronicles* (1578) (tales of English history) by Raphael Holinshed and others; they disseminated a patriotic version of English history to a largely illiterate and uneducated public. Early chronicle plays, which often strung together a series of incidents that occurred during a single ruler's reign, exhibited a very loose **structure** and tended to hold their audience's attention through a glitzy display of pageantry and battle scenes occasionally interrupted by comic interludes. Later chronicle plays showed greater literary sophistication, particularly as manifested by **character** portrayal and development.

EXAMPLE: William Shakespeare's *Henry IV* (1597–99) plays, memorable for their portrayals of fat Falstaff and his bad influence on the young Henry, Prince of Wales, the King's son.

class (and literary studies): A matter of birth in some older, socially stratified cultures; since the Industrial Revolution, a term more generally used to refer to social and, especially, economic groups. Karl Marx and Friedrich Engels, who together wrote *The Communist Manifesto* (1848), divided capitalist societies into two classes — the bourgeoisie and the proletariat — and saw the history and future development of such societies in terms of class struggle. Since then, social theorists from Max Weber (*Economy and Society* [1921]) to Pierre Bourdieu (*Distinction: A Social Critique of the Judgment of Taste* [1979]) have generally agreed that the **Marxist** paradigm, though helpful, does not adequately define the way in which classes are delineated, defined, and constructed in modern societies. Class status depends not only on economic production — whether one produces wealth as do laborers or enjoys surplus wealth as do the bourgeoisie — but also on patterns of consumption; ethnic, political, and national affiliations; social goals, expectations, opportunities, and so on.

Literary **texts** are among the most powerful forms of cultural **discourse,** and as such they may attest to, perpetuate, or critique the class divisions prevalent in a given culture at a given period of history. Indeed, a work of literature may simultaneously perpetuate and critique the class structure because, as Soviet critic Mikhail Bakhtin pointed out in works such as *Rabelais and His World* (1940), a literary text may be **dialogic** or even **polyphonic.** That is, it may contain two or more **voices** or discourses, one of which reinforces or reflects the values of the ruling class or dominant **ideology,** the other (or others) of which represents the priorities and values of the underprivileged class(es), the plebeian "second world" of commoners or **folk. Marxist critic** Michael Bristol undertook a Bakhtinian analysis when he argued in "'Funeral Bak'd Meats': Carnival and the Carnivalesque in *Hamlet*" (1994) that William Shakespeare's *Hamlet* (1602) not only gives voice both to royal figures and to poor gravediggers but also may be seen in light of class consciousness and **conflict.**

Although Marxist critics tend to see literature in terms of class and class conflict, some Marxists have cautioned against an overly simplistic view of class oppression and of literature's role in class struggle. In his *Prison Notebooks,* written during the period 1929–35 (and partially published in English as *Selections from the Prison Notebooks* [1971]), the Italian communist Antonio Gramsci argued that even working-class people have some power to struggle against the dominant ideology and change history. Louis Althusser, in works such as *For Marx* (1969) and *Lenin and Philosophy and Other Essays* (1971), saw ideology as being riven with **contradictions** that works of literature reflect but also expose; he followed Marx and Gramsci in believing that although literature must be seen in *relation* to ideology, it also has some independence from it. The British **cultural critic** Raymond Williams, in *Culture and Society 1780–1950* (1958) and *The Long Revolution* (1961), warned against viewing working-class people as the "masses," rather than as individuals, and viewed literary texts in the context of dynamically changing and evolving cultures of individuals.

Nonetheless, because class divisions are real — and because they unquestionably result in very different experiences for those they separate — most contemporary critics, particularly those practicing cultural criticism, argue that class, class distinctions, and class differences must be taken into account when we speak or write about literary texts. They hasten to add, however, that matters of class are inevitably intertwined with matters of **race, gender,** ethnicity, and nationality. The experiences of working- (or middle-) class women differ from those of working- (or middle-) class men, and those differences, compounded by differences of race, ethnicity, and/or nationality, are reflected in literary texts. Thus, a class-based, comparative reading of two novels published in 1989, *The Joy Luck Club,* by the Asian American novelist Amy Tan, and *Como agua para chocolate* (*Like Water for Chocolate*), by the Mexican novelist Laura Esquivel, should address racial and ethnic differences and the impact those differences have on not only the two women novelists but also the female and male **characters** who populate their fictions.

classic, classical: The term *classic* has an array of meanings. It may be applied to works from the ancient Graeco-Roman tradition or those written in **imitation** of it. The most common usage today, however, is a more general one. We say that a work is a classic when it has gained widespread and lasting recognition, that is, when readers and critics over a period of time agree that the work has merit that transcends the particular period in which it was written. Although some would generally define the classics as those frequently anthologized **texts** we associate with the Western **canon,** the word *classic* may be used to define an exceptional work arising out of any cultural tradition.

Classical has also had a number of meanings over the centuries. Its root (like the root of *classic* and **classicism**) is the Latin word *classicus,* referring to a person or thing of the first rank. A *scriptor classicus* was a writer whose audience was upper-class; thus, classical or classic literature first referred to works written for the nobility. Over time, however, this term came to signify any Greek or Roman works deemed particularly worthy, and subsequently Graeco-Roman writings in general. Still later it came to be used to refer to texts that imitated the Graeco-Roman tradition and even to ones that, although not written in imitation of the ancients (and perhaps even written in thematic or stylistic opposition to them), were deemed particularly worthy. *Classical* can also be used to describe works that exhibit the qualities or characteristics of classicism, a complex set of attitudes and standards that *classicists,* scholars of Graeco-Roman antiquity, believe to be reflected in the art, architecture, history, philosophy, politics, and literature of ancient Greece and Rome. Classicists believe that the ancients achieved a standard of excellence that has seldom been surpassed by more modern writers; as a result, the term *classical* carries the positive **connotations** of "excellence" and "achievement."

EXAMPLES: Classic works from the ancient Graeco-Roman tradition include Homer's Greek **epics** *The Iliad* (c. 850 B.C.) and *The Odyssey* (c. 850 B.C.); Greek **tragedies** including Aeschylus' *Agamemnon* (c. 458 B.C.), Sophocles' *Oedipus Rex* (c. 430 B.C.), and Euripides' *Electra* (c. 413 B.C.); and Virgil's Roman epic *The Aeneid* (c. 15 B.C.). Ancient classics arising out of other cultural traditions include the *Tao Te Ching* (sixth century B.C.), the works of Confucius (sixth–fifth century B.C.), and the *Kama Sutra* (fourth century A.D.). Works written in English that are commonly referred to as "classics" include William Shakespeare's play *Hamlet* (1602) and Charles Dickens's novel *Great Expectations* (1861).

Beatrix Potter's *The Tale of Peter Rabbit* (1902), Kenneth Grahame's *The Wind in the Willows* (1908), A. A. Milne's *Winnie-the-Pooh* (1926), and E. B. White's *Charlotte's Web* (1952; illustrated by Garth Williams) have long been regarded as children's classics, while J. K. Rowling's *Harry Potter* novels (1997–) are well on their way to achieving this status.

The songs "(I Can't Get No) Satisfaction" (1965) by the Rolling Stones and the Doors' "Light My Fire" (1967) are regularly referred to as "rock classics" or "classic rock." Classic rock albums include The Beatles' *Sgt. Pepper's Lonely Hearts Club Band* (1967) and U2's *The Joshua Tree* (1987).

classicism: A broad and general term (like **romanticism,** with which it is often contrasted) that refers to a complex set of beliefs, attitudes, and values presumed to be grounded in the cultures of ancient Greece and Rome. Some would even call classicism a doctrine or set of doctrines.

However, when used in connection with the arts or, more specifically, with literature, the term is somewhat less formidable. It is used to call to mind certain characteristics praised in the critical writings and found in the artistic achievements of the ancient Greeks and Romans. These include qualities such as simplicity, directness, order, clarity, **decorum,** balance, unity, and an emphasis on reason. Today *classicism* is not used exclusively to refer to Greek and Roman works; the term can be used in connection with any work that exhibits some combination of these qualities and that thereby captures something of the spirit of the ancient Graeco-Roman tradition. English literature has been strongly marked by classicism, the ideals and characteristics of which were resurrected most notably in the **Renaissance** and the subsequent movement we refer to as **neoclassicism.**

During the Renaissance, scholars and critics took a particular interest in two ancient **texts.** One was the *Poetics* (c. 330 B.C.) of the Greek philosopher Aristotle, who set forth rules governing **epic** and **tragedy,** argued that poetry properly imitates nature, and maintained that art has a salutary mental and moral effect. Most of the sixteenth-century commentators on Aristotle were Italians; of these, Julius Caesar Scaliger most influenced the emergence of classicism in England through his book *Poetice* (*Poetics*) (1561).

Renaissance commentators also focused on the *Ars Poetica* (*Art of Poetry*), written by the Roman poet Horace in the first century B.C. Horace emphasized the importance of craftsmanship and decorum in poetry; he defined a decorous poetic **style** as one that is appropriate to the character, **setting,** and/or situation depicted in a given work. Sixteenth-century critics responsible for perpetuating Horace's literary theory included the French poet Pierre Ronsard and the English poet Sir Philip Sidney. Ronsard, leader of the Renaissance literary group known as the Pléiade, argues in his *Défense et illustration de la langue française* (*Defense and Illustration of the French Language)* (1549) for the need to adapt French poetic tradition to a **classical** mold. In *An Apology for Poetry* (1595), Sidney maintains that the intellectually and morally formative power of poetry resides in its power to represent truths vividly.

If classicism was most effectively (re)theorized in the sixteenth century, it had its greatest impact on **imaginative** literature during the seventeenth century, as the Renaissance ended, and in the subsequent **Neoclassical Period,** which spanned the years 1660–1798. This is not to say that critical commentary on classicism ceased in the seventeenth and eighteenth centuries; indeed, some of the best-known restatements of classical principles are found in Pierre Corneille's discussion of the classical **unities** in *Discours* (*Discourses*) (1660), John Dryden's *An Essay of Dramatic Poesy* (1668), Nicolas Boileau's *L'art poétique* (*The Art of Poetry*) (1674), David Hume's *Of Tragedy* (1757), Johann Joachim Winckelmann's *Geschichte der Kunst des Alterthums* (*History of Ancient Art*) (1764), Samuel Johnson's *Preface to Shakespeare* (1765), Gotthold Ephraim Lessing's *Laocoön* (1766), and the *Discourses* (1769–90) of the English portrait painter and founding president of the Royal Academy, Sir Joshua Reynolds. Rather, classical **aesthetic** principles regularly showed up in *creative* as well as scholarly works.

In England, the influence of classicism was apparent in the plays of Ben Jonson, the poetry of John Dryden and Alexander Pope, the **satire** of Jonathan Swift, and the novels of Henry Fielding. In France, classicism most profoundly influenced the theater, as evidenced by the plays of Corneille, Racine, and Molière (Jean Baptiste Poquelin). In Germany, the poetry of Friedrich Hölderlin and various works in several **genres** by Johann Wolfgang von Goethe owe a debt to classicism (and Greek classicism in particular).

cliché: An expression used so often (and so often out of context) that it has become hackneyed and has lost its original impact. Many clichés were once hailed as striking **metaphors,** only to become denigrated over time due to over- and misuse.

EXAMPLES: Using "under the weather" to indicate feeling ill. "Don't rock the boat," "pushing the envelope," "just what the doctor ordered," and "have a nice day" are common clichés (as is the associated image of a yellow smiley face). Also common, but more contemporary, are overused phrases such as "been there, done that," "get a grip," "don't go there," "think outside the box," and "you go, girl!" The phrase "Show me the money!," prominently featured in the movie *Jerry Maguire* (1996), quickly became a sports cliché and subsequently invaded all facets of life.

The first line of Robert Burns's poem "A Red, Red Rose" (1796), "O my Luve's like a red, red rose," has become clichéd with overuse and the passage of time. Neil Young's song "Love Is a Rose" (1975) puts a twist on the "love is a rose" cliché by advising his listeners not to pick it!

In a July 11, 2000, essay in *The Wall Street Journal* entitled "Can 35 Million Book Buyers Be Wrong? Yes," noted critic Harold Bloom takes the unusual view that J. K. Rowling's *Harry Potter* books are "long on clichés, short on imaginative vision. They don't measure up to the classics of children's literature."

climax: The point of greatest tension or emotional intensity in a **plot.** In **drama,** the climax follows the **rising action** and precedes the **falling action.** Climax is one of five structural elements associated with **Freytag's Pyramid,** a model developed by Gustav Freytag for analyzing five-act plays (**tragedies** in particular). Climax is the point at which the **conflict** reaches its greatest height and the **crisis,** or turning point in the action, occurs.

Although the crisis and the climax generally occur together, *crisis* is sometimes distinguished from *climax* by critics who use the former term to refer to a purely structural element of plot and the latter term to signify the point of greatest emotional intensity. Critics who make this distinction would maintain that the climax may thus occur at points other than the crisis.

Sometimes *climax* is used to signify multiple minor emotional peaks in the plot, whereas *crisis* is reserved to refer to the single point at which the protagonist's fortunes change decisively for the better or the worse. Occasionally *climax* is used as a **rhetorical** term to refer to the last and most important in a series of items or terms organized progressively in order of importance.

closed couplet: Two successive lines of rhyming **verse** whose meaning is grammatically or logically complete, forming a statement that can stand meaningfully on its own.

EXAMPLES: John Dryden's "Epigram on Milton" (1688), a poem about three poets (Homer of Greece, Virgil of Rome, and John Milton of England), is suggestively composed of three closed couplets (the last of which involves an **eye-rhyme**):

> Three poets, in three distant ages born,
> Greece, Italy, and England did adorn.
> The first in loftiness of thought surpassed,
> The next in majesty, in both the last:
> The force of Nature could no farther go;
> To make a third, she joined the former two.

A more modern example of the closed couplet can be found in Elinor Wylie's "Fair Annet's Song" (1929), the first **stanza** of which follows:

> One thing comes and another thing goes:
> Frosts in November drive away the rose;
> Like a blowing ember the windflower blows
> And drives away the snows.

close reading: The thorough and nuanced analysis of a literary **text,** with particular emphasis on the interrelationships among its constituent elements (**allusions, images,** sound effects, etc.). Also referred to as **explication,** close reading is often associated with **the New Criticism.**

closet drama: A **drama,** often written in **verse,** that is meant to be read rather than performed, even though it includes **acts, scenes, dialogue,** and sometimes even stage directions. Many closet dramas have been written in **imitation** of dramatic works and **styles** of some earlier literary epoch or period.

Some scholars would include under the umbrella of closet drama other works that were once performed on the stage (or, at least, that were written to be so performed) but that are in our day viewed strictly as literary **texts** to be experienced by individual readers. Others would include works that, though still occasionally performed, make for better reading than theater, whether because of the staging problems they entail, the type or level of language used, or the antiquated and recondite nature of their **settings** or subjects.

EXAMPLES: John Milton's *Samson Agonistes* (1671), George Gordon, Lord Byron's *Manfred* (1817), Percy Bysshe Shelley's *The Cenci* (1819), Robert Browning's *Pippa Passes* (1841), and W. H. Auden's *The Sea and the Mirror* (1944) and *For the Time Being* (1944).

closure: The process by which a literary work is either brought to a logical conclusion or structured in such a way that the reader feels it is complete and coherent; alternatively, the apparent condition of completeness and coherence established at the end of a work. Closure provides a sense of wholeness, integrity, and finality to the relationships and events in **narratives** and to the arrangement of phrases, lines, and **images** in **lyric** poetry.

As early as the fourth century B.C., Aristotle argued that an artistic whole requires a beginning, middle, and end. The kind of ending that provides closure to a narrative often involves the resolution of a **conflict** or entails revelations that cause the reader or audience to feel no need for further information. Critic Barbara Herrnstein Smith has stated that "closure allows the reader to be satisfied by the failure of continuation or, put another way, it creates in the reader the expectation of nothing." According to the late-nineteenth-century novelist Henry James, a "proper ending" also provides a sense of thematic unity that makes the work seem like "a unified and organic whole."

As a term, *closure* need not refer to the conclusion of an entire work; rather, sentences, paragraphs, and poetic **stanzas** can themselves come to closure, as can the individual sections of a work. For example, according to **Freytag's Pyramid**, each of the five parts of a play (introduction, **rising action, climax, falling action,** and **catastrophe**) come to some degree of closure, with the last two parts bringing closure to the work as a whole. Even the rhyming of syllables that form poetic **couplets** creates closure at the subtextual level.

Writing on novelistic closure, **cultural critic** Marianna Torgovnick has developed terms to describe five types of relationships between the ending of a novel and its preceding parts: *circularity* refers to an ending that looks back to the beginning; *parallelism* to one that recalls numerous points in the narrative; *tangential* to one that introduces a new idea; *linkage* to one that anticipates a sequel; and *incompletion* to one that omits expected, important material, even if it exhibits some circularity or parallelism.

As Torgovnick's description of incompletion suggests, not all authors of literary works provide a sense of closure — or at least not one that most readers will agree on. For instance, in a meditative poem, closure may involve the restatement, in **imagery,** of an unanswerable question. Some "open-ended" texts — such as those identified by **reader-response critics** who view the making of meaning as a collaborative enterprise between reader and text — contain linguistic or structural **ambiguities** that cause readers (or disparate **interpretive communities**) to come to very different conclusions. Other unconventional works resist all attempts to "make sense," including and especially the effort to achieve closure. French **structuralist,** later **poststructuralist,** theorist Roland Barthes has contrasted *lisible* ("readerly") texts with *scriptible* ("writerly") ones, examples of which include the ***nouveau roman,*** or **antinovel.**

EXAMPLES: In the movies *The Sixth Sense* (1999) and *The Others* (2000), a surprising, final revelation provides a sense of closure that retroactively explains earlier, confusing **character** portrayals and **plot** developments. The ending of Virginia Woolf's *To the Lighthouse* (1927) is an example of circularity, for it transports Mr. Ramsay and his children to the very lighthouse that the late Mrs. Ramsay had promised to take their son James to at the beginning of the novel. The novel *The Magus* (1966) struck readers as being so open-ended that its author, John Fowles, revised the book in 1978 in part to achieve closure "less ambiguously."

The widely anthologized story "The Lady or the Tiger?" (1882), by Frank R. Stockton, exemplifies the kind of work that invites its readers to provide closure. The children's series "Choose Your Own Adventure" provides a twist on the idea of closure, situating young readers as **protagonists** who make choices about what actions to take — choices that can result in very different consequences and endings.

Percy Bysshe Shelley's **sonnet** "Ozymandias" (1818) — about a haughty, mocking king of the ancient world who built a monument to his own power — concludes with the following line:

The lone and level sands stretch far away.

This ending provides imagistic and **thematic** closure to the poem, suggesting that efforts by tyrants to immortalize themselves are pathetically doomed to failure.

codes: Organizing principles and assumptions underlying a **text** that facilitate (or occasionally resist) attempts to interpret its meaning. Although widely used by modern practitioners of **hermeneutics** (the **theory** of interpretation and interpretive methods), as well as by practitioners of various critical approaches, the term *codes* is most often associated with **structuralist critics** such as Roman Jakobson, Claude Lévi-Strauss, and Roland Barthes. **Structuralists** believe that all literary works — indeed, all elements of human culture — can be understood as part of a system of **signs** that includes numerous **conventions.** For instance, audiences aware of the fact that Shakespeare's *Hamlet* is a **revenge tragedy** and who understand the conventions of that **genre** know, even without reading or seeing the play, that the story will probably involve a son's quest to avenge his father's death as well as a dramatic and probably violent showdown between the **protagonist** and **villain.** Similarly, **Renaissance comedies** nearly always entail a happy ending involving marriage.

Jakobson has used the term *code* to refer to language, one of the elements of communication. According to Lévi-Strauss, codes are grounded in the **binary oppositions** that permeate Western **discourse,** including literary works. For instance, the opposition "head / heart" — and all the other dualities it implies — not only underlies countless texts, shaping the structure of their **plots,** the struggles of their **characters,** and the patterns of **symbols** they contain, but also drives our interpretations of those texts.

By contrast, Barthes's *S/Z* (1974) identifies five different types of codes: the *hermeneutic,* which comprises the binary questions and answers that serve to provide suspense in a **narrative;** the *semic,* which allows readers to distinguish characters and understand their behavior; the *symbolic,* which guides the reader's understanding of **figurative language,** including **metaphors** and symbols; the *proairetic,* which governs ideas regarding the work's plot and its likely development; and the *referential,* or *cultural,* which involves social assumptions, such as those concerning the tradeoff between tradition and change. Barthes identified several additional types of codes in his *Textual Analysis of Poe's 'Valdemar'* (1981) — the *metalinguistic,* the *socioethnic,* the *social,* the *narrative,* the *scientific,* and the *scientific-deontological* — but some if not all of these may simply be subsets of the types he previously identified.

In later writings, Barthes acknowledged that codes may not always be sufficient or reliable as interpretive tools. He recognized, for instance, that readers themselves bring to the hermeneutic process assumptions and experiences (including previous experiences with other texts) that affect reading outcomes. He also argued that experimental (***scriptible,*** or "writerly") texts may use language to create ambiguous and even contradictory references, thereby flouting conventional associations and expectations. This latter development in Barthes's theory of the interpretive process and ideas about **intertextuality** is one of many indications of his shift from structuralism toward **poststructuralism.**

Jacques Derrida, a leading theorist of poststructuralism closely associated with **deconstruction,** has suggested that the dichotomies forming the binary oppositions so firmly embedded in code-rich Western discourse are not simply oppositions but also valuative hierarchies in which one component is viewed as positive or superior while the other is considered negative or inferior, even if only slightly so. For instance, "active" is the more positive term in the opposition "active / passive."

Derrida's insight has made the term *code* increasingly useful to **feminist** and **gender critics** interested in the representation of **gender** and **sexuality,** as well as to **new historicist** and **cultural critics** interested in the literary representation of **race** and **class.** For instance, recurrent references to characters of one race or gender in terms of physical and emotional traits and to characters of another group in terms of intellectual traits can convey racist or sexist attitudes in cultural "code." That is because words and ideas associated with "body" and "feeling" within the pairs "mind / body" and "thought / feeling" generally carry inferior **connotations.**

These understandings of the term *code*, complex as they may seem, do not differ radically from what people think when they conclude that a statement like "I just want to be friends" is code for some other communication that the speaker wishes to be understood — but would prefer to leave unsaid.

See also **convention, sign, structuralism.**

collective unconscious: A term used by analytic psychologist Carl Jung to refer to a repository of unconscious memories dating back to the origins of human experience that Jung believed are shared by all members of the human race and that are manifested in dreams, **myths,** and literature.

See **archetypal criticism, Jungian criticism.**

Colonial Period (in American literature): An era in American literary history spanning the years 1607, when English settlers founded Jamestown, Virginia, to 1765, when the passing of the Stamp Act by the English parliament enraged the colonists in America, sparking opposition that led to the American Revolution some eleven years later in 1776.

To say that an "American" literature existed during the Colonial Period is somewhat misleading. Although the colonists came from a variety of countries, the influence of England on every "American" institution was overwhelming, and most colonial writers modelled themselves after English writers. Furthermore, the very fact that the colonists came from different lands and religious backgrounds with few unifying influences made it difficult to form any "national" literature. The geographic dispersal of the colonists into small, relatively insulated, and self-sufficient communities and the limited communication between the thirteen original colonies created additional obstacles.

Some have even suggested that the use of the term *literature* to describe works written during the Colonial Period is inappropriate. Literature as we often conceive of it today — as an artistic medium — did not thrive during the Colonial Period. Imaginative literature was banned in several colonies until the American Revolution, thanks in large part to the Puritans, who viewed drama and the novel in particular as paths to perdition. Drama was explicitly labeled an evil akin to cockfighting by the Continental Congress as late as 1774. Furthermore, the harsh conditions of frontier life in America and the nonexistence of a nation also inhibited the development of an artistic literature.

Colonial works were largely historical and **didactic,** intended to record, instruct, or even warn. Letters, journals, **narratives,** and histories were popular forms of writing. John Smith's *A True Relation of Occurrences and Accidents in Virginia* (1608) is sometimes called the first "American" book, but given that Smith was an Englishman who returned home only two years after writing this work, it is somewhat misleading to call it "American." Other writers, however, migrated to America and remained there. Political figures such as William Bradford and John Winthrop wrote histories of Plymouth and New England, respectively. William Byrd wrote about a border dispute between North Carolina and Virginia. Mary Rowlandson told of being captured and held for several months by "Indians" in her book *A Narrative of the Captivity and Restauration of Mrs. Mary Rowlandson* (1682). Many colonial writers, preoccupied with issues of day-to-day survival, expressed hostility and fear toward Native Americans, including a strong opposition to miscegenation (mixing of the races).

Many colonial works were also polemical or religious in nature. *The Bay Psalm Book* (1640), the first book published in America, was a compilation of psalms altered so that they could be sung. Sermons, philosophical pieces, and theological tracts were some of the most common forms of written expression; a number of ministers who were members of Massachusetts's famous Mather family delineated the dictates of Puritanism. Calvinist preacher and theologian Jonathan Edwards is perhaps most famous for his awe-inspiring if terror-inducing sermon "Sinners in the Hands of an Angry God" (1741).

Although poetry was not a major focus of colonial expression, a few poets emerged during the Colonial Period. Anne Bradstreet inaugurated **lyric** poetry in America with the publication of a volume entitled *The Tenth Muse Lately Sprung Up in America* (1650). Edward Taylor wrote a number of religious poems, but his work remained unpublished until 1937. Michael Wigglesworth was perhaps the most well-known poet of the time; his poem *The Day of Doom* (1662), which set forth Calvinistic theology, was required reading for most schoolchildren of the day.

Nonreligious and nonhistorical prose was fairly rare, but among prose authors Benjamin Franklin — who incorporated Enlightenment ideas into many of his works — clearly stands out. Franklin's *Poor Richard's Almanac* (1732) remains famous today; Richard Saunders, a **character** in that work, is probably the first fully developed fictional character in American literature. A very different kind of nonreligious, nonhistorical prose was produced by John Cleland, author of the early erotic, softcore porn **classic** *The Life of Fanny Hill (or, Memoirs of a Woman of Pleasure)* (1749).

The first **slave narratives** were also written during the Colonial Period. These include *The Narrative of the Uncommon Sufferings, and Surprizing Deliverance of Briton Hammon, A Negro Man, — Servant to General Winslow of Marshfield, in New England* (1760) and *The Interesting Narrative of the Life of Olaudah Equiano, or Gustavus Vasa, the African, Written by Himself* (1789).

comedy: Broadly defined, any amusing and entertaining work; more narrowly defined, an amusing and entertaining **drama.** Comedy is often contrasted with **tragedy,** not only because it ends happily and presents the "lighter side" of life but also because it generally represents the experiences of ordinary people in common or vernacular language, whereas tragedy has traditionally depicted noble **characters** in a loftier literary **style.** Humor (or **wit**) is the essential element of any comedy. Comic effect may be subtle or coarse; it is typically achieved through some incongruity, whether physical, verbal, or conceptual (such as when a character is exaggerating what he has done or would be able to do if a given situation arose). Although comedies aim to evoke laughter, they may also have a serious purpose.

Ancient Greek comedy is typically subdivided into three categories. *Old Comedy,* represented by the works of Aristophanes, is characterized by a combination of political **satire** and **fantastic** elements. *Middle Comedy* apparently served as a bridge between Old and *New Comedy.* New Comedy, epitomized by the works of Menander, typically depicts two lovers who must overcome obstacles to live happily ever after.

During the **Middle Ages,** the term *comedy* was applied to any literary work that had a happy ending and a style less exalted than that ascribed to tragedy. Hence Dante Alighieri's great work was named *Divina commedia* (*The Divine Comedy* [1321]) even though it does not make particular use of humor.

Many types of comedy (and ways of classifying comedy) have emerged since the **Renaissance.** Some critics subdivide comedies into three categories: **romantic, satiric,** and *rogue.* Romantic comedies have a pair (or pairs) of lovers as their center of interest. William Shakespeare, who based his comedies on the prose **romances** of his time, is credited with the development of this form. Satiric comedies typically have a critical purpose, attacking philosophical or political notions through ridicule. They may also direct ridicule at those who depart from societal rules and norms, or at meddlesome characters who somehow interfere with a pair of lovers. In rogue comedies, the audience is entertained by the antics of clever but congenial miscreants. Other critics classify comedies as **realistic** (including satiric comedies and such forms as the **comedy of manners** and the **comedy of humors**), romantic, or **sentimental.** Still other critics classify the comedy of manners separately rather than subsuming it under the heading of realistic comedy.

Comedies may also be categorized as *low* or *high.* Low comedies typically rely on the crude or the obvious to evoke laughter; they include *situation comedies,* **farces,** and slapstick works. Situation comedies contain characters whose absurdities are revealed through some entertaining machination of the **plot.** Farces are based on ludicrous situations, such as those that develop in cases of mistaken identity. Slapstick comedies are perhaps the least subtle of all types of comedy, relying on physical action (brawls, spectacular but harmless falls, and two-fingered pokes in the eyes) to provoke loud guffaws from the audience. High comedies rely heavily on intellectual issues, viewpoints, and the incongruities between them to produce their comic effect. Often satiric in nature and serious in purpose, they tend to emphasize humanity's foibles and seldom appeal to the audience's emotions. Witty repartee is common and is perhaps epitomized in the **Restoration**-era comedy of manners. High comedy of more recent vintage is sometimes referred to as *intellectual comedy* or *comedy of ideas.*

EXAMPLES: Aristophanes' *The Frogs* (c. 405 B.C.) is an ancient Greek comedy. Nicholas Udall's *Ralph Roister Doister* (1553) is generally credited with being the first dramatic comedy in English. *Much Ado About Nothing* (1599) is a well-known later comedy by William Shakespeare. The seventeenth-century French playwright Molière (Jean Baptiste Poquelin) is considered by many to be the greatest of all comic dramatists. In the twentieth century, George Bernard Shaw was famous for intellectual comedies such as *Major Barbara* (1905). The television show *Three's Company* is a situation comedy (commonly abbreviated as "sitcom") that often makes use of slapstick humor; other popular sitcoms include *Seinfeld, Friends, Frasier,* and *Will & Grace.* Movies such as *When Harry Met Sally* (1989), *Groundhog Day* (1993), and *Notting Hill* (1999) are considered romantic comedies.

comedy of humors (comedy of humours): A type of **satiric comedy,** developed in the late sixteenth century by the playwrights Ben Jonson and George Chapman, that presents characters with personality types that lead them to behave in a ridiculous manner. The word *humor* in the phrase *comedy of humors* does not refer to humor as we understand it today. Rather the comedy of humors is based on a theory of human behavior, current during the **Middle Ages** and the **Renaissance,** that held that personality was determined by the relative amounts of each of the four fluids, or humours, in the body: blood, phlegm, yellow bile, and black bile. As long as the humours were in balance, the individual supposedly exhibited a perfect temperament and no illness, but an imbalance affected the behavior of the individual in a very specific way. That is, an excess of blood produced a sanguine (happy) personality, phlegm a phlegmatic (cowardly, passive) personality, yellow bile a choleric (argumentative, stubborn) personality, and black bile a bilious (melancholy) one. The comedy of humors is closely related to the **comedy of manners** and influenced **Restoration**-era comedies.

EXAMPLES: Ben Jonson's *Every Man in His Humour* (1598). Molière's (Jean Baptiste Poquelin's) comedy *Le misanthrope* (1666) features the melancholy Alceste, who continuously rails against humankind. The very subtitle of the work — *L'atrabilaire amoureux* — overtly evokes the theory of humors, "*L'atrabilaire*" meaning (according to the *Dictionnaire de l'Académie*), "Qui est plein d'une bile noire et aduste. Visage atrabilaire, humeur atrabilaire" (One who is full of black, burnt bile. Peevish countenance, peevish disposition).

comedy of manners: A **satiric** form of **comedy,** most often associated with **Restoration-Age drama,** that usually takes the artificial and sophisticated habits and doings of (generally aristocratic or high) society as its general **setting** and love (usually amorous intrigues of some sort) as its specific subject. The comedy of manners frequently satirizes **stock characters** who somehow fail to conform to the **conventions** of polite society. This sub**genre** is noted for **witty** repartee and a certain cynicism with regard to affairs of the heart. The perceived moral shortcomings of these plays eventually caused a backlash and a consequent upsurge in the number of **sentimental comedies** — relatively upbeat works that were deemed more wholesome by audiences tired of Restoration excesses. During the subsequent **Neoclassical Period,** however, the comedy of manners was revived; it later had an influence on nineteenth-century novels such as Jane Austen's *Emma* (1815) and James Fenimore Cooper's *The Pioneers* (1823).

EXAMPLES: George Etherege's *The Man of Mode, or, Sir Fopling Flutter* (1676), William Congreve's *The Way of the World* (1700), and Richard Brinsley Sheridan's *The School for Scandal* (1777) are early examples. Twentieth-century comedies of manners include plays such as Oscar Wilde's *The Importance of Being Earnest* (1895) and Noël Coward's *Private Lives* (1930).

Recent films that might be considered comedies of manners include Whit Stillman's *Metropolitan* (1990) and Amy Heckerling's *Clueless* (1995), a contemporary version of Jane Austen's *Emma* (1815) set in Beverly Hills.

comic relief: A humorous scene or passage inserted into an otherwise serious work. Comic relief is intended to provide an emotional outlet and change of pace for the audience as well as to create a contrast that further emphasizes the seriousness of the work.

EXAMPLES: William Shakespeare used the gravedigger scene in *Hamlet* (1602), the drunken porter in *Macbeth* (1606), and the **character** of Mercutio in *Romeo and Juliet* (1596) to provide comic relief. Ratso Rizzo, played by Dustin Hoffman, provides comic relief in John Schlesinger's darkly disturbing film *Midnight Cowboy* (1969).

Jim Crace's novel *Quarantine* (1998), which chronicles Jesus' forty days in the wilderness and which has been described (by critic R. Z. Sheppard in *Newsweek*) as "a serious and skillfully crafted novel about folly, faith and a radically new relationship between a people and its god," contains numerous scenes that provide comic relief, such as the one in which Musa, a trader whom Jesus has healed, orders that a dead donkey be pushed over a cliff above the cave in which Jesus is awaiting a sign from God.

commedia dell'arte: A form of **comedy** that developed in Italy in the sixteenth century and was performed by professional, travelling groups (guilds) of actors who often wore masks and traditional costumes. Much of the detail in *commedia dell'arte* was improvised, but certain, oft-repeated scenarios were rehearsed in advance. These plays feature **stock characters** (the braggart soldier and the buffoon) and often involve a young couple who manage to outwit an elder (often a rich father) with the help of servants, thereby achieving wealth and happiness. As such, they exhibit their indebtedness to the ancient Roman comedies of such playwrights as Plautus and Terence.

Commonwealth Age (in English literature): Also known as the *Puritan Interregnum* (literally, "between reigns"), an age often classified as the last of the literary eras within the **Renaissance Period** in English literature. The Commonwealth Age began with the beheading of King Charles I in 1649 and ended with the restoration of the Stuart monarchy via the coronation of Charles II in 1660. During this period, England was ruled by a Puritan-dominated Parliament led by Oliver Cromwell (Lord Protector, 1653–58) and briefly by his son Richard Cromwell (Lord Protector, 1658–59).

Writers of prose and nondramatic poetry dominated the literary arena during the Commonwealth Age. Prose writers of the epoch include Thomas Hobbes, Jeremy ·Taylor, Izaac Walton, and John Milton, whose "Tenure of Kings·and Magistrates" (1649) attempted to justify the execution of Charles I. Milton, a Puritan, was also one of the greatest poets of the era, although his major works (*Paradise Lost* [1667] and *Paradise Regained* [1671]) were published after the **Restoration.** Other well-known poets of the interregnum era include Abraham Cowley, Andrew Marvell, and Henry Vaughan.

Playwrights were constrained during the Commonwealth Age, due in part to the government's decision to close public theaters in 1642. Interregnum playwrights lacked the support that had enabled great dramatists — such as Christopher Marlowe, William Shakespeare, Ben Jonson, Sir Francis Beaumont, John Fletcher, Thomas Middleton, and John Webster — to flourish in the first half of the seventeenth century, during the **Elizabethan, Jacobean,** and **Caroline Ages.**

See also **Renaissance.**

communicative presumption: See **speech act theory.**

conceit: An elaborate and often surprising comparison between two apparently highly dissimilar things, from the Italian *concetto* (meaning idea or concept). Whether it involves strikingly original **images** or familiar things used in an unusual way, the conceit is most notable for its ingenuity. Although the term acquired a derogatory **connotation** in the eighteenth and nineteenth centuries, it is generally used today in a more neutral, descriptive sense and can thus be applied to effective comparisons as well as to overbearing or strained ones. Conceits often take the form of extended **metaphors.**

Two major types of conceits exist. The **metaphysical conceit** frequently uses esoteric or, alternatively, commonplace objects or references in a previously unthought-of or entirely unfamiliar way; it sometimes functions as the controlling image for the entire poem. The **Petrarchan conceit** (following the example of the fourteenth-century Italian poet Petrarch) typically employs analogy, **hyperbole,** or **oxymoron** to figure one or both lovers in an unequal love relationship, exaggerating the beauty and cruelty of the beloved female while rendering as unjust or pathetic the suffering of the lovestricken male who worships her. Many of the images associated with the Petrarchan conceit, though once highly original, have been repeated so often by lesser poets since the **Renaissance** that they have become standard and even **clichéd**.

EXAMPLES: In "The Flea" (1635), John Donne used a flea in a metaphysical conceit to figure the sexual union desired by the speaker-lover:

> Mark but this flea, and mark in this,
> How little that which thou deny'st me is;
> Me it sucked first, and now sucks thee,
> And in this flea, our two bloods mingled be;
> Confess it, this cannot be said
> A sin, or shame, or loss of maidenhead,
>   Yet this enjoys before it woo,
>   And pampered swells with one blood made of two,
>   And this, alas, is more than we would do.

Edmund Spenser frequently employed Petrarchan conceits in his poetry. In the thirtieth **sonnet** of his *Amoretti* (1595), he compared the frustrated lover to fire, the object of his love to ice. This comparison, although original at the time, has since become hackneyed:

> My love is like to ice, and I to fire;
> How comes it then that this her cold so great
> Is not dissolved through my so hot desire,
> But harder grows the more I her entreat!
> Or how comes it that my exceeding heat
> Is not delayed by her heart-frozen cold;
> But that I burn much more in boiling sweat,
> And feel my flames augmented manifold!
> What more miraculous thing may be told,
> That fire, which all thing melts, should harden ice;
> And ice, which is congealed with senseless cold,
> Should kindle fire by wonderful device!
>   Such is the power of love in gentle mind,
>   That it can alter all the course of kind.

See **metaphysical conceit** and **Petrarchan conceit** for additional examples of these terms.

concrete: See **abstract**.

concrete poetry: A modern term for *pattern poetry,* or *shaped verse,* a type of poetry that has existed since the time of the ancient Greeks but that is most often associated with the **Renaissance,** the seventeenth century, and the **Modern Period**. A pattern, shaped, or concrete poem is to be perceived as a visual object and is at least as notable for its graphic design as for its verbal meaning. Thus, concrete poems are not meant simply to be read; in fact, many cannot be read at all in the way we think of reading. Concrete poems rarely employ conventional sentence **structure** and are often made up of a single word or phrase, parts of which may be repeated, strategically placed on the page, or otherwise highlighted by the use of different colors, fonts, or sizes.

EXAMPLES: A poem about fish might be shaped like a fish; a poem about motion might place the letters in the word *motion* in a wavy pattern on the page. George Herbert's poem "Easter Wings" (1633) — which, when printed, visually suggests the wings of an angel — is perhaps the most famous pattern poem. The following poem by e. e. cummings (1958) is a concrete poem:

l(a

le
af
fa

ll

s)
one
l

iness

The poem characterizes loneliness by visually depicting the slow downward flutter of a single leaf in the phrase "(a / le / af / fa /ll / s)."

confessional poetry: A contemporary poetic mode in which poets discuss matters relating to their private lives. Confessional poets go beyond **romanticism's** emphasis on individual experience in the intimate detail and often **psychoanalytic** terms with which they describe even their most painful experiences. The reader is often addressed directly by the confessional poet, who typically expresses some very private confusion or sorrow.

EXAMPLES: Anne Sexton's *To Bedlam and Partway Back* (1960) and Pulitzer Prize–winning *Live or Die* (1960), as well as Sylvia Plath's *Ariel* (1965), are volumes of confessional poetry by pioneers of this poetic mode. The following excerpt is from Plath's poem "Daddy," included in the *Ariel* collection:

You stand at the blackboard, daddy,
In the picture I have of you,
A cleft in your chin instead of your foot
But no less a devil for that, no not

Any less the black man who
Bit my pretty red heart in two.
I was ten when they buried you.
At twenty I tried to die
And get back, back, back to you.

Jane Kenyon's "Having It Out with Melancholy" (from *Constance: Poems* [1993]) is also an example of confessional poetry. The first **stanza** reads as follows:

> When I was born, you waited
> behind a pile of linen in the nursery,
> and when we were alone, you lay down
> on top of me, pressing
> the bile of desolation into every pore.

conflict: A confrontation or struggle between opposing **characters** or forces in the **plot** of a **narrative** work, from which the action emanates and around which it revolves.

Conflict is usually broken down into three major categories: *physical, social,* and *internal* (or *psychological*) conflict. Physical conflict generally involves the "elemental" clash between a character and nature or the physical world. Social conflict takes place between humans competing or struggling against one another or against that overarching entity called society. Opposing forces are typically represented or embodied by the **protagonist** and the **antagonist**, but conflict need not involve two distinct people, entities, or institutions, as demonstrated by the third type of conflict. Internal, or psychological, conflict involves the inner divisions or turmoil of a single character. Conflicts of this sort may result from the character's attempt to decide between multiple alternatives for action or between opposing attitudes or beliefs. Some critics have spoken of a fourth kind of conflict — *metaphysical conflict* — involving the clash between a human character and fate or some type of deity.

In general, literary works employ more than one type of conflict in order to enrich the plot and avoid oversimplification.

EXAMPLE: In Herman Melville's *Moby-Dick* (1851), Captain Ahab's psychological conflict is played out in his metaphysical conflict with God or fate, his physical conflict with the whale, and his social conflict with an endangered crew.

conflicts: See **gaps**.

connotation: The association(s) evoked by a word beyond its **denotation,** or literal meaning. A connotation may be perceived and understood by almost everyone if it is a product of or reflects broad cultural associations, or it may be recognized by comparatively few readers or listeners who have certain knowledge or experience. A connotation may even be unique to a particular individual, whose personal experiences have led him or her to associate a given word with some idea or thing in a way that would not be familiar to the general populace.

EXAMPLES: The word *water* might commonly evoke thoughts or images of an ocean or lake, thirst, or even a water balloon. Less common would be thoughts of the Wicked Witch of the West (from L. Frank Baum's *The*

Wizard of Oz [1900]), who melted when Dorothy threw a bucket of water on her, or of Samuel Taylor Coleridge's "The Rime of the Ancient Mariner" (1798), which includes the famous lines "Water, water, everywhere, / And all the boards did shrink; / Water, water, everywhere, / Nor any drop to drink." A near-drowning victim might associate water with sheer terror, as would someone who was hydrophobic. A woman whose husband had proposed to her on a canoeing trip might associate water with her engagement ring or, more broadly, her personal happiness.

A passage from Alice Munro's story "Boys and Girls" (1968) explains *connotation* without explicitly using the term:

> The word *girl* had formerly seemed to me innocent and unburdened, like the word *child;* now it appeared that it was no such thing. A girl was not, as I had supposed, simply what I was; it was what I had to become. It was a definition, always touched with reproach and disappointment.

consonance: The repetition of a final consonant sound or sounds following *different* vowel sounds in proximate words (*made / wood*). Most scholars maintain that the repetition of initial or intermediate consonant sounds, when occurring in *addition* to repeated final consonant sounds, also constitutes consonance (*litter / letter, wade / wood*).

EXAMPLES: Emily Dickinson's poem #214 (c. 1860) uses consonance rather than **perfect rhyme** in the words *Pearl* and *Alcohol.* Consonance is also present in the words *brewed, scooped,* and *Yield.*

> I taste a liquor never brewed —
> From Tankards scooped in Pearl —
> Not all the Vats upon the Rhine
> Yield such an Alcohol!

Wilfred Owen's "Arms and the Boy" (1920) provides an example of consonance in which initial as well as final consonant sounds are repeated (in the words *blade* and *blood, flash* and *flesh*):

> Let the boy try along this bayonet blade
> How cold steel is, and keen with hunger of blood;
> Blue with all malice, like a madman's flash;
> And thinly drawn with famishing for flesh.

constative: See **performative.**

constructionism: See **feminist criticism, gay and lesbian criticism,** and **gender criticism.**

contextual criticism: A revolutionary offshoot of **the New Criticism** that incorporated and modified the basic analytical methods and underlying outlook of its parent form. Eliseo Vivas and Murray Krieger shaped and defined this mode of **criticism,** which emphasizes **close readings** of individual **texts** and evaluations of those texts based on their internal structure and **aesthetic** impact. Although by the late 1960s contextual criticism was no longer in vogue, some of its assumptions and analytical methods persist in more contemporary critical approaches, such as **deconstruction.**

contradictions: See **gaps.**

convention: A literary device, usage, **style,** situation, or **form** so widely employed that it has become accepted and even expected by knowledgeable readers or audiences. In order to function, conventions must be recognized and accepted by the audience, even though many conventions involve highly unrealistic devices, situations, **character** types, and so on. Conventions cause — and allow — us to look at the stage in a theater and view as real the events that take place on it, even when those events supposedly occur at a variety of places and times. Conventions also make it possible for us to accept the "fact" that a character has aged five years in five minutes (or pages). Works in which people speak in verse or that contain **soliloquies** or **dramatic monologues** make use of conventions as well, for people do not ordinarily speak in such a manner.

Some conventions gain acceptance because they facilitate the presentation of material or enhance the quality of the **aesthetic** experience. (Convention allows a single set of large *papier-mâché* cylinders to represent tree trunks in one scene of *As You Like It* and architectural columns in the next; think how much less interesting certain novels and films would be if the convention we call **flashback** didn't exist.) Sometimes an original story, character type, or **theme** will so speak to the fears, fantasies, or preoccupations of an age that it will be repeated in a variety of different works. Such stories (the **medieval** damsel in distress), character types (the mustachioed **villain** of **Victorian melodrama**), and themes (the **romantic** idea that we should "get back to Nature") become conventions and remain conventional as long as new writers rework them and new audiences accept them.

In the twentieth century, convention took on an even broader meaning, thanks in part to **structuralist critics** who consider every literary work to consist of a plethora of **codes.** The reader or viewer, structuralists have argued, "naturalizes" these codes by conforming them to those culturally determined perceptions and assumptions that he or she views as "natural."

EXAMPLES: William Shakespeare's frequent use of soliloquies, **asides,** and **stock characters** (such as the fool) are conventions. Equally conventional, in William Shakespeare's day and plays, was the practice of using male actors to play all the women's parts (and, therefore, the parts of women pretending to be men, like Viola in *Twelfth Night* [1599] and Rosalind in *As You Like It* [c. 1600]). **Renaissance** audiences thus accepted that Juliet was female, even though the actor playing her would have been a boy. In our own day, it is conventional for women to play women's roles in plays — including plays by William Shakespeare. Nonetheless, our appreciation of a play like *As You Like It* or *Twelfth Night* still depends upon conventions. Audiences accept the fact that the **heroines** of these two plays are mistaken for the men they pretend to be, even though the parts are played by women who look like women, masculine garb and hairstyle notwithstanding.

Corpus Christi play: See **mystery play.**

cosmic irony: See **irony.**

couplet: Two successive lines of rhyming **verse,** often of the same **meter** and generally either octosyllabic or decasyllabic.
EXAMPLES: The Duke in Robert Browning's poem "My Last Duchess" (1842) speaks of his dead young wife in couplets:

> Sir, 'twas all one! My favor at her breast,
> The dropping of the daylight in the West,
> The bough of cherries some officious fool
> Broke in the orchard for her, the white mule
> She rode with round the terrace — all and each
> Would draw from her alike the approving speech,
> Or blush, at least. She thanked men — good! but thanked
> Somehow — I know not how — as if she ranked
> My gift of a nine-hundred-years-old name
> With anybody's gift.

A more modern example of the couplet may be found in the following **stanza** of Robert Lowell's "Waking Early Sunday Morning" (1967):

> No weekends for the gods now. Wars
> flicker, earth licks its open sores,
> fresh breakage, fresh promotions, chance
> assassinations, no advance.
> Only man thinning out his kind
> sounds through the Sabbath noon, the blind
> swipe of the pruner and his knife
> busy about the tree of life. . . .

See also **closed couplet.**

courtesy book: See **Renaissance.**

courtly love: A philosophy of love prevalent in **medieval** literature that purported to describe — but more truly prescribed — certain codes of behavior between aristocratic men and women. Although courtly love has come to suggest an ideal, spiritual love beyond physical pleasure, the term still generally refers to a specific method of courtship and specific manner of amorous conduct.

Courtly love is believed to have had its origins in the **lyrics** of the **troubadours** of eleventh- and twelfth-century Provence (France). Important influences included the Roman poet Ovid, who wrote *The Art of Love*

(c. 1 B.C.) and *The Remedies of Love* (c. A.D. 1), and traditions involving the veneration of the Virgin Mary.

As its name suggests, courtly love refers to love as practiced among the nobility. It presumes that a nobleman (often a knight) meets a lady with such striking beauty that he instantly falls in love and begins to exhibit wretched symptoms of ill health and anxiety (such as pallor, loss of appetite, and fits of weeping). If the lady who is the object of his veneration accepts him as her lover, however, the man regains his health and well-being. He then subjects himself to her every caprice and obsequiously serves her. Courtly love does not lead to marriage, which for medieval aristocrats was generally arranged and based on political and economic considerations. Indeed, the lady involved in a courtly love relationship is usually a married woman who depends upon the discretion of her lover to keep their love a secret.

With regard to adultery, two traditions of courtly love exist. In the early days of the courtly love tradition, adultery was glorified to the point that it was represented as an almost religious experience; of course, the two lovers had to remain completely — and eternally — faithful to each other. The man was also inspired to perform great deeds and to follow rigorously Christian and chivalrous tradition in every other respect in order to be worthy of his lady's love. Beginning particularly with Dante Alighieri, however, courtly love often meant a **Platonic** (unconsummated) **love,** one in which the lady inspired her lover to achieve a higher spiritual state rather than to perform noble deeds.

Whether courtly love was purely a literary **convention** or whether it actually reflected aristocratic practice to any significant extent is still debated. Although **representations** of courtly love became less common toward the end of the so-called **Medieval Period,** the influence of the courtly love tradition persisted in the literature of subsequent eras, particularly in **Renaissance** love poetry influenced by the **sonnets** of Petrarch, a fourteenth-century Italian poet. The special spiritual status accorded to women and the **theme** of love's ennobling power are two aspects of the courtly love tradition that have continued to influence Western thought, perhaps even to this day.

EXAMPLES: Courtly love traditions are represented in "Le rossignol" by the twelfth-century French poet Marie de France, "La mort de Tristan et d'Yseult" (from *Les romans de Tristan*) by the twelfth-century Anglo-Norman poet known simply as Thomas, "The Knight's Tale" (c. 1387) by Geoffrey Chaucer, and *Morte d'Arthur* (1485) by Sir Thomas Malory.

Cowleyan ode: See **irregular ode.**

creolization: See **postcolonial literature and postcolonial theory.**

crime novel: See **detective fiction.**

crisis: The moment in a **plot** when the **conflict** has intensified to a level at which the **protagonist's** lot will change decisively, either for the better or for the worse. The crisis is sometimes called the *turning point* because it represents the pivotal moment when the protagonist's fortunes begin to turn. Though the crisis and **climax** of a work generally occur together, *crisis* refers to a purely structural element of plot, whereas *climax* also (and perhaps especially) signifies the height of emotional response evoked in the audience by the crisis. *Crisis* and *climax* are generally used to refer to the major, decisive event in a work, but the terms have been used by some critics to refer to multiple minor peaks in the plot that change or intensify the course of action. Critics are more likely to identify multiple climaxes than crises in a work; most critics limit the use of the term *crisis* to the plot's ultimate turning.

EXAMPLE: In the movie *Dead Poets Society* (1989), the main character, Neil, decides to perform in a play even though his father has forbidden him to do so. When the father finds out and shows up at the play, the crisis occurs. From this point, Neil's fortunes decline progressively, ending with his suicide.

criticism: Reflective, attentive consideration and analysis of a literary work. The term comes from the Greek *kritikos,* which refers to the ability to discern or judge. Given the **etymology** of the term, many critics assert that an evaluation of the work at hand is an essential element of criticism, though others maintain that examination and analysis are sufficient. In popular parlance, criticism refers to the practice of pointing out faults or shortcomings; as a result, it has a somewhat negative **connotation.** Literary criticism refers to a more balanced analysis; even when literary critics supplement analysis with appraisal, they generally discuss the merits as well as the faults of a work in order to arrive at a sound, deliberate assessment. If a critic approves of the work he or she is analyzing, the resulting appraisal may be far from critical, at least in the popular sense of the word. In addition to the assessment and analysis of works of literature, criticism may refer to the establishment of a general set of principles applicable to any number of works.

Many schools or types of literary criticism exist; in fact, some might argue that as many kinds of criticism exist as there are critics, especially given the proliferation of **theories** of criticism in Europe and North America since the 1970s. Some kinds of literary criticism involve close and detailed analysis of the **text,** others the biographical background of the writer or the historical contexts within which the work was written, and still others the reader's subjective response to the work. Each school or type of criticism **privileges** some aspect or aspects of the work over others, as well as particular strategies of reading or interpretation.

Types of criticism include **antithetical criticism, archetypal criticism, Chicago School, contextual criticism, cultural criticism, deconstruction, dialectical criticism, dialogic criticism, disability studies, ecocriticism,** expressive criticism, feminist criticism, formalism, gender criticism, Geneva School, gynocriticism, historicism, impressionistic criticism, judicial criticism, Jungian criticism, Marxist criticism, mimetic criticism, mythic criticism, the New Criticism, the new historicism, objective criticism, personal criticism, phenomenological criticism, postcolonial theory, poststructuralism, practical (applied) criticism, pragmatic criticism, psychological and psychoanalytic criticism, queer theory, reader-response criticism, rhetorical criticism, Russian formalism, structuralist criticism, textual criticism, and theoretical criticism.

critics of consciousness: See **Geneva School.**

cultural criticism, cultural studies: Critical approaches with roots in the British cultural studies movement of the 1960s. A movement that reflected and contributed to the unrest of that decade, it both fueled and was fueled by the challenges to tradition and authority apparent in everything from the antiwar movement to the emergence of "hard rock" music. Birmingham University's Centre for Contemporary Cultural Studies, founded by Stuart Hall and Richard Hoggart in 1964, quickly became the locus of the movement, which both critiqued elitist definitions of culture and drew upon a wide variety of disciplines and perspectives.

In Great Britain, the terms *cultural criticism* and *cultural studies* have been used more or less interchangeably, and, to add to the confusion, both terms have been used to refer to two different things. On one hand, they have been used to refer to the analysis of literature (including popular literature) and other art forms in their social, political, or economic contexts; on the other hand, they have been used to refer to the much broader interdisciplinary study of the interrelationships between a variety of cultural **discourses** and practices (such as advertising, gift-giving, and racial categorization). In North America, the term *cultural studies* is usually reserved for this broader type of analysis, whereas *cultural criticism* typically refers to work with a predominantly literary or artistic focus. In this entry, we adhere to North American usage and focus mainly on cultural criticism.

Examples of cultural studies include various recent analyses of consumerism indebted to the work of Hall, Michel de Certeau, and Dick Hebdige, whose 1979 book *Subculture: The Meaning of Style* paved the way for critics like John Fiske (*Television Culture* [1987]), Greil Marcus (*Dead Elvis* [1991]), and Rachel Bowlby (*Shopping with Freud* [1993]). These analyses have addressed topics such as the resistance tactics employed by television viewers, the influence of consumers on rock music styles, and the psychology of consumer choice. An example of cultural criticism is Mary Poovey's book *The Proper Lady and the Woman Writer* (1984) — in which eighteenth-century novels by women are viewed in light of conduct manuals, ladies' magazines, and the **patriarchal** system governing the ownership and inheritance of property. Patrick Brantlinger's *Rule of Darkness* (1988) is another example of cultural criticism. Brantlinger reads Joseph

Conrad's *Heart of Darkness* (1899) in the context of late-nineteenth-century imperialism, racism, the goals of the Congo Reform Association, **impressionism,** popular **romances** concerning love and adventure, and "exposé literature" (mis)representing cannibalism in Africa.

Cultural critics examine how literature emerges from, influences, and competes with other forms of discourse (such as religion, science, or advertising) within a given culture. They analyze the social contexts in which a given **text** was written, and under what conditions it was — and is — produced, disseminated, and read. Like practitioners of cultural studies, they oppose the view that culture refers exclusively to high culture, culture with a capital C, seeking to make the term refer to popular, **folk,** urban, and mass (mass-produced, -disseminated, -mediated, and -consumed) culture, as well as to that culture we associate with so-called great literature. In other words, cultural critics argue that what we refer to as a culture is in fact a set of interactive *cultures*, alive and changing, rather than static or monolithic. They favor analyzing literary works not as aesthetic objects complete in themselves but as works to be seen in terms of their relationships to other works, to economic conditions, or to broad social discourses (about childbirth, women's education, rural decay, etc.). Cultural critics have emphasized what de Certeau, a French theorist, has called "the practice of everyday life," approaching literature more as an anthropologist than as a traditional "elitist" literary critic.

Cultural critics are as willing to write about *Star Trek* as they are to analyze James Joyce's *Ulysses* (1922), a modern literary **classic** full of **allusions** to Homer's *Odyssey* (c. 850 B.C.). When they do write about *Ulysses,* they are likely to emphasize how it reflects and represents cultural forms common to Joyce's Dublin, such as advertising, journalism, film, and pub life. They also typically demonstrate how the boundary between high and low culture is transgressed in innumerable ways within works on both sides of the putative cultural divide.

Hence, a cultural critic might contrast a revered literary classic with a movie or even a comic strip version. The classic might also be seen in light of some more common form of reading material (a novel by Jane Austen might be compared to **Gothic** romances or ladies' conduct manuals). Alternatively, it might be seen as the reflection of common cultural **myths** or concerns (Mark Twain's *Adventures of Huckleberry Finn* [1884] might be shown to reflect and shape American myths about race and concerns about juvenile delinquency). Finally, a cultural critic might use a work to demonstrate how texts transgress the alleged boundary between low and high culture. For instance, some cultural critics have noted that although William Shakespeare's plays began as popular works enjoyed by working people, they were later considered "highbrow" plays that only the privileged and educated could appreciate. With the advent of film production, however, they have regained an increasingly popular audience. Recently, cultural critics, responding to a spate of Shakespeare plays turned into movies, have analyzed the "cultural work" accomplished by Mel Gibson and Franco

Zeffirelli in the latter's 1990 film production of Shakespeare's *Hamlet* (1602) and by Baz Luhrman's 1996 resetting of *Romeo and Juliet* (1595) in contemporary, crime-ridden America.

In combatting traditional definitions of what constitutes culture, cultural critics sometimes contest traditional definitions of what constitutes the literary **canon,** that is, those literary works given special status by a given culture (classics or "Great Books"). Indeed, these critics generally critique the very idea of canon, rather than seeking to substitute a counterculture canon for the traditional one or to add books (or movies or sitcoms) to the old list of texts that every "culturally literate" person should supposedly know.

Cultural critics eschew the notion that certain works are the "best" ones produced by a given culture. They seek to be more descriptive and less evaluative; they seek to relate, rather than rate, cultural products and events. They also aim to discover the (often political) reasons why one aesthetic or cultural product is more highly valued than another. This is particularly true when the product has been produced since 1945, for most cultural critics follow Jean Baudrillard (*Simulations* [1981]) and Andreas Huyssen (*The Great Divide* [1986]) in arguing that any distinctions that may have existed between "high," popular, and mass culture collapsed after World War II.

Cultural critics have also questioned other value hierarchies. Many have criticized the institution of the university, for it is in universities that the old definition of culture as high Culture (and as something formed, finished, and canonized) has been most vigorously defended and preserved. Cultural critics have been especially critical of the departmental structure of universities, which has kept the study of the "arts" relatively distinct from the study of history, not to mention television, advertising, journalism, **folklore,** current affairs, and gossip. By maintaining artificial boundaries, universities reassert the high/low culture distinction. By implicitly associating **aesthetics** with literature and propaganda with advertising, for instance, they impede recognition of the propagandistic aspects of a literary work and the aesthetic aspects of an ad. Cultural critics have consequently mixed and matched the analytical procedures developed in numerous disciplines, focusing on human consciousness rather than a body of works assumed to reflect a given culture. They seek to understand and demonstrate that consciousness is itself largely forged by cultural forces.

Although the United States has probably contributed more than any other nation to the media through which culture is currently expressed, and although many contemporary practitioners of cultural criticism are North American, the evolution of cultural criticism and, more broadly, cultural studies has to a great extent been influenced by theories developed in Great Britain and on the European continent.

Structuralists and **poststructuralists** are among the Continental thinkers whose work set the stage for the development of cultural criticism and cultural studies. Using a scientific approach and the **linguistic** theory of Ferdinand de Saussure, structuralists such as Roland Barthes and Claude Lévi-Strauss suggested that *all* elements of human culture, including literature, may be understood as parts of a system of **signs.** The ideas of structuralist **psychoanalytic** theorist Jacques Lacan have been particularly influential, serving as the theoretical underpinning for cultural critics who have sought to show how **subjectivities,** that is, our very identities, are produced by social discourses and practices. Lacan posited that the human unconscious is structured like a language and treated dreams as forms of discourse. He also argued that the **ego,** subject, or self that we think of as natural (our individual human nature) is in fact a product of the social order and its **symbolic** systems (especially, but not exclusively, language).

Poststructuralist French philosopher Jacques Derrida has also influenced the development of cultural criticism and cultural studies. In *De la grammatologie (Of Grammatology)* (1967), Derrida provocatively asserted that *"there is nothing outside the text."* In making this statement, Derrida refused to categorically distinguish world and text, simultaneously asserting that every human (worldly) product can be viewed as a text and that every text reflects and shapes the world we perceive. From the time that we learn to speak, we perceive and describe the world through language, assigning everything a name; our actions and practices (registering for the draft, practicing birth control) are dependent upon language and discourse. Even the very contravention of discourses depends upon those same discourses, for there is nothing to argue about if we have nothing to argue against. Cultural critics have used Derrida's **deconstruction** of the world / text distinction, like his deconstruction of so many of the hierarchical **binary oppositions** we habitually use to interpret and evaluate reality, to erase the boundaries between high and low culture, classic and popular literary texts, and literature and other cultural discourses.

Several thinkers influenced by **Marxism** have also powerfully affected the development of cultural criticism and cultural studies. The French philosophical historian Michel Foucault has perhaps had the strongest influence on North American cultural criticism and **the new historicism,** a type of literary criticism whose evolution has often paralleled that of North American cultural criticism. In works such as *Discipline and Punish* (1975) and *The History of Sexuality* (1976), Foucault studied cultures in terms of power relationships, a focus typical of Marxist thought. Unlike Marxists, however, Foucault did not see power as something exerted by a dominant **class** over a subservient one. For Foucault, power was more than repressive power: it was a complex of forces generated by the confluence — or conflict — of discourses; it was that which produces what happens.

Foucault approached everything from punishment to **sexuality** in terms of the widest possible variety of discourses. As a result, he examined texts that most traditional historians and literary critics would have overlooked, such as diaries, court records, and doctors' reports. Foucault sought to pinpoint the crossroads at which discourses and social practices were contravened and transformed. His interdisciplinary work acknowledged the viewpoints and histories of women and of racial, ethnic, and sexual minorities, groups seldom studied by those interested in culture with a capital C.

Prominent British — as opposed to Continental — influences include E. P. Thompson and Raymond Williams. Thompson, a Marxist historian and author of *The Making of the English Working Class* (1963), revolutionized study of the Industrial Revolution by writing about its impact on human attitudes, even human consciousness. He showed how a shared cultural view, specifically that of what constitutes a fair price, influenced crowd behavior, causing disturbances like the "food riots" of the eighteenth and nineteenth centuries. Williams, best known for his book *Culture and Society: 1780–1950* (1958), argued that culture is living and evolving rather than fixed and finished, further stating in *The Long Revolution* (1961) that "art and culture are ordinary."

Although Williams did not define himself as a Marxist throughout his entire career, he always followed the Marxist practice of viewing culture in relation to **ideologies,** which he defined as the "residual," "dominant," or "emerging" ways in which classes or individuals holding power in a given social group view the world. He avoided dwelling on class conflict and class oppression, however, focusing on people and the way they experience the conditions in which they find themselves and creatively respond to those conditions through their social practices.

Because cultural criticism and cultural studies have been heavily influenced by Marxism (some contemporary cultural critics even consider themselves **Marxist critics** as well), it is important to be familiar with certain Marxist concepts, particularly those advanced by Mikhail Bakhtin, Walter Benjamin, Antonio Gramsci, and Louis Althusser. Bakhtin was a Soviet critic so original in his thinking and wide-ranging in his influence that some would say he was never a Marxist at all. He viewed literary works in terms of discourses and **dialogues** *between* discourses. The **narrative** of a novel written in a society in flux, for instance, may include not only an official, legitimate discourse but others that challenge that official viewpoint. In *Problems of Dostoevsky's Poetics* (1929) and *Rabelais and His World* (1940), Bakhtin examined what he called **polyphonic** novels, each characterized by several voices or discourses. In works by Rabelais, for instance, Bakhtin found that the (profane) discourses of the **carnival** and of other popular festivities play against and **parody** the more official discourses of churches and magistrates. Cultural critics have found particularly compelling Bakhtin's suggestion that the dialogue involving "high" and "low" culture takes place not only between classic and popular texts but also between the **dialogic** voices that exist *within* classic texts.

The second Marxist thinker that practitioners of cultural criticism and cultural studies have drawn on is Walter Benjamin, a German Marxist who attacked fascism and questioned the superior value placed on certain traditional literary forms that he felt conveyed a stultifying "aura" of culture. He took this position in part because so many previous Marxist critics (and, in his own day, Georg Lukács — author of *The Historical Novel* [1937]) seemed to prefer nineteenth-century **realistic novels** to the **modernist** works of their own time. Benjamin, best known for his essay "The Work of Art in the Age of Mechanical Reproduction" (1936), not only praised modernist movements such as **Dadaism** but also hailed the development of new art forms involving mechanical production and reproduction, anticipating by decades the work of those cultural critics interested in mass-produced, mass-mediated, and mass-consumed culture. Forms such as photography, radio, and film could render the arts a more democratic, less exclusive domain.

Antonio Gramsci, an Italian Marxist whose 1929–35 *Prison Notebooks* were partially published in English as *Selections from the Prison Notebooks* (1971), critiqued the very concept of literature and, beyond that, of culture in the old sense. He stressed the importance of culture more broadly defined and the need for nurturing proletarian (working-class) culture. Gramsci also argued that all intellectual or cultural work is fundamentally political, relating literature to the ideologies — the prevailing ideas and beliefs — of the culture in which it was produced. He developed the concept of **hegemony,** which refers both to the process of consensus formation and the authority of ideologies to shape the way things look, what they mean, and, therefore, what reality *is* for most people. But Gramsci did not see people, even poor people, as the helpless victims of hegemony, as ideology's hapless robots. Rather, he believed that people have the freedom and power to struggle against and shape ideology, to alter hegemony, to break out of the weblike system of prevailing assumptions, and to form a new consensus.

The French Marxist Louis Althusser also explored the relationship between literature and ideology, in works such as *For Marx* (1969) and *Lenin and Philosophy and Other Essays* (1971). But unlike Gramsci, Althusser tended to portray ideology as controlling people, and not vice versa. He argued that ideology serves to reproduce the society's existing relations of production, even in literary texts. Many cultural critics reject Althusser's view of literature, however, for although he did argue that literature is relatively autonomous — more independent of ideology than the church, press, or state — he was referring to the literature we associate with "high culture." Popular fictions, Althusser assumed, were mere packhorses designed (however unconsciously) to carry the baggage of a culture's ideology, or mere brood mares destined to reproduce it.

Even those cultural critics who agree with Althusser's reflections on literature and ideology have rejected the narrow limits within which Althusser and some other Marxists (such as Georg Lukács) have defined literature. In "Marxism and Popular Fiction" (1986), Marxist cultural critic Tony Bennett uses *Monty Python's Flying Circus* and another British television show, *Not the 9 O'clock News*, to reject the Althusserian notion that all forms of culture are manifestations of capitalist ideology. Indeed, Bennett argues that "popular fiction" (books, films, television, etc.) often has the effect of "distancing" or separating the audience from — rather than rebinding the audience to — prevailing ideologies.

Most practitioners of cultural criticism and cultural studies, however, are not Marxists in any strict sense. Anne Beezer, who has analyzed advertisements and women's magazines, gives both the media she is concerned with and their audiences more credit than Althusserian Marxists presumably would. Whereas Althusserian Marxists might argue that such media make people what they are, Beezer points out that the same magazines that tell women how to please their men also offer women liberating advice about how to preserve their independence. And, she suggests, many advertisements advertise their status as ads, just as many people see advertising as advertising and interpret it accordingly.

Tania Modleski and Janice Radway have undertaken similarly complex analyses of paperback romance novels in *Loving with a Vengeance: Mass-Produced Fantasies for Women* (1982) and *Reading the Romance: Women, Patriarchy, and Popular Literature* (1984), respectively. Radway, a **feminist** cultural critic who incorporates some Marxist ideas, points out that many women read romances in order to carve out a time and space that is wholly their own. Although many such novels end in marriage, the marriage is usually between a feisty **heroine** and a powerful man she has "tamed." Radway's reading is typical of feminist cultural criticism in that it is political but not exclusively about oppression. Although the thinking of romance readers may be governed to some extent by what they read, these women also affect what is published, thus performing "cultural work" of their own. Romances in which heroines are degraded are not popular among romance readers and, therefore, are rarely produced.

The overlap between feminist and cultural criticism is hardly surprising, especially given the recent evolution of feminism into various femin*isms*. These typically focus on "majority" women of European descent, minority women in Western culture, and women living in Third World (preferably called postcolonial) societies. The culturalist analysis of value hierarchies has focused on **class, race, gender, sexuality,** and national origin; the terms of its critique have proved useful to contemporary feminists, many of whom differ from their predecessors insofar as they see *woman* not as an overarching category but rather as one of several contributing to identity, or "subject," formation. The influence of cultural criticism (and, in some cases, Marxist class analysis) can be seen in the work of contemporary feminist critics such as Gayatri Chakravorty Spivak, Trinh T. Minh-ha, and Gloria Anzaldúa, who stress that although all women are female, they are something else as well (working-class, lesbian, Native American), a facet that must be considered in analyzing their writings.

The expansion of feminism and feminist literary criticism to include multicultural analysis parallels a transformation of education in general. African American studies, a form of cultural studies, has grown and flourished; African American critics have pointed out that the North American white cultural elite has tended to view the oral-musical traditions of African Americans (jazz, the **blues,** sermons, **folk tales,** etc.) as entertaining but nonetheless inferior. In order not to be similarly marginalized, black writers have produced texts that, as Henry Louis Gates has noted, fuse the language and traditions of the white Western canon with a black vernacular and tradition derived from African and Caribbean cultures.

Interest in race and ethnicity has accompanied a new, interdisciplinary focus on colonial and postcolonial societies, in which issues of race, class, and ethnicity loom large. Practitioners of **postcolonial theory,** another form of cultural studies inaugurated by Edward Said's book *Orientalism* (1978), have, according to Homi K. Bhabha in an essay entitled "Postcolonial Criticism" (1992), revealed the way in which certain cultures (mis-) represent others in order to achieve and extend political and social domination in the modern world order. Thanks to the work of scholars like Bhabha, Said, Gates, Anzaldúa, and Spivak, education in general and literary study in particular is becoming more democratic, multicultural, and **decentered** (less patriarchal and Eurocentric) in its interests and emphases.

cultural materialism: A term popularized by **Marxist critic** Raymond Williams to signify the belief that economic forces and modes of production inevitably affect cultures and cultural products, such as literature. Cultural materialists have often argued that literary **texts** perform a "subversive" or otherwise politically charged function — not only in their own historical eras but also in subsequent epochs, when they take on different meanings and become the **sites** of new kinds of debate. This view of literature as persistently subversive is in keeping with the broader interest of most cultural materialists in transforming the existing sociopolitical order, which they tend to view as being exploitative along the lines of **class, gender,** and **race.** A number of British and American **new historicist** and **cultural critics** have borrowed the terminology of cultural materialists, either to emphasize their **Marxism** or as a means of relating their descriptions of the past to the politics of present-day **discourses** and institutions.

cultural poetics: See **new historicism, the.**

cyberfiction: A word coined in the late twentieth century that is used interchangeably with *cyberpunk* and *hypertext fiction* but that may also refer more broadly to any fictional **text,** whether **classic** or contemporary, published (in some cases exclusively) on the Internet. The term *cyberfiction* acknowledges the increasing influence of computer technology on literature, whether manifested in terms of **plot** (e.g., computer-oriented **science fiction**), medium of publication (e.g., any work of fiction now available on the World Wide Web), reader participation (e.g., interactive novels that invite the reader's creative involvement), or in some other way.

Cyberpunk refers to a type of science fiction that emerged in the mid-1970s and that gained popularity in 1984 with the publication of William Gibson's novel *Neuromancer.* The prefix "cyber" is taken from *cybernetics,* the study of the control systems of the human brain and nervous system and of analogous mechanical and electronic technology, and invokes the idea of the *cyborg,* a hybrid of human and machine. The "punk" component of the term refers to a counterculture movement that began in the 1970s and that is especially associated with a form of rock music characterized by extreme and even offensive expressions of anger and alienation.

Cyberpunk authors such as Gibson, Bruce Sterling, Rudy Rucker, and Neal Stephenson write novels and short stories about near-future societies populated by characters who are totally immersed in a "cyborg world" in which the distinction between human and machine has been blurred, if not erased. Life is experienced only through the virtual reality of *cyberspace,* a term coined by Gibson in 1984 to describe the **linked** network referred to as the "matrix." Characters are usually technologically proficient, self-serving loners, computer "console cowboys" who have no loyalty to governments, nations, or politics and who may also be violent and unethical. Human bodies are routinely injected with drugs, hormones, and serums, as well as surgically implanted with advanced microprocessors, prostheses, and memory-enhancing components such as silicon-based storage. In Gibson's novels, these hybrids, or cyborgs, see "life in the flesh" as dull and are satisfied only when freed from bondage to "the meat," their term for the human body.

Cyberpunk fiction sometimes deals with religious beliefs and the nature of divinity, and some commentators believe it may subtly forewarn of the negative effects of society's increasing dependence on technology. Unlike most classic science fiction of the 1930s and 1940s, however, cyberpunk does not present a view of the future that is either overtly positive or negative; rather, it presupposes that ethics and integrity have become irrelevant in a computer-dominated world. Cyberpunk is also characterized by a mix of conventional language and "cyberjargon," terms such as ICE ("intrusion countermeasure electronics," i.e., security programs), A.I. (artificial intelligence), and ROM (technically meaning "read only memory," but as cyberfiction jargon referring to recordings preserving a personality after death). Cyberpunk fiction, which has inspired movies such as *Universal Soldier* (1992), *The Matrix* (1999), and *A.I.* (2001), typically appears in traditional print media but may also be published online and even written as hypertext fiction.

Hypertext fiction generally refers to interactive novels, short stories, and poems that are available on the Internet, CD-ROMs, and floppy disks and that often include sound and graphic art. This type of nonlinear, fragmented text is said to be **decentered,** because readers are allowed to leave the primary document through **links** that provide access to additional texts. As Jay Bolter states in *Writing Spaces: The Computer, Hypertext, and the History of Writing* (1991), "the fluidity of the electronic medium allows the texts to be in a perpetual state of reorganization." Unlike traditional books printed on paper that compel the reader to follow a linear route through the text, hypertext fiction greatly expands the universe of possible perceptions and conclusions by allowing readers to navigate the text, to choose which paths to follow — and when. As a result, readers become active participants, and their relationship to the text changes significantly. Indeed, they may even become authors if asked to reach their own conclusion(s) based on the path(s) they have chosen in solving a problem or mystery encountered along the way — or even to contribute to the plot by submitting their own writings.

The continuing use of *cyberfiction* to refer to classic or contemporary literature published or republished on the Internet ensures that this term will, for the foreseeable future, be broad in its applicability, meaning different things to different users.

FURTHER EXAMPLES: Cyberpunk novels by Bruce Sterling include *Islands in the Net* (1988), *The Difference Engine* (1990) (coauthored with William Gibson), and *Holy Fire* (1996). Other cyberpunk titles include Neal Stephenson's *Snowcrash* (1992), *The Diamond Age* (1995), and *Cryptonomicon* (1999).

Examples of hypertext fiction include Michael Joyce's *afternoon, a story* (1989), which is about a writer who suspects that the accident he saw earlier in the day involved his ex-wife, and an interactive novel entitled *The Patchwork Girl* (1995), a post**feminist** revision of Mary Shelley's *Frankenstein* (1818) by Shelley Jackson that considers the possibility that Mary Shelley, rather than Dr. Frankenstein, could have created a female monster. (Both of these works are available, at this writing, through the Web site of Eastgate Systems, Inc., <www.eastgate.com>.) Well-known author John Updike has written a hypertext novel, entitled *Murder Makes the Magazine* (1997), for the Internet at the request of Amazon.com. Readers were invited, over a six-week period, to compete for a monetary prize by contributing to the book. An example of cyberfiction broadly defined is Stephen King's Web novel *Riding the Bullet* (2000), republished on audiocassettes in 2002.

See **hypertext.**

cyberpunk: See **cyberfiction.**

D

dactyl(ic): A metrical **foot** in poetry that consists of one **stressed** syllable followed by two unstressed ones.

EXAMPLES: pórtăblĕ, márgĭnăl, écstăsў. Numerous nursery rhymes contain dactyls ("Hígglĕdў pígglĕdў," "Pát-ă-cakĕ, pát-ă-cakĕ," "Ríngs ŏn hĕr fíngĕrs ănd bélls ŏn hĕr tóes," etc.). The following line from Archibald MacLeish's poem "Speech to Those Who Say Comrade" (1936) is dactylic:

Húngĕr ănd húrt arĕ thĕ gréatĕst bĕgéttĕrs ŏf brótherhŏod. . . .

Also dactylic is Alfred, Lord Tennyson's poem "The Charge of the Light Brigade" (1854):

> Cánnŏn tŏ ríght ŏf thĕm,
> Cánnŏn tŏ léft ŏf thĕm,
> Cánnŏn ĭn frónt ŏf thĕm
> Vólleyĕd ănd thúndĕred;
> Stórmed ăt wĭth shót ănd shéll,
> Bóldlў thĕy róde ănd wéll,
> Íntŏ thĕ jáws ŏf Déath,
> Íntŏ thĕ móuth ŏf héll
> Róde thĕ síx húndrĕd.

Silliness (a dactyl) best describes the sound of dactyls when repeated. Recognizing that fact, wits have invented the *double dactyl,* a humorous **verse** form consisting of eight lines, each of which must be composed of two dactyls. The first double dactyl must be a nonsense phrase; the second must be a person's name, and the seventh and penultimate double dactyl must come in the form of a single word. The following examples are taken from C. Webster Wheelock's unpublished history of the world in double dactyls, *History Gistory:*

> Monocle-bonocle
> Theodore Roosevelt
> Bullied his way to the
> Top of San Juan:
> Muscular buster of
> Trusts and a booster of,
> Incontrovertibly,
> Brains under brawn.

Arrogant paragon,
Katharine of Aragon
Hitched onto Henry's her
Marital star;
Thinking how blessed he was,
Hank never guessed she was
Gynecologically
Way below Parr.

The **classic** rock song "Lucy in the Sky with Diamonds" (1967) by the Beatles has a predominantly dactylic **rhythm.**

Dadaism: A movement founded by Tristan Tzara in Zurich, Switzerland, in 1916 to rebel against the "civilization" that produced World War I, a war seen by members of this movement as insane. The movement rapidly spread to other European countries, where its adherents sought to destabilize the art and philosophy of the time, offering in their place seemingly insane, nihilistic works designed to protest the madness of war. Dadaism was particularly well received in Paris, which became the capital of the movement. Dadaists self-consciously insisted on absolute artistic freedom, ignored standard logic and restraint, and made a point of making shocking statements and doing outrageous things.

Many Dadaists claimed that the term *Dadaism* was chosen arbitrarily. Some students of the movement accept this explanation, noting that *dada* means "hobbyhorse" in French and pointing out that it would be in keeping with the spirit of the movement to defy traditions and **conventions** by picking a name with no apparent relevance. Others, however, see greater significance in the name, arguing that the *dada* in *Dadaism* involves an allusion to fatherhood (*dada* rather than *mama*) and reflects the desire of Dadaists to inject masculinity rather than femininity into literature.

As a movement, Dadaism itself was fairly short-lived. It was, however, the immediate forerunner of the **surrealist** movement of the mid-1920s and an influence on other subsequent **genres,** such as **Absurdist** theater and the **antinovel.**

dead metaphor: A phrase once recognized as a **metaphor** (a direct comparison between two distinct things without *like* or *as*) that has become so familiar that it is no longer recognized as a metaphor. Because the **vehicle** of the metaphor (the **image** used to describe or in some way define the subject, or **tenor,** of the metaphor) is no longer recognized as such, the phrase is taken in an almost literal sense. Poets, known for their strikingly creative and original use of language, nonetheless sometimes use dead metaphors to create specific poetic effects.

EXAMPLES: Keel over, toe the line, keystone, know the ropes, the foot of the bed. In "Renovations" (1977), a poem about the everyday business of taking a shower, Robert B. Shaw uses a dead metaphor ("fiddling") to strike an appropriately casual tone: "A twist, a little fiddling / With temperature, then in." When we use the term *fiddled* ("I fiddled with the color on my TV set"), no one thinks of the activity we are describing in terms of playing the violin!

decadence: Broadly defined, a term referring to moral decline or to the decline of a great artistic or literary period. Its literary application refers to a lapse in the quality of works associated with a particular literary era or movement. Decadent phases tend to be characterized by a self-consciously refined **style** that elevates polish and ornamentation over substance. Emphasizing technique results in an artificiality that is only heightened by the bizarre and esoteric nature of the subject matter typically chosen by decadent writers.

Decadence also has a more specific meaning, however. When capitalized, it refers to a literary movement strongest in France but also prevalent in America and especially England toward the end of the nineteenth century. The Decadence is closely associated with the Aesthetic Movement; indeed, the term is often used to refer to the last phase or decline (depending on the user's perspective) of **Aestheticism.** Like members of the Aesthetic Movement, Decadents extolled *l'art pour l'art* (**art for art's sake).** In addition to rejecting traditional artistic and **aesthetic** norms, they sought to flout conventional morality in their dress, public behavior, and private sexual practices. Decadence is also closely associated with *fin de siècle* ("end of the century"), a term connoting the boredom and indolence that so many of the Decadent writers expressed. The Decadents published a short-lived journal entitled *Le décadent;* Théophile Gautier outlined many of the tenets of Decadence in his preface to an edition of Charles Baudelaire's *Les fleurs du mal* (1868).

EXAMPLES: "Silver age" Latin literature written during the reign of Trajan is often considered decadent in comparison to the "golden age" literature produced during the preceding reign of Augustus. English adherents of the Decadence include Aubrey Beardsley, Algernon Charles Swinburne, and Oscar Wilde; Baudelaire, Arthur Rimbaud, and Paul Verlaine were well-known French Decadents.

decenter: See **center.**

deconstruction: Deconstruction involves the **close reading** of **texts** in order to demonstrate that any given text has irreconcilably contradictory meanings, rather than being a unified, logical whole. As J. Hillis Miller, the preeminent American deconstructor, has explained in an essay entitled "Stevens' Rock and Criticism as Cure" (1976), "Deconstruction is not a dismantling of the structure of a text, but a demonstration that it has already dismantled itself. Its apparently solid ground is no rock but thin air." Deconstructing a text involves showing that it — like DNA with its double helix — can and does have intertwined yet opposite **discourses,** multiple and conflicting strands of **narrative,** threads of meaning that cross and contradict one another.

Deconstruction was both created and has been profoundly influenced by the French philosopher of language Jacques Derrida. Derrida, who coined the term *deconstruction,* argues that in Western culture people tend to think and express their thoughts in terms of **binary oppositions.** Something is white but not black, masculine and therefore not feminine, a cause rather than an effect. Other common and mutually exclusive pairs include beginning / end, conscious / unconscious, **presence / absence,** and speech / writing. Derrida suggests these dichotomies are not simply oppositions but also hierarchies in miniature, containing one term that Western culture views as positive or superior and another considered negative or inferior, even if only slightly so. (Presence, for instance, is more clearly preferable to absence than speech is preferable to writing.) Derrida doesn't seek to reverse these oppositions, however, because doing so would mean falling into the trap of perpetuating the same forms that he seeks to deconstruct. He instead aims to erase the boundary between binary oppositions — and to do so in such a way that the hierarchy implied by the oppositions is thrown into question.

Of particular interest to Derrida, perhaps because it involves the language in which all the other dichotomies are expressed, is the speech / writing opposition. Derrida argues that the **privileging** of speech, that is, the tendency to regard speech in positive terms and writing in negative terms, cannot be disentangled from the privileging of presence. (Postcards are written by absent friends; we read Plato because he cannot speak from beyond the grave.) Furthermore, the tendency to privilege both speech and presence is part of the Western tradition of **logocentrism,** the belief that a creative Beginning requires spoken words announced by an ideal, present God. Derrida has also used the word *phallogocentrism* to point out the connection between logocentrism and the **phallocentrism (patriarchal** structure) of a culture whose God created light, the world, and man before creating woman — from Adam's rib.

Derrida uses the theories of Ferdinand de Saussure, who invented the modern science of **linguistics,** to remind us that associating speech with present, obvious, and ideal meaning and writing with absent, merely pictured, and therefore less reliable meaning is suspect, to say the least. As Saussure demonstrated, words are not the things they name and, indeed, are only arbitrarily associated with those things. A tiger, for instance, need not be represented by the word *tiger;* any other word would do just as well. A word, like any **sign,** is what Derrida has called a "deferred presence" in an essay entitled "Différance" (1973); that is to say, the thing being **signified** is never actually present, and every signified concept invokes others in an endless string of **connotations.** Thus, neither spoken nor written words have positive, identifiable attributes in and of themselves. Indeed, they have meaning only by virtue of their *difference* from other words and, at the same time, their contextual relationship to those words. When reading, to know whether the word *read,* for example, is the present or past tense of the verb — that is, whether it rhymes with *reed* or *red —*

we need to see it in relation to some other word or words (for example, *yesterday*).

Derrida argues that all language is constituted by **différance,** a word he coined that puns on the French verb *différer,* which can mean either "to differ" or "to defer." He uses the term to demonstrate that words are only the deferred presences of the things they "mean," and the meaning of words is grounded in their difference from other words. The word *différance* also suggests the French noun *différence,* meaning "difference"; changing the second *e* in *différence* to an *a* in *différance* is itself a playful, witty challenge to the notion that writing is inferior or "fallen" speech, for this change can be seen in written French but cannot be heard in spoken French.

In *De la grammatologie (Of Grammatology)* (1967), Derrida begins to redefine writing by deconstructing some of the ways in which it has been defined. He uses Jean-Jacques Rousseau's *Confessions* (1783) to expose Rousseau's conflicting attitudes and behavior with respect to speech and writing, thereby demonstrating the contradiction between writing as a secondary, even treacherous supplement to speech and writing as necessary to (effective) communication. Although Rousseau condemned writing as mere **representation,** a corruption of the more natural, childlike, direct, and supposedly undevious speech, he admitted that he often blurted out exactly the wrong thing in public and expressed himself better in writing.

Although Derrida has deconstructed numerous texts, he does not claim to have explained or revealed their true meaning, at least not in any traditional sense. In fact, Derrida would deny that any one "true" meaning can be found. Those who seek to find a single, homogeneous, or universal meaning in a text are imprisoned by the structure of thought that insists that only one of various readings can be "right." Deconstructors believe that all works defy the laws of Western logic, the laws of opposition and noncontradiction. Texts don't say A and not B (or B and not A). They say A and not A (or B and not B). As Barbara Johnson notes in her translator's introduction to *Dissémination (Dissemination)* (1972), Derrida makes a typical deconstructive move to show that a text dismantles itself when he unearths "dimensions of Plato's *text* that work against the grain of (Plato's own) Platonism." Johnson also points out in *A World of Difference* (1987) that the word *deconstruction* is itself intended to "undermine the either / or logic of the opposition 'construction / destruction.'" Deconstruction is both, it is neither, and it reveals the way in which both construction and destruction are themselves not what they appear to be.

Although its ultimate aim may be to criticize Western idealism and logic, deconstruction arose as a response to **structuralism** and to **formalism,** two **structure**-oriented theories of reading. Structuralists believe that all elements of human culture, including literature, may be understood as parts of a system of signs. Using Saussure's linguistic theory, structuralists attempted to develop a **semiology,** or science of signs, arguing that anything people do or use to communicate information of any type constitutes a sign. Roland Barthes tried to recover literary language from the isolation in which it had been studied and to show that the same laws govern all signs, from road signs to handshakes to articles of clothing. Claude Lévi-Strauss, a structural anthropologist, found in **myths** what he called "mythemes," or building blocks (such as basic **plot** elements) that occur in similar myths from different cultures.

Derrida did not believe that structuralists could explain the laws governing human signification and thus provide the key to understanding the **form** and meaning of everything from an African village to Greek myth to Rousseau's *Confessions*. In his view, the scientific search by structural anthropologists for what unifies humankind amounts to a new version of the old search for the lost ideal. Derrida also rejected the structuralist belief that texts have **centers** of meaning, classifying it as a derivative of the logocentric belief that a reading of the text exists that accords with "the book as seen by God."

Deconstruction questions assumptions made about literature by formalists as well, although deconstruction and formalism are superficially similar. Formalist critics, such as **the New Critics,** assume that a work of literature is a freestanding, self-contained object whose meaning can be found in the complex network of relations between its parts (**allusions, images, rhythms,** sounds). Like deconstruction, formalism is a text-oriented approach whose practitioners often focus on **figurative language.** And formalists, long before deconstructors, discovered counterpatterns of meaning in the same text. But here, the similarities end.

Formalists, who associated literary with figurative language, ranked some figures above others in a valuative hierarchy. They preferred **symbols** and **metaphors** to **metonyms,** for instance, arguing that the former are less arbitrary figures than the latter. For formalists, metonyms involve associations that, however common in a given culture, are purely arbitrary; liquor may be referred to as "the bottle," but there is no inherent relationship between the two. A metaphor ("I'm feeling blue"), by contrast, supposedly involves a special, intrinsic, even "natural" relationship between **tenor** (the subject of the figure, the thing being represented, here the feeling of melancholy) and **vehicle** (the **image** used to represent the tenor, here the color blue); a symbol ("the river of life") involves a unique fusion of image and idea.

Deconstructors have questioned the formalist hierarchy of figures and the distinctions upon which hierarchical valuations are based. In "The Rhetoric of Temporality" (1969), Paul de Man deconstructs the distinction between symbol and **allegory;** elsewhere, he, Derrida, and Miller have questioned the distinction between metaphor and metonymy, arguing that all figuration is a process of linguistic substitution. In the case of a metaphor (or symbol), they claim, we have simply forgotten what juxtaposition or contiguity gave rise to the association that now seems mysteriously special. In an essay and book entitled, respectively, *La mythologie blanche (la métaphore dans le texte philosophique)* (*White Mythology:*

Metaphor in the Text of Philosophy) (1971) and *Allegories of Reading* (1979), Derrida and de Man have also challenged the priority of literal over figurative language; Miller has even denied the validity of the literal / figurative distinction, arguing in *Ariadne's Thread: Story Lines* (1992) that all words are figures.

Deconstructors also differ from formalists in evaluating the counterpatterns of meaning that can be found in any text. Formalists conceded that the resulting **ambiguity** is characteristic of literary texts, but they also believed that a complete understanding of the literary work was possible pending the objective resolution of ambiguities by the reader. Deconstructors, by contrast, argue that the conflicts are irreconcilable or "undecidable," embedded as they are within the text itself. *Undecidability,* as de Man came to define it, is a complex notion easily misunderstood. Many people (incorrectly) assume that it refers to readers who, when forced to decide between two or more equally plausible and conflicting readings, give up and decide that the choice can't be made. Undecidability, however, actually debunks the whole notion of reading as a decision-making process by readers. To say that we are forced to choose or decide — or that we are unable to do so — is falsely to locate undecidability within ourselves, rather than recognizing it as an intrinsic feature of the text.

Undecidability thus differs from the formalist concept of ambiguity. Deconstructors reject the formalist view that a work of literary art is demonstrably unified from beginning to end, in one certain way, or that it is organized around a single center that ultimately can be identified. (They also reject the concept of **irony** as simply saying one thing and meaning another thing that the reader will understand.) As a result, deconstructors see texts as more radically heterogeneous than do formalists. Formalists ultimately make sense of ambiguity, even if only by recognizing that it serves a definite, meaningful function; undecidability, by contrast, is never reduced, let alone mastered. Though a deconstructive reading can reveal the incompatible possibilities generated by the text, it is impossible for the reader to decide among them.

Deconstruction, then, is not really interpretation, the act of choosing between or among possible meanings. It is more accurately defined as reading, as long as reading is defined as de Man defined it: a process involving moments of **aporia** (irreconcilable uncertainty) and an act performed with the awareness that all texts are ultimately unreadable (that is, irreducible to a single, homogeneous meaning). In *The Ethics of Reading* (1987), Miller explains unreadability by saying that although moments of great lucidity in reading exist, each such moment itself contains a "blind spot" that must be elucidated, and so on. Miller's recognition of moments of lucidity suggests that critics practicing deconstruction know that their own insights — even their insights into what is or isn't contradictory, undecidable, or unreadable in a text — are hardly sacrosanct.

For deconstructors, the boundaries between any given text and that larger text we call language are always shifting. It was this larger text that

Derrida was referring to in *Of Grammatology* when he made his famous statement *"there is nothing outside the text."* In making this statement, Derrida refused to categorically distinguish world and text, simultaneously asserting that every human (worldly) product can be viewed as a text and that every text reflects and shapes the world we perceive. It is through language that we express ourselves and understand the world; the acts that constitute the "real world" (the Oklahoma City and World Trade Center bombings, the decision to marry) are both inseparable from the discourses out of which they arise and as open to interpretation as any work of literature. If no language or discourse existed, neither would tradition nor even disagreement. Terrorist acts such as the Oklahoma City and World Trade Center bombings would not occur were there no newspapers to report them and no clash between competing philosophies to incite them in the first place.

Since a text is always open to being seen in the light of new contexts, any given text can be different each time it is read. Furthermore, as Miller has shown in *Ariadne's Thread*, the various terms and families of terms we use in reading invariably affect the results. Whether we choose to focus on a novel's **characters** or its **realism,** for instance, leads us to view the same text differently; no single thread, as Miller puts it, serves to control and unify the whole. Even the individual words of narratives — words used to compose a mental picture of a character or place — usually have several (and often conflicting) meanings.

Deconstruction has been the target of considerable opposition, expressed not only in academic books and journals but also in popular magazines such as *Newsweek*. Attacks on deconstruction increased dramatically some four years after de Man's death in 1983, when numerous articles he wrote between 1941 and 1943 as a young journalist during World War II for *Le Soir*, a Nazi-controlled Brussels newspaper, and *Het Vlaamsche Land*, a collaborationist newspaper, were discovered. De Man's wartime journalism consists mainly of inoffensive literary pieces, but not entirely. In one article he assumes Germany will win World War II, places the German people at the center of Western civilization, and foresees a **mystical** era. In another article entitled *"Les Juifs dans la littérature actuelle"* ("Jews in Present-Day Literature"), de Man scoffs at the idea that Jewish writers have significantly influenced the literature of his day and, worse, considers the creation of a separate Jewish colony.

No one who came to know de Man after his immigration to the United States in 1948 remembers him as being illiberal or anti-Semitic. Furthermore, de Man spent his career in the U.S. "debunking" the kind of **ideological** assumptions (about the relationship between **aesthetics** and national cultures) that lie behind his most offensive earlier writings, arguing in *The Resistance to Theory* (1986) that literature must not become "a substitute for theology, ethics, etc." Either de Man changed radically after characterizing Germany and German culture as possessing magical integrity, or he never deeply believed the things he wrote in the 1940s.

Deconstruction's severest critics, however, have tried to use de Man's sometimes deplorable statements to prove that the entire critical movement of deconstruction is somehow morally as well as intellectually flawed. Examining some of the myths that have dogged deconstruction — and realizing why they are myths — helps us to understand deconstruction in an indirect, contrapuntal way that is in keeping with its spirit.

In *The Ethics of Reading,* Miller identifies and refutes two notions commonly repeated by deconstruction's detractors. First, critics of deconstruction often claim that deconstructors believe a text means nothing insofar as it means whatever the playful reader wants it to mean. Miller responds by pointing out that both Derrida and de Man have consistently argued that readers cannot make texts mean anything they want them to mean because texts do not support a single meaning or interpretation.

Second, Miller notes that deconstruction has been criticized as "immoral" insofar as it refuses to view literature traditionally, that is, "as the foundation and embodiment, the means of preserving and transmitting, the basic humanistic values of our culture." Miller rejects the notion that deconstructors shirk an ethical responsibility because they do not seek to (re)discover and (re)assert the values contained in the Western **canon,** finding it contingent upon "a basic misunderstanding of the way the ethical moment enters into the act of reading." Miller views reading as an act that leads to further ethical acts, decisions, and behavior. For these, the reader must take responsibility, as for any other ethical act.

Foes of deconstruction also object to its playfulness, to the pleasure its practitioners take in teasing out the contradictory interpretive possibilities generated by the words in a text, their **etymologies** and contexts, and their potential to be read figuratively or even ironically. In *The Post Card: From Socrates to Freud and Beyond* (1987), Derrida associates deconstruction with pleasure; in an interview published in his *Acts of Literature* (1992), he speculates that "it is perhaps that *jouissance* which most irritates the all-out adversaries of deconstruction." But adversaries misread deconstruction's *jouissance,* its pleasurable playfulness. Whereas they believe deconstructors view texts as boards upon which they can play delightfully useless little word games, Derrida claims that the pleasure of deconstruction arises from dismantling repressive ideas.

Perhaps the most common charge levelled at deconstructors is a claim that they divorce literary texts from historical, political, and legal institutions. Derek Attridge counters this charge in his introduction to *Acts of Literature* by noting that deconstructors like Derrida view literature not as a word-playground but, rather, as discourse "brought into being by processes that are social, legal, and political, and that can be mapped historically and geographically." Derrida also points out in *Memoires for Paul de Man* (1986) that deconstructors have pointedly questioned the tendency of historians to view the past as the source of (lost) truth and value, to look for explanations in origins, and to view as unified epochs (for example, the **Victorian Period,** 1837–1901) what are in fact complex and heterogeneous times in history. Derrida further notes that de Man's commentaries acknowledge that conflicting interpretations reflect and are reflected in the policies of institutions.

In addition to history and politics, deconstructors have recently focused on the law. In an essay on Franz Kafka's "Before the Law," Derrida has shown that for Kafka the law as such exists but can never actually be confronted. Miller has pointed out in *The Ethics of Reading* that the law "may only be confronted in its delegates or representatives or by its effects on us or others." The law's presence is continually deferred by narrative, that is, writing about the law which constantly reinterprets it in the attempt to reveal what it really is and means. This very act of (re)interpretation, however, serves to "defer" or distance the law even further from the case at hand, since the (re)interpretation takes precedence (and assumes prominence) over the law itself.

Because the facts about deconstruction are very different from the myths of its playful irreverence and irrelevance, a number of contemporary thinkers have found it useful to adapt and apply deconstruction in their work. For instance, a deconstructive theology has been developed, as has a deconstructive architectural theory. In the area of law, scholars associated with the Critical Legal Studies movement, such as David Kennedy, Gerald Frug, and Pierre Schlag, began to self-consciously utilize deconstruction (among a number of other nonlegal methodologies) in the early to mid-1980s. These scholars sought to critique the claims to rational coherence made by judicial and legal discourse and to criticize the way in which particular legal regimes affect justice between groups by highlighting the **gaps, conflicts,** and ambiguities in the law and legal discourse. Although Derridean concepts were not invoked by name until the 1980s, American legal theory has actually had a very developed practice of internal critique of legal concepts since the Realist movement of the 1930s, such that deconstructive methodologies (though not labeled as such) were fairly familiar.

In the field of literary studies, deconstruction's influence is apparent in the work of critics ostensibly taking some other, more "political" approach. In *The Critical Difference: Essays in the Contemporary Rhetoric of Reading* (1980), Johnson has put deconstruction to work for the **feminist** cause. She and Shoshana Felman have argued that chief among those binary oppositions "based on a repression of differences within entities" is the opposition man/woman. Johnson, Felman, and Gayatri Spivak have combined Derrida's theories with the **psychoanalytic** theory of Jacques Lacan to analyze the way in which **gender** and **sexuality** are ultimately textual, grounded in language and **rhetoric. Gay and lesbian critics** have followed their lead, hence Eve Kosofsky Sedgwick's recognition in *Epistemology of the Closet* (1990) that the "categories presented in a culture as symmetrical binary oppositions — actually subsist in a more unsettled and dynamic tacit relation." For instance, although most people think of sexual preference in binary terms (heterosexual/homosexual), sexuality is more accurately represented along a continuum.

In "Telling the Story of Deconstruction" (*The Pleasure of Babel: Contemporary American Literature and Theory* [1993]), Jay Clayton suggests that what began as theory in the late 1960s and 1970s has, over time, developed into a method employed by critics taking a wide range of approaches to literature — ethnic, feminist, **new historicist, Marxist** — in addition to critics whose focus is broader than literary studies, such as critical race theorists and **postcolonial theorists.** Edward Said, a scholar who inaugurated postcolonial criticism, is just one of many who have imported deconstruction from the literary to the nonliterary arena. In *Orientalism* (1978), Said deconstructed the East / West, Orient / Occident opposition and the stereotypes it entails, arguing that they not only facilitated colonization but still govern Western relations with Arab and Eastern countries today.

decorum: The idea, propagated especially in **classical** and **Renaissance** criticism, that authors should use a **style** suited to their purpose and work, a style that is suitable and fitting for a **character, setting,** or situation in the work.

EXAMPLE: Literary decorum dictates that a young chimney sweeper depicted by a **Victorian** novel should not speak in the elevated, high-mannered, and grammatically precise style of an Oxford don. Charles Dickens deliberately breaks the rules of decorum by giving the workhouse orphan Oliver Twist the speech of a young gentleman.

deep ecology: See **ecocriticism.**

deictic(s): A word that refers to another word or element in a **text** or passage and therefore relies on that latter word or element for its meaning. Deictics are often pronouns, adjectives, or adverbs, although any word that directly refers to and is contingent upon something else is a deictic.

EXAMPLE: The sentence, "Jack was shot here yesterday; he was a drug dealer, so it came as no surprise," contains four deictics: *here, yesterday, he,* and *it. He* and *it* are pronouns that clearly refer to *Jack* and the shooting respectively. *Here* could refer to a location (such as Chicago or a subterranean garage) or to the part of Jack's body the bullet entered (such as the head). If we are given the referent for *here* before we read or hear this sentence, we can easily understand what *here* refers to. If we are not given this information, *here* is a deictic that brings us into the narrative *in medias res* ("in the middle of things"); despite the lack of a named referent, *here* is still a deictic because it refers to something specific even if we do not know what that something is. The meaning of *yesterday* is similarly determined by whatever information, if any, we are given.

demotic: A term used by the critic Northrop Frye to refer to the unpretentious **style** of a certain type of literary work. An author using demotic (as opposed to **hieratic**) style employs the associations, **diction, rhythms,** and **syntax** of mundane (everyday) speech. Frye further distinguishes three categories — *high, middle,* and *low* — in both the demotic and hieratic styles.

See also **hieratic.**

denotation: A word's literal and primary meaning, independent of any **connotations** — emotional associations or secondary meanings — that a given individual might attach to it; the "dictionary definition" of a word.

dénouement: From the French for "unknotting," a term that both refers to the events following the **climax** of a **plot** and implies some ingenious resolution of the dramatic **conflict** and explanation of the mysteries or misunderstandings of that plot. Although *dénouement* may be applied to both **tragedy** and **comedy,** the term **catastrophe** is typically used with reference to tragedy.

EXAMPLE: The *dénouement* of the film *Finding Forrester* (2000) provides literary **closure** as well as a sense of **poetic justice** when Jamal Wallace — a poor African American student who was recruited by a fancy New York prep school to play basketball and then falsely accused of plagiarism — inherits the house, furniture, and books of his mentor, elderly New York writer William Forrester.

descriptive linguistics: The branch of **linguistics** that concerns itself with the classification of a language's various characteristics. Descriptive linguistics is different from *historical linguistics,* which concentrates on studying the development of a language over time.

detective fiction: A type of **fiction** featuring a crime (in most cases, a murder) that is solved by the **protagonist,** a detective, through the use of deductive reasoning from a series of clues. **Characterization, setting,** and description have often taken a backseat in detective fiction to the twists and turns of the **plot,** in which clues and "red herrings" alike are introduced to the reader as the detective comes across them. Although the **genre** has evolved through the years, allowing writers to stray from the strict principles established by the London Detection Club (founded in 1928), the basic elements of detective fiction have remained unchanged: a baffling crime that usually occurs at the beginning of the story, an often-eccentric sleuth who solves the case through an impressive display of logic, several suspects, and an unexpected conclusion. The poet W. H. Auden concisely defined detective fiction when he wrote: "A murder occurs; many are suspected; all but one suspect, who is the murderer, are eliminated; the murderer is arrested or dies."

Detective fiction should be distinguished from **mysteries** more generally, which are fictional works concerning any type of perplexing mystery, criminal or otherwise, and which may or may not involve a detective, deductive reasoning, or the other hallmarks of detective fiction. Thus, while detective fiction is a subset of mystery fiction, the terms are not coextensive.

Detective fiction should also be distinguished more specifically from the *crime novel*, another type of mystery that was heavily influenced by detective fiction. While both detective fiction and crime novels involve a crime or crimes, the focus of the crime novel is on the criminal, rather than a detective (though a detective may be involved), and on his or her psychological state, rather than on the crime solver's investigation and efforts to identify the criminal and solve the crime through logical, deductive reasoning.

Detective fiction may have its roots in works involving crime and criminal apprehension written as early as the mid-1700s. Such precursors include Voltaire's *Zadig* (1747), Tobias Smollett's *The Adventures of Ferdinand Count Fathom* (1753), William Godwin's *The Adventures of Caleb Williams* (1794), and Eugène François Vidocq's autobiography, *Les mémoires de Vidocq* (1828). The many editions of *The Newgate Calendar* — a collection of true crime stories first published in London in 1773, updated and reprinted for more than a century — are also viewed as forerunners of detective fiction. Two attorneys, Andrew Knapp and William Baldwin, produced an 1809 edition of *The Newgate Calendar* that was a best-seller for its day, but what became known as "Newgate Fiction" did not reach the height of its popularity until the 1830s.

Most scholars agree that the first true example of detective fiction is Edgar Allen Poe's "Murders in the Rue Morgue" (1841), a watershed work that both established the **codes** and **conventions** of the genre and introduced one of the first fictional detectives, Le Chevalier C. Auguste Dupin. Consequently, Sir Arthur Conan Doyle, himself a master of detective fiction, called Poe "the father of the detective tale." Other early detective stories by Poe include "The Purloined Letter" (1845) and "The Mystery of Marie Roget" (1850).

Other notable writers of nineteenth-century detective fiction include Wilkie Collins, an Englishman, and Frenchman Émile Gaboriau. In 1868, Collins published *The Moonstone*, a novel involving a diamond heist that is said to have influenced all subsequent detective fiction. The twentieth-century poet T. S. Eliot referred to Collins's work as "the first and greatest of English detective novels." Dorothy L. Sayers, a contemporary of Eliot's and herself an important detective novelist, wrote: "Taking everything into consideration, *The Moonstone* is probably the very finest detective story ever written." Gaboriau, author of the first full-length French detective novel (*Le crime d'Orcival* [1867]) and the first to make his detective, Lecoq, a policeman, is credited with establishing the *roman policier*, a French form of detective and crime fiction.

It was Doyle's short stories and novels, though, that made detective fiction a popular form of literary entertainment. When he introduced the extraordinarily observant and astute Sherlock Holmes in his first two **novellas**, *A Study in Scarlet* (1887) and *The Sign of the Four* (1890), he created the prototype for countless fictional detectives to come. (In Dr. James Watson, he also created the model confidant, or sidekick, another common element of detective fiction.) In 1891, short stories he published in the magazine *The Strand* vastly increased the market for detective fiction by appealing to a broad range of readers. Two collections of stories — *The Adventures of Sherlock Holmes* (1892) and *The Memoirs of Sherlock Holmes* (1894) — were followed by a novel, *The Hound of the Baskervilles* (1902), and several other Sherlock Holmes works. Doyle inspired a generation of British authors like Ernest Bramah, who created the first blind detective (Max Carrados); Arthur Morrison, who wrote about Investigator Martin Hewitt, a man of extraordinary technical and statistical knowledge; and R. Austin Freeman, who introduced the first scientific detective (Dr. John Thorndyke) and who anticipated the *inverted detective story,* a form of detective fiction in which the reader is aware of the killer's identity from the beginning of the story although the detective is not.

In America, the most prominent — and prolific — detective fiction authors following Poe were women. Anna Katherine Green, the first American female author of detective fiction, published her first novel, *The Leavensworth Case,* in 1878; Mary Rinehart published one of her best-known works, *The Circular Staircase,* thirty years later. Perhaps the most popular male author was S. S. Van Dine (a **pseudonym** for Willard Huntington Wright), whose *The Benson Murder Case* (1926) launched a series of similarly titled novels.

The period between World War I and World War II (1918–39) is generally considered to be both the "golden age" of detective fiction and its "classic" period. In 1928, G. K. Chesterton, a well-respected English poet and author of the Father Brown series of detective stories, became the first president of the London Detection Club, whose guiding principles may have been influenced by Van Dine's "Twenty Rules for Writing Detective Stories" (1928) and Monsignor Ronald Knox's "A Detective Story Decalogue" (1929). One of these principles, which prohibited authors from concealing any vital clue from readers, became part of the solemn oath taken by club members. Particularly important during the interwar period were four women — Agatha Christie, Ngaio Marsh, Dorothy L. Sayers, and Margery Allingham — referred to as the "Big Four." Christie, the creator of the memorable Belgian detective with the famous mustache, Hercule Poirot, and the dauntless English spinster, Miss Jane Marple, is still the best-known detective novelist of the twentieth century. Her eighty-plus novels, perhaps the most famous of which is *Murder on the Orient Express* (1934; adapted to film in 1974) have been translated into dozens of languages.

Other respected **classic** detective writers include Erle Stanley Gardner, the creator of lawyer-detective Perry Mason; Anthony Berkeley (a pseudonym for Anthony Cox, who also wrote as Frances Iles), a key figure in developing the inverted detective story; Nicholas Blake (pseudonym for C. Day Lewis, who is said to have based his detective on W. H. Auden); John Dickson Carr; E. C. Bentley; Michael Innes (pseudonym for J. I. M. Stewart); A. E. W. Mason; and Ellery Queen (pseudonym for two writers, Frederic Dannay and Manfred Lee). Widely noted post–World War II authors in the classic tradition include Stanley Ellin, Kenneth Fearing, Elizabeth Ferrars, P. D. James, Simon Nash, Ellis Peters, Ruth Rendell, Rex Stout, and Patricia Highsmith, whose novels *Strangers on a Train* (1949) and *The Talented Mr. Ripley* (1957) were both later adapted to film: *Strangers* in 1951 and *Ripley* first in 1960 (under the title *Plein Soleil,* or *Purple Noon*) and then again in 1999.

Although female writers of detective fiction played prominent roles throughout the history and development of the genre, there were few black practitioners until well after World War II (with the notable exception of Hughes Allison, who in 1948 wrote a novel about a black detective named Joe Hill). With the popularity of Chester Himes, who wrote in the 1950s, and John D. Ball, who in 1968 won the Edgar Award for his novel *In the Heat of the Night* (Sidney Poitier portrayed Detective Virgil Tibbs in the 1967 film version), however, African American writers gained a solid foothold on the terrain of detective fiction.

Shot through with hallucinatory violence, **grotesque** scenes and situations, and black humor (in both senses of the phrase), Himes's novels (e.g., *Cotton Comes to Harlem* [1965] and *Blind Man With a Pistol* [1969]) showed the influence of so-called *hard-boiled detective fiction,* a decidedly American subgenre that had appeared in the 1920s and began to eclipse classic detective fiction in America during the 1940s. Classic detective fiction regards society as an orderly world in which crimes are abnormal occurrences and order is restored by the crime-solving detective. But in the world of hard-boiled detective fiction, gangsters reign, chaos and violence are the norm, and the detective only temporarily provides relief from a dysfunctional world. Whereas classic **whodunits** typically take place at country estates, and whereas the police in such novels are honest (if often inept) servants of the law — the 2001 film *Gosford Park* exemplifies the world of classic detective fiction — hard-boiled detective stories are typically set on mean city streets, where the police force is usually corrupt.

Practitioners of hard-boiled stories found it difficult to gain recognition in part because such stories were not initially considered to be literature. Indeed, hard-boiled stories were first published in magazines printed on cheap paper made from wood pulp. *Black Mask,* one popular pulp magazine founded in 1920 by H. L. Mencken and George Nathan, offered writers like Dashiell Hammett, Raymond Chandler, and Carroll John Daly a penny per word to publish their stories. Daly's Race Williams was the prototype of the new American detective, but Hammett's Continental Op and Sam Spade and Chandler's Philip Marlowe were the best-known private eyes, or "dicks," of the hard-boiled subgenre. Also notable are stories by Raoul Whitfield, published in *Black Mask* in 1925, about a tough Filipino character named Jo Garr.

Writers James M. Cain, Mickey Spillane, and Jim Thompson continued the hard-boiled tradition in the ensuing decades. Ross Macdonald, who was first published in the 1940s and continued writing into the 1970s, patterned his novels after the fiction of Daly, Hammett, and Chandler but softened the violence and took a psychological approach to characters in order to attract sophisticated upper-middle-class readers. Other subsequent popular writers who further modified the hard-boiled style include Andrew Bergman, James Crumley, James Ellroy, Arthur Lyons, Robert B. Parker, and Roger L. Simon.

Hard-boiled detective fiction was introduced primarily by male authors and, perhaps for that reason, generally portrayed women as either good housewives or femmes fatales. Exceptions included the works of a few female authors who published in this style during its early years. In 1928 Katherine Brocklebank's "Tex of the Border Service," featuring a female detective, was published in *Black Mask*. Other early female "hard-boiled" writers include Leigh Brackett, Delores Hitchens (who sometimes published under male pseudonyms), and Dorothy B. Hughes.

Contemporary women who write hard-boiled detective fiction include Sara Paretsky, whose private eye is Victoria Iphigenia ("V.I.") Warshawski; Sue Grafton, who publishes a series of novels with alphabetical titles such as *"A" is for Alibi* (1983); and Janet Evanovich, who writes a series of novels with numbered titles such as *Hot Six* (2000) and *Seven Up* (2001). Evanovich writes in the hard-boiled style from the perspective of her heroine, Stephanie Plum, a sassy and irreverent bail enforcer who continually has to contend with a cast of offbeat characters including female members of her own family. Of course, not every woman — or man — writing contemporary detective fiction is a practitioner of the hard-boiled subgenre. P. D. James and Ruth Rendell, like many of their male counterparts, publish detective novels in the more traditional style.

Contemporary authors of hard-boiled detective fiction, many of whom have woven hard-hitting social and **racial** issues into the fabric of their stories, have led the way in resurrecting social **realism.** As writer Dennis Lehane, using the term "crime novel" broadly, has said, "Today's social novel *is* the crime novel." Novelist Walter Mosley is generally credited with starting this trend through his Easy Rawlins mystery series (1990–), a saga that has already chronicled several decades of black life in Los Angeles. Paula L. Woods has likewise incorporated black experience into her Charlotte Justice novels, in which the **protagonist** is a black woman in the mostly white, mostly male LAPD. In *Inner City Blues* (1999), Woods's debut novel, Justice comments, "I learned from my mother's experiences that life in America was a game called Pigmentocracy, color a card you played."

Whether hard-boiled, traditional, or hybrid in their approach, contemporary authors have tended to situate many or all of their stories in a particular historical period, professional environment, geographical setting, or cultural or religious context. For instance, the novels of Ellis Peters, who follows a classic approach, are set in a medieval English monastery, with the "detective" being a monk named Brother Cadfael, whereas murders committed in the novels of Amanda Cross (literary critic Carolyn Heilbrun) always occur in an academic setting. Nevada Barr's female park ranger, in novel after novel, solves murders that occurred in a national park; Julie Smith's policewoman Skip Langdon and lawyer Rebecca Schwarz solve crimes in New Orleans and San Francisco, respectively; Robert B. Parker's Spenser works out of Boston; and John Sandford's Lucas Davenport is a Twin Cities detective in the "Prey" series.

Tony Hillerman's detective novels are defined by a culture as well as a location, centered as they are in a Southwest reservation and featuring Native American detectives Jim Chee and Joe Leaphorn. Other novelists who also highlight culture and/or religion include Mosley, whose African American detective Ezekial "Easy" Rawlins struggles to obtain racial justice; Sandra Scoppetone, who writes about gay culture and a lesbian detective name Lauren Laurano; and Harry Kemelman, whose novels have a religious context and feature the detective Rabbi David Small.

The works of Patricia Cornwell and Jeffrey Deaver, as well as the 1976–83 television series *Quincy, M. E.,* and the more recent series *CSI* (2000–) reflect the growing interest in sophisticated professional crime scene investigators who use forensics and physical evidence found at the site of the murder. The popular "Cat Who" series (1966–) by best-selling author Lillian Jackson Braun even features a mystery-solving cat, K'ao Ko Kung, better known as Koko by readers and by his mustachioed owner Jim Qwilleran, a former reporter-turned-mystery solver who has been transplanted up north to Moose County from "Down Below."

Detective fiction for children is also popular, though it generally involves nonviolent crimes or at least not murders. Classic examples include Carolyn Keene's "Nancy Drew" stories, Franklin W. Dixon's "The Hardy Boys" series, and Donald J. Sobol's "Encyclopedia Brown" books.

See also **mystery fiction.**

deus ex machina: From the Latin for "god from a machine," a phrase referring specifically to the intervention of a nonhuman force to resolve a seemingly unresolvable **conflict** in a literary work. It also refers more generally to improbable or artificial resolutions of conflicts, such as those provided by unbelievable coincidences or unexpected strokes of good luck.

EXAMPLES: Toward the end of Molière's (Jean Baptiste Poquelin's) *Tartuffe* (1667), Orgon has lost all his property to the dissembling Tartuffe and, thanks to Tartuffe's treachery, has been arrested for disloyalty to the King (who, in Molière's day, would have been seen as God's representative on earth). Suddenly, an officer of the Crown appears, forgives Orgon, and restores his property, saying:

> Sir, all is well; rest easy, and be grateful.
> We serve a Prince to whom all sham is hateful,
> A Prince who sees into our inmost hearts,
> And can't be fooled by any trickster's arts.

In George Eliot's novel *Adam Bede* (1859), Hetty Sorrell — about to be hanged for the murder of her own illegitimate child — suddenly hears a shout in the street:

It was a shout of sudden excitement at the appearance of a horseman cleaving the crowd at full gallop. The horse is hot and distressed, but answers to the desperate spurring; the rider looks as if his eyes were glazed by madness, and he saw nothing but what was unseen by the others. See, he has something in his hand — he is holding it up as if it were a signal.

The Sheriff knows him: it is Arthur Donnithorne, carrying in his hand a hard-won release from death.

The arrival of Donnithorne with a document officially ordering that Hetty is to be deported, rather than hanged, amounts to something like *deus ex machina*. It is worth pointing out, however, that this **convention** has its limits in **realistic** fiction. Donnithorne is, after all, an interested party; he is the father of the dead baby Hetty has abandoned. Later in the novel, the reader learns that the same Hetty "rescued" by a deportation order died during her journey home.

Bertolt Brecht parodies the use of *deus ex machina* in *The Threepenny Opera* (1928), a play with music by Kurt Weill, in a **scene** in which Macheath, a **villain,** is saved from hanging by a pardon from the king.

diachronic: A term used in **linguistics** to refer to historical linguists' study of the evolution of a language or family of languages over time, that is to say, of changes in language(s) over time.

dialectic: Originally developed by Greek philosophers, mainly Socrates and Plato (in *The Republic* and *Phaedrus* [c. 360 B.C.]), a form and method of logical argumentation that typically addresses conflicting ideas or positions. When used in the plural, *dialectics* refers to any mode of argumentation that attempts to resolve the contradictions between opposing ideas.

The German philosopher G. W. F. Hegel described dialectic as a process whereby a **thesis,** when countered by an *antithesis,* leads to the *synthesis* of a new idea. Karl Marx and Friedrich Engels, adapting Hegel's idealist theory, used the phrase *dialectical materialism* to discuss the way in which a revolutionary **class** war might lead to the synthesis of a new socioeconomic order.

In literary criticism, *dialectic* typically refers to the oppositional ideas and/or mediatory reasoning that pervade and unify a given work or group of works. Critics may thus speak of the dialectic of head and heart (reason and passion) in William Shakespeare's plays. The American **Marxist critic** Fredric Jameson has coined the phrase *dialectical criticism* to refer to a Marxist critical approach that synthesizes **structuralist** and **poststructuralist** methodologies.

dialectical criticism: See **dialectic.**

dialectical irony (Socratic irony): See **irony.**

dialectical materialism: See **dialectic.**

dialogic: See **dialogic criticism, monologic.**

dialogic criticism: A method of literary **criticism** based on theories developed by Soviet critic Mikhail Bakhtin. Bakhtin developed his theories in the 1920s and 1930s, but they did not enter the mainstream of Western literary critical thought until the 1980s, when they were translated from Russian.

In *Problems of Dostoevsky's Poetics* (1929), Bakhtin spoke of works as being either comparatively **monologic** or *dialogic*. A monologic work, according to Bakhtin, is one that is clearly dominated by a single, controlling **voice** or **discourse,** even though it may contain **characters** representing a multitude of viewpoints. Contrary voices are subordinated to the authorial (and authoritative) voice, which is usually, though not always, representative of the dominant or "official" **ideology** of the author's culture. A dialogic work, by contrast, is one that permits numerous voices or discourses to emerge and to engage in **dialogue** with one another. In dialogic works, the culture's dominant social or cultural ideology may vie with the discourses of popular culture. In the book *Rabelais and His World* (1940), Bakhtin associated these discourses with **carnival,** a term he used to refer not only to such festivities as the extravagant (perhaps even excessive) Mardi Gras celebrations held in the Christian world before Lent — celebrations during which commoners (and the more privileged **classes**) were temporarily free to transgress all kinds of written and unwritten social and ecclesiastical laws — but also to "low" or popular culture in the more general sense, as exemplified by fairs and spontaneous **folk dramas** (including puppet shows).

Having made the distinction between monologic and dialogic works, Bakhtin also argued that no work can be completely monologic. That is because the **narrator,** no matter how authorial and representative of the "official" culture, cannot avoid **representing** differing and even contrary viewpoints in the process of relating the thoughts and remarks of the diverse group of literary characters that inevitably populate a credible fictional world. These other voices, which make any work **polyphonic,** or *polyvocalic,* to some degree, inevitably disrupt the authoritative voice, even though it may remain dominant. Thus, for Bakhtin, the monologic / dialogic opposition was not an absolute; some works are more monologic, others more dialogic.

In a later essay, "Discourse in the Novel," Bakhtin further developed his concept of the novel as a primarily dialogic literary form. Contravening Aristotle's privileging of **plot** in the *Poetics* (c. 330 B.C.), Bakhtin argued that discourse is the main element of a **narrative** work. According to Bakhtin, the multiple voices contained in any narrative work invariably represent diverse and often conflicting attitudes, philosophies, and ideologies. Regardless of the efforts of the author to establish an uncontroverted (or incontrovertible) narrative voice, any work thus remains open and indeterminate to some extent.

Contemporary dialogic critics base their interpretations of literary works on Bakhtin's argument that no work can be completely monologic, for every work contains myriad voices that contend for recognition and disrupt the authorial voice and the dominant or official ideology. Following Bakhtin, these critics view the concurrence of numerous and often contrary voices as the definitive feature of literary narratives, celebrating the diversity of viewpoints these voices inevitably engender. In keeping with their own outlook, dialogic critics openly acknowledge that their perspective is only one possible approach that must compete with many other viewpoints and theories.

In addition to dialogic critics, practitioners of other modes of contemporary criticism have used Bakhtin's ideas. A few **deconstructors** have relied on Bakhtin's theory that a single work contains contending and conflicting discourses in their effort to show the contradictions in — and the **undecidability** of — literary texts. **Marxist critics** have found hospitable and helpful Bakhtin's notion that even those works dedicated to perpetuating the existing power structure may be seen, on closer inspection, to contain subversive "carnivalesque" elements and perspectives. But Bakhtin's theory may have had its greatest impact on **cultural criticism,** which typically shows how the boundary we tend to envision between high and low forms of culture — forms thought of as important on the one hand and as relatively trivial on the other — is transgressed in all sorts of exciting ways within works on both sides of the putative cultural divide. Thus, a cultural critic might ground in Bakhtinian theory the argument that James Joyce's novel *Ulysses* (1922) reflects not only the **influence** of Homer's epic *The Odyssey* (c. 850 B.C.) but also the diverse cultural forms common to Joyce's Dublin, such as advertising, journalism, film, and pub life.

See also **discourse analysis.**

dialogue: Conversation between two or more **characters** in a literary work.

dibrach: See **pyrrhic.**

diction: Narrowly defined, a speaker's (or author's) word choice. The term may also refer to the general type or character of language used in speech or in a work of literature. In this broader sense, diction is typically divided into two components: vocabulary and **syntax.** By *vocabulary,* we mean the degree of difficulty, complexity, abstractness, formality, and currency of words used, as well as the origin of the words chosen (native or foreign, Latinate or Germanic, and so forth). *Syntax* refers to the arrangement — the ordering, grouping, and placement — of words within a phrase, clause, or sentence. The term may also be extended to encompass such things as the degree of complexity versus simplicity or fragmentation versus completeness manifested in a given arrangement of words. In critical circles, vocabulary is often described in terms of the "level" of the language used, whereas syntax tends to be discussed in terms of its "texture." Some use *diction* to refer to pronunciation, that is, to the perceived accuracy with which someone pronounces words.

Poetic diction refers specifically to the choice and phrasing of words suitable for **verse.**

didactic, didactic literature: Something that is didactic instructs or provides information for a particular purpose. Literature is considered didactic when its primary aim is to teach readers some lesson — whether moral, political, religious, ethical, or practical. It might be argued that most literary works are didactic, insofar as they have some purpose or idea that the author seeks to convey. However, works that are essentially imaginative rather than instructive are usually not considered didactic. When applied to a work of literature, the term may be pejorative or simply descriptive.

EXAMPLES: Religious works such as the New Testament letters of Paul to early Christians and the Muslim holy book the *Qur'an* (Koran) are primarily didactic, as are the following works: the *Kama Sutra* (a fourth-century A.D. ancient Indian erotic manual), Geoffrey Chaucer's "The Parson's Tale" (c. 1387), Alexander Pope's "An Essay on Criticism" (1711), and eighteenth-century English ladies' conduct manuals. Many people would say that William Bennett's anthology of moral tales entitled *The Book of Virtues* (1994) is a didactic work.

différance: A term coined by the French theorist of **deconstruction** Jacques Derrida, suggesting the French verb *différer,* which can mean either "to differ" or "to defer." Derrida has used this double meaning to demonstrate the impossibility of arriving at a single, definitive, and determinate interpretation of language, particularly of literary language. He argued that as we read or listen, we seek to derive meaning. The quest for meaning, however, is no simple one, because as the linguistic theorist Ferdinand de Saussure has pointed out: (1) the relationship between a word (the **signifier**) and what it signifies (the **signified**) is always an arbitrary one; and (2) a single word, or signifier, can connote any number of different signifieds. Since each word has **connotations** that themselves have connotations, however, every signified is also another signifier; hence, meaning is endlessly deferred as we seek to differentiate among an array of interpretive choices and to negotiate the **gap** between an ever-increasing number of signifiers and signifieds.

In addition to suggesting the French verb meaning both "differ" and "defer," Derrida's **neologism** *différance* connotes the French noun *différence,* meaning "difference." The difference between the homonyms *différance* and *différence* is one that can be seen in writing but not heard in speech, a fact that Derrida uses to subvert, or "deconstruct," the **privileging** of speech and **presence** over writing and **absence** in **logocentric** Western metaphysics, which understands Creation to have taken place when a present God spoke the words "Let there be light."

See also **deconstruction.**

dimeter: A line of **verse** consisting of two **metrical feet.**

EXAMPLES: The lines "The clock struck one / And down he ran" from the nursery rhyme "Hickory, Dickory, Dock." Thomas Hardy wrote a number of poems entirely in dimeter, such as "To Lizbie Browne" (1901):

> Dear Liz|bie Browne,
> Where are | you now?
> In sun, | in rain? —
> Or is | your brow
> Past joy, | past pain,
> Dear Liz|bie Browne?

Dionysian: An adjective describing writing that exhibits a passionate or even frenzied quality, derived from Dionysus (the Greek god of wine). Dionysian writing involves imaginative and sensual expression rather than rational, critical **discourse.** In *The Birth of Tragedy* (1872), Friedrich Nietzsche used *Dionysian* in conjunction with the term **Apollonian** (signifying reason and order) to refer to the delicate balance struck by the two sides of Greek **tragedy. Romantic** writing tends to draw on the passionate, Dionysian tradition, whereas Apollonian writing or qualities are often called **classical.**

See **Apollonian.**

direct discourse: See **discourse.**

dirge: A song or poem that may be sung at a funeral and that is written to commemorate and lament someone's death. *Dirge* and **elegy** are sometimes confused, but the terms are not synonymous. Although elegies may lament the death of a particular person, they may also lament loss or death more generally. In addition, elegies are typically more formal than dirges and are more reflective in character, intended to be read rather than sung.

EXAMPLES: Edna St. Vincent Millay's poem "Dirge Without Music" (1928). Peter Gabriel's song "Biko" (1980), lamenting the murder of South African civil rights leader Stephen Biko, is a more recent dirge.

disability: See **disability studies.**

disability studies: A movement within literary criticism and the humanities more generally that focuses on — and critiques — *disability* as it is commonly conceived, applying cultural, historical, social, and other humanities-oriented approaches to the study of disability in society. Many people associate disability with *in*ability — with physical or mental defects that abnormally define and limit — and with personal misfortune. Proponents of disability studies seek to transform these commonly held perceptions, to show that disability is a matter of identity, an ordinary human variation like **race** or **gender.**

Disability studies as a new, interdisciplinary, sociohumanistic field emerged in the latter half of the 1990s. It draws heavily on disciplines involving other types of identity studies, such as women's studies and African

American studies, with a focus on disability akin to the focus on race and gender in race studies and **gender criticism,** respectively. The movement challenges established biological and cognitive-sciences models of disability and builds upon a **cultural-studies** approach to disability that dates back to the early 1980s and that examined, among other things, the nature of stigma.

The development of a humanities-oriented approach to disability owes a great deal to the work of Michel Foucault, a French philosophical historian most often associated with **the new historicism,** a type of literary criticism that analyzes **texts** with an eye to history. Foucault's recognition of the power dynamics implicit in medicine and a medicalized approach to people laid the groundwork for *body criticism,* an approach that identifies and analyzes the imposition of cultural messages regarding the human body.

Disability studies seeks to overturn the medicalized understanding of disability and to replace it with a social model. Its proponents define disability not as a physical, mental, or developmental defect — a medical perspective they believe has had the effect of segregating people with disabilities — but, rather, as a way of interpreting human differences. Theorists such as Phyllis Rubenfeld, a professor of social work, point out that disability, unlike health, is a constant state akin to race, gender, and ethnicity — a matter of identity, as psychologist Simi Linton emphasizes.

Proponents of disability studies thus characterize disability as an identifying category and the disabled as a cultural minority. They reject the negative labels and **connotations** of abnormality, misfortune, and even deviance typically associated with disability and argue that disability is a social construct, a way of differentiating, evaluating, and classifying bodies. From the critical vantage point of disability studies, disability is a culturally significant interpretive and representational system, not just a medical problem or set of classified handicaps, and thus a subject appropriate for wide-ranging intellectual inquiry instead of a subspecialty within medicine, rehabilitation, or social work.

Disability studies examines the historical formation of the social identity "disabled," pointing out that it covers a wide range of physical, mental, and emotional variations such that it encompasses a large and diverse group of people who actually have little in common. Government expert and community visionary Benedict Anderson calls this the "imagined community" of the disabled, a social group that virtually all people will join if they live long enough. Disability studies also considers the history of how disability influences and is influenced by power, status, and distribution of resources; changes in the way disability has been interpreted over time and within varying cultural contexts; the impact of institutionalizing disabled persons versus integrating them into the community; the political and material implications for *all* people of the practice of assigning value to bodies; and how disability affects artistic production.

In assessing **sites** where a given culture defines and interprets disability, disability studies ranges across art and literature, religion and philosophy, history and politics, linking these fields with others as diverse as **aesthetics,** epistemology, and ethnic studies. Its practitioners have shown that **representations** of disability abound in the seminal texts of Western culture, from Sophocles' *Oedipus Rex* (c. 430 B.C.) to the Human Genome Project and beyond. These representations provide a **narrative** about human differences, an interpretation of physiological and mental traits, that can be critically examined and charted over time. Countering false constructs of disability — "disability fictions," as it were — is important because these narratives shape the material world, inform human relations, and mold our sense of who we and our fellow human beings are.

Critical analyses of disability flourish in literary criticism, often focusing on how disability operates **thematically** in the text and/or influenced the author's life and work. Practitioners have demonstrated the influence of disability on the literary production of countless writers, from the ancient Greeks, who made the lame Hephaestus the butt of jokes, to eighteenth-century writers Alexander Pope and Samuel Johnson, to more contemporary authors such as William Styron and Audre Lorde. Interestingly, unlike in the case of race and gender, many disabled authors are taught in classrooms without reference to their disability.

Literary analyses of disability have focused repeatedly on the works of **canonical** European writers such as William Shakespeare, Charles Dickens, and Gustave Flaubert. Critics have also pointed out the pervasiveness of disability in **classic** American literature: Anne Bradstreet imagines her book of poetry as a deformed child; Nathaniel Hawthorne **symbolizes** human imperfections through the marked bodies of the wife in the short story "The Birthmark" (1843) and of Roger Chillingworth in the novel *The Scarlet Letter* (1850); Ralph Waldo Emerson elaborates the ideal of the American individual in opposition to the figure of the "invalid"; Herman Melville figures human excess as disability through **characters** such as the one-legged Captain Ahab; Mark Twain uses deafness for humorous effect; and Toni Morrison constructs female characters whose disabilities ultimately enable them to avoid the subservient roles women often play in society and to find other, more independent paths. Critics have also shown that Henry David Thoreau's tuberculosis shaped his libertarian philosophy and that the category of illness is fundamental to Walt Whitman's poetry. Likewise, disabled figures and the concept of disability are central to American **sentimental** literature; abolitionist **discourse;** religious devotional literature; writings about philanthropy; the **modernist** Southern literature of the **grotesque** as developed by writers such as William Faulkner, Flannery O'Connor, and Carson McCullers; and Morrison's **postmodern** novels, in which racial and disability identity often converge.

A number of seminal texts and collections **theorizing** disability were published in the 1990s: Lennard J. Davis's *Enforcing Normalcy: Disability, Deafness, and the Body* (1995); *The Disability Studies Reader* (1997), edited by Davis; Thomas Couser's *Recovering Bodies: Illness, Disability and Life Writing* (1997); Rosemarie Garland-Thomson's *Extraordinary*

Bodies: Figuring Physical Disability in American Culture and Literature (1997); Linton's *Claiming Disability: Knowledge and Identity* (1998); Brenda Jo Brueggemann's *Lend Me Your Ear: Rhetorical Constructions of Deafness* (1999); and David T. Mitchell and Sharon L. Snyder's *Narrative Prosthesis: Disability and the Dependencies of Discourse* (2000). Snyder, Brueggemann, and Garland-Thomson subsequently published a collection of critical essays conducting literary analyses entitled *Disability Studies: Enabling the Humanities* (2002). Disability studies is also proliferating in the form of special issues of journals such as *Hypatia, Gay and Lesbian Studies,* and *The National Women's Studies Association Journal.*

As noted above, disability studies aims to integrate the concept of disability as a category of analysis not only into literary criticism but also into the humanities more generally. Just as scholars and teachers have learned that **class-,** race-, gender-, and **sexuality**-based analyses deepen our understanding of cultural texts, so they now recognize that disability expands and complicates the way in which we see the world. Proponents of disability studies seek to integrate disability as a concept and the disabled as a constituency in the American classroom and other institutions, in much the same way as issues involving race, gender, and sexuality have been integrated and assimilated.

Theorizing disability responds not only to the recent emphasis on discourse analysis, social constructionism, and the politics of inclusion but also to an increasing scholarly interest in representations of the body and the relationship of those representations to **subjectivity** and identity. Efforts to recover the history of disabled people are part of the shift in the practice of social history from studying the powerful and the elite to focusing on the perspectives and contributions of the previously marginalized.

Political activism, as embodied by the rallying cry "nothing about us without us," and bids to reclaim old derogatory terms such as "cripple" and "gimp" likewise aim to empower the disabled. Finally, emphasis on the importance of integrating disability and the disabled into society at large and into the curriculum and the classroom more specifically reinforces the humanistic commitment to acknowledging and serving underrepresented populations.

discourse: Used specifically, (1) the thoughts, statements, or **dialogue** of individuals, especially of **characters** in a literary work; (2) the words in, or text of, a **narrative** as opposed to its story line; or (3) a "strand" within a given narrative that argues a certain point or defends a given value system. Discourse of the first type is sometimes categorized as *direct* or *indirect.* Direct discourse relates the thoughts and utterances of individuals and literary characters to the reader unfiltered by a **narrator** speaking from a **third-person point of view.** ("Take me home this instant!" she insisted.) Indirect discourse (also referred to as **free indirect discourse**) is more impersonal, involving the reportage of thoughts, statements, or dialogue by a third-person narrator. (She told him to take her home immediately.)

More generally, *discourse* refers to the language in which a subject or area of knowledge is discussed or a certain kind of business is transacted. Human knowledge is collected and structured in discourses. Theology and medicine are defined by their discourses, as are politics, sexuality, and literary criticism.

Contemporary literary critics have maintained that society is generally made up of a number of different discourses or *discourse communities,* one or more of which may be dominant or serve the dominant **ideology.** Each discourse has its own vocabulary, concepts, and rules — knowledge of which constitutes power. The psychoanalyst and **psychoanalytic critic** Jacques Lacan has treated the unconscious as a form of discourse, the patterns of which are repeated in literature. **Cultural critics,** following Soviet critic Mikhail Bakhtin, use the word **dialogic** to discuss the dialogue between discourses that takes place within language or, more specifically, a literary **text.**

Some **poststructuralists** have used *discourse* in lieu of *text* to refer to any verbal structure, whether literary or not. Poststructuralists who emphasize discourse often do so in an attack on the **deconstructive** concept of the *general text.* Discourse, they argue, is influenced by historical circumstances, including social and cultural factors, unlike the general text, to which deconstructors claim historical categories, distinctions, and boundaries do not apply.

discourse analysis: An approach to literature developed in the 1970s that examines how language is used in more-or-less continuous **discourse,** that is, in a running spoken or written conversation or **dialogue.** Practitioners of discourse analysis, unlike critics using conventional **linguistics** or **stylistics,** concentrate on the larger pattern of discourse (the language, or totality of words, used in a given passage or conversation), rather than on smaller linguistic units such as individual words or phrases.

Speech-act theorist H. P. Grice played a major role in the development of discourse analysis. In his 1975 essay "Logic and Conversation," Grice coined the phrase **communicative presumption** to refer to the set of assumptions that he claimed are shared by speakers of any given language. These assumptions, Grice argued, form the baseline from and the framework within which we interpret what we read and hear. How we interpret any given statement depends on how it conforms — or fails to conform — to our expectations. Other language theorists have further explored Grice's theory of the communicative presumption, identifying a number of shared assumptions that function to make discourse comprehensible and meaningful. Such assumptions include the supposition that the speaker or writer seeks to communicate with others and thus employs language in a deliberate manner in accordance with commonly accepted rules and **conventions,** as well as the supposition that the meaning of any given statement can vary and must be examined in light of the situation at hand. What is a threat in one circumstance ("You're going to get it") may be a promise in another.

Discourse analysis has influenced the practice of **stylistics** as well as critical examination of dialogue in literary works. Those who analyze dialogue often seek to demonstrate how **characters** and readers alike manage to infer meanings from an utterance or utterances when those meanings are not directly revealed. Such critics typically draw on Grice's theory of communicative presumption and the subsequent work of other theorists, arguing that these inferences also depend on a set of shared assumptions, the agreement with or breach of which determines how a given phrase is interpreted. Discourse analysis has had a particular impact on **dialogic criticism,** whose practitioners examine the way in which contrary **voices** representing opposed social, political, and cultural viewpoints or perspectives often compete within **polyphonic** works. The multiple voices of a polyphonic work include those of the characters and, of course, the narrator's "authoritative" voice (which often, but not always, represents the prevailing or "official" **ideology** of the author's culture).

Influential discourse analysts include Malcolm Coulthard, Teun A. van Dijk, and Walter Kintsch.

discursive formation: See *epistémé.*

dissemination: Literally, "the sowing of seeds," usually used more generally to refer to other forms of scattering or dispersal, such as in the expression "the dissemination of ideas." In traditional literary criticism, the word *dissemination* has sometimes been used to refer to the way in which **texts** influence later texts across the generations, almost as if words were seeds carried by the winds of time from one literary era to the next.

Recently, *dissemination* has been used quite differently to refer to the way in which the meaning of a given word scatters, spreads, or disperses. This usage implies that any word or word-cluster inevitably means different things to different readers, in part because every word has a complex etymology and is embedded in a web of diverse (and often contradictory) associations. Jacques Derrida, the French theorist of **deconstruction,** has written about this kind of linguistic dissemination, maintaining that the meaning of any utterance is indeterminable due to the linguistic forces that operate within it. The act of using language, he has argued, inevitably produces a "surplus," a "spilling" of meaning. This proliferation of meanings thus precludes the definite ascension of any one meaning over another. For this reason, so-called deconstructors have spoken of the **undecidability** of the text.

dissociation of sensibility: A phrase that T. S. Eliot popularized in critical circles via his 1921 essay "The Metaphysical Poets." By "dissociation of sensibility," Eliot referred to a divergence of thought and feeling that he claimed emerged in seventeenth-century literature (particularly poetry) after the era of the **metaphysical poets** and that supposedly persisted in the writings of subsequent authors such as Robert Browning and Alfred, Lord Tennyson. For Eliot, earlier writers (John Donne in particular) possessed a "direct sensuous apprehension of thought"; their ideas, conversely, were played out in a range of emotions. The result was a unified poetic sensibility, which Eliot explains as follows:

> When a poet's mind is perfectly equipped for its work, it is constantly amalgamating disparate experience; the ordinary man's experience is chaotic, irregular, fragmentary. The latter falls in love, or reads Spinoza, and these two experiences have nothing to do with each other, or with the noise of the typewriter or the smell of cooking; in the mind of the poet these experiences are always forming new wholes.

Writers coming after John Milton and John Dryden, who in Eliot's view were among those responsible for dissociating thought from feeling, never quite managed to recover and attain that unity of perception characteristic of the metaphysical poets and their predecessors.

The New Critics borrowed this term from Eliot and used it widely, but since the 1950s, this notion has come under attack. Those who still agree with Eliot's ideas point not to Milton and Dryden but, rather, to the advent of scientific rationalism as the culprit that caused the dissociation of sensibility. Less sympathetic critics claim that the doctrine was largely contrived by Eliot to justify his own poetic preferences and to support his own political and social views (namely his disapproval of the course of English history beginning in the mid-seventeenth century). Some critics also point to Eliot's vagueness and historical inaccuracy, arguing that dissociation of sensibility can be found in the works of poets who wrote long before the so-called metaphysical poets — and that plenty of unified sensibilities have existed since their time.

dissonance: Harsh, discordant sounds in any type of writing. Some scholars use the terms *dissonance* and **cacophony** synonymously, but others differentiate them, using the latter term to refer to harsh or discordant sounds themselves and the former to refer to the use of cacophony to achieve a specific effect.

EXAMPLES: The following prose passage from Jonathan Swift's *Gulliver's Travels* (1726) conveys, through dissonance, the chaos and destruction of war:

> And being no stranger to the art of war, I gave him a description of cannons, culverins, muskets, carabines, pistols, bullets, powder, swords, bayonets, battles, sieges, retreats, attacks, undermines, countermines, bombardments, sea-fights; ships sunk with a thousand men, twenty thousand killed on each side; dying groans, limbs flying in the air, smoke, noise, confusion; trampling to death under horses' feet; flight, pursuit, victory; fields strewed with carcasses left for food to dogs, and wolves, and birds of prey; plundering, stripping, ravishing, burning, and destroying.

"The Lay of Ike," the twenty-third of John Berryman's *77 Dream Songs* (1964), contains dissonant sounds that overtly suggest political opposition to the policies (or lack thereof) of President Dwight D. Eisenhower:

> This is the lay of Ike.
> Here's to the glory of the Great White — awk —
> who has been running — er — er — things in recent — ech —
> in the United — If your screen is black,
> ladies & gentlemen, we — I like —
> at the Point he was already terrific — sick
> to a second term, having done no wrong —
> no right — no right — having let the Army — bang —
> defend itself from Joe, let venom' Strauss
> bile Oppenheimer out of use — use Robb,
> who'll later fend for Goldfine — Breaking no laws,
> He lay in the White House — sob!! — . . .

See also **cacophony.**

distance: See **aesthetic distance.**

dithyramb: Originally a **choral** song in honor of Dionysus (the Greek god of wine) and thought to have formed a basis for Greek **tragedy.** Now the word applies to any literary expression characterized by wild, passionate, excited, impetuous language.

EXAMPLES: John Dryden's *Alexander's Feast* (1697), a **stanza** of which follows:

> The praise of Bacchus then the sweet musician sung,
> Of Bacchus ever fair and ever young:
> The jolly god in triumph comes;
> Sound the trumpets, beat the drums;
> Flushed with a purple grace
> He shows his honest face;
> Now give the hautboys° breath; he comes, he comes!   *oboes*
> Bacchus, ever fair and young
> Drinking joys did first ordain;
> Bacchus' blessings are a treasure,
> Drinking is a soldier's pleasure;
> Rich the treasure,
> Sweet the pleasure
> Sweet is pleasure after pain.

The opening lines of "Jazz to Jackson to John" (1988), by Jerry W. Ward, Jr., provide a more modern (but similarly musical) example of dithyrambic verse:

> it must have been something like
> sheets of sound wrinkled
> with riffs and scats,

the aftermath of a fierce night
breezing through the grits and gravy;
or something like a blind leviathan
squeezing through solid rock,
marking chaos in the water
when his lady of graveyard love went
turning tricks on the ocean's bottom;
or something like a vision
so blazing basic, so gutbucket, so blessed
the lowdown blues flew out: jazz

doggerel: Poorly written or crude **verse** that usually has a comic quality, although humor may not be the poet's intent. The rough, irregular **style** and the choice of a sickeningly **sentimental** or trite subject may be either intentional (for comic effect) or unintentional (due to the poet's ineptitude).

EXAMPLE: The following **stanza** from James Whitcomb Riley's "The Doctor" (1907) is unintentional doggerel:

He is the master of emotions — he
Is likewise certain of that mastery, —
Or dare he face contagion in its ire,
Or scathing fever in its leaping fire?
He needs must smile upon the ghastly face
That yearns up toward him in that warded place
Where even the Saint-like Sisters' lips grow dumb.
Why not idealize the Doctor some?

domesticity: An aspect of the **patriarchal,** nineteenth-century doctrine of separate spheres, according to which a woman's place was in the privacy of the home whereas a man's place was in the wider, public world. Domesticity implied a wide range of "feminine" attitudes, behaviors, and character traits that were especially expected of middle- and upper-class women and that stood in stark contrast to the attitudes and activities (such as adventure, commerce, and intellectual inquiry) associated with "masculine" life.

In **Victorian** England, the phrase "angel in the house" was used to refer to the domestic ideal of womanhood. The phrase conjured up the image of a dutiful young wife and mother who embodied the virtues of marital fidelity, patience, kindness, self-control, submissiveness, and Christian charity. This ideal, domestic woman not only provided her children with a moral and religious education but also sought to make the family home a cheerful refuge for her hardworking husband. Sarah Stickney Ellis described this latter aspect of a woman's domestic duty in her book entitled *The Women of England: Their Social Duties and Domestic Habits* (1858), in which she explains that women should provide a "relief from the severer duties of life" so that men can "pursue the necessary avocation of the day" while "keep[ing] as it were a separate soul for his family, his social duty, and his God." Domesticity, and the larger doctrine of separate spheres for men and women implied by the domestic ideal, are relevant to literature and literary study for a number of reasons, many of which have been identified by practitioners of **feminist** and **gender criticism.** For one thing, the ideal of domestic femininity made it extremely difficult for women to become writers. Young women being prepared for a life of nurturing others within the home received a very different kind of education than did young men preparing for life outside its confines, and women who *did* manage to read widely and hone their writing skills were discouraged from pursuing writing careers, since writing was understood to be a public, and therefore masculine, activity. Furthermore, because writers tend to draw on their own knowledge and experience, many women who managed to write and publish in spite of societal discouragement confined themselves to domestic subjects and were careful to conform to stylistic proprieties. More ambitious women writers — such as George Eliot and the Brontë sisters — chose to publish their works under male **pseudonyms.**

The values associated with domesticity are also reflected in the content of nineteenth-century fiction and poetry. Nineteenth-century novels such as Jane Austen's *Emma* (1815) and Charlotte Brontë's *Jane Eyre* (1847) make it clear that, for a proper young woman, one of the few socially acceptable alternatives to being a wife and mother was the undesirable job of governess — a mother and teacher rolled into one, a kind of substitute angel in some rich person's great house. Poets, as well as novelists of the period, tended to depict women who were *not* wives, mothers, dutiful daughters, or good governesses as evil homewreckers (or even nation-wreckers). In *Woman and the Demon: The Life of a Victorian Myth* (1982), Nina Auerbach has argued that "women exist only as spiritual extremes: there is no human norm of womanhood, for she has no home on earth, but only among divine or demonic essences." Thus, the "loose woman" — as depicted by William Makepeace Thackeray (in *Vanity Fair* [1848]), Alfred, Lord Tennyson (in *Idylls of the King* [1859]), and Dante Gabriel Rossetti (in his poem "Jenny" [1870]) is only the flip side of the angel in the house, a dark manifestation of the **ideology** governing the doctrine of separate spheres and the ideal of domesticity.

The cult of domesticity, however, is not just manifested in literary works; it pervades nineteenth-century political **discourse** more broadly, as exemplified in the Supreme Court's 1876 majority opinion that one Myra Bradwell, though qualified in every way except sex, should not be allowed to practice law in the state of Illinois. "The civil law," Justice Bradley wrote,

> as well as nature herself, has always recognized a wide difference in the respective spheres and destinies of man and woman. Man is, or should be, woman's protector and defender. The natural and proper timidity and delicacy which belongs to the female sex evidently unfits it for many of the occupations of civil life. The constitution of the family organization, which is founded in the divine ordinance, as well

as the nature of things, indicates the domestic sphere as that which properly belongs to the domain and functions of womanhood. The harmony, not to say identity, of interests and views which belong or should belong to the family institution, is repugnant to the idea of a woman adopting a distinct and independent career from that of her husband. . . . The paramount destiny and mission of woman are to fulfill the noble and benign offices of wife and mother. This is the law of the Creator.

double rhyme: **Rhyme** involving words of two syllables in which identical, unstressed syllables follow rhyming, **stressed** syllables (*slaughter* and *daughter, rowing* and *showing, Paris* and *ferris*). Double rhyme, which is often used as a synonym for **feminine rhyme,** is actually a type of feminine rhyme, which involves words of two or more syllables. Feminine rhyme that extends over three syllables is called *triple rhyme.*

EXAMPLE: The first and third lines and the second and fourth lines of George Dillon's poem "The World Goes Turning" (1926) exemplify double rhyme:

> The world goes turning,
> Slowly lunging,
> Wrapped in churning
> Winds and plunging
> Rains.

drama: In today's usage, a serious literary work usually intended for performance before an audience. From the Greek *dran,* meaning "to do," drama as we know it is generally believed to have arisen from unrelated ancient Greek and **medieval** Christian religious ceremonies. Greek **comedy** originated in fertility rites, Greek **tragedy** (the word means "goat song") in rites of sacrifice. Following the decline of Rome, which had adopted the Greek dramatic tradition (but not its religious associations), drama virtually disappeared in the West, although miming and other ceremonies influenced by Greek comedy and tragedy may have kept a certain consciousness of drama alive. Medieval drama appears to have arisen independently in Western Europe, from Christian rituals commemorating the birth, death, and resurrection of Jesus. With the advent of the **Renaissance** came the rediscovery of **classical** works and a fusion of classical and later European traditions and **conventions.**

The term *drama* originally encompassed all works, whether **prose** or **verse,** written to be performed theatrically. Beginning with mid-eighteenth-century French productions of plays by Denis Diderot, however, the term came to be applied specifically to serious (as opposed to comic) plays that, whether they end happily or unhappily, treat some important (nontrivial) issue or difficulty. This usage is common today, although tragedy and comedy are still often defined as the two major divisions of drama.

Although **play** is the most common synonym for *drama,* a play is a drama intended for performance. Thus, although all plays are, broadly speaking, dramas, not all dramas are plays. W. H. Auden's *The Sea and the Mirror* (1944) and *For the Time Being* (1944) — though they involve **acts, characters,** and **dialogue** — are correctly referred to as **closet dramas,** not as plays, because they are meant to be read as poems rather than to be seen in a theater by an audience. In addition, contemporary usage permits the term *drama* to be applied to a wide range of serious works. Thus the movies *An Officer and a Gentleman* (1982), *Dances with Wolves* (1990), *The Shawshank Redemption* (1994), and *A Beautiful Mind* (2001) are typically classified in the drama section of video stores.

See also **play.**

drama of sensibility: See **sentimental comedy.**

dramatic illusion: See **aesthetic distance.**

dramatic irony: See **irony.**

dramatic monologue: A **lyric poem** in which the speaker addresses a silent listener, revealing himself or herself in the context of a dramatic situation. The speaker thus provides information not only about his or her personality but also about the time, the **setting,** key events, and any other **characters** involved in the situation at hand.

EXAMPLES: Robert Browning's "The Bishop Orders His Tomb" (1845), T. S. Eliot's "The Love Song of J. Alfred Prufrock" (1917).

dramatis personae: The cast of **characters.** In a play (and sometimes in other works such as novels), a listing of all the characters generally precedes the written work itself and is provided in a printed program when the work is being performed on the stage. This list may give short descriptions of the characters and their relationship to other characters in the work.

dream allegory: See **dream vision.**

dream vision (dream allegory): A type of **narrative** in which the **narrator** falls asleep, dreams, and relates the contents of the dream. Dream visions have an **allegorical** aspect (the narrator may meet figures bearing names like Hope or Remembrance, for instance), hence the generally equivalent term *dream allegory.* Dream visions were a popular form of storytelling in the **Middle Ages;** they are less common today, but authors still occasionally choose to relate narratives in this manner.

EXAMPLES: Jean de Meung and Guillaume de Lorris's *Le roman de la rose* (c. 1230, c. 1270) and Dante Alighieri's *Divina commedia* (*The Divine Comedy*) (1321) are famous **medieval** examples. John Keats's "The Fall of Hyperion: A Dream" (1819) and "La belle dame sans merci" (1820) offer **romantic** variations on the form. Lewis Carroll's *Alice's Adventures in Wonderland* (1865) and James Joyce's *Finnegans Wake* (1939) exemplify more modern developments, as does the 1939 movie version of L. Frank

Baum's story *The Wizard of Oz* (1900). A more recent movie that experiments with the **conventions** of the dream vision is Adrian Lyne's *Jacob's Ladder* (1990). The *Nightmare on Elm Street* series (1984–) of "slasher" movies also toys with many of the allegorical and narrative conventions of the dream vision.

dumb show: See **pantomime.**

dystopia: From the Greek for "bad place," the opposite of a **utopia.** A dystopia is usually set at some point in the author's future and describes a society in which we would not want to live. Writers presenting dystopias generally want to alert readers to the potential pitfalls and dangers of society's present course or of a course society might conceivably take one day. Accounts of dystopias inevitably conclude by depicting unpleasant, disastrous, or otherwise terrifying consequences for the **protagonists** as well as for humanity as a whole.

EXAMPLES: George Orwell's *1984,* written in 1948, describes a society in which "Big Brother" is always watching and in which one party not only governs a territory called Oceania (presumably North America, South America, and at least part of Europe) but also attempts to control everyone and everything within it. The government even tries to monitor thought using organizations such as "thinkpol" (the Thought Police) and tortures and brainwashes anyone who exhibits even a shred of independent thought or hostility to the Party.

Margaret Atwood's novel *The Handmaid's Tale* (1985), in which women of the future have lost their personal freedoms, also depicts a dystopia. Women are slotted into male-controlled categories: wives, servants (Marthas), breeders (handmaids), and women who enforce the repression of their peers (Aunts). Those who won't cooperate are shipped off to the Colonies to perform hazardous labor (cleaning up after nuclear accidents or toxic spills). Women are denied access to printed material to enforce their mental as well as physical repression.

E

Early National Period (in American literature): An era in American literary history roughly spanning the years 1790–1828, a period significantly shaped by the efforts to establish a new nation and sometimes called the *Federalist Age* (after the conservative federalists who dominated American government during this time). The federal government, formed in 1789, remained under the control of the federalists until the election of Andrew Jackson to the presidency in 1828, an event that has often been termed the "second revolution." Jackson, though a slaveholder who implemented sometimes brutal policies affecting Native Americans, has often been characterized as a proponent of frontier individualism and know-how and as a champion of common people.

The Early National Period witnessed the beginnings of a relatively independent and **imaginative** literature in America. Writers of the preceding **Colonial** and **Revolutionary periods,** who had chiefly modelled themselves after English precursors such as Alexander Pope, had produced **texts** that were generally polemical or **didactic** in nature. Except in the **genre** of **drama,** less imitative and more distinctively American voices began to develop with the formation of a new nation. William Cullen Bryant is perhaps the best-known poet of the time; Washington Irving, an essayist and storyteller, became the first American prose writer to achieve international fame with works such as *Knickerbocker's History* (1809) and *Sketch Book* (1820). The first long-running American magazine, the *North American Review,* was also established (1815).

Unlike the previous Colonial and Revolutionary periods, the Early National Period was one during which the novel flourished. Most of the novels of the time can be classified as either **sentimental** or **Gothic.** Sentimental novels generally claimed to set forth a "true" story for the purpose of moral instruction in general and for warning young ladies of the perils of seduction in particular. Hannah Webster Foster's *The Coquette* (1797) is an example of this genre, as is Catherine Maria Sedgwick's *Hope Leslie: or, Early Times in the Massachusetts* (1827). Gothic novels, in stark contrast to sentimental novels, were characterized by their focus on the **grotesque** or supernatural, their preoccupation with **horror,** suspense, doom, **mystery,** and passion. Charles Brockden Brown's *Wieland* (1798) is perhaps the most famous example of this genre during the Early National Period. Not all novelists wrote within the sentimental or Gothic genres, however. The career of James Fenimore Cooper, for instance, was launched through works like *The Spy* (1821) and *The Last of the Mohicans* (1826); Cooper continued to write well into the **Romantic Period.**

Other notable prose of the period consisted mainly of descriptive accounts of life on the frontier. A prime example of this kind of writing is St. John de Crèvecoeur's *Letters from an American Farmer* (1782).

Early Tudor Age (in English literature): Considered the first of five literary eras within the **Renaissance Period** in English literature, an age generally said to have begun in 1500 and ended in 1558 with the coronation of Elizabeth I, at which point the **Elizabethan Age** is said to have begun. The Early Tudor Age is best known for its poetry and nonfiction prose, although *Ralph Roister Doister,* often referred to as the first dramatic comedy in English, was initially performed in 1553.

John Skelton, the first major poet of the age, began his career imitating the work of the great **medieval** poet Geoffrey Chaucer but later developed an original, **satirical** style that he turned on both church and state. Later poets of note include Sir Thomas Wyatt — who **imitated** and translated poems (especially **sonnets**) he read while on diplomatic missions to Italy, France, and Spain — and Henry Howard, the Earl of Surrey. Surrey is generally credited with being the first English poet to: (1) write in **blank verse,** which he encountered in an Italian translation of Virgil's *The Aeneid* and used in his own (English) translation of that ancient Roman **epic;** and (2) adapt the **Italian,** or **Petrarchan, sonnet** to the English language, turning it from a poem consisting of an (eight-line) **octave** followed by a (six-line) **sestet** into a form characterized by three (four-line) **quatrains** plus one (two-line) **couplet.** (This **English sonnet,** first developed by Surrey during the Early Tudor Age, came to be called the **Shakespearean sonnet** during the Elizabethan period.) Important prose works of the Early Tudor Age include Sir Thomas Elyot's *The Boke Named the Governour* (1531), which describes the cultivation of a gentleman (highlighting especially the essential role of Greek and Roman **classics** in a proper education), and Sir Thomas More's *Utopia,* written in Latin in 1516 but not published in English until 1551. More's work, which depicts life in a **utopian** land where reason and justice prevail, shows the **influence** of Plato's *The Republic* (c. 360 B.C.).

Focus on the relationship between the individual and the state, respect for and use of **classical** works, and the tendency to import and adapt classically influenced literary forms from other countries are characteristic not only of the Early Tudor Age but also of the Renaissance Period in English literature and the **Renaissance** in general.

See also **Renaissance.**

eclogue: A term referring to a formal **pastoral poem,** originally from the Greek for "selection." Before Virgil wrote his *Eclogues* (c. 40 B.C.), the term referred to several types of verse. Since Virgil, *eclogue* has been used to refer to a pastoral **soliloquy** or **dialogue.** The subject matter of an eclogue (as understood since Virgil) varies, but commonly concerns courtship, disappointment in love, or death. Eclogues often involve a conversation or singing contest between two shepherds or a lament for a dead shepherd (an eclogue may be or may contain a eulogy). Sometimes *eclogue* is distinguished from *pastoral,* with the latter term used to refer to the **sentimental** content and the former term used to refer to the dramatic form of a poem. In recent times, eclogues have been used to express social and political commentary.

EXAMPLES: Edmund Spenser's *The Shepheardes Calendar* (1579) contains twelve eclogues, one for each month of the year. Percy Bysshe Shelley introduced his "Rosalind and Helen: A Modern Eclogue" (1819) by advising his readers that "[t]he story of *Rosalind and Helen* is, undoubtedly, not an attempt in the highest style of poetry. It is in no degree calculated to excite profound meditation; and if by interesting affections and amusing the imagination, it awakens a certain ideal melancholy favorable to the reception of more important impressions, it will produce in the reader all that the writer experienced in the composition."

W. H. Auden's long poem *The Age of Anxiety: A Baroque Eclogue* (1947) describes the attempt of four **characters** representing diverse personality types (or, perhaps, mental faculties) to journey from the modern condition of alienation, decay, and despair to a state of rejuvenation and harmonious reconciliation. Instead of taking them through rural, **conventionally** pastoral scenery, their quest takes them through landscapes **symbolically** suggestive of human anatomy.

ecocriticism: A type of literary criticism, sometimes popularly referred to as *green criticism*, that focuses on the relationship between nature and literature. Ecocriticism, which is grounded in ecology, natural history, and environmental studies, examines how people interact with nature and how these interactions inform and are forged by **symbolic representations** of nature. Ecocriticism may involve the study of *nature writing* specifically or the study of ecological implications and human relationships to nature in any type of **text.** Ecocritics often analyze: (1) the relationship between literary representations of nature and human interactions with the natural world; and (2) the role of literature and language in furthering — or hindering — agendas for changing humanity's relationship with the natural environment. Unlike other approaches to literary criticism, ecocriticism addresses the relationship between writers, texts, and the world from a truly global perspective — one in which the "world" is the entire ecosphere, not just human society.

The term *ecocriticism,* coined by William Rueckert in 1978 in an essay entitled "Literature and Ecology: An Experiment in Ecocriticism," did not gain currency in critical **discourse** until 1989, when Cheryll Glotfelty, a leading theorist in the field, suggested referring to all ecologically informed literary criticism as ecocriticism. Because ecocriticism involves a shared frame of reference rather than a particular methodology or **theoretical** perspective, some practitioners refer to their work as "ecological literary criticism," "the study of nature-oriented literature," or "literature-and-environment studies." Most, however, use the term *ecocriticism.*

Several early examples of ecocriticism, dating back to the 1970s, emphasize scientific concepts and employ relatively direct applications of ecological science to literature. Rueckert, for example, used biological concepts to construct what he termed "literary ecology," arguing, for instance, that "poems can be studied as models for energy flow, community building, and ecosystems." Similarly, Joseph Meeker employed physical models of ecosystems to analyze literary modes in his book *The Comedy of Survival: Studies in Literary Ecology* (1972).

Ecocritical works from the 1970s and early 1980s that focused on representations of the land, wilderness, and women's relationship to nature, however, ultimately had a greater impact on contemporary ecocriticism than explicitly scientific applications. Influential examples include Annette Kolodny's *The Lay of the Land: Metaphor as Experience and History in American Life and Letters* (1975) and *The Land Before Her: Fantasy and Experience of the American Frontiers, 1630–1860* (1984), both of which discuss representations of land in American culture; Carolyn Merchant's *The Death of Nature: Women, Ecology, and the Scientific Revolution* (1980), which investigates the interplay between representations of women and nature; and Roderick Nash's *Wilderness and the American Mind* (1982), which traces the concept of the wilderness throughout American intellectual and cultural history.

Awareness of ecocriticism as a movement in literary studies did not develop until 1989; in 1992, a group of scholars established the Association for the Study of Literature & Environment (ASLE), which publishes the journal *ISLE: Interdisciplinary Studies in Literature and Environment*. In *The Ecocriticism Reader: Landmarks in Literary Ecology* (1996), Glotfelty and coeditor Harold Fromm mapped the lineage and landscape of ecocriticism, which at that time was still largely focused on American nonfiction nature writing or on explicitly nature-oriented fiction and poetry. Accompanying the innovative studies of American nature writing that appeared in the late 1980s and early 1990s were a number of anthologies, including Thomas J. Lyons's *This Incomperable Lande: A Book of American Nature Writing* (1989), which was prefaced with a piece entitled "A Taxonomy of Nature Writing" in which Lyons detailed questions about the purpose of the **genre.** (Note that although nature has played a key role in the ancient literature of many peoples, including the Chinese, Japanese, Indians, Greeks, and Romans, nature writing as a genre refers to American and European nature-oriented literature dating back to Henry David Thoreau's *Walden* [1854].)

Many ecocritics work within one of two related but contrasting theoretical frameworks: *deep ecology* and *ecofeminism*. Deep ecology, first outlined by Norwegian philosopher Arne Naess in his book *Ecology, Community and Lifestyle* (1989), locates the source of contemporary environmental crises in Western **ideologies** characterized by *anthropocentrism,* the tendency to conceive of nonhuman nature primarily in terms of human interests. Deep ecologists advocate a complete return to nature, in contrast to more moderate environmentalists, who emphasize conservation. Deep ecologists, who contend that nature has value in and of itself, should thus be distinguished from social ecologists, who believe that nature must ultimately be approached in light of human needs.

Ecofeminists take an explicitly **feminist** approach to ecocriticism. While ecofeminists, like deep ecologists, locate the source of environmental problems in the tendency to **privilege** human interests, many argue more specifically that *androcentrism,* the tendency to conceive of nonhuman nature in terms of human *male* interests, has led **patriarchal** cultures, particularly in the West, to associate and exploit women and nature. For essays relating environmental problems to androcentric ideologies, see Greta Gaard and Patrick D. Murphy's *Ecofeminist Literary Criticism: Theory, Interpretation, Pedagogy* (1998). For an ecofeminist identification and analysis of women's contributions to natural history and nature writing, see Very Norwood's *Made from This Earth: American Women and Nature* (1993).

Some ecocritics incorporate **poststructuralism,** which addresses the relationship between our experience of the material world and the language we use to describe that world, into their analyses. For instance, SueEllen Campbell's 1989 essay "The Land and Language of Desire: Where Deep Ecology and Post-Structuralism Meet" describes the inherent tension between ecocritics' concern with the material effects of the relationship between language and the natural environment and poststructuralist views on how language mediates and even creates all of our experiences (including our experience of the material world). Neil Evernden's book *The Social Creation of Nature* (1992), as well as the essays collected in Michael E. Soule and Gary Lease's *Reinventing Nature?: Responses to Postmodern Deconstruction* (1995), likewise deal with issues involving nature, language, and poststructuralist theory.

Ecocritics also draw on **rhetorical** theory and on ideas and attitudes growing out of the global environmental justice movement to study political and literary discourse in the context of public debate about environmental problems. M. Jimmie Killingsworth and Jacqueline S. Palmer's *Ecospeak: Rhetoric and Environmental Politics in America* (1992), like many of the essays in Carl Herndl and Stuart C. Brown's *Green Culture: Environmental Rhetoric in Contemporary America* (1996), analyzes public debate about environmental issues, such as the spotted owl controversy in the Pacific Northwest.

Some ecocritics, influenced by the personal style of much nature writing, also employ **personal criticism** in analyzing literature. They may extensively discuss their own experiences, and they tend to exhibit the same kind of heightened appreciation of place and community that is the defining feature of many of the works they study. (Indeed, some ecocritics have argued that "place" should be a critical category akin to **race, class,** and **gender.**) For instance, in *Reading the Mountains of Home* (1998), John Elder alternates interpretations of Robert Frost's poem "Directive" with **first-person** accounts of his own life and exploration in Vermont's Green Mountains, where Frost once also lived. Likewise, in *American Indian Literature, Environmental Justice, and Ecocriticism: The Middle Place* (2001), Joni Adamson's **narrative** scholarship places her examination of Native American literature in the context of her personal experience in natural and human communities that have borne the brunt of environmental degradation.

Ecocritics aim to raise environmental consciousness and to remind us of our dependence on the earth and its resources. Aldo Leopold's concept of the "land ethic" — that is, of nature as a part of the community rather than as a commodity — has been particularly influential. In addition, interconnections between nature and culture are central to ecocritical analyses. As Glotfelty explains in the introduction to *The Ecocriticism Reader*, "all ecological criticism shares the fundamental premise that human culture is connected to the physical word, affecting it and affected by it." While some practitioners of **cultural studies** have reduced nature to little more than a linguistic construct, one among many texts for analysis, ecocritics counter that all human culture exists in the natural world and that any human act affecting nature ultimately affects culture.

Common **themes** in ecocritical analyses include the interrelation of all elements in an ecosystem, from natural phenomena to social and political factors; the need to monitor technologies and to pursue sustainable means of living; and the quest for environmental justice. To ecocritics, who are motivated by the conviction that earth's ecology is precarious — as former vice president Albert Gore posited in *Earth in the Balance* (1992) — values matter in the most fundamental way.

Ecocritics also aim to establish a "green" **canon,** so to speak, to identify the **classics** of nature writing, to offer ecological readings of these texts, and to explain why these texts and readings matter. They seek to identify nature's **aesthetic** and symbolic value, to show that nature is far more than the object of scientific scrutiny. Many ecocritics even regard science as something of an enemy, particularly insofar as technology has contributed to environmental degradation.

In working to establish a canon, ecocritics initially focused on mid-nineteenth- and twentieth-century American nature writing, even though **pastoral** works dating back to the **Renaissance** had glorified rural environments and **Romantic** writers of the late 1700s and early 1800s had extolled nature's divinity and deplored the mechanization of society associated with the Industrial Revolution. This initial focus on American texts was probably due in part to the fact that ecocriticism first emerged as a field of study in America and in part to the perception that Thoreau's *Walden*, which offered an intensely personal take on living in harmony with nature, launched nature writing as a genre. Lawrence Buell's *The Environmental Imagination: Thoreau, Nature Writing, and the Formation of American Culture* (1996) examines Thoreau's influence on American attitudes and writing about the natural world.

Other key works of nature writing often studied by ecocritics include Mary Austin's *Land of Little Rain* (1903), Aldo Leopold's *A Sand County Almanac* (1949), Rachel Carson's *Silent Spring* (1962), Edward Abbey's *Desert Solitaire* (1968), Annie Dillard's *Pilgrim at Tinker Creek* (1974), Barry Lopez's *Arctic Dreams* (1986), Gary Snyder's *Practice of the Wild*

(1990), and Terry Tempest Williams's *Refuge* (1991). Scott Slovic's *Seeking Awareness in American Nature Writing: Henry Thoreau, Annie Dillard, Edward Abbey, Wendell Berry, Barry Lopez* (1992), which analyzes the works of several of the aforementioned nature writers, investigates the common theme of seeking inner awareness through engagement with outer landscapes. Writers of nature poetry — such as Snyder, Berry, W. S. Merwin, and Mary Oliver — are increasingly referred to as *ecopoets,* their work as *ecopoetry.* J. Scott Bruson's *Ecopoetry: A Critical Introduction* (2002) assembles scholarly inquiries into the historical and cross-cultural roots of ecopoetry, as well as into recurrent themes such as extinction, genocide, the female and lesbian body, and **postcolonialism.**

Recently, ecocritics have recognized the need for ecocritical studies of works in other genres, art forms, and national and cultural contexts. For example, Karla Armbruster and Kathleen R. Wallace's *Beyond Nature Writing: Expanding the Boundaries of Ecocriticism* (2001) features essays discussing works dating from **medieval** Europe to the present day, ranging from canonical texts to digital simulations of landscapes. Similarly, Murphy's *Farther Afield in the Study of Nature-Oriented Literature* (2000) looks beyond Euro-American literary traditions to survey Asian, South American, African, and Australian works, and Terrell Dixon highlights urban environments in *City Wilds: Essays and Stories about Urban Nature* (2002). Contemporary ecocritics have also focused on the relationship between literature and the environment as seen by Native Americans and other indigenous cultures around the world.

Chicano and Chicana literature has been a particularly fertile ground for nature writing and ecocriticism. In *Borderlands/La Frontera: The New Mestiza* (1997), Gloria Anzaldúa testifies to the exploitative and destructive effect of patriarchal values on the land and on Mexicans living on both sides of the United States–Mexico border. In *The Brushlands* (1997), Arturo Longoria discusses the devastation of brushlands along the border, as well as the effects of this destruction on the human spirit. Other Chicano and Chicana texts that highlight the link between environmental degradation and marginalization along economic, ethnic, and class lines include Rudolfo Anaya's novel *Bless Me, Ultima* (1971) and the works of two ecofeminists: Ana Castillo's *So Far from God* (1993) and Helena María Viramontes's *Under the Feet of Jesus* (1995).

ecofeminism: See **ecocriticism.**

ecopoetry: See **ecocriticism.**

écriture **(writing):** See **text.**

écriture féminine: See **feminist criticism.**

Edwardian Age (in English literature): A brief epoch in the history of English literature named after King Edward VII, whose reign began with the death of Queen Victoria in 1901 and ended in 1910, four years before the outbreak of World War I. During the Edwardian Age, which is generally said to have ended with the outbreak of the "Great War," a number of well-known authors wrote in a variety of **genres** and **styles,** among which prose was dominant. Authors of the Edwardian Age include James Barrie, Arnold Bennett, Joseph Conrad, Ford Madox Ford, John Galsworthy, Thomas Hardy, Rudyard Kipling, Alfred Noyes, Arthur Symons, and H. G. Wells.

Although it refers to a specific chronological era, the *Edwardian Age* is relatively loose and unhelpful as a literary category. For one thing, many of the authors associated with it began writing during the **Victorian Period** or are also associated with the later **Georgian Age** or even the beginnings of **modernism.** (Thomas Hardy, whose career extended from 1865 to 1928, is a case in point.) In addition, works said to represent the Edwardian Age seem less united by an underlying or overriding worldview and **aesthetic** than the works generally affiliated with certain other literary periods, ages, or movements. (Edwardian works encompass everything from **romance** to **realism, science fiction** to **satire,** cloying **sentimentalism** to trenchant pessimism.) Finally, the term *Edwardian* is sometimes used with reference to American **realist** contemporaries (such as Henry James) and Irish writers (such as W. B. Yeats, Lady Gregory, Douglas Hyde, and J. M. Synge) associated with the **Celtic Renaissance**, a movement with its own **aesthetic** and political roots — and agenda.

ego: See **id.**

Einfühlung: See **empathy.**

Electra complex: See **Oedipus complex.**

elegy: In Greek and Roman times, the term *elegy* was used to refer to any **poem** composed in elegiac **meter** (alternating **dactylic hexameter** and **pentameter** lines). Since the seventeenth century, *elegy* has typically been used to refer to reflective poems that lament the loss of something or someone (or loss or death more generally), although in **Elizabethan** times it was also used to refer to certain love poems. Elegies written in English frequently take the form of the **pastoral elegy.**

EXAMPLES: Thomas Gray's *Elegy Written in a Country Churchyard* (1751) is a famous English elegy, as is Alfred, Lord Tennyson's *In Memoriam A. H. H.* (1850). A more modern example is W. H. Auden's "In Memory of W. B. Yeats" (1940). In "A Refusal to Mourn the Death, by Fire, of a Child in London" (1946), Dylan Thomas struggles to resist the temptation to write an "elegy of innocence and youth," concluding his poem with a **stanza** that is, nonetheless, eloquently elegiac in spirit and **tone:**

> Deep with the first dead lies London's daughter,
> Robed in the long friends,
> The grains beyond age, the dark veins of her mother,
> Secret by the unmourning water

> Of the riding Thames.
> After the first death, there is no other.

Although *elegy* is not generally used in reference to songs, Don McLean's "American Pie" (1971), which associates the death of singer Buddy Holly with the end of an idealistic and optimistic era, is elegiac in its subject and tone.

elision: The omission of part of a word (typically a letter). Elision most commonly involves replacing a word-ending vowel with an apostrophe when it is followed by another word that begins with a vowel. Often employed to make verse more **rhythmic** or to conform to a **metrical** pattern, elision appears in prose as well.

EXAMPLES: *E'er* and *o'er* involve elision in the general sense of the term. The line in John Milton's *Paradise Lost* (1667) in which the angel Michael tells Adam "All th'earth he gave thee to possess and rule" involves the omission of the first of two adjacent vowels.

In the first **stanza** of "Beauty" (1656), Abraham Cowley elides (omits) the letter *e* on numerous occasions:

> Beauty, thou wild fantastic ape,
>   Who dost in ev'ry country change thy shape!
> Here black, there brown, here tawny, and there white;
> Thou flatt'rer which compli'st with every sight!
>   Thou Babel which confound'st the eye
> With unintelligible variety!
>   Who hast no certan What, nor Where,
> But vari'st still, and dost thy self declare
> Inconstant, as thy she-possessors are.

Elizabethan Age (in English literature): An era in English literary history that spanned the duration of Elizabeth I's reign (1558–1603) and that is often said to have reached its pinnacle with the defeat of the Spanish Armada in 1588 by the English navy. Closely associated with the transnational and transcultural **Renaissance** (literally "rebirth") of Western European cultural experience said to have followed the supposedly "dark" **Medieval Period,** the Elizabethan Age is often identified as the second of five literary eras within the **Renaissance Period** in English literature. Although best known for its poets (such as Sir Philip Sidney and Edmund Spenser) and playwrights (such as Christopher Marlowe and William Shakespeare), the Elizabethan Age also produced prose writers such as Francis Bacon and Sir Walter Raleigh.

Literature produced during the subsequent **Jacobean Age** is often called Elizabethan, since many Elizabethan writers (William Shakespeare and Francis Bacon included) also lived into and wrote during the Jacobean Age. Conversely, a number of authors whose careers were not fully established until the Jacobean period (the poet John Donne and the playwright Ben Jonson, for instance) are often referred to as Elizabethans.

See also **Renaissance.**

ellipsis: See **anachrony, prolepsis.**

empathy (*Einfühlung*): The involuntary projection of ourselves into an object, that is, an identification with the object (be it a person, physical state, emotion, etc.) to such an extent that we *feel* what that object feels or undergoes. In other words, through empathy we in essence participate in the existence of and identify with the object of our empathy. The German concept of *Einfühlung,* literally a "feeling into," came into being in the nineteenth century and became current, although often debated, in English-language **criticism** in the twentieth century. Many would distinguish between the "feeling into" of empathy and the "feeling along" implied by the term *sympathy.* However, the difference between *empathy* and *sympathy* has been disputed by literary critics, many of whom argue that the two terms are essentially synonymous.

EXAMPLE: If you are terrified and cower, shoulders hunched, along with the hunted character in a movie, you are experiencing empathy, whereas if you simply feel sorry or afraid for the intended victim (but not fearful yourself), you are experiencing sympathy.

encomium (encomiastic): Originally, a **choral hymn** developed in ancient Greece praising heroic athletes of the Olympic games; later, any ancient Greek work written to glorify people, events, or objects. Pindar is famous for his encomiastic **odes.** Today encomiums may take the form of eulogies for people or of verse (often written as an ode) written to celebrate individuals, objects, or **abstract** ideas. Essays or speeches written in praise of a person or group of people are usually referred to by the term **epideictic** but are sometimes called **prose encomiums.**

end-rhyme: Rhyme that occurs at the end of lines in **verse.** In end-rhyme, the most common type of rhyme, the last word of a line rhymes with the last word of another line. End rhyme is distinguished from **internal rhyme,** which occurs within a line of verse.

end-stopped line: A line of **poetry** in which a grammatical pause (as indicated by some form of punctuation) and the physical end of the line coincide. The meaning or sense of the line is also complete in itself. End-stopped lines are distinguished from lines exhibiting ***enjambement*** (*run-on lines*).

EXAMPLES: Each of the four lines of this **stanza** from William Blake's "A Poison Tree" (1794) is end-stopped:

> I was angry with my friend:
> I told my wrath, my wrath did end.
> I was angry with my foe:
> I told it not, my wrath did grow.

In the first stanza of the poem "Oread" (1924) by H. D. (Hilda Doolittle), all but the third and fourth lines (which demonstrate *enjambement*) are end-stopped. The third line is not end-stopped because there is no grammatical pause after the word *pines;* the fourth line is not end-stopped because the meaning of the line is not complete in itself:

> Whirl up, sea, —
> whirl your pointed pines,
> splash your great pines
> on our rocks,
> hurl your green over us,
> cover us with your pools of fir.

English sonnet: See **Shakespearean sonnet.**

enjambement: French for "striding over," a **poetic** expression that spans more than one line. Lines exhibiting *enjambement* (or enjambment) do not end with grammatical breaks, and their sense is not complete without the following line(s). Such lines are also commonly referred to as *run-on lines* and are distinguished from **end-stopped lines.** The meaning of an end-stopped line, in which a grammatical pause marked by punctuation and the physical end of the line coincide, is complete in itself.

EXAMPLES: The second, third, and fourth lines of the following passage from a **sonnet** published in 1807 by William Wordsworth exemplify *enjambement* (as well as **simile** and **personification**):

> It is a beauteous evening, calm and free,
> The holy time is quiet as a Nun
> Breathless with adoration; the broad sun
> Is sinking down in its tranquility.

Thom Gunn's "Considering the Snail" (1956) also contains run-on lines and therefore exhibits *enjambement:*

> The snail pushes through a green
> night, for the grass is heavy
> with water and meets over
> the bright path he makes, where rain
> has darkened the earth's dark. He
> moves in a wood of desire,
>
> pale antlers barely stirring
> as he hunts. I cannot tell . . .

Imamu Amiri Baraka (LeRoi Jones) uses *enjambement* in his poem "An Agony. As Now" (1964):

> I am inside someone
> who hates me. I look
> out from his eyes. Smell
> what fouled tunes come in

to his breath. Love his
wretched women.

envoy (*envoi*): A concluding **stanza** (often a **quatrain** of a **poem** that is particularly associated with the French **ballade**). The envoy, a typical element of the ballade, a French **verse** form, is typically addressed to a patron or other important person and often has the **rhyme scheme** *bcbc*.

EXAMPLES: The envoy of François Villon's "Ballade des dames du temps jadis" (1498), quoted here in the original, fifteenth-century French:

> Prince, n'enquerez de sepmaine
> Ou elles sont, ne de cest an,
> Que ce refrain ne vous remaine:
> Mais ou sont les neiges d'antan?

Two nineteenth-century English poets, Algernon Charles Swinburne and Dante Gabriel Rossetti, creatively translated Villon's **ballads.** What follows is Rossetti's translation, in what he calls "The Ballad of Dead Ladies" (1870), of the envoy by Villon quoted above:

> Nay, never ask this week, fair lord,
> Where they are gone, nor yet this year,
> Except with this for an overword, —
> But where are the snows of yester-year?

epic: A long and formal **narrative poem** written in an elevated **style** that recounts the adventures of a **hero** of almost **mythic** proportions, who often embodies the traits of a nation or people. A distinction is generally made between traditional (or **folk** or primary) epics and literary (or art or secondary) epics. Traditional epics are derived from oral tradition and are not the invention of those who first commit them to writing, whereas literary epics are the work of a single poet, written in conscious **imitation** of the traditional style.

Epics typically share a wide variety of characteristics: (1) the **protagonist** is a hero of great stature and significance (whether historical or mythic) with the two traditional virtues of bravery (*fortitudo*) and wisdom (*sapientia*); (2) the **setting** is on a grand and vast scale, often encompassing the known world at the time of the epic's composition; (3) the action requires noble, fantastic, and even superhuman actions; (4) supernatural entities usually involve themselves in the action and in the affairs of the hero, who often must descend into some kind of underworld before he can claim victory; (5) the entire epic is written in an elevated style designed to complement and heighten the already mythic proportions of the **characters** and their actions.

Epics also generally involve many of the same **conventions.** These include: (1) invoking a **muse's** aid during the **argument** and posing the epic question to her; (2) starting the narrative *in medias res;* (3) introducing the roster of characters in a formal manner and giving them particular speeches revealing their principal characteristics and attitudes; and (4) using **epic similes.**

EXAMPLES: Homer's *The Odyssey* and *The Iliad* (c. 850 B.C.) are traditional epics, as are *Beowulf* (c. A.D. 700), an epic in Old English, and *La chanson de Roland* (*The Song of Roland* [c. 1100]), an epic in Old French. Virgil's *The Aeneid* (c. 15 B.C.), Dante Alighieri's *Divina commedia* (*The Divine Comedy* [1321]), and Ariosto's *Orlando furioso* (1516) are literary epics. James Joyce's novel *Ulysses* (1922) and Derek Walcott's long poem *Omeros* (1990) are twentieth-century works in the epic tradition. Both are based on *The Odyssey,* as is Francis Ford Coppola's lavish television movie by the same name (1997).

epic simile (Homeric simile): An extended and elaborate **simile** (comparison) in which the **vehicle** (the **image** used to describe or in some way define the subject, or **tenor,** of a **figure of speech**) is itself described at such length that it nearly obscures the tenor. The epic simile is sometimes called the *Homeric simile* because it is consciously patterned after the ornate similes composed by Homer in his **epics,** but epic similes appear in works other than epics.

EXAMPLE: The following **Spenserian stanza** from Edmund Spenser's *The Faerie Queene* (1590, 1596) uses an epic simile to describe two knights who have broken their weapons in combat:

> As when two rams, stird with ambitious pride,
> Fight for the rule of the rich fleeced flocke,
> Their horned fronts so fierce on either side
> Doe meete, that, with the terror of the schocke,
> Astonied,° both stand senceless as a blocke,   *Astonished*
> Forgetfull of the hanging victorie:
> So stood these twaine, unmoved as a rocke,
> Both staring fierce, and holding idely
> The broken reliques of their former cruelty.

The following passage from John Milton's *Paradise Lost* (1667), describing Satan's entry into Paradise, contains two back-to-back epic similes:

> As when a prowling Wolf,
> Whom hunger drives to seek new haunt for prey,
> Watching where Shepherds pen thir Flocks at eve
> In hurdl'd Cotes amid the field secure,
> Leaps o'er the fence with ease into the Fold:
> Or as a Thief bent to unhoard the cash
> Of some rich Burgher, whose substantial doors,
> Cross-barr'd and bolted fast, fear no assault,
> In at the window climbs, or o'er the tiles:
> So clomb this first grand Thief into God's Fold. . . .

epideictic: From the Greek word meaning "display," a term referring to **poems** (*epideictic poetry*), speeches (*epideictic rhetoric*), and **essays** (*epi-*

deictic prose) meant to edify an audience by demonstrating the strengths (or, on rare occasions, the weaknesses) of some person or persons through praise (or blame). Works of epideictic prose are sometimes referred to as **prose encomiums.**

EXAMPLES: Statius's *Silvae* (c. A.D. 75) is a famous, **classical** example of epideictic poetry; a more recent instance is Robert Hayden's poem "Frederick Douglass" (1962). Abraham Lincoln's "Gettysburg Address" (1863) is perhaps the best-known example of epideictic rhetoric, whereas Samuel Johnson's *Preface to Shakespeare* (1765), a prose encomium, exemplifies epidiectic prose.

epigram: Originally an "inscription" and then simply a short **poem,** now either a short poem with a brief, pointedly humorous, quotable ending or simply a terse, **witty** statement in and of itself.

EXAMPLES: Martial, a Roman poet, and Ben Jonson, the seventeenth-century English poet and playwright, are famous for their witty, often **satiric,** epigrams. The *Rubáiyát of Omar Khayyám,* known to English readers thanks to the 1859 translation by Edward FitzGerald, contains many epigrams.

In his "Postscript" to "Prologue: The Birth of Architecture" (1965), W. H. Auden epigrammatically combines an overt warning that he is a private person with a covert reminder of his sexual orientation:

> Some thirty inches from my nose
> The frontier of my Person goes,
> And all the untilled air between
> Is private *pagus*° or demesne°.   *district; domain*
> Stranger, unless with bedroom eyes
> I beckon you to fraternize,
> Beware of rudely crossing it:
> I have no gun, but I can spit.

Auden's volume of poetry *About the House* (1965) is full of witty little epigrams:

> Money cannot buy
> The fuel of Love:
> But is excellent kindling.

Equally epigrammatic is John Lennon's disingenuously innocent (and sharply witty) statement, "All these financial takeovers and things — it's just like Monopoly."

epigraph: A term that can be used to refer to an inscription on a coin, stone, statue, or building, but more commonly employed by literary scholars and critics to refer to a passage printed on the title page or first page of a literary work or at the beginning of each section of such a work. Epigraphs, which tend to set the **tone** or establish the **theme** of what follows, are generally taken from earlier, influential **texts** by other authors. Some **modernist** and **postmodernist** authors, however, have written their own epigraphs, presumably in an attempt to wrest control from the past of the way in which contemporary texts are read.

EXAMPLES: Two epigraphs precede T. S. Eliot's poem "The Hollow Men" (1925): "Mistuh Kurtz — he dead" and "A penny for the Old Guy." The first epigraph is taken from Joseph Conrad's *Heart of Darkness* (1899) and refers to the death of Kurtz, the morally hollow **antihero** of the work. The second epigraph refers to a line commonly heard in London on Guy Fawkes Day, when children go door-to-door for money and older revellers burn straw effigies of the man who plotted to blow up King James I and the Houses of Parliament in 1605. The two epigraphs are thematically connected; in concert, they suggest that Kurtz has become a hollow man, a man of straw, an effigy, and they set the tone for a poem about "stuffed men" without morals, without even the will to act shown by Kurtz or Guy Fawkes.

More recently, postmodernist novelist Kathy Acker has written her own epigraph to part 2 of *Don Quixote* (1986): "Being born into and part of a male world, she had no speech of her own. All she could do was read male texts, which weren't hers." Contemporary novelist A. Manette Ansay's *Midnight Champagne* (1999) begins with the following epigraph: "If you fear loneliness, then marriage is not for you" — Anton Chekhov.

epilogue: The concluding section of a work. Also the recitation by an actor of the concluding section of a **play** (in the form of a speech), often requesting the appreciation (applause) of the audience and kind reviews from critics.

EXAMPLE: The epilogue to William Shakespeare's *The Tempest* (c. 1611) is spoken by Prospero, who begins by saying:

> Now my charms are all o'erthrown
> And what strength I have's all my own

and ends by subtly suggesting that the audience applaud:

> As you from crimes would pardoned be,
> Let your indulgence set me free.

Contemporary works that contain epilogues include Paulo Coelho's **fable** *O alquimista* (*The Alchemist*) (1988), Jane Smiley's novel *A Thousand Acres* (1991), and Charles Frazier's novel *Cold Mountain* (1997).

epiphany: From the Greek for "manifestation" or "showing-forth," traditionally used to refer to the incarnation or manifestation of a divine being (in Christian circles, Jesus Christ in particular). The term was introduced into literary criticism by James Joyce, who in *Stephen Hero* (an early version of *A Portrait of the Artist as a Young Man* [1916]) uses *epiphany* more **figuratively** to describe the insight or revelation gained when one suddenly understands the essence of a (generally commonplace) object, gesture, statement, situation, moment, or mentality — that is, when one "sees" that commonplace for what it really is beneath the surface and perceives its inner workings, its nature. By *epiphany*, Joyce's Stephen Dedalus "meant a sudden spiritual manifestation, whether in the vulgarity of speech or of gesture or in a memorable phase of the mind itself. He believed that it was for the man of letters to record these epiphanies with extreme care, seeing that they themselves are the most delicate and evanescent of moments."

Although the term can describe secular experience, epiphany retains a **mystical,** almost religious, **connotation** due to the emphasis on the intuitive connections made during the epiphanic moment — associations so surprising and unusual as to seem almost unworldly. As Joyce wrote of the epiphanic object: "Its soul, its whatness, leaps to us from the vestment of its appearance. The soul of the commonest object . . . seems to us radiant. The object achieves its epiphany." Literary critics now regularly use *epiphany* to refer to a sudden revelatory experience; it sometimes also refers to a work in which such an experience occurs.

FURTHER EXAMPLES: Virginia Woolf's novel *Mrs. Dalloway* (1925) ends by depicting a party at which a late-arriving doctor tells of attending to a young, former soldier who has just committed suicide by throwing himself from a window onto a railing below. The doctor's story triggers an epiphanic moment for Clarissa Dalloway, the hostess. She retreats from her guests to an empty room, where she envisions the young man's death and suddenly has the strange and surprising sense that he may have preserved something by throwing his life away, something that slips away from those who merely hold on to life:

> He had thrown himself from a window. Up had flashed the ground; through him, blundering, bruising, went the rusty spikes. There he lay with a thud, thud, thud in his brain, and then a suffocation of blackness. So she saw it. But why had he done it? And the Bradshaws talked of it at her party!
>
> She had once thrown a shilling into the Serpentine, never anything more. But he had flung it away. They went on living (she would have to go back; the rooms were still crowded; people kept on coming). They (all day she had been thinking of Bourton, of Peter, and Sally), they would grow old. A thing there was that mattered; a thing wreathed about with chatter, defaced, obscured in her own life, let drop every day in corruption, lies, chatter. This he had preserved. Death was defiance. Death was an attempt to communicate; people feeling the impossibility of reaching the centre which, mystically, evaded them; closeness drew apart; rapture faded; one was alone. There was an embrace in death.

In Barbara Kingsolver's novel *The Poisonwood Bible* (1998), Orleanna Price, the wife of a Southern Baptist preacher who takes his family to the Congo as missionaries, experiences an epiphany during an embarrassing moment at a local market, as the villagers stare at her and her daughter Leah, who has just unwittingly violated a local taboo:

Until that moment, I'd thought I could have it both ways: to be one of them, and also my husband's wife. What conceit! I was his instrument, his animal. Nothing more. How we wives and mothers do perish at the hands of our own righteousness. I was just one more of those women who clamp their mouths shut and wave the flag as their nation rolls off to conquer another in war. Guilty or innocent, they have everything to lose. They *are* what there is to lose. A wife is the earth itself, changing hands, bearing scars.

episodic structure: The **form** of a work containing a series of incidents or episodes that are loosely connected by a larger subject matter or **thematic structure** but that could stand on their own. A work that has a sustained story line or that would not be a complete work without one of its parts does not exhibit episodic structure.

EXAMPLES: Tobias Smollett's **picaresque novel** *Roderick Random* (1748) is episodic, as is Laurence Sterne's **sentimental novel** *A Sentimental Journey* (1768). Most travel **narratives** are episodic (D. H. Lawrence's *Twilight in Italy* [1916], Lawrence Durrell's *Sicilian Carousel* [1977]), as are most erotic and pornographic **texts** (*Delta of Venus* [1969] by Anaïs Nin; the *Sleeping Beauty* trilogy [1983–85] by Anne Rice, writing under the ***nom de plume*** A. N. Roquelaure).

epistémé (discursive formation): Based on the Greek word *epistēmē*, which means knowledge, a term used by twentieth-century French philosophical historian Michel Foucault to refer to: (1) a network of discursive practices — of thoughts, concepts, and cultural **codes** — dominant during a given historical period; and (2) the rules governing the transformation of those practices. In *Les mots et les choses* (*The Order of Things*) (1970), Foucault himself defined *epistémé* as a "historical a priori, [which] . . . in a given period, delimits in the totality of experience a field of knowledge, defines the mode of being of the objects that appear in that field, provides everyday perception with theoretical powers, and defines the conditions in which one can sustain a discourse about things which is recognized to be true." Foucault subsequently substituted the term *discursive formation* for *epistémé* in *L'archéologie du savoir* (*The Archaeology of Knowledge*) (1969).

Epistémé governs the way that people perceive and approach the world at any given time. It is analogous to *paradigm,* as understood by historian of science Thomas Kuhn, since both are conceptual frameworks that govern systems of knowledge until they shift, break down, and are replaced by new frameworks. According to Foucault, only one *epistémé* can exist at any given time, and each is unique. Over time, a new *epistémé* develops that replaces the last one, ushering in a new era in which people think differently than they did before. So long as any given *epistémé* is in place, however, it governs the boundaries within which people think and the ways in which they gain, process, and pass on knowledge. Insofar as *epistémés* entail universally accepted positions, they also preclude challenges to those positions.

Foucault has identified a number of successive *epistémés* in his body of work. The **Renaissance** *epistémé* of the sixteenth century was based on the concept of similitude between things and on uncovering such resemblances, whereas the subsequent **neoclassical** *epistémé* of the seventeenth and eighteenth centuries was based on the quite opposite concept of differences and distinctions. Instead of thinking of words and things as inextricably and reliably linked, as was common in the Renaissance, the connection between them was severed in the **Neoclassical Period.** During the nineteenth century, the neoclassical *epistémé* was displaced by the concept of historical development and of history as a way to trace language, which was in turn displaced by the present *epistémé*, in which the human being is the center for knowledge. The next *epistémé*, Foucault argued, will involve a diminution and **decentering** of the human being's role.

Epistémé should be distinguished from **ideology,** the frequently unrecognized set of beliefs underlying the customs, habits, and practices of a given social group. (In the nineteenth century, Karl Marx introduced the concept that cultures are governed by certain "ruling ideas," a concept later developed by **Marxist, feminist,** and **cultural critics** into theories regarding ideology.) *Epistémé* refers to an even more dominant and deterministic system than ideology. Whereas the **gaps, conflicts,** and contradictions in ideologies can be exposed through creative and critical **texts,** there is simply no vantage point outside an *epistémé*, which sets the boundaries within which people think, and thus no way to critique its rules or suggest alternative **discourses.**

Foucault's concept of *epistémé* has been criticized on several grounds. First, critics contend that Foucault ignored relevant contradictory evidence in his quest to identify particular *epistémés*. Second, proponents of the concept cannot account for why discursive practices *do* change over time. Third, they cannot explain why the very concept of *epistémé* and all the commentary it has generated are not themselves products of the current *epistémé* and its all-governing, or "totalizing," laws of transformation.

FURTHER EXAMPLES: In *Folie et déraison* (*Madness and Civilization*) (1965), Foucault discussed the transition from the *epistémé* of the **classic** age to that of the Renaissance as **represented** by two Spanish artists: painter Diego Velásquez and novelist Miguel de Cervantes. He subsequently elaborated on this shift in *Les mots et les choses,* suggesting that whereas before the Renaissance the world was represented as a book whose **signifiers** could reliably be read, the assumed intrinsic relationship between words and world ("things") was later broken, leaving the human subject wandering through the wreckage but also free to form new connections.

In *Surveiller et punir: Naissance de la prison* (*Discipline and Punish: The Birth of the Prison*) (1975), Foucault discussed the shift in the understanding of the human "subject," or self. He argued that in Europe, prior to the eighteenth century, a subject was a *body* subject to the power of a monarch — and subject to being physically punished by that power. Later, however, the subject became the internalized sense of individual self, a *psychological* entity punished through incarceration. Likewise, in *Naissance de la clinique (The Birth of the Clinic)* (1963), Foucault focused on the shift in perception of the human body due to shifts in the "medical gaze" from one *epistémé* to the next.

epistle: A letter. As a literary form, an epistle is generally restricted to a formal (not conversational), thoughtfully composed letter that is intended for a distant individual or group of people. Although some of the most famous epistles come from the New Testament of the Bible, any such formal letter, regardless of religious or moral intent, is an epistle. Alexander Pope composed a number of verse epistles.

epistolary novel: A **novel** whose **plot** is entirely developed through letters, whether through an exchange of letters between multiple **characters** or through the correspondence of only one character. The form has been employed for the immediacy it lends to the **narrative** (that is, events are recounted just after — and occasionally even during — the moment of their occurrence), as well as the opportunity it provides to reveal the intimate, private thoughts of characters. The **genre** was extremely popular during the eighteenth century but became increasingly rare thereafter.

EXAMPLES: Samuel Richardson's *Pamela; or, Virtue Rewarded* (1740) and *Clarissa Harlowe* (1748) are early examples that are generally considered to have established this genre. Other examples include Tobias Smollett's *The Expedition of Humphry Clinker* (1771), Johann Wolfgang von Goethe's *The Sorrows of Young Werther* (1774), Isabelle de Charrière's *Les lettres de Mistriss Henley* (1784), Choderlos de Laclos's *Les liaisons dangereuses (Dangerous Liaisons)* (1784), Hannah Foster's *The Coquette: or, The History of Eliza Wharton* (1797), and Mariama Bâ's *Une si longue lettre (A Very Long Letter)* (1981). Nick Bantock cleverly adapted the epistolary form in *Griffin and Sabine* (1991) and *Sabine's Notebook* (1992), popular short works that include actual envelopes, removable letters, and postcards by two correspondents, one of whom may be the invention of the other. Contemporary writer Steve Thayer's novel *Moon over Lake Elmo* (2001) also contains a twist on the epistolary form, for the story is told through both letters and diary entries.

epitaph: An inscription on a tomb to commemorate the deceased. Epitaphs often contain basic **biographical** information as well as memorial phrases. The term *epitaph* can also refer to a poem, whether serious or humorous, that commemorates the deceased.

EXAMPLES: Ben Jonson's "Epitaph on Elizabeth, L. H." (1616), quoted here in part:

> Underneath this stone doth lie
> As much beauty as could die;
> Which in life did harbor give

> To more virtue than could live.
> If at all she had a fault,
> Leave it buried in this vault.

George Gordon, Lord Byron's epitaph for his dog Botswain, next to whom he intended to be buried, reads:

> To mark a friend's remains these stones arise;
> I never knew but one — and here he lies.

epithalamium (epithalamion): A **poem** written to celebrate a specific marriage, to celebrate the bride and groom. From the Greek for "at the bridal chamber," an epithalamium was originally sung just outside the room to which the bride and groom retired on their wedding night.

EXAMPLES: Edmund Spenser's *Epithalamion* (1595), written to celebrate his own marriage, is an English example, as is John Donne's "Epithalamion, or Marriage Song, On the Lady Elizabeth, and Count Palatine Being Married on St. Valentine's Day" (1613).

epithet: An adjective or phrase applied to a noun to accentuate a certain characteristic.

EXAMPLES: Charles le Chauve (Charles the Bald); Elizabeth, the Virgin Queen; blundering fool; that big ape John. The following sentence, taken from Oscar Wilde's novel *The Picture of Dorian Gray* (1891), contains an epithet describing what we may infer was a certain aristocrat's most distinctive character trait: "The ducal hat of Charles the Rash, the last Duke of Burgundy of his race, was hung with pear-shaped pearls, and studded with sapphires." In H. G. Wells's **science fiction** novel *The Time Machine* (1895), the **narrator** uses epithets to refer to all but one of the **characters** who frequent the Time Traveller's — itself an epithet — house every Thursday evening: the Medical Man, the Provincial Mayor, the Editor, the Psychologist, the Very Young Man, and so forth.

Professional athletes are commonly referred to epithetically, as are political figures. Examples include "Wilt the Stilt" Chamberlain, "Magic" Johnson, "Give 'em Hell" Harry (Truman), and "Tricky Dick" (Nixon). Former president George H. W. Bush's wife Barbara was sometimes referred to by the epithet "The Silver Fox."

epoché: See **phenomenology.**

epode: The third **stanza** of the **classical** Greek choral **ode.** After the **strophe** and the **antistrophe,** which involve movement, the **chorus** sang the epode while standing still. The epode is one of the stanza forms of the **Pindaric ode.** The term also refers to a poem in which a short stanza or line follows a long one.

Erziehungsroman: German for "novel of upbringing," a novel of upbringing or education. Although the term is often used synonymously with **bildungsroman,** it is more correctly used to refer to a category of bildungsroman, the more general novel of formation. The *Erziehungsroman* examines, as does the bildungsroman, the growth and development of a central **character** from youth to maturity.

EXAMPLES: Johann Wolfgang von Goethe's *Wilhelm Meister's Apprenticeship* (1796), George Eliot's *The Mill on the Floss* (1860), Evelyn Waugh's *Brideshead Revisited* (1946).

eschatology: Concern with the "ultimate" questions, last things — sthat is, what happens after humans die, or after the end of the world and life as we know it. Christian eschatology includes such concepts as heaven and hell, salvation and damnation, and God's judgment and forgiveness. **Medieval** Christian eschatologists developed the concept of Purgatory, one still espoused by the Roman Catholic Church but rejected by Protestants after the Reformation.

Eschatology is generally relevant to literary study insofar as **texts** from the biblical book of Revelation through Mary Shelley's *The Last Man* (1826), from medieval **mystery plays** about Creation and the Day of Judgment through Piers Anthony's novels in the *Intimations of Immortality* series (1983–90), have been concerned with first and last things, ultimate questions.

essay: Nonfiction compositions that usually explore a single **theme** or topic, although some essays take up multiple subjects. Most are relatively brief, but essays may range from less than a single page to novel length. They are generally written in **prose,** but a few have been composed in **verse** (most notably Alexander Pope's "An Essay on Criticism" [1711] and "An Essay on Man" [1733]). The form developed in **classical** times, but the term itself derives from the French *essai* (meaning "attempt"), first applied by the French writer Michel de Montaigne to his 1580 collection of informal compositions. Montaigne's use of the term *essai* was meant to reflect the uncertain and inquiring quality of his ruminations. In 1597, the term entered English when Francis Bacon applied it to his famous work *Essays* (1597–1625). The **etymology** of the term reminds us that essayists make no claim to an exhaustive and technical examination of a subject; rather, they seek to record their thoughts and ruminations on the topic at hand for a general audience.

Essays are often classified as *argumentative, descriptive, expository,* or **narrative,** although the categories exhibit considerable overlap. They may also be categorized as *formal* or *informal.* Authors of formal essays conduct a comparatively impersonal and analytical examination of their subject matter. Formal essays are often longer than informal ones; more dignified or solemn in **tone,** they are designed to declaim or instruct rather than to entertain. Writers of informal essays tend to adopt a tone that is lighter, more personal or conversational, and more humorous than that adopted by their more formal counterparts. Informal essayists also tend to incorporate more **anecdotes** and **aphorisms** into their work than do formal essayists.

Until the eighteenth century, most essays were published as collections in books. The development of the periodical in the early eighteenth century, however, made essay writing a more prevalent and popular form. It also had a standardizing effect, particularly on the informal essay, elevating the role of humor and restricting maximum length. In the nineteenth century, the formal essay was chiefly found in a handful of important literary magazines. The proliferation of periodicals — whether literary or popular — from the eighteenth-century *Tatler* to the present day *New Yorker* — has kept the essay in the forefront of literary **genres.** The *personal essay,* a type of informal essay, emerged with the continued development of the periodical in the nineteenth century; its most famous English exponents were Thomas De Quincey, William Hazlitt, and Charles Lamb. Personal essays stress **autobiographical** content and are often written in an urbane and intimate manner.

FURTHER EXAMPLES: Henry David Thoreau's "Civil Disobedience" (1849) is perhaps the best-known formal American essay; Ralph Waldo Emerson is generally considered to be the dean of American essayists. Contemporary American essayists whose works have been published as book-length collections include Joan Didion (*Slouching Towards Bethlehem* [1967], *The White Album* [1979]), Susan Sontag (*Against Interpretation, and Other Essays* [1966], *Under the Sign of Saturn* [1980]), and Calvin Trillin (*Uncivil Liberties* [1982], *Too Soon to Tell* [1995]). Writers who are not primarily essayists have also turned their attention to this form. The poet Nikki Giovanni and British novelist Julian Barnes have recently published book-length collections of essays entitled *Racism 101* (1994) and *Letters from London* (1995), respectively.

essentialism: See **feminist criticism, gay and lesbian criticism,** and **gender criticism.**

etymology: See **linguistics.**

euphony: Pleasing, harmonious sounds. Euphony is the opposite of **cacophony,** or discordant sounds. The pleasurable impression achieved may be due as much or more to the **images** invoked and described as it is to any inherent musicality in the sounds; terming a passage euphonious thus necessarily involves a subjective judgment.

EXAMPLES: The first **stanza** of Christina Rossetti's "Song" (1862):

> When I am dead, my dearest,
> Sing no sad songs for me;
> Plant thou no roses at my head,
> Nor shady cypress tree.
> Be the green grass above me
> With showers and dewdrops wet;
> And if thou wilt, remember,
> And if thou wilt, forget.

Trumbull Stickney's poem "Mnemosyne" (1902) alternates matter-of-fact, one-line stanzas with euphonious **tercets:**

> It's autumn in the country I remember.

> How warm a wind blew here about the ways!
> And shadows on the hillside lay to slumber
> During the long sun-sweetened summer days.

> It's cold abroad the country I remember.

> The swallows veering skimmed the golden grain
> At midday with a wing aslant and limber;
> And yellow cattle browsed upon the plain.

Prose can also be euphonious, as is the description of snow in the concluding sentences of James Joyce's story "The Dead" (1907):

> It lay thickly drifted on the crooked crosses and headstones, on the spears of the little gate, on the barren thorns. His soul swooned slowly as he heard the snow falling faintly through the universe and faintly falling, like the descent of their last end, upon all the living and the dead.

euphuism: An artificial literary **style,** particularly popular in late-sixteenth-century and seventeenth-century England, that made frequent use of **alliteration,** elaborate and extended **figures of speech,** rhetorical questions, and **parallel** or balanced constructs, including **antitheses.** The term is derived from the extended prose **narrative** *Euphues* (1579) by John Lyly, who did not create the style but did much to broaden its appeal by combining and elaborating on features developed by several predecessors. Although viewed as extravagant and thoroughly affected today, euphuism had a positive effect on the development of English prose, which had previously been ponderously Latinate in style and sentence structure and consequently thick and tedious to follow. Euphuistic writing, although artificial, brought imagination, **wit,** and greater clarity to English prose.

EXAMPLE: An example from Lyly's *Euphues* follows:

> But this grieveth me most, that thou art almost vowed to the vain order of the vestal virgins, despising, or at the least not desiring, the sacred bands of Juno her bed. If thy mother had been of that mind when she was a maiden, thou hadst not now been born to be of this mind to be a virgin. Weigh with thyself what slender profit they bring to the commonwealth, what slight pleasure to themselves, what great grief to their parents, which joy most in their offspring and desire most to enjoy the noble and blessed name of a grandfather. Thou knowest that the tallest ash is cut down for fuel because it beareth no good fruit, that the cow that gives no milk is brought to the slaughter, that the drone that gathereth no honey is contemned, that the woman that maketh herself barren by not marrying is accounted among the Grecian ladies worse than a carrion, as Homer reporteth. Therefore, Lucilla, if thou have any care to be a comfort to my hoary hairs or a

commodity to thy commonweal, frame thyself to that honourable estate of matrimony which was sanctified in Paradise, allowed of the Patriarchs, hallowed of the old Prophets, and commended of all persons.

exegesis (explication): Most specifically, the interpretation (and, by implication, the explanation) of difficult passages of the Bible. When applied more generally to the study of literature, it refers to the elucidation of a passage (and through a given passage, the work as a whole) by a **close reading** of the text. In French literary study, *explication de texte* (explanation of text) used to be the chief and continues to be a prominent method of exegesis. *Explication de texte* aims to reveal the meaning of a work first and foremost through close analysis of its language (**images** and **symbols, diction** and **tone, style,** etc.).

See *explication de texte* for further explanation of this exegetical method.

exemplum: Commonly classified as a type of **allegory,** a story that, though generally presumed to be true, is told to validate a general moral point. **Medieval** preachers made frequent use of this device — so much so, in fact, that they occasionally lost sight of their moral point while recounting their *exempla,* or "examples." This tendency was criticized by such well-known figures as Dante Alighieri. Although these stories seem rather ridiculous to modern readers, they held wide appeal for medieval audiences, who apparently appreciated their **concrete** details and general applicability to daily life.

EXAMPLES: *Exempla* can be found throughout Geoffrey Chaucer's *Canterbury Tales* (c. 1387). The "Nun's Priest's Tale" contains several *exempla,* and "The Pardoner's Tale" is itself an *exemplum.*

existentialism: A philosophical school whose proponents maintain that existence precedes essence. Existentialists concern themselves with humanity's very being, with its perpetual, anguished struggle to exist. They presume that individuals have free will and are thus entirely responsible for their actions. Even as existentialists reject deterministic systems of fate or predestination, they also reject notions that immutable or absolute value systems exist to guide humanity and that human reason can adequately explain the universe. Instead, existentialists assert that individuals freely construct and use (or choose not to use) their own value systems, forming their own sense of being and creating meaning in the process. As Jean-Paul Sartre argued, "man makes himself." However, the attempt to create meaning and morality in a world without defined guideposts and rules, combined with the belief that freedom and responsibility rest squarely with the individual, generates a particularly trenchant anxiety for the individual. Thus, although existentialism holds out the possibility of an improved existence by positing the individual as the engine of change, it also runs the risk of fostering despair, hopelessness, and nihilism.

Existentialism gained global eminence in the aftermath of World War II, particularly in Europe. Since World War II, existentialists have gathered into two major camps. In the vein of nineteenth-century philosopher Søren Kierkegaard, Christian existentialists such as Paul Tillich and Gabriel Marcel have emphasized that true freedom — including freedom from conflict and despair — may be found in God, who bridges the finite and the infinite. Some existentialists accept this general orientation while rejecting any specific theology. Martin Heidegger and Sartre pioneered a second approach, one that asserts an atheistic universe in which individuals may "make themselves" through exercising their free will, but that necessitates "engagement" in the social sphere, including (and perhaps especially) political struggle against repressive social institutions, laws, and **conventions.**

Existentialist works of the second type tend to stress the alienation of individuals as well as their essential — and inescapable — loneliness and uncertainty. They also explore the reactions of individuals to predicaments accentuating humanity's isolation, hence the earnest attempts by the responsible to face such situations even as the irresponsible unsuccessfully try to evade them. This approach has placed particular emphasis on the essential meaninglessness of the universe and on man's need to struggle to create meaning. Sartre has written a number of works that explore and expound this less theological brand of existentialist theory. His major philosophical work is *L'être et le néant: Essai d'ontologie phénoménologique* (*Being and Nothingness: An Essay in Phenomenological Ontology*) (1943); other influential existentialist works by Sartre include plays such as *Huis clos* (*No Exit*) (1943) and novels such as *La nausée* (*Nausea*) (1938). In addition to Sartre, Albert Camus, Simone de Beauvoir, and Franz Kafka are well known for their existentialist writings.

Existentialist criticism, as pioneered by Sartre in works such as *Qu'est-ce que la littérature?* (*What Is Literature?*) (1947), evaluated literary works based on how well they represent the modern condition in general and, in particular, the struggle of individuals to define themselves through responsible individual action and social engagement in spite (or perhaps because) of their isolation and alienation.

explication: See **exegesis.**

explication de texte: A method of literary analysis that originated in late-nineteenth-century France involving close and detailed textual analysis. Only elements that bear directly on the interpretation of the **text** and a further understanding of its meaning are considered; hence the practitioners of this method concentrate on such things as **style, symbolism, diction,** and **imagery.** *Explication de texte* entered English-language criticism with the help of **the New Critics,** who emphasized a text-only approach as the only valid method of analysis. Thanks to the New Criticism, *explication* has become established in English as a critical term referring to the nuanced and thorough **close reading** of textual **ambiguities,** complexities, and interrelationships.

expressionism: A critical term that has been used in both literary and artistic circles. Born in Germany in the late nineteenth century, expressionism reached its zenith as an artistic and literary movement in the 1920s. In general, expressionists hold that "objective" depictions of circumstances and thoughts (that is, from an external viewpoint) cannot accurately render an individual's "subjective" or emotional experience of these things. Expressionists thus reject **realism** and share (although perhaps with more intensity) the **impressionist** intention to present a personal vision through art. To render this personal vision artistically, expressionists depict their subjects as they feel or sense or experience them rather than as those subjects appear objectively. To expose the idiosyncratic and often extreme states of human consciousness and emotion, expressionist works tend to oversimplify and distort. In addition, the singularly "unreal" or even nightmarish **atmosphere** of these works accentuates the gulf between personal perception and objective reality.

Expressionism has a more precise meaning in art criticism than it does in literary criticism. In art, the term is most often used to refer to an early-twentieth-century German school of painters who believed that human consciousness or essence could not be represented adequately by simulating external reality. Famous practitioners include Oskar Kokoschka, Wassily Kandinsky, Käthe Kollwitz, Max Beckmann, and Georg Grosz. Literary expressionism also originated in Germany, in the plays of Frank Wedekind and Carl Sternheim. However, it quickly influenced poets (such as Franz Werful) and fiction writers (for example, Franz Kafka). In time, literary critics began to apply the term to virtually any twentieth-century **text** in which reality is purposely distorted. For these reasons, it has become as difficult to define literary expressionism exactly as it is to associate it with a single school or period (as is commonly done in the art world). Some critics do limit the term's application, however, using it to describe the early-twentieth-century German literary movement (especially as it was manifested in drama) that sought to explore the recesses of the human mind and to divulge its secrets, an interest inaugurated by the work of **psychoanalytic** theorists such as Sigmund Freud.

Although the German expressionist movement was suppressed in Nazi Germany in the 1930s, it continued to influence other European and American writers, as evidenced by the tendency of many critics to label any twentieth-century work exhibiting purposeful distortion of reality expressionist. Inheritors of the expressionist tradition include the **Beat writers** as well as Tennessee Williams, Joseph Heller, and Thomas Pynchon.

EXAMPLES: August Strindberg's *A Dream Play* (1902), Eugene O'Neill's *The Emperor Jones* (1921), and Elmer Rice's *The Adding Machine* are exemplary expressionist dramas; T. S. Eliot's poem *The Waste Land* (1922) and James Joyce's novel *Finnegans Wake* (1939) show the strong **influence** of expressionism. Henri Matisse's paintings contain expressionist elements; Edvard Munch's postimpressionist painting *The Scream* (1893) anticipates and heavily influenced the expressionist movement.

expressive criticism: See **pragmatic criticism, rhetorical criticism.**

expressive form, fallacy of: The belief — considered to be fallacious by **New Critics** such as R. P. Blackmur — that if poets feel strongly enough about their subjects, the intensity of their feelings will be transferred to their poems and felt by their readers. Great believers in craftsmanship, the New Critics suggested that poets relying solely on inspiration and on the intensity of personal emotion to move their audience are unable to judge accurately the effects that their works really have on readers, because they lack not only an understanding of techniques and their effects but also objective standards of judgment.

eye-rhyme: Words that appear to **rhyme** due to their spelling but that do not rhyme when actually pronounced.

EXAMPLES: *Laughter* and *slaughter, bough* and *cough* and *dough, demon* and *lemon.* Percy Bysshe Shelley's "Ode to the West Wind" (1820) ends by eye-rhyming *wind* and *behind.* William Blake uses eye-rhyme in the second and fourth lines of the first **stanza** of "The Sick Rose" (1794):

> O Rose, thou art sick.
> The invisible worm
> That flies in the night
> In the howling storm
>
> Has found out thy bed
> Of crimson joy,
> And his dark secret love
> Does thy life destroy.

Anne Bradstreet uses eye-rhyme in these lines from "A Letter to Her Husband, Absent upon Public Employment" (1678):

> Flesh of thy flesh, bone of thy bone,
> I here, thou there, yet both but one.

F

fable (apologue): A short, fictional (nonhistorical) prose or verse **tale** with a specific moral. As **allegorical** works, fables are told to illustrate a particular point or lesson, which is often explicitly expressed at the end of the tale via an **epigram.** Fables often feature animals (**personified**) as their principal **characters;** animal-centered or animal-dominant fables may also be called **beast fables.** Some critics have used the term *apologue* as a synonym for *beast fable,* but most consider it to be equivalent to the more general term *fable.* Fables are often considered to be children's literature, but their origins frequently lie in **folklore** told by, for, and to adults.

The term *fable* also has other **connotations.** It has been applied to lies, **legends,** unbelievable stories, and **myths,** but none of these are standard critical usages of the term. Fable (or, sometimes, *fabula*) was has also been used synonymously with **plot;** this usage, however, was largely limited to **neoclassical** critics. In the twentieth century, the term *fabula* was used very differently by **Russian formalists** to refer to the basic elements of a **story.** (Russian formalists used the word *syuzhet* to refer to plot.)

EXAMPLES: Aesop's *Fables* (c. 550 B.C.) are undoubtedly the most well known. Other famous fabulists (writers of fables) include the seventeenth-century French poet Jean de la Fontaine and the English writer Rudyard Kipling, who wrote the popular *Just So Stories* (1902). Paulo Coelho's *O alquimista* (*The Alchemist*) (1988), a magical story about an Andalusian shepherd boy who seeks a worldly treasure, is subtitled *A Fable about Following Your Dream.*

fabliau: A short verse **narrative,** generally composed in octosyllabic **couplets,** that has a humorous and frequently **satiric** purpose. *Fabliaux* were particularly popular in **medieval** France in the twelfth and thirteenth centuries and became well known in England around the fourteenth century. They often take humor to the point of ridicule and/or ribaldry, their favorite targets being the clergy, the cuckolded husband, and women. Unlike a *fable,* a *fabliau* is designed primarily to entertain. Furthermore, it employs human (as opposed to animal) **characters** and usually is not composed with a moralizing purpose or political intent, dealing instead with middle- and lower-class people and their concerns in a thoroughly **realistic** manner.

EXAMPLES: Geoffrey Chaucer's *Canterbury Tales* (c. 1387) includes such *fabliaux* as "The Miller's Tale" and "The Reeve's Tale."

fabula: See **fable, Russian formalism.**

fallacy of expressive form: See **expressive form, fallacy of.**

falling action: In a **tragedy,** that portion of the **plot** that follows the **climax** or the **crisis** and that leads to and culminates in the **catastrophe.** (In other **genres** — fiction, for example — the falling action leads to and culminates in the **resolution** of the plot.) Falling action is one of five **structural** elements associated with **Freytag's Pyramid,** a model developed by Gustav Freytag for analyzing five-act plays and tragedies in particular.

fancy: With the exception of some minor distinctions made by writers such as John Dryden and Joshua Reynolds, a term generally used synonymously with **imagination** and in opposition to *reason* until the publication of **romantic** poet Samuel Taylor Coleridge's *Biographia Literaria* (1817). Coleridge, however, distinguished between the two, assigning a much higher value to imagination than to fancy. He saw fancy as a mode of memory "emancipated" from the normal constraints of time and space and assigned to it the function of reordering the sensory **images** it receives. Coleridge thus denied fancy any creative capability, limiting its effects to a rearrangement of what already exists. He credited imagination with the loftier function of creation, arguing that it is the **organic** imagination that can dissolve and remake sensory images — essentially "re-birth" them — into something completely new and different. Imagination alone, unlike the **mechanical** fancy, has the ability to unify disparate and even contradictory elements into a vital and interdependent whole. William Wordsworth, also a romantic poet, had drawn a similar (though by no means identical) distinction between imagination and fancy two years before Coleridge in his preface to the 1815 edition of *Lyrical Ballads;* nonetheless, it is Coleridge who usually is credited with making the distinction because of his extensive and in-depth discussion in the *Biographia Literaria.*

Subsequent critics have continued to differentiate fancy from imagination, but most do not delineate the two in as judgmental a manner as Coleridge. Instead, they typically claim that fancy produces a lesser, lighter verse while imagination generates the higher, more serious work we attribute to greater artists.

EXAMPLES: Coleridge considered John Milton an imaginative writer and Abraham Cowley a fanciful one. Since Coleridge, most critics have assumed that **light verse,** such as **limericks,** results from the workings of fancy, whereas a poem like Walt Whitman's "Song of Myself" (1881) is the work of imagination.

fantastic: See **fantasy fiction.**

fantasy fiction: A type of **fiction** set wholly or in part in a vaguely **medieval** Arthurian or imaginary land populated by inhabitants subject to magic, as well as by magical figures, creatures, or beasts. Attempts to define the term more broadly are complicated by the overlap between fantasy fiction and other **genres,** such as **science fiction** and *horror,* and further compounded by the tendency of fantasy authors to import and mix elements of different genres. Examples of hybrid works include Piers

Anthony's fantasy–science fiction *Apprentice Adept* series (1980–90), Clive Barker's fantasy-horror novel *Weaveworld* (1987), and television's animated *He-Man* (1983–85, 2002–) and *She-Ra* (1985–88) cartoon series, which combine fantasy, science fiction, and action / adventure.

Fantasy should not be confused with *fantastic,* a related term applicable not only to fantasy fiction but also to other literary **forms,** such as **magic realism** and **cyberfiction,** that contain fanciful, supernatural, or otherwise incredible elements. As defined by theorist Tzvetan Todorov in *Introduction à la littérature fantastique* (*The Fantastic*) (1970), the fantastic mingles the marvelous (which concerns magical events and locales) with the uncanny (which can be explained as delusion), thereby creating "hesitation" (i.e., **ambiguity** and uncertainty) as to whether a natural or supernatural explanation underlies events in a **narrative.** It is this uncertainty that distinguishes fantastic **plots** from horror plots, which typically involve an unquestionably supernatural actor or element. Fantastic **texts** discussed by Todorov include works ranging from *The Arabian Nights* (also known as *The Thousand and One Nights* [c. 1450]) to Edgar Allan Poe's short stories (c. 1840s) to Henry James's *The Turn of the Screw* (1898).

Fantasy fiction, which has roots in **folk tales** and fairy tales, emerged as a modern literary mode in the mid-nineteenth century, during the **Victorian Period. Tales** translated into English in the first half of the nineteenth century from sources including *The Arabian Nights,* Hans Christian Andersen, and the Brothers Grimm proved particularly influential, as evidenced by works such as Charles Dickens's *A Christmas Carol* (1843), John Ruskin's *The King of the Golden River* (1851), George MacDonald's *Phantastes* (1858), Lewis Carroll's *Alice's Adventures in Wonderland* (1865), Oscar Wilde's *The Happy Prince and Other Stories* (1888), Arthur Machen's *Fantastic Tales* (1890), and William Morris's *The Roots of the Mountains* (1890). Illustrations for many of the fantasy narratives produced by these writers anticipate the extravagant visual aspects of some forms of present-day fantasy.

Other important influences on the development of fantasy fiction as a genre include **Romantic** poetry, **medievalism,** and Arthurian **legends.** Romantic poetry, which **privileged** the **imagination** and incorporated fantastic elements, as exemplified by Samuel Taylor Coleridge's "The Rime of the Ancient Mariner" (1798) and Percy Bysshe Shelley's "The Witch of Atlas" (1824), helped set the stage for the emergence of fantasy fiction, which by its very nature eschews "believable" events and **settings.** Medievalism — an interest in the art, history, and thought of the **Middle Ages** exhibited by several Romantic poets as well as writers and painters associated with the Victorian movement of **Pre-Raphaelitism,** such as Morris — provided fantasy writers with a source of **images, themes,** and settings that remain popular to this day. In this regard, the genre is especially indebted to Alfred, Lord Tennyson, whose influential narrative poem *Idylls of the King* (1859) repopularized traditional Arthurian legends, that is, tales of King Arthur and the Knights of the Round Table. Fantasies attesting to continuing interest in Arthurian lore throughout the twentieth century and beyond include T. H. White's *The Once and Future King* (1958), which compiles *The Sword in the Stone* (1938) and the three other novels comprising White's Arthurian tetrology; Mary Stewart's *Merlin* trilogy (1970–79); movies such as John Boorman's *Excalibur* (1981) and Jerry Zucker's *First Knight* (1995); and the 2001 TNT television production of Marion Zimmer Bradley's novel *The Mists of Avalon* (1982), which presents Arthurian materials from the perspective of female **characters.**

Nineteenth-century fantasy narratives were frequently meant primarily for children and young adults, but early in the twentieth century fantasy emerged as a form of popular literature with a more diverse audience. Influential fantasies from the first half of the twentieth century include E. R. Eddison's *The Worm Ourobouros* (1922); **Celtic Renaissance** novelist Lord Dunsany's *The King of Elfland's Daughter* (1924); J. R. R. Tolkien's *The Hobbit* (1937); and Mervyn Peake's **Gothic, grotesque** Gormenghast trilogy (1946–59), adapted to television by the BBC and aired by PBS in 2001. Notable short stories, published in the American magazine *Weird Tales,* include H. P. Lovecraft's "The Call of Cthulhu" (1928); Clark Ashton Smith's "A Rendezvous in Averoigne" (1931); and Robert E. Howard's "The Phoenix on the Sword" (1932), the first of the Conan the Cimmerian (better known as Conan the Barbarian) stories.

Ironically, it was two Oxford University scholars of the **Medieval Period** — Tolkien and C. S. Lewis — who contributed significantly to the expansion of fantasy fiction beyond medieval settings and Arthurian lore. Both writers sought to produce literary works distinct not only from **realism** but also from the **allusive,** complex **modernism** of writers such as T. S. Eliot and James Joyce, who drew heavily on **classical myths.** The characters in Lewis's seven-volume *Narnia* series (1950–56), an example of theological fantasy fiction, shift back and forth between the middle-class world of twentieth-century England and the alternative, imaginary world of Narnia. The characters in Tolkien's *The Hobbit* and his *Lord of the Rings* trilogy (1954–55), by contrast, exist solely in a second world, called "Middle Earth," that is heavily influenced by Scandinavian and Anglo-Saxon myths.

There are two basic narrative strategies typical of non-Arthurian fantasy fiction. The first, exemplified by Lewis, is to have characters shuttle back and forth between a "real" and a fantasy realm. The second, exemplified by Tolkien, is to set stories entirely in a "second world," one that is separate and different from historical reality, though it may contain familiar elements. (Responding to charges of escapism, Tolkien defended the creation of second worlds as a way to loosen the constraints of conventional thinking.) In either case, the fantasy narrative is generally linear, proceeding in a logical, chronological fashion.

Today, Tolkien is commonly regarded as the fountainhead of contemporary fantasy fiction. His essay "On Fairy-Stories" (1938) has figured significantly in discussions of fantasy's **aesthetic** and social value, and his *Lord of the Rings* trilogy, more than any other work, continues to define the **conventions** of the genre. Key among these conventions is a focus on the struggle between good and evil, often conceptualized as light and dark. Several scholars have characterized Tolkien's own depiction of this tension as ethnocentric, arguing that the struggle in Middle Earth is culturally twofold, with "good" characters — men, elves, dwarves, and hobbits — being identified with Western (and, more specifically, Anglo-Saxon) values, and "bad" ones — including subhuman trolls and goblins, as well as corrupted or mutated elves (orcs), humans (e.g., Nazgul), and hobbits (e.g., Gollum) — representing the nonwhite, non-Western **Other**. Other scholars, however, have argued that Tolkien's world is not so black and white, pointing out, for instance, that it is Gollum's fateful intervention, not that of the hobbit **hero** Frodo Baggins, that ultimately results in the destruction of the terrible Ring of Power.

Also conventional in fantasy fiction is the use of a male **protagonist** with traditional, **patriarchal** Western values and attitudes. The **archetypal** hero is typically unaware, at first, of his true identity and/or abilities, but his coming fulfills some prophecy; and his actions ultimately save his life, love, and community from the depredations of evil, magical, and often foreign enemies (or influences). Such fantasy hero-quests are sometimes called **epic**, or "high," fantasy.

Although religion and religious faith are seldom a focus of fantasy fiction, the protagonist's conduct rarely strays far from that prescribed by the Ten Commandments, and his battles are grounded in Judeo-Christian moral precepts. Archetypal heroes invariably strive to do the right thing, assiduously avoiding self-serving and decadent behavior and often avoiding intimate, sexual relationships as well. When such relationships do occur, they tend to be implied rather than expressly acknowledged and are almost always monogamous, or at least serially monogamous, like those of Conan, a typical "sword and sorcery" hero. Infidelity is almost always the result of bewitchment, and profanity usually takes the form of archaic English expressions or of words coined by gods. Violent action, although often described graphically, mainly affects the story's **antagonists;** the protagonist and his companions generally emerge relatively unscathed, though they may suffer greatly in the course of achieving their quests. Notably, when good characters do die, they are often resurrected in the final scene or scenes.

Fantasy fiction, while privileging magic, tends to de-emphasize technology and science and to emphasize sociopolitical structures characteristic of preindustrial societies. Unlike science fiction and cyberfiction, which feature computers, spaceships, and a variety of as-yet-only-imagined technological marvels, fantasy fiction is more likely to incorporate agrarian inventions such as aqueducts, catapults, and windmills. Where issues of politics and government are concerned, fantasy fiction tends to rely on feudal models involving peasants and kings, slaves and serfs, knights and lords.

Several additional fantasy conventions derive from the work of Ursula K. Le Guin, a popular writer of both fantasy and science fiction. For instance, the training of wizards, a fantasy **motif** extensively developed in J. K. Rowling's *Harry Potter* series (1997–), harks back to Le Guin's novel *A Wizard of Earthsea* (1968). Le Guin is also credited with creating an "economy" and "ecology" of magic, for her magicians pay a physical price for using their arcane powers. As one of the teachers at the wizardry school on the island of Roke explains in *A Wizard of Earthsea*, every act has its consequence: "To light a candle is to cast a shadow." These concepts of physical costs and consequences later came literally into play with the development of *Dungeons & Dragons*™, a role-playing fantasy game initially developed as a board game in 1973 in which players earn the ability to perform tasks by accumulating points upon surviving various adventures and must recover after casting a spell.

Le Guin, who, like Tolkien, is a theorist as well as novelist, has written extensively on fantasy and science fiction. In her 1973 essay, "Dreams Must Explain Themselves," she pointed out that fantasy is circular: "The snake devours its tail. Dreams must explain themselves." In a 1974 essay entitled "The Child and the Shadow," she characterized fantasy as "the language of the inner self," a vehicle for depicting and exploring the psychic and moral journey of self-knowledge.

In the last decades of the twentieth century, authors began to break with some of the long-standing conventions of fantasy fiction. One major shift has been in the **representation** of women in a genre that, given its tendency toward patriarchal models and male protagonists, has historically had few female writers and few powerful or good female characters. Women's roles within Tolkien's works, as Noelle Bowles and other **feminist** scholars have pointed out, were limited to those of peacekeepers and prizes for men's heroic efforts. Even Le Guin, a leader in feminist fantasy fiction, began her foray into the genre by implicitly accepting its patriarchal assumptions. In her first novel, *A Wizard of Earthsea*, for instance, men dominate not only the magical and mundane arenas but also the entire story line. More recently, however, Le Guin and some of her contemporaries have made a concerted effort to give the women of fantasy fiction a voice and a place of substance. Thus, while "weak [or wicked] as women's magic" are common sayings among the **folk** in the patriarchal world of Earthsea, women have emerged both as supporting and central characters in subsequent books of the *Earthsea* cycle (1968–2001). Likewise, Angela Carter's **burlesque** (and **picaresque**) novel *Nights at the Circus* (1984) features a nineteenth-century woman whose career is based on her wings and her ability to fly. Even computer and video games, traditionally male-oriented, have begun to incorporate female characters in meaningful ways. For example, the computer game *Diablo II* (expansion version), a role-playing game, permits players to choose among seven roles, including three female roles (sorceress, amazon, and assassin). Perhaps in recognition of changing social values, the recently released film version of *The Lord of the Rings: The Fellowship of the Ring* (2001) attempts to give women a larger, more influential part than they actually played in Tolkien's text.

Several contemporary authors have inverted the usual theme of the formulaically good hero succeeding on a conventionally moral quest. Stephen Donaldson's six-volume *Chronicles of Thomas Covenant* series (1977–83), for instance, involves a psychologically dysfunctional **antihero** who dies horribly without benefit of divine intervention, wrongs that are not magically righted, and characters who bear the scars of their hasty decisions. Donaldson's eponymous protagonist slips back and forth between the modern world of the reader and the second world of "The Land," a recognizably Tolkienesque **setting.** (A number of Donaldson's creatures, names, and geographies parallel those in *The Lord of the Rings.*) Unlike traditional fantasy heroes, however, Covenant doubts not only the goodness but even the reality of this second world and brutally rapes a young woman he thinks is only a figment of his imagination. Ultimately, he becomes the unwilling savior of the very realm in which he never fully believes.

Other contemporary fantasy fiction heroes have similarly faced internal antagonists as well as external evil. Robert Jordan's *Wheel of Time* series (1990–), for example, features Rand Al'Thor, a hero whose exposure to and use of magic drives him insane. Likewise, in *Final Fantasy VII,* a video and computer game, the line between good and evil is complicated by the hero's apparent delusions. Recent works incorporating sexual violence include Terry Goodkind's *Wizard's First Rule* (1994), in which the hero is subjected to sexual torture. Yet such variations remain the exception rather than the rule, so that most contemporary works still reinforce the expectation that the hero will be male and good, that evil will suffer, and that the traditional virtues of Western culture will triumph.

FURTHER EXAMPLES: Mark Twain's **satirical** fantasy novel *A Connecticut Yankee in King Arthur's Court* (1889) draws on Arthurian legends. Madeline L'Engle's science fiction fantasy *A Wrinkle in Time* (1962), Julie Andrews's fantasy *The Last of the Really Great Whangdoodles* (1974), and Piers Anthony's seven-volume *Incarnations of Immortality* fantasy series (1983–89) are examples of non-Arthurian fantasy novels.

The Princess Bride (1987), directed by Rob Reiner, is a well-known, lighthearted fantasy-fairy-tale film. By contrast, *The Company of Wolves* (1984), a film directed by Neil Jordan and written by Angela Carter, presents a much darker take on a traditional fairy tale — specifically, the story of Little Red Riding Hood — in casting a Freudian eye on the wolf-girl relationship.

Fantasy elements also play a significant role in magic realism and neo-Gothic works such as Anne Rice's *Interview with the Vampire* (1976), Salman Rushdie's *Midnight's Children* (1981), and Toni Morrison's *Beloved* (1987). The permeable nature of the boundary between forms of fantasy fiction is further demonstrated by the fact that *Dungeons & Dragons*™, a game influenced by Le Guin's novels, has in turn influenced later works of published fiction, such as those in the multiauthored *Dragonlance* novel series (1984–).

farce: From the Latin *farcire,* meaning "to stuff," a type of low **comedy** that employs improbable or otherwise ridiculous situations and mix-ups, slapstick and horseplay, and crude and even bawdy **dialogue.** The humor in a farce is by no means subtle; it smacks the audience full-force in the face, aiming simply to entertain and evoke guffaws. Comedies or dramas may contain farcical elements without being farcical themselves.

EXAMPLES: The play *Charley's Aunt* (1892), by Brandon Thomas, is the most frequently cited example of farce. More modern examples include Ray Cooney's 1984 bedroom stage farce *Run for Your Wife!* and the *Home Alone* movies (1990, 1992, 1997). The actor Leslie Nielsen has made a career of starring in farces, including *The Naked Gun* (1988) and *Spy Hard* (1996). *A Knight's Tale* (2001), in which Geoffrey Chaucer, author of *The Canterbury Tales* (c. 1387), is a character, is an action-packed film farce set in **medieval** times. The long-running television show *Saturday Night Live* (1975–)relies heavily on farcical skits.

Federalist Age: See **Early National Period (in American literature).**

feet: See **foot.**

feminine ending (light ending): A line ending that is characterized by an extra, un**stressed** syllable. This extra**metrical** syllable, which usually concludes an **iambic** or **anapestic** line, often provides **rhythmical** variety and movement.

EXAMPLE: The humorous, **half-rhymed,** generally anapestic lines in "A Fable for Critics" (1848), James Russell Lowell's poem about the mid-nineteenth-century American artistic scene, have feminine endings:

> Why, there's scarcely a huddle of log-huts and shanties
> That has not brought forth its own Miltons and Dantes;
> I myself know ten Byrons, one Coleridge, three Shelleys,
> Two Raphaels, six Titians, (I think) one Apelles,
> Leonardos and Rubenses plenty as lichens,
> One (but that one is plenty) American Dickens. . . .

See also **catalexis.**

feminine rhyme: **Rhyme** in which rhyming **stressed** syllables are followed by identical unstressed syllables. A feminine rhyme that extends over two syllables is called **double rhyme,** and one extending over three syllables is called **triple rhyme.**

EXAMPLES: *Slaughter* and *daughter* constitute a double rhyme. *Bantering* and *cantering* constitute a triple rhyme. The American poet Trumbull Stickney typically alternates feminine and **masculine rhyme.** In the first stanza of "The Violin" (1902), he alternates double feminine rhyme with an **eye-rhyme** that is masculine (*how* and *bow*):

> You came to teach me how the hardened fingers
> Must drop and nail the music down, and how

The sound then drags and nettled cries, then lingers
After the dying bow. —

feminist criticism: A type of literary **criticism** that became a dominant force in Western literary studies in the late 1970s, when feminist theory more broadly conceived was applied to **linguistic** and literary matters. Since the early 1980s, feminist literary criticism has developed and diversified in a number of ways and is now characterized by a global perspective. It is nonetheless important to understand differences among the interests and assumptions of French, British, and North American (used in this entry to refer to the United States and Canada) feminist critics writing during the 1970s and early 1980s, given the extent to which their works shaped the evolution of contemporary feminist critical **discourse.**

French feminist criticism garnered much of its inspiration from Simone de Beauvoir's seminal book, *Le deuxième sexe* (*The Second Sex*) (1949). Beauvoir argued that associating men with humanity more generally (as many cultures do) relegates women to an inferior position in society. Subsequent French feminist critics writing during the 1970s not only acknowledged Beauvoir's critique but focused on language as a tool of male domination, analyzing the ways in which it represents the world from the male point of view.

Drawing on the ideas of French **psychoanalytic** theorist Jacques Lacan, French feminist critics reminded us that language is a realm of public discourse. Children enter the linguistic realm just as they begin to understand that they are individuals, distinct from their mothers; boys also begin to identify with their father, the family representative of culture. All children then learn to speak a language structured in accordance with **binary oppositions** (dichotomous terms), such as masculine/feminine, father/mother, son/daughter, phallus/vagina, head/heart, active/passive, reason/emotion, light/dark. French feminist critics pointed out that terms listed first in these binary sets tend to be aligned, as are terms listed second. Hence masculinity is associated with qualities such as light, reason, and activity, whereas femininity recalls passivity and emotion. They also argued that these two sets of terms are hierarchically structured; reason, for instance, is valued over emotion by the masculine-dominated culture. They thus concluded that language is **phallocentric, privileging** the **phallus** and masculinity.

Many French feminist critics argued that language systematically forces women to choose between adopting the male-dominated discourse or opting out — and thereby remaining silent. Women may either imagine and **represent** themselves as men imagine and represent them (in which case they may speak but will speak as men) or they can choose "silence," becoming in the process "the invisible and unheard sex," as Ann Rosalind Jones argued in her essay "Inscribing Femininity: French Theories of the Feminine" (1985).

Some French feminist critics, however, maintained that language only seems to give women a narrow range of choices. These feminists suggested that women not only have different life experiences than men but also write differently, which led them to advocate embracing and developing a feminine language. Early French feminists such as Annie Leclerc, Xavière Gauthier, and Marguerite Duras spoke of this special, feminine language as *l'écriture féminine:* women's writing. More recently, Julia Kristeva (commonly considered a pioneer of French feminist thought even though she eschews the feminist label) has characterized feminine language as **semiotic,** not **symbolic,** as the male-dominated **canon** of "Great Books" is said to be. By *semiotic,* she means that feminine language is rhythmic and unifying; it does not rigidly oppose and rank qualities or elements of reality, nor does it symbolize one thing but not another in terms of a third. If from the male perspective it seems fluid to the point of being chaotic, that is a fault of the male perspective.

According to Kristeva, feminine language is derived from the pre**oedipal** period of fusion between mother and child, the period during which children do not recognize that they are separate from their mothers. Since feminine language is associated with the maternal rather than the paternal, it poses a threat to **patriarchal** culture. Kristeva's central claim — that truly feminist innovation in all fields requires an understanding of the relation between maternity and feminine creation — came paired with a warning, however: feminine or feminist writing that resists or refuses participation in "masculine" discourse risks being politically marginalized in a society that still is, after all, patriarchal.

Like Kristeva, other leading French feminist critics also associated feminine writing with the female body. Hélène Cixous, for instance, posited an essential (that is, natural rather than socially constructed) connection between women's bodies (whose sexual pleasure has been repressed) and women's writing. "Write your self. Your body must be heard," Cixous urged in an essay entitled "The Laugh of the Medusa" (1976). Cixous believed that recognizing this connection would enable women not only to realize their sexuality but to enter history and move toward a future based on a "feminine" economy of giving rather than the "masculine" economy of hoarding. Luce Irigaray focused on women's sexual pleasure (*jouissance*), arguing that it could not be expressed by the dominant masculine language. Irigaray explored the connection between women's sexuality and women's language through the following analogy in a book entitled *Ce sexe qui n'en est pas un (This Sex Which Is Not One)* (1977): Just as women's *jouissance* is more multiple than men's unitary, phallic pleasure ("woman has sex organs just about everywhere"), so "feminine" language is more diffusive than its "masculine" counterpart.

This emphasis on feminine writing as an expression of the female body drew criticism from other French feminists, many of whom argued that emphasizing the body either reduces "the feminine" to a biological essence or elevates it in a way that shifts the valuation of masculine and feminine but retains the binary categories. For Christine Fauré, Irigaray's celebration of women's difference failed to address the issue of masculine dominance.

Marxist-feminist Catherine Clément warned that "poetic" descriptions of the feminine do not challenge masculine dominance in the realm of production; the boys will still make the toys and decide who gets to use them. Monique Wittig even called for the abolition of sexual categories so that women could be redefined as political rather than sexual beings.

North American feminist critics of the 1970s and early 1980s shared with French critics both an interest in and a cautious distrust of the concept of feminine writing. In "Some Notes on Defining a 'Feminist Literary Criticism'" (1975), Annette Kolodny worried that the "richness and variety of women's writing" could be overlooked in the effort to celebrate only its "feminine mode" or "style." And yet Kolodny proceeded to point out that women do have their own style, which includes reflexive constructions ("she found herself crying") and particular, recurring **themes** (Kolodny mentions clothing and self-fashioning; other North American feminists have focused on madness, disease, and the demonic).

Interested as they became in the "French" subject of feminine language and writing, North American feminist critics began by analyzing literary **texts** — not by abstractly discussing language — via **close reading** and historical scholarship. Critics like Kate Millett, Carolyn Heilbrun, and Judith Fetterley developed a model for American feminist criticism that Elaine Showalter called the *feminist critique* of "male-constructed literary history" in an essay entitled "Toward a Feminist Poetics" (1985). Critics undertaking the feminist critique reviewed canonical works by male writers, embarking on a revisionist rereading of Western literary tradition. They examined how female **characters** are portrayed, exposing the patriarchal **ideology** implicit in the so-called **classics** and demonstrating that attitudes and traditions reinforcing systematic masculine dominance are inscribed in the literary canon. In *The Resisting Reader: A Feminist Approach to American Fiction* (1978), Fetterley urged women to become "resisting readers"; to notice how biased most male-authored texts are in their language, subjects, and attitudes; and to actively reject this bias so as to render reading a less "immasculating" experience.

Another group of North American feminist critics, including Sandra Gilbert, Susan Gubar, Patricia Meyer Spacks, and Showalter herself, created a different model, which Showalter dubbed **gynocriticism.** Whereas feminists writing feminist critique analyzed works written by men, gynocritics studied the writings of women who produced what Showalter called "a literature of their own," in a book by the same name (1977). In *The Female Imagination* (1975), Spacks examined the female literary tradition to find out how women writers across the ages have perceived themselves and imagined reality. In *The Madwoman in the Attic* (1979), Gilbert and Gubar focused on nineteenth-century women writers, arguing that similar concerns, **images,** and themes recur in their works because they lived "in a culture whose fundamental definitions of literary authority were both overtly and covertly patriarchal."

If one of the purposes of gynocriticism was to (re)study well-known women authors, another was to rediscover women's history and culture, particularly women's communities that nurtured female creativity. Another related purpose was to discover neglected or forgotten women writers and thus to forge an alternative literary tradition, a canon that better represents the female perspective. In *A Literature of Their Own*, Showalter outlined just such a tradition by providing a comprehensive overview of women's writing through three of its phases. She defined these as the "Feminine, Feminist, and Female" phases, phases during which women imitated a masculine tradition (1840–80), protested against its standards and values (1880–1920), and advocated their own autonomous, female perspective (1920–present).

With the recovery of a body of women's texts, attention returned to a question raised by Lillian Robinson in *Sex, Class, and Culture* (1978): shouldn't feminist criticism formulate a **theory** of its own practice, since without one feminist critics must rely on critical discourses that are themselves part of the patriarchal tradition? Some feminist critics worried that using approaches such as psychoanalytic theory, **formalism,** and **Marxism** would prevent feminist theory from being accepted as an equal, but others denied the need for a special or unifying theory of feminist practice. Kolodny, for instance, advocated a "playful pluralism" encompassing a variety of critical schools and methods. Nevertheless, critics such as Jane Marcus feared that if feminists incorporate too many approaches, they may relax the tensions between feminists and the educational establishment that spur political activism.

The question of whether feminist criticism should emphasize its separateness from other critical approaches — and stress the unity of women given their difference from men in a patriarchal society — was debated throughout the 1970s and early 1980s. North American feminist critics also disagreed about whether feminists should stress universal, essentialist feminine attributes (the feminine imagination, feminine writing, women's communities, the experience of women in patriarchal society, the representation of women in patriarchal texts) or focus on the political conditions experienced by certain groups of women at certain times in history. In retrospect, it is evident that this latter debate was dominated by critics who saw women in terms of their similarities, not in terms of their differences.

While it gradually became customary to refer to an Anglo-American tradition of feminist criticism, British feminist critics of the 1970s and early 1980s criticized the tendency of some North American critics to find universal feminine attributes, arguing that differences of **race, class,** and culture gave rise to crucial differences among women across space and time. They also argued that the North American opposition to male stereotypes that denigrate women often led to counterstereotypes of feminine virtue that ignore the important differences among groups of women and fail to challenge male domination of society.

British feminist critics regarded their own critical practice as more political than that of North American feminists, emphasizing an engagement with historical process in order to promote social change. They asserted that North American celebrations of individual **heroines** falsely suggest that certain individuals may be immune to repressive, patriarchal conditions and may even imply that *any* individual can go through life unconditioned by the culture in which he or she lives. Similarly, British critics like Judith Newton and Deborah Rosenfelt viewed the North American effort to recover women's history as an endeavor that obscured male oppression, implying that it created special opportunities for women. They thus suggested that simply discovering women writers and looking for common themes might divorce women's texts from their historical context, a context that necessarily affected any work. Most importantly, British feminist critics rejected the universalizing and essentializing tendencies of much North American practice and most French theory; they feared that celebrating sexual difference disguised women's oppression and enabled patriarchy to survive and thrive. Any argument that social conditions are rooted in sexual difference, they felt, implies that those conditions are unlikely to change, since sexual difference will not disappear.

By the early 1990s, the French, American, and British approaches had so thoroughly critiqued, influenced, and assimilated one another that nationality no longer automatically signaled a practitioner's approach. Today's critics seldom focus on "woman" as a relatively monolithic category; rather, they view "women" as members of different societies with different concerns. Feminists of color, **postcolonial** feminists, and lesbian feminists have asked whether the universal category of woman constructed during the 1970s and early 1980s by certain French and North American critics is appropriate to describe women in minority groups or non-Western cultures. Their interest in sexual difference encompasses an interest in other differences that also define identity, and they recognize that feminism may mean something different to different groups. These feminists stress that women are not defined solely by the fact that they are female; other attributes (such as religion, class, and **sexuality**) are also important, making the problems and goals of one group of women different from those of another. As Armit Wilson has pointed out, Asian women living in Britain are expected by their families to preserve Asian cultural traditions; thus, the expression of personal identity through clothing involves a much more serious infraction of cultural rules than it does for Western women. In *Borderlands: La Frontera / The New Mestiza* (1987), Gloria Anzaldúa, who grew up under the influence of both the Mexican and Anglo cultures, discusses the experience of many women living on the margins of Eurocentric North American culture.

Instead of being divisive, this evolution of feminism into femin*isms* has fostered a more inclusive, global perspective, a recognition that feminism comes in many forms and that feminist critics have a variety of goals. The emphasis on recovering women's texts — especially texts by white Western women — has been supplanted by an effort to recover entire cultures of women. In works such as *In Other Worlds: Essays in Cultural Politics* (1987) and *Outside in the Teaching Machine* (1993), the Indian feminist critic Gayatri Chakravorty Spivak has demonstrated that national political independence for postcolonial countries is not the simple and beneficial change metropolitan Westerners commonly assume it to be; rather, independence has complex implications for "subaltern" and "subproletarian" women (women with an inferior position, rank, or caste and nonwage-earning women whose material conditions are substantially inferior to those we associate with working-class life), who may end up worse off than they were under colonial rule.

Understanding woman not as a single, deterministic category, but rather as the nexus of diverse experiences, has led some white, Western, "majority" feminists like Jane Tompkins and Nancy K. Miller to advocate and practice **personal** or **autobiographical criticism.** Once reluctant to include their reactions and feelings in their analyses for fear of being labeled idiosyncratic, **impressionistic,** and **subjective,** some feminists are now openly skeptical of the claims to reason, logic, and **objectivity** made by male critics in the past.

An interest in women's autobiographical writings has accompanied the interest in personal feminist critical styles. Some feminist critics have argued that traditional **autobiography** is a gendered, "masculinist" **genre,** given that its established **conventions** emphasize action, triumph through **conflict,** intellectual self-discovery, and public renown. The body, reproduction, children, and intimate interpersonal relationships are generally relegated to the background and are often completely absent. Arguing that the lived experience of women and men differ — women's lives are often characterized by interruption and deferral (such as when women delay or take time off from their careers to have children) — Leigh Gilmore has developed a theory of women's self-representation in her book *Autobiographics: A Feminist Theory of Self-Representation* (1994).

Autobiographics and personal criticism are only two of a number of recent developments in contemporary feminist criticism. A feminist performance theory has developed based on Joan Riviere's 1929 essay "Womanliness as Masquerade," in which Riviere argued that all femininity involves masquerade. Feminist performance theorists have used this insight to argue that femininity is a social construct rather than a natural quality. A feminist film theory has developed as well; practitioners analyze films as vehicles that perpetuate and enshrine the perception of women as sex objects. As Teresa de Lauretis argued in *Alice Doesn't: Feminism, Semiotics, Cinema* (1986), movies represent "woman as spectacle — body to be looked at, place of sexuality, and object of desire." **Lesbian criticism** has also evolved. All three of these approaches, however, have been as often associated — if not more often associated — with **gender criticism** as with feminist criticism and are discussed in greater detail in that entry.

Gender criticism, an approach to literary criticism that focuses on — and critiques — **gender** as it is commonly conceived in order to expose its insufficiency as a category, has grown considerably since the mid-1980s. Feminist criticism arose before gender criticism and heavily influenced its practitioners, even as they vigorously opposed many basic tenets of the feminist approach. As the gender approach has continued to gain recognition, however, some critics have suggested that it has overshadowed — or even subsumed — the feminist approach, an assertion many would contest. Whether or not feminist criticism is giving way to gender criticism, many critics (including those like de Lauretis who are commonly associated with the gender approach) continue to self-identify with the feminist approach.

Many commentators have argued that feminist criticism is by definition gender criticism because of its focus on the feminine gender. But the relationship between feminist and gender criticism is, in fact, complex; the two approaches are certainly not polar opposites but, rather, exist along a continuum of attitudes toward sex, sexuality, gender, and language. Nonetheless, several distinctions can be made between adherents of the two approaches, even as practitioners of each continue to critique and influence those in the other. Feminist critics, for instance, tend to focus on women and women's issues, whereas gender critics have focused as much on men as women. Feminist critics have also tended to equate gender with sex and gender difference with sexual difference, whereas gender critics have viewed gender as a cultural construct distinct from biological sex. Many feminist critics hold **essentialist** views, a point **constructionist** gender critics would oppose since they believe differences between men and women are the products of culture rather than nature. Furthermore, many feminist critics have spoken of a feminine language grounded in sexual difference which many gender critics would reject; such critics would posit a relationship only between gender and writing, not biological sex and writing. Even given these differences, however, many feminist critics have as much — if not more — in common with certain gender critics than with their own colleagues. An essentialist **gay critic** who believes that sexual orientation is a matter of nature rather than culture (gay criticism is a major emphasis within gender criticism), for instance, may agree more with an essentialist feminist critic than with those gender critics who espouse constructionism.

See **gender criticism** for a detailed discussion of the relationship between the feminist and gender approaches, their similarities, and their differences.

fiction: In the broadest sense of the word, any writing that relates imagined **characters** and occurrences rather than recounting real ones. Defined more narrowly, *fiction* refers to prose **narratives** (specifically the **short story** and the **novel**), rather than to **verse** or nonnarrative **prose**.

The boundary between fiction and nonfiction is not always clear. **Autobiographical** fiction, in which the author passes off as inventions events that actually occurred, and the **historical novel,** in which the author makes use of real people or events in an invented **plot,** are instances of fiction that border on fact. Norman Mailer, the controversial novelist and nonfiction prose writer, coined the term *faction* to refer to works written on the blurred boundary between fiction and historical fact.

figurative language: Language that employs one or more **figures of speech** to supplement and even modify the literal, **denotative** meanings of words with additional **connotations** and richness. Figurative language adds color and immediacy to **imagery.** Although figurative language can be used for decorative or purely **aesthetic** purposes, it is used primarily to attain some specific effect on the reader.

EXAMPLES: In his novel *A Son of the Circus* (1994), John Irving writes, "Far from outside the church, the doctor was aware of the constantly passing mopeds — the snarling of their low-powered engines, the duck-like quacking of their infernal horns." In *Shelter,* published the same year, Jayne Anne Phillips uses figurative language to describe a group of girls at a summer camp walking "double time": "Alma watched from the rear as her compatriots hit the clearing and swung into action. The line of girls resembled a giant centipede in electroshock." In *The Shipping News* (1993), the novel that won the 1994 Pulitzer Prize for fiction, E. Annie Proulx uses figurative language to add color, immediacy, information, associations, and psychological impact to her **narrative:** "It began with his parents. First the father, diagnosed with liver cancer, a blush of wild cells diffusing. A month later a tumor fastened in the mother's brain like a burr, crowding her thoughts to one side. The father blamed the power station. Two hundred yards from their house sizzling wires, thick as eels, came down from northern towers."

In the cartoon from a *Far Side* calendar shown on page 166, Gary Larson uses his trademark brand of "off"-to-dark humor, in this case to highlight the difference between literal and figurative interpretations of a witch's statement to her friend that she has a baby "in the oven."

See also **figure of speech.**

figure of speech: A literary device involving unusual use of language, often to associate or compare distinct things. Figures of speech typically depart from the usual order of words or from their literal meaning to create an image in the reader's mind. Language that uses figures of speech is called **figurative language.**

Numerous figures of speech exist, and they are commonly divided into two general categories: **rhetorical figures** and **tropes.** Rhetorical figures use words in some special way to create an unexpected effect without significantly altering the words' meanings. (If your mother asks you to "Trot on down to the corner video store and check out *The Bridges of Madison County,*" she doesn't change the meaning of the word *trot,* but she may cause you to picture yourself as a horse.) Tropes, by contrast, fundamentally change the meanings of words. (If you say that someone is "hot to trot," or if you tell someone that you "plowed through the book version of

THE FAR SIDE® By GARY LARSON

"Oh, Helen! You're pregnant? That's wonderful! ...
At first, I was taking you quite literally when you
said you had one in the oven!"

The Bridges of Madison County before watching the video," you change the meaning of the words *trot* and *plow*.)

Figures of speech have also been categorized in other ways (according to whether or not they involve a comparison, for instance). Alternatively, they have been grouped in three classes, depending on whether they **foreground** imagined similarities (**simile**), associations (**synecdoche**), or appeals to the ear and eye (**alliteration**). Most critics, however, do not recognize devices in the third category as figures of speech.

Perhaps the best-known and therefore most readily recognizable figures of speech are the five principal tropes: simile, **personification, metaphor, metonymy,** and synecdoche. Other figures of speech include **allegory, conceit,** and **symbol. Deconstructive** critic Paul de Man viewed **irony** as a figure of speech.

fin de siècle: French for "end of the century," a phrase referring generally to works produced in the last years of any century but specifically to the transitional 1890s, when French, English, and American writers were beginning to break free from the constraints and polite **conventions** we associate with **Victorianism** in favor of bold techniques and bolder subjects. When used as a chronological marker indicating the period 1890–1900, *fin de siècle* encompasses works written by darkly **realistic** writers, members of the **Aesthetic Movement,** and authors of radical or revolutionary works envisioning an **apocalyptic** end to the old social order. The phrase is most often used, however, with reference to late-nineteenth-century French writers who participated in the **Decadence,** a literary movement known for works that evoked a sense of lassitude and boredom, rejected conventional social mores, and insisted that the value of art should not be tied to morality. The term has also come to signify a period of literary decline or confusion.

first-person point of view: See **point of view.**

flashback: A **scene** that interrupts the present action of a **narrative** work to depict some earlier event — often an event that occurred before the opening scene of the work — via reverie, remembrance, dreaming, or some other mechanism. The term may be used to refer to the scene itself or to its presentation.

Flashback is a form of **analepsis,** one of the three major types of **anachrony.** The device has its origins in the ancient **epic** tradition of beginning a work ***in medias res*** ("in the middle of things") and then moving back in time to tell the beginning of the story.

EXAMPLES: Daphne du Maurier's *Rebecca* (1938) begins with a flashback; the famous first sentence reads: "Last night I dreamt I went to Manderley again." In *The Naked and the Dead* (1948), a novel of World War II that depends upon the interplay between past and present, Norman Mailer repeatedly announces flashback sequences via the indented, boldfaced phrase "The Time Machine." Anne Tyler's more recent, comic novel *Breathing Lessons* (1988) flashes back and forth between the funeral and wedding of Max Gill, the husband of the **protagonist's** best friend. At the end of *The Accused* (1988), a film in which Jodie Foster stars as a woman who seeks justice after being gang-raped, one of the witnesses recounts the events of the rape at a trial. As he is testifying, the movie shifts back to the scene of the rape, which had not actually been shown until that point although it obviously preceded all of the events in the movie. (The opening scene of the movie showed Foster fleeing from the scene of the crime.) Other well-known movies that use flashback include *Casablanca* (1942) and *Pulp Fiction* (1994).

flashforward: See **anachrony, prolepsis.**

flat and round characters: Terms coined by E. M. Forster in *Aspects of the Novel* (1927) to refer to depth and complexity of **characterization.** *Flat* *characters,* Forster claims, are easily recognizable by their very lack of complexity. Such characters tend to be **caricatures** defined by a single idea or quality. Their essences can usually be summed up neatly in a single sentence. *Round characters,* which have the level of complexity and depth we associate with real people, have been fully developed by the author. They can surprise us convincingly, for they have full-blown personalities complete with **ambiguities** and quirks that make it almost as difficult to describe them reductively as it would be to describe a friend or family member in a single sentence. Forster notes that works must generally have a mixture of flat and round characters in order to represent the world as we tend to perceive it, so he does not assign automatically a pejorative **connotation** to flat characters.

EXAMPLE: Minor characters in the *Sweet Valley High* adolescent novel series (1983–) created by Francine Pascal tend to be flat characters; consistently described in the same way, they can be depended on to behave predictably, thereby fulfilling specific **plot** functions. Examples include Bruce Patman, an arrogant rich snob; Lila Fowler, a daddy's girl obsessed with her wealth and looks; and Enid Rollins, Elizabeth Wakefield's devoted, loyal, studious — and mousy — best friend. These characters become round characters in the books devoted to them; thus, the rare book featuring Bruce Patman as the **protagonist** can be counted on to reveal good qualities underlying and complicating his trademark snootiness.

foil: A **character** who, by his contrast with the main character (**protagonist**), serves to accentuate that character's distinctive qualities or characteristics.

EXAMPLES: Fortinbras is a foil to Hamlet in William Shakespeare's play *Hamlet* (1602): He takes decisive action while Hamlet vacillates. "Slasher movies" often use a less subtle foil. In films such as the *Halloween* series (1978–95) and the *Friday the 13th* series (1980–), promiscuous teenagers are murdered, often while they are having sex, thus highlighting the virginal purity of the **heroine,** who survives the killer's attacks.

folk: See **folklore.**

folk drama: As initially defined by **folklorists,** theatrical performances by the **folk,** that is, by ordinary people — including **plays, dramatic** renditions of religious stories and lore, and traditional ceremonies and activities (such as sword dances) associated with seasonal festivals. Folk drama originated in the fertility rites of ancient communities as a way to pay tribute to agricultural gods. Performances honoring Dionysus — the Greek god of fertility, vegetation, and, more specifically, wine — may have been forerunners of Greek **tragedy.** Some English folk dramas dating from the **Renaissance** — for example, *The Plough Monday Play* — are grounded in **medieval** traditions and still performed today.

Thomas Hardy's novel *The Return of the Native* (1878) preserves **dialogue** from an early folk drama known as *The St. George Play,* a so-called mummers' play involving masked actors, **pantomimes,** sword fights, and **fantastic** situations. In the twentieth century, the term *folk drama* was defined more broadly to include works written by playwrights and performed by professional actors, so long as the works express the culture, language, beliefs, and traditions of the folk. Accordingly, the plays of J. M. Synge, Lady Gregory, William Butler Yeats, and other writers of the **Celtic Renaissance** are considered to be folk drama.

The 2001 musical version of *The Best Little Whorehouse in Texas,* which tells the story of a small-town establishment that once accepted chickens in exchange for sexual favors, is not folk drama *per se* but is a play grounded in Texas folklore. Paul Green's historical plays — such as *The Common Glory,* which is performed each summer in Williamsburg, Virginia — reflect the regional experiences, values, and culture of ordinary people who settled in various areas of the United States.

See also **folklore.**

folklore: The beliefs, traditions, rituals, stories, and other creative expressions of ordinary people, or *folk,* that have been transmitted orally or shared by example through successive generations. Folklore encompasses a wide range of community traditions that tend to evolve over time and that may be articulated through **ballads, tales, epics, dramas, legends,** and **myths,** as well as through less "literary" forms such as **folk tales, folk dramas, folk songs,** folk dances, **proverbs, maxims,** riddles, nursery rhymes, superstitions, spells, and plant and animal lore. Social customs and rituals regarding key life events such as birth, death, courtship, and marriage are also aspects of folklore, as are the communal construction of quilts, houses, and barns.

Scholars today differ in their definitions of *folklore,* perhaps in large part because various individuals and groups have assigned the term different meanings over time. W. J. Thomas, a nineteenth-century English scholar, coined the word as an Anglo-Saxon alternative to the Latinate phrase "popular antiquities," which referred to the intellectual heritage of the peasant **class.** Subsequently, in the late 1800s, the Folklore Society of London treated folklore as a means as well as subject of study, asserting that folklore involves "the comparison and identification of the survivals of archaic beliefs, customs, and traditions in modern ages." Later, Alexander H. Krappe, who like the Folklore Society approached folklore as a discipline and not merely as a subject of study, asserted in *The Science of Folklore* (1930) that folklore allows us to understand the unwritten "spiritual history" of past civilizations by focusing on the sayings of common people rather than on histories written by intellectuals.

Over time, the term *folk* has come to refer not just to the lower classes but, more generally, to all people who lived before the industrial age. The scope of the term *folklore* has likewise been broadened. Increasingly, it is not limited to the traditions of earlier cultures but encompasses the distinctive traditions of any community, past or present, with widely shared interests, purposes, and attitudes toward everyday life. In addition, although these attitudes and their expression have generally been recognized as folklore only when conveyed orally, some scholars have recognized as "folkloric" certain traditions and customs transmitted in writing.

Although experts do not agree upon any one definition, most have acknowledged that folklore has five basic characteristics, the first three being the most important. Folklore must be: (1) primarily transmitted orally; (2) rooted in tradition; (3) available in different versions or texts; (4) anonymous; and (5) eventually standardized. Most scholars also agree that folklore is shared and passed on at the grass-roots level of society rather than being formally taught via societal institutions such as the government, schools, churches, and so on.

Although folkloric **genres** and traditions have customarily been distinguished from the literary, musical, and dance forms associated with so-called high culture, folk **conventions, motifs,** and lore are commonly incorporated into these more "sophisticated" forms.

EXAMPLES: Eliot Wigginton's *Foxfire* books — especially *The Foxfire Book* (1972) and *Foxfire 2* (1973) — extensively collected and preserved Appalachian folklore including ghost stories, snake lore, burial customs, and information about planting various crops in accordance with astrological cycles. **Urban legends** — a much more recent phenomenon — have been similarly collected by Jan Brunvand, a folklore professor whose most recent book is entitled *Too Good to Be True: The Colossal Book of Urban Legends* (1999). One of the best-known urban legends is the story of a man who, drugged at a party, awakens naked in a bathtub full of ice and finds a note (sometimes scrawled in lipstick on the mirror) warning him that one of his kidneys has been removed for sale on the black market.

As noted above, folklore comes in many forms. Folkloric superstitions include the beliefs that walking under a ladder, breaking a mirror, and crossing paths with a black cat bring bad luck, as well as the belief that throwing spilled salt over your shoulder will counter the bad luck entailed by the spill. Proverbs include such contradictory standbys as "absence makes the heart grow fonder" and "out of sight, out of mind." Maxims include the advice that "people who live in glass houses shouldn't throw stones" and "an apple a day keeps the doctor away." Children's folklore includes the sidewalk superstition "Step on a crack, break your mother's back" and nursery rhymes such as "Ring Around the Rosy" (c. 1350), which actually references a very serious subject: the bubonic plague, also called the Black Death, that swept across China, West Asia, and Europe in the fourteenth century and did not disappear until the 1600s. Folklore also comes in the form of scary campfire stories, such as the tale about a babysitter receiving a phone call from inside the house and the one about two people who, after parking in a locked car, find the hook of a one-armed convict hanging on the door handle.

The influence of ancient folklore traditions on **classical** literature is evident in works such as William Shakespeare's *King Lear* (1606), in which the **tragic hero** disinherits his honest daughter for saying she loves him only as a daughter should. With regard to more contemporary works, the Coen brothers' film *O Brother, Where Art Thou?* (2000) reflects the ancient folkloric **theme** of men bewitched by fairy women.

See also **folk drama, folk song, folk tale.**

folk song: A song of unidentified origin that has been orally transmitted through successive generations within a given community. Folk songs, which are usually accompanied by acoustic instruments, typically recount stories about everyday life and express the hopes and beliefs of ordinary people. Common types of folk songs include **ballads,** carols, lullabies, spirituals, work songs, hobo songs, drinking songs, songs of the sea, and songs of unrequited love.

In America, within the past century, the definition of folk song has broadened to include folksy lyrics written or popularized by musical artists such as Woody Guthrie; Pete Seeger; Peter, Paul, and Mary; Joan Baez; Judy Collins; Joni Mitchell; Bob Dylan; and Arlo Guthrie.

EXAMPLES: Anonymous religious songs such as "Kumbaya My Lord" — a slave song with African roots — and "Have-Na Gila," a popular Jewish folk song and dance. Folk songs that began as written compositions attributable to a specific person include works by Stephen Foster (1826–64) such as "Camptown Races" and "Oh! Susanna." Well-known folk songs popular during the twentieth century include Woody Guthrie's "This Land Is Your Land" (1940), Pete Seeger's "If I Had a Hammer" (1949; cowritten with Lee Hays) and "We Shall Overcome" (1963; Seeger's version of a **hymn**-based black folk song written anonymously in 1945), Bob Dylan's "Blowin' in the Wind" (1963) and "The Times They Are a-Changin'" (1964), and Steve Goodman's "City of New Orleans" (1970), a song popularized by Arlo Guthrie in 1972 about ordinary people on a lightly loaded passenger train by that name. Contemporary folk singers include Catie Curtis, Nanci Griffith, and Ani Difranco.

See also **ballad, folklore.**

folk tale: A short **narrative** that has been orally transmitted through successive generations within a given community and that typically evolves over time. Although folk tales usually begin as oral **tales** of unidentified origin, they are generally committed to writing at some point. Occasionally, the reverse happens: an original, published story by a specific, identified person comes to be thought of as a folk tale and thus enters the realm of **folklore.**

Folk tales may include **fables, legends, myths,** tall tales, ghost stories, stories about giants, fairy tales, stories about saints, and humorous **anecdotes.**

EXAMPLES: Stories about Paul Bunyan, Davy Crockett, Casey Jones, Daniel Boone, Pecos Bill, Jesse James, Annie Oakley, Sacajawea, and Johnny Appleseed are staples of American frontier folklore, as are stories about former slave John Henry, who was said to be the strongest steel-driver working the railroads. As the folk tale goes, Henry beat out a steam-powered drill in a contest of man against machine, only to die immediately thereafter of an aneurysm. People say that Henry's image can be seen — and his hammering heard — in the tunnel where he worked.

Many African American and Native American folk tales feature animals and recount stories of trickery or the origin of certain animal characteristics. Anansi (a spider), Brer Rabbit, and the tortoise are often clever tricksters in African American folk tales, whereas Coyote is one of the major tricksters in Native American folk tales. Stories explaining particular animal characteristics include the African American tale that pigs have short, square noses because God cut off the pig's nose to punish it for eating all of the food given to the animals and the Native American Caddo tale that dogs have long tongues because a hunter pulled on his talkative dog's tongue as punishment for gossiping about a hunt. For a collection of African American folk tales arranged by subject — such as preacher tales, fool tales, and mistaken identity tales — see Zora Neale Hurston's posthumously published *Every Tongue Got to Confess: Negro Folk-Tales from the Gulf States* (published 2001; collected in the 1920s).

The Grimm brothers' fairy tales, or *Märchen*, have been widely translated from German and include such favorites as Cinderella, Little Red Riding Hood, and Hansel and Gretel. In *The Tales of Uncle Remus* (1880), Joel Chandler Harris claimed to have recorded accurately the dialect and **plot** of tales told by slaves he encountered during his childhood in Georgia.

Washington Irving's "The Legend of Sleepy Hollow" (1819) is an example of a folk tale that began as a published literary work.

See also **folklore, tale.**

foot: A **rhythmic** unit into which a line of **metrical verse** is divided. In English verse, a foot may have any of several combinations of **stressed** and unstressed syllables, but usually consists of one stressed syllable (´) and one or two unstressed syllables (˘). Five types of feet are particularly common in English verse: **iamb** (˘´), **trochee** (´˘), **anapest** (˘˘´), **dactyl** (´˘˘), and **spondee** (´´). Other less common metrical feet are **pyrrhic** (˘˘), *amphibrach* (˘´˘), *amphimacer* (´˘´), **choriambus** (´˘˘´), and *paeon* (´˘˘˘).

EXAMPLE: Samuel Taylor Coleridge's poem "Metrical Feet — A Lesson for a Boy" (1834) exemplifies the five major forms of metrical feet, plus two less common forms:

Trŏchĕe trĭps frŏm lóng tŏ short . . .

From long to long in solemn sort

Slów spóndee stalks; stróng fóot! yet ill able.

Évĕr tŏ cóme ŭp wĭth Dáctylĕ trĭsýllăblĕ.

Ĭambĭcs márch frŏm short tŏ lóng;

Wĭth ă leáp ănd ă boúnd thĕ swĭft ánăpĕsts thróng;

Oñe sýllăble lóng, wĭth one short ăt each side,

Amphibrachus hastes with a stately stride;

First and last being long, middle short, Amphimacer

Strikes his thundering hooves like a proud high-bred Racer.

foregrounding: Giving prominence to something in a literary work that would not be accentuated in ordinary **discourse.** The notion of foregrounding comes primarily from the work of **Russian formalist** critics, who deemed foregrounding a necessary component of "**literariness,**" that is to say, of a specifically literary work. When Russian formalists spoke of foregrounding, they referred in particular to the foregrounding of "device," that is, all those aspects of verbal expression that are present in the literary work but are not functionally necessary to communication. Literary critics practice foregrounding as well, **privileging** those aspects of the work that they believe to be important.

EXAMPLES: In Laurence Sterne's *Tristram Shandy* (1760–67), the foregrounding of literary device is manifested in constant digressions and temporal discontinuities that violate the **conventions** of ordinary discourse. In his foreword to Zora Neale Hurston's *Every Tongue Got to Confess* (2001), a posthumously published collection of African American **folk tales** from the Gulf States, novelist John Edgar Wideman states that Hurston "foregrounds creolized language and culture in her fiction and nonfiction, dramatizing vernacular ways of speaking that are so independent, dynamic, self-assertive and expressive that they cross over, challenge and transform mainstream dialects."

foreshadowing: The technique of introducing into a **narrative** material that prepares the reader or audience for future events, actions, or revelations. Foreshadowing often involves the creation of a **mood** or **atmosphere** that suggests an eventual outcome; the introduction of objects, facts, events, or **characters** that hint at or otherwise prefigure a developing situation or **conflict;** or the exposition of significant character traits allowing the reader or audience to anticipate that character's actions or fate. Occasionally the **theme** or conclusion of a work is foreshadowed by its title. **Prolepsis,** the evocation in narrative of scenes or events that take place at a later point in the **story,** necessarily foreshadows that future event or action.

Foreshadowing is found in all narrative **genres** but is especially common in suspense literature, including **mysteries, Gothic novels,** and **detective fiction.** Although there are many methods of foreshadowing and many reasons to use this technique, its effect is to unify the **plot** by making its development and **structure** seem logical and perhaps even inevitable. As playwright Anton Chekhov once said, "if there is a gun hanging on the wall in the first act, it must fire in the last."

EXAMPLES: The mood created in the first few sentences of Edgar Allan Poe's *The Fall of the House of Usher* (1839) forewarns the reader of horrible events to come:

> During the whole of a dull, dark, and soundless day in the autumn of the year, when the clouds hung oppressively low in the heavens, I had been passing alone, on horseback, through a singularly dreary tract of country, and at length found myself, as the shades of the evening drew on, within view of the melancholy House of Usher.

Similarly, the discordant music prior to the shower scene in Alfred Hitchcock's *Psycho* (1960) prepares the audience for the grisly stabbing of the character played by Janet Leigh.

Early in his novel *Kingsblood Royal* (1947), Sinclair Lewis uses the technique of foreshadowing by character trait. By revealing the racism of Neil Kingsblood, a Minnesota banker researching his family's genealogy in hopes of discovering that he is descended from British royalty, Sinclair subtly foreshadows Kingsblood's eventual discovery of an African American ancestor. Likewise, in Charlotte Brontë's *Jane Eyre* (1847), the revelation that Mr. Rochester's mentally ill wife lives in the attic of Thornfield Hall is foreshadowed by the "demoniac laughter" that governess Jane Eyre hears in her room late one evening.

The titles of Thomas Mann's *Death in Venice* (1912) and Willa Cather's *Death Comes for the Archbishop* (1926) foreshadow the eventual demise of their respective **protagonists**, Gustav von Aschenbach and Archbishop Jean Marie Latour. The early presentation in *Death in Venice* of a minor character who, though old, from a distance looks young — thanks to rouge, cheap dentures, a bad wig, and a fake mustache — foreshadows Aschenbach's own, later, hopelessly self-destructive pursuit of youth in the form of a beautiful young stranger.

Attack of the Clones (2002), the second episode of the *Star Wars* series, makes use of foreshadowing when Obi-wan Kenobi says proleptically to his young Jedi apprentice: "You'll be the death of me." The apprentice, Anakin Skywalker, will eventually become Darth Vader and kill Obi-wan.

See also **prolepsis.**

form: Either the general type or the unique **structure** of a literary work. When used synonymously with general type, or **genre,** it refers to the categories according to which literary works are commonly classified (for example, the **ballad** form, the **sonnet** form, etc.) and may imply a set of **conventions** related to a particular genre. Form can also be used generally to refer to **rhyme** patterns, **metrical** arrangements, and so forth (the **quatrain** form, **anapestic** form, etc.). The term is often used more specifically, however, to refer to the structure of a particular work; in this case, form involves the arrangement of component parts, such as the sequence of events, **parallelism,** or some other organizational principle.

In the past, a rigid distinction was often made between form and content, as if the two were completely unrelated or, at least, entirely distinct and divorceable. Critics who made this distinction typically argued that form is the structure devised by the author to contain the content (and ultimately the meaning) conveyed by the work. Many contemporary critics feel that this distinction, while helpful as a descriptive and even analytical device, is often misleading or even blatantly inaccurate. Thus many critics speak of concepts like **aesthetic** form, which takes into account more than the external organizational qualities of form, extending consideration to the integration of structural elements as well. Form can thus be perceived as internal as well as external.

Some theorists (such as those associated with **the New Criticism**) have equated structure and form, whereas others (such as those associated with the **Chicago School**) have distinguished between these two terms, arguing that form is the emotional force or shaping principle that gives rise to the mechanics of structure. Others have debated whether or not form and **style** are the same, separate, or overlapping features of the work — and whether or not style and content are separable. Most contemporary critics argue that form, structure, style, and content are intertwined and that distinctions among them, though useful tools of literary analysis, tend to obscure the intimate interrelationships that are essential to the effectiveness of the literary **text** as a whole.

See **organic form and mechanic form** for the distinction between these two types of form.

formalism: A general term covering several similar types of literary **criticism** that arose in the 1920s and 1930s, flourished during the 1940s and 1950s, and are still in evidence today. Formalists see the literary work as an object in its own right. Thus, they tend to devote their attention to its intrinsic nature, concentrating their analyses on the interplay and relationships between the text's essential verbal elements. They study the **form** of the work (as opposed to its content), although *form* to a formalist can connote anything from **genre** (for example, one may speak of "the **sonnet** form") to grammatical or rhetorical **structure** to the "emotional imperative" that engenders the work's (more mechanical) structure. No matter which **connotation** of *form* pertains, however, formalists seek to be **objective** in their analysis, focusing on the work itself and eschewing external considerations. They pay particular attention to literary devices used in the work and to the patterns these devices establish.

Formalism developed largely in reaction to the practice of interpreting literary **texts** by relating them to "extrinsic" issues, such as the historical circumstances and politics of the era in which the work was written, its philosophical or theological *milieu,* or the experiences and frame of mind of its author. Although the term *formalism* was coined by critics to disparage the movement, it is now used simply as a descriptive term.

Formalists have generally suggested that everyday language, which serves simply to communicate information, is stale and unimaginative. They argue that **literariness** has the capacity to overturn common and expected patterns (of grammar, of story line), thereby rejuvenating language. Such novel uses of language supposedly enable readers to experience not only language but also the world in an entirely new way.

A number of schools of literary criticism have adopted a formalist orientation, or at least make use of formalist concepts. **The New Criticism,** an American approach to literature that reached its height in the 1940s and 1950s, is perhaps the most famous type of formalism. But **Russian formalism** was the first major formalist movement; after the Stalinist regime suppressed it in the early 1930s, the **Prague Linguistic Circle** adopted its analytical methods. The **Chicago School** has also been classified as formalist insofar as the Chicago Critics examined and analyzed works on an individual basis; their interest in historical material, on the other hand, was clearly not formalist.

formalism, Russian: See **Russian formalism.**

fourfold meaning (four levels of meaning / of interpretation): A method of analysis generally applied to biblical works (or **allegorical texts,** particularly religious ones) that divides the meaning of the work into four levels: (1) the literal level of meaning — that is, the **plot** (action) of the work; (2) the moral or tropological level, at which generally applicable principles of human behavior are revealed; (3) the allegorical level, at which the reader understands the religious (usually New Testament) truth signified by the literal level; and (4) the anagogical level, which contains the highest spiritual, often **eschatological,** meanings of the work (those having to do with questions about what happens to the individual after death and, even more generally, at the end of time, on the Day of Judgment). This method of **explication** was common in the **Medieval Period** and continued to be widely used well into the eighteenth century. It has also been applied to, and adapted for, secular material, particularly secular poetry.

Some authors, such as Dante Alighieri, have implied that their works have not four but two levels of meaning: the literal and allegorical. However, they have gone on to subdivide the latter category of meaning into three levels: the allegorical, moral, and anagogical.

fourteener: A line of **verse** that has fourteen syllables; such a line is usually written in **iambic heptameter.**
EXAMPLE: George Chapman's 1616 translation of Homer's *Iliad* (c. 850 B.C.) was done in fourteeners.

frame story: A **story** that contains another story or stories. Usually, the frame story explains why the interior story or stories are being told. For example, the frame story in *The Thousand and One Nights* (c. 1450) (also known as *The Arabian Nights*) explains that Queen Shahrazad tells her husband, King Shahryar, a story every night — each one ending with a reference to or preview of the story to be told the following night — because the King has had over a thousand previous wives executed the morning after the wedding night in order to ensure that they would never be unfaithful to him, as was his first wife.

The degree to which the frame story has a **plot** varies; that is, the frame story may be extremely sketchy or fairly well developed. The interior stories are likely to be fully developed **tales,** usually completely separate from one another (except insofar as they are linked by the **narrative** frame and sometimes by **theme** or subject matter).

FURTHER EXAMPLES: *Panchatantra* (c. A.D. 500; anonymous), Boccaccio's *Decameron* (1348–53), Geoffrey Chaucer's *Canterbury Tales* (c. 1387), Marguerite de Navarre's *Heptaméron* (1548), and Joseph Conrad's *Heart of Darkness* (1899). The film *Invasion of the Body Snatchers* (1956) also makes use of a frame story — the movie begins and ends with a **character** named Miles Binnell recounting his experiences to the authorities.

free indirect discourse: Discourse that is represented, rather than directly related, to the reader. *Free indirect discourse* (or, more simply, *indirect discourse*) is the English term for the French *style indirect libre,* in which the thoughts, statements, and even **dialogues** engaged in by **characters** are recounted to the reader in a "reportorial" narrative mode. An author employing free indirect discourse might write a sentence like this: "She came to the realization that he would never change and told him she was thinking about leaving him; he was devastated by the news but told her to go ahead and make his day." The French novelist Gustave Flaubert helped pioneer this **style** of writing in *Madame Bovary* (1857).

Free indirect discourse has become an important subject of analysis for those critics interested in the "grammar of narration," that is, in a grammatical analysis of **narrative.** Such critics study the ways in which firsthand accounts of thoughts and actions differ from impersonal narrative accounts of those same thoughts and actions.

free verse: From the French *vers libre,* literally meaning "free verse," **poetry** that lacks a regular **meter,** does not **rhyme,** and uses irregular (and sometimes very short) line lengths. Writers of free verse disregard traditional poetic **conventions** of rhyme and meter, relying instead on **parallelism,** repetition, and the ordinary cadences and **stresses** of everyday **discourse.** In English, notable use of free verse dates back to the King James translation of the biblical Psalms and Song of Solomon, but it was not really recognized as an important new form until Walt Whitman's *Leaves of Grass* (1855). Since World War I, nonrhyming and nonmetrical forms of **verse** have been used by most poets.

EXAMPLE: W. S. Merwin's "The Judgment of Paris" (1967), from which the following lines have been taken, is an example of free verse:

> in the quiver on Paris's back the head
> of the arrow for Achilles' heel
> smiled in its sleep
>
> and Helen stepped from the palace to gather
> as she would do every day in that season
> from the grove the yellow ray flowers tall

as herself
whose roots are said to dispel pain

French Symbolists: See **symbolism.**

Freytag's Pyramid: Gustav Freytag's conception of the **structure** of a typical five-act **play,** introduced in *Die Technik des Dramas* (1863). According to Freytag's analysis, such plays are divisible into five parts: the introduction (containing an "inciting moment" or "force"), **rising action, climax, falling action,** and **catastrophe.** These parts loosely correspond with the five **acts** of the drama, although rising action can occur during the first act and falling action usually includes the catastrophe or "closing action," which typically takes place in the fifth and last act. Freytag referred to the five acts — as opposed to the five parts — of a drama as "the act of introduction," "the act of the ascent" (in which the play's action intensifies as **conflicts** develop), "the act of the climax" (containing the play's most important **scene,** the one in which the rising action culminates), "the act of the return" (in which new **characters** are introduced and "fate wins control over the hero"), and "the act of the catastrophe."

Although Freytag confined his analysis to five-act plays (**tragedies** in particular, and especially William Shakespeare's), Freytag's Pyramid has been applied to other dramatic forms and even to fiction, including prose. In these applications, the term **resolution** is used instead of *catastrophe.*

full rhyme: See **perfect rhyme.**

G

gaps: When used by **reader-response critics** familiar with the **theories** of Wolfgang Iser, the term refers to "blanks" in **texts** that must be filled in by readers. A gap may be said to exist whenever and wherever a reader perceives something to be missing between words, sentences, paragraphs, **stanzas,** or chapters. Readers respond to gaps actively and creatively, explaining apparent inconsistencies in **point of view,** accounting for jumps in chronology, speculatively supplying information missing from **plots,** and resolving problems or issues left **ambiguous** or "indeterminate" in the text.

Reader-response critics sometimes speak as if a gap actually exists in a text; a gap, of course, is to some extent a product of readers' perceptions. One reader may find a given text to be riddled with gaps while another reader may view that text as comparatively consistent and complete; different readers may find different gaps in the same text. Furthermore, they may fill in the gaps they find in different ways, which is why, a reader-response critic might argue, works are interpreted in different ways.

Although the concept of the gap has been used mainly by reader-response critics, it has also been used by critics taking other theoretical approaches. Practitioners of **deconstruction** might use *gap* when explaining that every text contains opposing and even contradictory **discourses** that cannot be reconciled. **Marxist critics** have used the term *gap* to speak of everything from the gap that opens up between economic **base** and cultural **superstructure** to two kinds of **conflicts** or contradictions found in literary texts. The first of these conflicts or contradictions, they would argue, results from the fact that even **realistic** texts reflect an **ideology,** within which there are inevitably subjects and attitudes that cannot be represented or even recognized. As a result, readers at the edge or outside of that ideology perceive that something is missing. The second kind of conflict or contradiction within a text results from the fact that works do more than reflect ideology; they are also fictions that, consciously or unconsciously, distance themselves from that ideology.

gay and lesbian criticism: Forms of **gender criticism** focused on textual **representations** of and readings responsive to issues of homo- (and hetero-) sexuality. Gay and lesbian criticism (sometimes referred to as *sexualities criticism*) emerged in the mid-1980s with the publication of Eve Kosofsky Sedgwick's *Between Men: English Literature and Male Homosocial Desire* (1985). In this pioneering work, Sedgwick adapts **feminist** critical theory to analyze relationships between men, between male **characters** in literary works, and, most importantly, between **gender** and **sexuality.**

Some practitioners of gay and lesbian criticism have extended a debate between feminist and gender critics about whether there is such a thing as "reading like a woman" (or man) by arguing that there are gay and lesbian ways of reading. In *On Lies, Secrets, and Silence: Selected Prose, 1966–1979* (1979), lesbian poet-critic Adrienne Rich has read Emily Dickinson's poetry as a lesbian, thereby revealing a poet quite different from the one heterosexual critics have made familiar. In "Wilde's Hard Labor and the Birth of Gay Reading" (1990), Wayne Koestenbaum has defined "the (male twentieth-century first world) gay reader" as one who "reads resistantly for inscriptions of his condition, for texts that will confirm a social and private identity founded on a desire for other men. . . . Reading becomes a hunt for histories that deliberately foreknow or unwittingly trace a desire felt not by author but by reader, who is most acute when searching for signs of himself."

The debate over whether distinct gay and lesbian ways of reading exist is related to a debate among gay and lesbian critics as to whether sexuality is biologically or socially determined (a debate that itself stems from the debate between some feminist and gender critics as to whether gender is a product of nature or culture). Most gender critics are **constructionists,** viewing gender as a cultural construct, whereas many feminist critics are **essentialists,** viewing gender — masculinity and femininity — as innate. Some gay and lesbian critics follow the lead of their gender-oriented colleagues in arguing that sexuality, too, is culturally constructed. Others, however, argue that sexuality is biologically determined. Such critics believe that homosexuals and heterosexuals are essentially different by nature, just as a number of feminists believe men and women to be different.

Following the lead of Michel Foucault, a French theorist generally associated with **the new historicism,** some gay and lesbian critics have argued that the heterosexual / homosexual distinction is as much a cultural construct as is the masculine / feminine dichotomy. They have viewed sexuality as a continuum, not a fixed set of **binary oppositions,** recognizing not only that many individuals have felt attracted to members of both sexes even if they are predominantly hetero- or homosexual but also that sexuality is not restricted to these binary opposites. Rather, it encompasses a range of behaviors, including sadomasochism and transvestism. They have also critiqued heterosexuality as a norm, arguing that it has been an enforced corollary and consequence of what Gayle Rubin has referred to as the "sex / gender system" in an essay entitled "The Traffic in Women: Notes on the 'Political Economy' of Sex" (1975). (Those subscribing to this system assume that persons of the male sex are and should be masculine, that masculine men are attracted to women, and therefore that it is natural for men to be attracted to women and unnatural for them to be attracted to men.)

Lesbian critics have taken some of their feminist counterparts to task on the grounds that the latter proceed from fundamentally heterosexual and even heterosexist assumptions. Particularly offensive to lesbians have been those feminists who, following Doris Lessing, have implied that to affirm a lesbian identity is to act out feminist hostility against men. In an essay entitled "Compulsory Heterosexuality and Lesbian Existence" (1983), Rich rejects this assertion, noting that women from diverse cultures and historical eras have "undertaken the task of independent, nonheterosexual, women-centered existence" even in the face of economic uncertainty and social disapproval. Rich further suggests that "heterosexuality [is] a beachhead of male dominance," which, "like motherhood, needs to be recognized and studied as a political institution."

Lesbian critics have produced a number of compelling reinterpretations of works by authors as diverse as Dickinson, Virginia Woolf, and Toni Morrison. As a result of these provocative readings, significant disagreements have arisen between straight and lesbian critics as well as among lesbian critics. A famous example of this kind of interpretive controversy involves the claim by Rich and Barbara Smith that Morrison's novel *Sula* (1973) can be read as a lesbian text — and Morrison's counterclaim that it cannot. In an essay entitled "Toward a Black Feminist Criticism" (1985), Smith points to Nel and Sula's close friendship and what she identifies as Morrison's critique of heterosexual institutions such as marriage to support her claim, even though Morrison previously had emphatically rejected such claims in Claudia Tate's *Black Women Writers at Work* (1983).

Gay male critics have produced a body of readings no less revisionist and controversial, focusing on writers as staidly **classic** as Henry James and Wallace Stevens. In *Hero, Captain, and Stranger* (1986), Robert K. Martin suggests that triangles of homosexual desire exist in Herman Melville's *Moby-Dick* (1851) and *Billy Budd* (written 1891, published 1924). In the former novel, the **narrator-hero** must choose between a captain who represents the "imposition of the male on the female" and a "Dark Stranger" (Queequeg) who represents an "alternate sexuality," one less grounded in "performance and conquest."

The work of gay and lesbian critics who are more theoretically oriented than text-centered has come to be referred to as **queer theory,** an approach to literature and culture that assumes sexual identities are fluid, not fixed, and that critiques gender and sexuality as they are commonly conceived in Western culture. Queer theorists emphasize that sexuality is not restricted to homo- and heterosexuality, which are usually seen as mutually exclusive, binary opposites. They also proudly and defiantly embrace the term *queer*. As Judith Butler points out in *Bodies That Matter: On the Discursive Limits of Sex* (1993), *queer* may be a "discursive rallying point for younger lesbians and gays . . . and for bisexuals and straights for whom the term expresses an affiliation with antihomophobic politics." Other notable contributions to the field of queer theory include Sedgwick's *Epistemology of the Closet* (1991) and *Tendencies* (1993), a special "Issue on Queer Theory" edited by Teresa de Lauretis and published by the journal *differences* (1993), and Alan Sinfield's *Cultural Politics — Queer Reading* (1994).

See also **gender criticism.**

gender: A term referring to the socially constructed identities *man, woman, masculine, feminine.* Some contemporary **gender critics** also use the term to refer to various **sexualities** (for example, heterosexuality, homosexuality, bisexuality, etc.). Gender is distinguished from *sex,* the biological designation of male or female. Unlike sex, which is anatomical, gender is widely held to be a product of the prevailing mores, expectations, and stereotypes of a particular culture. Thus, what it means to be "masculine" or "feminine" (rather than "male" or "female") — what attributes and roles are assigned to each of these categorizations — is determined by culture (which is shaped primarily by the dominant group) and may vary from one culture to the next. Most critics agree that Western civilization has been predominantly **patriarchal** and has thus tended to devalue the feminine (to which it has assigned such traits as passivity and emotionality) while extolling the masculine (which is commonly associated with activity and rationality). "Feminine" and "masculine" in other cultures may be perceived entirely differently.

gender criticism: A type of literary **criticism** that focuses on — and critiques — **gender** as it is commonly conceived, seeking to expose its insufficiency as a categorizing device. Many people associate biological sex — male and female — with a range of characteristics encompassed by the words *masculine* and *feminine,* respectively. Furthermore, people typically assume that these associations are somehow natural — that men are (or should be) masculine, women feminine — and that any other alignment is abnormal. Gender critics reject the view that gender is something natural or innate, arguing instead that gender is a social construct, a learned behavior, a product of culture and its institutions.

Certain gender critics have even questioned the distinction between heterosexuality and homosexuality, arguing that they, too, are social constructs. Many of these critics would also agree that **sexuality** as it is commonly perceived — as containing only two possibilities, homosexuality and heterosexuality — ignores the myriad variations and differences among individuals. Most people are not exclusively homo- or heterosexual, these critics would argue. Such critics view sexuality as a continuum, not a fixed set of **binary oppositions;** they also recognize that sexuality encompasses a range of behaviors, from bondage to bestiality. Some gender critics (especially many gay and lesbian critics) also focus on sexuality but would disagree that it is culturally produced. These critics would argue that sexuality is innate, that homosexuals and heterosexuals are naturally different.

The connection between gender studies and **gay and lesbian criticism,** which has focused on the issue of sexuality, has proved to be both elusive and problematic. The alliance — or even identification — some critics see between gender criticism and gay and lesbian criticism makes it possible that the term *gender studies* may (incorrectly) become synonymous with gay and lesbian criticism. This definition presents an expansive rather than restrictive categorization of gender criticism, however, classifying gay and lesbian criticism as a major emphasis within gender criticism, although not all gay and lesbian critics would so categorize their work.

Gender criticism has also been associated with **feminist criticism.** Many commentators have argued that feminist criticism is actually a type of gender criticism, despite the fact that feminist criticism arose as an approach to literary criticism in the 1970s, a decade earlier than gender criticism. Gender critics have drawn heavily upon feminist **theory** and practice even as they have attacked many feminist concepts and claims. Insofar as feminist criticism focuses on the feminine gender, it may be defined as a type of gender criticism, but the relationship between the two approaches is complex; they are certainly not polar opposites but, rather, exist along a continuum of attitudes toward sex, sexuality, gender, and language.

In an essay entitled "Feminist and Gender Studies" (1992), critic Naomi Schor estimated that gender studies began to prevail over feminist criticism around 1985. As Schor has pointed out, 1985 also marks the publication of gender critic Eve Kosofsky Sedgwick's seminal book, *Between Men: English Literature and Male Homosocial Desire,* a book that has had tremendous impact both on gender criticism generally and on gay and lesbian criticism more specifically. Although many commentators would debate Schor's claim that feminist criticism has been giving way to gender studies, they likely would agree that the publication of *Between Men* signalled a new development in literary studies. In *Between Men,* Sedgwick adapts feminist theory in such a way as to analyze relationships between men, between male **characters** in literary works, and, most importantly, between gender and sexuality.

Gender critics have stressed the importance of differentiating gender from biological sexual difference while also recognizing their interrelatedness. As gender critic Teresa de Lauretis points out in *Technologies of Gender: Essays on Theory, Film, and Fiction* (1987), many feminists of the 1970s equated gender with sex, gender difference with sexual difference. As such, these feminists viewed gender differences as natural. Gender critics, however, view gender as a construct, a product of language, culture, and its institutions. De Lauretis, for instance, has argued that gender is "the product of various social technologies, such as cinema," not "a property of bodies or something originally existent in human beings." In *Epistemology of the Closet* (1991), Sedgwick likewise argued that "chromosomal sex," the physical differences between men and women, should be distinguished from what she identified as the cultural system of gender. But Sedgwick took this insight even further, arguing that gender should be distinguished from sexuality as well as sex since sexuality encompasses such a wide variety of acts and inclinations.

Gender theorist Judith Butler further complicated the sex-gender debate in *Gender Trouble: Feminism and the Subversion of Identity* (1990) by arguing that all sexual difference is culturally produced rather than natural.

Sex, for Butler, is as much a cultural construct as gender; furthermore, notions about sex are created as a byproduct of the cultural construction of gender. Humans have created such a vast construct that no one can really know how the body functions apart from the culture in which it lives.

Many gender critics (both those who would call themselves feminists and those who would not) hold **constructionist** views and take issue with those feminists who urge an **essentialist** approach. Stated simply, the word *essentialist* refers to the view that women are essentially — that is, naturally — different from men. The most essentialist feminists write as if no amount of enculturation could alter female nature, female difference. *Constructionist,* by contrast, refers to the view that most of the differences between men and women are characteristics not of the male and female sex (nature) but, rather, of the masculine and feminine genders (nurture). Some extreme constructionists (also called *postfeminists*) even argue that nature is in some sense a cultural construct; as Butler argued in *Gender Trouble,* "sex, by definition, will be shown to have been gender all along." Schor has tried to explain this position in "Feminist and Gender Studies" by writing, "there is nothing outside or before culture, no nature that is not already enculturated." In *Between Men,* Sedgwick voiced the concerns of many constructionists when she critiqued "radical feminism" for its essentialist framework, arguing that it upholds the status quo by denying "that the meaning of gender or sexuality has ever significantly changed." If sexual difference is at the root of gender differences, perceptions of masculinity and femininity will not change because sexual difference will always exist.

Constructionist gender critics vehemently disagree with those feminists who emphasize the female body, its sexual difference, and the manifold implications of that difference, especially French feminist critics who argue that the female body gives rise to a special feminine language, writing, and style and French-influenced North American feminist critics, like Toril Moi and Nancy K. Miller, who posit an essential relationship between sex and **text.** These feminist critics have argued that women have a special mode of writing by virtue of the fact that they are women. Miller, for instance, suggested in *Subject to Change: Reading Feminist Writing* (1988) that no man could write the "female anger, desire, and selfhood" that Emily Brontë inscribed in her poetry and in *Wuthering Heights* (1847).

Constructionist gender critics, by contrast, attribute differences in language, writing, and style to cultural influences, not to sexual difference between female and male bodies. For instance, Peggy Kamuf, one of the first critics to attack the notion of feminine writing, posits a relationship only between gender and textuality — between what most men and women become after they are born and the way in which they write. Kamuf is therefore less interested in whether an author was a woman writing than in whether the author was "Writing Like a Woman" (1980), as the name of one of her essays implies. Since the differences between men and women are culturally constructed rather than "natural," constructionist gender critics believe that it is possible for a man to write like a woman, a woman to write like a man, and for men to read as women, women as men.

Many gender theorists have found especially disturbing the inclination of some avant-garde French feminists to equate the female body with the maternal body; they worry that this association may **paradoxically** play into the hands of extreme conservatives and fundamentalists who seek to reestablish **patriarchal** family values. In a book entitled *The Reproduction of Mothering: Psychoanalysis and the Sociology of Gender* (1978), Nancy Chodorow admits that what we call "mothering" — not simply the biological ability to have and nurse babies but mothering more broadly conceived — is commonly associated not just with the feminine gender but also with the female sex, often considered nurturing by nature. But she challenges the assumption that it is in women's nature or biological destiny to "mother" in the broader sense, arguing that the separation of home and workplace brought about by capitalism and the ensuing Industrial Revolution made mothering appear to be essentially a woman's job in modern Western society.

Chodorow, like many other theorists, self-identifies with the feminist perspective, but much of her work has been classified as gender analysis. Whether such critiques of gender should be categorized as the work of feminist analysis or that of gender studies is open to debate. Sedgwick attempts to answer the question in an essay entitled "Gender Criticism" (1992), explaining that gender criticism, unlike feminist criticism, is "not criticism *through* the categories of gender" but a "criticism *of* them."

Although feminist criticism and gender criticism differ, neither school is monolithic, and many gender critics have more in common with certain feminists than with other gender critics. Although feminist criticism has often been associated with essentialism, some feminist critics advocate constructionism as adamantly as many gender critics.

Similarly, gender criticism also encompasses a variety of viewpoints. Many gay and lesbian critics, for instance, adhere to the essentialist point of view. These critics believe that homosexuals and heterosexuals are fundamentally different by nature, just as essentialist feminists believe men and women to be different. What makes the work of such gay men and lesbians gender criticism is their conception of sexuality as the issue that "troubles," to use Judith Butler's term from *Gender Trouble*.

In tackling topics that most confound traditional notions of gender, critics such as Sedgwick have argued that sexuality most obviously and insistently resists analysis. Sexuality has served both as a focal point of and as an impetus to gender criticism, helping to distinguish it from feminist criticism and to make it a wide-ranging and significant movement in literary studies. Insofar as the study of sexuality is concerned, many critics regard Michel Foucault, a French philosophical historian most often associated with **the new historicism,** as an important theoretical influence on gender criticism. Instead of critiquing the male / female or masculine / feminine dichotomy, Foucault examined distinctions between heterosexuality and homosexuality. In *Histoire de la sexualité* (*The History of Sexuality*) (1976), Foucault distinguished sexuality from sex, calling the former a "technology of sex." In *Technologies of Gender,* de Lauretis explains Foucault's use of "technology" by writing that sexuality is neither natural nor private; rather, it is "completely constructed in culture according to the political aims of the society's dominant class."

Foucault suggested that the Western conception of homosexuality was largely an invention of the nineteenth century. Prior to the nineteenth century, people spoke of "acts of sodomy" and of the individuals who committed them as "sodomites," but the sodomite was a "temporary aberration," not the "species" he became with the advent of the modern concept of homosexuality. In other words, sodomitic acts did not define people so markedly as the word *homosexual* does now; sodomitic *acts* have been replaced by homosexual *persons,* and in the process the range of acceptable relationships between individuals of the same gender has been further restricted. As Sedgwick notes in "Gender Criticism" (1992), "In the late twentieth century, if I ask you what your sexual orientation or sexual preference is, you will understand me to be asking precisely one thing: whether you are homosexual or heterosexual."

By historicizing sexuality, Foucault made it possible to argue that all the categories and assumptions that operate when we think about sex, sexual difference, gender, and sexuality are social (rather than natural) artifacts, the products of cultural **discourses.** Gender critics have used the very variety of possible sexual identifications and affiliations to challenge gender as we commonly think of it, to expose its insufficiency as a category. Many gender critics (gay and lesbian critics in particular) have explored the issues raised by a variety of sexualities: homo-, hetero-, trans-, bi-, and — to use the term now applied defiantly and proudly to forms of sexuality that do not serve reproductive heterosexuality — *queer*. **Queer theory,** an approach to literature and culture that assumes sexual identities are fluid, not fixed, and that critiques gender and sexuality as they are commonly conceived in Western culture, is more theoretical and less text-oriented than gay and lesbian criticism. It covers any form or manifestation of sexuality other than heterosexual vaginal sex, such as bestiality, sadism, and heterosexual anal sex. Queer theorists emphasize that sexuality is not restricted to homo- and heterosexuality, which are usually seen as mutually exclusive, binary opposites.

Following Foucault's lead, some gay and lesbian critics have argued that the heterosexual / homosexual distinction is as much a cultural construct as is the masculine / feminine dichotomy. These critics have been especially critical of heterosexuality as a norm, arguing that it is an enforced corollary and consequence of what Gayle Rubin describes in "The Traffic in Women: Notes on the 'Political Economy' of Sex" (1975) as the "sex /

gender system," a system that presupposes that men are masculine, that masculinity carries with it an attraction to women, and that it is therefore unnatural for men to be attracted to other men.

Other gay and lesbian critics have taken an essentialist point of view, celebrating homosexual difference, much as many feminist critics postulated the existence of and embraced female difference. Many have argued that gay and lesbian ways of reading exist and have reinterpreted works by authors as diverse as Henry James, Herman Melville, Emily Dickinson, and Virginia Woolf.

Gay and lesbian critics are not the only gender critics who have critiqued masculinity. Many gender theorists have analyzed masculinity as a complex construct that produces and reproduces a constellation of behaviors and goals such as performance and conquest, many of them destructive and most of them injurious to women. In an article entitled "Anti-Porn: Soft Issue, Hard World" (1983), B. Ruby Rich challenged the "legions of feminist men" who deplore the effects of pornography on women to find out "why men like porn (not, piously, why this or that exceptional man does *not*)." Stephen H. Clark, writing on T. S. Eliot's *The Waste Land* (1920) in an essay entitled "Testing the Razor" (1989), analyzes Eliot's address to a specifically masculine audience — "'You! hypocrite lecteur! — mon semblable, — mon *frère!*'" — by concluding that many of Eliot's poems articulate a masculine "psychology of sexual fear and desired retaliation."

Other gender critics focusing on masculinity have analyzed the "anthropology of boyhood," a phrase coined by Mark Seltzer in an article entitled "The Love Master" (1990), in which he comparatively reads, among other things, Stephen Crane's *Red Badge of Courage* (1895), Jack London's *White Fang* (1905), and the first handbook published by the Boy Scouts of America. Others have examined the fear men have that artistry is somehow unmasculine, a guilty worry that surfaces perhaps most obviously in "The Custom-House," Nathaniel Hawthorne's lengthy preface to *The Scarlet Letter* (1850). Still others have studied the **representation** in literature (and film) of subtly erotic disciple-patron relationships, relationships like those between Nick Carraway and Jay Gatsby, Charlie Marlow and Lord Jim, Doctor Watson and Sherlock Holmes.

The critique of gender as a category of analysis continues to make its distinctive contributions in increasingly varied and expanding areas of inquiry. Joan Riviere's essay "Womanliness as Masquerade" (1929), in which Riviere argues that all femininity involves masquerade, has sparked an interest in performance theory in both the feminist and gender approaches. Marjorie Garber, a **cultural critic,** has analyzed the constructed nature of gender by focusing on people who have apparently achieved gender identity through transvestism, transsexualism, and sexual role-playing (and reversal), which appear in cultural productions ranging from Shakespeare to Liberace to Elvis Presley, "Little Red Riding Hood" to *La Cage aux Folles* (1979) or, more recently, *The Birdcage* (1996).

Gender critics have established the significance of gender, however defined, not only in poems and novels, but also in video and on television and in everyday life. Sedgwick's book *Tendencies* (1993) begins with commentary on subjects as diverse — and connected — as the suicide rate among gay teenagers, American Christmas traditions, AIDS, queer reading, and contemporary journalism. Other gender critics have focused on film (as have many feminist critics), arguing that it plays a primary role in gender construction. These critics have analyzed films ranging from *Rebel Without a Cause* (1955) to *Tootsie* (1982) to last year's Best Picture to uncover the ways in which they reflect, perpetuate, and sometimes even challenge stereotypical gender roles and characteristics.

See **gay and lesbian criticism** and **queer theory** for more detailed introductions to these emphases within gender criticism.

See also **feminist criticism.**

generative linguistics: One of the two components of Noam Chomsky's theory of **linguistics** postulated in *Syntactic Structures* (1951). Chomsky attempts to account for what he calls the "rule-bound creativity" of any given language — that is, the fact that a native speaker who is speaking to another native speaker can utter an original sentence, a series of words that neither has heard in that exact form and order before, but that both of them nonetheless easily understand due to their linguistic competence. Chomsky argues that competence in a given language follows from mastery of a certain set of generative and transformational rules. Thus his theory is termed "generative" in its attempt to determine the set of rules that accounts for all the possible **syntactically** correct sentences in any given language. His theory is termed "transformational" in its belief that a certain set of transformative rules produces a plethora of variations on "kernel sentences" (basic sentences) in the "deep structure" of any given language.

See also **transformational linguistics.**

Geneva School: Also called *critics of consciousness,* Geneva School critics practiced a type of **expressive criticism** called **phenomenological criticism,** which flourished in the 1950s and 1960s. Geneva critics approached **texts** as if the purpose of the critical act was to "get into the author's head," to achieve an intuitive understanding of, perhaps even identification with, what we might call the author's mindset — his or her idiosyncratic way of perceiving and representing the world, which, unlike ideas, attitudes, and beliefs, is fundamentally consistent through time. These critics maintained that each individual (and therefore each writer) has a unique **phenomenology,** a kind of mental fingerprint or "mindprint." Just as every fingerprint is different, so is every mind, and Geneva critics sought to experience and describe its subjective *Weltanschauung* ("worldview"), which, they felt, must inevitably be manifested in creative enterprises (including but not limited to literary efforts). In opening themselves and the critical act up to the author's linguistic constructs, they tried to set aside their own worldview to become a better receptacle for the author's "intentionality" or awareness and to reproduce the author's consciousness (rather than their own) in their criticism. They thus eschewed any references external to the work. In their emphasis on the unique consciousness of the author, Geneva School critics recall nineteenth-century **romantics,** who elevated the author to a position of prime importance and who considered insight into the author's personality and creative genius a chief objective of literary analysis.

Geneva School critics were likely to base their analyses on structural or perceptual similarities found in poems, letters, and diary entries. Since they were not overly concerned with chronology — after all, they believed that early writings, like late ones, reveal the same mindprint — they could discuss an adolescent love letter, a poem written during a midlife crisis, and a late novel side by side. Many also concentrated on a single work, seeking to reconcile a variety of passages that, taken together, theoretically provide insight into the overall scheme of the author's thinking. Whatever approach they took, Geneva critics aimed first and foremost to describe the patterns of thought and, beyond that, the qualities of mind that lie behind a text or an *oeuvre* (the whole of a given author's life's work).

The Geneva critics were a close-knit group in life as well as in literary criticism. Many of its members were professors at the University of Geneva in Switzerland; many were also friends. The Geneva School included Albert Béguin, Georges Poulet, Marcel Raymond, Jean-Pierre Richard, Jean Rousset, and J. Hillis Miller (before his turn to **deconstruction** in the 1970s). Some of the most influential Geneva School works include Poulet's *The Metamorphoses of the Circle* (1966) and Miller's *Thomas Hardy: Distance and Desire* (1970).

By the early 1970s, the Geneva School's theory and practices came under increasing fire, especially from **structuralists** and **poststructuralist** deconstructors (who otherwise opposed one another). Structuralists found the approach of Geneva critics unscientific and excessively **subjective;** deconstructors viewed the text as **rhetoric** riven by cross currents and contradictions, not as something indelibly stamped with the unitary, unified, and unique pattern of an author's consciousness. Deconstructors, in fact, have called into question the very notion of the unified and static psyche or self on which the Geneva School and phenomenological criticism rest.

genre: From the French *genre* for "kind" or "type," the classification of literary works on the basis of their content, form, or technique. The term also refers to individual classifications. For centuries works have been grouped and associated according to a number of classificatory schemes and distinctions, such as **prose / poem, fiction / drama / lyric,** and the traditional **classical** divisions: **comedy / tragedy / lyric / pastoral / epic / satire.** More recently, Northrop Frye has suggested that all literary works may be grouped with one of four sets of **archetypal myths** that are in turn associated with the four seasons; for Frye, the four main genre classifications are comedy (spring), **romance** (summer), tragedy (fall), and satire (winter). Many more specific genre categories exist as well, such as **autobiography,** the **essay, Gothic,** the **picaresque novel,** the **sentimental novel.** Current usage is thus broad enough to permit varieties of a given genre (such as the **novel**) as well as the novel in general to be legitimately denoted by the term *genre*.

Traditional thinking about genre has been revised and even roundly criticized by contemporary critics. For example, the prose / poem dichotomy has been largely discarded in favor of a lyric / drama / fiction (or **narrative**) scheme. The more general idea that works of **imaginative** literature can be solidly and satisfactorily classified according to set, specific categories has also come under attack in recent times. Those who still employ rigid genre distinctions are often accused of overgeneralizing and of obscuring aspects of works that "cross" or "mix" genres. (It should be noted, however, that works that blur the boundaries between once-distinct genres are a fairly modern development; the mixing of genres was discouraged or even forbidden before the eighteenth century.) Although identifying genre may be a helpful step in analyzing a work, doing so does not account for or explain all the elements of that work, as was once commonly assumed. This is especially true if the work in question is of recent vintage, since authors no longer feel bound to follow the **conventions** governing the composition of works in their chosen genre. (By contrast, in seventeenth-century France, Pierre Corneille had to defend himself before the Académie Française against charges of breaking the classical rule of the three **unities** in his play *Le Cid* [1636].)

Contemporary theorists of genre tend to follow the lead of the philosopher Ludwig Wittgenstein, who thought of genre in terms of "family resemblances," a set of similarities some (but by no means all) of which are shared by those works classified together. Viewed this way, genre is a convenient, though arguably loose and arbitrary, categorizing and descriptive device that provides a basic vantage point for examining most historical and many modern and contemporary works.

The term *genre* has a specific application with regard to painting that should in no way be confused with its use in literary **discourse.** In art criticism, it refers to works that depict ordinary life in a **realistic** manner.

Georgian Age (in English literature): Sometimes used to refer to the period 1714–1830 — during which George I, George II, George III, and George IV reigned successively — but more commonly used today to refer to the years 1910–36, during which George V was king. When used as an adjective to describe the poetry of this latter era, *Georgian* usually refers to quiet, relatively formal, often **elegiac** and rurally oriented **lyrics** written during and after World War I by poets such as Richard Aldington, Rupert Brooke, W. H. Davies, Walter de la Mare, and John Masefield, although

Aldington and Brooke also wrote passionately about the war experience, as did lesser-known Georgians Siegfried Sassoon, Isaac Rosenberg, and Wilfred Owen. The term is not generally used to describe the poetry of other writers of the time whose work was more fragmented, **allusive,** and unconventional — in short, "modern." (Thus, although T. S. Eliot lived in England and wrote during the Georgian Age, he is almost never referred to as a Georgian poet.)

Where fiction is concerned, the term *Georgian does* refer to a wide range of works written between the outbreaks of the two World Wars. As such, it is relatively unhelpful as a category of British fiction. Many of the great novelists of the earlier Edwardian Age — Arnold Bennett, Joseph Conrad, John Galsworthy, and H. G. Wells — wrote well into the Georgian Age and are sometimes referred to as Georgian novelists; their brand of **realism,** however, bore little similarity to works written by bold new **modernist** authors such as James Joyce, D. H. Lawrence, Dorothy Richardson, and Virginia Woolf. The theater of the Georgian Age was equally diverse in its styles and purposes; George Bernard Shaw further developed the kind of serious, intellectual drama pioneered by the nineteenth-century Norwegian dramatist Henrik Ibsen, while Noël Coward developed the lighter **genre** known as the **comedy of manners.**

As should be evident, the Georgian Age coincides with a large portion of the **Modern Period,** which encompasses the years 1914–45. Authors living and writing around the same time may thus be characterized as either Georgian or modernist, depending on their style and preferred form of literary expression.

Gothic and Gothic novel: A word that originally referred to a Germanic tribe, the Goths, the term *Gothic* today is usually used to connote the **medieval** world in general and, in particular, a style of architecture that originated in France and that flourished during the **Medieval Period,** particularly during the thirteenth through fifteenth centuries. Gothic buildings are characterized by a wealth of ornamental and intricate detail, flying buttresses, pointed arches and vaults, narrow spires, stained glass windows, and prominent verticality. Depending on the building, or the part of the building, one is looking at, Gothic architecture can seem flamboyant, mysterious, or even frightening. (Gothic cathedrals are often adorned with carvings of **grotesque** people, monsters, or devils known as gargoyles.)

When applied to literature, *Gothic* has been used both positively and pejoratively to refer to a **genre** characterized by a general mood of decay, action that is dramatic and generally violent or otherwise disturbing, loves that are destructively passionate, and **settings** that are grandiose, if gloomy or bleak. To eighteenth-century **neoclassicists,** who valued simplicity and unity, the appellation *Gothic* was synonymous with "barbaric" or crude. For them, "Gothic" writing was untutored, unrestrained, and ridiculously extravagant, particularly in its reliance on foreign ornament. **Romantics,** however, found in the Gothic a freedom of spirit, variety, mystery, and instinctual authenticity (as opposed to reasoned and therefore artificial **discourse**) that meshed well with their own emphasis on individuality, **imagination,** and **sublimity.**

The Gothic novel arose in late-eighteenth-century England and remained popular into the nineteenth century throughout Europe and America; elements of the Gothic novel and Gothic literature in general have persisted to our own day. The Gothic novel is a **romance** typically written as a long prose **horror narrative** that exhibits the Gothic qualities of doom and gloom as well as an emphasis on chivalry and magic. Dark, mysterious medieval castles chock full of secret passageways and (apparently) supernatural phenomena are common elements used to thrill the reader. Gothic **heroes** and **heroines** tend to be equally mysterious, with dark histories and secrets of their own. The Gothic hero is typically a man known more for his power and his charisma than for his personal goodness; the Gothic heroine's challenge is to win his love without being destroyed in the process. Exaggeration and emotional language are frequently employed by Gothic writers, who typically emphasize **story** line and setting over **character** and **characterization.** They seek to evoke an **atmosphere** of terror, often from an unidentifiable source.

The Gothic novel, which made its first appearance with the publication of Horace Walpole's *The Castle of Otranto: A Gothic Story* (1764) and rose to literary eminence with Ann Radcliffe's *The Italian* (1797), has had particular **influence** on the works of many nineteenth- and early-twentieth-century writers. Authors ranging from Samuel Taylor Coleridge to the Brontë sisters to Henry James to Daphne du Maurier owe a huge debt to the Gothic novel; some critics have even applied the term *Gothic* to novels such as Charlotte Brontë's *Jane Eyre* (1847) and Emily Brontë's *Wuthering Heights* (1847), as well as James's *The Turn of the Screw* (1898) and du Maurier's *Rebecca* (1938). Even today, Gothic elements are common in literature (especially but not exclusively in the popular historical romances sometimes referred to as "bodice rippers") and in other art forms such as film. The number of contemporary works falling into the "Gothic" category is even larger if we follow the current trend of using the term to refer to any work that evokes an atmosphere of brooding and terror.

FURTHER EXAMPLES: Radcliffe's *The Mysteries of Udolpho* (1794) was one of the early Gothic novels. Mary Shelley's *Frankenstein* (1818) and Edgar Allan Poe's "The Fall of the House of Usher" (1839) are nineteenth-century examples of Gothic literature. Recent examples include the Gothic romances of Victoria Holt (*Mistress of Mellyn* [1960]) and Phyllis A. Whitney (*Thunder Heights* [1960]), much of Stephen King's fiction (*The Shining* [1977], *It* [1986]), and the novels of Anne Rice (*Interview with the Vampire* [1976], *The Witching Hour* [1990]).

Popular culture continues to feature the Gothic and Gothic horror. Ken Russell's *Gothic* (1987) luridly retells the famous episode in the lives of Mary Shelley, Percy Bysshe Shelley, and George Gordon, Lord Byron that inspired Mary's classic Gothic novel *Frankenstein.* "Goth Rock" (short for "Gothic Rock") enjoyed a vogue in the 1980s, when musical groups such as The Cure forged a series of majestic, foreboding rock albums awash with morbid sounds and **themes.** A more recent and extreme version of Goth Rock with a particularly provocative, even blasphemous, edge is purveyed by Marilyn Manson.

Graveyard School of Poetry: A group of eighteenth-century English poets who, unlike their "rational" **neoclassical** contemporaries, emphasized **subjectivity, mystery,** and melancholy. Death, (im)mortality, and gloom were frequent subjects or elements of their meditative poems, which were often actually set in graveyards. This school, which is in the **Gothic** tradition, is often said to have laid the groundwork for English **romanticism.**

EXAMPLES: Thomas Gray's "Elegy Written in a Country Churchyard" (1751) is the most famous example. Robert Blair, Edward Young, and Thomas Parnell were other notable members of this school.

green criticism: See **ecocriticism.**

grotesque: From *grotte,* the Italian word for "grottoes" or "caves," a term first used in English in the sixteenth century to refer to decorative paintings or sculptures mixing human, animal, and supernatural figures (such as griffins) in designs found in or **imitating** those discovered in recently excavated rooms of ancient Roman houses. Such rooms, which were popularly referred to during the **Renaissance** as *grotte,* were literally "grotto-esque," since they were open spaces long buried under more recent buildings and even ruins.

In the seventeenth century, *grotesque* came to be used more broadly to refer to strangely unusual things or artistic **representations,** particularly ones involving bizarre or unnatural combinations of characteristics or **images.** Poet John Milton's representation of Paradise in *Paradise Lost* (1667) as a "steep wilderness" with "hairy sides / With thicket overgrown, grotesque and wild" is itself, properly speaking, a grotesque description, combining as it does images of hair and plant material. With this broader application, the term came to be used as an adjective describing gargoyles, statues combining human, animal, and monstrous features designed to protect buildings, particularly **Gothic** churches and cathedrals. Today, in art and literary **criticism,** the term refers to an **aesthetic** category involving but also **parodying** Gothic elements and **themes** and consequently evoking both fear and laughter.

The humorous aspect of the grotesque is often grounded in an extreme physicality and a concern with sexuality. In *Rabelais and His World* (1940), Mikhail Bakhtin maintains that the grotesque is characterized by bodily descriptions and the theme of procreation. The grotesque, however, also elicits fear of those same characteristics that evoke laughter. Wolfgang Kayser, in his book *The Grotesque in Art and Literature* (1957), defines the grotesque as "the estranged world," insisting that unlike **tragedy** or the fairy tale, both of which are composed of elements that are distanced from the everyday reality of the reader, the grotesque necessarily evolves out of humorous representations of a world familiar to the reader, resulting both in alienation from that world and in an unwilling participation in it.

The paintings of Hieronymous Bosch and the writings of François Rabelais have long been considered grotesque. More recent literary works containing grotesque elements include the stories of Edgar Allan Poe, Franz Kafka's "The Metamorphosis" (1915), William Faulkner's *As I Lay Dying* (1930), Erskine Caldwell's *Poor Fool* (1930), Carson McCullers's *Reflections in a Golden Eye* (1941), and Pär Lagerkvist's *The Dwarf* (1945).

gynocriticism: A term coined by Elaine Showalter to refer to a type of **feminist criticism** that focuses on literary works written by women, rather than critiquing male-authored works or studying women as readers who must resist the predominantly **patriarchal ideology** that traditional **texts** reinforce. Showalter separates women's writing since 1840 into three separate phases, which she refers to as "Feminine," "Feminist," and "Female." During these phases, women first imitated a masculine tradition (1840–80), then protested against its standards and values (1880–1920), and finally advocated their own autonomous, female perspective (1920 to the present).

Gynocritics have devised a special framework within which to examine and evaluate all varieties, formal and informal, of female-authored works ranging from diaries to novels to poems. They examine the ways in which such writers have formed and benefitted from their own communities and traditions — "a world of their own" (in Showalter's phrase) that, in turn, has reinforced the attitudes and aspirations of their female readers and, ultimately, their literary successors. In their effort to demonstrate that a special and explicitly female tradition exists in literature, a tradition that has too often been ignored or denigrated, gynocritics have broadened the traditionally patriarchal literary **canon** to include long-overlooked works of extraordinary literary merit, such as Aphra Behn's *Oroonoko* (1688) and Kate Chopin's *The Awakening* (1899).

Gynocritics focus on so-called feminine subjects **privileged** by women authors (such as domestic life, intimate experiences, and personal and family relationships) that are usually excluded from or marginalized in works by male authors, which tend to privilege adventure, achievement, work outside the home, voyages of self-discovery, and other endeavors deemed active, and therefore "masculine." Gynocritics also often seek to demonstrate the existence of a special feminine **subjectivity,** or way of thinking about and experiencing the world. Some gynocritics have expanded this view to argue that women's special mode of perception leads them to speak and, especially, to write in a way different from men. These gynocritics assert the existence of a distinctive "woman's language," which in French feminist criticism is referred to as *écriture féminine.*

Influential gynocritics include Showalter, Patricia Meyer Spacks, Sandra Gilbert, and Susan Gubar.

H

hagiography: See **biography.**

haiku (hokku): A Japanese **verse** form consisting of three un**rhymed** lines that together contain a total of seventeen syllables. The three lines typically consist of five, seven, and five syllables in turn. Haiku, which was developed during the sixteenth century, typically takes nature as its subject, using association and suggestion to appeal to emotion and to generate a moment of spiritual awareness or discovery.

EXAMPLES: The following **classic** haiku is by the seventeenth-century Japanese poet Bashō:

> Kumo to hedatsu
> Tomo kaya kari no
> Ikiwakare

As translated into English by Makoto Ueda, Bashō's haiku reads:

> Clouds will separate
> The two friends, after the migrating
> Wild goose's departure.

Other noted Japanese poets who have written haiku include Yosa Buson, Kobayashi Issa, and Konishi Raizan.

Michael McClintock is a master of contemporary English language haiku, which often modifies the classic 5-7-5 syllabic format of the traditional Japanese haiku, as in the following untitled example (1975):

> a broken window
> reflects half the moon,
> half of me.

Amy Lowell, Ezra Pound, Gary Snyder, and William Carlos Williams have also experimented with the form.

half-rhyme: A form of **rhyme** in which words contain similar sounds but do not rhyme perfectly. Most half-rhyme (also called *approximate rhyme, imperfect rhyme, near rhyme, oblique rhyme, pararhyme,* and *slant rhyme*) is the result of either **consonance** or **assonance,** usually the former. Half-rhyme may be unintentional or intentional. Unintentional half-rhyme results from the poet's lack of rhyming skills; intentional half-rhyme is usually the product of **poetic license,** liberties taken by the poet to create specific sound effects.

EXAMPLES: *Rhyme / writhe, horse / hearse, summer / humble,* and *thin / slim.* Emily Dickinson made frequent use of half-rhyme. In the following passage from "In Winter in my Room" (c. 1860), *Room / Worm,* and *Worm / warm* are half-rhymes:

> In Winter in my Room
> I came upon a Worm
> Pink lank and warm.

Wilfred Owen also relied heavily on half-rhyme in his poetry. In "Strange Meeting" (1920), *hall / Hell, friend / frowned,* and *killed / cold* are examples:

> And by his smile, I knew that sullen hall, —
> By his dead smile I knew we stood in Hell. . . .

> "I am the enemy you killed, my friend.
> I knew you in this dark; for so you frowned
> Yesterday through me as you jabbed and killed.
> I parried; but my hands were loath and cold.
> Let us sleep now. . . ."

Philip Larkin's "Toads" (1954) strikes a less solemn note. The pair *life / off* constitutes a half-rhyme, whereas the pair *work / pitchfork* constitutes an **eye-rhyme** as well as a half-rhyme:

> Why should I let the toad *work*
> Squat on my life?
> Can't I use my wit as a pitchfork
> And drive the brute off?

Eye-rhymes are generally half-rhymes, but not all half-rhymes are eye-rhymes.

Selena's soft-rock **ballad** "I Could Fall in Love with You" (1996) alternates **perfect rhymes** (*how / now*) and half-rhymes (e.g., *feel / still*).

hamartia: From the Greek for "error," an error in judgment made by a **tragic hero,** whether resulting from a lack of knowledge or a moral flaw, that brings about the suffering, downfall, and often death of that hero. The term is often used synonymously with **tragic flaw,** but this usage is not strictly correct — the error involved in hamartia need not be one inherent in the tragic hero (a character flaw, such as **hubris**) but may instead result from the hero's ignorance of certain crucial facts or from something as simple as an accident. Sometimes the hamartia may even result from the exercise (with disastrous consequences) of a virtue (such as bravery). Thus, although the hamartia may and often does result from a tragic flaw, the two terms are not technically equivalent.

Aristotle notes that the hamartia must cause or otherwise bring about the reversal of fortune for the tragic hero. Such heroes should be neither eminently good nor evil so that we can identify with them. Thus the audience should simultaneously experience both pity (for the hero's plight) and fear (of one day falling prey to the same error).

hard-boiled detective fiction: See **detective fiction.**

Harlem Renaissance: A literary movement that began in the 1920s in the almost exclusively African American area of Harlem in New York City. Harlem had grown tremendously following World War I, when a mass migration of black Americans out of the South and into northern cities had taken place. Thanks to the Harlem Renaissance, African American culture was for the first time deliberately highlighted for a diverse national audience. The Harlem area became not only the nexus of black literature, theater, music, and dance but also, for a time, an intellectual and artistic nerve center for the entire nation. Writers as varied as Countee Cullen, W. E. B. Du Bois, Langston Hughes, Zora Neale Hurston, James Weldon Johnson, Claude McKay, and Jean Toomer captivated America, as did such musical legends as Duke Ellington.

EXAMPLES: Alain Locke's anthology *The New Negro: An Interpretation* (1925); Zora Neale Hurston's novel *Their Eyes Were Watching God* (1937). Arna Bontemps, a participant in the Harlem Renaissance, chronicled its history years later in a collection of **essays** he edited entitled *The Harlem Renaissance Remembered* (1972).

hegemony: Most commonly, one nation's dominance or dominant influence over another. The term was adopted (and adapted) by the Italian **Marxist critic** Antonio Gramsci to refer to the process of consensus formation and to the pervasive system of assumptions, meanings, and values — the web of **ideologies,** in other words — that shapes the way things look, what they mean, and therefore what reality is for the majority of people within a given culture. Although Gramsci viewed hegemony as being powerful and persuasive, he did not believe that extant systems were immune to change; rather, he encouraged people to resist prevailing ideologies, to form a new consensus, and thereby to alter hegemony.

Hegemony is a term commonly used by **cultural critics** as well as by Marxist critics.

heptameter: A synonym for **septenary,** a line of **verse** consisting of seven **metrical feet.**

EXAMPLE: The following lines from Rudyard Kipling's "Tommy" (1890) are **fourteeners** written in **iambic** heptameter:

> I went | into | a pub|lic-'ouse | to get | a pint | o' beer,|
> The pub|lican | 'e up | an' sez, | "We serve | no red|-coats here."|
> The girls | be'ind | the bar | they laughed | an' gig|gled fit | to die, |
> I outs | into | the street | again | an' to | myself | sez I. . . . |

hermeneutics and hermeneutic circle: Originally, *hermeneutics* was reserved for principles used in interpreting religious writings (often specifically the Bible), but since the nineteenth century, the term has been used to refer to the **theory** of interpretation in general (that is, how to determine textual meaning). Modern hermeneutics — which considers the interpretive methods leading to the perception, interpretation, and understanding of **texts** (and their underlying organizing principles, or **codes**) — is grounded in the terminology and strategies of modern **linguistics** and philosophy.

In 1819, German theologian Friedrich Schleiermacher first developed a **theory** of hermeneutics in the general sense of textual interpretation. Wilhelm Dilthey, a German philosopher, built upon and expanded Schleiermacher's views in the 1890s. Dilthey coined the term *hermeneutic circle* to refer to a procedure originally described by Schleiermacher, who was referring to the idea that to understand the parts of a whole, one must begin with some general conception of that whole and vice versa. While this may seem to be an impossibly circular task, Dilthey argued that our perception and, therefore, our interpretation of both the whole and its component parts are modified as we move through the work. Because of the interdependent relationship between our retrospective comprehension of a work's constituent parts and an evolving concept of the constituted whole, we can ultimately develop a legitimate interpretation of that work.

Hermeneutics came back into critical fashion during the mid-twentieth century, thanks to a renewed interest in language and meaning, an interest expressed not only by philosophers but also by various **formalists,** including **the New Critics.** In the latter half of the twentieth century, two major developments in hermeneutics occurred. E. D. Hirsch developed Dilthey's view that an author's meaning may be **objectively** determined, arguing that a text means what its author intended it to mean and that the search for the author's "verbal intention" appropriately limits the otherwise inexhaustible supply of interpretations that may be derived from a single text. Hirsch's argument, which is complex and difficult to summarize briefly, depends on the use of certain precise terms and distinctions. For instance, Hirsch distinguishes between the "verbal meaning" of the text (which he believes *can* be determined and therefore properly falls in the provenance of hermeneutics) and the "significance" of a text (which depends to some extent upon the reader's **subjective,** culturally determined response and which therefore, in Hirsch's view, *cannot* be determined and is *not* the proper subject of hermeneutic analysis).

A second major development in hermeneutics occurred when Hans Georg Gadamer, a student of the philosopher Martin Heidegger, argued in *Truth and Method* (1975) that language and the interpretive act pervade and characterize all aspects of living — not just the study of literary texts. For Gadamer, our being (what Heidegger called *Dasein,* or "being in the world") involves a sense of time — a history that is past and a future yet to come — a sense that each person individually possesses. That sense, or "pre-understanding," forms the "horizons" within which we interpret. Gadamer further believed that readers can interact with the text, produced as it is by another person operating and communicating from the common baseline of language and temporality. By interacting with the text almost as if it were another person — a "Thou" whom the reader may approach as an "I" — the reader can work with the text, so to speak, cooperatively producing meaning rather than tagging the text as a freestanding, independent, fixed object with a specific, predetermined meaning that the reader must uncover.

Gadamer's theory, which Hirsch attacked in his book *Validity in Interpretation* (1967), differs not only from Hirsch's (insofar as it denies the possibility of establishing verbal intentions and determinate interpretations) but also from hermeneutics as understood by most traditional theorists and practitioners of literary interpretation. The New Critics, for instance, believed that the text of a poem contains within it an intended meaning; in warning against the pitfalls of the **intentional fallacy,** they mainly warned readers not to assume that an author's intentions can be known by studying things external to the text (the author's letters, for instance). John Searle's **speech-act theory** similarly held out the possibility of definite, determinate interpretation; Searle's point was that in order for a speaker's intention to be known, his or her "**locution**" must conform to the rules and **conventions** governing **locutionary, illocutionary,** and **perlocutionary acts.**

Gadamer's theory is closer to that espoused by those **reader-response critics** who have viewed the meaning-making process as one carried out by the reader under the guidance of the text. It is also closer to the thinking of **deconstructors,** for whom the text consists of words inscribed in and inextricable from the myriad **discourses** that inform it. From the point of view of deconstruction, the text can hardly "contain" a single, determinable meaning, because the boundaries between any given text and that larger text we call language are constantly shifting and uncertain.

hero/heroine: Often considered synonymous with **protagonist,** a term referring to the chief **character** of the work. Sometimes a work is said to have both a hero and a heroine, even if there is a wide discrepancy between the importance of the two in that work. When this is the case, the chief character is the protagonist; the other may be either a major or minor character.

EXAMPLES: In the movie *Dances with Wolves* (1990), Lieutenant John Dunbar is the hero and the protagonist. His love interest, Stands with a Fist, is the heroine; although she is an important character, she is not the primary character and therefore not the protagonist. In Charlotte Brontë's *Jane Eyre* (1847), Jane is the heroine and Mr. Rochester is the hero, but Jane is the protagonist.

heroic couplet: A pair of **rhymed** lines written in **iambic pentameter.** Geoffrey Chaucer was the first to compose **verse** using heroic couplets, but their use did not become widespread until the seventeenth century, during which they tended to be composed of **closed couplets,** each of which comprised a complete grammatical unit expressing a complete thought.

EXAMPLE: The following lines from Alexander Pope's "The Rape of the Lock" (1712–14):

> Meanwhile, declining from the noon of day,
> The sun obliquely shoots his burning ray;
> The hungry judges soon the sentence sign,
> And wretches hang that jurymen may dine. . . .

heteroglossia: A term used by Soviet critic Mikhail Bakhtin to refer to the plurality of **voices** present in a literary work — including those of the author, **narrator,** and **characters** — as well as to the **dialogue** between these often competing voices or **discourses.** For instance, a novel that is more **dialogic** than **monologic** may contain explicit or implicit disputes between: (1) characters (especially different groups or classes of characters); (2) certain characters or character groups and the sometimes monologic (i.e., singular and controlling) author and/or narrator; (3) the "official" **ideology** of the author's culture and the subversive ideology that authors may directly or indirectly represent or express; and (4) the traditional mores of the literary **genre** in which the work is written and those exhibited by a given **text.**

Heteroglossia is a translation of the Russian word *raznorecie,* which means "other tongues" or "different tongues." As Bakhtin states in *The Dialogic Imagination* (a 1981 English-language publication compiling four essays posthumously published in Russian in 1975 but substantially composed during the 1930s and 1940s), heteroglossia "permits a multiplicity of social voices and a wide variety of their links and interrelationships (always more or less dialogized)." According to Bakhtin, all novels are somewhat **polyphonic,** or *polyvocalic,* since the speech, ideology, and discourse of certain characters will inevitably argue with and compete against the authorial voice.

The term *heteroglossia,* according to Bakhtin, "conceptualizes" the "place," or "locus," where "centripetal" (e.g., official monologic) and "centrifugal" (e.g., unofficial dialogic) forces collide. At these crossroads, or in this "matrix," new viewpoints form contextually in language, almost of their own impetus, as a range of voices interrelate, compete with, and sometimes override the monologic voice of an author or the predominant ideology of his or her culture.

Heteroglossia should be distinguished from the **structuralist**-turned-**poststructuralist** critic Roland Barthes's concept of **plurality,** which also encompasses a multiplicity of voices. Bakhtin's concept of heteroglossia, however, involves a continual interaction between statements, ideas, and meanings; celebrates this diversity of voices; and views this interactive diversity as a means of moving beyond or around **codes, conventions,** and the dominant social discourse.

See also **dialogic criticism, monologic, polyphonic.**

hexameter: A line of **verse** consisting of six **metrical feet.** In **classical** (Greek or Latin) hexameter, this verse pattern was rigidly constructed; it consisted of four **dactyls** or **spondees** followed by a dactyl and then a spondee or **trochee**. Since true spondees are fairly rare in English, the classical hexameter is infrequently used by English poets.

EXAMPLE: The following lines from William Butler Yeats's "The Lake Isle of Innisfree" (1893):

> I will a|rise and | go now, | and go | to Inn|isfree,|
> And a small | cabin | build there, | of clay | and wat|tles made. . . . |

hieratic: Derived from a Greek word meaning "priestly" and originally used to describe a particularly conventional and stylized form of ancient Egyptian writing. *Hieratic* has been used by Northrop Frye to describe the **style** of certain more recent literary works. An author using hieratic (as opposed to **demotic**) style intentionally employs the **figures of speech, rhetorical figures,** and other **conventions** associated with **literariness** that elevate language to a level of formality exceeding that of ordinary speech. Frye further distinguishes three categories — *high, middle,* and *low* — in both the hieratic and demotic style.

See also **demotic**.

historical linguistics: See **descriptive linguistics**.

historical novel: A **novel** that makes use of historical personages or events in a fictitious **narrative**. True-to-life elements may be added to lend a sense of authenticity to the novel, but in serious examples of this **genre**, historical events, processes, and issues are central to the story line rather than providing peripheral or decorative touches. Historical novels are often vehicles for their authors' insights into historical figures and their influences or into the causes and consequences of historical events, changes, or movements.

EXAMPLES: Sir Walter Scott's *Waverley* (1814); William Makepeace Thackeray's *Barry Lyndon* (1844) and *The History of Henry Esmond* (1852). Herman Wouk (*The Winds of War* [1971]), Aleksandr Solzhenitsyn (*August 1914* [1971]), and Gore Vidal (*1876* [1976]) are famous twentieth-century historical novelists. Contemporary novelist Patrick O'Brian's Aubrey-Maturin series (including *The Commodore* [1994]) features Napoleonic naval history and even incorporates Incan history. Writer and jazz musician James McBride's novel *Miracle at St. Anna* (2002), which was inspired by the Buffalo soldiers of the 92nd Division (a division of African American soldiers who fought in Italy during World War II — not the Buffalo soldiers of the 1800s), as well as by an event that occurred in the village of St. Anna dei Stazzema, weaves a story of people caught up in war. The novel, which is set in Italy during World War II, focuses on the experiences of four African American soldiers, the villagers of St. Anna, a group of partisans, and an Italian boy and includes a soldier's participation in the liberation of a concentration camp.

historical romance: See **romance**.

historicism: A type of literary **criticism** that examines literary works within their diverse and interrelated historical contexts. In analyzing a **text,** historicists consider cultural and social forces that influenced and are revealed through the text. They sometimes assess the impact a literary work has had on readers in eras subsequent to the one in which it was written. In doing so, their goal is to understand how the perceived meaning and social significance of a work evolve over time. Historicists thus examine not only the influence of social, cultural, and historical circumstances on the work, but also the reception and significance of that work in the past and the present.

Historicists may incorporate a number of perspectives, including: (1) the **aesthetic** perspective (from which the work is viewed as a **representation** simultaneously shaped by and shaping its own era and fully understandable only in that context); (2) the *metaphysical* or *Hegelian* perspective (from which it appears to be part of a transcendental continuum); (3) the *nationalistic* perspective (from which it is seen as a cultural product influenced by nationally held norms and ideals); and (4) the *naturalistic* perspective (from which it is viewed as a means of gaining insight into contemporary social values). Above all else and no matter what specific approach to historicism is emphasized, historicists stress that literary works are produced by, reflect, and in some sense alter the social, cultural, and historical forces that were operative during their composition.

See also **new historicism.**

history play: A **drama** that makes use of historical events, personages, places, or times. Such plays have a greater tendency than **historical novels** to "document" a particular event or the life of a particular person. Sometimes the term *history play* is used more specifically to refer to Elizabethan **chronicle plays.**

EXAMPLES: Christopher Marlowe's *Edward II* (1593); William Shakespeare's *Henry V* (1599).

hokku: See **haiku.**

Homeric epithet: A short descriptive phrase, often involving compound adjectives, repeated so often that a more or less permanent association between the phrase and noun it was originally meant to modify is created.

EXAMPLES: Some examples from Homer himself include "swift-footed Achilles" and "Odysseus, sacker of cities."

See also **epithet.**

Homeric simile: See **epic simile.**

Horatian ode: Named for the Roman poet Horace, an **ode** that is usually composed of equal-length **stanzas** having the same **rhyme scheme** and **meter.** The term *Horatian* is sometimes also applied to writing with a "Horatian" — that is, meditative, quiet, and informal — **tone** like that found in Horace's odes.

EXAMPLE: John Keats's "To Autumn" (1820).

Horatian satire: A type of formal **satire** that pokes fun at human foibles with a **witty,** even indulgent **tone** rather than the dignified denunciations characteristic of **Juvenalian satire,** the other major type of formal satire. Horatian satire is so named for the Roman satirist Horace, who sought "to laugh people out of their vices and follies."

horror: See **fantasy fiction, mystery fiction.**

hubris (hybris): Greek for "insolence," excessive pride that constitutes the **protagonist's tragic flaw** and leads to a downfall. Disastrous consequences result when hubris causes the protagonist to ignore a wise warning from a god or other important figure, to violate some moral rule, or to try to transcend ordinary limits.

EXAMPLES: Macbeth in William Shakespeare's *Macbeth* (1606) and Creon in Sophocles' *Antigone* (c. 441 B.C.) are commonly cited as hubristic **characters.** Macbeth's hubris (specifically, his proud ambition) leads him to murder King Duncan in order to ascend to the throne. This act, in flagrant and bloody violation of divine and moral rules, ultimately results in Macbeth's own death. Creon, ruler of Thebes, explicitly rejects the prophet Tiresias's warning of impending death should he unjustly condemn Antigone. Convinced that he knows best, Creon condemns Antigone for disobeying him, knowing that she did so following the dictates of the gods. He consequently experiences the suicides of his wife and son as well as the death of Antigone just before he can reverse his decision. Contemporary movie protagonists who are taken down by hubris include the title character (played by Klaus Kinski) in Werner Herzog's *Aguirre, the Wrath of God* (1972) and the idealist father (played by Harrison Ford) in Peter Weir's *The Mosquito Coast* (1986; based on Paul Theroux's 1982 novel of the same name).

Hudibrastic verse: Deliberate **doggerel** in octosyllabic **couplets** composed in **iambic tetrameter,** modeled on Samuel Butler's **mock heroic** poem *Hudibras* (1663). Like all intentional doggerel, Hudibrastic verse aims for outrageous humor, deploying an arsenal of unlikely and therefore ridiculous-sounding **half-, double,** and **triple rhymes.** Such verse also often **satirizes** individuals or institutions.

EXAMPLE: A passage from Butler's *Hudibras* follows:

> Beside 'tis known he could speak *Greek,*
> As naturally as Pigs squeek:
> That *Latin* was no more difficile,
> Then to a Blackbird 'tis to whistle.
> Being rich in both he never scanted
> His Bounty unto such as wanted;
> But much of either would afford

To many that had not one word.
For *Hebrew* Roots, although th' are found
To flourish most in barren ground,
He had plenty, as suffic'd
To make some think him circumcis'd. . . .

humours: A physiological **theory** subscribed to during ancient times, the **Medieval Period,** and the **Renaissance** that held that the relative amounts of or balance between the four main fluids (humours) of the body — blood, phlegm, yellow bile, and black bile — determined an individual's state of health and even general personality. The four humours were also associated with the four elements: blood with air (hot and moist), phlegm with water (cold and moist), yellow bile with fire (hot and dry), and black bile with earth (cold and dry). The term *humour* comes from the Latin *humor,* meaning "moisture."

Adherents of this popular theory believed that the humours emitted vapors that rose to the brain, thus affecting both behavior and health. As long as the humours were in balance, the individual supposedly exhibited a perfect temperament and no illness, but an imbalance affected behavior in a very specific way. That is, an excess of blood produced a sanguine (happy) personality, phlegm a phlegmatic (cowardly, passive) personality, yellow bile a choleric (argumentative, stubborn) personality, and black bile a bilious (melancholy) one. Just as an imbalance produced a distinct behavioral effect, so would it produce illness and disease.

This theory was so commonly accepted that it made its way into popular culture and literature. Individuals (or literary **characters**) came to be classified according to their humour, and the word *humour* itself came to signify a variety of things from disposition or mood to peculiarity or affectation, particularly in **Elizabethan** times. Many works of literature even relied on this theory for **characterization** and to provide convincing **motivation** for the characters' actions.

See also **comedy of humours.**

hybris: See **hubris.**

hymn: A song of praise, usually written in **verse.** The word *hymn* comes from the Greek *hymnos,* meaning a song of praise to a god, human hero, or idea. Religious hymns praise God or another deity. Literary hymns may make religious references or employ religious terminology but are frequently written solely in praise of some secular ideal, attitude, person, figure, or object. Literary hymns are often very similar to **odes** and are meant to be read rather than sung. The widespread use and popularity of hymns had a significant impact on **versification,** particularly in English, German, and the Romance languages.

EXAMPLES: "Onward Christian Soldiers" (1871) is a religious hymn, whereas Algernon Charles Swinburne's "Hymn to Proserpine" (1866) is a literary hymn, even though it is ostensibly addressed to a goddess.

hyperbaton (anastrophe): A **rhetorical figure** involving a reversal of word order to make a point. The most famous example is Sir Winston Churchill's **witty** example of how grammatical propriety — in this case, the rule that says sentences should never end with prepositions — can produce terrible results: "This is the sort of English up with which I will not put!"

hyperbole: A **figure of speech** that uses deliberate exaggeration to achieve an effect, whether serious, **comic,** or **ironic.** Some critics refer to hyperbole as *overstatement.*

EXAMPLES: The following statement, made with reference to the murderous Lady Macbeth in William Shakespeare's **tragedy,** *Macbeth* (1606), is an example of hyperbole: "All the perfumes of Arabia / Will not sweeten this little hand." Oscar Wilde used hyperbole in this comment about Walter Pater's *The Renaissance* (1873–93): "It is my golden book; I never travel anywhere without it. But it is the very flower of decadence; the last trumpet should have sounded the moment it was written." Hyperbole and overstatement are staples of popular music, especially love songs. In the 1960s, Skeeter Davis lamented that the world ended the day her boyfriend said goodbye; in the 1980s, Modern English swore they would "stop the world" and "melt" in love's embrace; in the 1990s, the Proclaimers asserted they would "walk five hundred miles" for a lover. The title of Bruce Springsteen's song "57 Channels (And Nothin' On)" (1992) pointedly exemplifies hyperbole.

hyperlinks: See **linking.** See also **cyberfiction.**

hypertext: In its most common usage as a computer term, a document retrieval network that permits the user to access any of a group of linked documents by clicking on a jump marker, or **link structure.** Each of the documents contained in this network appears in full-text form on the computer screen; once users access one document, they can jump to other documents at will.

Increasingly, hypertext is providing literary scholars with the means of storing and conveniently linking textual editions and textual variants, not only with one another but also with contextual (including visual) materials. Jerome J. McGann's "hypermedia environment" archival edition of *The Complete Writings and Pictures of Dante Gabriel Rossetti,* available on the World Wide Web as The Rossetti Archive (2000–) and on a CD-ROM by the University of Michigan Press, is a good example of hypertextual scholarship.

Hypertext is as much the **site** of theoretical debate as it is the locus of new scholarly initiatives. Ted Nelson coined the term *hypertext* in 1965 to refer to computer-presented documents that represent ideas in a nonlinear, as opposed to an authorially organized, way. Nelson contrasted hypertext with the linear mode of presentation typically used in other media: most notably books, movies, and speeches. Adapted to the literary arena, *hypertext* refers to writing that is nonlinear or nonsequential.

Contemporary literary critics and theoreticians have increasingly expressed an interest in the application of hypertext — or, perhaps more precisely, in the amalgam of linked, yet nonlinear, elements it represents — to literary theory. They have explored the connection between hypertext and literary theory generally, as well as between hypertext and specific theoretical approaches, such as **deconstruction, narratology, the new historicism, and cultural criticism.** Although these critics often differ in their emphases and applications, most agree that the very existence and concept of hypertext alters our conception of the **text,** which traditionally has been thought of as a linear construct with a beginning, middle, and end determined by the author. As Gunnar Liestøl wrote in an essay entitled "Wittgenstein, Genette, and the Reader's Narrative" (1994), the "facilities of manipulation, individual navigation, and freedom from given, authoritative structures provide us with new practices of reading and writing." Liestøl is quick to note, however, that traditional print-age reading and writing have always been "subject to complications and oppositions."

Hypertext portends a much more active role for the reader and, in tandem, a less controlling one for the author, although the author does retain some modicum of control, if only because someone must set up the **links** and nodes that the reader will use.

See also **cyberfiction.**

hypertext fiction: See **cyberfiction.**

hypotaxis, hypotactic style: See **style.**

hysteron proteron: A **figurative** device involving achronology or an apparent chronological reversal.

EXAMPLE: In William Shakespeare's *Antony and Cleopatra* (1607), Mark Antony's friend Enobarbus says that retreating ships "fly and turn the rudder." Presumably, the ships turned around before retreating.

I
---

iamb(ic)(us): A **metrical foot** consisting of two syllables, an unaccented syllable (˘) followed by an **accented** one (´). The iamb is the most common metrical foot in English poetry.

EXAMPLES: afloat, respect, in love. In "A Slumber Did My Spirit Seal" (1800), one of his famous "Lucy" poems, William Wordsworth alternates iambic **tetrameter** and iambic **trimeter:**

> A slumber did my spirit seal;
> I had no human fears:
> She seemed a thing that could not feel
> The touch of earthly years.
> No motion has she now, no force;
> She neither hears nor sees;
> Rolled round in earth's diurnal course,
> With rocks, and stones, and trees.

Countee Cullen, a poet associated with the **Harlem Renaissance,** mainly employs iambic **pentameter** in "Yet Do I Marvel" (1925).

icon: A type of **sign** that signifies what it **represents** by its inherent similarity to that object, person, or place. A drawing of a bird could be an icon for *bird,* a miniature model ship could be an icon for *ship,* and a map or diagram could be an icon of a particular geographical area. The term also has a specialized religious application, one that refers to a depiction (such as a portrait or a statue) of a religious leader or figure. *Icon* is distinguished from *index,* a term used to refer to another type of sign, in that an index does not have an inherent similarity to what it signifies so much as it has some natural cause-effect relation to it. Thus a drawing of a fire would be an "icon-sign" for *fire,* but smoke would be an "index-sign" for it.

In the **lexicon** of computer technology, icons are pictorial signs indicating files, applications, and especially programs and groups of programs.

iconography: The **representation** of biblical (or, more broadly, any religious) figures in painting and sculpture with an eye to **symbolic** significance. Iconography in most religions encompasses a set of established **conventions** to which the artist must adhere in the portrayal of the subject matter. Iconography can also refer to the study of any subject (not just religious) represented in the visual arts, the conventions governing its representation, and the symbolic significance of the resulting work of art.

id: According to Austrian psychoanalyst Sigmund Freud, the component of the psyche that generates our instinctual physical, especially libidinal, desires. The id itself is often described as insatiable and pleasure-seeking (whether seeking food, sexual gratification, etc.); it does not consider the consequences or the implications of its desires or the actions it would take to satisfy those desires.

Freud believed the psyche has two other components. The *superego,* the component of the psyche that has internalized the mores and norms of society, is the opposite of the id. The *ego* attempts to mediate between the id and the superego in the context of reality and the demands and possibilities it creates for the individual.

ideology: A set of beliefs underlying the customs, habits, and practices common to a given social group. To members of that group, the beliefs seem obviously true, natural, and even universally applicable. They may seem just as obviously arbitrary, idiosyncratic, and even false to those who adhere to another ideology. Within a society, several ideologies may coexist; one or more of these may be dominant.

Ideologies may be forcefully imposed or willingly subscribed to. Their component beliefs may be held consciously or unconsciously. In either case, they come to form what Johanna M. Smith has called "the unexamined ground of our experience." Ideology governs our perceptions, judgments, and prejudices — our sense of what is acceptable, normal, and deviant. Ideology may cause a revolution; it may also allow discrimination and even exploitation.

Ideologies are of special interest to politically oriented critics of literature because of the way in which authors reflect or resist prevailing views in their **texts.** Some **Marxist critics** have argued that literary texts reflect and reproduce the ideologies that produced them; most, however, have shown how ideologies are riven with contradictions that works of literature manage to expose and widen. Other Marxist critics have focused on the way in which texts themselves are characterized by **gaps, conflicts,** and contradictions between their ideological and anti-ideological functions. Fredric Jameson, an American Marxist critic, argues that all thought is ideological, but that ideological thought that knows itself as such stands the chance of seeing through and transcending ideology.

Not all of the politically oriented critics interested in ideology have been **Marxists.** Certain non-Marxist **feminist critics** have addressed the question of ideology by seeking to expose (and thereby call into question) the **patriarchal** ideology mirrored or inscribed in works written by men — even men who have sought to counter sexism and break down sexual stereotypes. **New historicists** have been interested in demonstrating the ideological underpinnings not only of literary **representations** but also of our interpretations of them.

idyll (idyl): A **narrative** work — usually short, descriptive, and composed in **verse** — that depicts and exalts **pastoral** virtues and scenes. The subject of the simple shepherd's life is a typical one. The term *idyll* derives from the *Idylls* of Theocritus, a third-century B.C. Greek poet who composed idealized depictions of rustic life in the Sicilian countryside. **Renaissance** writers imitated the **classical** tradition, but several poets of the **Romantic Period** tried to reduce the artificiality of the **genre** by introducing elements that more **realistically** depicted the problems, passions, and expressions of rural people. Alfred, Lord Tennyson, whose *Idylls of the King* (1859–72) is renowned, rejected the idyll's traditional pastoral mode but retained the concept of an ideal life away (in time as well as place) from the hustle and bustle of a complex contemporary society. Idylls often have a formal or artificial quality because they tend to be composed from the viewpoint of a "civilized" society that longs for some more primal, natural, or innocent place untouched by the pace and stresses of civilized life. Movies in which the idyllic setting is **thematically** important include Frank Capra's *Lost Horizon* (1937), Joshua Logan's *South Pacific* (1958), and the Brooke Shields vehicle *The Blue Lagoon* (1980).

illisible **(unreaderly):** See **poststructuralism, text.**

illocutionary act: A term used in John R. Searle's expansion of John Austin's **speech-act theory** to refer to a **locution** (the utterance of a statement) that performs a particular function. The statement may assert something, or it may order, promise, question, threaten, and so forth.

The illocutionary act is one of four types of speech acts; the other three are the **utterance act** — saying something; the **propositional act** — referring to an object upon which something is predicated (saying something about something else); and the **perlocutionary act** — an illocutionary act that affects the state of mind and/or the actions of the person to whom it has been directed (when an illocutionary act is both understood and has some type of effect on the hearer, it is also called a perlocutionary act).

EXAMPLE: A bully says to Bart, "If you tell the secret, I'll kill you." As an illocutionary act, this statement is a threat. The locution "I'll take the children with me" has multiple illocutionary possibilities. It could simply be an assertion of truth, or it could be a promise. If a man says this to an ex-wife who has sole custody of their children, however, the ex-wife would probably perceive this as a threat. If the statement scared her or caused her to move to another city, a perlocutionary act would have occurred as well.

image: Most commonly, a visual, physical **representation** of something (such as a photograph) or a mental picture of some visible thing or things. Images can also involve senses other than sight and sensations such as movement and pressure. The sound of musical chords, the smell of freshly cut grass, or the heat of the sun can contribute as much to an image we may have of ourselves playing the guitar outside on a hot summer's day as the visible shape of the guitar or the greenness of the grass. At its extreme, *image* may be used to mean "idea" or even "vision"; in speaking of a slave living in the antebellum South, for instance, one might speak of his or her image of Canada. Used in that way, *image* refers not to the way Canada looks but, rather, the way the slave perceives Canada intellectually — as a place of freedom.

As an artistic term, *image* usually refers to an artistic representation of the visible world (for example, "Monet painted images of water lilies") and to the mental impressions conjured up by such a representation. When used specifically as a literary term, *image* most often **denotes** descriptive terms or **figurative language** used to produce mental impressions in the mind of the reader — and to the impressions themselves. Often these impressions or pictures are visual in nature, but not always, as the following sentence from Jayne Anne Phillips's novel *Shelter* (1994) aptly demonstrates:

> She felt the tug of memory, an image that pulled at her consciousness like a fish on a line.

The following **stanza** from John Keats's "Ode to a Nightingale" (1819) also demonstrates that images can involve a wide range of sensory perceptions and sensations:

> I cannot see what flowers are at my feet,
>   Nor what soft incense hangs upon the boughs,
> But, in embalmèd darkness, guess each sweet
>   Wherewith the seasonable month endows
> The grass, the thicket, and the fruit-tree wild;
>   White hawthorn, and the pastoral eglantine;
>   Fast fading violets cover'd up in leaves;
>   And mid-May's eldest child,
>   The coming musk-rose, full of dewy wine,
>   The murmurous haunt of flies on summer eves.

In its artistic and literary as well as in its more general usage, the term *image* may be used to mean "vision" or "idea"; one can speak of an artist's or author's "image" of something (such as life and death, suffering, or marriage) to mean his or her conception of that thing.

imagery: A term used to refer to: (1) the actual language that a writer uses to convey a visual picture (or, most critics would add, to create or **represent** any sensory experience); and (2) the use of **figures of speech**, often to express **abstract** ideas in a vivid and innovative way. Imagery of this second type makes use of such devices as **simile, personification,** and **metonymy,** among many others.

Imagery is a central component of almost all **imaginative** literature and is often said to be the chief element in poetry. Two major types of imagery exist — the literal and the **figurative.** Literal imagery is purely descriptive, representing an object or event with words that draw on or appeal to the kind of experiences gained through the five senses (sight, sound, touch, taste, and smell). Figurative imagery may call to mind real things that can be perceived by the senses, but it does so as a way of describing something else — often some abstract idea that cannot be literally or directly described (for example, Emily Dickinson's "'Hope' is the thing with feathers"). Whether literal or figurative, however, imagery is generally intended to make whatever the author is describing **concrete** in the reader's mind, to give it some tangible and real existence rather than a purely intellectual one. Imagery also provides the reader with a sense of vividness and immediacy.

Imagery also has a specific and special relation to **symbolism.** All symbols depend on **images,** images that are often repeated to give the symbol cogency and depth. In Toni Morrison's novel *Beloved* (1987), the repeated description of Sethe's scarred back as wrought iron or as a tree serves to make her a symbol of the slave's extraordinary physical and spiritual suffering and strength. Some critics have suggested that the key to unlocking the meaning of a work lies in identifying its image patterns and understanding how they work together to suggest or symbolize larger meanings or **themes.** These critics believe that the pattern of imagery in a work more truly reveals the work's meaning than anything explicitly stated by a speaker, **narrator,** or author. **The New Critics,** in particular, have examined and analyzed the interrelation among images and their relevance to interpretation.

FURTHER EXAMPLES: In his poem "Fish" (1922), D. H. Lawrence uses striking imagery to create the visual picture (and tactile sensation) of a fish on a line. The speaker says that he has:

> Unhooked his gorping, water-horny mouth,
> And seen his horror-tilted eye,
> His red-gold, water-precious, mirror-flat bright eye;
> And felt him beat in my hand, with his mucous, leaping
>   life-throb.

In her poem "The Fish" (1946), Elizabeth Bishop also uses imagery to describe a hooked fish. However, whereas Lawrence almost humanizes his subject with the image of the "horror-tilted eye," Bishop's imagery involves figurative comparisons with inanimate objects in the world above the surface:

> I looked into his eyes
> which were far larger than mine
> but shallower, and yellowed,
> the irises backed and packed
> with tarnished tinfoil
> seen through the lenses
> of old scratched isinglass.
> They shifted a little, but not
> to return my stare.

Marianne Moore, who has also written a poem entitled "The Fish" (1921), uses imagery that conveys a precise verbal picture while at the same time figuring her undersea subjects in such a way as to relate them to the terrestrial world:

> The Fish
> wade
> through black jade.
>   Of the crow-blue mussel-shells, one keeps
>   adjusting the ash-heaps;
>   opening and shutting itself like
> an
> injured fan.

Imaginary order: Along with **the Real** and the **Symbolic order,** one of the three orders of **subjectivity** according to the **psychoanalytic** theorist and critic Jacques Lacan. The Imaginary order is most closely associated with the five senses (sight, sound, touch, taste, and smell). The human infant, who is wholly dependent on others for a prolonged period, enters the Imaginary order when it begins to experience a unity of body parts and motor control that is empowering. This change, in which the child anticipates mastery of its body, occurs between the ages of six and eighteen months, during what Lacan called the "mirror stage," or "mirror phase," of human development. At the onset of the mirror stage — that is, upon entering the Imaginary order — the child identifies with the image of wholeness (that is, seeing its own image in the mirror, experiencing its mother as a whole body, and so on). This sense of oneness, and also of difference from others (especially the mother or primary caretaker), is established through an **image** or a vision of harmony that is both a mirroring and a "mirage of maturation" (a false sense of individuality and independence).

The Imaginary is a **metaphor** for unity, is related to the visual order, and is always part of human **subjectivity.** Because the subject is fundamentally separate from others and also internally divided (conscious / unconscious), the apparent coherence of the Imaginary, its fullness and grandiosity, is always false, a *mis*recognition that the ego (or "me") tries to deny by imagining itself as coherent and empowered.

The Imaginary, which operates in conjunction with the Real and Symbolic, is not a "stage" of development equivalent to Freud's "preoedipal stage," nor is it prelinguistic. The concept of the Imaginary — like Lacan's "schema" and terminology more generally — has proved useful to psychoanalytic and **poststructuralist** critics analyzing the unities and disunities within **texts.**

See also **the Real, Symbolic order.**

imagination: A term that has meant different things at different times, *imagination* was associated in the **Renaissance** with poetry and was understood to be the opposite of *reason.* In the later, **Neoclassical Period** the term was used simply to refer to the mind's power to call up **images** (especially visual images). Then, in the late eighteenth century, imagination once again came to be seen primarily in opposition to reason and as a source of **aesthetic** pleasure. **Romantic** theorists such as William Wordsworth and Samuel Taylor Coleridge gave imagination a much greater value, however, **privileging** it above **fancy** as the creative and unifying faculty of the mind, the faculty that reveals higher truths through **organic** rather than **mechanical** processes.

See **fancy** for Coleridge's distinction between imagination and fancy.

imagism: A school of **poetry** that flourished in North America and England, and especially in the United States, at the beginning of the twentieth century. Imagists rejected the **sentimentalism** of late-nineteenth-century verse in favor of a poetry that relied on **concrete imagery.** Ezra Pound originally led the movement, which drew upon T. E. Hulme's poetic theory, but Amy Lowell soon became its most famous proponent; "Amygism" was first used by the displaced Pound to refer derogatorily to the movement.

In a collection of imagist poems that Lowell edited called *Some Imagist Poets* (three volumes, published annually from 1915 to 1917), she formally outlined the major objectives or criteria of the Imagists, who believed that poetry should: (1) regularly use everyday speech, but avoid **clichés;** (2) create new **rhythms;** (3) address any subject matter the poet desired; and (4) depict its subjects through precise, clear **images.** Imagist poems, which are typically written in **free verse,** are generally short since Imagists seek above all else to write concentrated poetry. They seek to render the poet's response to a visual impression as concisely and precisely as possible; in this, at least, the influence of such short nature poems as the Japanese **haiku** is obvious. Those taking part in the imagist movement included H. D. (Hilda Doolittle), Carl Sandburg, F. S. Flint, Richard Aldington, D. H. Lawrence, and William Carlos Williams.

Imagism itself, although comparatively short-lived as a movement, had a wide-ranging **influence** on subsequent poetry of the twentieth century, which continues to employ and juxtapose precise images.

EXAMPLE: William Carlos Williams's "The Red Wheelbarrow" (1923) presents a single concrete image that exemplifies his edict about poetry, "No ideas but in things":

> so much depends
> upon
>
> a red wheel
> barrow
>
> glazed with rain
> water
>
> beside the white
> chickens.

imitation: As a literary term, (1) a synonym for *mimesis*, a Greek term used by literary critics to refer to the **representation** of reality in literature; (2) the practice of modeling one's writing after the established **forms** and **styles** of a particular **genre.**

The mimetic sense of imitation derives from the *Poetics* (c. 330 B.C.) in which Aristotle discusses the transference of human action through the vehicle of poetry, which he subdivides under headings such as **comedy, tragedy,** and **epic.** Aristotle also discusses what types of action ought to be "imitated" (presented via verbal art to the reader), as well as how (and in what form) imitation should be accomplished, noting especially that the poet should present actions that show the relationship between life and art. Briefly put, Aristotle argued that art imitates nature, but that it should do so in a selective manner. A good part of the poet's artistry goes into choosing and arranging the events and elements that ought to be **narrated;** one does not simply represent any action in any manner or mimic that action precisely as one views or experiences it. This view of poetry as a special imitation of human actions prevailed until the **Romantic Period,** although critics disagreed about the details (such as which actions were worthy of being represented). By the nineteenth century, however, a new view of poetry had begun to emerge that placed a premium on poetry not as a translation or record of human actions but rather as the personal, private expression of a poet's feelings and imaginings.

Imitation as used in the second sense was a common and acceptable practice up until the Romantic Period, which championed originality and individual expression. Writers were encouraged to imitate the established forms and styles of the genre in which they were writing in order to learn the art of composition. Our romantic heritage (and attendant definitions of plagiarism) inclines us to disparage imitation as a literary practice today, but it was regarded throughout most of literary history as a proper and useful practice. However, simple copying has never been considered art, and critics have long believed that no writer could achieve the form and spirit of the **classics** without a certain cultivated talent.

imperfect rhyme: See **half-rhyme.**

implied author: A term used by critic Wayne C. Booth in place of the term **voice** (what Aristotle called *ethos*) to refer to the unique and pervasive human **presence** that the reader senses is the driving force behind a literary work. Booth distinguishes the implied author from the real author, arguing that the implied author is as much a creation of the real author as any other element in the work. As Booth puts it, the implied author is an "ideal, literary, created version" of the real author. In a sense, the implied author is the **character** or **persona** that the real author creates to **represent** himself or herself to the reader.

implied reader: A phrase coined by **reader-response critic** Wolfgang Iser and used by other reader-response critics in contradistinction to the phrase "actual reader." Whereas the actual reader could be any individual who happens to have read or to be reading the **text,** the implied reader is the reader intended, even created, by the text. Iser calls this implied reader a "construct" of the text who "embodies all those predispositions necessary for a literary work to exercise its effect." Unlike the implied reader, real readers bring their own experiences and preconceptions to the text — and thus their own idiosyncratic modes of perception and interpretation. Other reader-response critics seeking to describe the implied reader have used other terms. Stanley Fish has spoken of the "informed reader" and Gérard Genette and Gerald Prince have referred to the "narratee," who is "the necessary counterpart of a given narrator."

impressionism: As a literary term, writing that seeks to capture fleeting impressions of **characters, settings,** and events, depicted **subjectively** as they appear through the filter of the writer's moods and personal perceptions. Impressionist works thus tend to be short on **objective, concrete** details of the kind we associate with conventional settings and **plots** but detailed in their presentation of characters' emotions, thoughts, and perceptions. The **French Symbolists,** other writers active in the **Aesthetic Movement,** and **stream-of-consciousness** novelists have all been termed impressionists or, at least, impressionistic in their writing.

Literary impressionism took its name from the famous nineteenth-century French movement in painting. Artists such as Édouard Manet, Claude Monet, and Edgar Degas believed that an individual's subjective impression of any given thing is a legitimate artistic subject, indeed, that it is more important for painters to render their impressions of objects, people, and scenery than to produce technically precise representations of them. Impressionist painters often worked directly from nature, seeking to capture fleeting moments on canvas in accordance with the artist's subjective experience of "seeing." These painters also emphasized visual sensations, using bright color and striving to depict the ephemeral effects of light.

impressionistic criticism: A type of **criticism** that centers on the critic's **subjective** impressions, that is, on the feelings elicited and associations prompted by the experience of the work rather than on the thoughts arising from a rigorous, intellectual analysis of it. Anatole France has said that impressionistic criticism records "the adventures of a sensitive soul among masterpieces."

incremental repetition: A device commonly used in **ballads** that involves the repetition of lines or phrases in successive **stanzas** or within a stanza itself with subtle modifications or additions to advance the story line. Incremental repetition sometimes employs a question-and-answer format, and the incremental repetition is often found in the last line of each stanza.

EXAMPLES: The **refrain** of each stanza of Emily Brontë's poem "November, 1837" exhibits incremental repetition:

The night is darkening round me,
The wild winds coldly blow;
But a tyrant spell has bound me
And I cannot, cannot go.

The giant trees are bending
Their bare boughs weighed with snow,
And the storm is fast descending
And yet I cannot go.

Clouds beyond clouds above me,
Wastes beyond wastes below;
But nothing drear can move me;
I will not, cannot go.

Trumbull Stickney's **euphonious** poem "Mnemosyne" (1902) also utilizes incremental repetition:

It's autumn in the country I remember.

How warm a wind blew here about the ways!
And shadows on the hillside lay to slumber
During the long sun-sweetened summer days.

It's cold abroad the country I remember.

The swallows veering skimmed the golden grain
At midday with a wing aslant and limber;
And yellow cattle browsed upon the plain.

It's empty down the country I remember.

I had a sister lovely in my sight:
Her hair was dark, her eyes were very sombre;
We sang together in the woods at night.

index: See **icon.**

indirect discourse: See **free indirect discourse.**

influence: A term used by literary historians to describe the effect of a writer or writers (whether disparately or as part of a school) on subsequent writers and their work. The later writer typically adopts some of the features (**style,** choice of subject matter, etc.) characteristic of the influential, earlier writer's work while slightly or radically modifying others. Walter Jackson Bate's *The Burden of the Past in English Poetry* (1970) revitalized the study of literary influence. More recently, revisionist critic Harold Bloom has challenged conventional conceptions of influence in his book *The Anxiety of Influence* (1973), in which he suggests that the writing of all strong poets involves the rewriting of earlier strong poets and that this rewriting always and inevitably involves one or another form of misprision, a kind of misreading that allows the later writer's creativity to emerge.

See also **anxiety of influence.**

in medias res: Latin for "in the middle of things," the technique of beginning a **narrative** in the middle of the action. Crucial events that occurred before the point at which the narrative actually begins are related at some appropriate later time, generally through one or more **flashbacks.** Beginning *in medias res* is a **convention** associated primarily with the **epic,** but the technique has also been used in other types of literary works to "hook" the reader or audience.

EXAMPLES: Book 1 of John Milton's *Paradise Lost* (1667) opens in hell, into which Satan and other fallen angels have been hurled as a result of an unsuccessful attempt to overthrow God in Heaven. This civil war between Satan's forces and those of God is not described until Book 6, which means that Milton's epic begins *in medias res,* in the middle of things.

A more contemporary example of a work beginning *in medias res* is the movie *The Usual Suspects* (1995), which opens with Verbal, the rather **ironically** named **narrator,** recounting an incredible story involving the elusive Keyser Soze to the local district attorney. As Verbal narrates the story, the movie flashes back to the events themselves.

intention: Long used by literary scholars and critics to refer to an author's stated or unstated purpose in writing a work, the term was given particular meaning by the German philosopher Edmund Husserl and **hermeneutical theorists** of interpretation such as E. D. Hirsch.

Husserl used *intention* in connection with **phenomenology,** a philosophical school of thought and method of analysis that holds that objects attain meaning only as they are perceived in someone's consciousness. In analyzing human consciousness, Husserl argued that consciousness is intentional, that is, directed toward an object; as long as we are conscious, we are perceiving something. Husserl's use of *intentional* does not accord with the traditional dictionary definition, "deliberate." Rather, intentionality in phenomenology simply refers to awareness of an object. Husserl further argued that awareness of the object brings us into a reciprocal relationship with it.

Hirsch uses *intention* differently in his books *Validity in Interpretation* (1967) and *The Aims of Interpretation* (1976). He relates what he calls the author's "verbal intention" to the interpretation of a work, building his argument that "a text means what its author meant" on the nineteenth-century philosopher Wilhelm Dilthey's assertion that readers can in fact arrive at **objective** and valid interpretations of expressed authorial meaning. He does not equate intention with the author's mental state while writing but rather with the fundamental goal of creating something out of words that will mean a certain thing or things to readers familiar with the extant rules, **conventions,** and norms of reading and interpretation. In determining an author's verbal intentions, readers must gather evidence from a variety of sources. Biographical, historical, and cultural contexts are important, as are other works by the same author. Knowledge of the conventions governing the **genre** in which the work is written is essential. Without reference to intentions and conventions, Hirsch argued, meanings remain elusive or even indeterminate, since no justifiable grounds exist for choosing one meaning over another. The Italian theorist Emilio Betti follows a similar line of argument.

See also **hermeneutics.**

intentional fallacy: A term coined by William K. Wimsatt and Monroe C. Beardsley, in an essay first published in the 1940s, to refer to the practice of basing interpretations on the expressed or implied **intentions** of authors, a practice they judged to be erroneous. As proponents of **the New Criticism,** a type of **formalism,** they argued that a work of literature is an object in itself and should be studied as such. They believed that it is sometimes helpful to learn what an author intended, but the critic's real purpose is to show what is actually in the **text,** not what an author intended to put there.

See also **authorial intention.**

interior monologue: A mode of **narrative** intended to reveal to the reader the **subjective** thoughts, emotions, and fleeting sensations experienced by a **character.** Interior monologue is a type of **stream of consciousness,** in which a character's subjective and ever-flowing mental commentary and observation are presented, usually through **free indirect discourse.** The ebb and flow of the psyche revealed by interior monologue typically exists at a pre- or sublinguistic level; this interior life is expressed more powerfully through **images** and the **connotations** they evoke than through straightforward, **denotative** narrative. Interior monologue functions much as **soliloquy** does in drama, rendering individual thought processes that go unexpressed in conversation or **dialogue.**

An interior monologue can be either *direct* or *indirect.* In a direct interior monologue, the author presents the character's inner thoughts and emotions transparently in a seemingly uninterrupted, random manner straight from the character's inner mind. When indirect interior monologue is used, the author selects — and may comment upon — elements from the stream of consciousness.

EXAMPLES: An early example of interior monologue is Laurence Sterne's *Tristram Shandy* (1760–67). Édouard Dujardin is usually credited with the first sustained use of this technique, which he relied upon heavily in his pioneering novel *Les lauriers sont coupés* (*We'll to the Woods No More*) (1888). The end of James Joyce's *Ulysses* (1922) consists of an interior monologue by Molly Bloom.

internal rhyme: Rhyme that occurs within a line of **verse.**

EXAMPLES: Edward Lear uses internal rhyme to achieve a comic effect in the following lines from his poem "The Owl and the Pussycat" (1942): "They took some honey, and plenty of money / Wrapped in a five pound note."

The following **stanza** from William Wordsworth's "We Are Seven" (1798), in which a child being questioned by an adult describes the graves of her brother and sister, contains three internal rhymes (*green* and *seen, more* and *door, side* and *side*) in addition to one **end-rhyme** (*replied* and *side*):

> "Their graves are green, they may be seen,"
> The little maid replied,
> "Twelve steps or more from my mother's door,
> And they are side by side."

interpretive communities: A term used by **reader-response critic** Stanley Fish to acknowledge the existence of multiple and diverse reading groups within any large reading population. Fish argues that the meaning of a given **text** may differ significantly from group to group. (College students reading novels in academic courses form an interpretive community that is likely to read a famous work of **detective fiction** differently from the way it would be read by retirees living in adult communities.) Different interpretive communities, Fish argues, share different reading goals and strategies; whether a given interpretation appears correct or logical to members of an interpretive community will depend greatly on whether it fits in with their shared assumptions, motives, and methods. Thus, Fish suggests, no interpretation is likely to be considered valid by everyone; multiple interpretations are not only possible, but probably inevitable. On the other hand, certain interpretations are likely to be shared by most members of a given interpretive community. In formulating the concept of interpretive communities, Fish substantially moderated a stand he had taken earlier while developing a different concept, that of **affective stylistics.** At that time, Fish had suggested that meaning is an "event" that takes place in the mind of an individual reader during the act of reading. In developing the theory of interpretive communities, Fish came to view affective stylistics as one of several possible reading strategies.

intertextuality: The condition of interconnectedness among **texts,** or the concept that any text is an amalgam of others, either because it exhibits signs of **influence** or because its language inevitably contains common points of reference with other texts through such things as **allusion,** quotation, **genre, style,** and even revisions. The critic Julia Kristeva, who popularized and is often credited with coining this term, views any given work as part of a larger fabric of literary **discourse,** part of a continuum including the future as well as the past. Other critics have argued for an even broader use and understanding of the term *intertextuality*, maintaining that literary history per se is too narrow a context within which to read and understand a literary text. When understood this way, *intertextuality* could be used by a **new historicist** or **cultural critic** to refer to the significant interconnectedness between a literary text and contemporary, nonliterary discussions of the issues represented in the literary text. Or it could be used by a **poststructuralist** to suggest that a work of literature can only be recognized and read within a vast field of **signs** and **tropes** that is like a text and that makes any single text self-contradictory and **undecidable**.

EXAMPLES: In his article "Ben Okri's *The Landscapes Within*: A Metaphor for Personal and National Development" (1988), Abioseh Michael Porter explores how Nigerian writer Ben Okri draws on and plays off a variety of other sources, including Ayi Kwei Armah's *The Beautiful Ones Are Not Yet Born* (1968) and James Joyce's *A Portrait of the Artist as a Young Man* (1916), in his **Künstlerroman** *The Landscapes Within* (1981).

Covers from *The New Yorker* magazine frequently exhibit intertextuality. For an example, see page 221.

intrigue: See **plot**.

intrusive narrator: See **narrator, omniscient point of view**.

invocation: A direct and explicit request for help in writing (usually verse) made to a divine or supernatural entity. **Classical convention** typically required such an address to the **muses** (in the **epic**, the address was usually directed to Calliope, the muse of epic poetry, or to Clio, the muse of history). Invocations remained relatively common through the **Neoclassical Period** but are rare today.

EXAMPLE: At the beginning of his cosmic seventeenth-century epic *Paradise Lost* (1667), John Milton invokes Urania, the muse of astronomy in antiquity, remade by Christian writers of the **Renaissance** into a heavenly, Christian muse.

Irish Literary Renaissance, Irish Revival: See **Celtic Renaissance**.

irony: A contradiction or incongruity between appearance or expectation and reality. This disparity may be manifested in a variety of ways. A discrepancy may exist between what someone says and what he or she actually means, between what someone expects to happen and what really does happen, or between what appears to be true and what actually is true. Furthermore, the term *irony* may be applied to events, situations, and even structural elements of a work, not just to statements. Irony is commonly employed as a "wink" that the listener or reader is expected to notice so that he or she may be "in on the secret." An irony that goes unnoticed, after all, fails to achieve its effect. Speakers and authors may even use irony as a general mode of expression rather than to make discrete ironic statements. In this sense, one might describe an author's very **tone** as ironic.

Irony comes from the Greek *eiron*, which itself derives from *eironeia*, meaning "dissembling." In Greek drama, the *eiron* was a **character** who, although weaker than his opponent, the braggart *alazon*, nevertheless de-

intertextuality: The January 8, 2001, cover of *The New Yorker* shown above, which depicts a baby wrapped in a "2001" banner who is reaching up to a giant monolith, intertextually alludes to Arthur C. Clarke's *Space Odyssey* series (1968–97), Stanley Kubrick's film *2001: A Space Odyssey* (1968), the tradition of New Year's Eve parties, the **convention** of **representing** the new year as a baby, and the **discourses** of millennialism.

feated him by misrepresenting himself in some way. The *eiron* often acted foolish or stupid, for instance, in order to fool the truly foolish and stupid *alazon*. **Meiosis,** or understatement, was perhaps the *eiron*'s most potent — and, to the audience, humorous — weapon. To this day, irony often depends on understatement, which requires the audience to recognize that the author, speaker, or character has purposely described something in a way that minimizes its evident significance.

Irony often gives the impression of deliberate restraint. Instead of flatly stating a point, the ironist's speech is often tongue-in-cheek, deliberately polished and refined. The ironist's approach to his or her subject may even seem unemotional, a wry illustration of his or her point. For this reason, irony has often been called the subtlest **rhetorical** form, for the success of an ironic statement or passage depends upon the audience's recognition of the discrepancy at issue. The ironist wears a mask that must at certain points be perceived as a mask. Irony's **paradoxical** nature makes it one of the most difficult forms to master.

Irony has also been called the subtlest **comic** form. Although understatement may give rise to raised eyebrows or even outright laughter, irony that evokes these reactions is more likely to be achieved through the use of **hyperbole,** or overstatement, which involves deliberate exaggeration. For instance, a speaker who ultimately sought to show up another's wartime record as inferior to his own might actually downplay his own Purple Heart even as he wildly extols his rival's promotion from private to corporal.

Irony should not be confused with either **sarcasm** or **satire;** although both sarcasm and satire frequently employ irony, the terms are all distinguishable. Sarcasm, which often involves an exaggerated form of irony, is at once more obvious, blunt, and nastier; a sarcastic remark is typically directed at a specific person, with the intent to wound and to ridicule. Irony is often directed toward a situation rather than toward a specific person; even when directed toward a person, irony generally lacks a hurtful aim. Furthermore, whereas sarcasm typically operates by heaping crude — and unfelt — praise on the individual, irony often employs blame. Irony must also be distinguished from satire, which ridicules human weaknesses in order to spur reform. The satirist derides humanity primarily in an effort to better it. Satire may involve irony, but irony typically lacks satire's ameliorative intent.

Several types of irony exist, all of which may be classified under one of three broad headings: *verbal irony, situational irony,* and *structural irony.*

Verbal irony, also called *rhetorical irony,* is the most common kind of irony. Verbal irony is characterized by a discrepancy between what a speaker or writer says and what he or she believes to be true. More specifically, a speaker or writer using verbal irony will say the opposite of what he or she actually means. For instance, imagine that you have come home after a day on which you failed a test, wrecked your car, and had a fight with your best friend. If your roommate were to ask you how your day went and you replied "Great day. Best ever," you would be using verbal irony. Similarly, the slang habit, popularized by the movie *Wayne's World* (1992), of adding "Not!" to the end of a patently false statement explicitly reveals the speaker's ironic (or sarcastic) intent. Usually, however, the clues are not quite so obvious, as when the **narrator** of Charles Dickens's *Oliver Twist* (1837) says that "the parish authorities magnanimously and humanely resolved that Oliver should be 'farmed,' or, in other words, dispatched to a branch workhouse some three miles off."

Verbal irony is sometimes viewed as one of the **tropes,** which are **figures of speech,** since it is a rhetorical device that involves saying one thing but meaning the opposite. Verbal irony can be the most difficult rhetorical device to master, since successful usage requires recognition by the reader or audience, even as it may demand authorial subtlety. Missing a verbal irony may lead the reader or audience to adopt a belief opposite to the one intended by the author. Tone probably keys the listener in to the irony more than any other element, but knowledge of the circumstances surrounding the statement may also spur recognition of the speaker's true meaning. The roommate from the aforementioned example might, for instance, pick up on the irony either via the speaker's tone or because he or she knew that the speaker had suffered one or more calamities that day. Since readers do not have the benefit of hearing a particular speaker's tone, knowledge and the general tone of the work play a greater role in accurately identifying ironic statements.

Situational irony, also called *irony of situation,* derives primarily from events or situations themselves, as opposed to statements made by any individual, whether or not that individual understands the situation as ironic. It typically involves a discrepancy between expectation and reality. For instance, situational irony existed when college-bound men in the Vietnam War era celebrated their avoidance of the draft, unaware that their exemption as college students was about to be revoked by Congress. Situational irony continued to exist even after the men learned about the revocation, provided that their college applications had been motivated solely by a desire to avoid the draft, the exemption was revoked after they went through the trouble of applying, and they actually got drafted. The scenarios described by Alanis Morissette in her song "Ironic" (1995) also exemplify situational irony: dying the day after you win the lottery; working up the courage to take your first airplane flight and then crashing; finding the man of your dreams only to discover that he has a beautiful wife; and so forth.

Literary examples of situational irony include O. Henry's "The Gift of the Magi" and the **mythic** story of King Midas. In "Gift of the Magi," both husband and wife give up their most prized possessions in order to give something to complement the other's most prized possession. The woman sells her beautiful long hair to buy a platinum fob chain for the man's watch; the man sells his watch to buy the woman tortoiseshell combs to hold up her hair. In the story of King Midas, Bacchus grants the king's wish that everything he touch be turned to gold; much to his chagrin, the king finds that this power does anything but enhance his *true* wealth when he hugs his beloved daughter, thereby (inadvertently) turning her to gold as well. A poetic example of situational irony is Percy Bysshe Shelley's "Ozymandias" (1818), in which "a traveller from an antique land" tells of coming upon a ruined statue, the pedestal of which reads "My name is Ozymandias, King of Kings: Look on my Works, ye Mighty, and despair!"

Three types of irony — *dramatic irony, tragic irony,* and *Socratic irony* — can be classified as situational irony. The term *dramatic irony* may be used to refer to a situation in which the character's own words come back to haunt him or her. However, it usually involves a discrepancy between a character's perception and what the reader or audience knows to be true. The reader or audience possesses some material information that the character lacks, and it is the character's imperfect information that motivates or explains his or her discordant response. The character may respond to a statement or situation in three ways: by making a statement, forming an expectation, or taking some action. A verbal response involves dramatic irony when a character fails to recognize the true import of his or her words; characters with partial information may thus assign meanings to their words that differ from the meanings assigned by the reader or audience. Expectation and action involve dramatic irony when they are inappropriate under the circumstances that actually exist. Characters may even accurately assess a situation without realizing it, attributing to someone or something a truth that they do not recognize as such.

Dramatic irony has often been used synonymously with *tragic irony,* but this usage is incorrect. Dramatic irony occurs in a wide variety of works, ranging from the **comic** to the **tragic.** Tragic irony is a type of dramatic irony marked by a sense of foreboding. As with all dramatic irony, tragic irony involves imperfect information, but the consequences of this ignorance are **catastrophic,** leading to the character's tragic downfall. The reader or audience experiences a sense of foreboding while anticipating this downfall. In Sophocles' *Oedipus Rex* (430 B.C.), for instance, Oedipus, the King of Thebes, vows to find the murderer of the prior king, only to find out something the audience knew all along: that Oedipus himself is the guilty party. Incidentally, neither dramatic nor tragic irony is limited to plays; both types of irony may appear in novels, movies, and other literary forms.

Socratic irony, also called *dialectical irony,* is, loosely speaking, situational in nature. The term stems from Plato's depiction of Socrates. In his early-fourth-century B.C. dialogues, Plato recounts Socrates' habitual practice of acting foolish or naive when questioning his fellow citizens. Having assumed the role of the *eiron,* Socrates successfully forced his "opponents" to recognize the irrationality or preposterous implications of their positions by using their own responses against them. For instance, when Euthyphro, a citizen of Athens who is about to turn his father in for murder, says that this is obviously the right thing to do, Socrates pretends to be really impressed by Euthyphro's moral certainty. He subsequently asks naive-seeming questions demonstrating not that Euthyphro is wrong to turn his father in, but rather that his grounds for doing so are irrational and self-contradictory.

The third major category of irony is structural irony. Works that exhibit structural irony contain an internal feature that creates or promotes a discrepancy that typically operates throughout the entire work. Some element of the work's **structure** (or perhaps even its **form**), unrelated to the **plot** *per se,* invites the audience or reader to probe beneath surface statements or appearances. Authors most commonly use **narration** to tip off the reader or audience. For instance, the author may employ a **naive** or otherwise **unreliable narrator** whose flaw the audience or reader readily recognizes. A naive narrator means what he or she says, but having recognized the narrator's flaw, the audience or reader mistrusts that narrator's perceptions or version of events. The reader or audience thus searches for and derives a different meaning that reflects the author's **intention.** For instance, the reader of Jonathan Swift's "A Modest Proposal" (1729) quickly recognizes that its narrator — an economist who advocates cannibalism, specifically, selling poor Irish infants to the wealthier English to solve Ireland's perpetual, cyclic problems of poverty, overpopulation, and starvation — is fallible. Since no reasonable reader would take this work at face value, discovering Swift's true view and purpose in using a fallible narrator becomes the reader's task. Swift's title is itself ironic, though this can be viewed as irony of a verbal rather than situational nature; calling such a proposal "modest" involves understatement, to say the least.

Structural irony should not be confused with situational irony. The former involves some sustained feature that makes up part of the very frame of the work, whereas the latter involves an event or comment keyed to the plot rather than to the work's structure. Granted, this difference sometimes seems more one of degree than absolute, as in the case where a plot element underlies the entire work. In Oscar Wilde's *The Importance of Being Earnest* (1895), a misunderstanding about identity serves as the basis of the comic plot and pervades the work. Similarly, in *Oedipus Rex*, Oedipus' ignorance that a man he murdered in the past was the prior King of Thebes underlies the plot and leads to his tragic fall from grace. Although both of these works are based on their **protagonists'** lack of crucial knowledge, both involve situational rather than structural irony, for the ironic discrepancies arise from the story line rather than the structure or form of the work itself.

Two types of irony — *cosmic irony* and *romantic irony* — can be classified as structural irony. Cosmic irony, also called *irony of fate,* arises from the disparity between a character's (incorrect) belief in his or her ability to shape his or her destiny and the audience's recognition that an external, supernatural force has the power to manipulate or even control that character's fate. Just as the unreliable narrator serves as a structural device giving rise to structural irony, so the supernatural force of cosmic irony makes the irony structural rather than situational in nature. The use of cosmic irony is more than a matter of plot.

Cosmic irony is characterized by four elements. First, it typically involves some powerful deity (or, sometimes, fate itself) with the ability and the desire to manipulate or even control events in a character's life. Second, the character subject to this irony believes — erroneously — in free will. Whether or not the character acknowledges the deity's existence, he or she persists in attempting to control or at least affect events. Third, the deity toys with the character much as a cat might with a mouse; the outcome is clear to the disinterested observer, but the mouse hopes desperately for escape. The deity may permit — or even encourage — the character to believe in self-determination, thereby raising false hopes that the audience knows or at least suspects will be dashed. Fourth, cosmic irony inevitably involves a tragic outcome. Ultimately, the character's struggle against destiny will be for naught; he or she will have to succumb to forces larger than him- or herself. Cosmic irony is notably apparent in Thomas Hardy's *Tess of the d'Urbervilles* (1891), the last chapter of which contains the statement "the President of the Immortals . . . had ended his sport with Tess."

Romantic irony, as defined by nineteenth-century German philosopher Friedrich Schlegel, is present in poems and prose works whose authors or speakers at some point reveal their narration to be the capricious fabrication of an idiosyncratic and highly self-conscious creator. Romantic ironists typically "give up the game" only after they have carefully constructed some vision of "reality," however. They may reveal their narrator to be a liar, for instance, or they may speak directly to the reader as an author. As a result, they wreak havoc with the reader's or audience's usual **suspension of disbelief,** debunking as illusion the normal operating assumption that the narration is a believable **representation** of reality. Romantic ironists *want* their readers or audiences to "see through" them, that is, to appreciate the manipulative nature of their art and the slightly comic quality of even their most serious artistic endeavors. In Henrik Ibsen's *Peer Gynt* (1875), for example, one of the characters says "One cannot die in the middle of Act Five." Authors as different as Geoffrey Chaucer; Miguel de Cervantes; George Gordon, Lord Byron; Luigi Pirandello; and Vladimir Nabokov have been called romantic ironists. A modern example of romantic irony is Nabokov's *Pale Fire* (1962), a novel thinly disguised as a nine-hundred-and-ninety-nine-line poem composed by a fictional poet named John Francis Shade, with a foreword, two-hundred-page commentary, and index by an equally fictional friend named Charles Kinbote. ("Kinbote" gives away Nabokov's game in the foreword, where he writes that although his commentary and index, "in conformity with custom, come after the poem, the reader is advised to consult them first," since "without my notes Shade's text simply has no human reality at all.") Referring to *Pale Fire* in a review, novelist Mary McCarthy wrote: "Pretending to be a curio, it cannot disguise the fact that it is one of the very great works of art of this century, the modern novel that everyone thought dead and that was only playing possum."

More recent examples of romantic irony include Steven Millhauser's *Edwin Mullhouse: The Life and Death of an American Writer, 1943–1954, by Jeffrey Cartwright* (1972) — the fictional **biography** of a cartoon-crazy preadolescent supposedly written by his best friend — and David Leavitt's *The Term Paper Artist* (1997), a **novella** that disguises fiction as **autobiography** insofar as its protagonist is the author of books bearing the same titles as Leavitt's own works.

FURTHER EXAMPLES: Sometimes several types of irony come into play at once. The following passage from Euripides' *Iphigenia at Aulis* (c. 405 B.C.) illustrates both dramatic irony and rhetorical irony. Agamemnon has brought his daughter Iphigenia to Aulis to be sacrificed to the gods; Iphigenia thinks a marriage has been arranged for her at Aulis with Achilles. Agamemnon's comments exemplify rhetorical irony; there is a discrepancy between his literal words and what he really means — and this discrepancy is readily perceived by the audience. Dramatic irony is exemplified by Iphigenia's failure to understand the true import of her words:

> Iphigenia: It's a long journey then; and you're leaving me behind!
> Agamemnon: Yours is a long journey too, like mine.
> Iphigenia: We could travel together then. You could arrange it.
> Agamemnon: No, your journey is different. You must remember me.
> Iphigenia: Will my mother sail with me? Or must I travel alone?
> Agamemnon: You'll sail alone . . . without father or mother.
> Iphigenia: Have you found me a new home, Father? Where is it?
> Agamemnon: That's enough . . . There are some things young girls
>   shouldn't know.
> Iphigenia: Sort the Phrygians out quickly, Daddy, and come back to me.
> Agamemnon: I must perform a sacrifice, before I go.
> Iphigenia: Of course you must! The right sacred rituals.
> Agamemnon: You'll be there too. By the holy water.
> Iphigenia: Shall I be part of the ceremonies at the altar?

In Hardy's *Tess of the d'Urbervilles,* cosmic and situational irony coexist in the scene in which Angel Clare confesses to his new bride Tess that he once "plunged into eight-and-forty hours' dissipation with a stranger." This confession prompts Tess, who incorrectly believes that Angel knows about her own past from a letter she slipped under his door (but which he did not receive because that letter also slid under his rug), to allude reassuringly to the child she had out of wedlock. Upon hearing about Tess's past for the first time, Angel subsequently announces that he cannot possibly live with her because "the woman I have been loving is not you." We can say that both cosmic and situational irony operate in this scene because, although the newlyweds' conversation grows out of the tragic situation created when a letter slipped under a rug as well as a door, the situation somehow seems fated. Hardy's novel, after all, describes the earth as a "blighted star" (Phase the First), Tess as being "doomed to receive" a dark stain for reasons unintelligible to "analytical philosophy" or our "sense of order"

(Phase the Second), and "The President of the Immortals" as "sport[ing] with Tess" (Phase the Seventh).

irony of fate: See **irony.**

irregular ode (Cowleyan ode): Named for Abraham Cowley, the seventeenth-century English inventor of this form, the irregular ode follows neither the **Pindaric** nor the **Horatian ode** pattern. The **rhyme scheme,** number of **stanzas,** and stanzaic form are irregular and at the poet's discretion. This form can allow for greater variability and adaptability to a range of subjects and **moods.**
EXAMPLE: William Wordsworth's "Ode: Intimations of Immortality" (1807).

Italian sonnet (Petrarchan sonnet): A fourteen-line **sonnet** consisting of two parts: the **octave,** eight lines with the **rhyme scheme** *abbaabba,* and the **sestet,** six lines usually following the rhyme scheme *cdecde* (or sometimes *cdcdcd*). The octave often poses a question or dilemma that the sestet answers or resolves.

The Italian sonnet originated in Italy in the thirteenth century, but its best-known proponent is the fourteenth-century poet Petrarch, hence its alternative name. English poets who have used this form have tended to take greater liberties with the rhyme scheme.
EXAMPLE: Dante Gabriel Rossetti's "Vain Virtues" (1870), a poem that scandalously assaulted **Victorian** pieties and morals, is one of the rare, nearly perfect Italian, or Petrarchan, sonnets in English:

> What is the sorriest thing that enters Hell?
>   None of the sins, — but this and that fair deed
>   Which a soul's sin at length could supersede.
> These yet are virgins, whom death's timely knell
> Might once have sainted; whom the fiends compel
>   Together now, in snake-bound shuddering sheaves
>   Of anguish, while the pit's pollution leaves
> Their refuse maidenhood abominable.
> Night sucks them down, the tribute of the pit,
>   Whose names, half entered in the book of Life,
>   Were God's desire at noon. And as their hair
> And eyes sink last, the Torturer deigns no whit
>   To gaze, but, yearning, waits his destined wife,
>   The Sin still blithe on earth that sent them there.

─────────── **J** ───────────

Jacobean Age (in English literature): An age spanning the reign of James I (1603–25) and often classified as the third of five literary eras within the **Renaissance Period** in English literature. The Jacobean Age derives its name from "Jacobus" (the Latin source of the name James) and succeeds the **Elizabethan Age** (named after Elizabeth I). Many famous Jacobean authors (such as Francis Bacon, John Donne, Michael Drayton, Ben Jonson, and William Shakespeare) began their careers during the Elizabethan era. Writers who began their careers during the Jacobean Age include the poet George Herbert and dramatists Sir Francis Beaumont, John Fletcher (Beaumont and Fletcher have been credited with developing the **genre** known as **tragicomedy**), Thomas Middleton, and John Webster. Famous prose works of the Jacobean Age include the King James translation of the Bible (1611) and Robert Burton's *Anatomy of Melancholy* (1621).

See also **Renaissance.**

jouissance: Jacques Derrida, a French philosopher of language, has used the term *jouissance* to refer to the attitude of pleasurable playfulness with which practitioners of **deconstruction** approach literary **texts.** Deconstructors seek to show that every text dismantles itself because each text contains opposed strands of meaning or conflicting **discourses** that cannot be reconciled, making it impossible to discern or establish any one, "true" meaning. Derrida has claimed in *Acts of Literature* (1992) that the "subtle and intense pleasure" deconstructors experience arises from the "dismantl[ing] of repressive assumptions, representations, and ideas — in short, from the lifting of repression" that occurs during this reading process. Foes of deconstruction have often objected to its playfulness, to the pleasure its practitioners take in teasing out the contradictory interpretive possibilities generated by the words in a text, their **etymologies** and contexts, and their potential to be read **figuratively** or even **ironically.**

Jouissance has also been used in **feminist criticism** to refer to sexual as well as textual pleasure or, more precisely, to a feminine, linguistic *jouissance* grounded in women's sexual potential and pleasure. As French feminist critic Luce Irigaray has argued in *Ce sexe qui n'en est pas un* (*This Sex Which Is Not One*) (1977), not only is a woman's *jouissance* more diffusive and diverse than a man's — she writes that "woman has sex organs just about everywhere," unlike men, whose *jouissance* is concentrated in the **phallus** — it cannot be expressed by the dominant, masculine language. Irigaray, like many other feminist critics, has connected this difference in bodily sensation and experience to a difference in the way women and men write. She has both postulated and celebrated the existence of a "feminine language" that is — like women's *jouissance* — more diffusive and fluid than its "masculinist" counterpart.

judicial criticism: A type of **practical criticism** involving the critic's individual assessment of and response to a work. Judicial critics seek not only to set forth their own reactions and evaluations but also to explain them in light of the author's general **style,** technique, and choice of subject. Judicial critics also attempt to justify their readings in light of commonly accepted standards of literary achievement.

Jungian criticism: A type of literary **criticism** based on the **theories** of Carl Jung, a psychiatrist who was originally a disciple of Sigmund Freud. Jung later developed his own theory of analytical psychology, a theory that differs markedly from the **psychoanalytic** theory of Freud. Consequently, it has had an effect on literary criticism quite distinct from that of Freud's psychoanalytic theory. Freud focuses on the individual unconscious and its manifestations; Jung identifies and concentrates on a **collective unconscious** that, he claims, is universally shared by people across cultures. According to Jung, this collective unconscious contains racial memories and **archetypes,** primordial **images** and patterns, that reflect the elemental content of human experience from its earliest beginnings.

Like Freud, Jung applied his psychoanalytic theory to literature, suggesting that the works that speak to generation after generation express the archetypes and racial memories contained in the collective unconscious; thus, great authors are great largely because they can tap into the elemental grounds of the human psyche and transcribe its contents for the reader. **Texts** that have become **classics** have universal appeal; their universality lies in the fact that they harness the collective unconscious much as do those **myths** that transcend individual cultures. Jungian criticism has influenced **myth criticism** and **archetypal criticism** in substantial ways.

Juvenalian satire: A type of formal **satire,** characterized by its harshness and pointed **realism,** that denounces human vice and error in solemn **tones.** Juvenalian satire is named for the Roman satirist Juvenal, noted for his dignified attacks on vice, which seek to evoke contempt or indignation from the reader. Juvenalian satire is distinguished from **Horatian satire,** the other major type of formal satire, by the latter's **witty,** even indulgent, tone, which is aimed at evoking laughter rather than derision.

K

katharsis: See **catharsis.**

kenning: A type of **periphrasis,** or circumlocution, in which an embellished **figurative** phrase is used in place of a simpler or more common term. Kennings were particularly common in Old English and Old Norse poetry.

EXAMPLES: The hyphenated nouns "whale-road" and "swan-road," used to refer to the sea in *Beowulf* (c. A.D. 700), are kennings, as are the phrases "storm of swords" (for "battle") and "oar-steed" (for "ship"). A more contemporary example of a kenning is referring to tuna fish as the "chicken of the sea."

Künstlerroman: A category of **bildungsroman,** this "novel of the artist" examines the development of the artist from childhood to the point when the subject realizes his or her artistic potential and mission. Such novels typically depict the struggles of sensitive **protagonists** to overcome bourgeois values and other obstacles, thereby realizing their creative potential.

EXAMPLES: Charles Dickens's *David Copperfield* (1868), James Joyce's *A Portrait of the Artist as a Young Man* (1916), Zelda Fitzgerald's **autobiographical** novel *Save Me the Waltz* (1932), Brian Moore's *An Answer from Limbo* (1962), Ben Okri's *The Landscapes Within* (1981), William T. Vollman's **satire** *You Bright and Risen Angels* (1987), and Shelley Jackson's **hypertext** work *My Body: A Wunderkammer* (1997). Elizabeth Barrett Browning's *Aurora Leigh* (1857), an **epic lyric** (written in verse, but with the length of a novel), has been called the first female *Künstlerroman.*

L

lai (**lay**): Initially, a term used to refer to **lyric** or, more commonly, short **narrative** poems composed in what is now France during the twelfth and thirteenth centuries and based on traditional songs and **legends.** Narrative *lais* of this period were usually written and recited in Old French in octosyllabic **couplets;** the **tales** they related typically dealt with **themes** of love and adventure. Lyric *lais* had a more varied poetic **form** and **structure,** were sung rather than read or recited, and were typically addressed to a lady or to the Virgin Mary. Most lyric *lais* were *Provençal lais*.

The *Breton lai* was a form of **verse** narrative that drew mainly on Celtic, including Arthurian, legends. Fairies or other supernatural agents often play a role, and faithful love — as opposed to **courtly love,** in which adulterous love is permissible — is extolled. Marie de France, who wrote in Old French at the English court toward the end of the twelfth century, pioneered the Breton *lai*.

The fourteenth-century English *lay*, which imitated the Breton *lai* with a few changes, came to be called the *Breton lay*. Over time, as this Anglicized term was applied to any short English verse narrative in the vein of a Breton *lai*, the meaning of *lay* expanded. Increasingly, the subject matter for Breton lays ranged beyond Celtic legends to include those of other traditions (even the "Oriental"), and the **tail-rhyme stanza** was used more often than octosyllabic couplets. Since the sixteenth century, the English word *lay* has been still more generally employed to describe any song or comparatively short verse narrative. For instance, in the nineteenth century, it was occasionally used to refer to short historical **ballads.**

EXAMPLES: Marie de France's "Le rossignol" ("The Nightingale"), "Le lai des deux amants" ("The *Lai* of Two Lovers"), and "Chèvrefeuille" ("Honeysuckle") are Breton *lais* dating from approximately 1175. Notable fourteenth-century Breton lays include *Lay of Launfal, Sir Orfeo, Havelok the Dane,* and Geoffrey Chaucer's "The Franklin's Tale" (c. 1387). No lyric *lais* from the **medieval** era appear to have survived, but the oldest such works were composed by Gautier de Dargiès in the early thirteenth century. Sir Walter Scott's *Lay of the Last Minstrel* (1805) and Thomas Macaulay's *Lays of Ancient Rome* (1842) are nineteenth-century examples of historical ballads referred to as lays (in these examples by the authors themselves).

An example of a lay from a non-European tradition is *The Lay of King Tongmyông*, which recounts an ancient Korean legend regarding the birth of Tongmyông and the founding of his kingdom.

lampoon: A **satiric**, often vicious, attack on an individual (or occasionally an institution or society in general). Lampoons were common — and popular — in seventeenth- and eighteenth-century England, but with the development of libel laws became legally risky for their composers and thus decreased in frequency as the vehicle of choice for satirizing specific people. However, public figures have remained vulnerable to lampoons.

EXAMPLES: In his poetic "Epistle to Dr. Arbuthnot" (1735), Alexander Pope satirizes Joseph Addison and John Gay in the fictional guises of Atticus and Bufo respectively; by contrast, he lampoons John, Lord Hervey, effeminate courtier and confidant of Queen Caroline, through an attack far more personally derogatory than his treatments of Addison and Gay. He portrays Hervey through the character of Sporus, whom he calls a "thing of silk," a "mere white curd of ass's milk," a "painted child of dirt that stinks and stings," and a "vile antithesis" (presumably a reference to Hervey's allegedly androgynous qualities).

The television show *Saturday Night Live* has long lampooned noted political figures, including Dan Quayle, Bill Clinton, George H. W. Bush, and George W. Bush. Two-time presidential candidate H. Ross Perot has been lampooned in Calvin Trillin's poem "The Ross Perot Guide to Answering Embarrassing Questions" (1992; adapted to song by Pete Seeger). Garry Trudeau, who has long satirized the American political landscape in his cartoon series *Doonesbury*, here lampoons the speech of teenagers in the 1990s.

The American family has been lampooned in a series of films starring Chevy Chase: *National Lampoon's Vacation* (1983), *National Lampoon's European Vacation* (1985), *National Lampoon's Christmas Vacation* (1989), and *National Lampoon's Vegas Vacation* (1997).

langue: See **semiotics.**

lay: See *lai.*

lecture (**reading**): See **text.**

legend: See **folklore, myth.**

leitmotif: An **image** or phrase that recurs throughout a work, each time evoking past associations in such a way as to serve as a subtly unifying element of the work as a whole. Meaning "leading motive" in German, *leit-motif* is typically used in music criticism to refer to a brief musical phrase that is introduced early and often repeated. (The first four notes of Beethoven's Fifth Symphony provide the leitmotif of the entire work.) The leitmotif is not necessarily the predominant musical statement or poetic image; rather, it is a repeated feature of the work that casts a revealing light on central **themes** and issues.

EXAMPLES: In George Eliot's novel *Middlemarch* (1872), Mr. Brooke's recurring comment, "I looked into that at one time but found you could go too far," serves as a leitmotif. "Rosebud" (as manifested in word, in image, and in variations on word and image) is the leitmotif of Orson Welles's movie *Citizen Kane* (1941). The leitmotif of Alfred Hitchcock's *Vertigo* (1958) is the image of a vortex, visible both in the swirl of Kim Novak's hair and in the effect created by a camera tracking back quickly while zooming forward.

See also **motif.**

leonine rhyme: A type of **internal rhyme** in which the last **stressed** syllable before the **caesura** rhymes with the last stressed syllable at the end of the line. Leonine rhyme is named for Leoninus of St. Victor in Paris, who frequently employed this type of **rhyme** in his verse.

EXAMPLE: The following **stanza** from Samuel Taylor Coleridge's "The Rime of the Ancient Mariner" (1798) exhibits leonine rhyme in the first and third lines:

> "Fly, brother, fĺy! ‖ more high, more hígh!
> Or we shall be bḙlated:
> For slow and slów ‖ that ship will gó,
> When the mariner's trance is abated."

lesbian criticism: See **gay and lesbian criticism.**

lexicography: The writing of dictionaries, or **lexicons.** Lexicography would seem to date back to Roman times and has evolved from the explanation of difficult words in simpler terms to the elaborate system we have today, in which everything from **etymology** to spelling to proper usage may be included, along with the actual meaning of the word being defined.

lexicon: A list or book of words and their corresponding **denotative** meanings; a dictionary. The term may also be used to refer to the vocabulary of a particular **class,** activity, and so on (for example, the lexicon of the upper class, the lexicon of sailing).

light ending: See **feminine ending.**

light verse: A term encompassing many different forms of **verse,** all of which aim to entertain the reader. Forms of light verse include **limericks,**

vers de société, nursery rhymes, **parodies,** and **nonsense verse.** Although always designed to entertain, humor in light verse may be **satiric, witty,** or simply playful. Light verse is distinguished from other verse by its **tone** rather than by its subject matter.

EXAMPLES: The light verse of Ogden Nash, a famous twentieth-century practitioner, is exemplified by his short poem, "Reflections on Ice-Breaking" (1945):

> Candy
> Is dandy
> But liquor
> Is quicker.

Dorothy Parker, perhaps best known for her statement "I'd rather have a bottle in front of me than a frontal lobotomy," has written light verse on a topic usually considered "heavy" in a poem entitled "Résumé" (1926):

> Razors pain you;
> Rivers are damp;
> Acids stain you;
> And drugs cause cramp.
> Guns aren't lawful;
> Nooses give;
> Gas smells awful;
> You might as well live.

Shel Silverstein, author of such children's **classics** as *The Giving Tree* (1964) and *The Missing Piece* (1976), wrote numerous illustrated collections of light verse including *Where the Sidewalk Ends* (1974), *A Light in the Attic* (1981), and *Falling Up: Poems and Drawings* (1996). Silverstein's poems have been popular with both adults and children. Examples from *A Light in the Attic* include "Reflection," in which a child looks at his reflection in a puddle of water, sees an "Upside-Down Man," and wonders who is really upside down and right side up;" "The Meehoo with an Exactly-watt," a take-off on the "knock, knock, who's there?" jokes; and "The Man in the Iron Pail Mask," which **alludes** to Alexandre Dumas's story *The Man in the Iron Mask* (1846; adapted to film in 1998). In "Sick," Silverstein's most famous poem (from *Where the Sidewalk Ends*), young Peggy Ann McKay reels off a list of ailments ranging from "instamatic flu" to a belly button that's caving in as reasons why she can't go to school — until she learns it's Saturday and announces she's going out to play!

limerick: A short, humorous **poem** that consists of five **anapestic** lines **rhyming** *aabba.* The first, second, and fifth lines are **trimeter** while the third and fourth lines are **dimeter.** The two shorter dimeter lines are sometimes combined into one line; when they are, the rhyme is **internal.** This type of **light verse** is one of the few to have become genuinely popular in

English and is still often composed extemporaneously. The humor in limericks often crosses over into the bawdy and absurd.

EXAMPLES: Edward Lear, famous for his **nonsense verse,** is renowned for limericks such as the following:

> There was a great sculptor named Phidias
> Whose knowledge of art was invidious.
> He carved Aphrodite
> Without any nightie,
> Which outraged the purely fastidious.

Countless off-color limericks have been inspired by a famous one about Nantucket Island, first printed in the Princeton *Tiger* in 1924:

> There once was a man from Nantucket,
> Who kept all his cash in a bucket,
> But his daughter, named Nan,
> Ran away with a man,
> And as for the bucket, Nantucket.

limited point of view: See **point of view.**

linguistics: The application of scientific principles to the study of language. Linguistics has several divisions, which include **syntax** (the arrangement of words), *semantics* (the meaning of words), **morphology** (the study of the form of words and their smallest meaningful parts, called **morphemes**), *etymology* (the derivation of words), and **phonology** (the study of basic sounds, called **phonemes**).

linking: The process by which documents in **hypertext** systems are interconnected so that readers can move, or "jump," from one to another or access a multitude of new documents through the use of *link structures.* Sometimes referred to as a *hyperlink* or "jump marker," *link structure* is defined as an **icon, image,** word, or phrase (usually highlighted or underlined) that enables the user to navigate through myriad **texts** on the World Wide Web.
See also **cyberfiction, hypertext.**

link structures (hyperlinks): See **linking.**

lisible **(readerly):** See **poststructuralism, text.**

literariness: A term used by **Russian formalists** and their followers in the **Prague Linguistic Circle** to refer to what makes a work specifically a literary work as opposed to some other kind of work. In 1921, Roman Jakobson wrote that "The object of study in literary science is not literature but 'literariness,' that is, what makes a given work a literary work." Jan Mukarovsky and Victor Shklovsky further argued that literariness requires the **foregrounding** of language in such a way as to make its "background" (the world it usually refers to) virtually disappear. The effect of this foregrounding is the temporary separation, or "estrangement," of the reader, not only from the familiar language of everyday **discourse** but also from the world as ordinarily perceived. According to formalist theory, by giving linguistic prominence, or "palpability," to something in a literary work that would not normally be accentuated in everyday discourse, the author of a **text** characterized by literariness frees readers to experience language and the world in a fresh way.

literature of sensibility: An emphasis on emotional sensitivity and charitable feelings in eighteenth-century literature, as manifested especially in the **sentimental comedy** and the **sentimental novel.** The literature of sensibility developed largely in reaction to seventeenth-century stoicism and in opposition to Thomas Hobbes's theory that humanity is inherently selfish. Sentimental poems, novels, and comedies exalted humanity's inherently benevolent nature, as demonstrated by the capacity for and expression of sympathy for the plights and joys of other human beings.

See **sensibility.** See also **Age of Johnson.**

literature of the absurd: See **Absurd, the.**

litotes: From the Greek for "simple" or "meager," a form of **meiosis** (*understatement*) that involves making an affirmative point by denying its opposite. Litotes is the opposite of **hyperbole** and is often used to achieve an **ironic** effect.

EXAMPLES: The common phrases "not a bad idea" (meaning "good idea") and "not many" (meaning "a few"). Litotes is commonly used in the Bible, as evidenced by lines such as "I will multiply them, and they shall not be few; I will make them honored, and they shall not be small" (Jer. 30:19) and "A prophet is not without honor, except in his own country, and among his own kin, and in his own house" (Mark 6:4).

Aphra Behn used litotes in the following phrase in *Oroonoko* (1688) to stress the great melancholy Prince Oroonoko feels on being invited to return to the Court after the death of his beloved Imoinda: "He obeyed, tho' with no little Reluctancy."

J. D. Salinger employed litotes in the following lines from *The Catcher in the Rye* (1951): "It isn't very serious. I have this tiny little tumor on the brain."

local color: The depiction of the distinctive characteristics (dialect, dress, mannerisms, culture, etc.) of a particular region, usually in prose writing. Fiction in which the local color provides the story's chief interest is termed *local color writing.* Often used to provide mere decoration or as a vehicle for **sentimentality,** local color has nonetheless been used by some **realists** as an aid in developing **character.** Rather than rendering picturesque scenes of unusual charm, these writers use local color to depict the tawdry-to-sordid breeding grounds of vice and temptation. Local color thus helps the reader to envision and understand the moral dilemmas faced by ordinary people.

The use of local color was particularly popular in the United States following the Civil War. Until the (re)discovery of her novel *The Awakening* (1899), Kate Chopin was thought of mainly as a local color writer, notable for her depictions of Creole life in New Orleans. Sarah Orne Jewett, Hamlin Garland, and George Washington Cable were famous for their meticulous **representations** of New England, the Midwest, and the South, respectively. Much local color writing, especially of the less serious kind, has been done in sketches and short stories, often for magazine publications. Even Robert Frost, a more modern figure — and a poet rather than a prose author — has been linked to this tradition by an epithet commonly used to describe him: "a poet of New England."

locution: A term used by philosopher John Austin in **speech-act theory** to refer to the utterance of a statement.

locutionary act: See **utterance act.**

logocentric, logocentrism: French theorist Jacques Derrida used the term *logocentric* to describe and characterize Western thought, language, and culture since the time of Plato. To understand what Derrida meant by *logocentric,* it is important to know that the root word, *logos* (which in Greek means "word," "speech," and "reason"), has in Western philosophical and theological tradition come to signify law, truth, and even ultimate Truth. The suffix *-centric* is generally used to suggest the privileged status of that to which the root refers. Thus, defined narrowly, *logocentric* means centered on and revolving around the word (or speech or reason). More broadly, the term implies a belief in the centrality and, more important, the determinability of ultimate Truth. It is this latter meaning that Derrida uses when he at once characterizes and critiques Western traditions as being hung up on the notion that words contain present truth or Truth.

It is difficult to disentangle Derrida's use of *logocentric* from his concept of **presence.** (In biblical tradition, *logos* refers to the creating, spoken word of a present God who, "In the beginning," said "Let there be light.") In arguing that the Western conception of language is logocentric, Derrida has also argued that it is grounded in "the metaphysics of presence," the prevalent tendency to believe that **linguistic** systems are grounded in "ultimate" foundations or "referents" (God, some **Platonic** or otherwise foundational "Idea," deep **etymological** word "roots") making possible an identifiable and correct meaning or meanings for any potential statement that can be made within that system. Far from supporting this Western, logocentric view of language, however, Derrida argues that there are no such ultimate referents; thus, presence turns out to be an arbitrary, rather than an inherent, intrinsic, or true foundation for language. Since presence is not an "ultimate referent," it cannot guarantee determinable (much less determinate) meaning. That is, presence no more makes it possible to determine meaning than it makes it possible to select one particular meaning with confidence in its correctness.

According to Derrida, Western logocentrism is due in part to Western *phonocentrism,* that is, the Western tendency to **privilege** the spoken over the written. Derrida argues that the privileging of speech — that is, the tendency to regard speech in positive terms and writing as comparatively negative — cannot be disentangled from the privileging of presence. (We write postcards, for instance, when the people with whom we wish to communicate are **absent;** similarly, we read Plato because he cannot speak from beyond the grave.) Just as Derrida debunks logocentrism, so he interrogates the privileged status granted to speech in Western metaphysics and culture.

long measure (L. M.): A type of **stanza,** common in **hymns,** in which all four lines of the **quatrain** are written in **iambic tetrameter.** The **rhyme scheme** may be either *abab* or *abcb.*
EXAMPLE: The hymn "O God, Beneath Thy Guiding Hand" (1793):

> Ŏ Gód, bĕneáth thў guídĭng hánd
> Our exiled parents crossed the sea
> And when they trod the wintry strand,
> With prayer and psalm they worshiped thee.

loose sentence (nonperiodic sentence): A sentence characterized by its informal or conversational **style;** the opposite of a **periodic sentence.** A loose sentence typically contains independent clauses connected by coordinating conjunctions (*and, or, but*) or an independent clause followed by one or more dependent clauses. Consequently, a loose sentence can generally be divided easily into two or more sentences, unlike a periodic sentence, which is not **syntactically** complete until its very end. Works predominantly containing loose sentences usually exhibit **paratactic style.**
EXAMPLES: "Kelly berated her subordinates on a regular basis, but she was not a very good worker herself; everyone thought she should be fired."
"Ronald was a B-grade actor who preached the virtues of 'family values'; of course, he never gave a thought to his own divorce, much less the fact that his children despised him."
The first sentence of J. D. Salinger's *The Catcher in the Rye* (1951) is also loose in construction:

> If you really want to hear about it, the first thing you'll probably want to know is where I was born, and what my lousy childhood was like, and how my parents were occupied and all before they had me, and all that David Copperfield kind of crap, but I don't feel like going into it, if you want to know the truth.

Lost Generation: A phrase used to describe the generation of young writers disillusioned by the experience and aftermath of World War I. These writers generally felt that the traditional values they were brought up with were a sham, given the senselessness of the war and the consequent devaluation of human life. As a group, they rejected what they viewed as a hypocritical society that falsely espoused puritanical virtues. Many American members of the Lost Generation became expatriates in the 1920s, clustering especially in Paris and London. Most of these expatriates returned in the 1930s, during the social and political upheavals caused by the Depression and the controversial policies of President Franklin Delano Roosevelt's New Deal.

The origin of the phrase *Lost Generation* has been a matter of dispute, but there is no doubt that it entered literary and popular circles with the publication of Ernest Hemingway's *The Sun Also Rises* (1926), in which Hemingway used the phrase in an **epigraph** that states, "You are all a lost generation." Hemingway borrowed this statement from American expatriate writer Gertrude Stein, who at some earlier point in the 1920s told him that "All of you young people who served in the war . . . [y]ou are all a lost generation." Hemingway himself declared in *A Moveable Feast* (1964), his **memoir** of his life in Paris, that he considered the phrase to be merely "splendid bombast"; he also indicated that Stein herself did not coin the phrase but, rather, borrowed it from the owner of a garage.

EXAMPLES: Jake Barnes, **protagonist** of Hemingway's *The Sun Also Rises*, epitomizes the Lost Generation, confused and disillusioned by the horrors of the Great War and its terrible aftermath. Other writers of the Lost Generation have traditionally been said to include F. Scott Fitzgerald, John Dos Passos, Hart Crane, and William Slater Brown. But Shari Benstock, in her book *Women of the Left Bank* (1986), has rediscovered the importance of Djuna Barnes, Jean Rhys, Sylvia Beach, and Janet Flanner.

lyric: Today, a brief melodic and **imaginative poem** (as opposed to a **narrated tale**) characterized by the fervent but structured expression of private thoughts and emotions by a single speaker who speaks in the **first person.** The term derives from the Greek for *lyre,* a type of musical instrument, and once designated any poem designed to be sung while accompanied by a lyre. During ancient Roman times, poets such as Horace wrote lyrics meant to be read, unaccompanied by music.

The lyric is one of the oldest, most popular, and most enduring forms of literary expression in the English language. Over the centuries, it has diversified into several subcategories, including such forms as the **ballad,** the **sonnet,** and the **ode.** Throughout its diversification, it has retained the basic qualities that originally characterized it, especially the **subjective** expression of thought and emotion, the individualistic and imaginative focus, and the subtly melodic **tone.**

Today, the plural form of the term (*lyrics*) also refers to the words of any song.

EXAMPLES: The American poet Sara Teasdale's "Wisdom" (1916) is a lyric:

> It was a night of early spring,
>   The winter-sleep was scarcely broken;
> Around us shadows and the wind
>   Listened for what was never spoken.
>
> Though half a score of years are gone,
>   Spring comes as sharply now as then —
> But if we had it all to do
>   It would be done the same again.
>
> It was a spring that never came;
>   But we have lived enough to know
> That what we never have, remains;
>   It is the things we have that go.

Other examples of the **genre** include Ralph Waldo Emerson's "Two Rivers" (1858), Emily Dickinson's "Because I could not stop for Death" (1863), and Robert Frost's "Stopping by Woods on a Snowy Evening" (1923).

M

madrigal: A short **lyric** sung *a capella* — that is, without musical accompaniment. The origins of the madrigal, which generally treats an amatory or **pastoral theme,** are Italian, but the form also became popular in England during the **Elizabethan Age.** Specific rules governed the number of lines contained in (and the number of singers involved in performing) the Italian madrigal, but when used in connection with **Renaissance** literature in English, the term refers more generally to any short, sung lyric about beauty or love.

EXAMPLE: The following song from William Shakespeare's *Much Ado About Nothing* (1599):

> Sigh no more, ladies, sigh no more,
>   Men were deceivers ever,
> One foot in the sea, and one on shore,
>   To one thing constant never.
>   Then sigh not so,
>   But let them go,
>   And be you blithe and bonny,
> Converting all your sounds of woe
>   Into hey nonny, nonny.
>
> Sing no more ditties, sing no more,
>   Of dumps° so dull and heavy;   *sad songs*
> The fraud of men was ever so,
>   Since summer first was leavy.
>   Then sigh not so,
>   But let them go,
>   And be you blithe and bonny,
> Converting all your sounds of woe
>   Into hey nonny, nonny.

magic realism: From the German *magischer Realismus,* a phrase used in 1925 by Franz Roh to describe the quasi-**surrealistic** work of a group of German painters in the 1920s.

Although *magic realism* was applied to a short-lived Italian literary movement of the 1920s known as *stracittà,* the term was not otherwise associated with literature until the latter half of the 1940s. In time, the term came to be applied to fictional prose works that are characterized by a mixture of **realistic** and **fantastic** elements. Realistic details and esoteric knowledge are intertwined with dreamlike sequences, abrupt chronological shifts, and complex, tangled **plots.** Magic realists also frequently incorporate fairy tales and **myths** into their works. Although the term has most often been applied to Latin American writers such as Jorge Luis Borges and Gabriel García Márquez, novelists such as Italo Calvino, John Fowles,

Günter Grass, and Salman Rushdie have also been called magic realists, as has Banana Yashimoto, who combines magic realism with **postmodernist** attitudes and styles.

EXAMPLES: Gabriel García Márquez's *Cien años de soledad (One Hundred Years of Solitude)* (1967) and *El amor en los tiempos del cólera (Love in the Time of Cholera)* (1985), Laura Esquivel's *Como agua para chocolate (Like Water for Chocolate)* (1989), Salman Rushdie's *Midnight's Children* (1981) and *The Moor's Last Sigh* (1995).

The 2001 film *Amélie* contained many elements of magic realism: talking lamps, paintings, and photographs; a winking statue; and a **protagonist** who literally melts when her love interest leaves the restaurant in which she works without asking her for a date.

malapropism: The erroneous substitution for the correct word of a word similar in sound but very different in meaning; a form of **catachresis.** This term is derived from Mrs. Malaprop, a **character** in Richard Sheridan's play *The Rivals* (1775), who consistently uses words incorrectly. Sheridan may have derived the name of his famous character from the French phrase "*mal à propos*," which roughly translates as "bad for the purpose."

EXAMPLES: In *The Rivals,* Mrs. Malaprop tells Sir Anthony Absolute that she would "by no means wish a daughter of mine to be a progeny of learning." (Here she erroneously substitutes "progeny" for "prodigy.") Mrs. Slipslop, an amorous older character in Henry Fielding's *Joseph Andrews* (1741), speaks in malapropisms to her beloved young Joseph, saying at one point, "Do you intend to *result* my passion . . . ? Must you treat me with *ironing*? Barbarous monster! how have I deserved that my passion should be *resulted* and treated with *ironing*. . . . Do you *assinuate* that I am old enough to be your mother?" (emphasis added).

The characters Latka on the TV show *Taxi* and Archie Bunker of *All in the Family* spoke in comic malapropisms. Movie mogul Samuel Goldwyn spoke malapropistically of blockbusters as creating "an excitement that will sweep the country like wildflowers."

The last word of the following passage from Isabel Allende's *The House of the Spirits* (1982) is a malapropism: "Nana pulled her hair back in a bun and took her to buy her first corset, her first pair of silk stockings, her first grown-up dress, and a collection of miniature towels for what she continued to call 'demonstration.'"

The character Rachel, in Barbara Kingsolver's novel *The Poisonwood Bible* (1998), is wildly malapropistic, referring to her "feminine wilds" and saying things like "I revert my eyes," "I prefer to remain anomolous," and "we Christians have [a] system of marriage called monotony." One of the characters who people Ruben Santiago-Hudson's one-man show *Lackawanna Blues* (2001) frequently uses malapropisms, referring to the "Statue of Delivery" and the "Entire State Building," opining that "beauty is in the behind of the beholder," and explaining that he has "de roaches of the liver," for which his doctor wrote him a "description."

Marxism: A school of thought founded by Karl Marx, a German philosopher known for works such as *Das Kapital* (*Capital*) (1867) and two works he wrote with Friedrich Engels, *The German Ideology* (1846) and *The Communist Manifesto* (1848).

Marx believed that historical change was primarily the result of **class** struggle and that the State, for as long as it has existed, has used its power to oppress and exploit the laboring masses for the benefit of a wealthy elite. He thus posited an oppositional relationship between the proletariat (the working class) and the capitalist bourgeoisie (those who own the means of production). In Marx's view, economic factors and the class divisions they reflect and reinforce play a primary role in determining social institutions and actions.

Marx believed that the capitalist-run system would eventually and inevitably break down, due to the chasm of inequalities it engenders between the privileged few and the deprived, overworked many. He thought that a dictatorship of the proletariat would temporarily emerge in the wake of capitalism and ultimately be succeeded by a socialist, classless society without need or use for any such government.

Marx, who was himself a literary critic, wrote **theoretically** about the relationship between economics, politics, and the arts. In *The German Ideology*, he and Engels argued that economics provides the **base** of society, from which emerges a **superstructure** consisting of law, politics, philosophy, religion, and art (including literature).

Marx's ideas have had a profound effect upon a range of subsequent thinkers, from political philosophers to literary critics. In all corners of the globe, adherents have greatly expanded on and modified them in various (and sometimes contradictory) ways. For instance, Nikolai Lenin and Mao Tse-tung developed quite different forms of political organization that drew upon the heritage of Marxist thought. Marx's ideas about literature and the other arts have powerfully informed the work of leading critics in Western Europe and the United States as well as in the former Soviet Union. As a result, Marxism has played a distinct and important role not only in the development of governments as different as China's and Cuba's, but also in the development of critical methodologies as different as those we associate with **the new historicism,** the Birmingham School of **cultural studies, dialogic criticism,** and post-Althusserian Marxist criticism. What Marxist approaches to literature have in common is the tendency to view the literary work as the product *of* work, as being ultimately rooted or based in the realm of economics and production.

See also **Marxist criticism.**

Marxist criticism: A type of **criticism** in which literary works are viewed as the product of work and whose practitioners emphasize the role of **class** and **ideology** as they reflect, propagate, and even challenge the prevailing social order. In light of the rapid reform of Soviet-style communism in the former USSR and throughout Eastern Europe, one might suppose that Marxist literary criticism would have become an **anachronism** in a world turning toward market capitalism. In fact, however, Marxist criticism has not disappeared. It is, after all, a phenomenon distinct from Soviet and Eastern European communism; Marxist literary analysis originated nearly eighty years before the Bolshevik revolution. Furthermore, since the 1940s, the approach has thrived mainly in the West — not as a form of communist propaganda but rather as a form of critique, a **discourse** for interrogating *all* societies and their **texts** in terms of certain specific issues. Those issues — including **race,** class, and the attitudes shared within a given culture — are as timely as ever, not only in contemporary Russia but also in the United States.

Marxist criticism may even have been strengthened by the collapse of Soviet-style communism. At one time, few self-respecting Anglo-American journals would use Marxist terms or models, however illuminating, to analyze Western issues or problems. With the collapse of the Kremlin, however, old taboos began to give way. Even the staid *Wall Street Journal* now uses phrases like "worker alienation" to discuss the problems plaguing the American business world.

The assumption that Marxist criticism will die on the vine of a moribund political system rests in part on another mistaken assumption — namely, that Marxist literary analysis is practiced only by people who would like to see society transformed into a Marxist-communist state, one created through land reform, the redistribution of wealth, a tightly and centrally managed economy, the abolition of institutionalized religion, and so on. In fact, it has never been necessary to be a communist political revolutionary to be classified as a Marxist literary critic. (Many of the critics discussed in this entry actually fled communist societies to live in the West.) Nor is it necessary to praise only those literary works with a radical social vision or to condemn books that represent or even reinforce a middle-class, capitalist worldview. It is necessary, however, to adopt what most students of literature would consider a radical definition of the purpose and function of literary criticism.

More traditional forms of criticism, according to Marxist critic Pierre Macherey, "set . . . out to deliver the text from its own silences by coaxing it into giving up its true, latent, or hidden meaning." Marxist critics, however, do not seek to unearth "hidden" meanings in texts, for they see silences as evidence of what the text fails to say, what the text cannot say because of its particular ideology. Rather than viewing texts as repositories for hidden meanings, they view texts as material products to be understood in broadly historical terms. In short, literary works are viewed as products *of* work (and hence of the realm of production and consumption we call economics). For instance, in *Criticism and Ideology* (1978), Marxist critic Terry Eagleton outlined the complex relationship between the soaring cost of books in the nineteenth century, the growth of lending libraries, the practice of publishing "three-decker" novels, and the changing content of those novels. Other Marxist critics have examined the way in which literary works do identifiable work of their own — work that usually enforces and reinforces the prevailing ideology, the network of **conventions,** values, and opinions to which the majority of people uncritically subscribe.

Marxism began with Karl Marx, the nineteenth-century German philosopher best known for writing *Das Kapital* (*Capital*) (1867), the seminal work of the communist movement. Marx was also the first Marxist literary critic, writing critical essays in the 1830s on writers such as Johann Wolfgang von Goethe and William Shakespeare (whose **tragic** vision of **Elizabethan** disintegration he praised). Even after Marx met Friedrich Engels in 1843 and began collaborating on overtly political works such as *The German Ideology* (1846) and *The Communist Manifesto* (1848), he maintained a keen interest in literature. He and Engels argued about the poetry of Heinrich Heine, admired Hermann Freiligrath (a poet critical of the German aristocracy), and faulted playwright Ferdinand Lassalle for writing about a reactionary knight in the Peasants' War rather than about more progressive aspects of German history.

As these examples suggest, Marx and Engels seldom thought of **aesthetic** matters as being distinct and independent from politics, economics, and history. In fact, they believed the alienation of the worker in industrialized, capitalist societies had grave consequences for the arts. Mechanized and assembly-line production not only resulted in mass-produced, identical products bearing no relation to the people who produced them, but also served to "reify" those producers (in essence, to turn them into things themselves). Marx and Engels wondered how such workers could possibly be expected to recognize, produce, or even consume things of beauty. And they worried that the shortage of consumers would result in a shortage of producers, especially in an age in which production (even of something like literature) meant *mass* (and therefore profitable) production.

In *The German Ideology,* Marx and Engels discussed the relationship between the arts, politics, and basic economic reality in terms of a general social theory. Economics, they argued, provides the *base,* or infrastructure, of society, from which a *superstructure* consisting of law, politics, philosophy, religion, and art emerges. Although Marx later modified his view of the interplay between base and superstructure, admitting that changes in economics may not be reflected by immediate changes in ethics or literature and that **gaps** sometimes open up between economic forms and those produced by the creative mind, he retained his emphasis on economics and its relationship to superstructural elements of society. Central to Marxism and Marxist literary criticism was and is the following "materialist" insight: Superstructural elements such as art owe their existence to consciousness, but consciousness is the product rather than the source of social forms and economic conditions.

Marx and Engels, drawing upon the philosopher G. W. F. Hegel's theories about the **dialectical** synthesis of ideas from **theses** and **antitheses,** believed that a revolutionary class war (pitting the capitalist class against a proletarian, antithetical class) would lead to the synthesis of a new socioeconomic order. They believed revolution might occur in the United States,

Great Britain, or Germany, a revolution that would work a secular and material salvation of humanity. Marx and Engels rejected the Hegelian dialectic insofar as it anticipated divine intervention, embracing instead a theory of **dialectical materialism** that emphasized revolution. And they believed that the communist society eventually established would produce new forms of consciousness and belief and, ultimately, great art.

The revolution anticipated by Marx and Engels did not occur in their century, let alone in their lifetime. When it did occur, in 1917, it did so in a place unimagined by either theorist: Russia, a country long ruled by despotic czars but also enlightened by the works of powerful novelists and playwrights, including Anton Chekhov, Alexander Pushkin, Leo Tolstoi, and Fyodor Dostoyevsky. Perhaps because of its significant literary tradition, Russia produced revolutionaries like Nikolai Lenin, who shared not only Marx's interest in literature but also his belief in its ultimate importance. But it was not without hesitation that Lenin endorsed texts written before the revolution. Well before 1917 he had questioned what the relationship should be between a society undergoing revolution and the literature of its bourgeois past.

Lenin attempted to answer that question in a series of essays he wrote between 1908 and 1911 on Tolstoi. Tolstoi — the author of *War and Peace* (1864–66) and *Anna Karenina* (1876–77) — was an important nineteenth-century Russian writer whose views did not always accord with those of the revolutionaries. Nevertheless, Lenin reasoned that continuing interest in a writer like Tolstoi was justified given the primitive and unenlightened economic order of the society that produced him. Since superstructure usually lags behind basc (and is therefore usually more primitive), the attitudes of a Tolstoi were relatively progressive when viewed in light of the monarchical, precapitalist society out of which they arose. Lenin also reasoned that the writings of the great Russian **realists** would have to suffice, at least in the short run, because a great proletarian literature was unlikely to evolve until the educational system had produced a literate proletariat. In essays like "Party Organization and Party Literature" (1905), Lenin looked forward to the day in which new artistic forms would be produced by progressive writers with revolutionary political views and agendas.

Leon Trotsky, Lenin's comrade in revolution, took a strong interest in literary matters as well, publishing a book called *Literature and Revolution* (1924) that is still viewed as a **classic** of Marxist literary criticism. Trotsky also worried about the future of Marxist aesthetic theory, responding skeptically to groups like Proletkult, which opposed tolerance toward pre- and nonrevolutionary writers and sought to establish a new, proletarian culture. He warned of the danger of cultural sterility, pointing out that there is no necessary connection between the quality of a literary work and its author's politics.

In 1927, Trotsky lost a power struggle with Josef Stalin, a man who believed that writers should be "engineers" of "human souls." After Trotsky's expulsion from the Soviet Union, the views of groups like Proletkult

and the Left Front of Art (LEF) and theorists such as Nikolai Bukharin and
A. A. Zhdanov became more prevalent. At the First Congress of the Union
of Soviet Writers in 1934, Soviet author Maxim Gorky called for writing
that would "make labor the principal hero of our books." **Socialist realism,** an art form glorifying workers and the revolutionary State, was made
Communist party policy and the official literary form of the USSR at this
same Congress. Under the Stalinist regime, the Soviet literary scene degen-
erated to the point that the works of writers like Franz Kafka were no
longer read, either because they were viewed as **decadent, formalist** experiments or because they "engineered souls" in "nonprogressive" directions.
Officially sanctioned works were generally ones in which artistry lagged
far behind politics.

Of those critics active in the USSR after the expulsion of Trotsky and
the triumph of Stalin, two stand out: Mikhail Bakhtin and Georg Lukács.
Many of Bakhtin's essays were written in the 1930s and 1940s but were
not translated or published in the West until the 1980s. His work reflects
an engagement with the Marxist intellectual tradition as well as an indirect, even hidden, resistance to the Soviet government. Bakhtin viewed language — especially literary texts — in terms of discourses and **dialogues.** A
novel written in a society in flux, for instance, might include an official, legitimate discourse, as well as one infiltrated by challenging comments. In a
1929 book on Dostoyevsky and a 1940 study entitled *Rabelais and His
World,* Bakhtin examined what he called **polyphonic** novels, characterized
by many **voices** or discourses. Marxist critics writing in the West have used
Bakhtin's theories to decode submerged social critique, especially in early
modern texts; other critics have used his theories as the basis for a method
of literary criticism called **dialogic criticism.** Bakhtin has also influenced
modern **cultural criticism,** showing that the conflict between "high" and
"low" culture occurs between classic and popular texts as well as between
the **dialogic** voices that exist within them and is accentuated in works containing **carnivalesque** elements.

Lukács, a Hungarian who began his career as an "idealist" Hegelian
critic and converted to Marxism in 1919, also survived Stalin's dictatorship and his repressive policies. Lukács was far less narrow in his views
than the strident Stalinist Soviet critics of the 1930s and 1940s. He disliked
much socialist realism and appreciated prerevolutionary, realistic novels
that broadly reflected cultural "totalities" and were populated with **characters** representing human "types" of the author's place and time. But like
his more censorious contemporaries, he refused to accept nonrevolutionary, **modernist** works like James Joyce's *Ulysses* (1922). He condemned
movements like **expressionism** and **Symbolism,** preferring works with content over more decadent, experimental works characterized mainly by
form.

Fortunately for the Marxist critical movement, politically radical critics
outside the Soviet Union were free of its narrow, constricting policies and,
consequently, able to develop the thinking of Marx, Engels, and Trotsky.

These non-Soviet Marxists kept Marxist critical theory alive in discussing all kinds of literature, written across the entire historical spectrum.

Perhaps because Lukács was the best of the Soviet communists writing Marxist criticism in the 1930s and 1940s, non-Soviet Marxists tended to develop their ideas by publicly opposing his. German dramatist and critic Bertolt Brecht countered Lukács by arguing that art ought to be viewed as a field of production, not as a container of content. Brecht also criticized Lukács for his attempt to enshrine realism at the expense not only of the other "isms" but also of poetry and drama, which Lukács had largely ignored.

Even more outspoken was Brecht's critical champion Walter Benjamin, a German Marxist who, in the 1930s, attacked conventional and traditional literary forms for conveying a stultifying "aura" of culture. Benjamin praised new art forms ushered in by the age of mechanical reproduction. Forms such as radio and film offered hope, he felt, for liberation from capitalist culture, for they were too new to be part of its ritualistic traditions.

Of all the anti-Lukácsians outside of the USSR who contributed to the development of Marxist criticism, the most important was probably Theodor Adorno. Leader since the early 1950s of the Frankfurt school of Marxist criticism, Adorno attacked Lukács for his dogmatic rejection of nonrealist modern literature and for his elevation of content over form. Art does not equal science, Adorno insisted, and should not be measured by or tied to empirical forms of knowledge. He also argued that the **interior monologues** of modernist works reflect the fact of modern alienation in a way that Marxist criticism ought to find compelling.

In addition to opposing Lukács and his overly constrictive **canon,** non-Soviet Marxists took advantage of insights generated by non-Marxist critical theories being developed in post–World War II Europe. **Structuralism,** a scientific approach to the study of humankind whose proponents believed that all elements of culture, including literature, could be understood as parts of a system of **signs,** was one such movement. Lucien Goldmann, a Romanian critic living in Paris, combined structuralist principles with Marx's base-superstructure model in order to show how economics determines the mental structures of social groups, which are reflected in literary texts. Goldmann rejected the idea of individual human genius, choosing instead to see works as the "collective" products of "trans-individual" mental structures.

Unlike Goldmann, who combined Marxism and structuralism, French Marxist Louis Althusser drew on the ideas of the **psychoanalytic** theorist Jacques Lacan and the Italian communist Antonio Gramsci, who discussed the relationship between ideology and **hegemony,** the pervasive system of assumptions and values that shapes the perception of reality for people in a given culture. Like Gramsci, Althusser viewed literary works primarily in terms of their relationship to ideology, the function of which, he argued, is to (re)produce the existing relations of production in a given society and, hence, to ensure that the proletariat remains subordinate to the dominant class. Althusser conceded that working-class people have some freedom to struggle against ideology; he even conceded that ideology was riven with **contradictions** that works of literature sometimes expose and that litera-ture — like all social forms — has some degree of autonomy. But he fol-lowed Marx and Gramsci in suggesting that literature must be seen in *rela-tion* to ideology.

Althusser's followers included Macherey, who in *A Theory of Literary Production* (1966) developed Althusser's concept of the relationship be-tween literature and ideology. A realistic novelist, he argued, attempts to produce a unified, coherent text, but instead ends up producing a work containing lapses, omissions, and gaps. Why? Because within any ideology there are subjects that cannot be covered, things that cannot be said, con-tradictory views that aren't recognized as contradictory. (The critic's chal-lenge, in this case, is to supply what the text cannot say, thereby making sense of gaps and contradictions.) Furthermore, works don't simply reflect ideology (which Goldmann referred to as "myth" and which Macherey identified as a system of "illusory social beliefs"); they are also "fictions," works of art, products of ideology that offer what Goldmann would call a "world-view." What kind of product, Macherey implicitly asked, is identi-cal to the thing that produced it?

A follower of Althusser, Macherey is sometimes called a *post-Althusserian Marxist*. Eagleton, too, is often described that way, as is his American contemporary, Fredric Jameson. Jameson and Eagleton, both post-Althusserians, are also among the few Contemporary Anglo-American crit-ics who have closely followed and significantly developed Marxist thought. Previously, Marxist interpretation in English was limited to the work of a handful of critics who generally eschewed Continental Marxist thinkers like Althusser: Christopher Caudwell, Christopher Hill, Arnold Kettle, E. P. Thompson, and Raymond Williams. Of these, Williams — a critic often associated with **cultural criticism** — was the most influential and per-haps the least Marxist in orientation: He felt that Marxist critics unduly isolated economics from culture; that they overlooked individualism, opt-ing instead to see people as "masses"; and that they had become an elitist group. Williams preferred to talk about "culture" instead of ideology; he argued in works such as *Culture and Society: 1780–1950* (1958) that cul-ture is "lived experience" and, as such, an interconnected set of social properties, all grounded in and influencing history.

Eagleton's *Criticism and Ideology* (1978) is in many ways a response to the work of Williams. Eagleton proposed an elaborate theory about how history — in the form of "general," "authorial," and "aesthetic" ideology — enters texts, which in turn may revivify, open up, or critique those same ideologies, setting in motion a process that may alter history. He showed how texts by Jane Austen, Matthew Arnold, Charles Dickens, George Eliot, Joseph Conrad, and T. S. Eliot address **conflicts** at the heart of the ideologies behind them: conflicts between morality and individualism, indi-vidualism and social organicism and utilitarianism.

As all this emphasis on ideology and conflict suggests, a modern British Marxist like Eagleton, even while acknowledging the work of a British predecessor like Williams, tends to develop the ideas of Continental Marxists. Modern American Marxists like Jameson also make far more use of Lukács, Adorno, Althusser, and non-Marxist structuralist, psychoanalytic, and **poststructuralist** critics.

In *Marxism and Form* (1971), Jameson takes up the question of form and content, arguing that the former is "but the working out" of the latter "in the realm of superstructure." (In making such a statement, Jameson opposes not only the tenets of **Russian formalists,** for whom content had merely been the fleshing out of form, but also of so-called vulgar Marxists, who tended to define form as mere ornamentation or window-dressing.) In *The Political Unconscious* (1981), Jameson uses what in *Marxism and Form* he had called a **dialectical criticism** to synthesize a set of complex arguments out of structuralism and poststructuralism, Freud and Lacan, Althusser and Adorno.

The fractured state of societies and the isolated condition of individuals, Jameson argued, may be seen as indications that an unfallen state that may be called "primitive communism" originally existed. History — which records the subsequent divisions and alienations — limits awareness of its own contradictions and of that lost, Better State via ideologies and their manifestation in texts, which essentially contain and repress desire, especially revolutionary desire, into the **collective unconscious.** For instance, Jameson argues that in Joseph Conrad's *Lord Jim* (1900), the knowledge that governing classes don't deserve their power is contained and repressed by an ending that metaphysically blames Nature for Jim's tragedy and that **melodramatically** blames wicked Gentleman Brown. Such textual strategies of containment and concealment may be discovered by the critic, but only by the critic practicing dialectical criticism, that is, a criticism aware of its own status as ideology. All thought, Jameson concludes, is ideological; only through ideological thought that knows itself as such can we see through ideologies and eventually transcend them.

masculine ending: A line of **verse** ending with a **stressed** syllable is said to have a masculine ending.
EXAMPLE: Every line of this **stanza** from Stevie Smith's "Our Bog is Dood" (1950) has a masculine ending:

> Our Bog is dood, our Bog is dood,
> They lisped in accents mild,
> But when I asked them to explain
> They grew a little wild.
> How do you know your Bog is dood
> My darling little child?

masculine rhyme: Rhyme involving **stressed,** single-syllable words.
EXAMPLES: The first and second (*Jill / hill*), as well as the fourth and fifth (*down / crown*), lines of this nursery rhyme contain masculine rhyme:

> Jack and Jill
> Went up the hill
> To fetch a pail of water.
> Jack fell down
> And broke his crown
> And Jill came tumbling after.

Sun/run and *meat/sweet* are masculine rhymes in Langston Hughes's "Harlem" (1951):

> What happens to a dream deferred?
>
> Does it dry up
> like a raisin in the sun?
> Or fester like a sore —
> And then run?
> Does it stink like rotten meat?
> Or crust and sugar over —
> Like a syrupy sweet?
>
> Maybe it just sags
> like a heavy load.
>
> *Or does it explode?*

mask: See **masque.**

masque (mask): A lavish form of courtly entertainment that flourished in England in the sixteenth and seventeenth centuries (more specifically, during the reigns of Elizabeth I, James I, and Charles I) until it was brought to an abrupt halt by the Puritan Revolution in 1642. The masque generally had a very thin **plot** line, typically dealing with **mythological** or **allegorical** figures, which served only to provide a framework (or excuse) for the dancing, music, elaborate costumes, and general spectacle that were its main features. The dancers and speaking **characters** wore masks, hence the name *masque.* Noble or even royal amateurs were the actors and dancers in these productions; commoners were only permitted to perform in the **antimasque,** a **grotesque** or bawdy interlude developed by Ben Jonson, a noted masque writer, as a **foil** to the elegant masque. Many **Elizabethan** playwrights also used the masque as an element of their popular dramas.

Over time, the masque developed from pure spectacle to spectacle with a more artistic or literary purpose. The essential masque, the early form, placed the greatest emphasis on astounding the eye and ear with its parade of beautiful and fabulous figures and rapidly changing **scenes,** all accompanied by appropriate music. With the development of the antimasque, the literary and dramatic qualities of the performance increased significantly, to the point that poetic effect and significant action became elements of the masque. The masque achieved its greatest height under Jonson and the architect Inigo Jones, who designed the visual aspects (sets, stage machinery, costumes, etc.) for performances of Jonson's plays.

EXAMPLES: John Milton's *Comus* (1634) is a masque. William Shakespeare's *The Tempest* (1610–11) includes a masque in Act 4. Peter Greenaway's movie *Prospero's Books* (1991) also includes a masque.

maxim: See **aphorism**. See also **folklore**.

mechanic form: See **organic form and mechanic form**.

medieval: From the Latin meaning "middle age," an adjective now used broadly to refer to that period of European history alternatively called the *Middle Ages* or, more specifically, to aspects and products of that same period. Thus one may refer not only to the *Medieval Period* but also to medieval art, architecture, attitudes, history, literature, philosophy, and theology. The term *Middle Ages* — or its equivalent in languages other than English — was first used during the **Renaissance** by writers who felt more artistic, intellectual, and spiritual affinity with the **classical** world of ancient Greece and Rome than with Europe as it had evolved, after the fall of the Roman Empire, under the control of what we now call the Catholic Church. The term *medieval* (originally spelled *mediaeval*) was not introduced into English until the nineteenth century, a period of heightened interest in the art, history, and thought of the Middle Ages. This interest, exhibited in the work of certain **romantic** poets and furthered (during the **Victorian Period**) by the poets and painters associated with **Pre-Raphaelitism**, came to be called *medievalism*.

There is some disagreement about whether the Middle Ages, or Medieval Period, began in the third, fourth, or fifth century A.D., although most scholars associate the period's beginnings with the Roman Empire's collapse. That collapse, which began in A.D. 410 as tribes of Germanic "Visigoths" poured southward through Italy and into Rome, was complete by A.D. 476, when the Emperor Romulus was swept out of power by a German tribal chief named Odoacer. Scholars also debate when the Medieval Period ended. Some maintain that it came to a close in 1453 — when Turkish forces conquered Constantinople, thereby causing the migration of Greek scholars into Western Europe. Others take the more general view that the Middle Ages ended with the rise of the Renaissance, which spread beyond Italy throughout Europe during the fifteenth century. Scholars generally agree, however, that the persistent popular assumption that centuries associated with the Medieval Period can be accurately represented by the phrase *Dark Ages* is misleading at best and grossly inaccurate at worst.

The tribes of Visigoths, or Goths (from whom we get the word **Gothic**), that had defeated the armies of Rome also penetrated westward into Gaul (now France) and Spain. Later, the Goths were themselves defeated by Moorish Africans who landed in Spain in A.D. 711 and subsequently introduced sophisticated elements of Arabic civilization throughout Spain and other parts of southern Europe. In the meantime, from Italy northward to Germany — under the influence of a Church that, though centered in Rome, had survived and then thrived following the empire's collapse —

medieval societies developed that were anything but barbaric and chaotic, artless and ignorant.

The Church successfully conveyed to a diverse group of peoples (many of whom had lived in wandering tribes) the value of a stable moral and civil order. Indeed, the foundations of several modern European nations were laid during medieval times. Charlemagne ("Charles the Great") not only conquered vast areas of what is now France but also set out to organize, educate, and unify the people living in the areas he ruled as King of the Franks beginning in A.D. 768 and as Emperor of the West from 800 until his death in 814. In England, a group of noblemen united in 1215 to dilute the power of King John, forcing the autocratic monarch to sign a list of rights and provisions guaranteeing, among other things, that taxes could only be "levied with the consent of a council of prelates and greater barons" and that "no freeman shall be arrested, imprisoned, or deprived of property except by judgment of his equals or the law of the land." This list, known as the Magna Carta, or "Great Charter," limited the power of King John and subsequent English monarchs over their subjects and pointed the way toward more democratic government.

Certain historical developments identified with medieval history were unquestionably uncivilized; bloody Inquisitions designed to root heretics out of the Church are among the reasons the Middle Ages have been referred to as the Dark Ages. However, chivalric ideals (such as courtesy) and highly "civilized" **courtly love** traditions and **conventions** were also developed during the Middle Ages. Furthermore, some of the imperialistic military initiatives, such as the Crusades, led to new markets and some degree of cultural cross-fertilization between Western Europe on the one hand and Arabic, Jewish, and Byzantine civilizations on the other. Perhaps as a result, **medieval romances** paint a portrait of Western Europe delicately marked by Eastern influences, such as those of the Persian **tale**.

Medieval art encompasses sophisticated media developed by persons of extraordinary talent whose work made Renaissance art possible. It includes gorgeously colored, "illuminated" manuscripts produced from the seventh through the fifteenth century A.D., the paintings of Giotto (1266?–1337), sculptures by Claus Sluter (1350–1406), and architecturally dazzling cathedrals such as the ones at Chartres (France) and Cologne (Germany), begun in the 1100s and 1200s, respectively. Outstanding medieval literary works include Boethius's "Consolation of Philosophy" (A.D. 524), the Anglo-Saxon **epic** *Beowulf* (c. A.D. 700), numerous medieval dramas (spanning the period 900 through 1400), Icelandic sagas (such as *Grettirsaga* and *Volsunsaga,* c. 1100–1200), *Le roman de la rose* (c. 1230, 1270) by Guilliame de Lorris and Jean de Meung, Dante Alighieri's *The Divine Comedy* (1321), Petrarch's sonnets (c. 1350), and Geoffrey Chaucer's *The Canterbury Tales* (c. 1387).

When referring to medieval literature in English, scholars typically divide the Medieval Period into the **Old English Period** and the **Middle English Period**.

See also **Middle English Period (in English literature), Old English Period (in English literature).**

medievalism: See **medieval.**

Medieval Period: See **medieval.**

medieval romance (chivalric romance): A **narrative,** written in prose or verse and concerned with adventure, **courtly love,** and chivalry. Popular during the **Middle Ages,** these **tales** often revolve around love as ideally practiced by the nobility and relate exciting occurrences ranging from the slaying of dragons to jousting in tournaments to the casting of spells. A typical story line might involve an adventurous young knight who takes up a quest to accomplish a particular goal, but whose progress is impeded by a variety of **fantastic antagonists** and obstacles. Some medieval romances are more religious in story line, **motivation, theme,** and **symbolism** than are others; all, however, are written in praise of both religious and chivalric ideals (such as courage, manners, piety, and loyalty).

The medieval romance developed as a narrative verse form in twelfth-century France before spreading to other parts of Europe, where it displaced the **epic** (in France, it overshadowed the epic form called the *chanson de geste*) and other forms of **heroic** narrative. The era of the epic, with its emphasis on the heroic (matters associated with tribal warfare), ended with the birth of the **romance,** which stressed the chivalric (matters associated with courtly traditions). Particular stories or **legends** from four traditions were recycled as subject matter. These traditions included Celtic lore (sometimes referred to as *Matter of Britain*), the history and legends of **classical** times (*Matter of Rome*), material involving Charlemagne and his era (*Matter of France*), and stories about Germanic / English **heroes** (*Matter of England*). English medieval romances, which appeared in the thirteenth century, tended to draw on all these traditions except for the "Matter of France." The French tradition drew and elaborated on the Celtic "Matter of Britain," especially the stories involving Arthurian legend, by adding such figures as Tristram and Lancelot not present in the original legends. On occasion, "Oriental" (Arabian or Persian) legend was also used in these romances.

EXAMPLES: Medieval metrical romances (that is, romances composed in verse) include Chrétien de Troyes's twelfth-century French romances *Lancelot* and *Perceval,* the anonymous thirteenth-century English romance *King Horn,* Wolfram von Eschenbach's thirteenth-century German romance *Parzifal,* and the anonymous fourteenth-century English romance *Sir Gawain and the Green Knight.* Sir Thomas Malory's fifteenth-century English medieval romance *Morte d'Arthur,* unlike the romances mentioned above, was written in prose.

meiosis: From the Greek for "lessening," a term referring to the use of *understatement.* The author using meiosis typically describes something in a way that, taken literally, minimizes its evident significance or gravity.

Authors often use meiosis for humorous, **ironic,** or even **satiric** effect. **Litotes,** a type of meiosis, involves making an affirmative point by denying its opposite.

The use of a simple, unadorned statement to underscore the **pathetic** or **tragic** has also been referred to as meiosis by certain critics.

EXAMPLES: In "The Open Window" (1928), a short story by Saki (H. H. Munro), a fifteen-year-old girl terrorizes a neurotic new neighbor, Framton Nuttel, who has come calling on her aunt. She does so by telling him a story in which her aunt's husband and two brothers were drowned in a bog while hunting, their bodies never recovered — a story designed to make Nuttel believe that the three hunters striding toward the window by which he sits are the ghosts of the dead men. The last sentence of "The Open Window," which refers to the girl, affords an example of meiosis: "Romance at short notice was her specialty."

For a graphic example of meiosis, see page 257.

melodrama: Originally, any **drama** accompanied by music used to enhance the emotional impact and **mood** of the performance. The term derives from the Greek *melos,* which means "song." In early-nineteenth-century London, melodramas became increasingly popular as a method of circumventing the Licensing Act, a law authorizing only the Drury Lane and Covent Garden theaters to present so-called legitimate plays but permitting musical entertainments to be performed elsewhere.

In the **Victorian Period,** melodrama came to emphasize the **conflict** between pure good and evil. Its **heroes** and **heroines** were inevitably completely moral and upright but terrorized, harassed, or otherwise troubled by thoroughly despicable **villains.** No matter what the ostensible subject matter, the chief concern of melodrama was to elicit the desired emotional response from the audience. To this end, writers frequently employed improbable situations, malevolent **intrigue,** and stock elements to produce feelings in the audience ranging from pity to terror to joy to moral indignation. Romantic **plots** twisted by a scheming villain were typical, as were ultimately unbelievably happy endings in which **poetic justice** required that evil be punished and good rewarded.

Today, *melodrama* and *melodramatic* are generally used pejoratively, although they may still be used in a purely descriptive sense for any work that relies on sensational events and improbabilities for dramatic effect.

EXAMPLES: Alexandre Dumas's *The Count of Monte Cristo* (1844–45) is a melodramatic novel.

Although Charles Dickens pokes fun at "modern melodramas" in *Oliver Twist* (1837), contemporary critics would say that that novel is itself a Victorian melodrama, thanks to scenes like the famous one in which Oliver finishes his gruel, extends his empty bowl to the workhouse master, and says, "Please, sir, I want some more."

The contemporary popular novelist Danielle Steele also writes melodramatic novels. Her novels contain such melodramatic elements as the embattled but thoroughly good heroine pitted against some evil force or nasty situation through no fault of her own, improbable plot twists that provoke **stock responses** of anger and compassion from the reader, and the traditionally happy ending wherein the heroine gets married and has a baby.

Jean Cocteau's play *Les parents terribles* (1939) simultaneously exemplifies and **parodies** the excesses of melodramatic **convention.**

meiosis: The above cartoon from Matt Groening's *The Big Book of Hell* (1990) represents a humorous use of meiosis, but with a more serious satirical dimension. The little bunny's passive construction, "Mistakes were made," is a comical attempt to distance himself from the mess he has created and is also an **allusion** to a political scandal of the mid-1980s, when President Ronald Reagan used the same words to refer to his administration's involvement in the Iran-Contra arms-for-hostages deal.

memoir: A **narrative** account typically written by an individual that depicts things, persons, or events the individual has known or experienced. Memoirs combine elements of **biography** and **autobiography** but are nonetheless distinguishable from both of these **genres.**

Memoirs differ from biographies in their focus on personal recollection—that is, on relating subject matter personally known or experienced by the writer. Thus, they tend to be far more **subjective** than biographies, which are typically the product of extensive research.

Memoirs differ from autobiographies in their degree of outward focus. While they can be considered a form of autobiographical writing, their personalized accounts tend to focus more on what the writer has witnessed than on his or her own life, character, and developing self.

Some novels purport to be or to include the memoirs of **characters** or other **fictional** persons whose writings have been discovered, recorded, or otherwise preserved.

EXAMPLES: William Godwin's *Memoirs of Mary Wollstonecraft* (1798) (a memoir about the life and loss of Wollstonecraft, author of *A Vindication of the Rights of Woman* [1792], by her anarchist husband); John Edgar Wideman's *Brothers and Keepers* (1984) (a memoir about Wideman's brother Robby, who was convicted of murder because his partner killed someone while the two were committing a robbery, and Wideman's efforts to come to terms with Robby's conviction and its consequences); Jung Chang's *Wild Swans: Three Daughters of China* (1991) (an **epic** account of three generations of Chang family women); Frank McCourt's *Angela's Ashes* (1996) (an account of the McCourt family—especially McCourt's mother, Angela—and of growing up poor in Ireland); James McBride's *The Color of Water* (1996) (a book that focuses on McBride's mother, a Polish Jew who married a black Baptist minister and raised twelve children); Marian Wright Edelman's *Lanterns: A Memoir of Mentors* (1999) (a tribute to those who helped shape Edelman's life); and critic and novelist John Bailey's *Iris and Her Friends* (2000) (Bailey's account of his life with his wife, novelist Iris Murdoch, begun as she moved into the last stages of Alzheimer's disease). That the boundary between memoirs, biographies, and autobiographies can be blurry is demonstrated by works such as *The Color of Water* and *Angela's Ashes,* which have also been categorized, respectively, as biography and autobiography.

Arthur Golden's *Memoirs of a Geisha* (1997) is an example of a **historical novel** that purports to be a memoir; in the fictive "Translator's Note" to the book, we learn that one Jakob Haarhuis, the Arnold Rusoff Professor of Japanese History at New York University, was granted permission to record the memoirs of Nitta Sayuri (born Chiyo Minoru), a geisha in Kyoto, Japan, before and after World War II, and to publish them after her death. In discussing the nature of a memoir, the fictional Professor Haarhuis opines that "[a] memoir provides a record not so much of the memoirist as of the memoirist's world. It must differ from biography in that a memoirist can never achieve the perspective that a biographer possesses as a matter of course. Autobiography, if there really is such a thing, is like asking a rabbit to tell us what he looks like hopping through the grasses of the field. How would he know?"

Anita Shreve's novel *The Weight of Water* (1997) is composed of alternating narratives: the **first-person** account of Jean Janes, a newspaper photographer who in 1995 travels to an island off the Maine coast to research a century-old double murder; the fictional private memoir of Maren Hortvedt, a third woman who was in the house when the murders occurred but who survived; and the actual court records regarding the trial of a man eventually convicted of the crime on which the novel is based.

Menippean satire: A type of indirect prose **satire** punctuated with verse and framed by a loose **narrative** story, named for its creator, the Greek Cynic philosopher Menippus (fl. 250 B.C.). None of Menippus' own works, which included "The Sale of Diogenes" and "Necromancy," survives.

Menippean satires frequently feature banqueting scenes or other **settings** in which extended and ridiculous debates take place. Far from being fully developed **characters,** the debaters are often little more than **caricatures** who merely serve to represent the ideas they expound. Particularly in shorter works, this type of satire emphasizes intellectual **conflict,** and the absurdity of some of the arguments and viewpoints expressed is a characteristic feature. In longer works, Menippean satirists often introduce a dizzying range of facts but subordinate them to some organizing principle or **theme,** thereby making clear their own general perspective.

Menippean satire is also called *Varronian satire,* so named for one of Menippus' imitators, the Roman writer Varro. In his book *The Anatomy of Criticism* (1957), Northrop Frye refers to this type of writing, centered around opposing ideas and erudite argument, as "anatomy"; he took the term from the title of a famous Menippean satire, Robert Burton's *Anatomy of Melancholy* (1621).

EXAMPLES: Lewis Carroll's *Alice's Adventures in Wonderland* (1865) and *Through the Looking Glass* (1872).

metafiction: A literary term popularized by Robert Scholes to describe novels that specifically and self-consciously examine the nature and status of **fiction** itself and that often seek to test fiction as a **form** in one way or another. (As a word, *metafiction* means something like "fiction about fiction.") In *Metafiction: The Theory and Practice of Self-Conscious Fiction* (1984), theorist Patricia Waugh described metafiction as "fictional writing which self-consciously and systematically draws attention to its status as an artifact in order to pose questions about the relationship between fiction and reality." Novelist and theorist John Barth said that metafiction is a "novel that imitates a novel rather than the real world." Most metafictions cannot be easily classified in the conventional categories of **realism** or **romance** and in fact flout the rules and conventions of these **genres.**

EXAMPLES: Barth's *Lost in the Funhouse* (1967), Richard Brautigan's *Trout Fishing in America* (1967), John Fowles's *The French Lieutenant's Woman* (1969), Raymond Federman's *Double or Nothing: A Real, Fictitious Discourse* (1971), Umberto Eco's *Il nome della rosa* (*The Name of the Rose*) (1980), Donald Barthelme's *Overnight to Many Distant Cities* (1983), Robert Coover's *Gerald's Party* (1985), and Salman Rushdie's *Midnight's Children* (1981) and *The Moor's Last Sigh* (1995). Japanese novelist Yasutaka Tsutsui, who shifted toward **cyberfiction** in the 1990s, has written numerous metafictional works. Fowles's *Mantissa* (1982) is a metafictional **parody** of metaficiton.

Michael Faber's *The Crimson Petal and the White* (2002) is a **postmodern,** metaphysical version of **Victorian** fiction. **Influenced** by the novels of Charles Dickens, it features **characters** who are writing books of their own.

metaphor: A **figure of speech** (more specifically a **trope**) that associates two distinct things; the representation of one thing by another. The **image** (or activity or concept) used to represent or "figure" something else is the **vehicle** of the figure of speech; the thing represented is called the **tenor.** For instance, in the sentence "That child is a mouse," the child is the tenor, whereas the mouse is the vehicle. The image of a mouse is being used to represent the child, perhaps to emphasize his or her timidity.

Metaphor should be distinguished from **simile,** another figure of speech with which it is sometimes confused. Similes compare two distinct things by using a connective word such as *like* or *as*. Metaphors use no connective word to make their comparison. Furthermore, critics ranging from Aristotle to I. A. Richards have argued that metaphors equate the vehicle with the tenor instead of simply comparing the two.

This identification of vehicle and tenor can provide much additional meaning. For instance, instead of saying, "Last night I read a book," we might say, "Last night I plowed through a book." "Plowed through" (or the activity of plowing) is the vehicle of our metaphor; "read" (or the act of reading) is the tenor, the thing being figured. (As this example shows, neither vehicle nor tenor need be a noun; metaphors may employ other parts of speech.) The increment in meaning through metaphor is fairly obvious. Our audience knows not only *that* we read but also *how* we read, because to read a book in the way that a plow rips through earth is surely to read in a relentless, unreflective way. Note that in the sentence above, a new metaphor — "rips through" — has been used to explain an old one. This serves (which is a metaphor) as an example of just how thick (another metaphor) language is with metaphors!

Metaphors may be classified as *direct* or *implied*. A direct metaphor, such as "That child is a mouse" (or "He is such a doormat!"), specifies both tenor and vehicle. An implied metaphor, by contrast, mentions only the vehicle; the tenor is implied by the context of the sentence or passage. For instance, in the sentence "Last night I plowed through a book" (or "She sliced through traffic"), the tenor — the act of reading (or driving) — can be inferred.

Furthermore, certain types of metaphors are given special names. A **dead metaphor** is a phrase that — although a metaphor — is no longer recognized as such because it has become so familiar. "Getting the hang of things" is a common phrase that few people think of as a metaphor today. A *mixed metaphor* exists when more than one vehicle is used to represent the same tenor. What makes this type of metaphor truly "mixed" is the (sometimes incongruous) presence of multiple — and very different — vehicles. In his essay "Politics and the English Language" (1946), George Orwell gives as an example of mixed metaphor the sentence "The fascist octopus has sung its swan song."

Traditionally, metaphor has been viewed as the most significant of the five principal tropes, the others being simile, **metonymy, personification, and synecdoche.**

FURTHER EXAMPLES: **Victorian** poet Matthew Arnold rather obviously makes the sea a metaphor for religious faith in his poem "Dover Beach" (1867):

> The Sea of Faith
> Was once, too, at the full, and round earth's shore. . . .

Modernist poet D. H. Lawrence uses metaphor less obtrusively in his poem "Cypresses" (1923) in which the tall, thin, blackish-green trees so familiar in European paintings are metaphorically transformed into "supple, brooding, softly-swaying pillars of dark flame."

Novelists, as well as poets, use metaphor extensively; in his Pulitzer Prize–winning novel *Rabbit, Run* (1960), John Updike's metaphors draw comparisons while also revealing the obsessions and anxieties of his **protagonist,** a twenty-six-year-old car salesman feeling trapped by marriage and domesticity. At one point Henry "Rabbit" Angstrom thinks of Chinese food metaphorically: "Candy. Heaped on a smoking breast of rice." In a later passage, while driving from his mistress's apartment to his wife's house, Rabbit thinks of himself in metaphorical terms as a knife:

> The car smells secure: rubber and dust and painted metal hot in the sun. A sheath for the knife of himself. He cuts through the Sunday-stunned town, the soft rows of domestic brick, the bannistered porches of calm wood.

In Carrie Fisher's *Postcards from the Edge* (1987), the protagonist is told that

> In India, they say that the body is the envelope of the spirit, and the spirit, I guess, is essentially who you are. Well, we live in a city of envelopes. The thing that's terrific about you is that *you* are a *letter*. I mean, it takes a letter to know a letter, and I can see we're really two letters in a town of envelopes. . . .

In the following passage from the Pulitzer Prize–winning novel *The Shipping News* (1993), E. Annie Proulx combines several metaphors with a single simile comparing the sea to milk:

It seemed the bird was trying to break from the closed room of sea and rock and sky into the vastness of his bare chamber. The whisper of his feet on the floor. Beyond the glass the sea lay pale as milk, pale the sky, scratched and scribbled with cloud welts. The empty bay, far shore creamed with fog.

Tom Petty's song title "Love Is a Long, Long Road" (1989) is metaphorical, as is the Rolling Stones' title "She's So Cold" (1980). In the latter, a reference to a bleeding volcano mixes two vehicles (wound and eruption) to represent one tenor (emotional overflow).

See **metonymy** for a discussion of the distinction (or lack thereof) between metaphor and metonymy.

metaphysical conceit: An extended **figure of speech** most commonly associated with **metaphysical poetry.** The metaphysical conceit involves the use of **paradox, images** from arcane sources not usually drawn upon by poets, and an original and usually complex comparison between two highly dissimilar things. The originality of a metaphysical conceit often derives from ordinary or esoteric materials used in a previously unthought-of way. A single metaphysical conceit may function as the controlling **image** for the entire poem.

After the seventeenth century, the metaphysical conceit fell into disuse. It regained popularity during the early decades of the twentieth century, however, thanks to the revival of interest in the metaphysical poets as paragons of intellectual precision and psychological analysis. H. J. C. Grierson, T. S. Eliot, and **the New Critics** were largely responsible for this revaluation of the metaphysical poets, who had for hundreds of years been considered quirky, esoteric writers at best.

EXAMPLE: The following **stanzas** from John Donne's "A Valediction: Forbidding Mourning" (1640), a poem about lovers parting, typify metaphysical poetry. They exhibit an analytical approach to subject matter ("therefore," "though," "if," "yet"), contain striking images ("like gold to airy thinness beat"), and use highly original comparisons (between couples and drawing compasses) to register complex thoughts colored by emotion:

> Our two souls therefore, which are one,
>   Though I must go, endure not yet
> A breach, but an expansion,
>   Like gold to airy thinness beat.
>
> If they be two, they are two so
>   As stiff twin compasses are two;
> Thy soul, the fixed foot, makes no show
>   To move, but doth, if th' other do.
>
> And though it in the center sit,
>   Yet when the other far doth roam,
> It leans and hearkens after it,
>   And grows erect, as that comes home.

The extended comparison between lovers and a compass is perhaps the most famous and acclaimed of all metaphysical conceits.

metaphysical poetry: A term that can be applied to any **poetry** that deals with philosophical or spiritual matters but that is generally limited to works written by a specific group of seventeenth-century poets who wrote in the manner of the poet John Donne. Aside from Donne, the poets commonly referred to as metaphysical poets include John Cleveland, Abraham Cowley, Richard Crashaw, George Herbert, Andrew Marvell, and Henry Vaughn.

Metaphysical is, in fact, something of a misnomer when applied to these writers, since they tend to be more concerned with how to regard God and women than with the essence of reality, the true domain of metaphysical concern. Nonetheless, the label has stuck ever since Samuel Johnson (following John Dryden, who first applied the adjective *metaphysical* to Donne specifically) used it to describe this group of poets.

The metaphysical poets are linked not so much by a common *Weltanschauung* ("worldview") as by **style** and modes of poetic organization that stemmed from their reaction against idealized **Elizabethan** love poetry. Their poems frequently take the form of arguments that yoke **wit** and originality with powerful emotions. Common elements include the following: (1) an analytical approach to subject matter (and an accompanying intellectual **tone**); (2) colloquial language; (3) **rhythmic** patterns that are often rough or irregular; and (4) the **metaphysical conceit, a figure of speech** used to capture thought and emotion as accurately as possible.

meter (metre): The more or less regular pattern of **accented** and unaccented syllables in **poetry.** Four basic kinds of meter exist: *quantitative, accentual, syllabic,* and *accentual-syllabic.* English verse is generally written in accentual-syllabic **rhythm,** in which both the number of syllables and the number of stressed and unstressed syllables are relatively consistent from line to line. The metrical unit of a line of verse is called a **foot** and usually consists of one stressed syllable and one or more unstressed syllables. Standard English feet include the **iamb, trochee, anapest, dactyl, spondee,** and **pyrrhic.**

Meter is typically described by using the dominant type of foot, the number of feet per line, or a combination of these two factors. When scholars describe meter based on the type of foot used in a passage, they refer to the meter as iambic, trochaic, anapestic, dactylic, spondaic, pyrrhic, and so forth. Of course, few poems are written using only one type of foot; poets generally vary the metrical pattern to avoid sounding singsongy or like a metronome. Identifying the poem's meter thus requires identifying the dominant type of foot used. Alternatively, scholars may describe the meter based on the number of feet per line. Standard English lines ranging, respectively, from one to eight feet per line include **monometer, dimeter, trimeter, tetrameter, pentameter, hexameter, heptameter,** and **octameter** (though monometer and octameter are rare). Finally, scholars may use a combination of the dominant type of foot and the number of feet in a line to describe the meter of a passage. Common metrical lines include iambic pentameter and trochaic tetrameter.

metonymy: From the Greek for "change of name," a **figure of speech** in which one thing is represented by another that is commonly and often physically associated with it. Referring to someone's handwriting as his or her "hand," or calling a monarch "the crown," involves use of a metonymic figure.

Metonymy is one of the five principal **tropes,** figures of speech in which a word or phrase is "turned" or "twisted" to make it mean something else. Certain **structuralists,** such as Roman Jakobson, have emphasized the difference between metonymy and **metaphor,** a trope in which two distinct things are associated or equated (for example, silence and gold in the phrase "silence is golden"). Such theorists argue that metonymy entails a contiguous association between **vehicle** and **tenor,** whereas metaphor involves a similarity that is perceived as more fundamental. (The vehicle is the **image,** activity, or concept used to represent or "figure" something else — for example, hand or gold — whereas the tenor is the thing being represented — for example, handwriting or silence.)

Certain contemporary critics, particularly those associated with **deconstruction,** have taken issue with the characterization of metonymy as involving an intrinsic association between vehicle and tenor. Deconstructors, who maintain that *all* figuration is arbitrary, contend that the vehicles of metonyms and metaphors alike are arbitrarily (rather than intrinsically) associated with their tenors. For instance, they would say that there is no special, intrinsic likeness or relationship between crowns and monarchs; it's just that crowns traditionally sit on monarchs' heads and not on the heads of university professors. In addition, deconstructors including Paul de Man and J. Hillis Miller have questioned the **privilege** that structuralists grant to metaphor — commonly viewed as the most significant of the five principle tropes — and have challenged the metaphor / metonymy distinction or "opposition," suggesting that all metaphors are really metonyms.

EXAMPLES: The opening line of the Pledge of Allegiance, "I pledge allegiance to the flag," exhibits metonymy, given that the Stars and Stripes are being used to represent the United States of America.

In Joseph Conrad's *Lord Jim* (1900), the alcoholic chief engineer of the ill-fated ship *Patna* is said to have been "shut . . . up with a supply of bottles in an upstairs room" of "Mariani's billiard-room and grog shop." What the engineer is really "shut up with," of course, is a supply of "grog," or liquor, which just happens to be stored in bottles in most cultures. Thus, in this passage, "bottles" is a metonym for booze, with which it is commonly, but arbitrarily (that is, not intrinsically), associated.

The following sentence from the opening paragraph of George Eliot's *Adam Bede* (1859) also involves metonymy:

> With this drop of ink at the end of my pen, I will show you the roomy workshop of Mr. Jonathan Burge, carpenter and builder, in the village of Hayslope, as it appeared on the eighteenth of June, in the year of our Lord 1799.

A "drop of ink," of course, cannot describe the workshop to readers, but the words used by a writer can. The "drop of ink" thus serves as a metonym for "words."

In Shirley Hazzard's *The Transit of Venus* (1980), a character named Ted Tice says "Paul Ivory is marrying that castle," by which he means metonymically that Paul — engaged to a daughter of an English lord — is marrying neither a building nor a woman but, rather, the British aristocracy, with all the rights and liabilities that pertain.

metre: See **meter.**

metrical accent: See **accent.**

metrics: The study of **rhythm** and **accent** (and their patterns) in **verse.**

Middle Ages: See **medieval, Middle English Period (in English literature).**

Middle English Period (in English literature): An era usually said to span the years 1100–1500. The grammatical system of **Old English** began undergoing changes that laid the groundwork for a new linguistic phase even before the arrival in England of the Norman invaders in 1066. During the early part of the Middle English Period, a transitional form of the language — one bridging Old and Middle English — competed first with Anglo-Norman and then with French, the official language of the court and a productive literary language in its own right. (Latin was used in legal and ecclesiastical documents.) Middle English literature thus cannot be said to have existed, properly speaking, before 1200; furthermore, the influence of French was substantial throughout the entire period, particularly in words "imported" from French into English.

Both Anglo-Norman and Middle English were the vehicles of prose chronicles, **chronicle plays, romances,** saints' lives (or **legends**), and **lyric** poetry. In the latter half of the fourteenth century, Middle English poetry flourished in different dialects. William Langland wrote *Piers Plowman* (1366–87) in the West Midlands dialect, which was also employed, albeit with some differences, by the anonymous *Pearl*-poet in both the **dream vision** *Pearl* and the **chivalric romance** *Sir Gawain and the Green Knight* (c. 1400). Both of these poets wrote **alliterative** verse. Geoffrey Chaucer wrote in the London East Midlands dialect. Influenced by Continental writers, however, he experimented with a variety of **genres** and **end-rhymed** verse forms. He is credited in his *Canterbury Tales* (c. 1387) with the first efforts at humor based on dialect, particularly in the *Reeve's Tale.*

The later Middle English Period is renowned for its drama as well as its poetry. **Mystery plays** and **miracle plays** were sponsored by religious and trade guilds, which staged the productions on wagons that moved throughout **medieval** towns, particularly during the summertime festival of Corpus Christi; unfortunately, no texts of these plays survive from earlier than the late fifteenth century. Both types of plays have a long and complex history; both Chaucer in the fourteenth century and William Shakespeare in the sixteenth century had the opportunity to see them.

Middle English prose also came into its own in the last one hundred fifty years of the period and was the vehicle of the earliest known efforts of women writers in English. Noted works include the religious prose of Richard Rolle (c. 1350); the *Showings* of the religious recluse Julian of Norwich (c. 1393); the recorded spiritual **autobiography** of Margery Kempe (c. 1435); and the correspondence of the landowning Paston family of Norfolk, England, commonly referred to as "The Paston Letters" (1422–1509). The most famous secular prose work is Sir Thomas Malory's *Works* (c. 1440), his encyclopedic synthesis of almost three hundred years of the Arthurian literary tradition, edited and printed by William Caxton, the first English printer, as *Morte d'Arthur* (1485).

mimesis: See **imitation.**

mimetic criticism: A type of **criticism** inaugurated by Plato that assumes literary works to be reflections or **representations** of life and the world in general. Mimetic critics evaluate works based on whether they accurately portray their subject matter. Representations of the subject should be "true," according to this school of thought; consequently, **realism** would be among the more modern **genres** meeting with the approval of mimetic critics.

miracle play: A **drama** that recounts the life of a saint, a miracle performed by Christ, or a miracle performed by God through a saint's faith or actions; some, but not all, of these stories come from the Bible. Some scholars make a distinction between miracle plays and **mystery plays,** limiting the former to nonbiblical material (stories about the lives of saints and the miraculous deeds they performed) and reserving the latter for biblical material. Other scholars use the term *miracle play* to refer to a drama in which a miracle is performed by Christ or one of the saints, whether or not the miracle is described in scripture.

Originally developed within the **medieval** Christian Church and written in Latin, miracle plays served as a dramatized part of the liturgical service. With the addition of secular material, they became the province of the towns (in France) and trade guilds (in England), which sponsored and staged them during religious holidays and festivals. In England, miracle plays composed in the vernacular flourished for about four hundred years, their height reached in the fifteenth and sixteenth centuries when they came to include comic elements such as buffoonery and ribaldry to appeal to a popular audience. **Scenes** or episodes were staged by local religious and trade guilds on separate wagons, each of which moved sequentially through a publicized number of places in the town in order to make the drama available to everyone.

EXAMPLES: *Lazarus,* from the Wakefield cycle (c. 1350); the Digby play of *Mary Magdalene* (c. 1480).

See also **mystery play.**

mixed metaphor: See **metaphor.**

mock epic and mock heroic: A type of high **burlesque,** the mock epic is a lengthy **poem** written in the lofty and exalted **style** of the **epic** but that deals with an utterly trivial subject. Mock epics are not generally intended to mock the epic **form** or style, but rather to mock the subject by treating it with a dignity it does not deserve. As numerous scholars and critics have pointed out, however, mock epics inevitably "cut both ways"; that is to say, when ordinary events are described in lofty terms using **classical conventions,** the reader is to some extent made aware of the amusing inappropriateness of heroic language and style as a means of representing life in the world as most human beings have experienced it.

Mock heroic is often used synonymously with *mock epic,* but the former term refers more broadly to any work (not just the epic) in which a trivial subject is **satirized** or ridiculed by discussing it in a lofty or grandiose manner. In this sense, the mock heroic is a style of writing that may be applied to any work burlesqued in this manner.

examples: Alexander Pope's mock-epic poem "The Rape of the Lock" (1712, 1714), which concerns the cutting and theft of a lock of a lady's hair, begins with an invocation to a muse and later describes a card game as if it were a major military battle.

In *Joseph Andrews* (1741), Henry Fielding uses the mock-heroic style to describe the battle waged by "the heroic youth" Joseph Andrews with nine hounds who have set upon the Reverend Abraham Adams. Challenging "those . . . that describe lions and tigers, and heroes fiercer than both" to "raise their poems or plays with the simile of Joseph Andrews, who is himself above the reach of any simile," Fielding proceeds by describing Joseph's dogfight in the following manner:

> Now Rockwood had laid fast hold on the parson's skirts, and stopt his flight; which Joseph no sooner perceived than he levelled his cudgel at his head, and laid him sprawling. Jowler and Ringwood then fell on his greatcoat, and had undoubtedly brought him to the ground, had not Joseph, collecting all his force, given Jowler such a rap on the back that, quitting his hold, he ran howling over the plain: A harder fate remained for thee, O Ringwood! Ringwood the best hound that ever pursued a hare, who never threw his tongue but where the scent was undoubtedly true; good at "trailing," and "sure in a highway"; no "babler," no "overrunner"; respected by the whole pack; for, whenever he opened, they knew the game was at hand. He fell by the stroke of Joseph. Thunder, and Plunder, and Wonder, and Blunder, were the next victims of his wrath, and measured their lengths on the ground. Then Fairmaid, a bitch which Mr. John Temple had bred up in his house, and fed at his own table, and lately sent the squire fifty

miles for a present, ran fiercely at Joseph, and bit him by the leg; no dog was ever fiercer than she, being descended from an Amazonian breed, and had worried bulls in her own country, but now waged an unequal fight, and had shared the fate of those we have mentioned before, had not Diana (the reader may believe it or not, as he pleases) in that instant interposed, and, in the shape of the huntsman, snatched her favourite up in her arms.

mock heroic: See **mock epic and mock heroic.**

modernism: A revolutionary movement encompassing all of the creative arts that had its roots in the 1890s (the *fin de siècle*), a transitional period during which artists and writers sought to liberate themselves from the constraints and polite **conventions** we associate with **Victorianism.** Modernism exploded onto the international scene in the aftermath of World War I, a traumatic transcontinental event that physically devastated and psychologically disillusioned the West in an entirely unprecedented way. A wide variety of new and experimental techniques arose in architecture, dance, literature, music, painting, and sculpture.

As a literary movement, modernism gained prominence during and, especially, just after World War I; it subsequently flourished in Europe and America throughout the 1920s and 1930s. Modernist authors sought to break away from traditions and conventions through experimentation with new literary **forms,** devices, and **styles.** They incorporated the new **psychoanalytic** theories of Sigmund Freud and Carl Jung into their works and paid particular attention to language — both how it is used and how they believed it could or ought to be used. Their works reflected the pervasive sense of loss, disillusionment, and even despair in the wake of the Great War, hence their emphasis on historical discontinuity and the alienation of humanity. Although modernist authors tended to perceive the world as fragmented, many — such as T. S. Eliot and James Joyce — believed they could help counter that disintegration through their works. Such writers viewed art as a potentially integrating, restorative force, a remedy for the uncertainty of the modern world. To this end, even while depicting disorder in their works, modernists also injected order by creating patterns of **allusion, symbol,** and **myth.** This rather exalted view of art fostered a certain elitism among modernists.

Modernism encompassed a number of literary paths, many of which became known as movements in their own right, such as **Dadaism, expressionism, formalism,** and **surrealism.** Modernist works are often called *avant-garde,* an appellation that has also been applied to more radically experimental **postmodernist** works written in the devastating wake of World War II. Many literary scholars distinguish between "old" (or modernist) *avant-garde* works and "new" (or postmodernist) ones. A modernist surrealist work is easily differentiated from a postmodernist **Absurdist** one.

Modern and *modernist* are not synonymous. The term *modern* broadly refers to that which is contemporary, that which pertains to the present day. *Modernist* refers to the complex of characteristics shared by those who embraced or participated in the modernist movement.

EXAMPLES: T. S. Eliot's *The Waste Land* (1922), James Joyce's *Ulysses* (1922), and Virginia Woolf's *To the Lighthouse* (1927) are famous modernist literary works. Modernist art includes the cubist and surrealist paintings of Pablo Picasso (such as *Three Musicians* [1921] and *Three Dancers* [1925], respectively) and the surrealist works of Salvador Dalí. Igor Stravinsky's *Le sacre du printemps* (*The Rite of Spring*) (1933) is an example of modernist music.

Modern Period (in English and American literature): A period in English and American literary history beginning in 1914 with the outbreak of World War I and ending in 1945 with the conclusion of World War II. The term *modern* in the phrase *Modern Period* should not be confused with *modern* as it is more commonly used, that is, to refer to recent or contemporary times. The Modern Period is noted for works characterized by a transnational focus, stylistic unconventionality, or interest in repressed sub- or unconscious material; it includes works written in just about every established **genre** (as well as in new, hybrid forms) by writers such as W. H. Auden, H. D. (Hilda Doolittle), T. S. Eliot, William Faulkner, Robert Frost, James Joyce, D. H. Lawrence, Doris Lessing, Marianne Moore, Eugene O'Neill, Ezra Pound, Dorothy Richardson, George Bernard Shaw, Gertrude Stein, Wallace Stevens, William Carlos Williams, Virginia Woolf, and W. B. Yeats.

Although the beginning of the Modern Period in English literature coincides with the beginning of the **Georgian Age** in English literature, the term *Georgian* is usually used in connection with relatively traditional **pastoral** or **realistic** poems written during and after World War I by writers such as Rupert Brooke, W. H. Davies, Walter de la Mare, Ralph Hodgson, and John Masefield. A number of the Georgian poets had been horrified by the tragic results of World War I and wrote poems attacking the absurdity of war in general. Many English writers not usually associated with the Georgian Age had also been deeply disturbed by the so-called Great War and, more generally, by the increasingly chaotic and absurd nature of modern life, but they expressed their alienation through radically unconventional, experimental literary forms or highly unusual subject matter rather than through traditional **styles** and realistic **representations.**

Virginia Woolf experimented with **stream of consciousness,** a style of writing reflecting a **character's** flow of perceptions, thoughts, memories, and feelings. Stream-of-consciousness **narrative** often exemplifies the way in which the modern mind attempts, consciously or, more commonly, unconsciously, to find or make coherence in a fragmented, apparently senseless world. Other writers turned to **myth** (as did Joyce) or even created their own strange visionary mythologies or **symbol** systems (as did Yeats) in order to express the psychological dis-ease of modern life or to wrest meaning from an otherwise meaningless cosmos. In "The Second Coming" (1921), Yeats alludes to his vision of historical cycles, or "gyres":

> Turning and turning in the widening gyre
> The falcon cannot hear the falconer;
> Things fall apart; the centre cannot hold;
> Mere anarchy is loosed upon the world.

Yeats's poem ends with a combination of **apocalyptic** and mythological elements that combine to announce the advent of a dark antichrist: "And what rough beast, its hour come round at last, / Slouches towards Bethlehem to be born?"

The United States, an isolationist nation before World War I, was characterized by significant tension between political isolationism and international involvement during the postwar period. As the country in general became increasingly isolationist (as evidenced, for instance, by the Congressional defeat of American involvement in the League of Nations), American authors marched to the beat of a different drummer. They exhibited a growing interest in European authors, including the seventeenth-century English **metaphysical poets,** the **French Symbolists** of the nineteenth century (writers who had themselves been **influenced** by the American writer Edgar Allan Poe), and writers of their own times (such as Joyce and the French novelist Marcel Proust).

American writers of the period who felt disillusioned by the experience and aftermath of World War I quickly came to be termed the **Lost Generation.** These writers generally viewed the "traditional" American values of their youth as a sham, given the senselessness of the war and its devaluation of human life. As such, members of this group deliberately rejected American culture as hypocritical; many even became expatriates in Europe during the 1920s, participating in movements such as **Dadaism** and **surrealism.** Expatriate members of the Lost Generation, who gathered around Gertrude Stein, included the following authors: F. Scott Fitzgerald, Ernest Hemingway, e. e. cummings, Sherwood Anderson, and William Slater Brown.

The **Harlem Renaissance,** centered in the almost exclusively African American area of Harlem in New York City and one of the high points of the Modern Period in American literature, also developed and flourished during the 1920s. For the first time in American history, African American culture was deliberately highlighted for a diverse national audience via literature, theater, music, and dance. Arna Bontemps, Countee Cullen, Langston Hughes, Zora Neale Hurston, and Jean Toomer are just a few of the figures associated with the Harlem Renaissance.

Other writers commonly associated with the Modern Period in American literature include Hart Crane, Amy Lowell, Sinclair Lewis, Edna St. Vincent Millay, Eleanor Wylie, and the **Agrarians,** a group of Southern poets and critics who repudiated capitalist industrialism and advocated establishing an agricultural base for the American economy. The Agrarians collectively published poetry and criticism in a literary periodical entitled *The Fugitive* between 1922 and 1925.

Although many English and American writers of the Modern Period rejected realism, a significant minority did not. English writers including D. H. Lawrence, E. M. Forster, and Graham Greene adapted realistic **narrative conventions** to represent new literary subjects, ranging from orgasm (Lawrence) to colonial India (Forster) to **postcolonial** Mexico (Greene). American novelist Willa Cather wrote a type of fiction often termed *genteel realism* for its effort to depict life as it really is and yet avoid vulgar or otherwise unpleasant or depressing subject matter. Cather's *My Antonia* (1918) and *Death Comes for the Archbishop* (1927) are two of her better-known works. Booth Tarkington also continued the **sentimental** vein of the realist tradition with works such as *The Magnificent Ambersons* (1918).

Works by a number of innovative English and American dramatists also appeared during the Modern Period. Of the former group, George Bernard Shaw (author of *Saint Joan* [1923]) had written plays during the preceding **Victorian** and **Edwardian** periods, and John Galsworthy (*The Skin Game* [1920], *The Forsyte Saga* [1906–21]) had become famous for realistic novels that bridged the Edwardian and Modern periods. Foremost among American playwrights of the Modern Period was Eugene O'Neill, author of *The Emperor Jones* (1920), *Mourning Becomes Electra* (1931), and *The Iceman Cometh* (1939).

The distinction between English and American writers of the Modern Period is difficult to make, as exemplified by the fact that one of the most important American writers of the period (Eliot) became a British subject, and one of the most important British writers of the period (Auden) became a U.S. citizen. It is equally difficult to distinguish between English and American writers of the Modern Period on the one hand and their Continental counterparts on the other; Proust experimented with stream of consciousness, and the German writer Thomas Mann used mythology to reveal disturbed psychic conditions. Similarly, one can compare the **themes** and formal experiments characteristic of modern literary works with those evident in musical works, paintings, and sculpture produced during the period between World War I and World War II. Like **neoclassicism** and **romanticism, modernism** was in fact a transnational, even transcultural movement that encompassed all of the arts.

See **modernism.**

monody: A **poem** of lamentation, sometimes intended to be sung, in which one individual grieves and mourns for another. Monody may be viewed as a type of **elegy,** a term with numerous meanings but most commonly used to refer to reflective poems that lament the loss of someone or something. Monodies, however, are elegies with one **narrator,** the mourner.

EXAMPLES: Matthew Arnold's "Thyrsis" (1867), subtitled "A Monody, to Commemorate the Author's Friend . . . ," an elegy on Arthur Hugh

Clough; John Milton's "Lycidas" (1638), written to lament Edward King's death.

monologic: A term used by Soviet critic Mikhail Bakhtin to describe works containing **characters** representing multiple **points of view** but clearly dominated by a single, controlling **voice** or **discourse,** one representing the dominant or "official" **ideology** of the author's culture. Bakhtin contrasts monologic with **dialogic** works, which are characterized by **dialogue** between the culture's dominant ideology and the discourses of popular culture, which Bakhtin associated with **carnival,** the extravagant celebrations associated with Mardi Gras but also with the values held by underprivileged or plebeian commoners, or **folk.** Having made a distinction between monologic and dialogic works, however, Bakhtin further argued that no work can be completely monologic because the **narrator,** no matter how authorial and indoctrinated in the "official" culture, inevitably represents the thoughts and remarks of others in some manner in the process of relating them and thus discloses a range of viewpoints. Bakhtin thus posited the monologic / dialogic opposition more as a tendency than as an absolute.

EXAMPLES: Bakhtin draws a comparison between the works of Leo Tolstoi and Fyodor Dostoyevsky in *Problems of Dostoevsky's Poetics* (1929). He calls Tolstoi a monologic writer in comparison to the more dialogic Dostoyevsky.

It could be argued that beginning in the late 1960s and early 1970s, television became a dialogic medium with the advent of characters and shows that challenged traditional mores and the political status quo. This trend has continued in recent years with shows such as *Roseanne, Married with Children, The Simpsons, Beavis and Butt-head, South Park,* and *The Osbournes.*

monologue: An extended **narrative,** whether oral or written, delivered uninterrupted and exclusively by one person (although it may be heard or witnessed by others). An **interior monologue** is a type of monologue in which the inner thoughts and workings of a **character's** mind are revealed or represented. A **soliloquy** is a type of monologue performed onstage as part of a play in which a single speaker reveals his or her inner thoughts out loud but while alone.

EXAMPLE: The following lines from Emily Brontë's *Wuthering Heights* (1847), spoken by Catherine Earnshaw to Nelly Dean, constitute a monologue:

> I cannot express it, but surely you and everybody have a notion that there is, or should be an existence of yours beyond you. What were the use of creation if I were entirely contained here? My great miseries in this world have been Heathcliff's miseries, and I watched and felt each from the beginning; my great thought in living is himself. If all else perished, and *he* remained, I should still continue to be; and if all

else remained, and he were annihilated, the Universe would turn into a mighty stranger. I should not seem a part of it. My love for Linton is like the foliage in the woods. Time will change it, I'm well aware, as winter changes the trees — my love for Heathcliff resembles the eternal rocks beneath — a source of little visible delight, but necessary. Nelly, I *am* Heathcliff — he's always, always in my mind — not as a pleasure, any more than I am always a pleasure to myself — but as my own being — so, don't talk of our separation again — it is impracticable. . . .

See **interior monologue.** See also **soliloquy.**

monometer: A line of **verse** consisting of one **metrical foot.**
EXAMPLES: Robert Herrick's "Upon His Departure Hence" (1648):

> Thus I
> Pass by
> And die.
> As one,
> Unknown,
> And gone:
> I'm made
> A shade,
> And laid
> I'th grave,
> There have
> My cave.
> Where tell
> I dwell,
> *Farewell.*

Many poems by William Carlos Williams also contain monometer lines. "Poem" (1934) provides one example:

> As the cat
> climbed over
> the top of
>
> the jamcloset
> first the right
> forefoot
>
> carefully
> then the hind
> stepped down
>
> into the pit of
> the empty
> flowerpot

montage: Based on a Russian word derived from the French verb *monter* ("to mount"), a composite of several different and typically unrelated elements that are juxtaposed and arranged to create or elicit a particular **mood,** meaning, or perception. A montage may be composed of film clips, photographs, **texts,** musical fragments, or other such elements and is compiled by photographers, art designers, cinematographers, writers, and musical composers.

Montage is a product of **modernism,** an early-twentieth-century movement led by authors and artists seeking to break away from traditions and **conventions** through experimentation with new literary **forms,** techniques, and **styles.** Following World War I, Georg Lukács, a Soviet **Marxist critic** who favored **realism** and realistic **representation,** criticized montage, which he viewed as **decadent** and concerned mainly with form rather than content. German playwright and Marxist critic Bertolt Brecht, however, countered that art is a field of production, not a container of content, and thus argued that progressive modes of expression should replace the conventional ones associated with representational art and literature. The ensuing debate between advocates of these two views came to be known as the "Brecht-Lukács" debate.

Although montage involving whole photographs, or parts thereof, manipulated to produce a design began to appear just before World War I, German artist John Heartfield is usually credited with developing photomontage as an art form in 1916, together with his colleagues Georg Grosz and Hannah Höch. Heartfield, who changed his name from Helmut Herzfeld in protest against rising German nationalism, became a political activist following the war and eventually employed photomontage as propaganda to attack Hitler and the Nazi party. Photomontage is still used today as a political medium, though it is also used by visual artists and advertising designers.

Another form of montage, the *Kuleshov effect,* was pioneered during the 1920s by three Russian film directors — Lev Kuleshov, Sergei Eisenstein, and V. I. Pudovkin — following Kuleshov's discovery that viewers will interpret two unrelated shots in terms of a larger context by inferring some type of relationship, so long as those unrelated shots are shown in succession. For instance, in one of Kuleshov's editing experiments, which involved splicing together shots including a waiting man, a walking woman, and a gate, viewers concluded that the man and woman met in front of the gate even though the shots were filmed in different times and places. The new editing technique derived from Kuleshov's discovery involved the juxtaposition of contrasting separate shots, often in rapid succession, to suggest new and different associations and **connotations.** The process is described by David A. Cook in *A History of Narrative Film* (1996) as one "whereby logically or empirically dissimilar images could be linked together synthetically to produce metaphors, to produce, that is, non-literal meaning." Eisenstein's use of the Kuleshov effect in his first film, *Strike* (1924), led to its recognition as an important cinematic editing device. Sometimes referred to in America as "dynamic cutting," montage has been used extensively ever since, particularly in polemic documentaries and propaganda films.

Literary montage, a technique used by authors experimenting with unconventional styles of writing, was developed by the German author and

Marxist critic Walter Benjamin in his drafts of the *Passagenwerk* (1927–39), an assemblage of quotations, illustrations, and comments regarding the cultural history of nineteenth-century Paris. Benjamin coined the term when he described his method as "literary montage. I have nothing to say only to show."

Today, because of sophisticated software, scanners, and digitized film, photographic, cinematic, and literary montage can all be computer-generated. Graphics, photographs, texts, film clips, and even music may easily be consolidated to create a **hypertext** montage.

EXAMPLES: **Dadaist** Hannah Höch's gigantic "Cut with the Kitchen Knife DADA through the Last Weimar Beer Belly Cultural Epoch of Germany" (1919–20) is an early example of photomontage.

In 1935, the U.S. government produced the photomontage shown below to promote "Suburban Resettlement housing projects" among "typical American families with limited incomes."

Editors of school yearbooks have also long employed photomontage, arranging snapshots to memorialize the past year. Photomosaic puzzles,

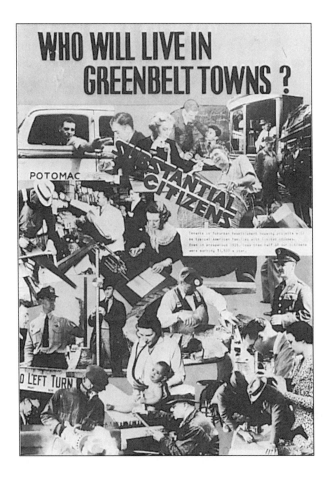

which consist of hundreds or thousands of pictures used to create one larger picture, are popular examples of visual montage.

Examples of the Kuleshov Effect include the **classic** "Odessa Steps scene" in *The Battleship Potemkin* (1925), directed by Eisenstein and Grigori Aleksandrov, as well as the famous "shower scene" in Alfred Hitchcock's *Psycho* (1960), which was assembled from approximately one hundred different film cuts.

In his modernist novel *Ulysses* (1922), James Joyce uses literary montage, as does T. S. Eliot in his modernist poem *The Waste Land* (1920). To suggest both the fragmentation of modern life and possibilities for reconnection and renewal, Eliot combines his own poetry with lines from several **Renaissance** plays, **lyrics** from nineteenth-century opera and twentieth-century popular songs, words from the Buddha's "Fire Sermon" and a Hindu *Upanishad*, advertising slogans, and the traditional closing call used in British pubs. Christiane Paul's *Unreal City: A Hypertextual Guide to T. S. Eliot's The Waste Land* (1996) offers a hypertext montage commentary on Eliot's famous poem. Shelley Jackson's *The Patchwork Girl* (1995) is a work of **hypertext fiction** employing literary montage

mood: Defined by some critics as synonymous with **atmosphere,** by others as synonymous with **tone,** and by still others as synonymous with both. *Tone* refers to the attitude of authors toward their readers, toward their subject matter, and even toward themselves; *atmosphere* refers to the general feeling created in the reader by the work at a given point, which may be entirely different from the tone. The atmosphere of a work may be oppressive without its tone being so, although the two inevitably affect one another. Mood is probably closer to atmosphere than to tone, but as a general term, it can correctly be applied to either. One could say that an author creates a somber mood (thereby using it as a synonym for *atmosphere*), and one could also say that an author's mood is somber (thereby using it as a synonym for *tone* to describe the author's attitude toward the audience or subject matter).

morality play: A **medieval drama** using **allegory** to make a moral point, whether it be religious, **didactic,** political, or doctrinal. Most such plays were religiously oriented, with a **protagonist** who represents humanity and other **characters** who fill out the cast of angels, demons, and **personified** abstractions (such as vices and virtues) struggling for the protagonist's soul. The comic as well as sinister characters Vice and Death became particularly well-developed, influencing the development of later **comedy** and the *interlude,* a type of English drama that influenced the development of **realistic** comedy. The morality play, which appeared around the fourteenth century, incorporated two sources: medieval religious drama and medieval allegory; the **genre** persisted well into the sixteenth century, when its popularity declined.

EXAMPLE: The fifteenth-century play *Everyman.*

morpheme: The smallest meaningful parts of words. Morphemes are composed of **phonemes,** the smallest basic speech sounds in a language.

EXAMPLE: The word *unworthy* is composed of three morphemes: *un, worth,* and *y. Worth* is a morpheme that is also a word — and the root of the word *unworthy* — in itself. Trying to further break up the word *worth* into smaller phonemic groups would in fact make it meaningless. *Un* is a morpheme that is a negator and *y* is a morpheme that transforms the word *unworthy* into an adjective.

morphology: A division of **linguistics,** the study of the form of words and of **morphemes,** the smallest meaningful parts of words.

motif: A unifying element in an artistic work, especially any recurrent **image, symbol, theme, character** type, subject, or **narrative** detail. Although scholars have variously traced the term *motif* back to French, Italian, and **medieval** Latin sources, the root words typically mean "motive." A given motif may be unique to a work or it may appear in numerous works (by the same author or different authors). In fact, a motif may be so widespread that it serves as the kernel for works typically associated with different **genres** or fields, such as literature, art, music, architecture, **myth,** and **folklore.**

EXAMPLES: Specific colors such as green and white serve as motifs in F. Scott Fitzgerald's *The Great Gatsby* (1925). A **Storm and Stress** motif is woven through numerous **romantic** works, such as Mary Shelley's *Frankenstein* (1818) and Emily Brontë's *Wuthering Heights* (1847). The egg — which comes either from heaven or from a woman impregnated by the sun and which is venerated, feared, or abandoned — is a recurring motif in founding **legends** of the three ancient Korean kingdoms. Examples of this motif can be found in *The Lay of King Tongmyông* and *The Legend of Pak Hyôkkôse.* Native American **tales** draw on the trickster motif. Folklorists have identified and even indexed hundreds of motifs including ones involving twin births, abandoned children, perilous journeys, and kindness rewarded.

The movie *Pretty Woman* (1990) is a modern-day version of the age-old Cinderella motif (a poor, mistreated, beautiful, kind girl is rescued by a dashing, kind, rich man). Another common motif is the starving artist unrecognized during his short, unhappy lifetime.

motivation: The mixture of situation and personality that impels a **character** to behave the way he or she does. When an author fails to establish plausible motivation, the character seems unconvincing and the action or work itself fails the test of plausibility; when the author does lay a reasonable foundation, the action or work makes sense in light of a particular character's situation and personality.

muckraker: See **naturalism.**

mummers' play: See **folk drama.**

muses: According to Greek **myth,** the nine daughters of Zeus and Mnemosyne (memory), each holding sway over a division of the arts and sciences. Poets have traditionally invoked one or more of these muses for inspiration; those especially relevant to verse are Calliope (**epic** poetry), Erato (love poetry), Euterpe (music and **lyric** poetry), and Polyhymnia (sacred poetry). The others are Clio (history), Melpomene (**tragedy**), Terpsichore (dance), Thalia (**comedy**), and Urania (astronomy). During the sixteenth century, the French poet Guillaume du Bartas transformed Urania from a pagan muse into a Christian, "Heavenly" muse. In recent times, the term *muse* has come to have a more general meaning. It is now used to refer to any person, entity, or spirit — real or imaginary — invoked for guidance and inspiration.

EXAMPLES: John Milton invokes Urania at the beginning of Book 7 of his epic *Paradise Lost* (1667):

> Descend from Heav'n *Urania*, by that name
> If rightly thou art call'd, whose Voice divine
> Following, above th' *Olympian* Hill I soar,
> Above the flight of *Pegasean* wing.
> The meaning, not the Name I call: for thou
> Nor of the Muses nine, nor on the top
> Of old *Olympus* dwell'st, but Heav'nly born. . . .

John Fowles's erotically charged novel *Mantissa* (1982) is about an author's alternately energizing and frustrating relationship with his muse. More recently, Albert Brooks has resurrected one of the ancient Greek muses in his film *The Muse* (1999), in which Brooks's **character** Steven Phillips seeks the aid of "Sarah," a muse who has found her way to Hollywood and who inspires creativity in her clients, provided that they furnish her with a variety of lavish perks.

mystery fiction: Popular fictional **narratives** with **plots** revolving around puzzling or frightening situations that create and even exploit a sense of uncertainty, suspense, or fear in the reader or audience. The word *mystery* has divergent **connotations,** suggesting the kind of divine or miraculous events recounted by **medieval miracle plays** and **mystery plays,** as well as baffling problems or enigmas demanding a solution or explanation. It is this latter usage of *mystery* that is operative in mystery fiction, which some scholars have traced back to Egyptian, Greek, and biblical "riddle stories" or puzzles. The term *mystery fiction* encompasses **Gothic** literature; **detective fiction; horror** literature; and *thrillers,* including **crime novels,** *spy novels,* and certain **psychological novels,** *suspense novels,* and adventure stories. *Mystery fiction* can also be used to refer to a broad range of works revolving around various sorts of puzzles, problems, or secrets.

Eighteenth- and nineteenth-century Gothic works, which are often set on aristocratic estates and which involve relationships clouded by suspicion, fear, and danger, are widely viewed as the forerunners of twentieth-century mystery **classics** such as Victoria Holt's *Mistress of Mellyn* (1960) and Phyllis A. Whitney's *Thunder Heights* (1960). Such Gothic works include Ann Radcliffe's *The Mysteries of Udolpho: A Romance* (1794), Charlotte Brontë's *Jane Eyre* (1847), and Henry James's *The Turn of the Screw* (1898). Horror and suspense novels — also descendants of Gothic fiction — are today written by authors like Mary Higgins Clark (*Where Are the Children?* [1975]) and Dean Koontz (*Phantoms* [1983]). Other contemporary novelists who incorporate Gothic suspense and horror include Stephen King (*The Shining* [1977], *The Green Mile* [1996]) and Anne Rice (*The Witching Hour* [1990], *Merrick* [2000]).

With the publication of Edgar Allan Poe's "Murders in the Rue Morgue" (1841), the category of mysteries broadened to comprise detective fiction, which includes a number of subgenres such as classic whodunits and hard-boiled detective fiction. Authors of classic whodunits, which feature plots in which a particular crime — usually a murder — is solved, thereby restoring order to society, include Agatha Christie, who wrote prolifically for more than five decades; Michael Innes; P. D. James; Ngaio Marsh; Ellery Queen; and Dorothy Sayers. Hard-boiled detective stories, which are set in the world of the criminal underground rather than in respectable society, have been published by writers like Raymond Chandler, Dashiell Hammett, Ross Macdonald, Sara Paretsky, and Mickey Spillane.

Crime novels, which are generally associated with thrillers, have greatly influenced and, in turn, been influenced by, detective fiction. Although often involving a detective, they emphasize the criminal's **motivation** and behavior rather than the detective's attempt to solve the crime. In fact, the identity of the criminal in a crime novel — unlike that of the culprit of a detective story — is often known from the beginning. Pioneered in such works as William Godwin's *The Adventures of Caleb Williams* (1794) and Charles Brockden Brown's *Wieland, or The Transformation* (1798), crime fiction was further developed by Wilkie Collins in *The Woman in White* (1860). Anthony Cox, who published crime novels under the **pseudonym** Frances Iles and detective fiction under the pseudonym Anthony Berkeley, is credited with pioneering the modern crime novel in works such as *Malice Aforethought: The Study of a Commonplace Crime* (1931).

As the crime novel became established, persistent subjects and **themes** emerged, such as criminal motivation and forensic theory and techniques. Most, if not all, crime-novel mysteries are psychological novels, such as Scott Turow's *Presumed Innocent* (1987) and Elizabeth George's *Deception on His Mind* (1997), and many psychological crime novels, such as Thomas Harris's *Silence of the Lambs* (1988) and Kathy Reichs's *Déjà Dead* (1997), focus specifically on fictional serial killers. Examples of novels concerned with pathological clues discovered at the crime scene by forensic investigators include Patricia Cornwell's *Postmortem* (1990) and Jeffrey Deaver's *The Bone Collector* (1997). Jonathan Kellerman, whose **protagonist** is a psychologist-detective working closely with the police, has written a series of mysteries including *Private Eyes* (1992) and *Flesh and Blood* (2001) that combine elements of the psychological novel, detective fiction, and the crime novel.

Mysteries also include spy novels, which can be traced back to James Fenimore Cooper's *The Spy* (1821). Spy fiction was further developed by William Le Quiex's *Guilty Bonds* (1890), a work that purported to offer a detailed inside account of the world of late-nineteenth-century espionage, and in Rudyard Kipling's *Kim* (1901). Subsequent notable twentieth-century spy novels include Ian Fleming's "James Bond" series (1953–65) and the novels of John LeCarré, which include *The Spy Who Came in from the Cold* (1963) and *The Honorable Schoolboy* (1977). More recent examples are Victor O'Reilly's *Games of the Hangman* (1991) and Robert Ludlum's *The Bourne Identity* (1980) and *The Prometheus Deception* (2000).

Certain suspenseful contemporary novels about lawyers, politicians, and military professionals are also classified as mysteries. Writers whose works often revolve around military action include Tom Clancy (*The Hunt for Red October* [1984]) and Nelson DeMille (*The Charm School* [1988]). Mystery novels involving the legal profession include John Grisham's *The Firm* (1991), *The Runaway Jury* (1996), and *The Testament* (1999). Some of Turow's psychological crime novels, such as *Burden of Proof* (1991), also qualify as legal mysteries.

FURTHER EXAMPLES: Contemporary movies involving perplexing mysteries include *The Usual Suspects* (1995), *Primal Fear* (1996), *L.A. Confidential* (1997), *The Sixth Sense* (1999), and *The Others* (2001).

See also **detective fiction, Gothic and Gothic novel.**

mystery play: A **medieval** religious **drama** that recounted a story from the Old or the New Testament of the Bible. The term *mystery play* is derived from the French word *mystère,* used to refer to plays based on the Scriptures that dramatized the basic "mysteries" of the faith as represented in the Bible (such as the Virgin Birth and the Ascension of Christ). Mystery plays were the most important type of medieval drama in Western Europe; in England, they were prevalent during the period ranging from the late **Middle Ages** into the **Renaissance.**

Like **miracle plays,** mystery plays were performed in the streets and squares of medieval towns. **Scenes** or episodes were staged by local religious and trade guilds on wagons, each of which moved sequentially through a publicized number of places, in order to make the drama available to everyone. Sometimes individual plays mounted on separate wagons formed a series of linked plays so that a *cycle* depicting biblical events from the Creation to the Last Judgment could be dramatized for the people of the town. Many of these cycles take their names from the towns in which they first gained renown; well-known examples include the Coventry and Wakefield cycles. Mystery plays were typically performed on religious holidays, particularly during the festival of Corpus Christi; consequently, they are sometimes referred to as *Corpus Christi plays.*

Mystery plays generally fall into one of three categories: (1) Old Testament plays about Adam and Eve, the patriarchs, and the prophets; (2) New Testament plays involving stories about the birth and early life of Christ; and (3) New Testament plays recounting Christ's death and resurrection. The terms *mystery play* and *miracle play* are used synonymously by some, but others make a distinction between the two, assigning plays based on Scripture itself to the category of mystery play and those based on the lives of saints or depicting miracles performed by Christ or by God through the saints to that of miracle play.

EXAMPLES: The following fourteenth-century English plays: *The Resurrection* from the York Pageant (c. 1340) and *Noah and the Ark* and *The Second Shepherd's Play* (about the birth of Christ) from the Wakefield Cycle (c. 1350).

See also **miracle play.**

mysticism: The belief that some kind of knowledge or special awareness can be acquired only through extrasensory means. In other words, such knowledge cannot be attained through the five senses, nor can it be gained by an exercise of logic or intellect. Rather, this exceptional knowledge is acquired intuitively; it involves insight into something beyond what is discernible through thought or normal sensory perception. People have sought to achieve the mystical state (or the ecstasy that often accompanies it) in a variety of ways, ranging from ascetic deprivation (of food, sleep, etc.) to mind-altering drugs (for example, peyote) to continuous whirling (Sufi dancing, for instance) to meditation. Whatever the means by which it is induced or attained, the mystical experience is generally considered to be so intensely personal that it cannot be readily described.

Since the experience sought by mystics often involves knowledge of the divine, mysticism frequently has an explicitly spiritual or religious character. Almost every religious tradition has a mystical branch or branches. There are Buddhist, Christian, Islamic, Jewish, and Hindu mystics, among others. Mysticism comes in many forms, however, not all of which are religious. Mystics may seek knowledge of "reality," for instance, a quest that may or may not involve a deity. **Transcendentalism** is a form of mysticism often said to draw on the spiritual tradition even though its primary emphasis is literary, not religious, and on Nature rather than God *per se.*

Mysticism has two components that may seem incongruous or even conflicting to nonmystics but that mystics view as complementary. The first component is speculative, asserting the existence of a divine essence or ultimate reality that lies beyond knowledge. The second component is pragmatic, asserting that this essence can and should be known. A nonmystic might ask how people can know that which is beyond knowledge; a mystic might respond **paradoxically** by stating that what is beyond us and our traditional ways of knowing is also immanent (dwelling within us) and thus can be found through self-discovery. For example, an ancient Hindu story posits that humanity was once divine. When other, more powerful gods decided to rob human beings of their godliness, they debated about where to hide human divinity so that it would never be found. After concluding that humankind would eventually travel to the tops of the highest mountains and the deepest troughs of the sea, they decided to bury human divinity where it would never be discovered: within the heart and soul of each individual.

Although the speculative side of mysticism has been termed its philosophical side and the practical side of mysticism its religious side, mysticism has historically been rejected by mainline philosophers and theologians. Mystics have typically acquiesced in this rejection, since they tend to position themselves outside the mainstream of philosophical and theological thought, viewing philosophical systems and religious rituals or dogmas as the petrified remains of some originally vital search for truth or a sense of divinity.

Mysticism is an ancient phenomenon in the Middle East, India, and the Far East and a more recent development in the West. Although mysticism was not evident in **classical** Greece, a form of Christian mysticism known as **Neoplatonism** was developed in Greece in the third century A.D. by the philosopher Plotinus. He developed Plato's conception that things must be understood in relation to ideas — and that all ideas emanate from The One, The Good, and the Idea of Good — into a quasi-Christian, mystical philosophy / religion allowing for ecstatic coalescence with a transcendent deity, The One, through a process of self-repudiation that begins with the rejection not only of the body but also of intellectual thought. Greek Neoplatonism was further developed by Dionysius Aeropagiticus and Maximus the Confessor in the fifth and seventh centuries, respectively.

Other **medieval** versions of Christian mysticism were espoused in what is now France during the twelfth and thirteenth centuries by Bernard of Clairvaux, Hugh of St. Victor, and Bonaventura, who described union with God in terms of mystic intuition. During the fourteenth century, Christian mysticism was developed by Meister Eckhart in Germany and by Jan van Tusbrock in the Netherlands. Some Protestant theologians have treated the mystics of Germany and Holland as precursors of the Reformation, and, indeed, many of the Christian mystics who lived during the **Renaissance** did define themselves in opposition to the growing rigidity and ritualism of what we now refer to as the Catholic Church. Christian mystics, however, were not as interested in Church reform as they were in finding and defining a nondogmatic, meditative way that would lead outside of and beyond traditional ecclesiastical teachings. Christian mysticism typically asserts that mystical knowledge of God can be acquired by progressing not through any learnable theological system but, rather, through a difficult, disciplined, and potentially perilous journey of the individual soul, one involving cleansing self-denial, an illuminative awareness of God's love, and, ultimately, a spiritual union with or marriage to God.

The tendency of mystics, Western and Eastern, to posit the simultaneous existence of transcendent power(s) and an indwelling power to commune with such power(s) has characterized the thinking of any number of poets, some of whom have been consciously aware of mystical traditions, others of whom have independently established a meditative mode aimed at communion with the ineffable through the indirection of **figurative language.**

Mysticism pervades the work of William Blake; it also plays a role in works by authors as various as Richard Crashaw; William Wordsworth; Samuel Taylor Coleridge; Alfred, Lord Tennyson; the American transcendentalists (especially Ralph Waldo Emerson); Herman Melville; Walt Whitman; T. S. Eliot; and D. H. Lawrence. Although **the New Critics** and other **formalists** practicing during the mid-twentieth century viewed mysticism and mystical writings as unclear and imprecise, recent practitioners have been more appreciative, finding in mystical **texts** such things as unusual experimentation with **form; symbolic** or other figurative language that responds to **psychoanalytic** or **poststructuralist** theory or analysis; and **mythic** or **archetypal images,** figures, and patterns that pervade the religious and secular texts of separate and diverse cultures.

FURTHER EXAMPLES: Christina Rossetti's poetry, as exemplified by her collection *Goblin Market and Other Tales* (1862), is infused with mysticism. Ralph Waldo Emerson's poems "Each and All" (1839), "Hamatreya" (1846), and "Brahma" (1857), show the **influence** of Eastern mysticism. That influence may also be found in T. S. Eliot's *The Waste Land* (1922), which ends with the line "Shantih shantih shantih." In a note, Eliot says that "our equivalent" to the word *Shantih* is the phrase "The Peace which passeth understanding" and that, "repeated as here," the word forms "a formal ending to an Upanishad" (a work of Hindu theology expounding mystical knowledge). In "The Dry Salvages" (1941), a later poem written after he embraced Christianity, Eliot "wonder[s] if that is what the Krishna meant" before postulating that "the way up is the way down, the way forward is the way back." But the poem, one of the *Four Quartets* (1943), comes closest to achieving the spirit of mysticism in lines treating "the intersection of the timeless / With time":

> For most of us, there is only the unattended
> Moment, the moment in and out of time,
> The distraction fit, lost in a shaft of sunlight,
> The wild thyme unseen, or the winter lightning
> Or the waterfall, or music heard so deeply
> That it is not heard at all, but you are the music
> While the music lasts. These are only hints and guesses,
> Hints followed by guesses; and the rest
> Is prayer, observance, discipline, thought and action.

Hermann Hesse's novel *Siddhartha* (1951) and Lawrence Durrell's series of novels *The Alexandria Quartet* (1957–60) are well-known twentieth-century works of fiction in which the influence of mysticism is pervasive.

A December 4, 2000, *Time* magazine review of singer-songwriter Erykah Badu's *Mama's Gun* stated that her earlier, "spectacular debut album, *Baduizm* (1997) blended hip-hop realism with soul-sister mysticism."

myth: A traditional anonymous **story,** originally religious in nature, told by a particular cultural group in order to explain a natural or cosmic phenomenon. Individual myths are typically part of an interconnected collection of such **tales,** known as a culture's *mythology.* Myths generally offer supernatural explanations for the creation of the world (whether seen as the planet alone or the universe generally) and humanity, as well as for death, judgment, and the afterlife. Myths that explain the origins of humanity often focus on the cultural group telling the myth; that group may even be portrayed, as in many Native American myths, as "the people," or the "true" people. Stories chronicling the adventures of gods and other supernatural forces, especially stories about their various feuds and encounters with mortals, are also common fare, as are tales about the fictional humans who must interact with them. Achilles is as much a mythic figure as Zeus.

Myths are different from *legends,* which detail the adventures of a human cultural **hero** (such as Robin Hood or Annie Oakley) and tend to be less focused on the supernatural. Whereas a legend may exaggerate — perhaps even wildly — the exploits of its hero, it is likely to be grounded in historical fact. Myths also differ from **fables,** which have a moral, **didactic** purpose and usually feature animal **characters.**

Myths that originally served to explain mysterious natural phenomena have been rejected as "false" as cultures have gained scientific knowledge. One does not, for instance, need to explain winter as the months Persephone spends in the underworld if one realizes that the seasons are determined by the tilt of the earth's axis in relation to its orbit around the sun. Even when a culture no longer believes that its myths are true explanations, however, these stories often survive as receptacles of important cultural values.

A comparison of myths produced by different cultures reveals that myths are strikingly similar in the types of phenomena they seek to explain and the types of questions they address, a point that led Carl Jung, a noted psychiatrist and the founder of analytic psychology, to argue that myths reveal a **collective unconscious,** a common inheritance among all human beings. Many writers have accorded myths a similarly evocative power and have either incorporated myths into their works or created their own mythic frameworks in an attempt to reach their audiences at a universal or primal level of human thought, emotion, and experience. William Blake and William Butler Yeats are among the best known **mythopoetic** writers. Led by Northrop Frye, the so-called **myth critics** of the mid-twentieth century have also looked beyond the idiosyncratic surfaces of individual **texts** to find mythic figures, forces, patterns, implications, and structures. Myth critics maintain that certain myths are so deeply ingrained in most cultures that literary works typically rehash the same general mythic formulas.

The term *urban legend,* or *urban myth,* referring to bizarre events erroneously believed to have occurred in modern city life, surfaced during the 1980s.

EXAMPLES: An ancient Babylonian myth elaborated in the **epic** poem *Enuma Elish* ("When on High") explains the emergence of Marduk as the chief god in tandem with the creation of earth and sky. According to this creation myth, Marduk (originally a minor god) struck a bargain with the other gods to kill Tiamat, a fearsome she-dragon, and her husband Kingu. In return for killing Tiamat, the other gods agreed to recognize Marduk as the supreme god and to create the earth and sky by splitting Tiamat's body in half. They were also obligated to use Kingu's blood to create humankind and then to organize the universe.

A **classic** Greek myth, said to explain the origin of the seasons, is the story of Persephone (the daughter of Zeus and Demeter), who is abducted by Hades and brought to his underground kingdom to be his wife. According to the myth, Demeter is so consumed by grief and rage that she punishes the earth's inhabitants with cold and wind so that nothing can grow. Only when Herakles negotiates a compromise so that Persephone can return to earth for part of the year does spring come again, and when Persephone returns to Hades, winter also returns.

In the Roman version of the myth, Proserpina is abducted by Pluto and tempted to eat her favorite fruit, the pomegranate, while in the underworld. Unaware that any live mortal who eats while in the underworld has to stay there, Proserpina eats six pomegranate seeds. Her mother, Ceres, grieving the loss of her daughter, neglects to care for the fields and crops, and winter falls. Only when Proserpina's father, Jupiter, sends Mercury to negotiate a compromise between Pluto and Ceres can Proserpina return to earth, and then only six months per year, since the compromise calls for her to spend one month per year in the underworld for each seed she ate.

Ancient Greek legend has it that the poet Sappho, who taught girls the arts on the island of Lesbos, threw herself into the sea due to unrequited love.

An example of urban legend or myth is the commonly told story of a man who, drugged at a party, awakens naked in a bathtub filled with ice and finds a note (sometimes scrawled in lipstick on the mirror) warning him that one of his kidneys has been removed for sale on the black market. Another such urban legend is the assertion that author Kurt Vonnegut gave a commencement speech at MIT advising new graduates to "wear sunscreen." In reality, Vonnegut neither gave nor wrote any such address; rather, the text that has been attributed to him, widely circulated on the Internet as a "forward" and made into a popular song by filmmaker Baz Luhrmann, was actually written by Mary Schmich as a column published by the *Chicago Tribune* in 1997.

myth critics and mythic criticism: An interpretive approach to literature that analyzes mythic **structures** and **themes** as they are recurrently manifested in literary **genres** and individual works. A myth critic writing on John Milton's *Paradise Lost* (1667) and Joseph Conrad's *Heart of Darkness* (1899), for instance, might see both in terms of the "night journey" common to any number of **myths, epics,** and heroic **tales.** Myth critics argue that certain basic mythic figures and situations both permeate and transcend individual cultures; they find such universal patterns in works from cultures throughout the world. Northrop Frye is perhaps the best-known myth critic.

Myth criticism has much in common with **archetypal criticism,** but the two approaches to literature are not identical. Myth critics focus specifically on identifying and analyzing recurrent mythic structures and themes in literary works, whereas archetypal critics approach works from a broader perspective, identifying **archetypes,** those cross-cultural **images,** figures, and story patterns manifested in a wide variety of literary works. Archetypes are often expressed in myths and in literary works using mythic structures and themes, hence the overlap between mythic and archetypal criticism.

See also **archetypal criticism, archetype, myth.**

mythology: See **myth.**

mythopoesis (mythopoeia): The creating of **myths** or of a mythic framework for a literary work.

EXAMPLES: Eighteenth-century poet William Blake and **modernist** poet W. B. Yeats both undertook to create their own personal mythic systems. Blake wove his mythic framework into his poems; Yeats set his forth openly in a work entitled *A Vision* (1926).

naive hero: A **protagonist,** generally the **narrator** of a work, who consistently misinterprets the events or situations he or she witnesses or experiences because of some character trait such as innocence, stupidity, or insensitivity. A naive hero who also narrates the work is a type of **unreliable narrator,** a narrator whose opinions the reader recognizes as fallible and, therefore, untrustworthy.

An author may use a naive hero for **ironic** purposes, in which case the irony is **structural** because the **hero** or **heroine** fails to perceive what author and reader readily recognize. Furthermore, an author may use a naive hero to achieve **pathos,** often by having an innocent child-hero relate events of a horrifying nature that the child does not fully understand but that the reader does. (When a naive hero is employed for this purpose, the pathos thus exhibited is still structurally ironic.) A naive child-hero may also be used to achieve a humorous effect.

EXAMPLES: Lemuel Gulliver, the narrator of Jonathan Swift's *Gulliver's Travels* (1735), is the best-known naive hero in English literature and the source and linchpin of the work's structural irony. Gulliver is so impressed by the talking horses he meets in Houyhnhnmland that he can see none of their faults and, as a result, none of the virtues of humankind. The young chimney sweep in William Blake's short poem "The Chimney Sweeper" (1789) is a naive hero who also serves to create a pathetic effect. A modern example of the naive hero is Forrest Gump, the decidedly obtuse narrator of Winston Groom's novel *Forrest Gump* (1986; adapted to film in 1994).

narration: The act or process of recounting a **story** or other **narrative.**

narrative: A **story** or a telling of a story, or an account of a situation or event. Narratives may be fictional or true; they may be written in either prose or verse. Some critics use the term even more generally; Brook Thomas, a **new historicist,** has critiqued "narratives of human history that neglect the role human labor has played."

EXAMPLES: A novel and a **biography** of a novelist are both narratives, as are newspaper accounts and psychoanalyst Sigmund Freud's case histories.

narratology: The analysis of the **structural** components of a **narrative,** the way in which those components interrelate, and the relationship between this complex of elements and the narrative's basic **story** line. Narratology incorporates techniques developed by other critics, most notably **Russian formalists** and French **structuralists,** applying in addition numerous traditional methods of analyzing narrative fiction (for instance, those methods outlined in the "Showing as Telling" chapter of Wayne Booth's *The Rhetoric of Fiction* [1961]). Narratologists treat narratives as explicitly, intentionally, and meticulously constructed systems rather than as simple or natural vehicles for an author's **representation** of life. They seek to explain how an author transforms (or how authors in general transform) a story line into a literary **plot** by analyzing the "rules" that generate plot from story. They pay particular attention to such elements as **point of view;** the relations among story, teller, and audience; and the levels and types of **discourse** used in narratives. Certain narratologists concentrate on the question of whether any narrative can actually be neutral (like a clear pane of glass through which some subject is **objectively** seen) and on how the practices of a given culture influence the shape, content, and impact of "historical" narratives. Mieke Bal's *Narratology: Introduction to the Theory of Narrative* (1980) is a standard introduction to the narratological approach.

narrator: A speaker through whom an author presents a **narrative,** often but not always a **character** in the work. Every narrative has a narrator; a work may even occasionally have multiple narrators or a main narrator with subnarrators. An author's choice of **point of view** influences the kind of narrator used. A work written from the **third-person point of view** often has an **omniscient** narrator, whereas a work written from the **first-person point of view** is either narrated by a character or, if **autobiographical,** the author. An omniscient narrator may be *intrusive* (opinionated) or **unintrusive** (detached); a fictional, first-person narrator may turn out to be **naive** or **unreliable.** Third-person narrators (particularly omniscient ones) generally have a more authorial-seeming sound and function and are more likely to comment upon the action in addition to recounting it.

Wilson, the soccer ball addressed by Chuck Noland, the marooned character played by Tom Hanks in the film *Cast Away* (2000), is a narrative device used to inform the audience of the thoughts and feelings of the isolated, lonely **protagonist.**

naturalism: When used with reference to the arts in general, a term referring to a mode of **representation** that is detailed, detached, and **objective.** When applied to literature, however, *naturalism* usually refers to a literary movement of the late nineteenth and early twentieth century in America, England, and France that produced a type of "realistic" fiction. Naturalism is not, however, synonymous with or even really a subtype of **realism.** In realism, **characters** have at least some degree of free will, which they are able to exercise to affect their situations; naturalism assumes humans have little if any control over what happens. In naturalistic works, which tend to stress either biological or socioeconomic determinism, things happen *to* people, who are at the mercy of a variety of external and internal forces as if they were marionettes whose movements are entirely determined by forces beyond their control.

Naturalists claim to present their subjects objectively. They do not, for example, comment on the morality or the fairness of the situations in which characters find themselves. Their works, however, are written in strict accordance with a highly deterministic philosophical viewpoint, one that was heavily influenced by emergent scientific theories, such as Charles Darwin's theory of evolution and its corollary, "survival of the fittest." Since naturalists believe that everything that is real is found in nature and is subject to scientific investigation and (eventual) verification, they reject supernatural explanations of situations and events. From their essentially pessimistic perspective, humans are but higher-order animals fully subject to the forces of heredity and environment, and life in general is an inescapable trap.

Naturalism has also been used to designate works by **nature writers** (William Wordsworth, for example), but this is a less common application of the term and one that is increasingly viewed as incorrect.

EXAMPLES: Émile Zola's *Le roman experimental* (*The Experimental Novel*) (1880) best delineates the tenets of naturalism; Zola himself is generally considered the greatest of naturalistic writers. Other noted naturalists include the English writer George Gissing and the Americans Stephen Crane, Frank Norris, Theodore Dreiser, and Eugene O'Neill.

Naturalistic Period (in American literature): A period in American literary history commonly said to have begun around 1900 and to have ended with the outbreak of World War I in 1914. **Naturalism** has sometimes been called an exaggerated form of **realism.** Naturalistic writers, who drew on Social Darwinism, Friedrich Nietzsche's doctrine of the superman, and the pessimistic determinism of French writer Émile Zola, tended to represent **characters** as victims both of their instinctual drives and of society. Thus, environment and social background play a much larger role than free will in determining characters' fates. Naturalistic novels typically center around a social problem or vice affecting the lower **classes** of society and use a case study method to analyze how particular individuals fared under the circumstances.

Stephen Crane is most frequently credited with pioneering American naturalism, although several works by **romantic** novelist Herman Melville also exhibited the pessimistic attitude characteristic of the **genre.** Crane's *Maggie: A Girl of the Streets* (1893) evidenced a fascination with life in New York's Bowery district; Maggie, the **heroine,** becomes a prostitute after being abandoned by a man and eventually commits suicide. Other noted naturalistic novels include Theodore Dreiser's *Sister Carrie* (1900), Frank Norris's *The Octopus* (1901), and Jack London's *The Call of the Wild* (1903).

Not all novelists of the Naturalistic Period took such a dark view of life, however. William Dean Howells, Henry James, and Mark Twain, for instance, continued to write realistic novels. James in particular brought realism to its high water mark with novels such as *The Ambassadors* (1903). Novelist Edith Wharton, too, continued the realistic tradition in works such as *The House of Mirth* (1905) and *Ethan Frome* (1911).

Modern American poetry is often said to have begun during the Naturalistic Period. *Poetry,* a magazine devoted to poetry and criticism, was established in 1912 by Harriet Monroe. **Imagism** also began to develop, though it flourished primarily during and after World War I. The careers of a number of **modernist** poets such as H. D. (Hilda Doolittle), T. S. Eliot, Robert Frost, Ezra Pound, Carl Sandburg, and William Carlos Williams all began during this period.

Significant American drama finally began to develop during this period as well. The Little Theater Movement, developed in France in 1887 to encourage the writing and production of plays with serious literary value, appeared in Chicago in 1906 and quickly spread to other American cities, bringing drama to many more people than ever before.

Muckraking magazines and exposés were common during the Naturalistic Period. Muckrakers usually sought to expose the existence of an alliance between capitalist big business and corrupt politicians, who they believed created (and then covered up or ignored) numerous social problems. Two such exposés, published in 1904, were Ida Tarbell's *The History of the Standard Oil Company* (1904) and Lincoln Steffens's *The Shame of the Cities* (1904). Upton Sinclair's *The Jungle* (1906), a novel that exposed the disgusting conditions and rampant corruption of Chicago's meat-packing plants, is perhaps the best-known muckraker work.

See **naturalism.**

nature writing: See **ecocriticism.**

near rhyme: See **half-rhyme.**

negative capability: A term coined by John Keats (in a letter to his brothers on December 21, 1817) to describe the capacity to be "in uncertainties, mysteries, doubts, without any irritable reaching after fact and reason." Keats believed that few possess this ability and that most people, in their quest to categorize and rationalize every uncertain thing, distort and reduce reality instead of openly and actually perceiving it. For Keats, the great poet has to be able to accept intuitive insights for what they are, instead of trying to incorporate them systematically into some rational, explanatory scheme. Writers possessing this ability have the capability to negate their own personalities — to get outside of themselves — in order to perceive reality (especially human reality) in its manifold complexity. Keats cited Samuel Taylor Coleridge as a poet lacking this ability and praised William Shakespeare as one possessing it in great measure. Subsequent critics have developed Keats's insight by making two other observations: first, that authors should maintain **aesthetic distance** from their subject matter, thereby making impersonality and some degree of **objectivity** possible; second, that literature should not be held to ordinary standards of morality and truth in cases where the beauty of artistic **form** is paramount.

Neoclassical Period (in English literature): See **neoclassicism.**

neoclassicism: A **style** of Western literature that flourished from the mid-seventeenth century until the end of the eighteenth century and the rise of **romanticism.** The neoclassicists looked to the great **classical** writers for inspiration and guidance, considering them to have mastered the noblest literary forms, **tragic** drama and the **epic.** Many practiced **imitation** of the "masters" — and their preferred literary forms such as **satire** and the **ode** — in order to perfect their own work and foster proper modes of expression. (Neoclassicists recognized that the creation of art requires individual inspiration and talent, but they also maintained that, except for the rare genius, long and careful study is equally essential to the production of great work.)

Neoclassical writers shared several beliefs. They thought that literature should both instruct and delight and that the proper subject of art was humanity. (Their emphasis was more on humanity in general than on the individual.) Unlike some of the more idealistic, optimistic, and expansive writers who preceded them during the **Renaissance** (and followed during the **Romantic Period**), neoclassicists started from the assumption that humanity is imperfect and limited. However, certain neoclassicists found cause for optimism, particularly in the power of reason to perfect human civilization gradually.

The **Restoration** (of the monarchy) in 1660 marked the beginning of the *Neoclassical Period* in Great Britain, whose writers included John Dryden, Henry Fielding, Samuel Johnson, Alexander Pope, and Jonathan Swift. But neoclassicism was by no means an exclusively British phenomenon; the movement flourished throughout Europe, particularly in France and Germany. Perhaps the most notable French neoclassical writer is Jean Racine, a dramatist, whose *Phèdre* (1677) exemplifies neoclassical qualities. Molière's play *Tartuffe* (1667) is another enduring French example. In Germany, this movement was simply called *die Klassik,* or classicism. Notable works include Friedrich Schiller's play *Don Carlos* (1787), Johann Wolfgang von Goethe's *Iphegenie auf Tauris* (1787), and Friedrich Hölderlin's long poem *Brot und Wein (Bread and Wine)* (c. 1800). German classicism developed one major difference from Graeco-Roman **classicism:** the absolute, uncompromisable integrity of the human being.

Neoclassicism stressed rules, reason, harmony, balance, restraint, order, serenity, **decorum, realism,** and **form** — above all, an appeal to the intellect rather than emotion. The twentieth century witnessed a revival of neoclassical qualities in such writers as W. H. Auden, T. S. Eliot, Robert Frost, and Ezra Pound. Many critics have viewed this revival as a corrective reaction to the excesses of **romanticism,** whose conventions, styles, and traditions nonetheless still influence our literary landscape.

neologism: A new word or phrase that has been coined to express economically a meaning not conveyed by any single word in the dictionary. "Nannygate" — a neologism referring to the scandal that erupted when candidates for high-ranking government positions were found to have employed illegal immigrants as childcare providers and to have violated tax laws by not paying social security and other taxes on these workers — is based on "Watergate," which refers to the scandal that ultimately led to the resignation of President Richard M. Nixon. As a literary term, *neologism* refers to an original word or phrase invented by an author to convey an idea or create an effect that no existing word could convey or create. Poets writing in the **euphuistic** style were especially inclined to use neologisms.

EXAMPLES: The second line of the following passage from Jerry W. Ward Jr.'s poem "Jazz to Jackson to John" (1988) ends with a neologism:

> yeah, brother, it must have been something
> striking you like an eargasm,
> a baritone ax laid into soprano wood,
> like loving madly in hurting silence,
> waiting to fingerpop this heathen air
> with innovations of classical black
> at decibels to wake the deaf, the dumb, and the dead. . . .

The Beatles' use of "snide" as a verb in "I Am the Walrus" (1967) is neologistic. Rapper Snoop Doggy Dog employs what has come to be called "Snoop Latin," which involves inserting "izz" or "izzay" into monosyllabic words, thereby creating neologisms like "fizzake" and, more famously, "bizznatch," which combines "bitch" and "snatch" using the "izz" connector. As outrageous as these neologisms seem, they are in fact quite similar to the kind pioneered by James Joyce in *Finnegans Wake* (1939).

Neoplatonism: A school of thought, originating in the third century A.D. in Alexandria, Egypt, and persisting until the fifth century, whose proponents believed in the superiority of mind over matter and concerned themselves with fundamental human aspirations and problems. They especially developed Plato's theory of beauty, arguing that the Absolute (the One, the Infinite Being, the source of all value and being) radiates all the beauty (and goodness and truth) that exists in this world. Neoplatonism, whose best-known proponent is the third-century A.D. philosopher Plotinus, incorporated certain elements of Christianity, gnosticism, and Oriental **mysticism** into **Platonic** thought to create a relatively optimistic, if vaguely defined, philosophical system. Later Christian thinkers were greatly influenced by the Neoplatonists, particularly by their concept of the Absolute and their understanding of beauty. Subsequently, during the **Renaissance,** Neoplatonism was revived by thinkers who stressed that the material world is a path to the spiritual world, rather than an obstacle to or diversion from it. Writers influenced by this version of Neoplatonism often wrote about lovers practicing a version of **Platonic love** that is in fact Neoplatonic; although the lovers' ultimate goal is to apprehend Divine Beauty, they appreciate the bodily beauty of their earthly lover, believing it to signify a higher, more ethereal beauty, the experience of which, in turn, will further their spiritual quest. (Neo)platonic love and lovers appear in the **courtesy books** of Baldassare Castiglione (*The Courtier* [1528]) and in the poetry of Dante Alighieri, Petrarch (Francesco Petrarca), and Edmund Spenser.

New Criticism, the: A type of **formalist** literary **criticism** that reached its height during the 1940s and 1950s and that received its name from John Crowe Ransom's 1941 book *The New Criticism.* New Critics treat a work of literary art as if it were a self-contained, self-referential object. Rather than basing their interpretations of a **text** on the reader's response, the author's stated **intentions,** or parallels between the text and historical contexts (such as the author's life), New Critics perform a **close reading,** concentrating on the relationships within the text that give it its own distinctive character or **form.** New Critics emphasize that the **structure** of a work should not be divorced from meaning, viewing the two as constituting an "organic unity." Special attention is paid to repetition, particularly of **images** or **symbols,** but also of sound effects and **rhythms** in poetry. New critics especially appreciate the use of literary devices, such as **irony** and **paradox,** to achieve a balance or reconciliation between dissimilar, even conflicting, elements in a text.

Because of the importance placed on close textual analysis and the stress on the text as a carefully crafted, orderly object containing observable formal patterns, the New Criticism has often been seen as an attack on **romanticism** and **impressionism,** particularly **impressionistic criticism.** It has sometimes even been called an **objective** approach to literature. New Critics are more likely than certain other critics to believe and say that the meaning of a text can be known objectively. For instance, **reader-response critics** see meaning as a function either of each reader's experience or of the norms that govern a particular **interpretive community,** and **deconstructors** argue that texts mean opposite things at the same time.

The foundations of the New Criticism were laid in books and essays written during the 1920s and 1930s by I. A. Richards (*Practical Criticism* [1929]), William Empson (*Seven Types of Ambiguity* [1930]), and T. S. Eliot ("The Function of Criticism" [1933]). The approach was significantly developed later, however, by a group of American poets and critics, including R. P. Blackmur, Cleanth Brooks, John Crowe Ransom, Allen Tate, Robert Penn Warren, and William K. Wimsatt. Although we associate the New Criticism with certain principles and terms (such as the **affective fallacy** and the **intentional fallacy** as defined by Wimsatt and Monroe C. Beardsley), the New Critics were trying to make a cultural statement rather than to establish a critical dogma. Generally Southern, religious, and culturally conservative, they advocated the inherent value of literary works (particularly of literary works regarded as beautiful art objects) because they were sick of the growing ugliness of modern life and contemporary events. Some recent theorists even link the rising popularity after World War II of the New Criticism (and other types of formalist literary criticism such as the **Chicago School**) to American isolationism. These critics tend to view the formalist tendency to isolate literature from **biography** and history as symptomatic of American fatigue with wider involvements. Whatever the source of the New Criticism's popularity (or the reason for its eventual decline), its practitioners and the textbooks they wrote were so influential in American academia that the approach became standard in college and even high school curricula well into the 1970s.

See also **affective fallacy, intentional fallacy.**

new historicism, the: A type of literary **criticism** that developed during the 1980s, largely in reaction to the text-only approach pursued by **formalist** New Critics and the critics who challenged **the New Criticism** in the 1970s. New historicists, like formalists and their critics, acknowledge the importance of the literary **text,** but they also analyze the text with an eye to history. In this respect, the new historicism is not "new"; the majority of critics between 1920 and 1950 focused on a work's historical content and based their interpretations on the interplay between the text and historical contexts (such as the author's life or **intentions** in writing the work).

With the advent of the text-oriented New Criticism, however, historically oriented critics faded into obscurity. New Critics treated literary works as self-contained, self-referential objects; they examined relationships within the text to uncover its **form** and meaning, focusing on **symbolism, imagery, rhythm,** and the like. In the 1970s, **reader-response critics** (who believe that the meaning of a work is cooperatively produced by reader and text) and **poststructuralists** (who, following Jacques Derrida, argue that texts are inevitably self-contradictory) roundly attacked the New Critics. Like the New Critics, however, these critics focused on the text itself (or the reader), ignoring the historical context within which literary works are written and read.

Around 1980, however, a form of historical criticism practiced by Louis Montrose and Stephen Greenblatt began to transform the field of **Renaissance** studies and to influence the study of American and English **romantic** literature (from which the distinct but related approach of **political reading** would arise). In 1981, American **Marxist critic** Fredric Jameson began his book *The Political Unconscious* with the following two-word challenge: "Always historicize!" By 1987, when Brook Thomas published an essay entitled "The Historical Necessity for — and Difficulties with — New Historical Analysis in Introductory Courses," the new historicism was flourishing. New historicist critics were rediscovering the value of history in literary analysis. Thomas, for instance, suggested that discussions of John Keats's "Ode on a Grecian Urn" (1820) begin by considering where Keats would have seen such an urn — and how a Grecian urn came to rest in an English museum. Important historical and political realities, Thomas suggested, underlie and inform Keats's definitions of art, truth, beauty, the past, and timelessness.

"History," as Herbert Lindenberger wrote in an essay entitled "Toward a New History in Literary Study" (1984), was "making a powerful comeback." The historical criticism practiced in the 1980s, however, was not the same as the historical criticism of the 1930s and 1940s. Indeed, if the word "new" still serves any useful purpose in defining contemporary historical criticism, it is in distinguishing it from such older forms of **historicism.** New historicists believe that criticism should incorporate diverse **discourses;** the new historicism is informed by the poststructuralist and reader-response theory of the 1970s, as well as by the thinking of **feminist, cultural,** and Marxist critics whose work was also "new" in the 1980s. New historicist critics assume that works of literature both influence and are influenced by historical reality, and they share a belief in referentiality, that is, a belief that literature both refers and is referred to by things outside itself. They are also less fact- and event-oriented than historical critics used to be, perhaps because they have come to wonder whether the truth about what really happened can ever be purely and **objectively** known. They are less likely to see history as linear and progressive, as something developing toward the present, and they are also less likely to think of it in terms of specific eras, each with a definite, persistent, and consistent *Zeitgeist* (spirit of the times). Hence, they are unlikely to suggest that a literary text has a single or easily identifiable historical context.

New historicist critics also tend to define the discipline of history more broadly than did their predecessors. They view history as a social science and the social sciences as being properly historical. In *Historical Studies and Literary Criticism* (1985), Jerome McGann spoke of the need to make sociohistorical subjects and methods central to literary studies; in *The Beauty of Inflections: Literary Investigations in Historical Method and Theory* (1985), he linked sociology and the future of historical criticism. Lindenberger found anthropology particularly useful in the new historicist analysis of literature, especially anthropology as practiced by Victor Turner and Clifford Geertz.

Geertz, who related theatrical traditions in nineteenth-century Bali to forms of political organization that developed during the same period, has influenced many critics writing the new historical criticism. Due largely to Geertz's influence, new historicists have asserted that literature is not distinct from the history that is relevant to it. The old historicism did make such a distinction, viewing historical contexts as "background" information necessary to appreciate fully the separate world of art. New historicists reject not only this distinction but also the separation of artistic works from their creators and audiences. They have used what Geertz calls **thick description** to blur distinctions, not only between history and the other social sciences but also between background and foreground, political and poetical events. They have erased the line dividing historical and literary materials, showing not only that the production of one of William Shakespeare's **history plays** was both a political act and a historical event, but also that the coronation of Elizabeth I was carried out with the same care for staging and **symbol** lavished on works of dramatic art.

New historicists remind us that it is treacherous to reconstruct the past as it really was — rather than as we have been conditioned by our own place and time to believe that it was. And they know that the job is impossible for those who are unaware of that difficulty, insensitive to the bent or bias of their own historical vantage point. Historical criticism must be "conscious of its status as interpretation," Greenblatt asserted in *Renaissance Self-Fashioning from More to Shakespeare* (1980). Hence, when new historicist critics describe a historical change, they are highly conscious of (and even likely to discuss) the **theory** of historical change that informs their account. They know that the changes they notice are ones that their (historically determined) theory allows or helps them to see and describe. They seek to minimize the distortion inherent in their perceptions and **representations** by acknowledging their preconceived notions.

In *The Beauty of Inflections,* McGann suggested that new historicists follow a set of basic, scholarly procedures. These procedures — "practical derivatives of the Bakhtin school," as McGann referred to them — assume that new historicist critics will study a literary work's "point of origin" via **biography** and bibliography. Critics must then consider the expressed **intentions** of the author, because, if published, these intentions have modified the developing history of the work. Next, the new historicist must learn the history of the work's reception, as that body of opinion has become part of the platform on which we are situated when we study the work at our own particular "point of reception." Finally, McGann urged the new historicist critic to point toward the future, toward his or her own audience, defining for its members the aims and limits of the critical project and injecting the analysis with a degree of self-consciousness that alone can give it credibility.

In his introduction to a collection of new historical writings on *The New Historicism* (1989), H. Aram Veeser stressed the unity among new historicists, not by focusing on common critical procedures but rather by outlining certain "key assumptions" that "continually reappear and bind together the avowed practitioners and even some of their critics." These include the following: that "expressive acts" cannot be separated from "material" conditions; that the boundary between "literary and nonliterary texts" is a false one; that neither "imaginative" nor "archival" (historical) discourse "gives access to unchanging truths nor expresses inalterable human nature"; that historical critiques tend to depend on the methods they condemn; and that — more specifically — critical discourses "adequate to describe culture under capitalism participate in the economy they describe."

These same assumptions, it should be pointed out, are shared by a group of historians practicing what is now commonly referred to as the *new cultural history.* Influenced by so-called *Annales*-school historians in France and post-Althusserian **Marxists,** these historians share with their new historicist counterparts an interest in anthropological and sociological subjects and methods; a creative way of weaving stories and **anecdotes** about the past into revealing thick descriptions; a tendency to focus on nontraditional, non**canonical** subjects and relations (historian Walter Laqueur is best known for *Making Sex: Body and Gender from the Greeks to Freud* [1990]); and the tendency to invoke or engage the writings of Michel Foucault.

A French philosophical historian, Foucault brought together incidents and phenomena from areas normally seen as unconnected, encouraging new historicists and new cultural historicists to redefine the boundaries of historical inquiry. Foucault's views of history were influenced by the philosopher Friedrich Nietzsche's concept of a *wirkliche* ("real" or "true") history. Like Nietzsche, Foucault refused to see history as an evolutionary process, a continuous development toward the present. Neither did he view history as an abstraction, idea, or ideal, as something that began "In the beginning" and that will come to THE END, a moment of definite **closure,** a Day of Judgment. No historical event, according to Foucault, has a single cause; rather, each event is tied into a vast web of economic, social, and political factors. Foucault urged historians to be aware that they are themselves historically "situated," making it difficult to see present cultural practices critically and extremely difficult to enter bygone ages.

Like Karl Marx, Foucault saw history in terms of power, but his view of power probably owed more to Nietzsche than to Marx. Foucault viewed power not simply as a repressive force or a tool of conspiracy but rather as a complex of forces that produces what happens. Not even a tyrannical aristocrat simply wields power, for the aristocrat is himself empowered by discourses and practices that constitute power.

Discipline and Punish: The Birth of the Prison (1975) illustrates some of Foucault's key ideas. The book opens with a description of the public execution of a Frenchman who had attempted to assassinate King Louis XV, then details rules that govern the daily life of modern Parisian felons. What has happened to torture, to punishment as public spectacle? Foucault asks. What network of forces made it disappear? In seeking to understand this "power," Foucault notes that in the early years of the nineteenth century, crowds would sometimes identify with the prisoner and treat the executioner as if he were the guilty party. But Foucault sets forth another reason for keeping prisoners alive, moving punishment indoors, and eliminating physical torture in favor of mental rehabilitation: colonization. As time passed, people were increasingly needed to establish colonies and trade, and prisoners could be used for that purpose. They could also be used as infiltrators and informers. Foucault even relates modern-day rehabilitation of prisoners to the old form of punishment, which began with a torturer extracting a confession. Contemporary psychologists now probe the minds of prisoners with a scientific rigor that Foucault considers a different kind of torture, a kind that our modern perspective does not allow us to see as such.

A number of new historicist literary critics owe a great debt to Foucault. Greenblatt, a founding editor of *Representations* (a journal published by the University of California Press that is still considered today to be the mouthpiece of the new historicism) and perhaps the quintessential new historicist, is arguably still most famous for his essay entitled "Invisible Bullets" (1981). There, he followed Foucault's lead in interpreting literary devices as if they were continuous with all other representational devices in a culture; he therefore turns to scholars in other fields in order to better understand the workings of literature.

In *Learning to Curse: Essays in Early Modern Culture* (1990), Greenblatt also acknowledged the influence of Marxist cultural critic Raymond Williams upon his intellectual development. While studying under Williams's tutelage in England, Greenblatt was exposed to topics excluded from his Yale education in literary criticism. Questions about "who controlled access to the printing press, who owned the land and the factories, whose voices were being repressed as well as represented in literary texts, what social strategies were being served by the aesthetic values we constructed — came pressing back in upon the act of interpretation." Greenblatt returned to the United States determined to incorporate such matters in literary investigations. Blending what he had learned from Williams with poststructuralist thought about the **undecidability,** or indeterminacy, of meaning, he developed a critical method that he has called *cultural poetics,* a term that he prefers to "the new historicism." More tentative and less overtly political than cultural criticism, it involves what Brook Thomas called "the technique of montage" in an article entitled "The New Literary Historicism" (1995). Thomas wrote: "Starting with the analysis of a particular historical event, it cuts to the analysis of a particular literary text. The point is not to show that the literary text reflects the historical event but to create a field of energy between the two so that we come to see the event as a social text and the literary text as a social event." Montrose explained in "Professing the Renaissance" that this new historicist criticism aimed to show the "historicity of texts and the textuality of history."

The cultural poetics practiced by many new historicists and the cultural criticism associated with **Marxism** share common elements, but one must understand the difference between the two approaches to understand the new historicism. Cultural criticism is in many ways more compatible with the old historicism than with the new. Cultural critics posit that history is driven by economics, that it is determinable even as it determines the lives of individuals, and that it is progressive, its **dialectic** one that will bring about justice and equality. By contrast, new historicists such as Greenblatt do not **privilege** economics in their analyses, arguing instead that individuals possess considerable productive power. Optimism about the individual, however, should not be confused with optimism about either history's direction or any historian's capacity to foretell it. Like a work of art, a work of history is the negotiated product of a private creator and the public practices of a given society.

Although new historicists do not see history melioristically or teleologically — that is, in terms of a progressive development toward some final purpose — this does not mean that they ignore historical change or that they are uninterested in describing it. Indeed, in works from *Renaissance Self-Fashioning* (1980) to *Shakespearean Negotiations* (1988), Greenblatt has written about Renaissance changes in the development of both literary **characters** and real people. But his view of change — like his view of the individual — is more "Foucauldian" than Marxist. He believes that any one change is connected with a host of others, progressive or regressive, repressive or enabling.

Not all new historicist critics are as Foucauldian as Greenblatt. Some owe more to Marx than Foucault, and others, like Thomas, have been more influenced by German Marxist Walter Benjamin, best known for essays such as "The Work of Art in the Age of Mechanical Reproduction" (1936) and "Theses on the Philosophy of History" (1940). Still others — McGann, for example — have followed the lead of Soviet critic Mikhail Bakhtin, who viewed literary works in terms of **polyphonic** discourses and **dialogues** between the official, legitimate voices of a society and other, more challenging or critical voices echoing popular culture.

Although Foucault has clearly had a powerful impact on the new historicism, other reasons also militate against considering him the single or even central influence. First, he so critiqued the old-style historicism that he ended up being antihistorical, or at least ahistorical, in the view of many new historicists. Second, his commitment to a radical remapping of the relations of power and influence, cause and effect, may have led him to adopt too cavalier an attitude toward chronology and facts. Finally, the very act of identifying and labeling *any* primary influence goes against the grain of the new historicism. Its practitioners have sought to **decenter** the study of literature, not only by incorporating historical studies (defined broadly to include anthropology and sociology) but also by struggling to see history itself from a decentered perspective. That struggle has involved recognizing that a historian's position is itself historically determined (and hence biased) and that events seldom have any single or central cause.

Throughout the 1980s, many hypothesized that the ongoing debates about the sources of the new historicism, the importance of Marx and Foucault, Benjamin and Bakhtin, and the exact locations of all the complex boundaries between the new historicism and the other "isms" (such as Marxism and poststructuralism) were due to the new historicism's very newness. In the initial stages of their development, new intellectual movements are often difficult to outline clearly because they invariably respond to disparate influences and include thinkers from diverse backgrounds. Now, however, it seems that the inchoate quality of the new historicism is characteristic of the movement rather than a function of newness. Its boundaries are fuzzy because it must always be subject to revision and redefinition as historical circumstances change. The fact that so many new historicist critics are working right at the border of Marxist, poststructuralist, cultural, **postcolonial,** feminist, and a new form of reader-response (or at least reader-oriented) criticism is evidence of the new historicism's multiple interests and motivations rather than of its embryonic state. New historicists themselves advocate and even stress the need to perpetually re-define categories and boundaries — whether disciplinary, generic, national, or racial — not because definitions are unimportant but because they are historically constructed and thus subject to change.

new novel: See *nouveau roman.*

New Wave: See **science fiction.**

Noble Savage: See **primitivism.**

nom de plume: From the French, an author's "pen name." The term is used most commonly to refer to entirely fictitious names, in which case it is synonymous with **pseudonym,** but it has been used by some scholars to refer to whatever name under which an author chooses to write. When used in this latter sense, an author's *nom de plume* may heavily resemble or even be identical to his or her legal name.

Pen names are generally used by authors who (1) wish to keep their identities private or even secret; or (2) wish to publish writings differing in kind or quality under different names (in which case, one or both names may be a *nom de plume*). In the nineteenth century, when women writers were not taken seriously, they sometimes published under fictitious men's names.

Although the term *nom de plume* is taken from the French, the French themselves tend to use the phrase *nom de guerre.*

EXAMPLES: Benjamin Franklin wrote under the *nom de plume* Richard Saunders in his serial *Poor Richard's Almanack,* published from 1733 to 1758; French novelist Marie-Henri Beyle wrote under a single *nom de guerre:* Stendhal. The real name of Mark Twain was Samuel Clemens. The philosopher Søren Kierkegaard wrote under numerous pen names. Amandine Aurore Dupin and Mary Ann Evans were the real names of George Sand and George Eliot, respectively. Charlotte and Emily Brontë pub-lished under the names Currer and Ellis Bell, respectively. Harriet Jacobs, who escaped from slavery and subsequently told her story in a **slave narra-tive** entitled *Incidents in the Life of a Slave Girl* (1861), published under the pseudonym Linda Brent. Michael Crichton also writes as Jeffery Hudson and John Lange and has coauthored a book with brother Douglas Crichton under the single joint *nom de plume* of Michael Douglas. Anne Rice (author of *Interview with the Vampire* [1976] and *The Witching Hour* [1990]) has writen pornography under the name A. N. Roquelaure.

nonperiodic sentence: See **loose sentence.**

nonsense verse: A type of **light verse** that emphasizes rhythmic and sound effects over meaning. It also frequently makes use of absurd or un-likely situations or ideas. Writers of nonsense verse often make up words and string them together in such a way as to frustrate or entertain the reader. Although difficult if not impossible to paraphrase, nonsense verse is seldom meaningless.

EXAMPLES: Edward Lear and Ogden Nash are two writers noted for their nonsense verse. Lear's *Book of Nonsense* (1846) is a collection of **limericks** for children. Lewis Carroll's "Jabberwocky" (1871) is one of the most famous English examples of nonsense verse. The first two **stanzas** follow:

'Twas brillig, and the slithy toves
Did gyre and gimble in the wabe;
All mimsy were the borogoves,
And the mome raths outgrabe.

"Beware the Jabberwock, my son!
The jaws that bite, the claws that catch!
Beware the Jubjub bird, and shun
The frumious Bandersnatch!"

An Alliterative Alphabet Aimed at Adult Abecedarians (1947) is composed of nonsense verse and illustrations by husband-and-wife team Huger Elliot and Elizabeth Shippen Green.

The Beatles' song "I Am the Walrus" (1967) provides a more recent example of nonsense verse, as does Spike Milligan's "On the Ning Nang Nong" (1959; from his collection *Silly Verse for Kids*), which in 1998 was voted the most popular nonsense verse in England:

On the Ning Nang Nong
Where the cows go Bong!
And the Monkeys all say Boo!
There's a Nong Nang Ning
Where the trees go Ping
And the tea pots Jibber Jabber Joo.
On the Nong Ning Nang
All the mice go Clang!
And you just can't catch 'em when they do!
So it's Ning Nang Nong!
Cows go Bong!
Trees go Ping!
Nong Nang Ning!
The mice go Clang!
What a noisy place to belong,
Is the Ning Nang Ning Nang Nong!

The following nursery rhyme is also an example of nonsense verse:

Hey diddle diddle,
The cat and the fiddle,
The cow jumped over the moon.
The little dog laughed to see such sport,
And the dish ran away with the spoon.

nouveau roman: Literally, "new novel," the French term for a type of twentieth-century experimental fiction often referred to in English as the **antinovel.** Writers of *nouveaux romans* typically violate established literary **conventions.** Standard elements such as **setting, characterization,** or even **plot** are often jettisoned or used in a minimal or unusual way. As a result, readers — especially those who are unfamiliar with the **genre** — may experience confusion. It is the responsibility of the reader to struggle to make sense of this kind of novel, which often appears to be little more than a loose association of perceptions and textual fragments. (Ironically, making sense of the *nouveau roman*'s achronological and alogical **narrative** sequences usually requires employing the conventional reading strategies we use to understand standard narratives.)

EXAMPLES: Novels by Nathalie Sarraute, Philippe Sollers, Marguerite Duras, and, especially, Alain Robbe-Grillet, whose 1957 *La jalousie* (*Jealousy*) is the best-known example of the genre.

See also **antinovel.**

novel: A lengthy **fictional prose narrative.** The novel is distinguished from the **novella,** a shorter fictional prose work that ranges from roughly fifty to one hundred pages in length, from which many scholars have argued the novel developed. The greater length of the novel, especially as compared with even briefer prose works such as the **short story** and the **tale,** permits authors to develop one or more **characters (characterization),** to establish their **motivation,** and to construct intricate **plots.** Some authors and critics maintain that it is possible to write a *nonfiction,* or *documentary, novel;* novelist Norman Mailer has used the word *faction* to refer to such works. However, the stories recounted in novels are usually and perhaps essentially products of the **imagination,** despite the presence in many novels of historical facts, situations, and personages.

Scholars disagree about when the novel first appeared on the literary scene. Some bestow this distinction on Shikibu Murasaki, a Japanese court lady, for her *The Tale of Genji* (c. A.D. 1000), a long story about the life, particularly the love life, of a young prince. Others argue that the French writer Madame de Lafayette's *La princesse de Clèves* (1678) is the first novel fully recognizable as such, by which they mean that it contains many of the elements characteristic of the novel form as it was first undeniably established in the eighteenth century, particularly in England. Still others argue that Aphra Behn, the first Englishwoman to support herself as a writer, produced the first novel when she wrote *Oroonoko* (1678), her account of the adventures of a real African prince by the same name. Behn was undeniably a precursor of the great English novelists to follow; the noted nineteenth-century historian Thomas Babington Macaulay compared her prose fiction to the novels of Daniel Defoe.

Of all the novelistic prototypes advanced as the first novel, however, Miguel de Cervantes's *Don Quixote de la Mancha* (part 1, 1605; part 2, 1615) is cited most often. Even scholars who do not believe that novels were written until the eighteenth century would agree that *Don Quixote* qualifies as an ancestor of the first novel. Certainly, it was the most famous and influential of the **picaresque narratives** often viewed as transitional works linking the prose tale and the novel in Western literary history. Picaresque narratives can be seen as a **framed** set of tales; **episodic** in structure, they recount a series of events linked by the presence of a single, usually roguish, **protagonist,** or main character. Although works like *Don Quixote* lack the sustained focus on characterization typical of later novels, they undeniably played a special role in the development of the novel (especially the **realistic novel**) by debunking the idealized forms of the **romance** and by legitimizing a fairly systematic examination of a specific **theme** or problem.

In describing other influences on the development of the novel, some scholars trace the **genre's** roots back to **classical** times, to narrative **epics** written in **verse** that tell a sustained story and feature a single protagonist. (Verse narratives have declined in popularity over time to the point that they are virtually nonexistent today; with this decline has come a corresponding increase in the popularity of prose narratives.) Other scholars who focus on classical precedents for the novel have emphasized classical Greek romances that date as far back as the second century A.D. These works, which are fairly lengthy, typically center on a pair of lovers who have to overcome various obstacles before living happily ever after. **Medieval romances** (sometimes called *chivalric romances*) and romances written subsequently during the **Renaissance** also exhibit the length characteristic of the novel, as well as an intricate plot, which typically features stories of adventure involving quests, chivalry, and the **fantastic** or supernatural. Although early examples of the medieval romance (such as Chrétien de Troye's twelfth-century *Lancelot*) were composed in verse, later examples (such as Thomas Malory's fifteenth-century *Morte d'Arthur*) were written in prose.

As mentioned previously, the novella, though distinct from the novel, is widely viewed as an influential forerunner; it is also the form on which English writers most often drew for their subject matter. In fact, whereas the French word for novel (*roman*) associates the form with the romance, the English word *novel* derives from the Italian *novella,* itself taken from the Latin *novella narrātiō,* meaning a "new kind of story." Although *novella* is now used to refer to any fictional prose work ranging from fifty to one hundred pages in length, it has traditionally been used to refer to the short Italian and French tales written between the fourteenth and sixteenth centuries — works such as the prose narratives included in Boccacio's *Decameron* (1348–53) and Marguerite de Navarre's *Heptaméron* (1548).

Whatever its origins, the novel became established definitively as a genre in early-eighteenth-century England with the work of Daniel Defoe, Samuel Richardson, and Henry Fielding. Defoe's novels *Robinson Crusoe* (1719) and *Moll Flanders* (1722) are largely episodic in structure, but they differ from picaresque and romance narratives on the one hand and Italian and French novellas on the other because of the convincing solidity of their characters and the circumstances in which those characters find themselves. Whereas Defoe emphasized the action undertaken by his main characters, Richardson established what we have come to call the *psychological novel*. In works such as *Pamela; or, Virtue Rewarded* (1740) and *Clarissa Harlowe* (1747–48), he focused on motivation and character development, rather than the latest vagary of the plot. Like many other eighteenth-century novels, both *Pamela* (a phenomenal success) and *Clarissa* employed the **epistolary** form (narratives presented and propagated entirely through letters written by one or more characters).

Fielding's nonepistolary works *Joseph Andrews* (1742) and *Tom Jones* (1749) managed to synthesize many of the best characteristics of Defoe's and Richardson's novels. Packed with adventure, they also develop character sensitively and sympathetically and are philosophically undergirded by the tenets of **neoclassicism,** a broad-based movement whose proponents believed that the proper subject of art is humanity in the broadest sense and that literature should both instruct and delight. ("I describe not men, but manners," says the **narrator** of *Joseph Andrews,* "not an individual, but a species.")

A tremendous growth in literacy — and a related explosion in novel publication — occurred between 1750 and 1900. Reflecting the evolving concerns and tastes of their historical place and time, new generations of novelists wrote about new subjects using innovative **styles** and **structures** and published their works in new media designed to reach a growing audience. (These media included the three-volume editions developed for lending libraries and the installment style of publication typical of literary periodicals and popular magazines.) In particular, the novel allowed women to break into the literary profession, which historically had been almost exclusively a male domain. Several of the best and most famous women novelists, however, fearing that their work would not be taken seriously, assumed masculine pen names, or **noms de plume.** As a result of these changes in audience, authorship, and production, the novel took on new forms and contributed dynamically to the development of evolving literary movements, some of which overlapped chronologically but involved very different **aesthetic** principles and assumptions.

One of the new novelistic forms that emerged during the period 1750–1800 was the **picaresque novel,** which grew out of picaresque narrative. Tobias Smollett, through works such as *Peregrine Pickle* (1751), was instrumental in developing this type of novel, in which a physically vigorous but morally imperfect **hero** gets into a series of hair-raising adventures. Through works such as *Wilhelm Meister's Apprenticeship* (1796), Johann Wolfgang von Goethe helped usher in another new form: the **bildungsroman,** a type of novel that recounts the psychological and sometimes spiritual development of an individual from childhood to maturity. Other novelistic forms that developed during the latter half of the eighteenth century include the **sentimental novel** and the **Gothic novel.** The sentimental novel — as exemplified by Laurence Sterne's *A Sentimental Journey* (1768) — exalted the emotions, particularly those of sympathy and generosity, and portrayed their expression as the most reliable marks of human virtue. The Gothic novel — as exemplified by Horace Walpole's *The Castle of Otranto: A Gothic Story* (1764) and Ann Radcliffe's *The Italian* (1797) — also represented and relied on emotional expression. But fear and horror, rather than sympathy and generosity, were the emotions most often appealed to by these novels, which are typically set in mysterious castles full of secret passageways and supernatural occurrences.

Often associated not only with the romance but also with **romanticism** — the late-eighteenth- and early-nineteenth-century literary movement associated with writers who emphasized imagination and feeling over logical thought — the Gothic novel was further developed during the nineteenth century by writers such as Mary Shelley, author of *Frankenstein* (1818). Several nineteenth-century works commonly associated with the Gothic novel, however, do not fit neatly within the genre's confines. Jane Austen's *Northanger Abbey* (1818), for instance, is actually a gentle **parody** of Gothic fiction. Emily Brontë's *Wuthering Heights* (1847) blends Gothic and, more generally, romance elements with the emerging interests of **realism,** a nineteenth-century literary movement emphasizing the **objective** presentation of ordinary places and events rather than the **subjective** presentation of personal feelings and imaginings associated with romanticism.

Traditionally, literary historians have distinguished two overarching categories of novelistic prose fiction: the *realistic novel* (sometimes called *the novel proper*) and the *romance novel*. Realistic novelists seek to attain verisimilitude in their depictions of ordinary characters, situations, and **settings;** in other words, they seek to construct believable, plausible stories. Romance novelists, on the other hand, make little claim to verisimilitude. Instead, their novels generally focus on adventure, involve heroes and **villains** who are larger than life, and often feature improbable, though imaginative, situations.

The nineteenth century has often been called the age of the **realistic novel;** fiction writers whose works broadly exemplify the tenets of realism include Honoré de Balzac, Anthony Trollope, George Eliot, Gustave Flaubert, Fyodor Dostoyevsky, William Dean Howells, and Henry James. Well-known examples of the realistic novel include Balzac's *Le père Goriot* (*Father Goriot*) (1835), Dostoyevsky's *Crime and Punishment* (1866), and James's *The Portrait of a Lady* (1881). Within the general category of realism, moreover, particular types of realistic fiction were developed. These include **local color writing,** a type of writing that depicts the distinctive characteristics (dialect, dress, mannerisms, etc.) of a particular region; the *roman à clef,* a type of novel in which real people are represented in the guise of novelistic characters bearing fictional names; and the **historical novel,** in which historical personages (bearing their own names) and events are worked into a fictitious narrative. Sarah Orne Jewett's representation of New England in *The Country of the Pointed Firs* (1896) is an example of local color writing. George Meredith's *roman à clef Diana of the Crossways* (1885) depicts the English prime minister Lord Melbourne as a character named Lord Dannisburgh. An example of the nineteenth-century historical novel is William Makepeace Thackeray's *The History of Henry Esmond* (1852), in which Queen Anne, the Pretender, and noted essayists Joseph Addison and Richard Steele appear.

Not all nineteenth-century fiction writers were realists, however. François-René de Chateaubriand, author of *Atala* (1801) and *René* (1805), is commonly classified as a romantic. Sir Walter Scott, the author of *Waverley* (1814) and *Ivanhoe* (1819), built so many romance elements into his historical settings that, despite his reputation for being the first historical novelist, scholars more commonly associate him with the romance novel than with the realistic novel. (The same may be said of Alexandre Dumas, author of *The Three Musketeers* [1844] and *The Count of Monte Cristo* [1845].) Nathaniel Hawthorne's *The Scarlet Letter* (1850), though steeped in colonial American history, was originally subtitled *A Romance*. James Fenimore Cooper's *The Deerslayer* (1841), like Herman Melville's *Moby-Dick* (1851) and *Billy Budd* (written in 1891, published posthumously in 1924), are also generally viewed as examples of the romance novel.

Some of the most acclaimed and influential novelists of the nineteenth century, however, cannot be clearly identified either with the romance novel or the realistic novel. Some of these writers, such as the Brontë sisters, combined romantic and realistic elements in their works. Others produced novels associated with a major genre (**comedy, tragedy,** or **satire**) that predates realism and, indeed, the novel itself. Charles Dickens was as much a satirist as a realistic novelist; comic and **autobiographical** early novels were followed by major works, such as *Bleak House* (1852–53) and *Our Mutual Friend* (1864–65), that contain far more **caricature, symbolism,** and **allegory** — also more absurd, fantastic and **grotesque** elements — than are common in realistic works. Other novelists wrote works that contributed to the development of **naturalism,** a literary movement whose adherents pessimistically depicted pathetic protagonists with little if any control over their destinies. Thomas Hardy consistently employed the tragic genre but also adapted it in a naturalistic manner in novels such as *The Mayor of Casterbridge* (1886), *Tess of the d'Urbervilles* (1891), and *Jude the Obscure* (1896). Other, purer examples of the naturalistic novel include Émile Zola's *Germinal* (1885), Stephen Crane's *Maggie: A Girl of the Streets* (1893), Frank Norris's *McTeague* (1899), and several novels published early in the twentieth century by Theodore Dreiser.

With the advent of the twentieth century and, shortly thereafter, the rise of **modernism,** the novel became ever more diverse in its development and increasingly difficult (if not impossible) to fit into the general categories of romance and realism. To be sure, the romance form did not die out (Daphne du Maurier's *Rebecca* [1938] is a twentieth-century romance **classic**), nor did realism. Modern writers including E. M. Forster, F. Scott

Fitzgerald, D. H. Lawrence, Ernest Hemingway, and Graham Greene adapted the **conventions** of realism to represent new literary subjects ranging from colonial India (Forster, in *A Passage to India* [1924]) to the "Roaring Twenties" (Fitzgerald, in *The Great Gatsby* [1925]) to sexual relationships (Lawrence, in *Lady Chatterley's Lover* [1928]) to World War I (Hemingway, in *A Farewell to Arms* [1929]), to **postcolonial** Mexico (Greene, in *The Power and the Glory* [1940]). In works such as Zora Neale Hurston's *Their Eyes Were Watching God* (1937), Richard Wright's *Native Son* (1940), and Ralph Ellison's *Invisible Man* (1947), African American writers associated with the **Harlem Renaissance** wrote with psychological realism about the black experience in the United States.

The writers most closely associated with modernism, however, ignored both romance conventions and realism's emphasis on objectivity to carry out radical experiments with style, structure, and subject matter. In works such as *Swann's Way* (1913), *Ulysses* (1922), *To the Lighthouse* (1927), and *As I Lay Dying* (1930), Marcel Proust, James Joyce, Virginia Woolf, and William Faulkner, respectively, experimented with **stream of consciousness,** a literary technique reflecting a character's jumbled flow of perceptions, thoughts, memories, and feelings. Joyce also turned to **myth** in order both to contrast his age with heroic times past and to suggest the timeless, universal qualities of certain situations, problems, and truths. Other twentieth-century novelists used mythical contexts and structures differently; in works ranging from the novella *Death in Venice* (1911) to his novel *The Magic Mountain* (1924), Thomas Mann used mythology to reveal disturbed psychic conditions within his characters.

Following the **Modern Period,** fiction writers associated with **postmodernism** experimented even more radically with conventional literary forms and styles. While preserving the spirit and even some of the themes of modernist literature (such as the alienation of humanity and historical discontinuity), they rejected the order that a number of modernists attempted to instill in their work via mythology and other patterns of **allusion** and **symbol.** Postmodernists include William Burroughs, Donald Barthelme, John Barth, Kathy Acker, and Thomas Pynchon, the author of *V* (1963) and *Gravity's Rainbow* (1973).

Within postmodernist fiction, a special type of novel developed: the **antinovel,** referred to in French as the ***nouveau roman*** (literally, "new novel"). "New" or "anti" novelists largely dispensed with standard novelistic elements such as setting, characterization, or even plot, forcing the reader to struggle to make sense of a seemingly fragmented **text.** They also aimed to depict reality without recourse to a moral frame of reference and to avoid the kind of subjective narrative evaluation that creeps into realistic, naturalistic, and modernist works. John Hawkes's *The Blood Oranges* (1971) and Alain Robbe-Grillet's *La jalousie* (*Jealousy*) (1957) are commonly cited as examples of the antinovel and *nouveau roman,* respectively. Other practitioners of the *nouveau roman* include Nathalie Sarraute, Philippe Sollers, and Marguerite Duras.

Magic realism also emerged (mainly in Latin America) as a postmodernist innovation in the late 1940s. When applied to novels, the term *magic realism* refers to works characterized by a mixture of credible and utterly fantastic elements. Realistic details, esoteric knowledge, fairy tales, myths, and dreams are intertwined in a complex, even tangled plot that often involves abrupt chronological shifts. Gabriel García Márquez's *Cien años de soledad* (*One Hundred Years of Solitude*) (1967) and Laura Esquivel's *Como agua para chocolate* (*Like Water for Chocolate*) (1989) are examples of realism; Isabel Allende blended magic realism and political realism in her novel *La casa de los espíritus* (*The House of the Spirits*) (1982).

The emergence of new categories of fiction — such as magic realism and the antinovel — does not mean that most or even many of the most critically acclaimed novels written since World War II fall into those categories. Space does not permit an exhaustive list of novelists whose major works are *not* significantly associated with magic realism, the antinovel, or postmodernism more generally, but an inevitably eclectic and idiosyncratic short list might include (in alphabetical order): Margaret Atwood, A. S. Byatt, Robertson Davies, Margaret Drabble, Ernest Gaines, William Golding, John Irving, Norman Mailer, Bernard Malamud, Toni Morrison, Iris Murdoch, Vladimir Nabokov, Joyce Carol Oates, Nelida Piñon, E. Annie Proulx, Wallace Stegner, Amy Tan, Anne Tyler, John Updike, and Herman Wouk. Also worthy of mention are a few of the novelists, such as James Clavell and James Michener, whose works are considered "popular" rather than "serious" fiction. Noted authors associated with some well-defined subgenres of popular fiction include Isaac Asimov, Ray Bradbury, and Ursula Le Guin (**science fiction**); Piers Anthony, Terry Brooks, Le Guin, and Anne McCaffrey (**fantasy fiction**); and John Le Carré, Robert Ludlum, and Tom Clancy (**spy fiction**). Authors of **detective fiction** influenced by the pre-1950 work of Raymond Chandler, Dashiell Hammett, Dorothy Sayers, and Agatha Christie include writers such as Ross Macdonald, John D. MacDonald, Sue Grafton, Tony Hillerman, and Sara Paretsky. Laura Esquivel's *La ley del amor* (*The Law of Love*) (1995) has been called the first multimedia novel, involving as it does a musical CD keyed to the plot.

novelette: See **novella.**

novella: As commonly used today, a term referring to a **fictional prose narrative** ranging from fifty to one hundred pages in length, that is, a work longer than a **short story** but shorter than a **novel.** When used in this contemporary sense, the term is synonymous with *novelette*. Due to the dimestore connotations that have grown up around the term *novelette*, however, it is rarely used today, except disparagingly.

Before the twentieth century, *novella* had a different meaning. When used strictly, it referred specifically to Italian and French **tales** written between the fourteenth and sixteenth centuries, some of which were as short as two pages long. Famous examples include the prose narratives found in Boccaccio's *Decameron* (1348–53) and Marguerite de Navarre's *Heptaméron* (1548), which contains stories ranging from approximately three hundred words to fifty pages in length. Used more generally, *novella* could refer to later works written in other languages, but only to those exhibiting specific characteristics found in early Italian and French examples of the **genre.**

As traditionally understood, the novella focuses on some narrowly circumscribed occurrence, situation, or **conflict.** In representing the **protagonist's** reaction to a particular development or in working out the resolution of a particular conflict, many practitioners of the early novella form place a premium on suspense and surprise. Traditional novellas, like those comprising *Heptaméron*, are also often encompassed by a "cornice," or **frame story,** explaining why the various "interior" stories are recounted. (Most frame stories linking novellas and their **narrators** involve a shared journey, disaster, refuge, or condition of exile; the story framing the *Decameron* tells of ten young people who escape from plague-ridden Florence to their country villas, where they pass the time telling tales.) However, Miguel de Cervantes, known as "the Spanish Boccaccio," dispensed with the frame story in his collection of novellas entitled *Novelas ejemplares* (*Exemplary Novellas*) (1613).

The traditional novella had a powerful influence on narrative poetry (Geoffrey Chaucer's *Canterbury Tales* [c. 1387] has been viewed as a series of novellas organized by a frame story about pilgrims on a pilgrimage), on drama (the plot of Shakespeare's *All's Well That Ends Well* [1602–1603], like that of other **Renaissance** plays, is derived from a tale in the *Decameron*), and on the development of the novel. The terms *novel* and *novella* are both derived from the Italian word *novella*, which itself derives from the Latin *novella narrātiō*, meaning "new kind of story."

Although certain **characters** (the betrayed husband, the corrupt clergyman, the clever merchant) and **plots** (adulterous plans foiled, patience overcoming all odds, **wit's** triumph over force) common to the traditional novella recur in works by novelists from Fielding through Faulkner and beyond, the aspect of the traditional novella that most significantly influenced the novel's development was the frame story. The frame story demonstrated: (1) how disparate but related **stories** (like those of the **medieval romance**) could be unified into a larger but nonetheless coherent structure; and (2) that narrators can be characters and vice versa. The former demonstration paved the way for the **picaresque narrative** and eventually the eighteenth-century **picaresque novel;** the latter contributed to the development of many features of the modern novel, including that of the **first-person** narrator and the **unreliable narrator.**

Since the nineteenth century, the Germans have been the most avid practitioners of the novella form, which they term the *Novelle*. Johann Wolfgang von Goethe, borrowing from the Italian term *novella*, introduced the term into German in 1795, the same year in which he wrote the first German *Novelle,* or, more properly, the first collection of German *Novellen.* Entitled *Unterhaltungen deutscher Ausgewanderten (The Recreations of the German Immigrants),* this work involves seven stories linked by a frame story about a group of German refugees awaiting news about French army movements. Typical of the traditional novella are the two stories related by a priest. One involves a man who is unexpectedly pursued by a young lady in the absence of her husband; another involves a man who unintentionally discovers how to open a secret compartment in his father's desk.

After Goethe, nineteenth- and early-twentieth-century German-language writers of the *Novelle* played with and strayed from the novella tradition, creating what are essentially very long short stories, the length of which allowed for background information, descriptions of nature, and character development (all of which were largely absent from the traditional novella). These German authors in a sense created the modern understanding of *novella,* a term now commonly applied to lengthy, descriptive, psychologically nuanced stories such as Thomas Mann's *Death in Venice* (1911) and Franz Kafka's *The Metamorphosis* (1915).

The novella, however, has by no means been an exclusively German form since the advent of the nineteenth century. The Frenchwoman Amandine Aurore Dupin, writing under the male **nom de plume** George Sand, wrote several novellas, such as *Marianne* (1876). Fyodor Dostoyevsky's *Notes from the Underground* (1866) and Leo Tolstoi's *The Death of Ivan Ilyich* (1886) are Russian examples of the novella. English-language examples include Henry James's *The Turn of the Screw* (1898), Joseph Conrad's *Heart of Darkness* (1899), Edith Wharton's *Ethan Frome* (1911), and Ernest Hemingway's *The Old Man and the Sea* (1952). Though novellas in the contemporary sense, some of these works also contain elements of the traditional novella, whether it be resolution of a single and simple plot conflict (*The Old Man and the Sea*), the **theme** of illicit temptation (*Ethan Frome*), or a frame story surrounding the main story (*Heart of Darkness*). More recent examples of the novella in English include Mark Helprin's *Ellis Island* (1981), Jane Smiley's *Ordinary Love* (1989), and A. S. Byatt's *Angels and Insects* (1991).

objective correlative: A term popularized by T. S. Eliot in his 1919 essay "Hamlet and His Problems" to refer to an **image,** action, or situation — or, more often, to a pattern of images, actions, or situations — that somehow evokes a particular emotion from the reader without expressly stating what that emotion should be. As Eliot wrote, "The only way of expressing emotion in the form of art is by finding an 'objective correlative'; in other words, a set of objects, a situation, a chain of events which shall be the formula of that *particular* emotion; such that when the external facts, which must terminate in sensory experience, are given, the emotion is immediately evoked." According to Eliot, when writers fail to find objective correlatives for the emotions they wish to convey, readers or audiences are left unconvinced, unmoved, or even confused. Eliot applied his theory to William Shakespeare's play *Hamlet* (1602), arguing that it is an "artistic failure" because occurrences in the play do not justify Hamlet's depth of feeling and thus fail to provide convincing **motivation.** *Objective correlative* was first used in a mid-nineteenth-century art lecture given by the American poet and painter Washington Allston, but it was not until Eliot redefined the term that it elicited widespread interest and debate in critical circles, especially among **the New Critics.**

objective criticism: A type of **criticism** that views any given literary work as freestanding, independent of external references to its author, audience, or the environment in which it is written or read. That is, the work is viewed as authoritative and sufficient in and of itself, or even as a world-in-itself. Objective critics, therefore, evaluate and analyze works based on internal criteria rather than by external standards of judgment. They consider, for instance, whether a work is coherent or unified and how its various components relate to one another rather than how the work is or was received by the public. Many of the tenets of objective criticism were articulated by the philosopher Immanuel Kant in his *Critique of Aesthetic Judgment* (1790). In the twentieth century, objective criticism has evolved through the work of several groups of **practical critics,** especially those **formalists** associated with **the New Criticism.**

objective theory of art: A term used by M. H. Abrams to refer to the theory of literature that prizes literary works as objects in and of themselves above all other considerations, including the effect they have, the conditions under which they were written and published, the author's **intentions,** and so forth.

See **objective criticism** for an example of such a theory.

objectivity: A term referring to the presentation of **characters** and **plot** in a literary work without overt comment or judgment by the author. Objectivity is the opposite of **subjectivity,** in which the personal opinions and emotions of the author are evident and even paramount. Writers attempting to achieve objectivity try to suppress their personal feelings and opinions in order to present the most impersonal, neutral view possible. Such writers, for instance, would not address the reader via **apostrophe,** nor would they comment upon a character's behavior or **motivation.** Although some writers are much more objective than others, most critics would agree that no author can be completely objective; for one thing, the very choice of what to present and what not to present in a story involves a subjective decision. Thus, objectivity and subjectivity tend to be viewed as two ends of a continuum, with infinitely subtle gradations in between.

EXAMPLES: Novelist Ernest Hemingway is often cited for his objective style. The following passage from Carl Hiassen's novel *Strip Tease* (1993) is written in an objective manner:

> Shad went to Sears and purchased two jumbo outdoor garbage buckets with clip on lids. Then he drove to a snake farm near the Tamiami Airport, west of Miami. The man who owned the snake farm called himself Jungle Juan. He told Shad that most of his reptile stock had been wiped out by the hurricane. His insurance company still hadn't paid him off.

object-relations theory: See **psychological criticism and psychoanalytic criticism.**

oblique rhyme: See **half-rhyme.**

occasional verse: Verse written to celebrate or commemorate a particular occasion or event. Poetry of this type may range from joyous to somber in **tone.** In the past, occasional (or *topical,* as it is sometimes called) verse has often been used to honor royalty or praise **heroes,** although it can be used in response to any event such as births, deaths, marriages, and military victories. Occasional poems tend to have a short life span since they are written for a specific event, but those that have unusual literary merit have survived.

EXAMPLES: The poem "On the Pulse of Morning" was written by Maya Angelou for President Bill Clinton's 1993 inauguration; her reading of the poem was meant to recall to the public memory President John F. Kennedy's inauguration, at which Robert Frost read a poem written for that occasion entitled "Gift Outright of 'The Gift Outright'" (1962). "Candle in the Wind 1997," sung by Elton John at Princess Diana's funeral, commemorated Princess Diana's death. Paul McCartney's anthem "Freedom" (2001) commemorated the terrorist attacks of September 11, 2001; "Let's Roll" (2001), by Neil Young and Booker T. Jones, more specifically memorialized the heroics of passengers on ill-fated Flight 93, who struggled with hijackers to prevent them from using the plane to hit a populated target and lost their lives when the plane crashed in a Pennsylvania field. Poet Galway Kinnell's "When the Towers Fell" (2002) — containing a **pastiche** of quotations from poems by François Villon, Hart Crane, Paul Celan, Aleksander Wat and Walt Whitman — was published in *The New Yorker* to mark the first anniversary of the September 11th tragedy.

occultatio: See **paralipsis.**

occupatio: See **paralipsis.**

octameter (octometer): A line of **verse** consisting of eight **metrical feet.**
EXAMPLES: Robert Browning's poem about old Venice entitled "A Toccata of Galuppi's" (1855):

Did young | people | take their | pleasure | when the | sea was | warm in | May?
Balls and | masks be|gun at | midnight, | burning | ever | to mid|day,
When they | made up | fresh ad|ventures | for the | morrow, | do you | say?

Alfred, Lord Tennyson's "Locksley Hall" (1842):

Comrades, | leave me | here a | little, | while as | yet 'tis | early | morn;
Leave me | here, and | when you | want me, | sound u|pon the | bugle | horn.

'Tis the | place, and | all a|round it, | as of | old, the | curlews | call,
Dreary | gleams a|bout the | moorland | flying | over | Locksley | Hall. . . .

Both of the preceding poems are written in **trochaic** octameter; in each, the final foot consists of one **accented** syllable rather than a complete trochaic foot, in which the accented syllable is followed by an unaccented one.

octave (octet): Any eight-line **stanza,** but a term most frequently applied to the first eight lines of an **Italian sonnet,** which **rhymes** *abbaabba* and terminates with a full stop before the succeeding **sestet.** The octave may pose a question or dilemma that the sestet answers or resolves.

octet: See **octave.**

octometer: See **octameter.**

ode: A relatively long, serious, and usually meditative **lyric poem** that treats a noble or otherwise elevated subject in a dignified and calm manner. Odes come in three varieties — the *regular,* or **Pindaric;** the **irregular,** or *Cowleyan;* and the **Horatian.** Its lineage traceable back to the Greek poet Pindar, the ode was originally a choral poem intended to be sung at a public event. Odes were composed in a trifold **stanzaic** form involving a **strophe** to be sung while the **chorus** danced in one direction, an **antistrophe** to be sung while it moved in the opposite direction, and an **epode** to be sung while standing still. The strophe and antistrophe exhibited the same **meter,** which was different from that of the epode.

EXAMPLES: John Dryden's "A Song for Saint Cecilia's Day" (1687), Samuel Taylor Coleridge's "Dejection: An Ode" (1802), John Keats's "Ode to a Nightingale" (1819). Most **modernist** poems called odes (Robert Penn Warren's "Ode to Fear" [1944] and W. H. Auden's "Ode to Gaea" [1954], for example) are odes only in the formal, Horatian sense; that is, they contain stanzas of similar length, **rhyme scheme,** and **rhythmical** pattern. Poems that exemplify the ode more broadly defined include Allen Tate's "Ode to the Confederate Dead" (1928) and Frank O'Hara's "Ode to Joy" (1960).

See also **Horatian ode, irregular ode, Pindaric ode.**

Oedipus complex: A **psychoanalytic** term used by Sigmund Freud to describe the sexual desire that a young boy (typically aged three to six) feels for his mother and the rivalry and hostility the child correspondingly feels toward his father. This sense of competition is so intense that the child may fantasize about ways in which the father might be removed from the family so that the child can become the focal point of his mother's attention and affection. Whether the child imagines killing his father or envisions his father's removal by some passive cause (such as disappearance or death in a car accident), he aims to take possession of his mother for himself alone. Freud coined the term *Oedipus complex* in reference to the Greek Oedipus **myth** dramatized in Sophocles' play *Oedipus Rex* (c. 430 B.C.), a tragedy in which the **protagonist,** Oedipus, blinds himself after discovering that the man he killed years ago was his father and the woman he married is his mother.

Freud viewed the manifestation of this complex as a universal, and therefore normal, experience. In fact, Freud argued that all children, female as well as male, experience sexual desire for the parent of the opposite sex. Since Freud, the term *Electra complex* has replaced what Freud referred to as the "female Oedipus complex," the situation in which a girl feels desire for her father. *Electra complex* refers to the Electra myth, the source of *Electra* plays by Aeschylus, Euripides, and Sophocles in which Electra, the daughter of Agamemnon and Clytemnestra, successfully urges her brother Orestes to kill their mother.

Although Freud identified the Oedipus complex as a normal experience, he also argued that adult neuroses would result should the conflict remain unresolved. Most children, however, successfully resolve the conflict, according to Freud, by eventually identifying with the same-sex parent.

EXAMPLES: Shakespeare's play *Hamlet* (1602) and D. H. Lawrence's novel *Sons and Lovers* (1913) have been said to portray protagonists with unresolved oedipal complexes. The Brazilian film *The Dolphin* (1987) — based on the Amazonian **legend** of (and **folklore** surrounding) Bufeo Colorado, a dolphin-man from a race of water gods who live in underwater cities — likewise concerns a **character** with an unresolved Oedipus complex. In the movie, the son of a human female and a pink river dolphin who turns into a man when there is a full moon has an oedipal fixation that leads him to track and haunt his mother.

Old English Period (in English literature): Also referred to as the *Anglo-Saxon Period* by historians, an era usually said to have begun in the first half of the fifth century A.D. with the migration to Britain by members of four principal Germanic tribes from the European continent: the Frisians, the Jutes, the Saxons, and the Angles (whose name, by the seventh century, was used to refer to all of the Germanic inhabitants of "Engla-land," hence, England). *Old English* refers to the synthetic, or fairly heavily inflected, language system of these peoples, once they were separated from their Germanic roots.

By the time the Germanic tribes arrived, the British Isles had been inhabited for centuries by Celtic peoples, who had been under Roman occupation for nearly four hundred years (A.D. 43–410). While some of these native British had learned the Latin language, their Celtic language and culture had remained intact. Christianity had also been introduced under the Roman occupation, and a British (as well as Irish) church flourished almost completely independent of Rome, helping to sustain the literate and learned traditions of the Latin West when non-Christian Germanic peoples swept into the Roman Empire.

According to the monk historian Bede, writing circa A.D. 730, long after the collapse of Rome, the Celts, abandoned by the Romans, invited help from the Saxons against the marauding Picts and Scots to the north. Once in Britain, the mercenaries decided to stay. King Arthur — if he ever existed — may have been a Romano-British war leader (perhaps nicknamed "Arcturus," Latin for "The Bear") and is credited with holding off the first waves of Germanic invader-immigrants in the early fifth century. But the Anglo-Saxons soon drove the native British into Wales and Cornwall. The invaders were themselves converted to Christianity after the arrival of Augustine (not to be confused with his famous predecessor of the same name, the fifth-century Bishop of Hippo) in 597, whose mission from Rome also included bringing the British Christian clergy into the Roman Catholic sphere. Christianity brought literacy to the orally based culture of the Anglo-Saxons; by the eighth century, Anglo-Saxon monks were prominent scholars and leading missionaries among the Germanic peoples on the Continent.

England was invaded several more times during the Old English Period by Germanic cousins of the Anglo-Saxons: Danes, Norwegians, and Swedes, all of whom were called "Vikings" by the English. These peoples were not Christianized when they arrived, beginning in the late eighth and early ninth centuries, and again in the tenth century, but eventually, like the Anglo-Saxons, they settled the lands they took and adopted the religion of their inhabitants. The Norman conquest of England in 1066 — at the hands of still other Germanic peoples, the "Northmen" who had settled the northern area of modern France and whose language was a dialect of Old French — is generally said to have ended the Old English Period and to have inaugurated the subsequent **Middle English Period** (1100–1500).

King Alfred, often referred to by the **epithet** "Alfred the Great," is the best-known figure of the Old English Period because of his success in unifying the Anglo-Saxons against the Vikings during the ninth century. Alfred also sponsored the translation of several Latin works into Old English and inaugurated the *Anglo-Saxon Chronicle,* a record of events in England that was kept through the twelfth century. Under his influence, West Saxon, the language of almost all of the period's surviving manuscripts, emerged as a sort of "standard" among the four principal dialects.

The **epic** *Beowulf,* parts of which may have taken shape in early Germanic oral tradition, but which was written down in Old English after A.D. 1000, is the period's most famous literary work and is concerned exclusively with Scandinavian peoples and events. Other notable poems, most of which were committed to writing in the eleventh century, include "Deor," "The Seafarer," "The Wanderer," and "The Dream of the Rood" (or Cross). This last poem comes from the less well-known but large body of verse that is explicitly religious in **theme,** including stories from Genesis and Exodus, as well as saints' lives and prose sermons. Although these works were put in writing in a Christianized culture, they nonetheless represent the pre-Christian Germanic past of the Anglo-Saxons. The work of a few poets, such as Cynewulf and Cædmon (we know nothing more about Cædmon than what Bede tells us in his *Ecclesiastical History of the English People* [c. A.D. 730]), was more obviously Christian in subject. Most of the writing of the period that was predominantly religious consisted of biblical **narratives** and saints' lives retold in Old English verse and homilies or sermons in Old English prose, alongside and in communication with a flourishing Latin literature.

omniscient point of view: A **third-person point of view** in **fictional** writing that permits the author to present not only external details and information through an all-knowing **narrator** but also the inner thoughts and emotions of all of the **characters** of a work. The omniscient narrator is frequently described as "godlike." Authors writing from the omniscient point of view may reveal — or conceal — at their discretion; their presentation of material to the reader is limited only by their own choices. Shifts in time and place as well as shifts from the viewpoint of one character to another are common. The omniscient point of view enables an author to comment openly upon the action or **theme** of the work in addition to simply recounting events. An omniscient narrator who makes valuative judgments is considered **intrusive,** whereas one who generally refrains from doing so is called **unintrusive.** A large number of the works that have traditionally been considered **classics** are written from the omniscient point of view — for example, Charles Dickens's *A Tale of Two Cities* (1859), and Leo Tolstoi's *War and Peace* (1864–66). Moreover, many such "Great Books" are written from the intrusive omniscient point of view — for example, Henry Fielding's *Joseph Andrews* (1741) and George Eliot's *Middlemarch* (1872).

See also **point of view.**

onomatopoeia: The creation or use of words that, however we explain it, sound like what they mean or, perhaps more accurately, seem to signify meaning through sound effects. The significance of an onomatopoetic word, in other words, is somehow inseparable from its pronunciation.

EXAMPLES: *Hiss* and *sizzle* are common examples, as are *spurt* and *suck*. "Suck was a queer word," the child Stephen Dedalus thinks to himself in James Joyce's *A Portrait of the Artist as a Young Man* (1916):

> The sound was ugly. Once he had washed his hands in the lavatory of the Wicklow Hotel and his father pulled the stopper up by the chain after and the dirty water went down through the hole in the basin. And when it had all gone down slowly the hole in the basin had made a sound like that: suck. Only louder.

Theodore Roethke's "The Storm" (1958) also makes use of onomatopoeia:

> A thin whine of wires, a rattling and flapping of leaves,
> And the small street lamp swinging and slamming against the lamp pole.

oppositions: See **binary oppositions.**

oration, oratory: *Oration* refers to a carefully crafted oral presentation, usually written with a large audience in mind and designed to emotionally move as well as intellectually persuade a body of listeners. Alternatively, it signifies the practice of writing and delivering such speeches. The term *oratory* can refer to a private place for prayer, usually a small chapel within a large church or cathedral, or to a musical composition for solo voices, choir, and orchestra; when used by literary scholars, however, it usually refers to the use of eloquent language, the art of oration, public speaking, lecturing.

In **classical** Greek and Roman times, skillful orators were widely respected, and oration was a preferred mode of public **discourse**. Specific rules governed the construction of a formal oration, which, according to Corax of Syracuse (a fifth-century B.C. Greek), had five parts but which, by Roman times, had seven: the *exordium* (an attention-grabbing opening); a **narration** of facts; a subsequent *exposition,* or explanation, of the situation that needs to be addressed; a statement (called the *proposition*) of the speaker's **point of view** (literally, of what the orator intends to "prove"); the *confirmation* (in which the speaker attempts to prove his point(s), convincing the audience to adopt the expressed point of view); *refutation* of some real or possible opponent's point of view; and a *peroration,* or summing up, sometimes called the **epilogue** or conclusion.

Orations are seldom heard today, and those that are delivered are rarely constructed according to classical rules. (Exceptions might include the valedictory and salutatory addresses still given in Latin at the commencement exercises of a handful of schools, colleges, and universities.) The closest thing to an oration that most of us are likely to hear would be a president's inaugural (or State of the Union) address; an impassioned speech given on the Fourth of July by a hopeful politician; the closing arguments made in a highly publicized trial (such as the murder trial of O. J. Simpson); a sermon given to tens of thousands of people attending a Billy Graham–style evangelistic "crusade"; or a speech meant to inspire a large group marching on Washington, such as the one given by Louis Farrakhan to the multitude of African American men who took part in the 1995 Million Man March.

organic form and mechanic form: Following German critic A. W. Schlegel, English poet and critic Samuel Taylor Coleridge elaborated upon and popularized the distinction between organic and mechanic form in attempting to defend William Shakespeare from **neoclassical** critics who claimed that Shakespeare's plays lacked **form.** Coleridge defined organic form as "innate" form, which depends upon, unfolds from, and evolves according to the subject matter of the work. Organicists commonly use the analogy of a plant growing from a seed to explain how the form of an organic work develops from a seminal insight into a subject. By contrast, mechanic form is shaped externally by rules and **conventions,** rather than developing out of the subject's essence. Organic works are in a sense inseparable from authors and their choices of subjects; mechanic works, while often the product of creative thinking, depend more heavily on tradition.

Mechanic form, it should be pointed out, has its defenders (although most of them would reject the adjective *mechanic*). Critics championing the neoclassical literature of the **Augustan Age** have suggested that if **romantic** works are like plants, then neoclassical works are like cities, which is to say that their authors are freed by their "nonorganic" conceptions of art not only to **imitate** the best of what has been done before but also to revise and improve what they themselves have done: razing, redeveloping, and replacing whole concepts, **stanzas,** chapters, and so forth, none of which have to be viewed as an intrinsic or inevitable part of some thoroughly interdependent, living form.

EXAMPLE: The contrast between Coleridge's "Kubla Khan" (1816) (the structure of which reflects the struggle to recapture a drug-induced hallucination in language) and John Dryden's "Absalom and Achitophel" (1681) (a political **narrative** poem written in **heroic couplets**) points up the difference between poetry with and without organic form.

orientalism: A term most closely associated with Edward Said, a **postcolonial** and **cultural critic** who, in his book *Orientalism* (1978), uses the term to refer to the historical and **ideological** process whereby false **images**

of and **myths** about the Eastern or "oriental" world have been constructed in various Western **discourses,** including that of **imaginative** literature. These images and myths have sometimes involved positive idealizations and fantasies of Eastern differences (for instance, family loyalty and hospitality to strangers). Usually, however, orientalism involves denigrating fictions (for instance, deceptive "inscrutability" and loose sex). In *Orientalism,* Said demonstrates how Eastern and Middle-Eastern peoples have for centuries been stereotyped systematically by the West and how this stereotyping facilitated the colonization of vast areas of the globe by Europeans. Said has been **influenced** by the work of Michel Foucault, a French theorist often associated with **the new historicism** who examined the ways in which power is manifested and exercised through discourses.

The panel shown below, which was taken from a **classic** comic book — *Scream Cheese and Jelly* (1979) — that teaches American children about humor and puns, also reinforces some of the more benign stereotypes associated with orientalism.

See also **postcolonial literature and postcolonial theory.**

Other, the: In **psychoanalytic criticism,** that which defines and limits the **ego,** subject, or self and from which the subject seeks confirmation of its existence and agency. To put it another way, the subject only exists in relation to the Other, which both defines the self through differences and engenders a yearning for unification. Language, **ideology,** and other **symbolic** systems function as **discourses** of the Other. According to psychoanalytic theorist Jacques Lacan, who contends that humans have no sense of self separate from the world surrounding them until they reach the "mirror stage" of childhood, the unconscious itself is a discourse of the Other.

Outside psychoanalytic criticism, the term *the Other* (or, sometimes, *an Other*) refers to any person or category of people defined as different from — and viewed as functioning outside the **conventions** of — the dominant social group. Virtually any ideology involves the identification of some group as the Other, whether by virtue of language, ethnicity, **race, class, gender,** or **sexuality.** The recent emergence of **disability studies** has increased awareness of the way in which societies construct an Other composed of persons with unrelated physical, mental, and developmental differences.

EXAMPLES: In H. G. Wells's *The Time Machine* (1895), the Time Traveller, a denizen of the nineteenth century, comes to realize that there are two species of humans in A.D. 802,701, the year to which he has been transported by his time machine: the innocent, childlike, playful Eloi, which he perceives as the **privileged,** and the shadowy, subterranean Morlocks, which he perceives as the Other:

> But, gradually, the truth dawned on me: that Man had not remained one species, but had differentiated into two distinct animals: that my graceful children of the Upper-world were not the sole descendants of our generation, but that this bleached, obscene, nocturnal Thing, which had flashed before me, was also heir to all the ages.

ottava rima: A form of **verse** that originated in Italy with the fourteenth-century poet Boccaccio. The English version of ottava rima is a **stanzaic** form consisting of eight lines written in **iambic pentameter** with the **rhyme scheme** *abababcc.*

EXAMPLE: The following stanza from George Gordon, Lord Byron's *Don Juan* (1819):

> They looked up to the sky, whose floating glow
> Spread like a rosy ocean, vast and bright;
> They gazed upon the glittering sea below,
> Whence the broad moon rose circling into sight;
> They heard the waves splash, and the wind so low,
> And saw each other's dark eyes darting light
> Into each other — and, beholding this,
> Their lips drew near, and clung into a kiss.

overdetermined: A term derived from psychoanalysis, where it has been applied to symptoms and dreams, and used in literary criticism to describe situations in which multiple causal factors give rise to two or more plausible, coexisting interpretations. Things that are overdetermined are hard to explain without reference to various factors, rendering meaning indeterminate in the sense that no one meaning or interpretation can be said to be definitive.

The term *overdetermined* (*überdeterminiert*) was introduced by psychoanalyst Joseph Breuer, who in *Studies on Hysteria* (1895) attributed it to fellow psychoanalyst Sigmund Freud, asserting that "Such symptoms are invariably 'overdetermined,' to use Freud's expression." By this, Breuer meant that hysterical symptoms have more than one provoking cause.

Freud, too, subscribed to this view, arguing that multiple causation of hysterical symptoms was typical. According to Freud, the onset of such symptoms is often delayed, triggered not by an initial traumatic event, however serious, but by some later, similar trauma.

Freud also applied the concept of multiple causation to dreams. In *The Interpretation of Dreams* (1900), he described the overdetermined character of dream content, arguing that such content may arise from diverse "dream-thoughts." Freud maintained that the elements of any dream "have been represented in the dream-thoughts many times over." As a result, the elements of dream content cannot be traced to a single source, and no single element or source is determinate of meaning. As Freud explained, multiple interpretations "are not mutually contradictory, but cover the same ground; they are a good instance of the fact that dreams, like all other psychological structures, regularly have more than one meaning."

French **Marxist** Louis Althusser subsequently applied the term *overdetermined* to the analysis of certain historical events. In *For Marx* (1969), Althusser argued that events resulting from multiple or conflicting factors are overdetermined and cannot be explained adequately by reference to principles of economic determinism (the belief that human events and choices result primarily from economic causes). By combining this insight with preexisting understandings of overdetermination, several post-Althusserian **Marxist critics** and **cultural critics** have analyzed, or "unpacked," textual **sites** marked by the confluence of economic, historical, literary, and psychological forces.

Literary critics have used the term *overdetermined* primarily to discuss the nature and function of **symbols.** Symbols are overdetermined insofar as they are **metaphors** in which the **vehicle** — the **image,** activity, or concept used to describe the **tenor,** or subject — refers to a variety of things. For instance, the sea, a common symbol in literary works, may represent hope or despair; anger, love, or indifference; vastness, emptiness, or endless possibilities. It may be all-encompassing or isolating, the means of sustaining life or ending it, or any and all of these things at once. In short, the sea as an image or symbol may take on more than one meaning, in which case it is said to be overdetermined.

EXAMPLES: The **character** of Edgar in William Shakespeare's play *King Lear* (1606) is overdetermined. Lear's description of Edgar as a "learned Theban" suggests he is a skeptical, materialist philosopher. But seen from the perspective of English social history, he looks like a "Bedlam" or "Poor Tom" figure, a wandering beggar dispossessed by sixteenth-century laws that allowed landowners to privatize semipublic lands. And viewed in light of literary history, he exemplifies the "trickster" who turns out to be the bearer of truth. Notably, all of these "takes" on Edgar can and do coexist, such that none is mutually exclusive. And yet none sufficiently elucidates important aspects of his character, such as his relationship with his father, which remains inexplicable notwithstanding the explanation Edgar himself advances.

In an essay entitled "Introduction to the *Danse Macabre:* Conrad's *Heart of Darkness*" (1989), **psychoanalytic critic** Frederick Karl treats Joseph Conrad's depiction of the jungle in his **novella** *Heart of Darkness* as overdetermined, pointing out that the jungle symbolizes both what people fear and what they destroy.

overstatement: See **hyperbole.**

oxymoron: From the Greek *oxymoros* ("pointedly foolish"), a **figure of speech** that juxtaposes two opposite or apparently contradictory words to present an emphatic and dramatic **paradox** for a **rhetorical** purpose or effect.

EXAMPLES: Wise fool, bittersweet, eloquent silence, painful pleasure. Isabelle de Charrière uses the phrase "extrême modération" in her **novella** *Les lettres de Mistriss Henley* (1784). In William Shakespeare's *Much Ado About Nothing* (1599), Claudio uses two oxymorons in accusing his fiancée, Hero, of infidelity and unchastity as they stand at the altar on their wedding day: "Thou pure impiety and impious purity. . . ." In her **slave narrative** *Incidents in the Life of a Slave Girl* (1861), Harriet Jacobs defines slavery as a "living death." The following line from Adrienne Rich's poem "Toward the Solstice" (1977) contains an oxymoronic sentiment: "I long and dread to close."

P

paeon: See **foot.**

palimpsest: From the Greek for "scraped again," a piece of parchment, papyrus, or other manuscript writing material from which the original **text** has been removed so the material may be reused. Since good, suitable writing surfaces were difficult and expensive to produce in ancient and early **medieval** times, before paper became a common commodity, old surfaces were washed and scrubbed so they could be written on a second (and sometimes even a third) time. Scholars have been able to recover some of these original texts, however, either because they were not completely erased or because the older texts have shown through the newer ones with the passage of time. Modern chemical technology has also sometimes made it possible to uncover older texts. *Palimpsest* has been used **metaphorically** by some literary critics to refer to the multiple meanings of any word and the multiple layers or levels of meaning in any text.

With reference to the pictorial arts, the term is used to refer to a re-painted canvas bearing one or more paintings covered over by another painting or paintings.

EXAMPLE: The idea of the palimpsest functions on several levels in Salman Rushdie's novel *The Moor's Last Sigh* (1996). The plot involves a painter who continually paints portraits of a woman he once loved, subsequently covering them over with hackneyed commercial works that he sells at extravagant prices.

palindrome: Writing — such as a word, sentence, or poetic line — where the letters are exactly the same whether read forward or backward (ignoring punctuation and spaces). *Word palindromes* are lines or sentences that read the same way whether the words are read forward or backward. Given that the letters or words on either side of the midpoint of a palindrome mirror one another, a palindrome is a type of **chiasmus.**

Palindromes may also be *numeric.* Adding a number (e.g., 47) to its reverse form (e.g., 74) often results in a number that is itself a palindrome (e.g., 121).

EXAMPLES: Words such as *civic, racecar, radar,* and *Xerox*™ are palindromes, as are the sentences "Madam, I'm Adam" and the **apocryphal** line falsely attributed to Napoleon, "Able was I ere I saw Elba." An example of a word palindrome is the sentence "First ladies rule the state and state the rule 'Ladies first.'"

Adah Price, one of the **characters** and **narrators** in Barbara Kingsolver's novel *The Poisonwood Bible* (1998), makes frequent use of palindromes, such as "Amen, enema" and "Evil, all its sin is still alive." Adah even laments the spelling of her name, for without the "h," it would be a palindrome.

palinode: From the Greek for "singing over again," a work written to retract a previous written statement. Generally, both the original "offensive" or "incorrect" writing and the retraction are written in verse. During the **classical, Medieval,** and **Renaissance periods,** writing palinodes was a fairly common practice.

EXAMPLE: Geoffrey Chaucer's palinode *The Legend of Good Women* (c. 1385) was written to recant — or at least balance out — his negative presentation of women as unfaithful in *Troilus and Criseyde* (c. 1383) and other works.

pantomime: In its purest and original form, acting without words. In pantomimes, the **characters** do not speak; instead, they act out stories and convey their thoughts and emotions solely through body movements, facial expressions, gestures, and posture. Costumes may also play a role, particularly in the miming of circus clowns. Pantomimes as we know them today date back to **classical** times, when they were a form of entertainment involving elements of both drama and dance.

The term *pantomime* is also often associated with the *dumb show,* a feature of **tragedies** by the Roman playwright Seneca and of **Elizabethan** dramas written in the **Senecan** tradition. A dumb show is an episode of pantomime performed in a play that otherwise involves speech. Dumb shows often occur when the literary device of a play-within-a-play is used, such as in *Hamlet* (1602).

Pantomime has also come to be used to refer to a particularly extravagant type of drama that emerged in eighteenth-century England. This type of English pantomime typically tells a **folkloric** story (for example, Dick Whittington and his cat), includes figures from the *commedia dell'arte,* and uses a great deal of theatrical machinery and numerous **scene** changes for spectacular dramatic effect. As its name suggests, pantomime includes silent passages, but it also employs a variety of songs and dances. Perhaps in keeping with their slapstick comic nature, these extravagant hybrids often feature girls in boys' roles and men playing elderly women. Such pantomimes, which are still performed in England during the Christmas season, are usually intended for the entertainment of children.

In the twentieth century, pantomime enjoyed a brief revival with the advent of the silent movie. Charlie Chaplin is by far the best-known cinematic pantomimist. Circus clowns make frequent use of miming as well. French mimes, such as Marcel Marceau, have also kept up the pantomime tradition, as have street performers in some American cities, especially New York and San Francisco.

parable: A short, **realistic,** and illustrative **story** intended to teach a moral or religious lesson; a type of **allegory.** The parable differs slightly from the **fable** and the **exemplum,** two other types of allegory also designed to make a point, insofar as a true parable is composed or told in response to a specific situation and addresses that situation, at least implicitly, in an allegorical manner. The most famous parables in Western literature are those told by Jesus and include the parables of the talents, the prodigal son, the rich man and Lazarus, the young rich ruler, and the lost sheep.

paradigm: See *epistémé.*

paradox: A statement that seems self-contradictory or nonsensical on the surface but that, upon closer examination, may be seen to contain an underlying truth. As a **rhetorical figure,** paradox is used to grab the reader's attention and to direct it to a specific point or **image** that provokes the reader to see something in a new way. The term has been used much more broadly by **the New Critics** to refer to any unexpected deviation from ordinary **discourse** or expectations. As such, New Critic Cleanth Brooks maintained that poetic language is fundamentally paradoxical.

When two opposite words are juxtaposed, thereby presenting a paradox for **rhetorical** effect, the author or speaker is said to use **oxymoron.**

EXAMPLES: The **metaphysical poets** made frequent use of paradox. The speaker of John Donne's poem "Lovers' Infiniteness" (1633) tells his beloved:

> Thou canst not every day give me thy heart;
> If thou canst give it, then thou never gavest it. . . .

The Friar in William Shakespeare's *Much Ado About Nothing* (1599) tells Hero, "Come, lady, die to live. The wedding day / Perhaps is but prolonged." By this statement, he means that by pretending to die, Hero may have her best chance of living a happy life. Unjustly accused of unchastity and infidelity, Hero has been vilified and abandoned at the altar by her betrothed, Claudio, who mistakenly believes he has seen her with a lover.

The following statement, attributed to Pyrrhus, King of Epirus, after defeating the Romans in battle at the cost of near-catastrophic losses of soldiers, provides another example of paradox: "One more such victory and we are lost." By contrast, a United States military officer in Vietnam attempted to justify the devastating effect of war through the following paradoxical, and much criticized, statement: "We had to destroy the village to save it."

In Richard Bach's *Jonathan Livingston Seagull* (1970), Jonathan's reproach to his friend Sullivan involves the paradoxical idea that friends can see each other "in the middle of Here and Now" by overcoming space and time:

> If our friendship depends on things like space and time, then when we finally overcome space and time, we've destroyed our own brotherhood! But overcome space, and all we have left is Here. Overcome time, and all we have left is Now. And in the middle of Here and Now, don't you think that we might see each other once or twice?

The opening chapter of Piers Anthony's **fantasy** novel *On a Pale Horse* (1983) introduces the reader to a store proprietor seeking to sell a "Death-stone" to the hero, Zane. The stone, the proprietor advises Zane, "merely advises the wearer of the proximity of termination, by darkening. The speed and intensity of the change notifies you of the potential circumstance of your demise — in plenty of time for you to avoid it." Zane replies, "But isn't that paradox?" The proprietor assures his potential customer that it is not, calling it "Merely adequate warning." But, in fact, Anthony's Death-stone is a paradox, since it performs its function by warning of the immi-nence of something that does not subsequently occur.

Other examples of paradox include the Zen koan "what is the sound of one hand clapping?" and the Zen spiritual principle that "the higher you go, the more excrement you are willing to clean up."

paralipsis (praeteritio): A **rhetorical figure** involving a speaker's assertion that he or she will not discuss something that he or she in fact goes on to dis-cuss. (The Latin term *paralipsis* **denotes** "leaving aside," the Greek *praeteri-tio* "going beyond." If a paraliptic statement involves an attempt to conceal the speaker's true motive in speaking, it may be referred to more specifically as *occultatio*. Moreover, if a speaker claims that he or she is otherwise occu-pied or is too busy to address a topic, the paralipsis may be called *occupatio*.

EXAMPLES: The following statement involves paralipsis, occultatio, and occupatio: "Since I need to finish warming up because the marathon is about to begin, I won't take the time to tell you that I came in first in our age category in each of the last three races."

The **narrator** of Geoffrey Chaucer's *Troilus and Criseyde* (c. 1383) regu-larly discusses the subject of love after refusing to discuss it, citing his own status as a failed lover and deferring to the expertise of his audience.

Marc Antony's famous speech in William Shakespeare's play *Julius Cae-sar* (1598) begins with a paralipsis ("Friends, Romans, countrymen, lend me your ears; / I come to bury Caesar, not to praise him") and proceeds with an occultative paralipsis:

> ... if I were dispos'd to stir
> Your hearts and minds to mutiny and rage,
> I should do Brutus wrong, and Cassius wrong,
> Who, you all know, are honorable men.
> I will not do them wrong; I rather choose
> To wrong the dead, to wrong myself and you
> Than I will wrong such honorable men.

Anthony nonetheless goes on to praise Caesar and to rile up the crowd against Brutus and Cassius.

parallelism: A **rhetorical figure** used in written and oral compositions since ancient times to accentuate or emphasize ideas or **images** by using grammatically similar constructions. Words, phrases, clauses, sentences, paragraphs, and even larger structural units may be consciously organized into parallel constructions, thereby creating a sense of balance that can be meaningful and revealing, as when two **antithetical** ideas of comparable importance are juxtaposed. By using parallelism, authors or speakers implicitly invite their readers or audiences to compare and contrast the parallel elements. Parallelism that only involves the exact repetition of words or phrases at the beginning of successive lines or sentences is called **anaphora.**

Repetition often plays an important role in establishing parallelism. Sometimes a word, line, or other grammatical unit is repeated verbatim. The **refrain,** or **chorus,** of a song, for instance, is usually repeated after each **stanza.** Often, however, repetition is not this strict. The repetition may be **incremental,** as when the same basic line recurs with subtle variation throughout a poem. Repetition may also occur when one grammatical unit essentially reinforces another, saying the same thing, but in different words. To say that a woman is lovely, then to describe her as beautiful, and then to present an **image** depicting this beauty is to use repetition of this latter sort.

Parallelism has been a particularly important device in oral composition, such as speeches and sermons, and in Hebrew (and thus biblical) poetry. In biblical poetry in particular, parallelism often involves the restatement of the same idea in slightly different words rather than the juxtaposition of related or antithetical ideas.

EXAMPLES: William Blake and Walt Whitman commonly employed parallelism in their poetry. Charles Dickens consciously used parallelism to emphasize **antithetical** but balanced ideas in the opening lines of his novel *A Tale of Two Cities* (1859), where the **narrator** speaks of the year 1775:

> It was the best of times, it was the worst of times, it was the age of wisdom, it was the age of foolishness, it was the epoch of belief, it was the epoch of incredulity, it was the season of Light, it was the season of Darkness, it was the spring of hope, it was the winter of despair, we had everything before us, we had nothing before us, we were all going direct to Heaven, we were all going direct the other way.

The poet H. D. (Hilda Doolittle) employed parallelism in her lyric "The Helmsman" (1916):

> We forgot — we worshipped,
> we parted green from green,
> we sought further thickets,
> we dipped our ankles
> through leaf-mould and earth,
> and wood and wood-bank enchanted us —
>
> and the feel of the clefts in the bark,
> and the slope between tree and tree —
> and a slender path strung field to field
> and wood to wood
> and hill to hill
> and the forest after it.

Gitanjali (1910), a book of poetry written in Bengali and translated into English by Nobel laureate Rabindranath Tagore, contains a short poem — the thirty-fifth in the volume — as familiar to Indian schoolchildren as the "Pledge of Allegiance" is to their American counterparts:

Where the mind is without fear and the head is held high;
Where knowledge is free;
Where the world has not been broken up into fragments by narrow domestic
　walls;
Where words come out from the depth of truth;
Where tireless striving stretches its arms towards perfection;
Where the clear stream of reason has not lost its way into the dreary desert
　sand of dead habit;
Where the mind is led forward by thee into ever widening thought and
　action—Into that heaven of freedom, my Father, let my country awake.

pararhyme: See **half-rhyme.**

parataxis, paratactic style: See **style.**

Parnassians: A group of French and English poets active during the latter half of the nineteenth century who rejected **romanticism** and influenced **aestheticism;** a literary movement that glorified **art for art's sake** rather than for any purported moral value. Parnassianism arose in France, where several poets **influenced** by Théophile Gautier and led by Leconte de Lisle strove to produce impersonal, **objective** poetry that exalted **form** and minimized the author's **presence** and preferences. Followers included Théodore de Banville, François Coppée, and Sully Prudhomme. During the 1870s, the movement spread to England, where writers known as the English Parnassians (such as Edmund Gosse, Andrew Lang, and Algernon Charles Swinburne) **imitated** the French School, placing particular emphasis on matters of form.

parody: As a literary term, a form of high **burlesque** popular since ancient times that **imitates** a specific literary work or the **style** of an author for comic effect, usually to ridicule or criticize that work, author, or style. The literary counterpart to **caricature,** which is also designed to ridicule (through an exaggerated depiction of an individual's features or characteristics), parody is often used to make a **satiric** (and even a political) point. Although the subject of an existing work has occasionally been parodied, parodies that debase the subject of the original generally do so not to ridicule that subject so much as to poke fun at the author or style of the work being parodied.

When used broadly, the term *parody* may also be applied to certain other artistic forms, such as film, song, and painting.

EXAMPLES: In "Aged, Aged Man" (1871), Lewis Carroll parodies William Wordsworth's "Resolution and Independence" (1807), especially Wordsworth's figure of the old leech-gatherer:

> I shook him well from side to side,
>   Until his face was blue:
> 'Come, tell me how you live', I cried,
>   'And what it is you do!'
>
> He said 'I hunt for haddocks' eyes
>   Among the heather bright,
> And work them into waistcoat buttons
>   In the silent night.'

J. K. Stephen parodies Walt Whitman in his poem "Of W. W. (Americanus)" (1891):

> The clear cool note of the cuckoo which has ousted the legitimate
>   nest-holder,
> The whistle of the railway guard dispatching the train to the inevitable
>   collision,
> The maiden's monosyllabic reply to a polysyllabic proposal,
> The fundamental note of the last trumpet, which is presumably D
>   natural;
> All these are sounds to rejoice in, yea to let your very ribs re-echo with:
> But better than them all is the absolutely last chord of the apparently
>   inexhaustible pianoforte player.

Algernon Charles Swinburne, known for writing ultrasensuous poems characterized by exceedingly **alliterative, anapestic** lines, had the good humor to write a self-parody entitled "Nephelida" (1880):

> From the depth of the dreamy decline of the dawn through a notable
>   nimbus of nebulous noonshine,
> Pallid and pink as the palm of the flag-flower that flickers with fear at
>   the flies as they float,
> Are they looks of our lovers that lustrously lean from a marvel of mystic miraculous moonshine,
> These that we feel in the blood of our blushes that thicken and threaten
>   with throbs through the throat?

Stephen Crane parodied the American **genre** we refer to as the "Western" in his short story "The Bride Comes to Yellow Sky" (1897); the Western genre has also been parodied in Mel Brooks's movie *Blazing Saddles* (1974).

Film was a popular medium for parodists in the latter half of the twentieth century. Woody Allen parodied the Russian **realistic novel,** and Leo Tolstoi's *War and Peace* (1869) in particular, in his movie *Love and Death* (1975). *Airplane!* (1980) specifically parodied the television drama *Zero Hour* (1957), written by Arthur Hailey. More generally, *Airplane!* parodied the four *Airport* movies produced during the 1970s and based on Hailey's 1968 novel of the same name. Novels and films featuring the **hard-boiled detective** were parodied in *Dead Men Don't Wear Plaid* (1982), starring Steve Martin. Other movie parodies include *Spaceballs*

(1987), *Hot Shots!* (1991), and *Hot Shots!: Part Deux* (1992), which parody *Star Wars* (1977) and *Top Gun* (1986), respectively.

Rob Reiner's movie *This Is Spinal Tap* (1983) parodied the "rock documentary" (or "rockumentary"), as exemplified by *The Last Waltz* (1978), a film directed by Martin Scorsese about the last concert given by the seventies rock group The Band. *The Brady Bunch Movie* (1995) offered a tongue-in-cheek parody of the television show *The Brady Bunch* (1969–74). T. Coraghessan Boyle parodied another famous and long-running TV show, *Lassie,* in his short story "Heart of a Champion" (1974).

Grant Wood's painting *American Gothic* (1930), featuring a severe-looking, elderly couple with a pitchfork, has been parodied many times. In music, "Weird" Al Yankovich made fun of Michael Jackson's hit song "Beat It" (1983) in his parody "Eat It" (1984).

More recently, Alice Randall parodied Margaret Mitchell's *Gone With the Wind* (1936) in her "unauthorized" novel *The Wind Done Gone* (2001) by exploring life at Tara and in the Old South more generally from an illegitimate mulatto slave's **point of view.**

See also **burlesque.**

parole: See **semiotics.**

paronomasia: See **pun.**

pastiche: A term used in art criticism to refer to a work that borrows heavily from a master's recognizable **style** and in music criticism to refer to a medley of known melodies, songs, or musical **themes.** *Pastiche* can be used in either way by literary critics, although the former usage is more common. (Most critics use the term descriptively, but some use it to derogate an author's efforts. When used dismissively, the term describes a work that is deemed highly derivative of someone else's work or style.) *Pastiche* may have a humorous, **satirical,** or serious purpose, but sometimes authors write *pastiche* simply as a literary exercise. *Pastiche* should not be confused with plagiarism, in which one author steals a passage or idea from another, passing it off as his or her own and failing to credit the original source. Plagiarism is characterized by deceptive intent; *pastiche* involves open and intentional **imitation** or borrowing.

Pastiche is also French for **parody;** when used as a synonym for *parody* rather than in its more general, imitative sense, the term refers to a satirical presentation, usually one involving a sustained, parodic imitation of a particular author's style or technique.

EXAMPLES: Some of Carl Sandburg's poetry could be referred to as "Walt Whitman *pastiche.*" The American Telephone and Telegraph (AT&T) headquarters building in New York City, designed by noted American architect Philip Johnson, has been referred to as *pastiche.* So closely does the top resemble a Chippendale cabinet that the building has, since opening in 1982, been referred to as the "Chippendale building." ("Chippendale" was a style of furniture fashionable in the third quarter of the eighteenth century and named after the English cabinetmaker Thomas Chippendale.)

The setting of the film *Moulin Rouge* (2001) is Paris at the end of the nineteenth century, but the movie's **anachronistic** musical score is a *pastiche* of late-twentieth-century popular songs such as Elton John's "Your Song" and Sting's "Roxanne."

Through use of the technique known as "sampling" — borrowing riffs from other, well-known songs — rap artists have also created works that involve pastiche in the sense of "medley."

pastoral: (1) As an adjective, a term that can be applied to any work with a rural **setting** and that generally praises a rustic way of life; (2) as a noun, a term that refers to a literary mode historically and conventionally associated with shepherds and country living. Pastoral life has been associated by many poets (especially the ancient Greeks and Romans) with a variety of eras considered as the Golden Age of humankind. The third-century B.C. Greek poet Theocritus wrote the first pastorals, which he ostensibly based on the lives of Sicilian shepherds. The Roman poet Virgil, who **imitated** Theocritus and established the pastoral as a popular literary form, set many of the **conventions** of the **genre.** Traditional pastoral verse typically involves a singing contest between two shepherds, a **monologue** praising someone or something or lamenting the loss of love, or a lament for a dead shepherd and friend.

The pastoral became so popular that it evolved into new, hybrid forms including **pastoral elegy,** pastoral **drama,** pastoral **romance,** and even the pastoral **novel.** Pastoral elements, settings, and **themes,** moreover, began to crop up in a variety of nonpastoral works (William Shakespeare's plays, for instance). The use of the term *pastoral* has been extended by the critic William Empson, in *Some Versions of Pastoral* (1935), to refer to any work that cloaks complexity in simple garments (for instance, urban **characters** in a rural setting) and that praises values associated with simplicity.

FURTHER EXAMPLES: Edmund Spenser's *The Shepheardes Calendar* (1579). William Wordsworth's *Michael* (1800) is subtitled *A Pastoral Poem.* Still later examples of works containing pastoral elements include Thomas Hardy's *Far from the Madding Crowd* (1874) and Isak Dinesen's *Out of Africa* (1937; adapted to film in 1985).

See also **eclogue.**

pastoral elegy: A serious formal **poem** in which a poet grieves the loss of a dead friend (often another poet). Composed in an elevated, dignified style, pastoral elegy, as its name implies, combines the forms and traditions of **elegy** with those of **pastoral,** specifically pastoral **eclogue.** In this type of elegy, the poet-mourner **figures** himself and the individual mourned as shepherds who have lived their lives in a simple, rural **setting,** tending their flocks. The dead shepherd is traditionally given a Greek name in recognition of the fact that the earliest examples of this **genre** were written in ancient Greece. The Greek poet Theocritus is usually credited with creating the form, an early example of which is Moschus's "Lament for Bion" (c. 150 B.C.). The genre became so popular in Europe at various points during the sixteenth through nineteenth centuries that it has become common for any type of elegy on another poet to contain pastoral elements.

The pastoral elegy is highly **conventional,** generally opening with an **invocation** that is followed by a statement of the poet's great grief and a subsequent description of a procession of mourners. (In addition to people and supernatural beings, this procession may include Nature, plants and animals, and even things to which the dead poet gave imaginative existence. For instance, in "Adonais" [1821], Percy Bysshe Shelley's elegy for John Keats, the procession includes "All he had loved and moulded into thought.") The pastoral elegy also usually involves a discussion of fate, or some similarly philosophical topic, and, ultimately, a statement by the speaking poet to the effect that all is well and has turned out as it should. (In Christian elegies, such statements imply or explicitly involve affirmations of belief in an afterlife.) Expressions of bewilderment, invectives against death, belief in immortality, arrangements of flowers, and the **pathetic fallacy** are also conventional elements of the pastoral elegy.

FURTHER EXAMPLES: John Milton's "Lycidas" (1638) (for Edward King), Matthew Arnold's "Thyrsis" (1866) (for Arthur Hugh Clough).

pathetic: See **pathos.**

pathetic fallacy: A term coined by John Ruskin in *Modern Painters* (1856) to describe the attribution of human emotions to inanimate nature. Ruskin used the term pejoratively, believing that such attribution was a sign of artistic weakness. Today the term is used neutrally.

Pathetic fallacy is distinguished from **personification,** a **figure of speech** that bestows human characteristics upon anything nonhuman. Since the pathetic fallacy bestows such characteristics only on inanimate nature, it covers a much narrower range of subjects than personification, which can apply to animals, plants, synthetic materials, and so forth. Furthermore, the "humanizing" **characterization** of objects effected by the pathetic fallacy is typically less sustained than that brought about by personification.

EXAMPLES: Ruskin cited this phrase from Charles Kingsley's *Alton Locke* (1850) as an example of pathetic fallacy, noting that "The foam is not cruel, neither does it crawl":

> They rowed her in across the rolling foam —
> The cruel, crawling foam.

William Wordsworth uses the pathetic fallacy in his "Ode: Intimations of Immortality" (1807):

> Ye blessed Creatures, I have heard the call
> Ye to each other make, I see
> The heavens laugh with you in your jubilee. . . .

Modern poets tend to avoid the pathetic fallacy, but that hardly means it is absent from modern language and writing. Our habit of naming hurricanes after people and of representing their results as purposeful is a good example of the modern, journalistic use of pathetic fallacy. An August 1995 headline in the *Miami Herald* read: "Killer Storm Swirls Toward Open Seas: East Coast May Be Spared Luis's Fury." A month later, a hurricane-related headline in the *Boston Sunday Herald* ("Hurricane Marilyn Pounds Virgin Islands") was followed by the pathetically fallacious lead-in line, "With ferocious winds, story-high waves and lightning-forked storms, Hurricane Marilyn raged through the Virgin Islands and Puerto Rico yesterday, tearing apart homes, tossing aside airplanes, and toppling towers."

See also **personification.**

pathos: From the Greek for "emotion," "passion," or "suffering," a quality in a work or a portion thereof that makes the reader experience pity, sorrow, or tenderness. Pathos is distinguished from **tragedy** in that pathetic characters are generally helpless, innocent victims suffering through no fault of their own. Tragic figures, by contrast, possess a heroic grandeur and are in some way at least partially responsible for their fates. Works involving the misuse, abuse, or death of children are almost inevitably pathetic, although an unskilled writer can easily slip into **bathos** from pathos if the effect is exaggerated or **anticlimactic.**

EXAMPLES: Charles Dickens achieves pathos in his description of the death of Paul Dombey in *Dombey and Son* (1846–48), but most critics would say he slips into bathos in describing the death of Little Nell in *The Old Curiosity Shop* (1840). Toni Morrison's *Beloved* (1987), which relates the story of a woman who deliberately kills her child to save her from being returned to slavery, is a novel of intense emotion and immense pathos. **Sentimental** Hollywood movies that target women as their main audience have a mixed record in achieving pathos rather than bathos. Most critics agree that the death scene in *Terms of Endearment* (1983) touches the right pathetic chords but are not as impressed by a similar scene in *Steel Magnolias* (1989).

patriarchal: A term used by **feminist critics** who consider Western society to be "father-ruled," that is, dominated and generally controlled by men upholding and promoting masculine "values" that, in turn, maintain men in positions of power. Use of this term implies the corollary that men use their positions of power in the major institutions of society to subordinate women. In all cultural areas, from the family to religion to government to the arts and beyond, women are thereby relegated to a sort of cultural wasteland where they are presumed to contribute little or nothing of importance to society. Having been defined as **Others,** that is, in **binary opposition** to the "superior" male and his masculine characteristics from ancient times to the present day, women have been conditioned to accept the patriarchal **ideology** that devalues them and all things labeled "feminine."

pattern poetry: See **concrete poetry.**

pen name: See *nom de plume.*

pentameter: A line of **verse** consisting of five **metrical feet.** Pentameter is the most commonly used line length in English verse.

EXAMPLE: The last lines of Wallace Stevens's "Sunday Morning" (1915) are written in pentameter:

> Deer walk | upon | our moun|tains, and | the quail |
> Whistle | about | us their | sponta|neous cries;|
> Sweet ber|ries ri|pen in | the wil|derness;|
> And, in | the i|sola|tion of | the sky,|
> At eve|ning, cas|ual flocks | of pi|geons make|
> Ambi|guous un|dula|tions as | they sink,|
> Downward | to dark|ness on | extend|ed wings.|

perfect rhyme (true or full rhyme): Rhyme in which the final **accented** vowels and all subsequent sounds are identical. *Perfect rhyme* has been used as a synonym for two different types of rhyme: *true* (or *full*) *rhyme* and *rime riche.*

When used as a synonym for true (or full) rhyme, which is the more common usage, *perfect rhyme* refers to rhyme in which the initial sounds of the rhyming words must be different (for instance, *hit / pit*). Thus, perfect rhyme does not occur when two or more words are pronounced exactly alike. Other sounds preceding the final accented vowel of the rhyming words, however, may or may not be different. Both *brim / trim* and *skim / trim* are perfect rhymes.

When used in the sense of *rime riche,* however, *perfect rhyme* refers to words that do sound exactly alike but that have different meanings. Although *rime riche* and true or full rhyme are obviously not the same thing, the term *perfect rhyme* can be used as a synonym for both, since it is defined as occurring when rhymed sounds correspond exactly to each other.

EXAMPLES: The following are perfect rhymes in the sense of true or full rhymes: *brother* and *mother; coat, moat,* and *smote; lingering* and *fingering. Doe* and *dough* are perfect rhymes in the sense of *rime riche.* The first eight lines of John Crowe Ransom's poem "Dead Boy" (1927) contain perfect (true or full) rhymes. All of these rhymes except "tree" and "me" are also examples of **feminine rhyme:**

> The little cousin is dead, by foul subtraction,
> A green bough from Virginia's aged tree,
> And none of the county kin like the transaction
> Nor some of the world of outer dark, like me.
>
> A boy not beautiful, nor good, nor clever,
> A black cloud full of storms too hot for keeping,
> A sword beneath his mother's heart — yet never
> Woman bewept her babe as this is weeping.

performative: A term used by John Austin, a **speech-act theorist,** in *How to Do Things with Words* (1962) to distinguish between two classes of **locutions.** *Performative* locutions, Austin states, are sentences that actively "do" something, such as question or admonish. Austin opposes performative locutions to *constative* locutions, which are sentences that state something that can be determined to be true or false. After establishing these two types of locutions, Austin goes on to prove that they are not mutually exclusive, that is, that a sentence can involve both elements simultaneously.

EXAMPLES: An example of a performative is the statement, "Don't touch that cookie jar!" whereas a related constative is "He didn't touch that cookie jar."

periodicity: The idea that there are distinct periods or ages within the literature of a nation or culture. Scholars and critics who adhere to the concept of periodicity maintain that writers within a given historical era (for example, the **Augustan Age** or the **Romantic Period**) — even writers working in different **genres** — can be shown **objectively** to have more in common in terms of **themes, styles,** and **structures** of works than writers of different timeframes, even those that are chronologically adjacent.

Recently, critics of periodicity have pointed out that the parameters of literary periods are arbitrarily drawn and have little, if anything, to do with literature. For instance, the **Victorian Period** is said to span the years 1837–1901 because those are the years of Queen Victoria's reign in England, but why should we assume that Victoria's reign made Alfred, Lord Tennyson's *Poems* (1830) less like the poems of John Keats (1795–1821) and Percy Bysshe Shelley (1792–1822) than like Thomas Hardy's *fin de siècle* novel *Jude the Obscure* (1895)? Critics of periodicity also point out that many writers span periods; Hardy (1840–1928), for instance, wrote during the Victorian Period and the **Modern Period,** and William Shakespeare wrote plays during the **Elizabethan Age** and the **Jacobean Age.** This means that the works of writers like Hardy and Shakespeare — to the extent that they are **aesthetically** and thematically consistent — undermine the claims of scholars and critics who would differentiate the periods during which such works were written.

Few scholars and critics today explicitly advocate periodicity. Somewhere between those who do and those who debunk its distinctions as false or, at best, arbitrary are scholars and critics who argue that it is *useful* to think of works as falling within chronological periods loosely defined, insofar as **texts** are inevitably rooted in historical contexts, however broadly those roots may extend and however slippery or unreliable our definitions of those contexts may be. These somewhat traditional literary historians thus might defend preservation of a university literature curriculum consisting of courses that group literary works under traditional chronological rubrics (courses such as "**Restoration Age** Drama"). And they undoubtedly would defend the inclusion in this glossary of entries defining the various **Periods in English literature** and **Periods in American literature.** Those most radically opposed to periodicity, on the other hand, would argue that it is misleading and thus intellectually harmful to organize a literary curriculum around periods. They might even argue that this glossary, in defining those periods traditionally, perpetuates and preserves a set of distinctions causing readers to see textual similarities — and differences — that are highly suspect and easily contradicted.

periodic sentence: A sentence that is not **syntactically** complete until its very end; the opposite of a **loose sentence.** Periodic sentences are typically used in formal, as opposed to conversational, writing and are often used to heighten suspense since their meanings are not fully revealed until the last word. Periodic sentences include at least one dependent clause and/or **parallel** construction (and often several of each) before the final independent clause, which completes the sentence and provides its grammatical close as well as its meaning. Works predominantly containing periodic sentences usually exhibit **hypotactic style.**

EXAMPLES: Shivering in anticipation of the next thunderbolt, and huddled in the dark recess of the staircase as the rain battered against the window and the tall grass bent in the wind that whistled through the gnarled oaks, Norma's old mongrel whimpered.

The following sentence from Jonathan Swift's *Gulliver's Travels* (1726) is periodic in its construction:

> And it must be confessed, that from the great intercourse of trade and commerce between both realms, from the continual reception of exiles, which is mutual among them, and from the custom in each empire to send their young nobility and richer gentry to the other, in order to polish themselves, by seeing the world, and understanding men and manners, there are few persons of distinction, or merchants, or seamen, who dwell in the maritime parts, but what can hold conversation in both tongues.

So is this sentence from John Stuart Mill's *On Liberty* (1859):

> If all mankind, minus one, were of one opinion, and only one person were of the contrary opinion, mankind would be no more justified in silencing that one person than he, if he had the power, would be justified in silencing mankind.

Periods in American literature: See **Colonial Period, Revolutionary Period, Early National Period, Romantic Period, Realistic Period, Naturalistic Period, Modern Period (in English and American literature), Postmodern Period (in English and American literature).**

Periods in English literature: See **Old English Period, Middle English Period, Renaissance Period** (including **Early Tudor Age, Elizabethan Age, Jacobean Age, Caroline Age,** and **Commonwealth Age**), **Neoclassical Period** (including **Augustan Age, Restoration Age,** and **Age of Johnson**), **Romantic Period, Victorian Period, Edwardian Age, Georgian Age, Modern Period**

(in English and American literature), Postmodern Period (in English and American literature).

periphrasis (pleonasm): A **rhetorical figure** involving elevated language, redundancy, or circumlocution; alternatively, speaking or writing that is unintentionally and unnecessarily wordy and roundabout. When used intentionally, periphrasis provides emphasis or creates a comic effect. For instance, an author comically undercuts a **character** by having him or her speak in unbearably inflated, periphrastic prose. Alternatively, writers may employ a periphrastic **style** in an effort to avoid unpleasant or mundane expression; unfortunately, verbosity or pomposity may be an unintended result. When used to avoid offending others or to sugarcoat the truth, periphrasis may even become euphemism. As an element of **poetic diction,** periphrasis has perhaps been most often used — with varying degrees of success — in an effort to transform the ordinary into the extraordinary, to render **images** and even language itself more elegant, special, and unique.

EXAMPLES: The advertising slogan "Raid™ kills bugs dead." A teacher calling roll reads off John Doe's name; he replies "I am present at this moment in time in this classroom" instead of simply "Here." Alexander Haig, deputy assistant to President Nixon for national security affairs, chief of staff under the Ford administration, and secretary of state under President Reagan, used periphrasis in calling a lie a "terminological inexactitude."

Alexander Pope's reference to fish as "the finny tribe" in his poem "The Rape of the Lock" (1712) is periphrastic. William Shakespeare's Constable Dogberry from *Much Ado About Nothing* (1599) is an unwitting master of periphrasis. When Don Pedro asks him "Officers, what offense have these men done?" Dogberry replies:

> Marry, sir, they have committed false report; moreover, they have spoken untruths; secondarily, they are slanders; sixth and lastly, they have belied a lady; thirdly, they have verified unjust things; and to conclude, they are lying knaves.

Don Pedro mockingly replies:

> First, I ask thee what they have done; thirdly, I ask thee what's their offense; sixth, and lastly, why they are committed; and to conclude, what you lay to their charge.

Although some critics have described as poetic the following passage from Joseph Conrad's *Heart of Darkness* (1899), others have found it a wordy and pompous — hence periphrastic — way of saying that a jarring memory suddenly intruded upon the mysterious stillness of the present:

> There were moments when one's past came back to one, as it will sometimes when you have not a moment to spare to yourself; but it came in the shape of an unrestful and noisy dream, remembered with wonder, amongst the overwhelming realities of this strange world of plants, and water, and silence. And this stillness of life did not in the

least resemble a peace. It was the stillness of an implacable force brooding over an inscrutable intention.

Some critics have suggested that Conrad's periphrasis is intentional, a way of poking light fun at the **narrator,** Marlow. Others believe that the fault is one of Conrad's occasionally overbearing style.

perlocutionary act: A term used in John R. Searle's expansion of John Austin's **speech-act theory** to refer to an **illocutionary act** that actually affects the hearer. An illocutionary act is the utterance of a statement that performs a particular function, such as ordering, promising, and so on. When such a statement is not only understood by the hearer but also produces a change in his or her actions or state of mind, it is also classified as a perlocutionary act.

The perlocutionary act is one of four types of speech acts; the other three are the **utterance act** (saying something), the **propositional act** (referring to an object upon which something is predicated, or saying something about something else), and the **illocutionary act.** While Searle believes that speaking (or writing) necessarily involves the first three speech acts, he holds that the perlocutionary act may or may not occur, depending on whether the illocutionary act actually produces a change in the hearer's actions or state of mind.

EXAMPLE: A bully says to Bart, "If you tell the secret, I'll kill you." As an illocutionary act, this statement is a threat. If Bart just hears what the bully is telling him and doesn't care (that is, if he is not affected by the statement — if neither his actions nor frame of mind change), no perlocutionary act exists. If Bart becomes scared or decides not to tell the secret because of the threat, the statement becomes a perlocutionary act.

persona: Generally, the speaker (the "I") in any **first-person** poem or **narrative.** The term derives from the Latin word for "mask" and literally refers to that through which sound passes. Although the persona often serves as the "voice" of the author, it nonetheless should not be confused with the author, for the persona may not accurately reflect the author's personal opinions, feelings, or perspective on a subject.

Persona has also been used to refer to the public "face" an individual presents to others, as opposed to his private (and, by implication, true) self.

EXAMPLES: Notable literary personae include a wife-murdering Duke who speaks in the poem "My Last Duchess" (1842); Mr. Lockwood, the lonely and loveless invalid who tells the simmering story of Heathcliff and Cathy's love in *Wuthering Heights* (1847); Pip, the selfish young social climber who **narrates** the novel *Great Expectations* (1861); J. Alfred Prufrock, who wonders if he "dare[s] to eat a peach" in "The Love Song of J. Alfred Prufrock" (1917); and Tashi, who submits to genital mutilation in order to experience cultural unity with her people in *Possessing the Secret of Joy* (1992). Few readers would confuse these speakers with Robert

Browning, Emily Brontë, Charles Dickens, T. S. Eliot, or Alice Walker, respectively.

personal criticism: A type of **feminist criticism** developed in the early 1990s that is generally associated with Jane Tompkins and Nancy K. Miller, who in books such as Miller's *Getting Personal: Feminist Occasions and Other Autobiographical Acts* (1991) have urged women not to exclude their personal reactions and even histories from their readings of literary **texts.** Personal criticism is sometimes referred to as *autobiographical criticism.* Once reluctant to reveal themselves in their analyses for fear of being labeled idiosyncratic, **impressionistic,** and **subjective,** personal critics, like many other feminist critics, are now openly skeptical of the claims to reason, logic, and **objectivity** made in the past by male critics (particularly those practicing **the New Criticism** or other types of **formalist** criticism).

Although personal criticism is sometimes contrasted with the politically engaged work of feminists associated with **cultural criticism** or **postcolonial theory,** the emphasis on **race, class,** and ethnicity brought to bear by the latter group made personal, or autobiographical, feminist criticism possible by demonstrating that *woman* is not a single, monolithic, or deterministic category but rather an umbrella term covering a vast range of identities and experiences.

With the advent of more personal feminist critical styles has come a new interest in women's autobiographical writings. Some feminist critics have pointed out that the **conventions** of traditional **autobiography** emphasize action, triumph through **conflict,** intellectual self-discovery, and public renown and relegate the body, reproduction, children, and interpersonal relationships to the background, if they are included at all. Accordingly, these critics have argued that autobiography as commonly conceived is a **gendered,** "masculinist" **genre.** One such critic, Leigh Gilmore, has asserted that the lived experiences of men and women differ, largely because women's lives are characterized by interruption and deferral to a much greater extent than are men's. Women, for instance, often delay or take time off from their careers to have and raise children. To facilitate the understanding of women's lives and experiences, Gilmore has developed a **theory** of women's self-**representation** in her book *Autobiographics: A Feminist Theory of Self-Representation* (1991).

Increasingly, practitioners of **ecocriticism** influenced by the personal style of much **nature writing** have employed personal criticism in analyzing their own experiences of places, communities, and literary texts.

See also **ecocriticism, feminist criticism.**

personification: A **figure of speech** (more specifically a **trope**) that bestows human characteristics upon anything nonhuman, from an **abstract** idea to a physical force to an inanimate object to a living organism.

Prosopopoeia is typically used as a synonym for *personification,* but some scholars have used *prosopopoeia* more narrowly, limiting its application to situations in which the personified figure can and does speak.

Personification is distinguished from the **pathetic fallacy,** in which human emotions are attributed to inanimate nature. Since the pathetic fallacy refers only to inanimate nature, it covers a much narrower range of subjects than personification, which covers anything nonhuman, including animals, plants, synthetic materials, and so forth. Furthermore, the "humanizing" **characterization** of the subject brought about by the pathetic fallacy is typically less sustained than that effected by personification.

EXAMPLES: Examples of personification include using the word *blind* to describe love, using *kind* or *gentle* to describe a slight breeze, describing raindrops as tears from a sad sky, or saying that a tree patiently grows and waits. In his "Elegiac Stanzas Suggested by a Picture of Peele Castle in a Storm, Painted by Sir George Beaumont" (1807), William Wordsworth personifies the castle in the following lines, using the pathetic fallacy to characterize the storm:

> And this huge Castle, standing here sublime,
> I love to see the look with which it braves,
> Cased in the unfeeling armor of old time
> The lightning, the fierce wind, and trampling wave.

In his poem "The Mother Mourns" (1901), Thomas Hardy uses prosopopoeia, personifying Nature as a parent who speaks her sad "accents" in a "dirge-like refrain":

> "My leopardine beauties are rarer,
>   My tusky ones vanish,
> My children have aped mine own slaughters
>   To quicken my wane.
>
> "Let me grow, then, but mildews and mandrakes,
>   And slimy distortions,
> Let nevermore things good and lovely
>   To me appertain. . . ."

In his poem "Chicago" (1916), Carl Sandburg personifies an entire city by directly addressing it as "you":

> They tell me you are wicked and I believe them, for I have seen your
>   painted women under the gas lamps luring the farm boys.
> And they tell me you are crooked and I answer: Yes, it is true I have seen
>   the gunman kill and go free to kill again.

See also **pathetic fallacy.**

Petrarchan/Petrarchan conceit: *Petrarchan* is an adjective derived from the name of the fourteenth-century Italian poet Petrarch (Francesco Petrarca). Petrarch was particularly noted for his elaborate **imagery** and **figures of speech,** as well as for his elevated and formal language and **style.** A

Petrarchan conceit is a **conceit** that presents an exaggerated portrait of the beauty and cruelty of a woman and the suffering, lovestricken man who worships her. Analogy, **hyperbole,** and **oxymoron** are literary devices commonly used in the elaborate comparisons found in Petrarchan conceits. Since Petrarch, this kind of conceit has been imitated both seriously and **satirically;** certain standard comparisons, such as that of the lover to a ship in a stormy sea, are so common that they have become **clichés.**

EXAMPLE: The fifty-fourth **sonnet** from Edmund Spenser's *Amoretti* (1595) contains a Petrarchan conceit:

Of this world's theatre in which we stay,	
My love like the spectator ydly° sits;	*idly*
Beholding me that all the pageants° play,	*roles*
Disguysing diversly my troubled wits.	
Sometimes I joy when glad occasion fits,	
And mask in myrth lyke to a comedy:	
Soone after when my joy to sorrow flits,	
I waile and make my woes a tragedy.	
Yet she, beholding me with constant eye,	
Delights not in my merth nor rues° my smart:	*pities*
But when I laugh she mocks, and when I cry,	
She laughs and hardens evermore her heart.	
What then can move her? if not merth nor mone,°	*moan*
She is no woman, but a sencelesse stone.	

Petrarchan sonnet: See **Italian sonnet.**

phallocentric: Centered around or **privileging** the masculine, a nonnatural characteristic ascribed to institutions (including literature) and culture more generally by certain **deconstructors, feminist critics,** and **psychoanalytic critics.** When used by feminists, the term is almost synonymous with **patriarchal.** Psychoanalytic critics usually use the term to suggest that psychic life is conditioned by the **phallus** as understood by psychoanalytic theorist Jacques Lacan. Deconstructors often prefer philosopher Jacques Derrida's term *phallogocentric,* which through the insertion of an **allusion** to the word *logos* (Greek for "word," "speech," and "reason") implies that the masculine **gender** is privileged in Western language and thought, which Derrida has described as being **logocentric.**
See **phallus.** See also **deconstruction, logocentrism.**

phallogocentric: See **phallocentric.**

phallus: A **symbol** or **representation** of the penis, particularly when used to signify power. Freud identified the stage in which children become interested in their own sexual organs as the phallic stage, a normal stage in the development not only of libidinal desire but also of human **subjectivity** more generally. **Psychoanalytic critic** Jacques Lacan viewed the phallus as the representative of a fraudulent power (male over female) whose "law" is a principle of psychic division (conscious / unconscious) and sexual differ-ence (masculine / feminine). The **Symbolic order** is ruled by the phallus, which in itself has no inherent meaning; rather, power and meaning are as-cribed to the phallus by individual cultures and societies, as represented by the father as namer and lawgiver.

phenomenological criticism: A type of literary **criticism** based upon **phenomenology,** a philosophical school of thought and method of analysis founded by German philosopher Edmund Husserl whose proponents pos-tulate that objects attain meaning only as they are perceived in someone's consciousness. In other words, phenomenologists reject the notion that ob-jects have inherent meaning and instead argue that objects have whatever meaning a given subject perceives in them. They also believe that all con-sciousness is **intentional,** that is, directed toward an object.

Roman Ingarden, a Polish thinker, was one of the first critics to incor-porate phenomenology into literary theory. In *The Literary Work of Art* (1931) and *The Cognition of the Literary Work of Art* (1937), Ingarden borrowed the phenomenological concept of intentionality in arguing that a literary work: (1) has its beginnings in the intentional acts of its author's consciousness; and (2) represents those acts, that consciousness, so that the reader apprehends them by experiencing the work both as an object and as his or her own consciousness. According to Ingarden, readers must, however, perform "active readings" to "concretize" works; the author's perceptions are not automatically transferable — and therefore com-prehensible — to the reader. Instead, the reader must engage in a "co-creative" reading that bridges **gaps** and may even resolve **ambiguities** in the work. For Ingarden, then, readers are not passive receptacles of an au-thor's perceptions but active partners in realizing the work in their own consciousness.

Phenomenological criticism is most often associated with the **Geneva School,** a close-knit group of critics united by their method of analyzing lit-erary works. These critics typically sought to experience the **text** passively, sympathetically, and meditatively in an intuitive attempt to discover the web of patterns and relationships that manifests the unique consciousness of its author. They attempted to disregard any references external to the text, including their own presuppositions and beliefs, in order to experi-ence the author's *Weltanschauung,* or worldview, more completely and ac-curately.

See **Geneva School** for further explanation of this group's method of analysis.

phenomenology: A philosophical school of thought and method of analysis founded by German philosopher Edmund Husserl whose propo-nents postulate that objects attain meaning only as they are perceived in someone's consciousness. Husserl argued that human consciousness is **in-tentional** (directed toward an object) as well as unitary (in a reciprocal relationship with the object). As Husserl noted, phenomenology emphasizes the psychical realm of awareness; the phenomenologist analyzes the object as it is perceived, suspending judgments or presuppositions that are not part of the analyst's own consciousness. Husserl used the term *epochē* to refer to this suspended, or "bracketed," moment.

Phenomenologists acknowledge that objects exist in the space-time continuum, but they believe that active awareness on the part of some subject is required for an object to be intelligible. Phenomenologists thus reject any preconceived notions about epistemology or ontology (the studies of knowledge and being, respectively), since they argue that an object carries the meaning that any given subject perceives in (or for) it, rather than an inherent meaning.

Phenomenology provides the basis for **phenomenological criticism,** a form of literary criticism usually associated with the **Geneva School.** Geneva School (or Geneva) critics try to analyze a literary work without any external references, experiencing the **text** passively, sympathetically, and meditatively to discover the patterns and relationships that make up the unique consciousness of its author.

philology: The study of language and literature. When referring to the study of language, the term refers to the study of the historical and comparative development of languages, whereas the term **linguistics denotes** the scientific study of language (how it functions as a system).

phoneme: A basic sound unit (unit of pronunciation) in a language. If one such unit of a word is replaced with another phoneme, the word changes. For instance, change the *f* sound in *phaser* to an *l* sound, and the result is *laser*. Phonemes may thus be seen as the building blocks of words. Each basic sound unit can be distinctly articulated, as so often happens when a child is learning to read (phoneme: *f-ō-n-ē-m*), and yet one must move smoothly from one phoneme to the next in any given word in order to enunciate that word properly.

An alphabetic letter is not equivalent to a phoneme. For instance, *f* and *ph* represent a single phoneme, for the sound they signify is always the same. Similarly, *k* and *ck* represent a single phoneme, as can *oo* and *ou* (if pronounced as in *doodle* and *you* or *through*). *Ou*, when followed by *gh*, itself represents at least five phonemes, as in the following series of words: *dough, cough, through, bough, slough*. The letter *c* may signify the phonemic sound represented by the letters *k* or *s*, as in the words *cool* and *cereal*. Many letters, when followed by the letter *h* in our linguistic system, produce entirely different phonemes than those we most commonly associate with the letters themselves: *church, thanks, rough, trophy*. *K* only represents one sound (although that sound is also represented by *ck* or *c*). It is important to remember, however, that even single letters may represent different phonemes, as is the case with *c* and with every vowel. *E*, for instance, may be long or short, as in *reed* and *red*, respectively.

The number of phonemes in any linguistic system is limited. English, for example, has about 45 discrete sound units, or phonemes.

phonocentrism: See **logocentric, logocentrism.**

phonology: A division of **linguistics,** phonology is the study of basic sounds, called **phonemes.**

picaresque narrative: See **picaresque novel.**

picaresque novel: From the Spanish *pícaro,* meaning "rogue," a **novel** that **realistically** recounts the adventures of a carefree but engaging rascal who always manages to escape by the skin of his or her teeth. The picaresque novel is **episodic** in **structure,** its unity resulting from the near-constant presence of the central **character,** who comes from a low social class and generally lives by his or her wits rather than by honest, hard work. *Pícaros,* though adept at trickery, generally do not engage in serious criminal behavior; furthermore, they do not change, evolve, develop, or grow in the way that more conventional novelistic **protagonists** do. In general, picaresque novels are told from the **first-person point of view** and have **satiric** intent (often toward the **class** structure). True-to-life **settings** and details — many of which are coarse and bawdy — give the **genre** a realistic **texture.** Influenced by the *Satyricon* (c. A.D. 50) of the ancient Roman writer Petronius, the picaresque novel emerged as a genre in sixteenth-century Spain with the publication of the anonymous *La vida de Lazorillo de Tormes* (*The Life of Lazorillo de Tormes*) (c. 1555) and played an important role in the development of the novel through its rejection of the **romantic,** idealized depictions so popular in **medieval romances,** which featured chivalrous knights as **heroes.**

FURTHER EXAMPLES: Thomas Nashe's *The Unfortunate Traveller; or, The Life of Jack Wilton* (1594) is the first English example of the genre. The French writer Alain-René Lesage's *Gil Blas* (1715–35), Daniel Defoe's *Moll Flanders* (1722), and Mark Twain's *Adventures of Huckleberry Finn* (1884) are other **classic** examples. More modern works in which picaresque heroes and **antiheroes** appear, respectively, include Saul Bellow's *Henderson the Rain King* (1959) and John Kennedy Toole's *A Confederacy of Dunces* (1980); the works in which these heroes appear are more tightly structured than picaresque novels, strictly defined.

Television series, monthly comic books, and daily comic strips provide a continuing episodic structure hospitable to the picaresque genre. The time-travelling protagonist of the long-running TV series *Quantum Leap* is an example, as is the eponymous hero of the less successful Western spoof *Briscoe County Jr.* Jamie Hewlett and Alan Martin's *Tank Girl,* who roams a bizarre post**apocalyptic** world accompanied by a genetically altered kangaroo, is a comic-book picaresque heroine.

Pindaric ode (regular ode): Named for the fifth-century B.C. Greek poet Pindar, a type of **ode** that consists of **strophes, antistrophes,** and **epodes,** a triadic structure corresponding to the movement of the ancient Greek **chorus.** The strophes and antistrophes share the same **stanzaic** form, while the epodes have another. Pindaric odes, rare in English, are typically characterized by a ceremonious or even exalted **tone.**
    EXAMPLE: Thomas Gray's "The Progress of Poesy" (1757).

plaisir: See **poststructuralism.**

Platonic criticism: A type of **criticism** that judges a work by its extrinsic purpose rather than by any intrinsic (artistic) value, as in Aristotelian criticism. Platonic critics determine the value of a work by assessing whether it has a useful nonartistic purpose or application, such as promoting morality.

Platonic love: A philosophy of love set forth by Plato in his *Symposium* and *Phaedrus* (c. 360 B.C.) and attributed to the female sage Diotima, who supposedly related it to Socrates. This **theory** was further developed in the third through fifth centuries A.D. by **Neoplatonist** Roman philosophers such as Plotinus; it evolved still further during the **Renaissance,** when it informed the writings of Church fathers and love poets alike. Platonic philosophy dominated Western thinking about love until the **Medieval Period,** when the competing **courtly love** tradition emerged.
    The lover of beauty, according to Platonic love philosophy, should not reserve his admiration for purely physical beauty, although appreciating an attractive body can be the first step toward worshipping beauty of a more spiritual nature. (Incidentally, the masculine pronoun has been used deliberately in the preceding sentence because the Platonic lover has traditionally been conceived of as — and specified to be — male, perhaps because in the *Phaedrus,* Socrates specifically talks about male-male relationships, asserting the superiority of nonsexual male friendships over merely physical homosexual relationships.) According to the philosophy of Platonic love, which, since Plato, has been applied primarily to heterosexual relationships, we should progress from contemplating physical to mental to conceptual to spiritual beauty (and so forth) until we have attained a vision of beauty at the highest level, namely, the eternal and true Ideal Beauty from which the soul is normally separated and next to which all worldly beauty pales. The Platonic lover admires the beauty in a human body as a sign of or step toward higher spiritual beauty and ultimately the absolute and perfect beauty in and of God. This doctrine also postulated that, by achieving the highest vision of beauty, the Platonic lover could actually create in his beloved a higher, more soulful beauty. Today, most people use the phrase *Platonic love* to refer to love that does not involve sexual relations, without realizing that the term has a much deeper and more complex significance.
    EXAMPLES: The following lines from Percy Bysshe Shelley's "Epipsychidion" (1822) express the philosophy of Platonic love:

Warm fragrance seems to fall from her light dress
And her loose hair; and where some heavy tress
The air of her own speed has disentwined,
The sweetness seems to satiate the faint wind;
And in the soul a wild odour is felt,
Beyond the sense, like fiery dews that melt
Into the bosom of a frozen bud. —
See where she stands! a mortal shape indued
With love and life and light and deity,
And motion which may change but cannot die;
An image of some bright Eternity;
A shadow of some golden dream; a splendour
Leaving the third sphere pilotless; a tender
Reflection of the eternal moon of love. . . .

The relationship between Jude Fawley and Sue Bridehead in Thomas Hardy's *Jude the Obscure* (1896) is essentially Platonic. Theirs was "not an ignoble, merely animal feeling" but rather "an extraordinary affinity, or sympathy . . . which somehow took away all flavor of grossness"; they "seem to be one person split in two."

Today's simpler use of *Platonic* is conveyed by the following joke: *He:* "Come over to my place for some scotch and sofa?" *She:* "No — but maybe a gin and platonic."

Platonism: A body of thought associated with the fourth-century B.C. Greek philosopher Plato that includes three major doctrines concerning ideas, love, and recollection. Plato's idealistic doctrines, unlike much of Aristotelian thought, are not easily pinned down, for Plato did not explicitly codify his thinking; rather, he wove it (along with **antithetical** views) through his various **dialogues,** which take the form of discussions among Socrates and other speakers on the nature of various problems.

The doctrine of ideas postulates that the materiality of the visible world (what we think of as "reality") emanates from a higher ideal realm. Plato believed that true reality lies in this invisible and universal spiritual realm and that humans should use their intellect to attempt to understand this world of ideas. For Plato, ideas were the source of everything, hence the corollary that humanity should aspire to the ideas of justice, friendship, and morality that it discovers in this unseen realm. The doctrine of love, known more commonly as **Platonic love,** equates beauty and virtue, holding that the proper appreciation and understanding of beauty can lead to a more spiritual level of being. The doctrine of recollection postulates that the soul has many incarnations and is, therefore, immortal. Although the soul "forgets" most of what it learned in higher realms during those periods in which it resides in a physical body, it does "recollect" certain ideas and **images,** which are the basis for knowledge.

Followers of Plato have so modified his doctrines over the centuries that it can be difficult to separate true Platonism (if such a thing exists) from its offshoots. Two particularly important schools of **Neoplatonism,** however, have emerged from Platonic thought. The first is the Alexandrian school (associated with the Roman Plotinus), which accentuated the **mystical** elements in Platonism and which functioned nearly as a religion. The second is Italian **Renaissance** Neoplatonism (associated with Marsilio Ficino), which developed a mystical system intended to fuse Christian doctrine with Platonic thought.

See also **Neoplatonism, Platonic love.**

play (drama): A **story,** in verse or prose, that is generally intended to be performed onstage (in a theater and in the presence of an audience) by actors who deliver the **dialogue,** perform the actions, and follow the stage directions written by the author. Although *drama* is often used as a synonym for *play,* the two terms differ slightly in meaning. A play is a drama intended for performance before a theatrical audience. Although all plays are, broadly speaking, dramas, not all dramas are plays; for instance, some dramas (properly called **closet dramas)** are meant not to be performed but, rather, to be read as poems. The word *drama* may also be used in a narrower sense to refer to a serious play, movie, or television show.

See also **drama.**

pleonasm: See **periphrasis.**

plot: The arrangement and interrelation of events in a **narrative** work, chosen and designed to engage the reader's attention and interest (or even to arouse suspense or anxiety) while also providing a framework for the exposition of the author's message, or **theme,** and for other elements such as **characterization, symbol,** and **conflict.**

Plot is distinguished from **story,** which refers to a narrative of events ordered chronologically, not selectively, and with an emphasis on establishing causality. Story is the raw material from which plot is constructed. Crafting a plot requires choosing not only which elements of a story to include — and what order to tell them in — but also relating the events of a story to one another so that causality may be established convincingly. As novelist E. M. Forster explained in *Aspects of the Novel* (1927), to say that "the king died and the queen died" is to tell a story. Adding three simple words — "The king died and then the queen died of grief" — transforms the story into a plot by including and emphasizing causality. **Russian formalists** made a similar distinction between plot and story, which they referred to as *syuzhet* and *fabula,* respectively. Unlike Forster, however, they did not emphasize causality. Rather, they argued that the literary devices (such as **rhythmic** patterns, **syntax,** and **imagery**) used by an author convert a story into a plot. Recent critics who have sought to explain this transformation from story line into plot by analyzing the "rules" that generate plot are called **narratologists.**

Plot, unlike story, frees authors from the constraints of chronology and enables them to present their chosen subjects in whatever way they see fit to elicit the desired emotional response from readers. Despite this authorial freedom (to use **flashbacks** or **anachronisms,** for instance, or to begin a narrative *in medias res* ["in the middle of things"]), most critics agree with Aristotle's argument (made in the *Poetics* [c. 350 B.C.]) that effective plots must have three relative parts — a beginning, a middle, and an end — that are complete in themselves. Of course, these parts need not correlate temporally with the story — for instance, when the beginning of a plot does not correspond with the chronological beginning of the story but rather begins *in medias res.* Michael Ondaatje's novel *The English Patient* (1992) begins with a nurse named Hana caring for a hideously burned, nameless man in a war-torn Italian villa. The plot subsequently tells, through interspersed flashbacks, the story of that man — Count Laszlo de Almasy, an explorer and mapmaker — and his love affair with Katherine Clifton, the wife of a colleague. At the same time, the plot includes the present story of Hana, a drifter named Caravaggio, and a Sikh bomb-disposal expert named Kip.

Aristotle's tripartite conception of plot, which he considered the primary dramatic element, still sets the parameters of discussion today. Aristotle also argued that a plot must have unity such that if any of its parts, or incidents, are removed, something seems to be missing. If a part of a work can be removed without affecting the whole, then the work is **episodic** rather than plot-based (and, according to Aristotle, inferior). This is not to say that a work must only have one story line and, thus, that subplots render a work episodic. Rather than detracting from a work's unity, a well-crafted subplot may enhance the main plot by providing a **foil** to the main plot.

Aristotle's identification of plot as a work's chief element faced increasing challenge in the nineteenth and twentieth centuries. Many critics have focused on characterization as the defining element of a literary work, viewing plot as a mere framework for showcasing character. Following this **theory,** the plot of Emily Brontë's *Wuthering Heights* (1847), composed of a carefully arranged story line, nonetheless serves primarily as a structure and spotlight for the development of Cathy Earnshaw and her volatile and brooding soul mate, Heathcliff.

Many critics and writers conceive of plot in the terms used by Gustav Freytag to describe the structure of a typical five-act play, especially a **tragedy. Freytag's pyramid,** his enumerated sequence of events, includes the introduction, **rising action, climax, falling action,** and **catastrophe.** Alternative and additional terms such as **crisis, resolution,** and *dénouement* have come into vogue, but Freytag's terms and sequence are still often used to describe and analyze elements of plot.

Conflict plays a central, often defining, role in plot. Some critics even maintain that plot does not exist in the absence of conflict. As the confrontation or struggle between opposing **characters** or forces, conflict usually sets the plot in motion; it is the element from which the action emanates and around which it revolves. In the first scene of William Shakespeare's *Romeo and Juliet* (1596), the swordfight between Benvolio,

Tybalt, and their respective servants — staged in Baz Luhrman's 1996 film version as a gas-station shootout — deepens the divide between the Montague and Capulet families that turns Romeo Montague and Juliet Capulet into "star-crossed lovers."

Sometimes the word *intrigue* (which comes from the French *intrigue*, meaning "plot") is confused with *plot*. As an English literary term, however, *intrigue* refers to a type of plot in which the outcome of some scheme depends on the ignorance or credulity of its targets.

plurality: See **heteroglossia.**

poem: See **poetry.**

poetaster: An unskilled poet who tries but doesn't quite cut it. In short, a bad poet.

poetic diction: Diction — the choice and phrasing of words — deemed suitable to **verse.** Since the time of Aristotle, poets and critics have disagreed about what constitutes proper poetic diction. Those who believe that verse is, or should be, essentially different from **prose** advocate the use of language that is particularly **imaginative,** elevated, or otherwise different from everyday **discourse.** They celebrate diction that rises above the level of ordinary speech. Others, such as the **romantic** poet William Wordsworth, feel that poets should speak in ordinary language like their contemporaries.

From the **Renaissance** through the eighteenth century, elaborate and elevated poetic diction was a key feature of much poetry. Poets frequently used **archaisms** and **periphrasis** (circumlocution) to distinguish poetic discourse from that of prose. Twentieth-century poets have generally promoted the widest possible range of expression for poetry and have even adopted diction and discourse patterns typically associated with prose.

EXAMPLES: Words such as *ere* (for *before*), *thrice* (for *three times*), and *thou* (the formal address for *you*) are commonly associated with poetic diction. John Keats uses poetic diction in his poem "The Eve of St. Agnes" (1820) when he writes "Of all its wreathéd pearls her hair she frees." In ordinary discourse, the subject ("she") would precede the verb ("frees"), which would be followed by the direct object ("her hair") and its prepositional modifier ("of all its wreathéd pearls").

poetic justice: The idea that virtuous and evil actions are ultimately dealt with justly, with virtue rewarded and evil punished. Poetic justice occurs, for instance, when a misunderstood **protagonist** is praised after a long struggle or when his or her **antagonist** is cast out from the community.

Thomas Rymer, a seventeenth-century English critic who coined this term, used it specifically with reference to poetic works (including dramatic **tragedies**). Rymer also viewed poetic justice as a device conducive to achieving what he viewed as literature's ultimate goal: furthering morality.

Today, the term is used with reference to all types of literary works — as well as life in general. Furthermore, contemporary critics almost uniformly reject Rymer's view that literature should provide moral instruction.

Used colloquially, the term *poetic justice* is often applied specifically to situations in which the **hero** and **villain** get their "just deserts" at a pivotal moment for both of them, as when the villain is shot while trying to shoot the hero or unmasked at the height of his apparent glory, resulting in the hero's vindication.

EXAMPLES: In Charles Dickens's *Oliver Twist* (1837), when villain Bill Sykes envisions the eyes of Nancy, the girlfriend he has viciously murdered, he accidentally hangs himself by a rope he had intended to use to escape from an angry crowd seeking vengeance for her death.

In the movie *The Fugitive* (1993), the villain, Dr. Charles Nichols, promotes a "wonder drug" worth millions of dollars that the hero, Dr. Richard Kimble (played by Harrison Ford), discovers to be ineffective. In order to prevent disclosure of Kimble's discovery, the evil doctor has Kimble's wife murdered; Kimble is subsequently wrongly convicted of this murder and becomes a fugitive from justice. In his quest to find the real murderer (and the motive behind the killing), Kimble uncovers this sinister plot and ultimately reveals Nichols's role in the "wonder drug" scam at a medical convention dinner intended to honor Nichols.

poetic license: Narrowly defined, the linguistic liberty taken by poets in composing **verse.** This liberty typically involves deviations from normal patterns of speech and prose for poetic effect or to meet the demands of **prosody.** Poets may use unusual **syntax, archaic** words or **neologisms, wrenched accent, eye-rhymes** or **half-rhymes** rather than **perfect rhymes,** and so forth. Defined more broadly, poetic license refers to any non-linguistic liberty, such as **anachronism** or extreme coincidence, taken by a poet or by any writer that violates reality (or reality as it is generally perceived) or accepted standards of **discourse.** Poetic license is acceptable so long as it maintains or heightens the impact of the work in which the artistic liberties have been taken; when misused, poetic license is the mark of a **poetaster** or other incompetent writer.

poetics: The **theory** or principles of the nature of **poetry** or its composition; writing that expounds such theory or principles. Although the term may be used as a singular noun (critics sometimes speak of a "poetic"), this usage is uncommon. Today, the term also refers to the **aesthetic** principles of any literary **genre,** including prose forms (it is perfectly acceptable to speak of "the poetics of fiction"). The term has also been used occasionally to denote the study of **versification.**

EXAMPLE: Aristotle's *Poetics* (c. 330 B.C.).

poetry: Generally said to be one of the three or four major literary **genres,** a term defined and described in so many different ways that one might easily argue that there are as many ways to characterize it as there are people. However, there is general agreement about what poetry is not.

First, poetry is frequently distinguished from **verse** — broadly speaking, any **rhythmical** or **metrical** composition. Poetry is a subset of verse, from which it is distinguished (and to which it is considered superior) by virtue of its **imaginative** quality, intricate **structure,** serious or lofty subject matter, or noble purpose.

Second, poetry is often contrasted with **fiction.** This distinction, however, has proved more problematic because some poets and literary historians have characterized poetry *as* fiction (or even as the "supreme fiction"), as that which is not essentially tied to fact, to history. Seen from this angle, any imaginative artistic work might be called poetic.

Third, poetry has frequently been contrasted with **prose.** Aside from the obvious difference in **form,** many critics argue that, although it is possible to restate the meaning of a prose passage, the meaning of a poetic passage cannot be so easily paraphrased. While poetry can be approached intellectually, it is equally an emotional experience; one might even say that poetry is meant to be experienced rather than simply read. Poetry is rich with a suggestiveness born from the interplay of words and sounds. The **connotations** of words and the relationships among words, phrases, and ideas all add to the purely **denotative** meanings of the poet's language, giving it a richness greater than that found in most prose. Furthermore, auditory elements — the sounds and rhythms of letters, words, phrases, and lines — are key aspects of the poem and play a large role in how that poem is read and understood.

Although rhythm is an essential, in fact an indispensable, element of poetry, **rhyme** is not. Prose, too, may have rhythm, but without the marked regularity and integral importance found in poetry. A poem typically contains some basic rhythmic pattern; variations on the pattern create auditory interest but also may introduce a new or different idea or viewpoint. Rhyme is often used, perhaps because it is a chief contributor to establishing rhythm. When used unskillfully, however, rhyme can detract from poetry since it can easily sound singsongy or contrived. Although rhyme was often used in **Romance-** and English-language poetry in the last several centuries, much twentieth-century poetry dispensed with rhyme. Modern poets have similarly dispensed with **poetic diction,** the special "poetic" vocabulary used heavily in the past (for example, *thou* as a form of address, even to an old Grecian urn, or the use of *ere* for *before*), and instead write poems in the language and cadences of everyday speech.

The care with which poets choose their words also distinguishes poetry from prose. This is not to say that authors writing in prose choose their words carelessly; rather, prose authors can afford to be more discursive than poets since prose works are typically much longer than poems. Since poets must be more economical, each word in a poem tends to be packed with meaning. The brevity of poetry, in contrast to prose, affords it a particular intensity.

Finally, poetry tends to be more **concrete**, replete with specific and detailed **images**. The suggestive essence of poetry means that poets commonly make use of **figurative language** and **symbolism**. **Tropes,** such as **metaphor, metonymy, personification, simile,** and **synecdoche,** as well as other **figures of speech,** such as **allegory** and **conceit,** enhance both the **imagery** and the sensory impact of the poem.

There are also differing schools of thought regarding the aim of poetry, though everyone agrees that poetry has a special meaning or significance for humanity. Some see a **didactic** purpose, an aim to instruct. Some argue that poetry's chief goal is to provide pleasure to the reader. Others argue that poetry provides a special, even unique, insight not possible in prose. In many ways, these differing conceptions of what poetry is and what purpose it serves reflect differing views of what poetry should be.

Poetry appears to have originated as a collective endeavor, or at least for a collective purpose. Many of the earliest literary (and often religious) works are poems. Notably, poetry played a major role in religious and other ceremonial events and helped to preserve a tribe's or group's history and its traditions, which were often passed down orally from generation to generation — a process that continues in some groups even today.

Over time, however, the collective use of poetry diminished. Poetry became the vehicle for **drama** and then specifically for individual expression. Today, poetry is seen as a highly individualistic endeavor; perhaps no other form of expression is deemed so intensely personal, and therefore unique. No subject is off-limits to the poet. To call poetry a discipline seems limiting in itself, but poetry is surely the one literary area in which anything goes, as long as the poet's emotions have been aroused.

point of view: The vantage point from which a **narrative** is told. A narrative is typically told from a *first-person* or *third-person point of view;* the *second-person point of view* is extremely rare. Novels sometimes, but infrequently, mix points of view.

In a narrative told from a first-person perspective, the author tells the story through a **character** who refers to himself or herself as "I." Such a **narrator** is usually (but not always) a major participant in the action. This first-person narrator recounts events as he or she experiences, remembers, or hears about them. First-person narrators are sometimes **unreliable narrators** — and they may also be **naive heroes** — who color or distort matters in ways that the reader (at least eventually) detects. Occasionally, works written from the first-person point of view contain multiple narrators, each of whom personally recounts his or her story. In Amy Tan's novel *The Joy Luck Club* (1989), several mothers and daughters convey varied perspectives on life in recounting their own histories.

Third-person narratives come in two types: **omniscient** and *limited.* An author taking an omniscient point of view assumes the vantage point of an all-knowing narrator able not only to recount the action thoroughly and reliably but also to enter the mind of any character at any time in order to reveal his or her thoughts, feelings, and beliefs directly to the reader. (Such a narrator, it should be pointed out, can conceal as well as reveal at will.) An author using the limited point of view recounts the story through the eyes of a single character (or occasionally more than one, but not all or the narrator would be an omniscient narrator). The reader is thus usually privy to the inner thoughts and feelings of only one character and receives the story as that character understands and experiences it, although not in that character's own voice. Such a narrator is generally an observer of or a participant in the action.

In a narrative told from the second-person point of view, the narrator addresses a "you"; thus, a narrative that reads "If you really want to know New Orleans, you need to walk Bourbon Street at midnight . . ." would be an example of second-person narrative, as would a story a parent told to and about a child ("Early in the morning, you set out alone for Grandma's house . . .").

FURTHER EXAMPLES: The concluding chapter of Charlotte Brontë's *Jane Eyre* (1847), a novel written from the first-person point of view, begins:

> Reader, I married him. A quiet wedding we had: he and I, the parson and clerk, were alone present. When we got back from church, I went into the kitchen of the manor-house, where Mary was cooking the dinner, and John cleaning the knives, and I said —
> "Mary, I have been married to Mr. Rochester this morning."

Stephen Crane's *The Red Badge of Courage* (1895), by contrast, is narrated from the omniscient point of view:

> The cold passed reluctantly from the earth, and the retiring fogs revealed an army stretched out on the hills, resting. As the landscape changed from brown to green, the army awakened, and began to tremble with eagerness at the noise of rumors. It cast its eyes upon the roads, which were growing from long troughs of liquid mud to proper thoroughfares. A river, amber-tinted in the shadow of its banks, purled at the army's feet; and at night, when the stream had become of a sorrowful blackness, one could see across it the red, eyelike gleam of hostile camp fires set in the low brows of distant hills.

Katherine Mansfield's short story "Miss Brill" (1922) is written from the limited point of view:

> She thought of the old invalid gentleman to whom she read the newspaper four afternoons a week while he slept in the garden. She had got quite used to the frail head on the cotton pillow, the hollowed eyes, the open mouth and the high pinched nose. If he'd been dead she mightn't have noticed for weeks; she wouldn't have minded.

Jay McInerney's *Bright Lights, Big City* (1984) is an example of a novel told from the rarely used second-person point of view:

> Monday arrives on schedule. You sleep through the first ten hours. God only knows what happened to Sunday.

At the subway station you wait fifteen minutes on the platform for a train. Finally a local, enervated by graffiti, shuffles into the station. You get a seat and hoist a copy of the New York *Post*. The *Post* is the most shameful of your several addictions. You hate to support this kind of trash with your thirty cents, but you are a secret fan of Killer Bees, Hero Cops, Sex Fiends, Lottery Winners, Teenage Terrorists, Liz Taylor, Tough Tots, Sicko Creeps, Living Nightmares, Life on Other Planets, Spontaneous Human Combustion, Miracle Diets and Coma Babies. The Coma Baby is on page two: COMA BABY SIS PLEADS: SAVE MY LITTLE BROTHER.

political readings: A term used in **the new historicism,** specifically by new historicists of **romantic** (as opposed to **Renaissance**) literature, to describe their critical method of reading a literary **text.** New historicists who perform political readings rely on terms borrowed from **deconstruction** and **psychoanalytic criticism** (such as *substitution* and *suppression*) to describe how writers may unconsciously conceal or ignore the **contradictions** of their own time and in their own works. Political readers analyze these suppressions and substitutions in order to discover the historical and political realities that the text elides or covers up. For political readers, the true subjects of a literary work are the difficulties and **conflicts** papered over by the **ideological discourses** permeating its language.

polyphonic (polyvocalic): Meaning "many-voiced," a term used to refer to what Soviet critic Mikhail Bakhtin called **dialogic texts,** that is, ones in which several viewpoints or **discourses** are in **dialogue** with one another. Like *polyvocalic,* with which it is synonymous, *polyphonic* is closely associated with Bakhtin's **theory** of **heteroglossia** (literally, "other tongues" or "different tongues"), which holds that most if not all literary works involve a multiplicity of voices that interact and compete, thereby representing and generating social debate. According to Bakhtin, all novels are to some degree polyphonic, since they represent the diverse viewpoints and **ideologies** of various **characters;** the **narrator** or narrators; and the author, whose generally more **monologic** (i.e., singular, controlling, "official") voice is disrupted by other discourses. Even characters and narrators who engage in disruptive dialogue may be polyphonic if they voice inconsistent attitudes and beliefs.
See also **dialogic criticism, heteroglossia.**

polyvocalic: See **polyphonic.**

portmanteau word: A word coined by combining two other words, encompassing the original meanings of both component parts. (A portmanteau is a suitcase that opens up into two compartments.) Lewis Carroll invented the term in 1872, explaining it as follows: "You see, it's like a *portmanteau* . . . there are two meanings packed up in one word." Some portmanteau words have become commonplace in English vocabulary.

EXAMPLES: *Smog,* coined from *smoke + fog,* has become a familiar word today, as have *brunch (breakfast + lunch)* and *squiggle (squirm + wiggle).* Contemporary portmanteau words include *spork* (a spoon and a fork combined in a single utensil), *splurchase* (a splurged-on purchase), and *Spanglish* (a "tossed salad" of Spanish and English). *Chunnel (Channel + tunnel),* which refers to the Eurotunnel, the long-anticipated rail link between Britain and the European continent, is also a portmanteau word. An extensive compilation of portmanteau words can be found in Dick Thurner's *Portmanteau Dictionary: Blend Words in the English Language, Including Trademarks and Brand Names* (1993).

The word *slithy,* from Lewis Carroll's poem "Jabberwocky" (1871), is made up by combining *slimy* and *lithe,* as Humpty Dumpty explains to Alice in Carroll's *Through the Looking Glass* (1872). *Galumph,* said to be a combination of *gallop* and *triumph,* is another portmanteau word created by Carroll, as is *chortle (chuckle + snort).* James Joyce made extensive use of portmanteau words in *Finnegans Wake* (1939).

In the 1980s, comedian Rich Hall found an audience (on television and with his novelty books) for portmanteau words he called "sniglets"; for instance, Hall defined "hozone" (hosiery zone) as a place "where socks go when they disappear in the dryer." In his book *Playing the Future* (1996), Douglas Rushkoff coined the term *screenagers* to refer to teenagers raised on television, movies, and computer games. A 1997 article in the *Dallas Morning News* referred to Plano, a suburb home to numerous high-tech businesses and industries, as a "technoburb" of Dallas.

positivism: A philosophical school emphasizing facts and the description of phenomena. Positivists have developed a mode of empirical investigation based on that of physical scientists pursuing factual, descriptive knowledge. Positivists also reject speculation, especially about matters of "ultimate concern," arguing that philosophy and the pursuit of knowledge ought to be concerned with humanity and its condition rather than with metaphysical issues.

Positivism has its roots in the writings of the eighteenth-century philosophers George Berkeley and David Hume, but its strongest proponent was the nineteenth-century Frenchman Auguste Comte, who coined the term. The positivist philosophy is pervasive in works by John Stuart Mill, such as *On Liberty* (1859).

In the twentieth century, positivism was further redefined and refined into a philosophy known as *logical positivism,* which was championed chiefly by Ludwig Wittgenstein. Wittgenstein redefined the goal of positivism as the use of logic to elucidate human thought systematically. Logical positivism incorporates elements of experimental scientific and mathematical methods.

Although positivism has had its most direct impact on philosophical and scientific methods, critics readily acknowledge the widespread impact it has had indirectly on literature and its analysis. The development of positivism coincided with the rise of **realism** and, subsequently, **naturalism,** literary movements whose practitioners attempted to observe, organize, and present reality logically and **objectively** to readers who, in turn, were expected to approach **texts** empirically, viewing descriptions, statements made by **characters,** and **plot** developments as evidence leading to some viewpoint or interpretive conclusion. This essentially empirical approach to texts is shared by several schools of literary criticism, most of which require interpreters to provide evidence (textual, historical, psychological, and so forth) for their analyses. **Impressionistic criticism, personal criticism,** and **deconstruction** are among the critical schools that have resisted the influence of positivism.

postcolonial literature and postcolonial theory: *Postcolonial literature* refers to a body of literature written by authors with roots in countries that were once colonies established by European nations, whereas *postcolonial theory* refers to a field of intellectual inquiry that explores and interrogates the situation of colonized peoples both during and after colonization. Postcolonial literature and theory are often, but not always, anti-imperialist in character.

As with **postmodernism** and **poststructuralism,** the prefix *post-* in *postcolonial* implies opposition as well as chronological sequence; that is, *postcolonial* not only **denotes** the period after a former colony has become independent but also typically **connotes** political and moral attitudes opposed to colonization. By extension, works produced during the colonial period can be **anachronistically** viewed as postcolonial in character if they express, even implicitly, resistance to colonialism and in some way project the potential for independence, whether **utopian** or **dystopian.**

The term *postcolonial* is sometimes also extended to refer to situations that share material characteristics with postcolonial conditions but that do not actually involve a former colony. The situations of African Americans and of the Irish, who were long under English domination, are cases in point. Thus, both African American works and works by nonblack authors about slaves and their free descendants may include postcolonial perspectives and invite interpretations that draw on postcolonial theory. Moreover, critics applying postcolonial theory to works by writers ranging from Toni Morrison to William Faulkner tend to view the situation of African Americans as a result of domestic colonization that is historically tied to European empire building through the slave trade. Postcolonial readings of Irish literature have had to take into account Ireland's status as a colony in all but name — but one that, unlike colonies such as India, was near the center of empire with regard not only to location but also **race** and language.

As a literary category, postcolonial literature has displaced and expanded narrower rubrics such as "Commonwealth literature" and "literature of the Third World" (which is usually subdivided into anglophone literature, francophone literature, and so forth). Postcolonial literature includes works by authors with cultural roots in South Asia, Africa, the Caribbean, and other places in which colonial independence movements arose and colonized peoples achieved autonomy in the past hundred years. Works by authors from so-called settler colonies with large white populations of European ancestry — such as Australia, New Zealand, Canada, and Ireland — are sometimes also included. (Note that a postcolonial author need not reside in the former colony and may well live in the capital of the former empire or in some other industrialized region.) In practice, most of the works currently studied by scholars of postcolonial literature and by postcolonial theorists are written in English; that is, they are addressed, either implicitly or explicitly, to an international audience of English speakers rather than to a national or regional audience that speaks a non-European language.

Critical readings of postcolonial literature regularly proceed under the overt influence of postcolonial theory, which raises and explores historical, cultural, political, and moral issues surrounding the establishment and disintegration of colonies and the empires they fueled. As an interdisciplinary field, postcolonial theory routinely crosses perceived boundaries between literary **criticism,** history, anthropology, and other subjects, in part because postcolonial theorists themselves analyze such a wide range of issues and in part because they believe that the strict division of knowledge into academic disciplines contributes to colonizing mindsets. Like its object of study, postcolonial theory is *in-between,* a word that some postcolonial theorists also routinely employ in their own analyses.

The most influential postcolonial theorists are Edward Said, Gayatri Chakravorty Spivak, and Homi K. Bhabha. Said, a politically active scholar of Palestinian descent who teaches in the United States, laid the groundwork for the development of postcolonial theory in general, as well as specifically identifying and analyzing the process of **orientalism,** in his book *Orientalism* (1978). In this study, Said, who was influenced by French philosophical historian Michel Foucault, analyzed European **discourses** concerning the exotic, arguing that stereotypes systematically projected on peoples of the East contributed to establishing European domination and exploitation through colonization. Although *Orientalism* focuses on colonialist discourses, both Said and other postcolonial theorists have applied its insights in interpreting the aftermath of colonialism.

Spivak, an Indian scholar, has highlighted the ways in which factors such as **gender** and **class** complicate our understanding of colonial and postcolonial situations. In essays such as "Can the Subaltern Speak?" (1988), Spivak challenges postcolonial theory to address the silencing of women and other subaltern subjects not only by and in colonial discourses but also in postcolonial responses to those discourses. (*Subaltern,* a British military term that refers to a low-ranking, subordinate officer, is used in postcolonial theory to designate the colonized, whom Europeans considered to be subject races. Spivak also uses the term to refer to voiceless groups within colonies or former colonies, such as women, migrants, and the subproletariat, who are dominated by other groups inside the colonized culture.)

The issues Spivak raises concerning how agency — the ability to choose and to speak independently — can survive the impact of long-term hierarchical situations are central to the difficulties facing not only postcolonial theory but also individuals and groups in postcolonial contexts. Some of these difficulties have been addressed by the Subaltern Studies Group through the production of revisionary historical accounts of life as experienced by once-silent or silenced colonial subjects. Ranajit Guha's "The Prose of Counter-Insurgency" (1988), for example, provides a critical alternative to accepted historical **narratives** by contrasting official documents with personal ones, contemporary accounts with retrospective ones, and European views with indigenous ones.

Bhabha, another Indian scholar, has shown how colonized peoples have co-opted and transformed various elements of the colonizing culture, a process he refers to as *hybridity.* In his essay "Of mimicry and man: The ambivalence of colonial discourse" (1987), he sketches the process by which colonized peoples turn the tables on the colonizing culture through imitation that produces a difference. In "DissemiNation: Time, narrative and the margins of the modern nation" (1990), Bhabha himself mimics and transforms the title of poststructuralist theorist Jacques Derrida's *Dissemination* (1972). The concept of hybridity — which suggests a crossover or amalgamation that produces something unalterably new and independent and which characterizes a contradictory, in-between "location of culture" that enables the emergence of postcolonial nationhood and individual agency — has been widely embraced by postcolonial theorists.

Hybridity also has implications akin to the biological, cultural, and linguistic connotations of *creolization,* a term used by Caribbean writer Edward Kamau Brathwaite in *The Development of Creole Society in Jamaica 1770–1820* (1971). Both *hybridity* and *creolization* attempt to give name to the coexistence of seemingly incompatible elements, a coexistence that frequently characterizes postcolonial societies and writing. The terms are not, however, synonymous, since *creolization* evokes more historical and regional specificity than does *hybridity.*

Important antecedents of postcolonial theorists include writers from former colonies, such as Brathwaite, Chinua Achebe, Aimé Césaire, and Frantz Fanon, who have reflected as critics both on their societies and on the predicament of postcolonial intellectuals, especially in relation to the history of colonialism. For example, in "An Image of Africa" (1977), Achebe, a Nigerian writer, perceives racism and condescension in Joseph Conrad's **representation** of the Belgian Congo in *Heart of Darkness* (1899), a book he considers "offensive and deplorable." Césaire, who experienced colonial life in the Caribbean and who founded the pan-national "Negritude" movement, writes vividly about the barbarism of the colonizer in *Discours sur le colonialisme (Discourse on Colonialism)* (1950). Fanon, a French-trained psychiatrist from Martinique who practiced in the

French colony of Algeria during the war for independence and who was the foremost precursor of postcolonial theory, wrote a series of essays (based on his experiences) commenting on the problems and needs of colonized peoples and advocating independence movements. Of particular importance are the essays collected in *Les damnés de la terre* (*The Wretched of the Earth*) (1961), including "Spontaneity," which addresses spontaneous violence and national consciousness, and "On National Culture," which describes the native intellectual's role in the stages by which a postcolonial national identity — and by implication the intellectual's own identity — can develop.

Postcolonial theory has also been influenced by poststructuralist approaches including **deconstruction,** though it diverges from poststructuralism in its attention to history and politics. Deconstruction's challenge to hierarchical, **binary oppositions** has provided postcolonial theory with conceptual strategies for undermining the ostensible difference between center and margins that is frequently at work in the relationship of the colonizing culture to the colonized. Insofar as postcolonial theorists such as Spivak and Bhabha have focused on such abstract argumentation derived from European tradition, however, they have come under fire from other postcolonial theorists. For example, in *Beyond Postcolonial Theory* (1998), Epiphanio San Juan, Jr., a scholar of Philippine descent who teaches in the United States, takes to task postcolonial theorists whom he considers too abstract and insufficiently committed to effective political action.

Because of diverse historical, geographical, linguistic, and intellectual factors, postcolonial literature and postcolonial theory are still developing as categories of writing. Neither looks the same as it did around 1990, when the terms first gained wide currency. Matters such as the character and effects of diaspora — the dispersion of peoples from their homelands — have only begun to be explored. Moreover, postcolonial theorists have begun to study the differences among various postcolonial experiences. Postcolonial situations vary widely, in part because of the idiosyncratic character of the many European countries that had imperial ambitions and in part because of the global dispersion of their colonies. Postcolonial theorists have also recognized that the cultural location of the writer — whether author, theorist, historian, or literary critic — also makes a difference. The writer's angle of vision varies (as does the reader's), depending on factors such as gender, class, and cultural roots, whether in a former colony, in Europe, or in the United States.

To date, postcolonial literature and theory have been strongly influenced by theorists primarily concerned with the Middle East and the Indian subcontinent. Many of their insights and concepts regarding postcolonial writing cannot, however, be transferred to other regions without significant revision due to sharp regional and historical differences. Accordingly, it is likely that African, Caribbean, Hispanic, and Irish voices, among others, will increasingly give postcolonial literature and theory new inflections.

See also **orientalism.**

postmodernism: A term referring to certain radically experimental works of literature and art produced after World War II. *Postmodernism* is distinguished from **modernism,** which generally refers to the revolution in art and literature that occurred during the period 1910 through 1930, particularly following the disillusioning experience of World War I. The postmodern era, with its potential for mass destruction and its shocking history of genocide, has evoked a continuing disillusionment similar to that widely experienced during the **Modern Period.** Much of postmodernist writing reveals and highlights the alienation of individuals and the meaninglessness of human existence. Postmodernists frequently stress that humans desperately (and ultimately unsuccessfully) cling to illusions of security to conceal and forget the void over which their lives are perched.

Not surprisingly, postmodernists have shared with their modernist precursors the goal of breaking away from traditions (including certain modernist traditions, which, over time, had become institutionalized and **conventional** to some degree) through experimentation with new literary devices, **forms,** and **styles.** While preserving the spirit and even some of the **themes** of modernist literature (the alienation of humanity, historical discontinuity, etc.), postmodernists have rejected the order that a number of modernists attempted to instill in their work through patterns of **allusion, symbol,** and **myth.** They have also taken some of the meanings and methods found in modernist works to extremes that most modernists would have deplored. For instance, whereas modernists such as T. S. Eliot perceived the world as fragmented and represented that fragmentation through poetic language, many also viewed art as a potentially integrating, restorative force, a hedge against the **cacophony** and chaos that postmodernist works often imitate (or even celebrate) but do not attempt to counter or correct.

Because postmodernist works frequently combine aspects of diverse **genres,** they can be difficult to classify — at least according to traditional schemes of classification. Postmodernists, revolting against a certain modernist tendency toward elitist "high art," have also generally made a concerted effort to appeal to popular culture. Cartoons, music, "pop art," and television have thus become acceptable and even common media for postmodernist artistic expression. Postmodernist literary developments include such genres as **the Absurd,** the **antinovel, concrete poetry,** and other forms of *avant-garde* poetry written in **free verse** and challenging the **ideological** assumptions of contemporary society. What postmodernist theater, fiction, and poetry have in common is the view (explicit or implicit) that literary language is its own reality, not a means of **representing** reality.

Postmodernist **critical** schools include **deconstruction,** whose practitioners explore the **undecidability** of **texts,** and **cultural criticism,** which erases the boundary between "high" and "low" culture. The foremost theorist of postmodernism is Jean-François Lyotard, best known for his book *La condition postmoderne* (*The Postmodern Condition*) (1979).

Recently, modern science has been critiqued by postmodernist theorists who, in journals such as *Social Text,* have sought to "demystify" science by showing it to be: (1) a cultural construct whose **privileged** status among means of arriving at knowledge is undeserved; and (2) a tool of repressive ideologies that have favored the health, welfare, and interests of whites and males over people of color and females. Ironically, as *Scientific American*'s John Horgan pointed out in a *New York Times* article entitled "Science Set Free From Truth" (1996), "some of the most prominent scientists in the world traffic in hypotheses that are remarkably postmodern in character." Ever since Thomas Kuhn argued, in *The Structure of Scientific Revolutions* (1962), that what science tends to reveal is the prevailing scientific **paradigm** (which is subject to shifting), many leading scientists have been less hung up on the idea that they are producing objectively verifiable truths and more willing to speculate about "realities," the reality of which will probably remain unprovable.

Horgan cites artificial intelligence expert Marvin Minsky, who has argued that computers can think; chemist Ilya Prigogine, whose work led to the development of chaos theory; and physicists such as Sidney Coleman, Andrei Linde, and John Wheeler as examples of scientists who would agree that science has reached, in Prigogine's words, "the end of certitude." Coleman and Linde have suggested that our universe may be one of many, each with similar — or different — laws of physics; Wheeler, who coined the term *black hole,* has argued that reality is "participatory" in nature, that it is partially the product of the questions we pose about it and thus, in some sense, "a figment of the imagination."

FURTHER EXAMPLES: Postmodernist poets include John Ashberry, Maxine Chernoff, Jori Graham, Richard Howard, James Merrill, and Maureen Owen. Harold Pinter's *The Homecoming* (1965) and Edward Albee's *Three Tall Women* (1994) are examples of postmodernist theater. Robert Wilson's *Einstein on the Beach* (1979) has been called a postmodernist opera. Postmodernist novels include William Burroughs's *Naked Lunch* (1962), Donald Barthelme's *Come Back, Dr. Caligari* (1964), John Barth's *Lost in the Funhouse* (1967), Thomas Pynchon's *Gravity's Rainbow* (1973), David Shield's *Remote* (1996), and Kathy Acker's *Empire of the Senseless* (1988), which includes the statement "Get rid of meaning. Your mind is a nightmare that has been eating you: now eat your mind." Don DeLillo has written several postmodernist novels, including *White Noise* (1985), *Libra* (1988), and *Mao II* (1991). In a review, T. Coraghessan Boyle refers to Thomas Pynchon's *Mason & Dixon* (1997) as a postmodernist **historical novel,** explaining that "if the traditional historical novel attempts to replicate a way of life, speech and costume, the post-modernist version seeks only to be that, a version."

In 1996, *Social Text* published an article entitled "Transgressing the Boundaries: Toward a Transformative Hermeneutics of Quantum Gravity," in which physicist Alan Sokal argued that many existing laws of physics are social conventions and called for the development of an "emancipatory mathematics." Later, Sokal declared over the Internet that the article was a hoax intended to debunk postmodernist critiques of science, but some postmodernists still find more truth in the hoax than in Sokal's subsequent representation of it as "a melange of truths, half-truths, quarter-truths, falsehoods, and syntactically correct sentences that have no meaning whatsoever."

Postmodern Period (in English and American literature): Less coherent and less well defined than many other literary eras, a period usually said to have begun in both England and North America after World War II. The Postmodern Period follows the **Modern Period** in English and American literature, which began around 1914. Both **modernist** and **postmodernist** works tend to express feelings of anxiety and alienation experienced by individuals living in the twentieth century, but postmodernist works tend to be even darker, suggesting the meaninglessness of the human condition in general through radically experimental works that defy **conventions** of literary cohesion and even coherence. Postmodernist novels fitting this description are often referred to as **antinovels.**

See **postmodernism.**

poststructuralism: The general attempt to contest and subvert **structuralism** and to formulate new theories regarding interpretation and meaning, initiated particularly by **deconstructors** but also associated with certain aspects and practitioners of **psychoanalytic, Marxist, cultural, feminist,** and **gender criticism.** Poststructuralism, which arose in the late 1960s, includes such a wide variety of perspectives that no unified poststructuralist theory can be identified. Rather, poststructuralists are distinguished from other contemporary critics by their opposition to structuralism and by certain concepts they embrace.

Structuralism, briefly defined, is a science of humankind born in the theories of structuralist anthropologist Claude Lévi-Strauss and linguist Ferdinand de Saussure. Lévi-Strauss, who studied everything from the structure of villages to **myths,** looked for recurring, common elements that transcended the differences within and among cultures. Saussure founded **semiology,** a science of **signs,** and argued that any sign is composed of two parts: the **signifier** (the "sound-image") and the **signified** (the **abstract** concept represented by the signifier). Using Saussure's linguistic theory as a model and employing **semiotic** theory, structuralists claim that it is possible to analyze a **text** or other signifying structure systematically, even scientifically, to reveal the "grammar" behind its form and meaning.

Structuralists also follow Saussure's lead in believing that sign systems must be understood in terms of **binary oppositions,** contrary pairs such as light / dark and strong / weak. For instance, in analyzing myths and texts to uncover basic structures, structuralists argue that opposite terms modulate until they are finally reconciled by some intermediary third term. They typically believe that meaning(s) in a text, as well as the meaning of a text, can be determined with reference to the system of signification — the **codes** and **conventions** that governed the text's production and that operate in its reception. Poststructuralists, on the other hand, reject the possibility of such "determinate" knowledge. They believe that signification is an interminable and intricate web of associations that continually defers a determinate assessment of meaning. The numerous possible meanings of any word lead to **contradictions** and ultimately to the dissemination of meaning itself. Thus, poststructuralists contend that texts contradict not only structuralist accounts of them but also themselves.

To elaborate, poststructuralists have suggested that structuralism rests on a number of distinctions — between signifier and signified, self and language (or text), texts and other texts, and text and world — that are overly simplistic, if not patently inaccurate, and they have made a concerted effort to discredit these oppositions. For instance, poststructuralists have viewed the self as the subject, as well as the user, of language, claiming that although we may speak through and shape language, it also shapes and speaks through us. In addition, poststructuralists have demonstrated that, in the grand scheme of signification, all "signifieds" are also signifiers, for each word exists in a complex linguistic matrix and has such a variety of **denotations** and **connotations** that no one meaning can be said to be final, stable, and invulnerable to reconsideration and substitution. Signification is unstable and indeterminate, and thus so is meaning. Poststructuralists, who have generally followed their structuralist predecessors in rejecting the traditional concept of the literary "work" (as the work of an individual and purposeful author) in favor of the impersonal "text," have gone structuralists one better by treating texts as "intertexts": crisscrossed strands within the infinitely larger text called language, that networked system of denotation, connotation, and signification in which the individual text is inscribed and read and through which its myriad possible meanings are ascribed and assigned. (Poststructuralist psychoanalytic critic Julia Kristeva coined the term **intertextuality** to refer to the fact that a text is a "mosaic" of preexisting texts whose meanings it reworks and transforms.)

Poststructuralists have even viewed the world itself as a text. We desire a certain car, for instance, because it represents achievement, even though in most measurable ways it is indistinguishable from (or even inferior to) certain other cars. Thus, the car is deemed desirable not for reasons of safety, performance, comfort, gas mileage, or even agreed-on **aesthetic** values but rather because it has come to **symbolize** success according to the network of cultural **discourses** — "the text" — in which we live, think, and choose. The poststructuralist view of world as text has been set forth most powerfully and controversially by the deconstructive theorist Jacques Derrida in his book *De la grammatologie* (*Of Grammatology*) (1967), where he maintains that "*there is nothing outside the text.*" In order to understand what Derrida meant by that statement, consider the following: We know the world through language, and the acts and practices that constitute that "real world" (the Oklahoma City and World Trade Center attacks, the decision to marry) are inseparable from the discourses out of which they arise and as open to interpretation as any work of literature. Derrida is not alone in deconstructing the world / text opposition. Deconstructive theorist and critic Paul de Man viewed language as something this has great power in individual, social, and political life. Geoffrey Hartman, who was closely associated with deconstruction during the 1970s, once went so far as to claim that "nothing can lift us out of language."

Although poststructuralism has drawn from numerous critical perspectives developed in Europe and in North America, it relies most heavily on the work of French theorists, especially Derrida, Kristeva, Jacques Lacan, Michel Foucault, and Roland Barthes. Derrida's 1966 paper "Structure, Sign and Play in the Discourse of the Human Sciences" inaugurated poststructuralism as a coherent challenge to structuralism. Derrida rejected the structuralist presupposition that texts (or other structures) have self-referential centers that govern their language (or signifying system) without being in any way determined, governed, co-opted, or problematized by that language (or signifying system). Having rejected the structuralist concept of a self-referential **center,** Derrida also rejected its corollary: that a text's meaning is thereby rendered determinable (capable of being determined) as well as determinate (fixed and reliably correct). Lacan, Kristeva, Foucault, and Barthes have all, in diverse ways, arrived at similarly "antifoundational" conclusions, positing that no foundation or "center" exists that can ensure correct interpretation.

Lacan, a psychoanalytic critic whose theories have proved of interest to deconstructors and other poststructuralists, posited that the human unconscious is structured like a language. He treated dreams not as Freud treated them — as revelatory of symptoms of repression — but rather as forms of discourse. Lacan also argued that the **ego,** subject, or self that we think of as being necessary and natural (our individual human nature) is in fact a product of the social order and its various and often conflicting symbolic systems (especially, but not exclusively, language). The "ego-artifact," produced during what Lacan called the "mirror stage" of human development, seems at once unified, consistent, and organized around a determinate center. But the unified self, or ego, is a fiction, according to Lacan. The yoking together of fragments and destructively dissimilar elements takes its psychic toll, and it is the job of the Lacanian psychoanalyst to "deconstruct," as it were, the ego, to show its continuities to be contradictions as well.

Kristeva, another psychoanalytic critic, explores the relationship between a number of binary oppositions within Western culture (such as normal / poetic, conscious / unconscious, and, most importantly, semiotic / symbolic) in her work *La révolution du langage poétique* (*Revolution in Poetic Language*) (1974). Kristeva associates the semiotic with the chaotic, the irrational, the fluid, and argues that the semiotic has the capacity to undermine the symbolic, which is associated with the coherent and the logical. Kristeva's opposition of symbolic and semiotic seemingly contradicts the poststructuralists' challenge to binary oppositions, thereby reminding us that poststructuralism includes perspectives and practitioners whose principles and priorities diverge as much as they overlap. In another sense, though, the fluid "semiotic" language **privileged** by Kristeva's analysis is language unmarked by binary oppositions and without rigid, determinate, or determinable meaning. It could therefore be argued that the triumph of semiotic over symbolic language would ultimately fulfill the aims of post-structuralism by making unnecessary its more radical critical ambitions and methods. Kristeva, by the way, hints at a possible association of the semiotic with the feminine and the symbolic with the masculine, an idea this laid the groundwork for the feminist concept of *écriture féminine:* women's writing.

Foucault, yet another influential French critic now associated with post-structuralism, began his career by embracing **Marxism.** Although Foucault broke with Marxist thought after the French student uprisings of 1968, the influence of Marxism continued to be seen in his tendency to study cultures in terms of power relationships. Unlike Marxists, however, Foucault re-fused to see power in terms of simple, binary oppositions (as something ex-ercised by a dominant **class** over a subservient class). Indeed, he argued in *Surveiller et punir: Naissance de la prison (Discipline and Punish: The Birth of the Prison)* (1975) that power is not simply repressive power, that is, a tool of conspiracy by one individual or institution against another. Rather, power is a complex of interwoven and often contradictory forces; power produces what happens. Thus, even a tyrannical aristocrat does not simply wield power, for he is empowered by discourses (accepted ways of thinking, writing, and speaking) and practices that embody, exercise, and amount to power.

Barthes, both a structuralist and a poststructuralist over the course of his career, was one of the first to strip the author of the unique role ac-corded to him by Western culture and by traditional literary criticism. In *Le plaisir du texte (The Pleasure of the Text)* (1973), Barthes said that the author as an institution (that is, the author traditionally conceived as the source of knowledge, the controller of a text's meaning, and a chief object of critical interest) is dead. Along with Foucault and de Man, Barthes views the author not as an original and creative master and manipulator of the linguistic system but, rather, as one of its primary vehicles, an agent through which it works out new permutations and combinations. These theorists even criticize humanism insofar as it views the human "subject" as a consistent, creative, and purposive entity. Other important poststruc-turalist ideas elaborated by Barthes include the French concepts of *plaisir* (pleasure) and *jouissance* (which roughly translates as playful, ecstatic en-joyment) and the terms *lisible* and *scriptible*. In *S/Z* (1970), Barthes ar-gued that texts were either *lisible* ("readerly") or *scriptible* ("writerly"). *Lisible* indicates a certain dependence on convention, which facilitates in-terpretation. *Scriptible* implies a significant degree of experimentation, a flouting or modification of traditional rules that makes a text difficult to interpret and, occasionally, virtually incomprehensible. Works by writers such as Jorge Luis Borges, William Burroughs, James Joyce, Gertrude Stein, and Virginia Woolf tend to be *scriptible* and **illisible** (unreaderly). By this, we mean that works such as Borges's *Ficciones* (1956) and Burroughs's *Naked Lunch* (1962) will not make sense to readers who assume them to be governed by standard literary conventions and who, therefore, approach them according to standard rules of reading. *Illisible* texts, because they so obviously and radically violate ordinary reading conventions, implicitly and indirectly force us to realize the extent to which all texts are artistic fabrications and not (as *lisible* texts sometimes seem) realistic **representations** of reality.

Even as poststructuralists have radically reduced the author's role, they have also diminished the role of the reader, whom they view not as a stable, coherent, and consistent subject or self but rather as the locus of competing and often contradictory discourses. They concern themselves with "reading" (*lecture*), rather than with the reader per se. For poststructuralists, reading is a process that involves a "text" (an endless chain of signifiers with no fixed meaning), rather than a "work" (a literary production understood more traditionally to involve methodical authorial construction, inherent form or unity, and determinable, determinate meaning). Texts themselves may also be stripped of individuality, seen simply as part of writing-in-general (*écriture*) in which the boundaries between texts, and even between the various disciplines that have been developed to read various kinds of texts, melt away or (as many poststructuralists would say) "undergo erasure." Deconstructors have even spoken of a "general text" to which historical categories and distinctions do not apply. Some poststructuralist critics have gone so far as to reject the term *text* altogether, preferring *discourse,* which they broadly use to refer to any verbal structure, whether literary or not. Discourse, they argue, is influenced by historical circumstances, including social and cultural factors. Poststructuralists who emphasize discourse often do so in an attack on the concept of the "general text."

Poststructuralists have radically revised the traditional concept of **theory** even as they have elevated it to a position of prime importance (so much so that poststructuralist critics who want to be taken seriously must theorize their critical practices). Theory, as poststructuralists conceive of it, is vastly different from theory as defined in more conventional literary criticism (as a general set of principles applicable to the analysis or classification of a literary work). In the view of poststructuralists, theory has more than literature to account for, since everything from the unconscious to social and cultural practices is seen as functioning like a language; thus the goal of poststructuralist theorists is to understand what controls interpretation and meaning in all possible systems of signification. Not surprisingly, this novel and far-ranging concept has facilitated the development of theories that challenge the very underpinnings of traditional Western thought, especially the **logocentric** assumption that meaning is ultimately determinable and determinate. Although the poststructuralist concept of theory has been challenged by a number of other influential critics, including Steven Knapp, Walter Benn Michaels, Stanley Fish, and Jean-François Lyotard, theorizing one's critical practices remains imperative for poststructuralists, who also expect other types of critics to theorize their positions and who criticize those who do not.

Poststructuralism continues to flourish today. In fact, one might reasonably say that poststructuralism serves as the overall **paradigm** for many of the most prominent contemporary critical perspectives. Approaches ranging from **reader-response criticism** to **the new historicism** assume the "antifoundationalist" bias of poststructuralism. Many approaches also incorporate the poststructuralist position that texts do not have clear and definite meanings, an argument pushed to the extreme by those poststructuralists identified with deconstruction. But unlike deconstructors, who argue that the process of signification itself produces irreconcilable contradictions, contemporary critics oriented toward other poststructuralist approaches (**discourse analysis** or Lacanian psychoanalytic theory, for instance) maintain that texts do have real meanings underlying their apparent or "manifest" meanings (which often contradict or cancel out one another). These underlying meanings have been distorted, disguised, or repressed for psychological or **ideological** reasons but can be discovered through poststructuralist ways of reading.

Of the various critical approaches associated with poststructuralism, deconstruction has had the greatest impact on the theory and practice of literary criticism, perhaps because of its emphasis on the text as **rhetoric** requiring **close reading** that must be at once careful and playful. Deconstruction has not been without its detractors, however, including some powerful critical adversaries who have deplored everything from its emphasis on the text's **undecidability** to the wordplay with which some deconstructors have responded to what they call the *jouissance* of the text to the critique of history's essentially genealogical **narrative** advanced by Derrida, de Man, and J. Hillis Miller. Some have even maintained that deconstruction is a fundamentally nihilistic approach to literature whose advocates believe that texts are divorced from historical and political reality and ultimately mean nothing (in the sense that they mean whatever the reader wants them to mean). Derrida and Miller responded to these charges in their respective books *Memoires for Paul de Man* (1986) and *The Ethics of Reading* (1987).

See also **deconstruction**.

practical criticism (applied criticism): A type of **criticism** that emphasizes and responds to the characteristics of specific **texts**. Practical criticism differs from **theoretical criticism,** which emphasizes the formulation of general principles applicable to all texts rather than **explicating** individual works. Practical critics often apply **aesthetic** principles that theoretical critics have simply postulated. But rather than elaborating on the theoretical assumptions underlying their analyses, practical critics concentrate on performing a **close reading** of the text in discussing the work and its author. The term *practical criticism* was first employed by Samuel Taylor Coleridge but given broad usage by I. A. Richards, who in 1929 published a book entitled *Practical Criticism: A Study of Literary Judgment.*

Some critics distinguish between two types of practical criticism: (1) **impressionistic criticism,** which is based on the critic's **subjective** impressions and reaction to a work; and (2) **judicial criticism,** which not only provides but also attempts to explain impressionistic readings in light of the author's general manner (including elements of **style** and technique) and choice of subject. The line between impressionistic and judicial criticism is blurred and, not surprisingly, subject to debate.

See also **impressionistic criticism, judicial criticism, theoretical criticism.**

praeteritio: See **paralipsis.**

pragmatic criticism: A type of **criticism** going back to the Roman poet Horace, who in his *Ars Poetica (Art of Poetry)* (first century B.C.) emphasized the effect of a literary work on its audience. Pragmatic critics believe that authors structure works in such a way as to attain specific effects on and elicit certain responses from the reader or audience. These critics thus evaluate a work based on their perception of the success or failure of that work (or author) to achieve its objectives.

Pragmatic criticism is similar to **rhetorical criticism** in its emphasis on how — and how well — the work (or author) manages to "influence" the reader or audience (in the sense of inducing the reader or audience to respond in a particular way). Like rhetorical criticism, pragmatic criticism was practiced from **classical** times up through the eighteenth century, when its popularity fell with the rise of **expressive criticism,** which views literary works in light of their authors' thoughts and feelings. It lapsed into still deeper obscurity during the nineteenth century with the advent of **objective criticism.**

Prague Linguistic Circle: A group of scholars centered in Prague (in the former Czechoslovakia) who continued working in the vein of the **Russian formalists** after that school was suppressed by the Soviet government in the 1930s. Leading members included Roman Jakobson (a leader of the original Russian formalist school who emigrated to Czechoslovakia from Russia) and René Wellek.

See **formalism, Russian formalism.**

Pre-Raphaelitism: A literary movement propagated by a group of English writers of the **Victorian Period** who shared the **aesthetic** values of Pre-Raphaelite painters such as Dante Gabriel Rossetti (who was also a poet), Holman Hunt, John Everett Millais, Ford Madox Brown, and Edward Burne-Jones. What these and other members of the *Pre-Raphaelite Brotherhood* (formed in 1848) shared was the belief that European art in general and English art in particular were stuck in a rut of traditions that had dictated an increasingly tired aesthetic ever since the Italian High **Renaissance,** the birth of which they associated with the painter Raphael.

The Pre-Raphaelites greatly preferred the originality, simplicity, freshness, sharp lines, and strong colors of artists who painted before Raphael to the often idealized images and *chiaroscuro* coloration (involving the atmospheric mixture of light and shadows) characteristic of both the High Renaissance and those English painters whose work grew out of that tradition, such as Sir Joshua Reynolds (President of the Royal Academy), Sir George Beaumont, and Sir John Constable. In their own paintings, the Pre-Raphaelites strove to reveal truth through nature carefully observed and rendered brightly and precisely. Rossetti established his own version of Pre-Raphaelitism, one involving **medieval images** and **themes** and elevating beauty above all other values.

The literary tradition that emerged out of this artistic movement is noted on the one hand for its crisp descriptions and sensuous details and, on the other, for its power to suggest metaphysical states, to indicate philosophical and theological truths unobtrusively. In Pre-Raphaelite poetry, the sound of chairs being pushed back from a table, the sight of coins in a sleeping woman's hair, or the number of petals in a blossom can be **symbolically** suggestive, calling to mind the spiritual dimensions that lie behind the most commonplace objects or situations. The Pre-Raphaelite emphasis on sensuous detail led some critics to dub the movement as the "fleshly school of poetry."

Major writers associated with the movement included Dante Gabriel Rossetti, Christina Rossetti, Algernon Charles Swinburne, and William Morris, who was also a designer perhaps now best known for his lush wallpaper patterns and the still-popular "Morris Chair." Pre-Raphaelitism had a considerable **influence** on late-Victorian medieval revival and also on **Aestheticism,** the movement sometimes summarized by the rallying cry, **art-for-art's-sake.**

EXAMPLE: The following lines, spoken by Queen Guenevere in Morris's poem "The Defence of Guenevere" (1858), convey the spirit of Pre-Raphaelite painting and poetry. The medieval **setting,** the intensified experience of nature in the garden, the garden's subtly symbolic suggestiveness, the idea of weary thoughts giving way to sharp new perceptions, and the overriding emphasis on beauty all exemplify Pre-Raphaelitism:

> I was half mad with beauty on that day,
> And went without my ladies all alone,
> In a quiet garden walled round every way;
>
> I was right joyful of that wall of stone,
> That shut the flowers and trees up with the sky,
> And trebled all the beauty: to the bone,
>
> Yea right through to my heart, grown very shy
> With weary thoughts, it pierced, and made me glad. . . .

presence and absence: Words given a special literary application by French theorist of **deconstruction** Jacques Derrida when he used them to make a distinction between speech and writing. An individual speaking words must actually be present at the time they are heard, Derrida pointed out, whereas an individual writing words is absent at the time they are read. Derrida, who associates presence with "logos" (the creating spoken Word of a present God who "In the beginning" said "Let there be light"), argued that the Western concept of language is **logocentric.** That is, it is grounded in "the metaphysics of presence," the belief that any linguistic system has a basic foundation (what Derrida terms an "ultimate referent"), making possible an identifiable and correct meaning or meanings for any potential statement that can be made within that system. Far from supporting this common Western view of language as logocentric, however, Derrida in fact argues that presence is not an "ultimate referent" and that it does not guarantee determinable (capable of being determined) — much less determinate (fixed and reliably correct) — meaning. Derrida thus calls into question the **privileging** of speech and presence over writing and absence in Western thought.

primitivism: A doctrine postulating that, although humans are essentially good, they have been (and are still being) corrupted by "civilization." Primitivism emerged in the eighteenth century as a reaction against rationalistic **neoclassicism;** it was particularly popular in the eighteenth century and the subsequent **Romantic Period** but has persisted into the present day. Primitivists typically espouse a certain "back-to-nature" philosophy that has led to the glorification of both past eras and past (and present) peoples seen as "natural" in contrast to the largely urban culture that exists today.

Primitivism is often divided into two general categories — *cultural* and *chronological*. This distinction is fairly elastic, however; as a result, the categories frequently overlap. Cultural primitivism holds that what is perceived as natural is usually preferable or superior to what is perceived as artificial. "Nature" is lauded over "culture." The simple and the instinctual are preferred to the complex and the reasoned. Cultural primitivists thus typically see the practices of still-existing tribal groups as superior to the ways of urban civilization. Advocates of chronological primitivism, by contrast, typically emphasize some golden age of humanity that supposedly existed in the past. That is to say, chronological primitivists usually claim that such and such a time was the best in human history and that humanity, having subsequently lost the near-perfection it had attained during that period, has been in decline, perhaps progressive decline, ever since. Chronological primitivists have named eras as late as that of **classical** Greece as being the golden age of humanity.

In literary theory, primitivism has manifested itself in the belief that the best poetry is produced naturally or instinctively. Primitivists have sought to prove their theory by finding an "innate" talent for poetry in individuals who have had no formal education and among groups remote from civilization as we know it. Such searches and assertions were particularly common in eighteenth-century England and France. Jean-Jacques Rousseau, an eighteenth-century French writer, popularized primitivist concepts with his argument that humans are innately good but corrupted by the vices and influences of society. He also popularized the concept of the *Noble Savage,* the idea that humanity in its unspoiled, primitive state is possessed of superior intelligence, morality, and dignity.

The doctrine of primitivism has also been popular in America. In the nineteenth century, pioneers were viewed as Adamic **heroes** going back to living off the (Edenic) land, and in the late 1960s, so-called flower children advocated escaping the military-industrial complex through drugs and what might be called the primitivism of rock 'n' roll music. (In their song "Woodstock" [1970], Crosby, Stills, Nash, and Young speak of having to "get back to the land" to set their souls free; the song concludes with the line, "We've got to get ourselves back to the garden.") More recently, specific movements within the rock 'n' roll tradition, such as punk and grunge, have stressed directness and raw emotion, thus placing themselves in the larger, primitivistic tradition.

Primitivism has had an influence on classical as well as on popular music (Igor Stravinsky's *Le sacre du printemps* [*The Rite of Spring*] [1913] is a primitivistic, classical symphonic piece) and an even greater influence on twentieth-century novels, poems, paintings, and sculptures. Practitioners of each of these arts have made use of increasingly complex techniques and technologies to produce works that laud or mimic those produced in centuries, even millenia, past. These works, dependent upon modern methods for their creation, paradoxically reject "sophisticated" culture and civilization. Artists generally influenced by primitivist thought and expression range from the poet-novelist D. H. Lawrence to the painter Paul Gauguin (who went to Tahiti as a "missionary in reverse") to the sculptor Constantin Brancusi (*The Kiss* [1908]), who sought to capture the expressiveness of prehistoric stone carvings in his work. The English sculptor Henry Moore, a self-described "primevalist," created works suggestive of the monoliths of Stonehenge and statues of deities smoothed by centuries of weather and wear. More recently, the art of Jean-Michel Basquiat has been associated with primitivism, as has the contemporary vogue for "outsider art," a species of **folk** art. The work of graffiti artists such as Keith Haring also exhibits features characteristic of the primitivistic tradition. Others influenced by primitivism include those political and moral commentators who have argued in books, magazines, and newspapers that the modern condition corrupts, that it entails evils from which primordial humanity was exempt. Thus, although opposed by the doctrine of progress — which asserts that humanity has been improving throughout history thanks to advances in technology, science, art, and knowledge — primitivism has, nonetheless, had an important influence on the art and thought of the twentieth century.

privilege: As a verb, to address interpretively, in literary study, one set of textual or contextual issues before, and often instead of, others. Since no scholar or critic can account for all of the causes, contents, or **connotations** of even a single **text,** all interpretive acts involve some degree of privileging, which, in turn, involves the assumption or creation of priorities grounded in a hierarchy of values. **Marxist critics** privilege social **class** in analyzing texts; **reader-response critics** privilege readers' responses to literary works, as the name of the approach indicates; and **structuralists** privilege the idea that all elements of human culture, including literature, can be understood as part of a system of **signs. Feminist critics,** who have historically privileged **gender** — with special emphasis on women and the way in which literature reflects and reproduces **patriarchal** attitudes — have recently begun to extend almost the same degree of privilege to class and **race.**

As a noun, that status of authors, **narrators,** and **characters** which derives from their possession of information that is known — and perhaps available — to them alone. For example, **third-person omniscient** narrators have this kind of "authorial privilege," as do characters whose **first-person narratives** are privileged by hindsight (e.g., the Ancient Mariner in Samuel Taylor Coleridge's "The Rime of the Ancient Mariner" [1798] and Marlow in Joseph Conrad's *Heart of Darkness* [1899]).

As an adjective ("privileged"), the special status accorded to certain persons, works, ideas, **images, theories,** or forms of expression by a given culture. Texts considered **classics** are privileged, as are Ludwig von Beethoven's nine symphonies and Julia Child's French cookbooks. In the U.S., television is privileged over radio, drama over soap operas, football over soccer, cars over public transit, the individual over the group, and so forth.

prolepsis: The evocation in a **narrative** of scenes or events that take place at a later point in the **story.** One of the three major types of **anachrony,** *prolepsis* is sometimes equated with **flashforward,** but **reader-response critics** Gérard Genette and Gerald Prince have recently argued that it is in fact a more general term (much as its opposite, **analepsis,** is a broader term than **flashback**). For instance, prolepsis may involve an **image** that suggests something to occur in the future. More commonly, it involves a **figure of speech** in which an event or action that is anticipated is treated as if it has already occurred or is presently occurring, even though this is temporally impossible. Occasionally, a proleptic thought or dream disrupts the chronological flow of material being related, often manifesting itself in the conscious or subconscious thought processes of a **narrator** or of a protagonist whose mental processes are recounted by the narrative — for instance, via **free indirect discourse.**

As a **rhetorical** device in an argument or debate, prolepsis involves anticipating an opponent's arguments or rebuttals before they have been made.

EXAMPLES: The italicized clause in the following passage: "Linda had never seen such beautiful scarves. *Although she would later feel guilty having spent so much money,* she decided to buy one on the spot."

A **classic** literary example of prolepsis is found in John Keats's poem "Isabella" (1820):

> So the two brothers and their murder'd man
> Rode past fair Florence . . . .

The first paragraph of Carson McCullers's *Reflections in a Golden Eye* (1941) proleptically anticipates the ending of the novel: "There is a fort in the South where a few years ago a murder was committed. The participants of this tragedy were: two officers, a soldier, two women, and a horse."

In the movie *The Empire Strikes Back* (1980), Luke Skywalker says "I'm not afraid," to which Jedi master Yoda responds "You will be." *Terminator 2: Judgment Day* (1991) contains proleptic scenes of future nuclear devastation envisioned by a woman whose son is the target of a robot sent back in time to kill him.

See also **anachrony, analepsis.**

prologue: An introductory statement preceding a literary work; in Greek **tragedy,** the opening section of a **play,** preceding the first **choral ode.**

The prologue, which can be written in prose or verse, often gives information that helps the reader or audience understand the story that follows. It may establish the **setting,** introduce the **characters,** or indicate a **theme** or moral the writer wishes to convey. In a play, the prologue is usually a **monologue** delivered by one of the actors. Prologues written by the author may be explicitly presented as such or may be passed off as the work of a character in the drama. Some prologues, however, are actually written by another person, often a well-known writer who has agreed to introduce and thereby commend a particular work. Some critics would limit the use of *prologue* to plays, but writers of prose works have employed this device for centuries.

EXAMPLES: Marie de France's "Prologue" to her collection of twelfth-century *lais,* in which she, as a female poet, justifies her writing and her act of presenting her work to the King, ends with the following words:

> In your honour, noble king, you who are so worthy and courtly, you to whom all joy pays homage and in whose heart all true virtue has taken root, did I set myself to assemble lays, to compose and to relate them in rhyme. In my heart, lord, I thought and decided that I should present them to you, so if it pleased you to accept them, you would bring me great happiness and I should rejoice evermore. Do not consider me presumptuous if I make so bold as to offer you this gift. Now hear the beginning.

In *Plain and Simple* (1989), Sue Bender begins her account of her journey to the Amish with the following prologue: "I had an obsession with the Amish. Plain and simple. Objectively it made no sense. I, who worked hard at being special, fell in love with a people who valued being ordinary."

Other works that contain prologues include Willa Cather's *Death Comes for the Archbishop* (1926), Paulo Coelho's *Monte cinco* (*The Fifth Mountain*) (1998), and Michael Cunningham's *The Hours* (1998), in which Virginia Woolf wades into a river to drown herself even as her husband discovers her suicide note and rushes off to try and save her.

propositional act: A term used in John R. Searle's expansion of John Austin's **speech-act theory** to refer to a **locution** (the utterance of a statement) that says something about something else. A propositional act has two components: referring to an object and predicating something upon that object. The "referring expression," according to Searle, is "any expression that serves to identify any thing, process, event, action, or any other kind of 'individual' or 'particular'"; the object referred to in a locution may thus be the grammatical subject of that locution.

The propositional act is one of four types of speech acts; the other three are the **utterance act** (saying something), the **illocutionary act** (the utterance of a statement that performs a particular function, such as ordering, promising, etc.), and the **perlocutionary act** (an illocutionary act that affects the state of mind and/or the actions of the person to whom it has been directed).

EXAMPLE: In the locution, "The house is red," the house is the object to which the speaker refers, and the speaker predicates that it is red.

proscenium and proscenium arch: In a modern theater, the *proscenium* is the front part of the stage, that is, the part that lies between the curtain and the edge of the stage, which thrusts out toward the orchestra. The *proscenium arch* is the arch from which the curtain hangs, formally separating the audience from the stage proper. In the past, the term *proscenium* has been used to refer to the whole stage; even today, the word is sometimes used as a synonym for *stage*.

prose: From the Latin for "straightforward," ordinary written or spoken expression; as applied specifically to literature, non**poetic** expression, that is, expression that exhibits purposeful grammatical (including **syntactic**) design but that is not characterized by deliberate or regular **rhythmic** or **metrical** patterns.

The development of prose has generally followed that of verse. Poets tend to innovate; prose writers, by contrast, tend to **imitate,** making belated use of those poetic innovations that can be adapted to the prose environment. The more "artful" or "literary" the work of prose, the more it tends to employ poetic devices, such as rhythm, **imagery,** and sonority (achieved through **alliteration, assonance, consonance,** etc.). Nonfiction prose writers such as Walter Pater and fiction writers such as D. H. Lawrence and, more recently, Toni Morrison and Graham Swift have written poetic prose. Some creative prose writers adopt traditional poetic devices to such a great extent that the line between prose and poetry becomes blurred, hence the designation *prose poem.*

prose encomium: See **encomium, epideictic.**

prose poem: See **prose.**

prosody: The study of **versification,** particularly as it encompasses **meter, rhyme, rhythm,** and **stanzaic** form, and — to a lesser degree — sound patterns such as **alliteration.** Some say that prosody especially involves the study of **accent,** given its roles in meter, rhythm, and other poetic sound effects.

prosopopoeia: See **personification.**

protagonist: The most important or leading **character** in a work; usually identical to the **hero** or **heroine,** but not always. The term comes from the Greek for "first combatant" and referred to the first actor (the person with the leading role, supported by the **chorus**) in **classical** Greek **tragedy.** If the protagonist is in primary **conflict** with another character, that character is the **antagonist;** an evil antagonist is called a **villain.** Whatever the source of the conflict with which the protagonist struggles, that conflict sets the **plot** in motion.

EXAMPLES: Jane Eyre is the protagonist and heroine of Charlotte Brontë's *Jane Eyre* (1847); Emma Woodhouse is the protagonist but dubious heroine of Jane Austen's *Emma* (1815); Becky Sharp is the unheroic — and sometimes quasi-villainous — protagonist of William Makepeace Thackeray's *Vanity Fair* (1846).

Simon Winchester's *The Professor and the Madman* (1998), a best-seller about the origins of *The Oxford English Dictionary,* begins by describing a "controversy" about whether a literary work can have more than one protagonist.

Provençal lai: See *lai.*

proverbs: See **aphorism.** See also **folklore.**

pseudonym: See *nom de plume.*

psychic(al) distance: See **aesthetic distance.**

psychoanalytic criticism: See **psychological criticism and psychoanalytic criticism.**

psychological criticism and psychoanalytic criticism: *Psychological criticism,* which emerged in the first half of the nineteenth century, is a type of literary **criticism** that explores and analyzes both literature in general and specific literary **texts** in terms of mental processes. Psychological critics generally focus on the mental processes of the author, analyzing works with an eye to their authors' personalities. Some psychological critics also use literary works to reconstruct and understand the personalities of authors — or to understand their individual modes of consciousness and thinking. Many critics we would term psychological do not identify themselves as such; furthermore, although psychological critics may employ psychological techniques and methods of analysis, they often write in broadly un**theorized** terms.

Psychoanalytic criticism, a type of psychological criticism, is actually better known and more widely practiced than its "parent" approach. In fact, most critics who approach literature from a psychological perspective focus on readers as well as on authors and identify themselves specifically as psychoanalytic critics. They also tend to structure their analyses within a relatively well-defined theoretical framework.

Psychoanalytic criticism originated in the work of Austrian psychoanalyst Sigmund Freud, who developed a theory of human psychology. Freud also pioneered the technique of psychoanalysis, a therapeutic method designed to treat individual neuroses that has sometimes been called the "talking cure." Psychoanalysis is a long and complex process in which the patient and psychoanalyst meet in one-on-one sessions to explore and discuss the root cause(s) of the patient's problem(s).

Freud's theories are directly and indirectly concerned with the nature of the unconscious mind. Although Freud didn't invent the notion of the unconscious — others before him had suggested that even the supposedly "sane" human mind was conscious and rational only at times, and even then at possibly only one level — he expanded it, suggesting that the powers motivating men and women are mainly and normally unconscious.

Freud, then, powerfully developed an old idea: that the human mind is essentially dual in nature, operating both consciously and unconsciously. He also identified three components of the human psyche. He called the predominantly passionate, irrational, unknown, and unconscious part of the psyche the **id,** or "it." Freud viewed the id — insatiable and pleasure-seeking — as the source of our instinctual physical (especially libidinal) desires. Freud opposed the id to the **superego,** the part of the psyche that has internalized the norms and mores of society. Since the superego reflects societal beliefs, behaviors, and even pressures, it almost seems to be outside of the self, making moral judgments and telling us to make sacrifices even when such sacrifices may not be in our best interests. The third aspect of the psyche identified by Freud is the **ego,** or "I," which is predominantly rational, logical, orderly, and conscious. The ego must constantly mediate between the often competing demands of the id and the superego; roughly speaking, it must choose between (or balance) liberation and self-gratification on one hand and censorship and conformity on the other.

Freud argued that we often repress what the id encourages us to think and do — things the superego and ego correspondingly tell us not to think and do — thereby forcing these "unacceptable" wishes and desires into the unconscious. Hence, much of what lies in the unconscious mind has been put there by consciousness itself in its role as a censor. According to Freud, all of us have repressed wishes and fears. We are particularly likely to censor infantile sexual desires, which, repressed to an unconscious state, emerge only in disguised forms: in dreams, in language (so-called Freudian slips), in creative activity that may produce art (including literature), and in neurotic behavior.

Freud believed that a commonly repressed unconscious desire is the childhood wish to displace the parent of our own sex and take his or her place in the affections of the parent of the opposite sex. Freud referred to this complex of wishes and fears as "oedipal" (after the Greek **tragic** hero Oedipus, who unwittingly killed his father and married his mother). Because the feelings associated with the **Oedipus complex** are seen as taboo, they are viewed as unnatural, even though Freud considered them characteristic of human development.

Freud used dream analysis as a tool for uncovering our repressed feelings and memories. He believed that the repressed urges of the id surface in dreams, masked in **symbolic** form, and that analysis is therefore required to reveal their true meaning. Although Freud's belief in the significance of dreams was no more original than his belief that there is an unconscious side to the psyche, it was the extent to which he developed a **theory** of how dreams work — and the extent to which that theory helped him, by analogy, to understand far more than dreams — that made him unusual, important, and influential.

Many of the elements of psychology that Freud described and explained are present in the literary works of various ages and cultures, from Sophocles' *Oedipus Rex* (430 B.C.) to William Shakespeare's *Hamlet* (1602) to works being written today. The psychoanalytic approach to literature not only rests on the theories of Freud, it may even be said to have *begun* with Freud, who was especially interested in writers who relied heavily on symbols. Such writers regularly cloak ideas in **figures** that make sense only when interpreted, much as the unconscious mind of a neurotic disguises secret thoughts in dream stories or bizarre actions that need to be interpreted by an analyst. Freud's interest in literary artists led him to make some unfortunate generalizations about creativity; for example, in the twenty-third lecture in *Introductory Lectures on Psycho-Analysis* (1922), he defined the artist as "one urged on by instinctive needs that are too clamorous." But it also led him to write creative literary criticism of his own, including an influential essay on "The Relation of a Poet to Daydreaming" (1908) and "The Uncanny" (1919), a provocative psychoanalytic reading of E. T. A. Hoffmann's supernatural **tale** "The Sandman" (1817).

Freud's application of psychoanalytic theory to literature was imitated and then modified by numerous critics. In 1909, the psychoanalyst Otto Rank, in *The Myth of the Birth of the Hero*, theorized that the artist turns a powerful, secret wish into a literary fantasy; Rank used the Oedipus complex to explain the similarities between the popular stories of so many literary **heroes**. A year later, Ernest Jones also drew on the oedipal conflict in his analysis of William Shakespeare's tragedy *Hamlet* (1602), suggesting that Hamlet is a victim of strong feelings toward his mother, the queen. In the next forty years, many other critics adopted the new approach; some of the most influential included I. A. Richards, Kenneth Burke, and Edmund Wilson.

Freud exerted a great deal of influence over the approach to literature that he pioneered. As a result, psychoanalytic critics have had to contend with the Freudian heritage even when they have ultimately rejected it. Alfred Adler, for instance, believed that writers wrote out of inferiority complexes, not, as Freud believed, to express their personal, repressed wishes. Analytic psychologist Carl Jung, who had broken with Freud over Freud's emphasis on sex, developed a theory of the **collective unconscious,** a repository of shared unconscious memories dating back to the origins of human experience that he believed are manifested in dreams, **myths,** and literature. According to Jungian theory, a great work of literature is not a disguised expression of its author's repressed wishes; rather, it is a manifestation of desires once held by the whole human race (but that are now repressed because of the advent of civilization).

Several writers of poetry and fiction have relied on Freudian models. For instance, Conrad Aiken, W. H. Auden, and Robert Graves applied Freudian insights when writing critical prose. Novelists William Faulkner, Henry James, James Joyce, D. II. Lawrence, Toni Morrison, and Marcel Proust have written either criticism influenced by Freud or novels that conceive of **character, conflict,** and creative writing itself in Freudian terms. The poet H. D. (Hilda Doolittle) was actually a patient of Freud's and provided an account of her analysis in her book *Tribute to Freud* (1956). Writers such as these not only lent Freudian theory credibility among students of literature but also helped to endow earlier psychoanalytic criticism with a largely Freudian orientation; this orientation, however, has faced increasingly virulent challenges in the last two decades.

Probably because of Freud's characterization of the creative mind as "clamorous" if not ill, psychoanalytic criticism written before 1950 tended to psychoanalyze the individual author. Poems were read — sometimes unconvincingly — as fantasies that allowed authors to indulge repressed wishes, to protect themselves from deep-seated anxieties, or both. Marie Bonaparte's 1933 study of Edgar Allan Poe, for instance, found Poe to be so fixated on his mother that his repressed longing emerges in his stories in **images** such as the white spot on a black cat's breast (said to represent mother's milk). A later generation of psychoanalytic critics paused to analyze the characters in novels and plays before proceeding to their authors. Such critics still focused on psychoanalyzing authors, however, since they generally viewed characters (whether good or evil) as the authors' potential selves or projections of their psyches.

Psychoanalytic critics who have attempted to arrive at more psychological insights into an author than **biographical** materials can provide view a work of literature as a fantasy or dream — or at least as so analogous to daydreams or dreams that Freudian analysis can help explain the nature of the mind that produced it. Such critics maintain that the author writes to gratify secretly some forbidden wish, usually a repressed infantile desire, and employ Freud's dream-analysis procedures to reveal these subconscious motivations.

The literal surface of a work is sometimes called its "manifest content" and is treated as a Freudian analyst would treat a "manifest dream" or "dream story." Just as the analyst tries to figure out the "dream thought" behind the dream story—that is, the latent or hidden content—so the psychoanalytic literary critic tries to expose the "latent content" of a work. Freud used the words *condensation* and *displacement* to explain two of the mental processes with which the mind disguises its wishes and fears in dream stories. Condensation involves the consolidation of several thoughts or persons into a single manifestation or image; displacement involves the projection of an anxiety, wish, or person onto the image of another, with which it is loosely connected through a string of associations that only an analyst can unravel. Psychoanalytic critics treat **metaphors** as dream condensations; they treat **metonyms (figures of speech** in which one thing is represented by another that is commonly and often physically associated with it) as dream displacements. **Figurative language** is treated as something that evolves as the writer's conscious mind resists what the unconscious tells it to picture or describe. Daniel Weiss, for instance, defines a **symbol**—one type of figurative language—as "a meaningful concealment of truth as the truth promises to emerge as some frightening or forbidden idea."

In a 1970 article entitled "The 'Unconscious' of Literature," Norman Holland, a literary critic trained in psychoanalysis, sums up the attitudes held by critics who would psychoanalyze authors, but without explicitly admitting that the author is being analyzed: "When one looks at a poem psychoanalytically, one considers it as though it were a dream or as though some ideal patient [were speaking] from the couch in iambic pentameter." One "looks for the general level or levels of fantasy associated with the language. By level I mean the familiar stages of childhood development—oral [when desires for nourishment and infantile sexual desires overlap], anal [when infants receive their primary pleasure from defecation], urethral [when urinary pleasures are the locus of sexual pleasure], phallic [when the penis or, in girls, some penis substitute is of primary interest], oedipal." Holland then analyzes Robert Frost's poem "Mending Wall" as an oral fantasy, not unique to its author, involving "breaking down the wall between the individuated self" and "some 'Other'"—including and perhaps especially the nursing mother.

While not denying the idea that the unconscious plays a role in creativity, psychoanalytic critics such as Holland began to emphasize the ways in which authors create works that appeal to readers' repressed wishes and fantasies. Consequently, they shifted their focus away from the author's psyche toward the psychology of the reader and the text. Holland's theories, which have been concerned more with the reader than with the text, have helped to establish **reader-response criticism,** another school of critical theory.

R. D. Laing and D. W. Winnicott, like Holland, have revised Freud significantly in the process of revitalizing psychoanalytic criticism. Laing's controversial writings about personality, repression, masks, and the double or "schizoid" self have blurred the boundary between creative writing and psychoanalytic **discourse.** Critics influenced by Winnicott, an *object-relations theorist,* have questioned the tendency to see reader / text as an either / or construct; instead, they have seen reader and text (or audience and play) in terms of a relationship taking place in what Winnicott calls a "traditional" or "potential space" — a **site** in which **binary oppositions** like real/illusory and **objective / subjective** have little or no meaning. They see the transitional or potential reader / text (or audience / play) space as being *like* the space entered into by psychoanalyst and patient. They also see this space as similar to the space between mother and infant: a space characterized by trust in which categorizing terms such as *knowledge* and *feeling* mix and merge.

Although Freud saw the mother-son relationship in terms of the son and his repressed oedipal complex, object-relations theorists have stressed primacy of a still earlier relationship to the mother, one that (according to object-relations theorist Melanie Klein) dates back to the first days of infancy. And whereas Freud saw the analyst-patient relationship in terms of the patient and the repressed "truth" that the analyst could scientifically extract, object-relations theorists view this relationship, like the relationship between mother and infant, as being dyadic — that is, as being dynamic in both directions. Consequently, they don't depersonalize analysis or their analyses. Contemporary literary critics who apply object-relations theory to texts follow the lead of these theorists by refusing to depersonalize critics; they also refuse to categorize their interpretations as "truthful," given that interpretations are constructed from language, itself a transitional object.

Like Winnicottian critics, French psychoanalytic theorist Jacques Lacan has focused on language and language-related issues. In so doing, Lacan has done more than simply extend Freud's theory of dreams, literature, and their interpretation; he has added the element of language to Freud's emphasis on psyche and **gender.** Lacan treats the unconscious as a language; consequently, he views the dream not as Freud did (that is, as a form and symptom of repression) but rather as a form of discourse. Thus we may study dreams psychoanalytically in order to learn about literature, even as we may study literature in order to learn more about the unconscious. For instance, Lacan employed a psychoanalytic technique to arrive at a reading of Poe's story "The Purloined Letter" (1845). In the process, he both used and significantly developed Freud's ideas about the oedipal stage and complex.

Lacan points out that the pre-oedipal stage, in which the child at first does not even recognize its independence from its mother, is also a preverbal stage, one in which the child communicates without the medium of language, or — if we insist on calling the child's communications language — in a language that can only be called *literal.* ("Coos" cannot be said to be figurative or symbolic.)

While still in the pre-oedipal stage, the child enters the mirror stage, in which it comes to view itself and its mother (and, later, other people) as independent selves. At this point, the child begins to fear the aggressions of others, to desire what is recognizably beyond the self (initially, the mother), and, finally, to want to compete for the same, desired object. The child also learns to feel sympathy with another being who is being hurt by a third, to cry when another cries. All of these developments, of course, involve projecting beyond the self and, by extension, constructing one's self (or "ego" or "I") as others view one — that is, as *another*. Such constructions, according to Lacan, are just that: constructs, products, artifacts — fictions of coherence that in fact hide what Lacan calls the "absence" or "lack" of being.

The mirror stage, which Lacan associates with the **Imaginary order,** is fairly quickly succeeded by the oedipal stage. As in Freud, this stage begins when the child, having come to view itself as self and the father and mother as separate selves, perceives gender and gender differences between its parents and between itself and one of its parents. For a boy, gender awareness involves another, more powerful recognition, for the recognition of the father's **phallus** as the mark of his difference from the mother involves the recognition that his older and more powerful father is also his rival. The mother, who once seemed wholly his and even indistinguishable from himself, is in fact someone else's: something properly desired only at a distance and only in the form of socially acceptable substitutes.

Lacan finds significant the fact that the oedipal stage roughly coincides with the entry of the child into language. For the linguistic order is essentially a figurative or **Symbolic order;** words are not the things they stand for but, rather, are stand-ins or substitutes for those things. Hence boys, who in the most critical period of their development have had to submit to what Lacan calls the "Law of the Father" — a law that prohibits direct desire for and communicative intimacy with the mother — enter more easily into the realm of language and the Symbolic order than do girls, who have never really had to renounce that which once seemed continuous with the self. The **gap** opened up for boys, which includes the gap between **signs** and what they signify — the gap marked by the phallus and encoded with the boy's sense of his maleness — has not opened up for girls, at least not in the same way.

For Lacan, the father need not be present to trigger the oedipal stage; nor does his phallus have to be seen to catalyze the boy's transition into the Symbolic order. Rather, Lacan argues, a child's recognition of its gender is tied up with a growing recognition of the system of names and naming, part of the larger system of substitutions we call language. A child has little doubt about who its mother is, but who is its father, and how would one know? The father's claim rests on the mother's word that he is the father; the father's relationship to the child is thus established through language and a system of marriage and kinship — names — that form the basis of rules for everything from paternity to property law.

Lacan's development of Freud has had several important results. First, his sexist-seeming association of maleness with the Symbolic order, together with his claim that women cannot therefore enter easily into the order, has prompted **feminist critics** not to reject his theory outright but rather to examine the relationship between language and gender, language and women's inequality. Some feminists have suggested that the social and political relationships between males and females will not change until language itself has been radically changed.

Second, Lacan's theory has proved of interest to **deconstructors** and other **poststructuralists,** in part because it holds that the ego (which in Freud's view is as necessary as it is natural) is a product or construct. The ego-artifact, produced during the mirror stage, seems at once unified, con-

sistent, and organized around a fixed center. But the unified self, or ego, is a fiction, according to Lacan. The yoking together of fragments and destructively dissimilar elements takes its psychic toll, and it is the job of the Lacanian psychoanalyst to "deconstruct" the ego, to show its continuities to be **contradictions** as well.

Psychoanalytic theory has permeated modern-day life, including popular culture. A recent humor publication by Sarah Boxer, *In the Floyd Archives: A Psychic Bestiary* (2001), at once pays homage to and sends up psychoanalysis through its cartoons involving the duck Dr. (Sigmund?) Floyd. For an example, see page 382.

psychological novel: See **novel.**

pulp fiction: See **science fiction.**

pun (paronomasia): A play on words that capitalizes on a similarity of spelling and/or pronunciation between words that have different meanings. A pun may also employ one word that has multiple meanings. Although puns have been used for serious purposes in the past (and still occasionally are), since the beginning of the eighteenth century, most have been used to comic effect.

EXAMPLES: William Shakespeare's *Romeo and Juliet* (1596) contains a plethora of puns. One involves the words *maiden, head,* and *maidenhead* (which in **Renaissance** times referred to virginity):

> Sampson: When I have fought with the men, I will be civil with the maids — I shall cut off their heads.
> Gregory: The heads of the maids?
> Sampson: Ay, the heads of the maids or their maidenheads. Take it in what sense thou wilt.

Dylan Thomas's poem "Do Not Go Gentle into That Good Night" (1952) also contains a pun. "Grave" carries the **connotation** of "serious" as well as a more literal reference to an actual grave (i.e., burial, death):

> Grave men, near death, who see with blinding sight
> Blind eyes could blaze like meteors and be gay,
> Rage, rage against the dying of the light.

The 1997 cloning of a sheep named Dolly spawned countless journalistic puns, from "When Will We See Ewe Again?" to "Will There Ever Be Another Ewe?" to "Dolly's Creators Find Wolf in Sheep's Cloning."

Puritan Interregnum: See **Commonwealth Age (in English literature).**

purple patch: A passage that stands out from the prose or verse surrounding it by its ornateness and abundance of literary devices. From a phrase coined by the first-century B.C. Roman poet Horace in his *Ars Poetica (Art of Poetry),* this term is usually derogatory, although it may be used descriptively. A purple patch may result from the self-conscious effort of a **character** to speak — or author to write — eloquently.

EXAMPLES: Although full of red and green **images,** Macbeth's speech in Act 2, scene 2, of William Shakespeare's *Macbeth* (1606) is arguably a purple patch:

> Whence is that knocking?
> How is 't with me when every noise appalls me?
> What hands are here? Ha! They pluck out mine eyes!
> Will all great Neptune's ocean wash this blood
> Clean from my hand? No, this my hand will rather
> The multitudinous seas incarnadine°   *make red*
> Making the green one red.

The following passage from D. H. Lawrence's essay "Poetry of the Present" (1918) might also be considered a purple patch:

> Let me feel the mud and heavens in my lotus. Let me feel the heavy, silting, sucking mud, the spinning of sky winds. Let me feel them both in purest contact, the nakedness of sucking weight, nakedly passing radiance. Give me nothing fixed, set, static. Don't give me the infinite or the eternal: nothing of infinity, nothing of eternity. Give me the still, white seething, the incandescence and the coldness of the incarnate moment: the moment, the quick of all change and haste and opposition: the moment, the immediate present, the Now.

pyrrhic (dibrach): A **metrical foot** of **poetry** that consists of two unstressed syllables (˘˘). Some critics do not consider the pyrrhic to be a true foot, which they maintain requires the presence of at least one **stressed** syllable. Other critics who do not consider the pyrrhic to be a true foot object on opposite grounds. These critics argue that the prevailing meter of a poem invariably renders one of the two syllables stronger than the other, thereby making that syllable stressed and the foot either **trochaic** or **iambic.** The pyrrhic is relatively uncommon in English and virtually nonexistent as the base, or predominant, foot of a poem, occurring instead as an occasional foot substituting for some other kind of foot that serves as the basis for the poem's metrical pattern.

EXAMPLE: The thirty-eighth **sonnet** from Elizabeth Barrett Browning's *Sonnets from the Portuguese* (1850) contains a pyrrhic foot followed by four iambic feet (˘´):

> Ĭ hăve beĕn próud ănd sáid, 'Mў lóve, mў ówn.'

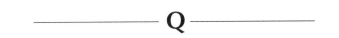

Q

quantitative verse: Verse whose **meter** is based on quantity, that is, the relative time it takes to pronounce a particular syllable in a poetic line. Various combinations of long and short syllables may make up a **foot** of quantitative verse. The meter of choice for **classical** Greek and Roman poets, quantitative verse is often contrasted with **accentual-syllabic verse,** the meter of choice for poets writing in English. In accentual-syllabic verse, both the number of syllables and the number of **stressed** and unstressed syllables are relatively consistent from line to line.

Few poems composed in English employ meter based on quantity, though poets such as Edmund Spenser; Alfred, Lord Tennyson; and Samuel Taylor Coleridge experimented with quantitative verse form. Quantitative verse is extremely difficult to sustain in English because of the strongly **accented** nature of the English language and the difficulty of determining the duration of its syllables.

quatrain: A **stanza** containing four lines. The term is also used, though less commonly, to refer to a four-line poem. No **rhyme scheme** need exist in a quatrain, but the following rhyme schemes are common: *abcb* (the **ballad stanza**), *abba*, and *abab*. The quatrain is the most common stanzaic form in English-language poetry.

EXAMPLES: Many of William Blake's *Songs of Innocence and of Experience* (1789–94) are composed in quatrains. In "Infant Sorrow," each quatrain exhibits an *aabb* rhyme scheme:

> My mother groan'd! my father wept.
> Into the dangerous world I leapt.
> Helpless, naked, piping loud;
> Like a fiend hid in a cloud.
>
> Struggling in my father's hands,
> Striving against my swaddling bands;
> Bound and weary I thought best
> To sulk upon my mother's breast.

Alfred, Lord Tennyson's **elegy** for Arthur Henry Hallam, "In Memoriam A. H. H." (1850), is written in quatrains with an *abba* rhyme scheme:

> Ring out the old, ring in the new,
> Ring happy bells, across the snow:
> The year is going, let him go;
> Ring out the false, ring in the true.

Josephine Miles often wrote in unrhyming quatrains. The following one is from her poem "Belief" (1955):

Mother said to call her if the H-bomb exploded
And I said I would, and it about did
When Louis my brother robbed a service station
And lay cursing on the oily cement in handcuffs.

queer theory: A contemporary approach to literature and culture that
assumes sexual identities are fluid, not fixed, and that critiques **gender** and
sexuality as they are commonly conceived in Western culture. Queer theorists, like **gender critics,** maintain that gender is a social **construct** — that
is, that masculinity and femininity are patterns of behavior rather than natural or innate. Those who embrace Jacques Lacan's **psychoanalytic theory**
have even contested the distinction between gender and biological sex, arguing that anatomical **signifiers** are themselves cultural products belonging
to the realm of what Lacan termed the **Symbolic.** As Judith Butler has written in *Gender Trouble* (1990), "perhaps this construct called 'sex' is as culturally constructed as gender; indeed, perhaps it was always already gender, with the consequences that the distinction between sex and gender
turns out to be no distinction at all."

Queer theorists further contend that sexuality, like gender, is socially
constructed, arguing that the **binary opposition** heterosexual / homosexual
is as much a product of culture and its institutions as the opposition masculinity / femininity. They also view sexuality as performative — that is, as
a process involving signifying *acts* (that may or may not be consistent)
rather than an externally defined "normative" identity. The AIDS epi-
demic, queer theorists note, tragically highlights the performative nature of
sexuality and the permeability of the "line" separating gay and straight
populations.

The term *queer* — long used pejoratively to refer to homosexuals, especially male homosexuals — has been reclaimed and embraced by queer theorists, who use it with respect to both sexual relations and critical practice.
When used to refer to sexual relations, *queer* encompasses any practice or
behavior that a person engages in without reproductive aims and without
regard for social or economic considerations. As a critical term, *queer*
refers to writings that question generally accepted associations and identities involving sex, gender, and sexuality. As queer theorist Annamarie
Jagose writes in her book *Queer Theory* (1996), "queer is less an identity
than a critique of identity." Queer theorists seek to keep the term *queer*
flexible and resist the tendency to turn it into a "pride word" simply meaning homosexual. Seeking to avoid the normalization of *queer,* David
Halperin wrote in 1995, "*There is nothing in particular to which it necessarily refers.*"

Queer theory is an outgrowth of gender criticism and, more specifically,
of **gay and lesbian criticism.** In fact, the term *queer theory* is generally
credited to gender theorist Teresa de Lauretis, who in 1992 edited a special
issue of the journal *differences* entitled *Queer Theory: Lesbian and Gay*

Sexualities. Queer theory diverges from gender theory, however, in its emphasis on sexuality and in its broader insistence that the multifaceted and fluid character of identity negates efforts to categorize people on the basis of any one characteristic. Queer theory differs from gay and lesbian criticism in that its approach is more **theoretically** oriented than **text**-centered and insofar as some gay and lesbian critics advance an **essentialist** view of sexuality—namely, that sexuality is biologically determined rather than socially constructed. Moreover, unlike practitioners of gay and lesbian criticism, who tend to assume that sexual identity defines textual **representations,** queer theorists argue that representations define the contours of sexual identity. Like most gender, gay, and lesbian critics, however, queer theorists acknowledge and draw on the work of French philosophical historian Michel Foucault, poet-critic Adrienne Rich, gender critic Judith Butler, and gender critic Eve Kosofsky Sedgwick.

In his *Histoire de la sexualité* (*The History of Sexuality*) (1976), Foucault suggested that the Western conception of homosexuality was largely an invention of the nineteenth century—as was heterosexuality, its "normal" opposite. (Before that time, people spoke of "acts of sodomy" but not of homosexual *persons*.) By historicizing sexuality, Foucault made it possible to argue that all the categories and assumptions that operate when we think about sex, sexual difference, gender, and sexuality are the products of cultural **discourses** and thus social, rather than natural, artifacts. For example, Halperin has recently argued in *Saint Foucault: Toward a Gay Hagiography* (1995) that "homosexual" is not a natural category but, rather, "a discursive, and homophobic, construction."

More than a decade earlier, Rich had extended Foucault's theories in an essay entitled "Compulsory Heterosexuality and Lesbian Existence" (1983), in which she claimed that "heterosexuality [is] a beachhead of male dominance" that, "like motherhood, needs to be recognized and studied as a political institution." Subsequently, Butler argued in *Gender Trouble: Feminism and the Subversion of Identity* (1990) that all sexual differences are culturally produced and thus indistinguishable from gender. Sedgwick, in her book *Between Men: English Literature and Male Homosocial Desire* (1985), adapted **feminist criticism** to analyze relationships between men, between male **characters** in literary works, and, most importantly, between gender and sexuality. She later specifically critiqued the gender category "sexual orientation" in *Epistemology of the Closet* (1990), stating that "it is a rather amazing fact that, of the very many dimensions along which the genital activity of one person can be differentiated from another..., precisely one, the gender of object choice, emerged...and has remained...*the* dimension denoted by the now ubiquitous category of 'sexual orientation.'"

Building on these insights, queer theorists have questioned the "solidarity" and "pride" aspects of homosexual liberation movements. They argue, among other things, that lesbians and gays should not be grouped together given that their separate histories are defined by gender differences. For example, lesbians, as women, have been more affected than gay men by pay discrimination issues. Moreover, queer theorists have taken the position that liberation movements that are specifically gay or specifically lesbian ultimately encourage the development of new sets of gender-based norms that divide more than they unite.

Queer theorists are wary of identity politics, believing as they do that identity is fluid and that categorization on the basis of a single shared characteristic is inappropriate. They question, for example, whether African American lesbians really have more in common with white, upper-middle-class lesbians than they do with heterosexual African American women. Queer theorists have also argued that identity politics tend to reinforce a web of heterosexual and heterosexist "norms." As such, some have even questioned whether it is wise to view "coming out" as the assumption of a "transformative identity."

Queer theorists, who favor coalition politics over what they view as exclusionary identity politics, seek to destabilize popular conceptions of normality and sexuality and to undermine the heterosexual / homosexual opposition. To this end, they focus attention on those who do not easily fit into the socially constructed categories of gender and sexuality (such as bisexuals, transvestites, transgendered persons, and transsexuals) and explore from a nonjudgmental perspective behaviors and practices that are often considered deviant (such as fetishes, autoeroticism, and sadomasochism). They ultimately aim to show that representations — whether in novels, movies, ads, or other media — are culturally dependent and fallible, not some sort of received or **objective** truth. By "queering the text" — by revealing within cultural representations the signs of what Rich has called "compulsory heterosexuality" and by showing that meaning is the relative product of prevailing discourses — queer theorists seek to show that the truly "queer" thing is how quick we are to label, categorize, and judge.

The tenets of queer theory are reflected in numerous works of literary and **cultural criticism.** Early examples include Thomas Yingling's *Hart Crane and the Homosexual Text* (1990), Jonathan Goldberg's *Sodometries* (1992), and Michael Moon's *Disseminating Whitman* (1993). Other critics whose analyses are informed by queer theory include Lauren Berlant, Richard Bozorth, Joseph Bristow, Christopher Craft, Lisa Duggan, Elizabeth Freeman, Christopher Lane, Jeff Nunokawa, and Michael Warner. Berlant and Freeman's "Queer Nationality," which appears in Berlant's collection *The Queen of America Goes to Washington City: Essays on Sex and Censorship* (1997), discusses the ways in which a national network of gay and lesbian affinity groups have sought to use everything from local rituals to mass-culture spectacles to alter America's self-perception as a heterosexual nation. Bozorth's book *Auden's Games of Knowledge: Poetry and the Meanings of Homosexuality* (2001) argues that Auden's poetry addresses and reflects the psychological and political meanings of same-sex desire. Given queer theory's view of identity as fluid rather than fixed, queer theorists such as Mimi Nguyen have even suggested that the approach readily lends itself to the "queering" of other socially constructed categories such as **race** and **class.**

See also **gay and lesbian criticism, gender criticism.**

quest romance: See **romance.**

R

race (and literary studies): Although anthropologists and biologists recognize physical variation across human populations, race, as we commonly think of it, has been shown by many of these scientists and other theorists to be a social or cultural **construct.** First, more variation generally exists within a given race than exists, on the average, between racial groups. Furthermore, race as we commonly think of it often involves cultural rather than biological differences and characteristics ranging from diet to music to dress to religion. Finally, race is to a great extent a social construct because, over the tens of thousands of years of human history, migration and the subsequent biological mixing of races have made racial categorization an extremely arbitrary business. Historically, different states in the United States have used very different racial percentages (ratios of black-to-white ancestry, for example) in determining the racial identity of citizens for census or other purposes. A much more startling example of race as a social construct is the fact that immigrants from the Indian subcontinent are said to be "black" in Great Britain but not in North America, where the term is reserved for people of African descent.

The cultural construction of race commonly involves the practice of stereotyping as biologically "natural" or "typical" what are in fact the cultural characteristics — eating habits, attitudes toward time, and so on — of persons viewed as outside of, and therefore as **Other,** by an **ideologically** dominant group. Thus, it is hardly surprising that the constructs or fictions of race respond to, reinforce, and at some level are responsible for racism — the destructive devaluation of one cultural group by another based on supposed (but in fact nonexistent or insignificant) differences.

Literary critics, particularly those practicing **cultural criticism,** have shown that race, the social and cultural construction of race, and racism are important to the study of literature. Literary **texts,** whether written by authors in the racial majority or minority, attest to and may effectively critique the racial and racist attitudes prevalent in a given culture at a given time. Furthermore, literature is among the most powerful forms of **discourse** in which race is constructed and racial or racist attitudes are expressed and perpetuated. Readers also bring their own racial and racist attitudes to any work, which necessarily affect their interpretation of the **text.**

Finally, because racial constructs result in very different experiences for the various groups kept distinct by racial stereotyping, race — like **class** and **gender** — must be taken into account when we speak or write about literary texts, especially when discussing texts produced by writers representing different racial and cultural groups. One can hardly imagine a race-blind critical comparison of Frederick Douglass's *Narrative of the Life of*

Frederick Douglass, An American Slave, Written by Himself (1845) and another famous nineteenth-century American text that deals with race and racism, Mark Twain's *Adventures of Huckleberry Finn* (1884). With regard to more recent texts, the noted African American scholar and critic Henry Louis Gates has pointed out that black writers until recently have had to fuse black **linguistic** and cultural **conventions** and traditions with those of the white Western literary **canon** in order to reach a wide audience and avoid marginalization.

reader-oriented criticism: See **reader-response criticism.**

reader-response criticism: Reader-response criticism encompasses various approaches to literature that explore and seek to explain the diversity (and often divergence) of readers' responses to literary works. Reader-response critics raise **theoretical** questions about whether our responses to a work are the same as its meaning(s), whether a work can have as many meanings as we have responses to it, and whether some responses are more valid than others. They also provide us with models that aid our understanding of **texts** and the reading process. Adena Rosmarin, for instance, suggested in 1987 that a literary text may be likened to an incomplete work of sculpture: to see it fully, we must complete it imaginatively but also responsibly, taking into account what exists.

Reader-response critics share not only questions but also goals and strategies. They show that a work gives readers something to do; they also describe what the reader does by way of response. To achieve these goals, the critic may make any of a number of what Steven Mailloux calls "moves" in his essay "Learning to Read: Interpretation and Reader-Response Criticism" (1979). A reader-response critic may cite direct references to reading in the text being analyzed in order to justify the focus on reading and show that the world of the text is continuous with the reader's world. Alternatively, the critic may show how other nonreading situations in the text nonetheless mirror the reader's situation. (Mailloux cites as an example reader-response critic Stanley Fish's observation that, in Book 11 of John Milton's *Paradise Lost* [1667], Michael's teaching of Adam parallels Milton's efforts to instruct the reader throughout the work.) Finally, the reader-response critic may demonstrate that the reader's response is analogous to the story's action or **conflict.** For instance, in his essay "On the Value of *Hamlet*" (1969), Stephen Booth calls *Hamlet* (1602) the **tragic** account of "an audience that cannot make up its mind."

Although reader-response criticism emerged in the United States in the 1970s, it is in one respect as old as the foundations of Western culture. The ancient Greeks and Romans tended to view literature as **rhetoric,** a means of making an audience react in a certain way. Although their focus was more on rhetorical strategies and devices than on the reader's (or listener's) response to those methods, the ancients by no means left the audience out of the literary equation.

In the twentieth century, several critics who wrote long before 1970 held attitudes that anticipate the thinking of reader-response theorists. One such critic, I. A. Richards, is usually associated with **formalism,** a supposedly **objective,** text-centered approach to literature that reader-response critics of the 1970s roundly attacked. Unlike his formalist contemporaries, who would have deplored the fact that readers' personal situations affect their readings, Richards argued in *Practical Criticism* (1929) that readers' feelings and experiences provide a kind of reality check, a way of testing the authenticity of emotions and events represented in literary works.

A decade later, Louise M. Rosenblatt published *Literature as Exploration* (1938). In that seminal book, Rosenblatt began developing a theory of reading that blurs the boundary between reader and text, subject and object. In a 1969 essay entitled "Towards a Transactional Theory of Reading," she summed up her position as follows: "a poem is what the reader lives through under the guidance of the text and experiences as relevant to the text." Recognizing that many critics would reject this definition, Rosenblatt wrote: "The idea that a *poem* presupposes a *reader* actively involved with a *text* is particularly shocking to those seeking to emphasize the objectivity of their interpretations."

Rosenblatt implicitly and generally refers to formalists (the most influential of whom are **the New Critics**) when she speaks of supposedly objective interpreters shocked by the notion that a "*poem*" is cooperatively produced by a "*reader*" and a "*text*." Formalists spoke of "the poem itself," the "concrete work of art," the "real poem." They had no interest in what a work of literature makes a reader "live through." In fact, in *The Verbal Icon* (1954), William K. Wimsatt and Monroe C. Beardsley used the term **affective fallacy** to define as erroneous the very idea that a reader's response is relevant to the meaning of a literary work.

Stanley Fish, whose early work is seen by some as marking the true beginning of contemporary reader-response criticism, also took issue with the tenets of formalism. In "Literature in the Reader: Affective Stylistics" (1970), he argued that any school of criticism that sees a literary work as an object, claiming to describe what it is and never what it does, misconstrues the very essence of literature and reading. Literature exists and signifies when it is read, Fish suggests, and its force is an affective force. Furthermore, reading is a temporal process, not a spatial one as formalists assume when they step back and survey the literary work as if it were an object spread out before them. Formalists may find elegant patterns in the texts they examine, but they fail to consider that the work appears very different to a reader in the act of reading, turning the pages and being moved, or affected, by each word. Fish then quotes a line from *Paradise Lost*, a line that refers to Satan and the other fallen angels, to illustrate his point: "Nor did they not perceive their evil plight." Whereas more traditional critics might say that the line means "They did perceive their evil plight," Fish relates the uncertain movement of the reader's mind to that half-satisfying interpretation and argues that this very uncertainty as to what "they" perceive is part of the line's meaning.

The emphasis on how reading affects readers (and how they respond) pervades the writings of most, if not all, reader-response critics. Stephen Booth, whose book entitled *An Essay on Shakespeare's Sonnets* (1969) greatly influenced Fish, describes the "reading experience that results" from a "multiplicity of organizations" in a **sonnet** by William Shakespeare. Sometimes these organizations don't make complete sense, Booth points out, and sometimes they even seem curiously contradictory. But that is precisely what interests reader-response critics, who, unlike formalists, are at least as interested in fragmentary, inconclusive, and even unfinished texts as in polished, unified works. For it is the reader's struggle to make sense of a challenging work that reader-response critics seek to describe.

German critic Wolfgang Iser has described that struggle in his books *The Implied Reader: Patterns of Communication in Prose Fiction from Bunyan to Beckett* (1974) and *The Act of Reading: A Theory of Aesthetic Response* (1976). Iser argues that texts contain **gaps** (or *blanks*) that powerfully affect the reader, who must explain them, connect what they separate, and create in his or her mind aspects of a work that aren't *in* the text but that the text incites. As Iser puts it in *The Implied Reader,* the "unwritten aspects" of a story "draw the reader into the action" and "lead him to shade in the many outlines suggested by the given situations." Such "outlines" influence how the **implied reader** subsequently reads the text.

In *Self-Consuming Artifacts: The Experience of Seventeenth-Century Literature* (1972), Fish reveals his preference for literature that makes readers work at making meaning. He contrasts two kinds of literary presentation. He uses the phrase *rhetorical presentation* to describe literature that reflects and reinforces opinions that readers already hold; *dialectical presentation* refers to works that prod and provoke. **Dialectical** texts, rather than presenting an opinion as if it were truth, challenge readers to discover truths on their own. A dialectical text, or self-consuming artifact, may lack the symmetry that formalist critics seek, containing contradictory units rather than a unified argument. Whereas a critic of another school might advance a contorted explanation to render the units coherent, the reader-response critic describes how the reader deals with the sudden twists that characterize the dialectical text. Readers may, for instance, refer to earlier passages and see them in an entirely new light.

With the redefinition of literature as something that only exists meaningfully in the mind of the reader, with the redefinition of the literary work as a catalyst of mental events, comes a redefinition of the reader. No longer is the reader the passive recipient of those ideas that an author has planted in a text. "The reader is *active*," Rosenblatt insists. Fish makes the same point in "Literature in the Reader": "reading is . . . something *you do*." Iser, in focusing critical interest on the gaps in texts, on what is not expressed, similarly redefines the reader as an active maker of meaning.

The reader is also "the *informed* reader," Fish argues in *Self-Consuming Artifacts.* The informed reader (whom Fish sometimes calls "the *intended* reader") is someone who is "sufficiently experienced as a reader to have internalized the properties of literary discourses, including everything from the most local of devices (figures of speech, etc.) to whole genres." The informed reader also possesses the "semantic knowledge" (knowledge of idioms, for instance) assumed by the text.

Other reader-response critics define the reader differently. Wayne Booth uses the phrase "the implied reader" to mean the reader "created by the work." Like Booth, Iser employs the term "the implied reader," but he also uses "the educated reader" when he refers to what Fish called the "informed reader." Others, like Gérard Genette and Gerald Prince, prefer to speak of "the narratee," which Susan R. Suleiman has defined as "the necessary counterpart of a given narrator, that is, the person or figure who receives a narrative."

Jonathan Culler, who has criticized Fish for his sketchy definition of the informed reader, set out in *Structuralist Poetics* (1975) to describe the educated or "competent" reader, by which he meant the competent reader of "literature," a reader who employs those reading **conventions** that make possible the understanding of poems and novels. (By "literature," Culler meant what schools and colleges mean when they speak of literature as being part of the curriculum.) Subsequently, critics such as Mailloux have pointed out that definitions of literary competence inevitably reflect the prevailing **ideology** (the opinions, attitudes, and practices of socially dominant groups and institutions).

Although Fish, following Rosenblatt's lead, contrasted reader-response criticism with formalism and, more specifically, the New Criticism, the formalism of the 1950s and early 1960s had a great deal in common with the reader-response criticism of the late 1960s and early 1970s. This has become increasingly obvious with the rise of subsequent critical approaches whose practitioners have proved less interested in the **close reading** of texts than in the way literature represents, reproduces, and resists prevailing ideologies concerning **class, race, gender,** and **sexuality.** In an essay entitled "The Turns of Reader-Response Criticism" (1990), Mailloux suggests that hindsight reveals a surprising degree of similarity between formalism's close reading and Fish's early practice of analyzing the **affective stylistics** of a text.

Since the mid-1970s, however, reader-response criticism (once commonly referred to as the "School of Fish") has diversified and taken on a variety of new forms, some of which truly are incommensurate with formalism, with its considerable respect for the integrity and power of the text. For instance, **subjectivists** like David Bleich, Norman Holland, and Robert Crosman have viewed the reader's response not as one "guided" by the text but rather as one motivated by deep-seated, personal, psychological needs. As Holland put it, readers find their own "identity theme" in texts; in "UNITY IDENTITY TEXT SELF" (1975), he argued that as readers we use "the literary work to symbolize and finally to replicate ourselves. We work out through the text our own characteristic patterns of desire." Subjective critics often find themselves confronted with the following question: If all interpretation is a function of private, psychological identity, then why have so many readers interpreted, say, William Shakespeare's *Hamlet* (1602) in the same way? Different subjective critics have answered the question differently. Holland has said that common identity **themes** exist, such as those involving an **oedipal** fantasy.

Meanwhile Fish, who in the late 1970s moved away from reader-response criticism as he had initially helped define it, came up with a different answer to the question about why different readers tend to read the same works in the same way. His answer, rather than involving common individual identity themes, involved common cultural identity. In "Interpreting the Variorum" (1976), Fish argues that shared "interpretive strategies," which "exist prior to the act of reading and therefore determine the shape of what is read," are held in common by **interpretive communities** such as the one composed by American college students reading a novel as a class assignment. In developing the model of interpretive communities, Fish truly made the break with formalist predecessors, becoming in the process something of a social, **structuralist,** reader-response critic. He has subsequently been engaged in studying reading communities and their interpretive conventions in order to understand the conditions that gave rise to a work's intelligibility.

Fish's shift in focus is in many ways typical of changes that have taken place within the field of reader-response criticism — a field that, because of those changes, is increasingly being referred to as *reader-oriented criticism.* Less and less common are critical analyses examining the transaction between the text and its individual reader. Increasingly, reader-oriented critics are investigating reading communities, as the reader-oriented **cultural critic** Janet Radway has done in her study of female readers of romance paperbacks entitled *Reading the Romance* (1984). They are also studying the changing reception of literary works across time, as Mailloux has done in his **pragmatic** readings of American literature in *Interpretive Conventions* (1982) and *Rhetorical Power* (1989). Some critics, including Mailloux and Jane Tompkins, identify themselves as practitioners of *reader-reception criticism,* an approach to texts generally viewed as a type or subset of reader-response or reader-oriented criticism.

An important catalyst of this gradual change and of the development of reception criticism was the work of Hans Robert Jauss, a colleague of Iser's whose historically oriented **reception theory** (unlike Iser's theory of the implied reader) was not available in English book form until the early 1960s. Rather than focusing on the implied, informed, or intended reader, Jauss examined actual past readers. In *Toward an Aesthetics of Reception* (1982), he argued that the reception of a work or author depends upon the reading public's "horizons of expectations," noting that, in the morally conservative climate of mid-nineteenth century France, *Madame Bovary*

(1857) was literally put on trial. Its author, Gustave Flaubert, was accused of glorifying adultery in passages representing the **protagonist's** fevered delirium through **free indirect discourse,** a mode of **narration** in which the thoughts and attitudes of a **character** almost seem to be those of the author, since they are reported to the reader by an **omniscient, third-person narrator.**

As readers have become more sophisticated and tolerant, the popularity and reputation of *Madame Bovary* have soared. Sometimes, of course, changes in a reading public's horizons of expectations cause a work to be less well received over time. As American reception critics influenced by Jauss have shown, Mark Twain's *Adventures of Huckleberry Finn* (1884) has elicited an increasingly ambivalent reaction from a reading public increasingly sensitive to demeaning racial stereotypes and racist language. The rise of feminism has prompted a downward revaluation of everything from Andrew Marvell's "To His Coy Mistress" (1681) to D. H. Lawrence's *Women in Love* (1920).

Some reader-oriented **feminist critics,** such as Judith Fetterley, Patrocinio Schweickart, and Monique Wittig, have challenged the reader to become what Fetterley calls "the resisting reader." Arguing that literature written by men tends, in Schweickart's terms, to "immasculate" women, they have adopted strategies of reading that involve substituting masculine for feminine pronouns and male for female characters in order to expose the sexism inscribed in **patriarchal** texts. Other feminists, such as Nancy K. Miller in *Subject to Change* (1988), have suggested that there may be **essential** differences between the way women and men read and write.

That suggestion, however, has prompted considerable controversy. A number of **gender critics** whose work is oriented toward readers and reading have admitted that there is such a thing as "reading like a woman" (or man) but have also agreed with Peggy Kamuf that such forms of reading, like gender itself, are cultural rather than natural constructs. **Gay and lesbian critics,** such as Wayne Koestenbaum, have argued that sexualities have been similarly constructed within and by social **discourse** and that there is a homosexual way of reading.

Some students of contemporary critical practice have concluded that reader-oriented theory has been absorbed by feminist, gender, gay, and lesbian theory. Others, like Elizabeth Freund, have suggested that **deconstruction** has taken over the reader-oriented approach. In fact, however, there are still critics who would define their approach as primarily reader-oriented, although their work has also been heavily influenced by other approaches, namely, **the new historicism** and cultural criticism.

Two critics whose work exemplifies this contemporary version of reader-oriented criticism are Mailloux and Peter Rabinowitz. In *Before Reading: Narrative Conventions and the Politics of Interpretation* (1987), Rabinowitz sets forth four conventions or rules of reading, which he calls the rules of notice, signification, configuration, and coherence — rules telling us which parts of a **narrative** are important, which details have a reliable secondary or special meaning, which fit into which familiar patterns, and how stories fit together as a whole. He then analyzes the misreadings and misjudgments of critics and shows that politics governs the way in which those rules are applied and broken. In subsequent critical essays, Rabinowitz shows how a society's ideological assumptions about gender, race, and class determine the way in which artistic works are perceived and evaluated.

Mailloux, who calls his approach "rhetorical reception theory" or "rhetorical hermeneutics," takes a similar tack, insofar as he describes the political contexts of (mis)interpretation. In the essay "Misreading as a Historical Act" (1993), he shows that a mid-nineteenth-century review by protofeminist Margaret Fuller of the *Narrative of the Life of Frederick Douglass, An American Slave, Written by Himself* (1845) seems to be a misreading until we situate it "within the cultural conversation of the 'Bible politics' of 1845." Woven through Mailloux's essay on Douglass and Fuller are philosophical pauses in which we are reminded, in various subtle ways, that all reading (including Mailloux's and our own) is culturally situated and likely to seem like misreading someday. Reading is, according to Mailloux, contingent upon history, affected by politics, and to a great extent defined and conditioned by the institutions (churches, schools, colleges, and universities) in which texts are regularly read and interpreted.

Real, the: Along with the **Imaginary** and **Symbolic orders,** one of the three orders of **subjectivity** according to **psychoanalytic** theorist and critic Jacques Lacan. The Real is the intractable and substantial world that resists and exceeds interpretation. The Real cannot be imagined, **symbolized,** or known directly; it constantly eludes our efforts to name it. Death, gravity, and the physicality of objects are examples of the Real, but the words signifying these realities ultimately and utterly fail to explain or make sense of their apparent inevitability. Because the Real cannot be known, imagined, symbolized, or named, it challenges both the Imaginary and Symbolic orders. The Real is fundamentally **Other,** the mark of the divide between conscious and unconscious, and is signaled in language by **gaps,** slips, speechlessness, and the sense of the uncanny. The Real is not what we call "reality." It is the stumbling block of the Imaginary, which thinks it can "imagine" anything (including the Real), and of the Symbolic, which tries to bring the Real under its laws. The Real is frightening; we try to tame it with the law of order, language, and differentiation — that is, with the law of the **phallus,** a culturally prevalent law of referentiality that takes the male sign as its ordering principle and determines an individual's entrance into the Symbolic — and call it "reality." The Real, however, exposes the "phallacy" of the law of the phallus, revealing both the Symbolic order's reliance on the male **sign** as a referent and demonstrating the inappropriateness of such reliance in a world where meaning and comprehension rest in gaps and on the margins of what we perceive. The concept of the Real — like Lacan's schema and terminology more generally — has proven useful to psychoanalytic critics in their analyses of language, literature, and the laws governing expression and interpretation.

See also **Imaginary order, Symbolic order.**

realism: (1) Broadly speaking, a term that can be applied to the accurate depiction in any literary work of the everyday life of a place or period. When the term *realistic* is applied to works that predate the nineteenth century, however, it usually refers more specifically to a writer's accuracy in portraying the speech and behavior of a **character** or characters from a low socioeconomic **class.** (2) A literary movement that developed in the latter half of the nineteenth century in America, England, and France in reaction to the excesses of **romanticism.** Writers associated with this movement tried to "write reality."

Realism differs from **romanticism** particularly in its emphasis on an **objective** presentation of details and events rather than a **subjective** concentration on personal feelings, perceptions, and imaginings of various characters. Realists also reject the idealized presentations, imaginative and exotic **settings,** and improbable **plot** twists characteristic of the **romance.** Realists often rely heavily on **local color,** deliberately attempting to portray faithfully the customs, speech, dress, and living and working conditions of their chosen locale. Realists also stress **characterization** as a critical (if not *the* critical) element of a literary work.

Realism should also be distinguished from **naturalism,** with which it is sometimes confused. Although naturalists' emphasis on the presentation of **concrete** details renders their fiction "realistic," naturalism cannot properly be classified even as a subtype of realism because of the deterministic outlook of its proponents. Naturalists view all individuals as being at the mercy of biological and socioeconomic forces, whereas realists hold that humans have a certain degree of free will that they can exercise to affect their situations.

Realists (especially nineteenth-century realists) often espouse democracy and pragmatism. They implicitly express these beliefs by choosing to depict lower- and middle-class subjects and characters more often than the noble ones associated with **classicism** or the fanciful ones characteristic of romanticism. Many early American realists depicted everyday life and the common person with a certain affection and respect; after the Civil War, however, a disillusioned strain developed in realistic fiction that portrayed ordinary men and women as having their share of petty vices.

Many realists, American and otherwise, have also embraced what might be termed *psychological realism* as they have turned from emphasizing the accuracy of external detail to reporting internal detail, the thought processes of the human mind or consciousness. Some authors, such as Virginia Woolf, have taken the reporting of internal detail to its extreme manifestation, using **stream-of-consciousness narration** to convey to the reader the jumble of thoughts and sensory impressions that flows unremittingly through the human mind.

Variants of realism that have developed in the twentieth century include **magic realism** and **socialist realism.** Magic realists mix realistic and **fantastic** elements; in fact, magic realists arguably use such hallmarks of realism as its emphasis on detail to make their presentations of the dreamlike, **mythic,** or otherwise fantastic more plausible to readers. Socialist realists employ the techniques associated especially with nineteenth-century realism but solely in the service of the proletarian cause. Early practitioners of socialist realism believed that, in order to appeal to most readers, works should depict the lives of average working-class citizens. After 1934, however, when socialist realism became the official form of the Soviet Union, it ceased to be a means of connecting with the masses and instead became chiefly a means of propagating doctrinally "correct" thinking.

Realists include Jane Austen, Honoré de Balzac, George Eliot, Gustave Flaubert, William Dean Howells, Henrik Ibsen, Henry James, Mark Twain, and Edith Wharton. Certain poems by Robert Browning, Walt Whitman, and Carl Sandburg can be referred to as realistic poems insofar as they capture real people, places, or situations by using an almost prosaic style. Pre-nineteenth-century writers who are generally realistic in their outlooks and depictions of life include Geoffrey Chaucer, William Shakespeare, and Henry Fielding.

realistic novel: A type of **novel** that depicts **characters, settings,** and events in accordance with reality or, at least, in accordance with reality as most readers perceive it. Realistic novelists seek to write fictional **narratives** that present a plausible world. To achieve this goal, they typically include a variety of **concrete** details meant to ground their story lines in human experience.

Realistic novelists emphasize **characterization.** They typically present well-developed, **round characters** whose experiences and interactions with other characters could occur in real life and situate these characters in a specific cultural group, locale, and historical era. Perhaps most importantly, they establish convincing **motivation** for the thoughts, emotions, and actions of the characters as well as for the turns and twists of the **plot.** A realistic novel might depict the daily drudgery of a working-class girl forced to labor twelve hours a day in an English garment factory to help support her family, or it might depict the plush and lavish life of the Hungarian count who owns the factory and spends his days hosting society luncheons or playing croquet on the well-tended lawns of his English estate. Whichever scenario a realistic writer adopts, he or she will strive to plausibly present the characters, activity, and milieu therein.

The realistic novel is most often contrasted with the **romance,** which eschews realistic verisimilitude in favor of fanciful or **fantastic** depictions. Nineteenth-century **realism,** in particular, developed largely in reaction to the idealized, **conventional** subjects, **themes,** and modes of **representation** associated with **romanticism.**

EXAMPLES: George Eliot's *The Mill on the Floss* (1860), Henry James's *The Portrait of a Lady* (1881), John Steinbeck's *Tortilla Flat* (1935). More recent examples of the realistic novel include John Fowles's *Daniel Martin* (1977) and Joyce Carol Oates's *Because It Is Bitter, and Because It Is My Heart* (1990). Other contemporary authors who draw on the tradition of the realistic novel include Margaret Drabble and Naguib Mahfouz.

Realistic Period (in American literature): A literary epoch spanning the years 1865 through 1900. In the wake of the devastation of the Civil War, forces including capitalist industrialization; Reconstruction; northern urbanization; and rapid advances in communications, science, and transportation contributed to a great change in American literature as well as American society and politics. The work of many writers continued to exhibit a **romantic** strain throughout much of this period, but **realism** unquestionably dominated the national literary scene by the epoch's end. Nevertheless, much of the work of the Realistic Period drew on both the romantic and realistic traditions. So-called romantic realists, for instance, essentially presented their subject matter accurately but wrote only about subject matter that was pleasant or positive.

Unlike romantic writers, who emphasized emotion, **imagination,** and individuality, realistic authors aimed to present life as it really is, in its nobility as well as its banality. Although realistic authors sought to represent their subject matter in an unidealized, un**sentimentalized** way, they did not set out to emphasize the negative, the distorted, or the ugly. Rather, they sought to create truthful portraits, unlike **naturalistic** writers who depicted life with a decidedly deterministic, pessimistic bent. Novelist William Dean Howells outlined the tenets of realism in a book entitled *Criticism and Fiction* (1891).

Some realistic poets, such as Walt Whitman and Emily Dickinson, began writing during the **Romantic Period.** Others, such as Thomas Bailey Aldrich, Stephen Crane, Richard Hovey, Sidney Lanier, and Edwin Arlington Robinson, wrote entirely during the Realistic Period, though Aldrich and Hovey chiefly **imitated** the English romantics. Crane's poems, written in **free verse,** anticipate the twentieth-century experiments of Ezra Pound and the **Imagists.** Lanier experimented with **versification** by introducing musical **meter;** he is one of many writers of the Realistic Period whose romantic leanings make his work hard to categorize strictly.

The Realistic Period was also a high water mark for the novel; aside from Howells, authors include Charles W. Chesnutt, Crane, Henry James, Mark Twain, and Edith Wharton. The works of these authors reflect some turbulence and disillusionment but nothing on the order of the pessimistic, naturalistic works that began appearing in the early 1900s. Crane was perhaps the realistic novelist whose work most anticipated naturalism, as evidenced by his best-known work, *The Red Badge of Courage* (1895). Twain, who began his career as a Western humorist, wrote a number of popular novels, such as *Adventures of Tom Sawyer* (1876) and *Adventures of Huckleberry Finn* (1884). He also worked with **satire,** however, disguising his merciless and cynical criticism under the guise of **historical romance** in works such as *A Connecticut Yankee in King Arthur's Court* (1889).

Local color literature (whether in the form of the novel, poem, or short story), which emphasizes the **setting,** customs, dialects, and other features peculiar to a given region of the country, also developed and thrived during the Realistic Period. Local color writers include Bret Harte, Sarah Orne Jewett, and Kate Chopin. Chopin, who wrote *The Awakening* (1899), is one of many female writers who have been "rehabilitated" by **feminist** scholars; as a result, her work is now viewed much more favorably and seriously than in times past.

Other prose writing of the Realistic Period includes the **historical novel,** works published in mass-circulation magazines, **short stories,** and **utopian literature.** Mark Twain's "The Celebrated Jumping Frog of Calaveras County" (1867) is one of the best-known short stories in American literature. Edward Bellamy's *Looking Backward: 2000–1887* (1888) is a utopian novel. (Although the appearance of utopian texts during an age of realism may seem to be **paradoxical,** the authors of such works in fact used some of the strategies of realism to make their depictions of the future convincing and credible.)

See **realism.**

reception theory: A type of **reader-response criticism** that examines the reception of a literary work — namely, how that work has been viewed by readers — since its initial publication. Hans Robert Jauss is the key figure associated with reception theory. Jauss used the term **aesthetic distance** to describe the difference between how a work was viewed when it was originally published and how that same work is viewed today. In his essay "Literary History as a Challenge to Literary Theory" (1967), he added a new twist to traditional reader-response criticism by exploring the diverse responses of readers over time to a given literary work; traditional reader-response critics tended to probe the individual contemporary reader's response. Jauss later elaborated on this new approach in his book *Aesthetic Experience and Literary Hermeneutics* (1977).

Jauss concurs with other reader-response critics in rejecting the theory that a single, correct meaning can be derived from any given **text,** noting that a text can be rationally interpreted in numerous ways. He argues that readers' responses are conditioned or even determined by the confluence and interplay of their "horizon of expectations" and textual elements that confirm or challenge those expectations. Jauss readily concedes that individual readers (with all of their idiosyncratic responses) contribute to the production of meaning in a text, but also notes that the elements of the text itself serve to limit and shape readers' interpretations. He thus strikes a balance between the contribution of the reader and that of the text in establishing meaning.

Unlike some traditional reader-response critics, however, Jauss emphasizes that readers' expectations change with the passage of time. These changing expectations, coupled with knowledge of (and reaction to) past readers' responses, combine to produce for each literary work a critical "tradition" that is continuously enriched and modified as new generations of readers emphasize different points or see old ones in a new light. Ultimately, Jauss proposes the existence of an active and evolving **dialogue** between texts and the continuous flow of readers over the course of time.

refrain: A line or lines that recur(s) throughout a **poem** or the **lyrics** of a song. The refrain may vary slightly but is generally exactly the same. It usually occurs at the end of a **stanza** or section but need not do so. When a refrain is intended to be repeated or sung by a group of people, it is called a **chorus.**

EXAMPLES: Every stanza but the last in Alfred, Lord Tennyson's "Mariana" (1830) concludes with the following two-line refrain:

> She said, "I am aweary, aweary,
> I would that I were dead."

The last stanza ends only slightly differently, with what is called an **incremental repetition** of the refrain:

> She wept, "I am aweary, aweary,
> O God, that I were dead!"

The refrain of Robert Burns's poem "Auld Lang Syne" (1896) is an entire stanza. Printed only once — after the first stanza and under the word *Chorus* — it is meant to be repeated after every subsequent stanza:

> CHORUS
> For auld lang syne, my dear,
>   For auld lang syne,
> We'll take a cup o' kindness yet,
>   For auld lang syne.

Each four-line refrain from the popular song "It's a Small World" (1963) by Richard and Robert Sherman **anaphoristically** repeats the song title three times. The theme song of the TV show *Friends* (The Rembrandts' "I'll Be There for You") similarly repeats the title in the refrain.

regular ode: See **Pindaric ode.**

Renaissance: Meaning "rebirth," a term referring to a transformation of Western culture that most scholars say took place after the **Medieval Period,** the so-called Dark Ages of European history. This transitional period, which bridges the **Middle Ages** and the beginnings of the modern world, began in fourteenth-century Italy; it did not reach England until well into the fifteenth century. Most scholars agree that the Renaissance ended during the latter half of the late seventeenth century.

A number of contemporary literary historians resist the concept of **peri-odicity,** the idea that there are distinct periods or ages within the literature of a nation or culture. They view historical and literary periods as arbitrary and misleading, questioning the usefulness of chronological categories such as "the Renaissance." For instance, some scholars have pointed out that the love of learning, literature, and the other arts associated with the Renaissance was significantly present during the Middle Ages, which, they argue, are improperly characterized by the adjective "dark." Others have challenged the validity of the Renaissance as a distinct epoch by erasing its other chronological boundary: the one separating it from the subsequent **Neoclassical Period.** After all, many features of Renaissance culture — renewed interest in the Greek and Roman **classics** and the reliance placed on human reason, to name only two — persisted into and similarly characterize this later period of "Enlightenment."

The Renaissance is probably more properly described as a period characterized by a changing *paradigm,* or ***epistémé*** — in this case, the shift in human perspective from a predominantly Christian to an increasingly secular point of view — than as a rebirth of Western culture. The importance of this change in emphasis, however, should hardly be downplayed, since humankind, rather than God, became the center of human interest as a result. And to the extent that this anthropocentric perspective characterized Greek and Roman culture, the Renaissance *did* amount to a demonstrable rebirth of a humanistic outlook that had characterized **classical** Graeco-Roman culture but that was uncommon during the Middle Ages.

Thus, although contemporary scholars correctly question the usefulness of specific categories and, indeed, the general concept of periodicity, the Renaissance is actually easier to defend as a distinct historical epoch and cultural category than are most other historical and literary periods. The changes associated with this cultural "rebirth" were so sweeping that they transcended national boundaries within Europe. Furthermore, they were revolutionary changes, altering the way in which life was lived and understood at least as profoundly as life has been altered in modern times by the development of nuclear physics and the invention of the computer. Aside from the general change from a theocentric to an anthropocentric perspective, these changes include: a cosmological revolution during which the Ptolemaic theory of an earth-centered universe was abandoned in favor of the Copernican understanding that the earth revolves around the sun; a dramatic schism within the Western (now known as Roman Catholic) Church that led to the Reformation and the rise of Protestantism; the discovery of the so-called New World; the emergence of nationalism and international commerce as we now know them and the rise of an imperialism that would culminate with Europe dominating the globe in the nineteenth century; and Johann Gutenberg's invention of the printing press, a device that made possible an unprecedented explosion of communication, knowledge, and scholarship.

The Renaissance was an age of scholarship even before the invention of movable type, which greatly facilitated book production. Beginning with Petrarch (Francesco Petrarca, 1304–74), classical scholars (later referred to as humanists) revitalized interest in the pagan authors and texts of ancient Greece and Rome, many of which were pre-Christian. By 1500, the works of Plato and Aristotle had been translated; within decades, Aristotle's ideas about biology, like Plato's philosophies of politics and love, were published in book form. Plato's writings about love in the *Symposium* (written during the fourth century B.C.), together with the **Platonic love** philosophies developed by subsequent Neoplatonist Roman philosophers such as Plotinus, proved particularly influential in the development of literature. They gave rise to a Renaissance **Neoplatonism** that colored a variety of works, including (and especially) Baldassare Castiglione's *Il cortegiano* (*The Courtier*) (1528), an early and extremely influential *courtesy book*. Courtesy books defined the relationships between aristocratic men and women specifically and the rules governing cultivated behavior (the behavior expected of the aristocratic class) generally.

With the development of printing and publication technology, courtesy books were published — first in Italy, then in France, and finally in England — throughout the sixteenth century. Courtesy books are particularly characteristic of the Renaissance in their praise of the accomplished, well-rounded individual (a "Renaissance man" or, more politically correctly, "Renaissance person") and, more generally, in their focus on the individual — and individual self-development. At the heart of most courtesy books is the idea that courtiers should carefully and deliberately cultivate a wide range of athletic, intellectual, artistic, conversational, and romantic capabilities. In his book *Renaissance Self-Fashioning: From More to Shakespeare* (1980), Stephen Greenblatt proposes an interesting corollary to the view that Renaissance art tended to **represent** individuals, not types. (It has long been noted that there is more variation among the Madonnas depicted in Renaissance paintings than among their **medieval** counterparts.) During the Renaissance, Greenblatt suggests, the human individual came to be seen *as* a work of art.

This focus on the developing individual is as characteristic of Renaissance religious **discourse** as it is of Renaissance works of art. Central to the Reformation, which was instigated by Martin Luther in Germany during the first half of the sixteenth century, is the idea that although ecclesiastical intermediaries may provide comfort and guidance, they are neither necessary nor sufficient for an individual's salvation. Protestant reformers insisted that believers are their own priests, capable of a direct personal relationship with God; consequently, they are empowered to confess their own sins, read scripture on their own, and interpret God's word in light of their own experience.

The questioning of authority — in this case the authority of the Church in Rome over certain religious and spiritual matters — spurred the onset of the Reformation. This spirit of questioning was as characteristic of the Renaissance as was the focus on the individual. The tendency to question received "truth" also lay behind the Copernican revolution in astronomy and, more broadly, led to a growing skepticism regarding supernatural and especially occult explanations for everyday occurrences and behaviors. Increasingly, scientists and nonscientists alike argued that all of known reality may be explained in accordance with natural laws, some of which are not yet known or understood but all of which are potentially knowable and provable.

As a result of this new attitude and outlook — and following famous early experiments by scientists such as Nicolaus Cusanus (1401–64), a German cardinal generally credited with proving that air has weight by showing that plants derive some of their own weight from the atmosphere — the Renaissance became an age of scientific testing. The printing press, which was made possible by scientific advances, in turn advanced science by making possible the publication of experimental results and scientific discoveries. Over time, scientific discourse entered the language of literature; in his great Renaissance **epic** *Paradise Lost* (1667), the Puritan poet John Milton acknowledges recent scientific discoveries and theories even as he questions the ultimate wisdom of the scientific ambition to know and understand everything.

Other artists of the Renaissance more openly welcomed scientific advances and, more important, the spirit of scientific discovery, seen as akin to the artistic spirit of the age. Indeed, the Renaissance was a period in which the arts and sciences developed in tandem, reinforcing one another. (Since the rise of **romanticism** in the late eighteenth century, the arts have tended to critique scientific and technological approaches to life.) During the early years of the Renaissance in Italy, Leonardo da Vinci established the link between the arts and sciences that became characteristic of the Renaissance. Through his work, Leonardo introduced the idea that visual representations should reflect correct geometric perspective. In the sciences, Leonardo's emphasis on accurate perspective inspired more careful study of living and nonliving things, which in turn led to new levels of geometric sophistication that made possible the idea of scientific or technological illustration and design as we now know them. Scholars have argued, for instance, that the design and development of the internal combustion engine would have been impossible without Leonardo's emphasis on perspective. Meanwhile, perspective in the visual arts allowed for the development of **realistic** representation, which remained a generally accepted **convention** of artistic representation until the rise of **modernism** in the twentieth century. Although art remained heavily dependent upon Church funding, artists were increasingly freed of religious restraints as secular painting — especially portraiture — became more acceptable and even embraced.

As the examples of Leonardo and Milton suggest, the Renaissance — with its emphasis on the individual and discovery — produced a number of individual geniuses, "Renaissance men" who have had a profound impact not only on the arts and sciences but also on how humanity conceives of itself, its capabilities, and its place in the universe. Michelangelo Buonarroti (1475–1564), perhaps the best-known painter of the Renaissance, was also an architect, engineer, poet, and sculptor. (His impact on sculpture is now generally recognized as being even greater than his influence on painting.) Raphael (1483–1520), a student of Michelangelo's, produced what many art critics have described as the world's greatest painting (the so-called Sistine Madonna); Raphael's work as an architect led Pope Leo X to appoint him chief architect of Saint Peter's Church in Rome. Galileo Galilei (1564–1642), imprisoned by the Church for agreeing with Copernicus that the earth revolves around the sun, was a painter, writer, musician, and scientist who is now considered the founder of modern experimental science due to his work in astronomy and physics. His ideas paved the way for Johannes Kepler (1571–1630), who discovered the laws of planetary motion, and Sir Isaac Newton (1642–1727), the mathematician and philosopher best known for describing gravitational laws. René Descartes (1596–1650), perhaps most famous for the statement *Cogito, ergo sum* ("I think, therefore I am"), also invented analytic geometry and subsequently had as great an impact on the evolution of mathematics as he did on the future of philosophy. The English physician William Harvey (1578–1657), who explained the workings of the heart and the circulation of human blood, is credited with having profoundly altered the course of Western medicine, much in the way that William Shakespeare (1564–1616) — actor, director, playwright, and poet — is generally acknowledged to have had an unparalleled influence on Western literature ever since the seventeenth century.

In addition to Shakespeare, notable Renaissance writers and their works include: Desiderius Erasmus (*In Praise of Folly* [1509]), Ludovico Ariosto (*Orlando furioso* [c. 1513]), Sir Thomas More (*Utopia* [1516]), Baldassare Castiglione (*Il cortegiano* [*The Courtier*] [1528]), Niccolò Machiavelli (*The Prince* [1532]), François Rabelais (*Pantagruel* [1532]), Michel de Montaigne (*Essais* [1580]), Edmund Spenser (*The Faerie Queene* [1590–96]), Miguel de Cervantes (*Don Quixote* [1605, 1615]), and John Milton (*Paradise Lost* [1667]).

Renaissance Period (in English literature): A period in English literary history spanning the years 1500 to 1660. The Renaissance Period, conceived broadly, is usually divided into five literary eras: the **Early Tudor Age** (1550–58); the **Elizabethan Age** (1558–1603); the **Jacobean Age** (1603–25); the **Caroline Age** (1625–49); and the **Commonwealth Age,** or *Puritan Interregnum* (1649–60).

Major poets of the period include John Donne, John Milton, Sir Philip Sidney, and Edmund Spenser. Notable prose writers include Sir Thomas More and Francis Bacon. William Shakespeare, poet and dramatist, has probably had the greatest impact on Western literature, profoundly influencing its course up to the present day.

See **Renaissance.**

representation: Generally speaking, the use of one thing to stand or substitute for another through some **signifying** medium. A representation of an event is not the event itself but rather a statement about or rendition of that event. An artistic representation is an **image** or likeness of something achieved through a medium such as language, paint, stone, film, etc.

Recently, this term has been given a more specific meaning by **new historicists,** who use it to refer to the **symbolic** constructions of a given society in a specific era. These constructions are predominantly but not exclusively verbal; for instance, the placing of a criminal on public view in "the stocks" could be viewed as a representation of the New England Puritan belief in the communal implications of individual sin and the consequent importance of public penance. New historicists view representations as both the products of and the means of propagating the culture's prevailing **ideologies** and power relations. In other words, representations maintain the status of the dominant **class** or classes by re-presenting the belief systems and preserving the institutions upon which their status and power depend.

EXAMPLE: William Shakespeare's play *Hamlet* (1602) and the coronation of Queen Elizabeth I may both be referred to as Renaissance representations because they served as elaborate, highly **figurative,** and powerfully significant (re)statements of their culture's predominant ideological thinking about power and hierarchy, **gender** and primogeniture, and law and order.

resolution: When used generally, the culmination of a fictional **plot;** when used specifically with reference to **tragic drama,** the concluding action, or **catastrophe,** one of five structural elements associated with **Freytag's Pyramid,** a model developed by Gustav Freytag for analyzing five-act plays, and tragedies in particular.

Restoration Age (in English literature): The Restoration Age is generally said to be the first of three literary eras within the **Neoclassical Period** in English literature, although only a few of its writers fully embraced the **classical** values of intellect, reason, balance, **decorum,** and order commonly associated with **neoclassicism.**

The Restoration Age began in 1660, when the House of Stuart (via Charles II) was restored to the English throne after the eleven-year **Commonwealth,** or **Puritan, Interregnum** (which means, literally, "between reigns"). It is generally, if arbitrarily, said to have ended in 1700. The libertine spirit of Restoration Age literature — which was noted for its focus on aristocrats, their amorous intrigues, and **witty** repartee — starkly contrasts with that of the preceding, Puritan-dominated era, during which public dancing had been virtually eliminated and public theaters closed. Playwrights such as William Congreve, Sir George Etherege, and William Wycherley wrote what came to be called *Restoration comedy,* a type of **comedy of manners.**

John Dryden, a famous poet who wrote not only comedies of manners but also prose pieces and a type of **tragedy** known as heroic drama, became the most noted critic of the age and the writer whose works most fully reflect the priorities and values associated with neoclassicism. In addition to Dryden, prose writers of the Restoration Age include John Bunyan and Samuel Pepys. John Milton, a poet who published his greatest works during this literary epoch, was a Puritan; as such, he is never referred to as a Restoration Age writer even though he was arguably the greatest writer of the time.

revenge tragedy: A type of popular **Elizabethan tragedy,** modelled loosely on the plays of the Roman playwright Seneca, in which revenge was featured and bloodshed was common. Revenge tragedies (the most extreme of which are sometimes referred to as *tragedies of blood*) generally deal with a son's quest to avenge his father's murder or vice versa.

A typical revenge tragedy includes the following elements: (1) the ghost of the murdered man who seeks revenge and implores or orders the **protagonist** to act; (2) hesitation on the part of the protagonist seeking revenge; (3) other delays that retard the accomplishment of the act of revenge; (4) some dissimulation (such as feigned insanity by the protagonist) to deceive the clever, scheming, and villainous murderer; (5) dramatic scenes of gore and horror, especially during the showdown between the protagonist and the **villain;** (6) **intrigue** and lurid incidents such as adultery, suicide, and incest; and (7) philosophical **soliloquies.**

Although fashioned in the **Senecan tragic** tradition, particularly insofar as they involve considerable violence and an occasional ghost, revenge tragedies actually diverge quite significantly from Seneca's plays. In Seneca's tragedies, horrifying events occur, but they occur offstage and are simply reported by the actors rather than witnessed by the audience. Violence in a revenge tragedy, by contrast, is brought onstage for the audience to see and experience in the most graphic, even **cathartic,** way possible.

EXAMPLES: Thomas Kyd's *The Spanish Tragedy* (1586) established the revenge tragedy as a popular **genre** in England. William Shakespeare's *Hamlet* (1602) is the best-known revenge tragedy written in English.

Revolutionary Period (in American literature): A literary epoch spanning the years 1765 to 1790. In 1765, the English Parliament passed the Stamp Act, igniting the first serious opposition in the American colonies to English rule. For the next twenty-five years, until the implementation of the United States Constitution in 1789, the majority of American writing was politically motivated, whether supportive of English rule or revolutionary in character.

Most of the poetry of the Revolutionary Period was **neoclassical,** composed in **imitation** of the English poet Alexander Pope. The poets of this period, such as Joel Barlow, Timothy Dwight, Philip Freneau, and John Trumbull, often used neoclassical forms and styles such as **burlesque, satire,** and **epic** for political ends, especially the patriotic political end of independence. All four poets were also part of the first American literary school, the *Yale Poets* (also known as the *Hartford Wits*). These poets consciously imitated Pope and his circle in their quest to establish a **classical** standard for American literature. A few poets diverged from neoclassicism, however, most notably those associated with the **Graveyard School** and those who emphasized an appreciation of nature, thereby **foreshadowing** early **romanticism.** And Phyllis Wheatley, an American slave and poet, inaugurated the African American literary tradition with her volume *Poems on Various Subjects* (1773).

Revolutionary prose was often polemical in nature, written to encourage and even inspire the movement for political independence from England and to promote national unification. Thomas Paine championed an absolute break with England in his revolutionary tract *Common Sense* (1776). Alexander Hamilton and James Madison contributed the majority of the essays that make up *The Federalist Papers* (1787–88), a collection that sets forth much of the political theory underlying the U.S. Constitution and argues for its ratification. Other major politically oriented prose authors of the period include Benjamin Franklin, who wrote his *Autobiography* in 1771, and Thomas Jefferson, who authored the Declaration of Independence (1776).

The first American novel was also written at the end of the Revolutionary Period. **Epistolary** in form, *The Power of Sympathy* (1789), by William Hill Brown, was supposedly based on the true story of a woman who was seduced by her brother-in-law, became pregnant as a result, and committed suicide after the birth of her illegitimate child. **Sentimental novels** like *The Power of Sympathy,* said to provide moral instruction and to warn unsuspecting women of the dangers of seduction, flourished in the succeeding **Early National Period.**

Drama also entered the American literary arena during the Revolutionary Period. The first play written by an American and acted in America was Thomas Godfrey's *The Prince of Parthia* (1767). The first American comedy, Royall Tyler's play *The Contrast* (1787), was performed in New York. Throughout the period, drama was most influential and widespread outside of New England, where the Puritan suspicion of the medium remained strong. Philadelphia, New York, and Charleston became magnets for playwrights, who modelled their works largely after those of neoclassical English dramatists Oliver Goldsmith and Richard Brinsley Sheridan. American drama was distinguished from the English, however, by its subject matter, which was chiefly historical, **didactic,** and patriotic in nature.

Several of America's most famous songs and **ballads** were also composed during this period. Edward Bangs's song *Yankee Doodle,* first printed as part of an instrumental medley entitled "The Federal Overture" (1795), is just one of many examples.

rhetoric: The art of persuasion through speaking and writing; one of the seven major **medieval** subjects of study (and, more specifically, part of the trivium, the other two members of which were logic and grammar).

Such well-known **classical** writers as Aristotle stressed the importance of the rhetorical arts, which in ancient times were seen as essential to effective argumentation and **oratory**. Classical theorists identified five components of rhetoric: (1) *invention* (the argument itself or its supporting evidence); (2) *disposition* (the arrangement of that evidence); (3) **style** (**diction**, patterns, **images, rhythms** of speech, etc.); (4) *memory*; and (5) *delivery*. They also identified three types of rhetoric: (1) *deliberative* (to persuade toward a course of action regarding public policy); (2) **epideictic** (to praise or blame, thereby demonstrating the rhetorical skill of the orator); and (3) *forensic* (to establish, through a forum-like setting — such as a court of law — either a positive or negative opinion of someone's actions).

Since the classical and medieval periods, rhetoric has acquired negative **connotations,** most of which are associated with its inherent neutrality toward truth and falsehood and the ensuing possibility that it may be used to promote lies or immorality. Used pejoratively, *rhetoric* connotes empty rhetoric — language that sounds good but is at best insubstantial and, at worst, a deliberately distorting medium.

rhetorical accent: See **accent.**

rhetorical criticism: A type of **criticism** emphasizing examination of the strategies and devices authors use to get readers to interpret their works in certain desired ways. Practitioners of rhetorical criticism specifically identify and analyze the devices of persuasion present in a work that are designed to elicit or even impose a particular interpretation of a work's **denotative** and **connotative** meanings. Rhetorical critics also study the interaction of author and reader and view the **text** as a means of communication between the two.

Rhetorical criticism is similar to **pragmatic criticism** in its emphasis on how — and how well — a work (or author) manages to influence the audience (in the sense of inducing the audience to respond to the work in a particular way). Like pragmatic criticism, rhetorical criticism was practiced from **classical** times up through the eighteenth century, when its popularity declined with the rise of *expressive criticism,* which views literary works in light of their authors' thoughts and feelings. It fell into still deeper obscurity during the nineteenth century with the advent of **objective criticism.** Recently, however, rhetorical criticism has been resurrected and revamped, in the work of critics associated with **reader-response** and **reader-oriented criticism.**

rhetorical figures: One of the two major divisions of **figures of speech,** the other being **tropes.** Unlike tropes, which turn one word or phrase into a **representation** of something else, rhetorical figures involve a less radical use of language to achieve special effects. **Antithesis, apostrophe, chiasmus, parallelism,** *rhetorical questions,* **syllepsis,** and **zeugma** are considered to be the major rhetorical figures. Other rhetorical figures include **amplification, anaphora, antonomasia, aposiopesis, asyndeton, hyperbaton,**

occultatio, occupatio, paralipsis (praeteritio), periphrasis (pleonasm), and **pun (paranomasia).**

rhetorical irony (verbal irony): See **irony.**

rhyme: Generally, the repetition of identical vowel sounds in the **stressed** syllables of two or more words, as well as of all subsequent sounds after this vowel sound. When most people speak of words as rhyming, they are referring to a specific type of rhyme — **perfect rhyme** — and, indeed, to a specific type of perfect rhyme — *true,* or *full, rhyme,* in which only the sounds preceding the first **accented** vowel in the rhyming sounds differ. Seventeenth-century poet John Milton's definition of rhyme as "the jingling sound of like endings" describes rhyme of this sort. *Bard / lard / shard / marred* are true (or full) rhymes, for instance, as are *thinking, drinking,* and *shrinking.* But *bard / barred* and *board / bored* are not; nor are *bard / hoard* or even *bard / beard / board.* These latter two word sets are examples of *rime riche* and **half-rhyme,** respectively. In *rime riche,* the second type of perfect rhyme, rhyming words sound identical; their meaning cannot be distinguished except through spelling and context. In half-rhyme, words contain similar sounds but do not rhyme exactly. Half-rhyme typically results from **consonance** or **assonance,** similarities in consonant and vowel sounds, respectively. When words appear to rhyme based on their spelling but sound completely different when pronounced — as in *dough / tough* — no rhyme exists; rather, this phenomenon is labeled **eye-rhyme.**

Perfect rhyme may further be classified as **masculine** or **feminine.** A masculine rhyme has one stressed syllable; a feminine rhyme has either two (**double rhyme**) or three (**triple rhyme**) syllables. Furthermore, a double feminine rhyme involves one stressed syllable followed by an identical-sounding unstressed syllable (*shatter / splatter*); in a triple feminine rhyme, one stressed syllable precedes two unstressed identical-sounding syllables (*clattering / flattering*). Some critics would argue that, although perfect rhyme may be masculine, not all masculine rhyme is perfect; masculine rhyme, they would maintain, may involve half-rhyme (*care / core*) or even eye-rhyme (*how / low*).

Finally, rhyme may be classified according to its placement within the poetic line. Rhyme can occur at the end of a line (**end-rhyme**), somewhere in the middle of a line (**internal rhyme,** including **leonine rhyme**), or at the beginning of a line (beginning rhyme).

Rhyme should be distinguished from **rhythm,** which refers generally to the measured flow of words in a passage or work and signifies a basic (though often varied) beat or pattern in language established by pauses and stressed and unstressed syllables. First, rhyme is generally limited to poetic works, whereas rhythm is a feature of both prose and poetry. Second, critics generally agree that rhythm, unlike rhyme, is an indispensable element of poetry. Of course, poets often use rhyme to establish or intensify the rhythm of a poem and to establish the unities and divisions within a given passage or work. A poet's **rhyme scheme,** or pattern of rhymes, for instance, may delineate **stanzas** and unify the poem as a whole through its recurrent regularity. To emphasize the distinction between rhyme and rhythm, some critics have suggested returning to an older spelling of *rhyme: rime.*

The trend in the twentieth century was toward dispensing with rhyme, or at least toward minimizing its use. Today, few poets compose using rhyme — at least of the conventional, perfect kind. As the use of perfect rhyme has declined, forms of rhyme such as half-rhyme have become increasingly popular. But even these forms have suffered as nonrhyming forms such as **free verse** have become the dominant means of poetic expression. Unrhymed verse written in English dates at least as far back as the sixteenth century, when **blank verse** (broadly defined, any unrhymed verse, but usually referring to unrhymed **iambic pentameter**) first appeared.

Despite the use of nonrhyming forms of verse such as blank verse and free verse, rhyme has been a popular poetic tool, especially of English-language poets. Rhyme, however, does not usually appear in ancient poetic works, such as those of **classical** Greece and Rome, or those written in Sanskrit and Hebrew. Some scholars have suggested that the origins of rhyme as we know it lie in the early Catholic Church and, more specifically, in the African church Latin that developed during the reign of the Roman emperor Tertullian (c. A.D. 160–230). Later, priests throughout Europe began introducing rhyme in order to make long passages of liturgy easier to listen to and remember. By the fourth century A.D., key liturgical readings and responses had evolved into rhymed poems; some of these, such as the "Stabat Mater" and "Dies Irae," are familiar to churchgoers today. Later, during the **Middle Ages, hymns** were composed that combined assonance and consonance, **alliteration** and end-rhyme.

Other scholars have theorized that the absence of rhyme can be traced to the very nature of the ancient languages of these cultures. The fewer syllables that follow a word's final, accented syllable, the easier rhyming becomes. *Can,* for instance, is more easily rhymed than *canister.* The language of classical and other ancient locales tended to be suffixal rather than prefixal — that is, to follow the root with numerous syllables rather than so preceding it — hence making rhyming more difficult. English, by contrast, is a prefixal language, which may account for the greater development of rhyme in English-language poetry than in various ancient languages.

rhyme royal (rime royal): Introduced by Geoffrey Chaucer in *Troilus and Criseyde* (c. 1383), a seven-line poetic **stanza** written in **iambic pentameter** with the **rhyme scheme** *ababbcc.* Rhyme royal is said to be named after King James I of Scotland (1394–1437), who used this form in writing his **dream vision** *The King's Quair* (*The King's Book*).

FURTHER EXAMPLE: The following stanza from Chaucer's *Troilus:*

And whoso seith that for to love is vice,
Or thraldom, though he feele it in destresse,
He outher° is envyous, or right nyce°   *either; foolish*
Or is unmyghty, for his shrewedness,°   *impotent because*
To loven; for swich manere folk, I gesse,   *of his nastiness*
Defamen Love, as nothing of him knowe.
They speken, but thei benten nevere his bowe!

rhyme scheme: The pattern of **rhyme** in a **poem.** A lower case letter is typically assigned to each new rhyming sound. Certain poetic forms, such as the **sonnet, triolet,** and **villanelle** — as well as **stanza** types, such as the **Spenserian stanza** — are **conventionally** composed in accordance with a specific rhyme scheme. Thus the rhyme scheme of an **Italian sonnet** is generally *abbaabbacdecde,* whereas that of a **ballad stanza** is *abcb.*

rhythm: From the Greek for "flow," a term referring to a measured flow of words and signifying the basic (though often varied) beat or pattern in language that is established by **stressed** syllables, un**stressed** syllables, and pauses.

Rhythm is distinguished from **meter.** When the pauses and stresses of rhythm are organized into a more formal, regular pattern of stress units with a dominant **foot** (what in music would be called a "beat"), this is called **meter. Accentual-syllabic** meter, which regulates both the number of syllables and the number of stressed and unstressed syllables in a line of verse, is the most common kind of meter in English. Other types of meter include the *accentual,* the *syllabic,* and the *quantitative,* the last of which was the meter used by the **classical** poets of ancient Greece and Rome.

Rhythm is also distinguished from **rhyme.** Though rhythm is essential to verse, rhyme is not. Rhythm is often accompanied and intensified by rhyme, however, since rhyme accentuates the rhythmic pattern(s) of any poem.

Rhythm can occur in prose as well as in poetry. Since rhyme is uncommon in prose, which approximates everyday speaking patterns, rhythm is generally established by imitating the rhythmic cadences of speech. **Parallelism, euphony,** repetition, and line length are also commonly used to establish and enhance rhythm.

rime riche: See **perfect rhyme.**

rime royal: See **rhyme royal.**

rising action: The part of a **drama** that follows the inciting moment (the event that gives rise to the **conflict**) and precedes the **climax** or the **crisis.** During the rising action, the **plot** becomes more complicated and the **conflict** intensifies. Rising action is one of five structural elements associated with **Freytag's Pyramid,** a model developed by Gustav Freytag for analyzing five-act plays, and **tragedies** in particular.

roman à clef: A **novel** that **represents** real people in the guise of novelistic **characters** bearing fictional names. Usually the author makes the identities of the characters readily apparent, at least to contemporary readers. This is particularly true when the novelist has written a *roman à clef* to **satirize** an individual or individuals, or some associated event.

EXAMPLES: Lady Caroline Lamb's *Glenarven* (1816) is a *roman à clef* about the poet George Gordon, Lord Byron, thinly disguised as the character Ruthven Glenarven. In Mary Shelley's **apocalyptic** novel *The Last Man* (1826), the characters of Adrian, Earl of Windsor, and Lord Raymond are portraits of Percy Bysshe Shelley (Mary Shelley's husband) and Byron, respectively. Many of the minor characters in *The Last Man* have also been linked to real people, such as the politician Ryland, widely acknowledged to be a **caricature** of popular journalist and editor William Cobbett. In Aldous Huxley's *Point Counter Point* (1928), real people such as D. H. Lawrence and critic Middleton Murry are barely disguised under thin fictional veneers.

In the novel *Primary Colors* (1996), the author Joe Klein (who covered the 1992 presidential race as a *Newsweek* correspondent and who was anonymous at the time of publication) essentially told the story of Bill Clinton's first campaign for the White House. Clinton is portrayed via a character named Jack Stanton; Orlando Ozio is former New York governor Mario Cuomo. A character named Henry Burton, though an African American, is recognizable as the ever-adaptable George Stephanopoulos, and Clinton's campaign director, James Carville, is Richard Jemmons — "a hyperactive redneck from outer space."

romance: A term that has been used at different times to refer to a variety of fictional works involving some combination of the following: high adventure, thwarted love, mysterious circumstances, arduous quests, and improbable triumphs. Although some scholars during and since the **Renaissance** have maintained that romances were first written in ancient Greece (Homer's *The Odyssey* [c. 850 B.C.] has been called a prototypical romance), most literary historians maintain that the romance originated in twelfth-century France. The term *romance* derives from the French word *roman* and was first used exclusively to refer to **medieval romances** (sometimes called *chivalric romances*) written in French and composed in verse. These **narratives** were concerned with knightly adventure, **courtly love,** and chivalric ideals. By the seventeenth century, the term was used to refer to any medieval romance, whether in verse or prose and regardless of country of origin.

Unlike the **epic,** a narrative form that exalts the struggles associated with a heroic era of tribal warfare, the romance pertains to a courtly era associated with chivalry. Romances represent the supernatural as characteristic of this world rather than of the gods or their will. They also tend to have what we would describe as a psychological interest or component; the landscapes of romance are often outward manifestations of the **hero's** or

heroine's inner state. Thus, a despairing character is likely to stumble into a cave, and temptation is likely to be encountered in a deep forest rather than on a broad, sunny plain. The *quest romance* was adapted and internalized by **Romantic** and **Victorian Period** poets, who in works like Percy Bysshe Shelley's "Alastor" (1816), John Keats's "La belle dame sans merci" (1820), and Robert Browning's "Childe Roland to the Dark Tower Came" (1855) turned the search for the Grail (or Girl) common in medieval and Renaissance romances into an often frustrated psychological quest for some ideal, forbidden, lost, or otherwise unreachable state or condition.

The meaning of *romance* broadened considerably over time, especially in the twentieth century. The term has been used to refer to any fictional work that features the supernatural, some sort of quest or "impossible dream," intense love, and unusual subjects and events. Today, *romance* is usually understood to refer to a fictional account of passionate love prevailing against social, economic, or psychological odds, but any **plot** that revolves around love can now be characterized as a romance. (*Romance* may even be used as a synonym for love, as in the sentence "Our romance had to end.") Love stories whose **characters,** situations, or events are given a historical **setting** are often referred to as *historical romances.* When romance **conventions** are overlaid, as is often the case, with the emotionally and supernaturally charged features of **Gothic** literature, the resulting works may be called *Gothic romances.* In a further broadening of this term's meaning, *romance* has been recently used to signify any work whose author rejects **realistic** verisimilitude in favor of fanciful or **fantastic depictions.**

Romance is also used in the phrase *Romance languages.* The five principal Romance languages, all of which are derived primarily from the Roman language Latin, are French, Italian, Portuguese, Romanian, and Spanish.

FURTHER EXAMPLES: Guillaume de Lorris and Jean de Meung's *Le roman de la rose* (*The Romance of the Rose*) (c. 1230, c. 1270) and Edmund Spenser's *The Faerie Queene* (1590, 1596) are romances in the original sense of the term, which, with varying levels of laxity and generality, may be used to describe Emily Brontë's *Wuthering Heights* (1847), Nathaniel Hawthorne's *The Scarlet Letter* (1850), William Morris's poem "Rapunzel" (1858), Margaret Mitchell's *Gone With the Wind* (1936), Erich Segal's *Love Story* (1970), any Harlequin paperback, Danielle Steele's books, and films like *Sleepless in Seattle* (1993) and *Notting Hill* (1999). The latter two works are examples of a hybrid **genre,** the **romantic comedy.**

romantic comedy: See **comedy.**

romantic irony: See **irony.**

romanticism: Broadly speaking, a term applicable to philosophy, politics, and the arts in general. Even when specifically applied to literature, *romanticism* cannot be strictly defined, for it has been used in a wide variety of ways. The diverse and even dissimilar nature of works commonly said to be romantic, however, is actually in keeping with romanticism's emphasis on **subjective** experience, innovation, **imagination,** and the individual.

The term *romantic* was first used to characterize **narratives** called **romances** that arose in **medieval** times; these stories often featured improbable **plots,** hence the (often pejorative) **connotation** of *romantic* as "implausible." In the eighteenth century, the term was frequently used to describe melancholy works with exotic **settings** and situations. Some critics viewed such works as imaginative; others viewed them as patently silly. German philosopher and critic Friedrich Schlegel was the first to apply the term to a literary movement that opposed **neoclassicism** (called *die Klassik* in German), which emphasized qualities such as reason, order, restraint, balance, and clarity in emulation of **classical** literature. Schlegel's application of the term quickly entered English and French usage. The so-called **Romantic Period** or movement is generally considered to extend from the end of the eighteenth century through much of the nineteenth century, depending on which country's romantic movement is being discussed. Most critics agree that romanticism arose first in Germany and England, followed by America and other European countries such as France. William Blake, William Wordsworth, Samuel Taylor Coleridge, John Keats, Percy Bysshe Shelley, Mary Shelley, and Emily Brontë were among the foremost romantic writers in England; famous American romantics include Emily Dickinson, Ralph Waldo Emerson, Nathaniel Hawthorne, Herman Melville, Edgar Allan Poe, Henry David Thoreau, and Walt Whitman. Johann Wolfgang von Goethe, Victor Hugo, and Alexander Pushkin were noted romantic writers in Germany, France, and Russia, respectively.

Reacting against neoclassicism, romantic writers valued emotions and expressed their ideas in everyday language and in their own individual styles, rather than in formal **imitation** of the ancient writers neoclassicists so admired. Romantics rejected many of the artistic **forms** and **conventions** associated with **classicism** and neoclassicism, considering them to be overly constricting and detrimental to the artistic mission. Deeming spontaneity in composition essential to a true **representation** of their subjective experience, they asserted their right to express themselves as they saw fit. This is not to say that the romantics ignored writings of the classical era; they read and respected ancient Greek and Roman authors, but they put a premium on original expression. The movement cannot be strictly defined, however; within it, authors (and critics) differed tremendously in their interests and emphases. Some urged a revival of **medievalism** (an interest in emulating certain aspects of the **Middle Ages**); others emphasized the importance of freedom from all traditions (from aristocracy to the restraints of classicism and neoclassicism in art). Still others tended to turn literature into a vehicle for the **fancy,** a mode of escapism. It is thus better to discuss several common characteristics than to attempt to paint a definitive "romantic profile."

Some romantic writers, such as Coleridge and Wordsworth, drew a distinction between fancy and imagination, **privileging** the latter as the source of creativity. In his *Biographia Literaria* (1817), Coleridge defined fancy as a mode of memory freed from the normal constraints of space and time and thus capable of reordering sensory **images.** He credited imagination with the ability to remake sensory images, however, and thus viewed it as the source of true creativity. Coleridge viewed fancy as **mechanic,** capable only of rearranging that which already exists, whereas he viewed imagination as **organic,** capable of unifying disparate and even contradictory elements into a complex whole.

In addition to believing in the power of imagination, romantics believed that humans are essentially good, namely that people are good by nature; they also believed that civilization corrupts this essential goodness. Closely related to the belief in humanity's original goodness is the romantic esteem, even reverence, for childhood and the **primitive,** the natural states unspoiled by society's influence. The importance romantics placed on emotion is similarly explicable in light of their belief in essential human goodness; if humans are by nature good, their emotions, the most "natural" of human manifestations, cannot be bad. In fact, romantics often regarded emotions as more reliable than reason, which they tended to view as a negative product of civilization, unlike the eighteenth-century Enlightenment philosophers who celebrated reason as the vehicle furthering and expanding human capabilities. The conception of civilization as a corrupting influence also led romantics to value nature and to give it a prominent place in their works. Nature was often seen as the **antithesis** of the materialism and artifice engendered by civilized society. Romantics so valued nature that they often imputed to it a **mystical** or even **sublime** quality. Observations on nature frequently served as an occasion for sustained reflection or meditation on the human condition and the individual human "self."

Romantics also prized individualism. Since they believed humans to be naturally good and their emotions to be reliable, they also believed in the sanctity of individual expression. They considered self-analysis especially constructive, particularly as it pertained to personal development. Romantic writers highly valued the exploration and evaluation of the inner self; they brought the review of and focus on self into the realm of literature.

With emphasis on the individual, the romantic was likely to oppose the established order, the bourgeois status quo. Many demanded political as well as moral change, which they believed was possible due to their faith in the perfectibility of humanity. Some looked to the French Revolution of 1789 as a political blueprint for improvement, at least before the excesses of the Reign of Terror became widely known; others focused on the unparalleled (if unfulfilled) possibilities for beneficial social change that the revolution engendered.

Romantic writers frequently perceived themselves as at once sensitive and unappreciated. (In fact, the romantics may be chiefly responsible for popularizing, and even glorifying, the **theme** of the suffering artist — the lonely, misunderstood artistic genius.) Although romantics recognized the potential represented by the new machinery and scientific developments so prized in the industrial era, they also felt undervalued (or even rejected) by a world increasingly fixated on progress and what Wordsworth called "getting and spending." The intensity of personal self-assessment and the pursuit of the spiritual or otherwise **fantastic** often seemed to create an unbridgeable chasm between the susceptible romantic poet and an increasingly commercial and technologically oriented society. The **heroes** and **heroines** of romantic literature often share their creators' perceptions of alienation and difference from the society at large.

Many romantics also felt an affinity with the **Gothic** and the **grotesque.** Gothic literature is typically characterized by a general mood of decay, action that is dramatic and generally violent, loves that are destructively passionate (like that of Cathy and Heathcliff in Emily Brontë's *Wuthering Heights* [1847]), and grandiose yet gloomy settings. Gothic literature often invokes the grotesque, artistic representations that are always strange — even bizarre or unnatural — and often disturbing (involving, as they often do, a mix of human, animal, and supernatural figures). Unlike the neoclassicists, who viewed such writing as crude or even barbaric, romantics found in the Gothic a freedom of spirit, mystery, and instinctual authenticity that meshed well with their own emphasis on individuality, imagination, and sublimity.

As with all other literary movements, a reaction against romanticism eventually set in. Beginning in the latter half of the nineteenth century, romanticism became the target of increasing (and increasingly vitriolic) criticism. The self-centeredness, **sentimentalism,** and improbability of many romantic works incited some of the harshest attacks, many of which came from **Victorian** writers and critics associated with movements as varied as **realism** and **aestheticism.** Walter Pater called Wordsworth a "brain-sick . . . mystic" and described Coleridge's work as representative of "that inexhaustible discontent, languor, and homesickness, that endless regret, the chords of which ring all through our modern literature. It is to the romantic element in literature that these qualities belong. One day, perhaps, we may come to forget the distant horizon, with full knowledge of the situation, to be content with 'what is here and now.'" Matthew Arnold argued that Percy Bysshe Shelley suffered from "the incurable want . . . of a sound subject-matter," characterizing him as an "ineffectual angel beating in the void his luminous wings in vain." John Ruskin attacked Shelley's lyrics as "false, forced, foul"; he not only criticized such poems as Shelley's "The Sensitive Plant" (1820) on the scientific grounds that "Sensitive plants can't grow in gardens! . . . Dew with a breeze is impossible" but also mounted a more personal attack on the poet, calling him a "blockhead — and he thinks himself wiser than God though he doesn't know the commonest law of evaporation!" Nonetheless, regardless of the ferocity of Victorian criticism, romantic elements continued to pervade nineteenth-century works and still play a major role in literature today, especially the emphasis on individual perspective and artistic originality.

Romanticism is frequently viewed in opposition to realism as well as in opposition to classicism and neoclassicism. Realism in fact developed in the latter half of the nineteenth century in reaction to the various excesses of romanticism. Unlike the romantics (and, to some extent, in criticism of them), realists tried to "write reality," to concentrate on **objectively** presenting details and events rather than personal feelings or perceptions.

The terms *classic* and *romantic* are also still frequently used in a general sense. *Classic* is associated with the rational, the unified, the orderly, the stately, the long-lasting or finite, whereas *romantic* is associated with the emotional, the energetic, the changing, the improbable, the visionary, the supernatural, the infinite, even the chaotic.

Romantic Period (in American literature): A literary epoch spanning the years 1828, when Andrew Jackson was elected to the presidency, to 1865, the year the Civil War ended. The limits of American unity were tested during this period, due to the rapid rate of westward expansion and, more importantly, the issue of slavery, which increasingly divided the nation. During this turbulent and often contentious time, the first truly American literature was produced, with significant works appearing in all areas except for drama, thereby giving rise to the appellation *American Renaissance.*

The Romantic Period has also been called the *Age of Transcendentalism.* Adherents of **transcendentalism,** an idealistic philosophical and literary movement that arose in New England, maintained that each person is innately divine, with the intuitive ability to discover higher truths. They rejected dogmatic religious doctrines, praised self-reliance, and gloried in the natural goodness of the individual. Transcendentalism is most closely associated with the poet and essayist Ralph Waldo Emerson, who outlined the movement in an essay entitled "The Transcendentalist" (1842). Other members of the movement include Amos Bronson Alcott, early feminist Margaret Fuller, and Henry David Thoreau, best known for his essay "Civil Disobedience" (first published in 1849 as "Resistance to Civil Government") and his book *Walden* (1854). Members of the Transcendental Club contributed writings to *The Dial,* the group's quarterly periodical.

Romantic writers generally emphasized emotion over intellect; the individual over society; inspiration, **imagination,** and intuition over logic, discipline, and order; the wild and natural over the tamed. American romantic novelists and poets were heavily influenced by English **romanticism** and yet produced the first truly distinctive American works.

Poetry flourished during the Romantic Period. Edgar Allan Poe took the novel step of formulating his own **theory** of poetry, based on which he produced a **symbolist** verse that would heavily **influence** post–Civil War poetry and the **Symbolist movement** in France. "The Raven" (1845) and "Annabel Lee" (1849) are perhaps his most famous poems. Walt Whitman challenged poetic **conventions** with the radically personal and informal **lyrics** he published in *Leaves of Grass* (1855). Whitman's poems are **or-**

ganic in **form,** composed of **free verse** of widely varying line lengths, and discuss subject matter deemed highly taboo at the time, such as sex. Emerson praised Whitman for his "free and brave thought" and "large perception," declaring that "it is the office of poets to suggest a vast wealth, a background, a divinity," for "if this religion is in the poetry, it raises us to some purpose." Other romantic poets included William Cullen Bryant, Emily Dickinson, Frances Ellen Watkins Harper, Paul Hamilton Hayne, Henry Wadsworth Longfellow, James Russell Lowell, Henry Timrod, and John Greenleaf Whittier.

Washington Irving and James Fenimore Cooper, novelists whose careers had begun during the preceding **Early National Period,** produced some of their best works during the Romantic Period. But it was writers like Nathaniel Hawthorne and Herman Melville who more truly exemplified novelistic romanticism. Hawthorne's *The Scarlet Letter* (1850) and Melville's *Moby-Dick* (1852) are among the most well-known American works. Margaret Fuller, William Gilmore Simms, William Brown, and Harriet Beecher Stowe are other notable writers of the period. Stowe's *Uncle Tom's Cabin* (1852) is not only credited with being America's first **sociological novel,** it is also often said to have instigated the Civil War by its depiction of slavery. Louisa May Alcott, who sold her first story in 1852 and published her first book in 1854, became world-famous for her novel *Little Women* (1868).

Other varieties of prose were also common in the Romantic Period. A group of Southern writers including John Pendleton Kennedy and William Alexander Caruthers developed a plantation tradition idealizing plantation life through **historical romances** and sketches. Western writers such as Davy Crockett chronicled the frontier life. Essayists including Oliver Wendell Holmes, Emerson, and Thoreau were also widely read. Short stories such as Hawthorne's "Young Goodman Brown" (1835) and Poe's "The Fall of the House of Usher" (1843) and "The Tell-Tale Heart" (1843) captivated readers. Poe also pioneered **detective fiction** through works such as "Murders in the Rue Morgue" (1841).

American literary criticism also began during the Romantic Period. Poe, who developed an analytical approach to literary criticism, is usually credited as being America's first real critic. Simms and Lowell are other noted critics of the time.

A number of new periodicals, which often reflected the sectional divisions that were tearing the country apart, were founded during the Romantic Period. The *Southern Review* and *Southern Literary Messenger* represented the views of the South; in the North, the *Atlantic Monthly* and *Harper's Magazine* joined the *North American Review*, which was established during the Early National Period.

Slave narratives and **autobiographies** also increased in number and became increasingly popular in the North, even as they were banned in the South. Frederick Douglass's *Narrative of the Life of Frederick Douglass* (1845) and Harriet Jacobs's *Incidents in the Life of a Slave Girl* (1861) are two of the most well-known examples of the slave-narrative **genre**. Abolitionist newspapers and pamphlets also sprang up, even though many of their editors and authors were persecuted. For instance, William Lloyd Garrison, editor of the *Liberator,* was attacked and dragged through the streets of Boston by a mob.

Drama, unlike other forms of literary expression, did not produce very distinctive works. Most dramatists continued to **imitate** English spectacles and romantic **tragedies** modelled on William Shakespeare's plays. Of particular interest were stage adaptations of well-known novels (such as *Uncle Tom's Cabin*) and short stories (such as Irving's "Rip Van Winkle" [1819]). Also popular was the star system, which, as its name suggests, subordinated both play and actors to one "star," one name actor.

See **romanticism.**

Romantic Period (in English literature): A watershed era in the history of English literature usually said to have commenced with the 1798 publication of Samuel Taylor Coleridge and William Wordsworth's *Lyrical Ballads,* a volume that included such well-known poems as Coleridge's "The Rime of the Ancient Mariner" and Wordsworth's "Lines Written a Few Miles Above Tintern Abbey." Some scholars, however, have maintained that the Romantic Period began before 1798, arguing that certain works published before that date (such as Robert Burns's *Poems* [1786]; William Blake's *Songs of Innocence* [1789]; Mary Wollstonecraft's *A Vindication of the Rights of Woman* [1792]; and various **Gothic works** published by writers like Ann Radcliffe, William Godwin, and Horace Walpole) exemplify the radical changes in political thought and literary expression commonly associated with English **romanticism.** Most scholars agree that the Romantic Period concluded in 1837 with the coronation of Queen Victoria, after whom the subsequent **Victorian Period** is named.

In addition to Coleridge, Wordsworth, and Blake (whose artistic career, unlike that of Burns, continued well past 1798), critic Charles Lamb and novelists Jane Austen and Sir Walter Scott are generally viewed as early or "first generation" romantics. Major "second generation" English romantic poets, who published their most important work after 1815, include George Gordon, Lord Byron (*Don Juan* [1819–24]); John Keats ("Ode on a Grecian Urn" [1820]); and Percy Bysshe Shelley ("Adonais" [1820]). Prose writers of this second phase of English romanticism include Thomas de Quincey (best known for his provocatively titled work *Confessions of an English Opium-Eater* [1821]), William Hazlitt (*Spirit of the Age* [1825]), and Walter Savage Landor (*Imaginary Conversations* [1824–29]).

Mary Shelley—Percy's wife and the daughter of Wollstonecraft and Godwin—was one of the major novelists of the later Romantic Period. Her novel *Frankenstein* (1818) shows the clear influence of the late-eighteenth-century Gothic tradition. In *Northanger Abbey,* a novel published the same year as *Frankenstein,* Austen adapted the **conventions** of the Gothic romance. Critics have pointed out, however, that in more critically acclaimed works such as *Sense and Sensibility* (1811) and *Emma* (1815), Austen reflects the priorities and values of the preceding **Neoclassical Period** as fully as she does those of romanticism.

In general, writers associated with the Romantic Period valued **imagination** and feelings as highly as reason and intellect; believed that humans are by nature good; felt that Nature is the source of sublime feeling, divine inspiration, and even moral action (Wordsworth speaks in "... Tintern Abbey" of Nature's being the source of "our little, nameless, unremembered acts of kindness and of love"); celebrated the individual rather than the social order and, indeed, critiqued oppressive, **class**-based political regimes and social forms; and rejected many of the artistic rules, forms, and conventions associated with **classicism** and **neoclassicism,** considering them to be **aesthetic** forms of repression or, at least, unnecessary constrictions detrimental to the individual artist's calling. Artistic and intellectual freedom combined to make the spirit of the age one of exploration and discovery. That spirit underlies countless lines of romantic poetry, from those in which Coleridge's Ancient Mariner declares "We were the first that ever burst / Into that silent sea" to those lines of *The Prelude* (1850) in which Wordsworth describes the "silent face" of a statue of Sir Isaac Newton as "The marble index of a mind for ever / Voyaging through strange seas of Thought, alone."

See **romanticism.**

rondeau/rondel/roundel: The *rondeau* is a French **verse** form consisting of fifteen lines (generally octosyllabic) in three **stanzas** with the **rhyme scheme** *aabba aabc aabbac.* The rondeau contains only two **rhymes** except for the **refrain,** here indicated by the letter *c.* This short refrain is identical to the first half of the first line and is repeated at the end of the second and third stanzas. Some critics do not count the refrains as lines and hence say the rondeau has thirteen lines.

The rondeau flourished in sixteenth-century France, thanks to poets such as Clément Marot. Variations on the form have subsequently been produced by poets writing in English, such as W. E. Henley. One of these, the *rondel,* consists of either thirteen or fourteen lines in three stanzas based entirely on two rhymes with the rhyme scheme *abba abab abbaa(b)* (depending on whether the fourteenth line is included). The first two lines are repeated as a refrain in the seventh and eighth lines (the last two lines of the second stanza). The first line is again repeated as the thirteenth line; if the fourteenth line is included, it is identical to the second line, making a complete refrain just as at the end of the second stanza. Unlike the rondeau, the rondel uses entire rather than partial lines for the refrain.

The term *roundel* is sometimes used synonymously with both *rondeau* and *rondel,* but it typically has a more specific meaning, that of the variation on the rondeau created by Algernon Charles Swinburne. Swinburne's roundel consists of eleven lines in three stanzas with the rhyme scheme *abaB bab abaB.* Like the rondeau, the roundel has a refrain (*B*) identical to the first half of the first line, but unlike the rondeau, the roundel contains a total of only two rhymes because the refrain has the same rhyme as the lines marked *b*. Again, some critics do not count the refrains as lines and thus say this form has nine lines.

round character: See **flat and round characters.**

run-on line: See *enjambement.*

Russian formalism: A school of literary **criticism** that originated during World War I, that flourished in the 1920s in the former Soviet Union, and whose practitioners focused on the **form** (rather than the content) of literary works. The school met with a great deal of opposition, particularly at its inception, and the term *formalism* was actually used by critics of the school to deride its elevation of form over content. Russian formalists argued that literary language has a special function: to reinvigorate language and to redeem it from the insipid and vapid state into which it sinks under the weight of everyday usage. They thus viewed literary language as fundamentally different from everyday speech, which serves simply to communicate information. They believed that **literariness,** by virtue of its capacity to overturn common and expected patterns (of grammar, of story line), could rejuvenate language. Using language in novel ways could, according to these critics, free readers to experience not only words, but even the world, in an entirely new way.

This emphasis on form and literariness was accompanied by an interest in the literary devices that make the **foregrounding** — and therefore rejuvenation — of language possible. Literary devices, for Russian formalists, were "deviations" from everyday speech; these critics studied the special **rhythmic** patterns, **syntax, structure, imagery,** and so forth that distinguish a literary work from other written or spoken **discourse.** That which was different or even strange was prized, for such devices triggered what Victor Shklovsky called *ostranenie* ("defamiliarization"), a dislocating experience for readers that wrenched them from the banality of everyday language, freeing them to contemplate the world afresh.

By so elevating form, literariness, and the literary devices upon which both of these depend, Russian formalists to a great extent relegated writers to the background, viewing them as manipulators of various techniques, **styles, motifs,** and **conventions.** By viewing works as freestanding, independent entities, they de-emphasized the author's status as a unique and independent creator. They understood the **text** to be an assemblage of literary devices and conventions, not the unique product of an individual author's thoughtful interaction with the external world and its influences.

Russian formalists made a number of contributions that have become widely accepted by literary critics of diverse theoretical orientations. For instance, they distinguished *syuzhet* (**plot**) from *fabula* (**story**), defining the first as how events are actually presented in a **narrative** and the second as how those events would be recounted chronologically. The literary devices employed by the author in converting a story into a plot fundamentally transform the story, making it a work of literature that has the capacity to provoke *ostranenie* and thus bring a fresh view of language and the world to the reader. Russian formalists also pointed out that **metrical** patterns and sound patterns developed through **alliteration** and **rhyme** serve to re-organize language itself rather than simply serving as window-dressing.

Russian formalism originally arose in Moscow and Petrograd (now St. Petersburg). The two groups chiefly responsible for its theoretical development were the Moscow Linguistic Circle (founded 1915) and OPOYAZ (the Society for the Study of Poetic Language, founded 1916). Influential practitioners of Russian formalism included Boris Eichenbaum, Roman Jakobson, Jan Mukarovsky, Victor Shklovsky, Boris Tomashevsky, and Yuri Tynyanov. The movement was suppressed in the Soviet Union in 1930 by the Stalinist regime, but it spread to other areas. **Formalism** flourished first in the former Czechoslovakia under the aegis of the **Prague Linguistic Circle** and then had an impact on American literary criticism when Jakobson and Prague Linguistic Circle critic René Wellek came to the United States in the 1940s. Russian formalism has chiefly affected American theories of **stylistics** and **narratology.** American formalism, primarily associated with **the New Criticism,** shares many characteristics with Russian formalism, but arose independent of the Russian school.

S

sapphic: A **verse** form consisting of **quatrains** (four-line **stanzas**) containing eleven syllables in each of the first three lines and five in the fourth. Named for the ancient Greek poet Sappho, the term also refers to the particular **quantitative** meter (combination of long [-] and short [ˇ] syllables) she used in poetic composition: ‑ˇ|‑ˇ|‑ˇˇ|‑ˇ or ‑ˇ|‑‑|‑ˇˇ|‑ˇ|‑‑ in the first three lines of each quatrain and ‑ˇˇ|‑ˇ or ‑ˇˇ|‑‑ in the last.

Catullus, an ancient Roman poet, is typically credited with introducing the sapphic **form** and **meter** into **classical** Latin poetry, whereas Horace, another ancient Roman poet, popularized *sapphics,* as compositions in the sapphic stanzaic form and meter were called. Poets writing in English who have experimented with sapphics include Sir Philip Sidney, Algernon Charles Swinburne, Ezra Pound, and e. e. cummings.

EXAMPLES: Swinburne's poem "Sapphics" (1865), about the goddess Aphrodite.

In Thomas Hardy's poem "The Temporary the All" (1898), the speaker lists the foolish assumptions and mistakes of his youth, one per sapphic stanza:

> 'Thwart my wistful way did a damsel saunter,
> Fair, albeit unformed to be all-eclipsing;
> "Maiden meet," held I, "till arise my forefelt
> Wonder of women."

sarcasm: Intentional derision, generally directed at another person and intended to hurt. The term comes from a Greek word meaning "to tear flesh like dogs" and signifies a cutting remark. Sarcasm usually involves obvious, even exaggerated **verbal irony,** achieving its effect by jeeringly stating the opposite of what is meant (for instance, false praise) so as to heighten the insult.

EXAMPLE: The following passage from Charles Dickens's *Oliver Twist* (1837), although not directed at any particular person, has a decidedly sarcastic **tone** and effect:

> Let it not be supposed by the enemies of the "system," that, during the period of his solitary incarceration, Oliver was denied the benefit of exercise, the pleasure of society, or the advantages of religious consolation. As for exercise, it was nice cold weather, and he was allowed to perform his ablutions, every morning under the pump, in a stone yard, in the presence of Mr. Bumble, who prevented his catching cold, and caused a tingling sensation to pervade his frame, by repeated applications of the cane. As for society, he was carried every other day into the hall where the boys dined, and there was sociably flogged as a public warning and example. And so far from being denied the advantages of religious consolation, he was kicked into the same apartment

every evening at prayer-time, and there permitted to listen to, and console his mind with, a general supplication of the boys, containing a special clause, therein inserted by authority of the board, in which they entreated to be made good, virtuous, contented, and obedient, and to be guarded from the sins and vices of Oliver Twist. . . .

satire: A literary **genre** that uses **irony, wit,** and sometimes **sarcasm** to expose humanity's vices and foibles, giving impetus to change or reform through ridicule. The satirist reduces the vaunted worth of someone or something to its real — and decidedly lower — worth. Although satire uses comic elements, it differs from **comedy** in that pure comedy primarily seeks to entertain and amuse. Satire may generate laughter but essentially has a moral purpose. It is typically directed at correctable instances of folly or immorality in humanity or human institutions. Its goal is not to abuse so much as to provoke a response, ideally some kind of reform. Thus satire would not be directed at characteristics individuals cannot change (such as physical deformities).

Satire falls into two major categories — *direct* and *indirect*. Direct satire uses a **first-person narrator** who either directly addresses the reader or another **character** in the work, called the *adversarius*. Types of direct satire include **Horatian satire,** which pokes fun at humble foils with a witty, even indulgent tone, and **Juvenalian satire,** which denounces human vice and error in dignified and solemn tones. In indirect satire, of which **Menippean satire** is the most common form, satiric effect is achieved not through direct condemnation but rather through modes of presentation and **representation.** For instance, authors may make their points through exaggeration and non sequitur. Furthermore, satire is often as pointed in what it doesn't say as in what it does.

Satire was a favored **classical** genre, and **neoclassicists,** attempting to reassert classical traditions, produced some of the most famous and effective satires in the seventeenth and eighteenth centuries. Satire persists today, particularly in works (including films) whose subjects are political figures, situations, or institutions.

EXAMPLES: Petronius' *Satyricon* (c. A.D. 50), Rabelais's *Pantagruel* (1533) and *Gargantua* (1535), Molière's *Tartuffe* (1667), Jonathan Swift's "A Modest Proposal" (1729), and Voltaire's *Candide* (1759) are all famous satiric works. Anthony Burgess's *A Clockwork Orange* (1962) is a satiric **dystopia** written against modern violence, police tactics, prisons, politicians, and psychologists. Its criminal adolescent **protagonist,** Alex, is temporarily "reconditioned" into a "model citizen" through the "Ludovico Technique" of behavior-modification therapy. Other twentieth-century literary satirists include Evelyn Waugh, George Orwell, Kingsley Amis, David Lodge, and David Sedaris.

Examples of twentieth-century cinematic satire include Charlie Chaplin's *Modern Times* (1936), Paddy Chayefsky's *The Hospital* (1971), Sidney Lumet's *Network* (1976), and Tim Robbins's political satire *Bob Roberts*

(1992), which in the words of *Time* magazine is a "pseudo-documentary account of a 1990 Pennsylvania senatorial race" that "pits a right-wing, folk-singing Yuppie touting 'family values' against an aging liberal incumbent who tries to talk about the issues while fending off rumors of a sexual liaison with a teenage girl." More recent film satires have involved politics at the presidential level: notably *Wag the Dog* (1997) and *Primary Colors* (1998), which was based on the novel *Primary Colors* (1996) by Anonymous (Joe Klein).

The examples shown below and on page 428, reprinted from the **parodic** newspaper *The Onion*, satirize the privatization of public services and the tendency of well-educated, upper-middle-class parents to believe that their children are perfect. In 2002, *Satire Wire*, an Internet site whose motto is "Because you can read, and we have a website," satirized the controversy over the inclusion of the phrase "under God" in the Pledge of Allegiance in an article characterizing God as the country's principal sponsor and suggesting possible commercial replacements such as McDonald's and Starbucks.

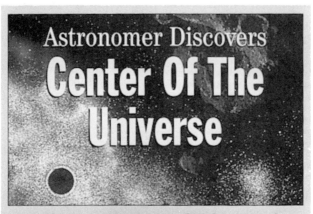

Astronomer Discovers Center Of The Universe

'It Is My Beautiful 9-Year-Old Son,' He Says

PASADENA, CA—California Institute of Technology astronomer Dr. James Shrifkin stunned the scientific and space-exploration communities Wednesday, when he announced that the center of the known universe is his 9-year-old son Brian.

"The universe revolves around him," Shrifkin told colleagues at the annual American Society Of Astronomers convention at Cal Tech. "He is the most precious and wonderful child in all known creation."

Shrifkin said he first suspected

Above: Brian Shrifkin, center of the known universe.

Brian, a straight-A student at Lakeside Elementary School, to be the center of the universe last Saturday, when he scored three goals in his soccer game.

"After the game, I went home and thought about the many quantifiable properties of goodness my son possesses, including kindness, generosity, and intelligence," Shrifkin said. "Formulating a rough Briancentric theory of space and time, I proceeded to gather more evidence, including the beautiful card he bought me last Father's see UNIVERSE page 136

scansion: The analysis, typically using visual symbols, of poetic **meter,** the more or less regular pattern of **stressed** and unstressed syllables in **poetry.** Meter is typically described in one of the following three ways: by citing the dominant type of **foot** (a poetic line's **rhythmic** unit, containing some combination of stressed and unstressed syllables), the number of feet per line, or a combination of these two factors.

Critics "scan" lines to determine a poem's predominant metrical pattern and to discover deviations from that pattern. Scanning verse typically involves the following steps: (1) determining whether each syllable in a given line is stressed or unstressed, using natural speech patterns; (2) dividing each line into feet, determining both the predominant type of foot and the number of feet per line; (3) indicating any major pause (**caesura**) in each line; and (4) determining the poem's **rhyme scheme,** if any such scheme exists. Most critics assume that the identification of a work's particular **stan-zaic** structure is part of the work of scansion.

Modern scansion was adapted from **classical** quantitative scansion, in which critics analyzed meter on the basis of the relative time required to pronounce each syllable of a poetic line. Various combinations of long and short syllables made up a foot of **quantitative verse,** whereas various combinations of stressed and unstressed syllables make up a foot of **accentual-syllabic** poetry in English.

Three types of scansion exist in English — the *graphic,* the *musical,* and the *acoustic* — but the graphic is the most commonly used method of analysis. The following marks are typically used in graphic scansion: | (separating one metrical foot from the next), ´ (indicating a stressed or **accented** syllable), ˘ (indicating an unstressed or unaccented syllable), and ‖ (indicating a caesura).

EXAMPLES: Scansion of the first two lines of a famous **sonnet** by John Keats reveals that it is written in regular **iambic pentameter,** a meter in which unstressed and stressed syllables alternate, respectively, in each five-foot line of the poem:

> Whĕn Í | hăve féars | thăt Í | măy céase | tŏ bé
> Bĕfóre | mў pén | hăs gléaned | mў téem|ĭng braín. . . .

Beginning in the late nineteenth century, poets began to experiment with irregular meter. Scansion reveals Edna St. Vincent Millay's "sonnet xli" (1923) to be an **Italian sonnet** (rhyme scheme *abbaabbacdcdcd*) in which seven lines are written in fairly regular iambic pentameter and the other seven exhibit highly irregular metrical patterns. (Only the irregular lines have been scanned below):

> Í, beĭng | bórn ă | wómăn | ănd dĭs|tréssed
> Bў áll | thĕ néed | ănd nó|tiŏns óf | mў kínd,
> Am urged by your propinquity to find
> Your person fair, and feel a certain zest
> To bear your body's weight upon my breast:
> Sŏ súbt|lў ĭs | thĕ fúme | ŏf lífe | desígned,
> To clarify the pulse and cloud the mind,
> And leave me once again undone, possessed.
> Thínk nót | fŏr thís, | hŏwévĕr, | thĕ pŏor | tréasŏn
> Ŏf mў | stóut blóod | ăgaínst | mў stágg|ĕrĭng braín,
> Í shăll re|mémbĕr | yóu wĭth | lóve, ŏr | séasŏn
> My scorn with pity, — let me make it plain:
> Ĭ fínd | thĭs frĕn|zy ín|sufficiĕnt | réasŏn
> For conversation when we meet again.

Contemporary poetry can be so irregular that scansion becomes a form of interpretation. It is often difficult, in other words, to be sure which syllables are intended to be stressed, and different readers are likely to scan the same lines somewhat differently. Our scansion of a stanza from Derek Walcott's poem "A Far Cry from Africa" (1962), for instance, is at points highly debatable; note, for instance, that we have scanned the line "Where shall I turn, divided to the vein" in such a way as to suggest that the "I" is unstressed. You (or Mr. Walcott) may read it as a stressed syllable:

> Ăgáin | brútĭsh nĕ|céssĭtў| wípes ĭts | hánds
> Ŭpŏn thĕ | nápkĭn | ŏf ă | dírtў | caúse, ă|gáin
> Ă wáste | ŏf oúr | cŏmpás|sĭŏn, ăs | wĭth Spáin,
> Thĕ gŏríl|lă wrést|lĕs wĭth | thĕ súp|ĕrmăn.
> Í whŏ ăm | poísŏned | wĭth thĕ blŏod | ŏf bóth,
> Whére shăll Ĭ | túrn, dĭ|vídĕd tŏ | thĕ véin?
> Í whŏ hăve | cúrsed
> Thĕ drúnkĕn | óffĭcĕr | ŏf Brít|ĭsh rúle, | hŏw chóose
> Bĕtwéen thĭs | Áfrĭcă | ănd thĕ | Énglĭsh | tóngue Ĭ | lóve?
> Bĕtráy | thĕm bóth, | ŏr gíve | báck whăt | thĕy gíve?
> Hŏw căn Ĭ | fáce sŭch | sláughtĕr ănd | bĕ cóol?
> Hŏw căn Ĭ | túrn frŏm | Áfrĭcă | ănd líve?

scene: Traditionally, a subdivision of an **act** in **drama**. Today, however, many playwrights dispense with acts and compose plays that involve a series of scenes. Transitions between scenes are usually indicated by logical breaks in the action and **dialogue** and by the lowering and raising of the curtain in a conventional **proscenium** theater. In the **classical** French tradition, the entrances and exits of **characters** delineate the scenes in a play, but English theater has been less consistent in this regard. Reconfigured scenery, a change of **setting,** or (especially) indications that time has passed may indicate the commencement of a new scene in English drama. Distinguishing between scenes in modern works is often difficult and, consequently, a catalyst of critical debate.

science fiction: A type of **narrative fiction** that is grounded in scientific or pseudoscientific concepts and that, whether set on Earth or in an alternate or parallel world, employs both **realistic** and **fantastic** elements in exploring the question "What if?" As novelist Kingsley Amis explains, science fiction deals with a situation that "could not arise in the world we know, but which is hypothesized on the basis of some innovation in science or technology, or pseudo-technology." Such situations may entail either wonders or disasters. Other topics and **themes** typical of the **genre** include **utopian** or **dystopian** societies, fantastic journeys to unknown worlds, time travel, alien invasions and encounters, wars involving mass destruction, the destruction or assimilation of cultures, questions of identity, and the (d)evolution of humanity.

The term *science fiction,* which was coined in 1851 by British author William Wilson and popularized in the late 1920s by science fiction novelist and publisher Hugo Gernsback (who coined the term *scientifiction*), encompasses such a wide variety of works that many have claimed it defies definition. Science fiction writer and editor Damon Knight has stated that *science fiction* "means what we point to when we say it." Ursula K. Le Guin, a leading author and theorist of both science fiction and **fantasy fiction,** wondered in her 1993 introduction to *The Norton Book of Science Fiction* whether "the non-definability of science fiction [is] perhaps an essential element of it."

Forerunners of science fiction typically recount **tales** of adventurers who have travelled to unknown worlds. For instance, *Vera Historia (True History),* written around A.D. 150 by Lucian of Samosata, included a journey to the sun and the moon. **Dream visions** of the **Medieval Period** were religious in nature, describing journeys to heaven, hell, and the limbo called purgatory. By the beginning of the sixteenth century, several authors had imaginatively written about flights into space, where utopian societies were sometimes discovered. Thomas More's *Utopia* (1516), in which a sailor speaks of an **idyllic** land beyond the sea, is an early example of utopian literature said to anticipate science fiction. Other early works about fantastic journeys include Bishop Francis Godwin's *The Man in the Moone* (1638), John Wilkins's *Discovery of a New World in the Moone* (1638), Cyrano de Bergerac's *L'autre monde (Voyages to the Moon and the Sun)* (c. 1640–50), Jonathan Swift's *Gulliver's Travels* (1726), and Ludwig Holberg's *Nicolai Klimii iter Subterraneum (A Journey to the World Underground)* (1741).

Most scholars view Mary Shelley's *Frankenstein* (1818) as the first major work in the development of the genre; some have even called it the first science fiction novel. *Frankenstein,* which involves an experiment gone horrifically awry — the creation of a monstrous creature from parts of human corpses — has inspired countless stories about the possible misuse of science and has been spun off into numerous novels, movies, and comic books.

The nineteenth century also saw a number of other early and influential science fiction narratives into print. Edgar Allan Poe incorporated science into short stories such as "The Balloon-Hoax" (1850) and "Mellonta Tauta" (1850). Jules Verne contributed to the development of the genre with novels such as *Voyage au centre de la terre (Journey to the Center of the Earth)* (1864) and *Vingt mille lieues sous les mers (Twenty Thousand Leagues Under the Sea)* (1869). Space travel and utopias continued to be popular subjects for science fiction, as evidenced by Gustavus Pope's *Journey to Mars* (1894) and *Journey to Venus* (1895) and Edward Bellamy's *Looking Backward: 2000–1887* (1888), a novel that inspired political movements in both England and America through its tale of a man who falls asleep in capitalist Boston in 1887 and awakens in 2000 in a society free from injustice. Another common theme, the death of civilizations, is exemplified by Shelley's *The Last Man* (1829) and Richard Jefferies's *After London* (1885). Other notable nineteenth-century authors who mixed science and fiction include Rudyard Kipling and Robert Louis Stevenson.

Although Shelley's *Frankenstein* appears in hindsight to have been the first science fiction novel, it is H. G. Wells who is generally credited with having engendered the recognition of science fiction as a literary genre. Wells not only wrote about fantastic journeys, utopian and dystopian societies, and scientific discoveries but also introduced new topics, such as the concept of intentional time travel popularized by his **novella** *The Time Machine* (1895). He also provided the prototype for alien invasion stories in *The War of the Worlds* (1898), which, when performed on a live radio broadcast by Orson Welles and his Mercury Theater Company in 1938, caused panic among thousands of listeners who believed that aliens had actually invaded New Jersey.

Following the mass destruction of World War I, science fiction addressing the interrelated topics of war and the end of civilization as we know it became particularly popular in Britain. Examples of works reflecting these themes include Edward Shanks's *People of the Ruins* (1920) and S. Fowler Wright's trilogy about a possible second world war (*Beyond the Rim* [1932], *Power* [1933], and *Prelude in Prague* [1935]). Works describing dystopian societies, perhaps the best known of which is Aldous Huxley's *Brave New World* (1932), also came into vogue, as did works incorporating the idea of a new human race, such as Olaf Stapledon's *Last and First Men* (1930).

Notable science fiction was also produced in the first few decades of the twentieth century in both continental Europe and Japan. Examples include the Russian Konstantin Tsiolkovski's novel *Beyond the Planet Earth* (1920); the German science fiction magazine *Kapitän Mors (Captain Mors)*, launched in 1909; the works of German author Hans Joachim Dominik, one of the most popular and prolific practitioners of the genre; the Frenchman André Maurois's stories, including *The Weigher of Souls* (1931); and the works of Japanese authors such as Komatsu Kitamura, Juza Uno, and Masami Fukushima.

It was the United States, though, that was to become the center of the science fiction universe, thanks to the emergence of the "dime novel" and *pulp fiction,* both of which featured invention themes and could be inexpensively produced. At the end of the nineteenth century, a fifteen-year-old American named Louis Philip Senarens inaugurated "invention stories" — which were published as dime novels and widely **imitated** — with his tales of a **character** named Frank Reade, Jr., whose worldwide adventures involved submarines, helicopters, and armored cars and trucks. While the popularity of dime novels gradually faded, given that most were poorly written, the invention theme remained popular, and publishers turned to magazines printed on cheap paper made from wood pulp as a new medium for publishing science fiction featuring technological innovations.

With the advent of this "pulp fiction," the popularity of science fiction grew much faster in America than in England, on the European continent, or in Japan. In fact, during the two decades following 1926 — the year in which Gernsback founded *Amazing Stories,* America's first science fiction magazine — the genre became predominantly American. Some established British authors — including Wells, Stapledon, and Huxley, as well as John Beynon Harris (who wrote as John Wyndham), George Orwell (*1984* [1949]), and Arthur C. Clarke (best known for his *Space Odyssey* series [1968–97]) — continued to write in the traditional style. But other British science fiction writers began adapting their efforts to an identifiably American style: *hard science fiction,* based on real scientific theories. While hard science fiction may explore "hot topics" on which scientists disagree, it is grounded in actual science and engineering and generally offers a scientific explanation for any technology introduced in the story. In her introduction to the *Norton Anthology of Science Fiction,* Le Guin describes hard science fiction more valuatively, both as **denoting** "a fiction using hi-tech iconology with strong scientific content, solidly thought out, well researched, tough minded" and as **connoting** "fiction whose values are male-centered, usually essentialist, often politically rightist or militaristic, placing positive ethical value on violence."

The person most responsible for shaping and defining hard science fiction was an American named John W. Campbell, Jr., who in 1937 became the editor of the science fiction magazine *Astounding* (later renamed *Analog*). Campbell, who argued that science fiction stories should involve predictions based solely on scientific facts and principles and provide inspiration for future scientific discoveries, himself published an influential story in *Astounding* entitled "Who Goes There?" (1938) that was adapted to film as *The Thing* (1951, 1982). He also recruited authors for the magazine including Canadian A. E. Van Vogt, whose *Slan* (serialized in 1940) inspired science fiction readers to call themselves "slans"; Isaac Asimov, an influential and prolific author perhaps best known for his *Foundation* series (1951–53, 1982), who has contended that "modern science fiction is the only form of literature that consistently considers the nature of the changes that face us, the possible consequences, and the possible solutions"; and Robert Heinlein, who in 1947 set forth five principles for science fiction writing. Heinlein, also an influential and prolific author, argued that science fiction should: (1) be set in a new world; (2) make this faraway environment an integral part of the story; (3) feature a human problem or dilemma that is the focus of the **plot;** (4) show that the developing problem relates to and results from the new situation; and, most importantly, (5) rely on accurate scientific facts. Other authors who wrote for Campbell include Ray Bradbury (who later authored the best-selling novel *Fahrenheit 451* [1953]); Lester Del Rey; L. Ron Hubbard, whose best-selling book

Dianetics: The Modern Science of Mental Health (1950) is the basis of Scientology; Henry Kuttner; Catherine L. Moore (who wrote as C. L. Moore); Clifford D. Simak; and E. E. Smith, Ph.D. (known as "Doc" Smith).

Another influential and independent group of American science fiction writers and fans known as the Futurians emerged in the 1930s. The group, which was based in New York and active from 1938 to 1945, held that science fiction fans "should be forward-looking ('futurian') and constructive." Members included James Blish, Damon Knight, Cyril Kornbluth, Robert A. W. Lowndes, Frederik Pohl, and Donald Wollheim (who was considered the group's leader in the 1930s). Asimov was also associated with the group.

In 1949 and 1950, respectively, two important new science fiction magazines appeared: *The Magazine of Fantasy and Science Fiction* and *Galaxy*. *Galaxy,* edited by Pohl and H. L. Gold, published a number of works in serial form that became particularly influential, including Heinlein's *The Puppet Masters* (1951), Pohl and Kornbluth's *The Space Merchants* (1952), and Asimov's *The Caves of Steel* (1953, 1954), which was adapted to film in 1984.

Hollywood's popularization of several recurring themes in science fiction further contributed to the popularity of the genre. Notable movies include *The Day the Earth Stood Still* (1951), a movie about the fear of the end of civilization; *Forbidden Planet* (1956), which adapted Shakespeare's play *The Tempest* (1611) into a cautionary tale about the power of scientists; and the cult favorite *Invasion of the Body Snatchers* (1956), which, through its depictions of "pod creatures" taking over human beings, has been said by some to reflect fears of communism and attacks on individual freedom.

Other science fiction authors who wrote during the 1950s and beyond include American authors Hal Clement, Philip José Farmer, Frank Herbert (best known for his *Dune* series [1965–85]), Walter M. Miller, and Robert Silverberg. Edgar Rice Burroughs, best known for his *Tarzan* series but who had begun writing space stories — including works in his *Mars* and *Venus* series — several decades earlier also continued to publish science fiction. In addition, — several authors otherwise unassociated with the genre produced notable science fiction works, as exemplified by British novelist Nevil Shute's *On the Beach* (1957), which was adapted to film in 1959, and American novelist Daniel Keys's *Flowers for Algernon* (1959), later adapted to film as *Charly* (1968).

In the 1960s, a new type of science fiction called *New Wave* writing appeared on the scene. The phrase "New Wave" — from *nouvelle vague,* a French phrase used in criticism — was adopted in 1963 by Michael Moorcock, a respected British science fiction author, in an editorial published by the British science fiction magazine *New Worlds*. Moorcock, who drew on the unconventional science fiction works of William Burroughs in formulating his ideas and who later became the editor of *New Worlds,* encouraged science fiction writers to break away from traditional science fiction and to experiment. Among other things, Moorcock recommended avoiding the themes of space travel and interplanetary warfare and concentrating instead on the mysteries of mind and body. In essence, "inner space," rather than outer space, became the focus, and this "soft" science fiction, with its emphasis on human psychology and emotion, challenged the "hard," which its practitioners viewed as being out of step with the turbulent times.

Moorcock handpicked several authors to advance his ideas, including J. G. Ballard, who wrote *The Four-Dimensional Nightmare* (1963) and *The Terminal Beach* (1964); John Brunner, author of *Stand on Zanzibar* (1968); and E. C. Tubb (who in 1997 published *The Return,* the thirty-second and last novel in his "Dumarest Saga"). Brian Aldiss also wrote in the New Wave style, though he expressed reservations about the tendency of the movement to de-emphasize **plot.** American authors who wrote British-style New Wave stories included Samuel R. Delaney, Philip K. Dick, Thomas M. Disch, Harlan Ellison, John Sladek, Norman Spinrad, and Theodore Sturgeon. The film *Minority Report* (2002), which is set in Washington, D.C., in the year 2054 and which involves a "precrime" department that relies on three humans called "precogs" to predict murders before they happen, is based on Dick's short story "Minority Report," first published in 1956 in the magazine *Fantastic Universe.*

While Moorcock was promoting his ideas, Americans were developing their own version of New Wave writing under the influence of Judith Merrill, a science fiction author, reviewer, and anthropologist who from 1955 until 1966 published an annual collection of science fiction stories entitled *Year's Best SF.* Merrill, like Moorcock, sought to improve science fiction by encouraging writers to incorporate contemporary literary techniques into their works. The American authors she most influenced tended to be already established writers such as Roger Zelazny, perhaps best known for *He Who Shapes* (1966); Kurt Vonnegut, whose *Slaughterhouse-Five* (1969) boosted science fiction's standing in the academic world; and Silverberg, the author of *Dying Inside* (1972).

While British and American New Wave writers such as Ballard, Brunner, Delaney, Ellison, and Silverberg remained popular throughout the 1970s, hard science fiction began to make a comeback. Writers like Clement, Fred Hoyle, Larry Niven, and others who had published in *Analog* resisted Moorcock and Merrill's philosophy. Although the New Wave movement eventually lost some of its influence, both in England and America, its guiding principles have continued to inspire new science fiction incorporating sophisticated literary techniques and topics related to the world's emerging political and moral problems.

The 1970s also marked a turning point for science fiction in terms of two other influences on the genre. First, many authors began to mix fantasy fiction — which generally differs from science fiction in featuring magic and the supernatural — and science fiction. Second, new themes such as the evolution of gender relations and roles emerged when female authors such as Le Guin, Marion Zimmer Bradley, Anne McCaffrey, Alice Sheldon, and Kate Wilhelm began contributing to a genre that had previously been dominated by men.

Toward the end of the twentieth century, a group of younger American authors influenced by William Gibson's novel *Neuromancer* (1984) started writing a new type of science fiction called **cyberpunk,** a mix of hard and soft science fiction that reflected the ideas and attitudes of the rebellious counterculture "punk" movement. Cyberpunk authors Rudy Rucker, Neal Stephenson, and Bruce Sterling write about future worlds populated by "cyborgs" — hybrid beings that are part human and part machine — living in societies dependent upon technology for their daily existence. But more traditional science fiction, now a blend of various influences of the past century, is still written and published in magazines like *Isaac Asimov's Science Fiction Magazine.*

Contemporary science fiction authors include Samuel R. Delaney (*Dahlgren* [1975]), Orson Scott Card (*Ender's Game* [1986]); Lucius Shepard (*Life During Wartime* [1987]); Lois McMaster Bujold (*Falling Free* [1989]); Kim Stanley Robinson (*Red Mars* [1992]); Paul J. McAuley (*Red Dust* [1993]), and Octavia E. Butler, who received a MacArthur Foundation grant, or "genius award," in 1995 and who is best known for *The Xenogenesis Trilogy,* comprising *Dawn* (1987), *Adulthood Rites* (1988), and *Imago* (1989), and reissued as *Lilith's Brood* in 2000. Authors who are not typically classified as science fiction writers but who have made significant contributions to the genre include Stephen King, author of *The Dead Zone* (1979); Doris Lessing, whose four-novel *Canopus in Argos* series (1979–83) considers the possibilities presented by a feminist utopia; Carl Sagan, whose novel *Contact* (1985) was adapted into a 1997 film starring Jodie Foster; and Michael Crichton, whose *Jurassic Park* (1990) became a blockbuster movie in 1993. Other popular science fiction movies from the past few decades include *Close Encounters of the Third Kind* (1977), the *Star Wars* movies (1977–), and *E.T.* (1982).

scriptible* (writerly):* See **poststructuralism, text.

second-person point of view: See **point of view.**

semantics: See **linguistics.**

semiology: Another word for **semiotics.** The term *semiology* was coined by Swiss linguist Ferdinand de Saussure in his 1915 book *Course in General Linguistics.*
See **semiotics.**

semiotics: A term coined by Charles Sanders Peirce to refer to the study of **signs,** sign systems, and the way meaning is derived from them. **Structuralist** anthropologists, psychoanalysts, and literary critics developed semiotics during the decades following 1950, but much of the pioneering work had been done at the turn of the last century by Peirce and by the founder of modern **linguistics,** Ferdinand de Saussure.

To a semiotician, a sign is not simply a direct means of communication, such as a stop sign or a restaurant sign or language itself. Rather, signs encompass body language (crossed arms, slouching), ways of greeting and parting (handshakes, hugs, waves), artifacts, and even articles of clothing. A sign is anything that conveys information to others who understand it based upon a system of **codes** and **conventions** that they have consciously learned or unconsciously internalized as members of a certain culture. Semioticians have often used concepts derived from linguistics, which focuses on language, to analyze all types of signs.

Although Saussure viewed linguistics as a division of semiotics (semiotics, after all, involves the study of all signs, not just linguistic ones), much semiotic theory rests on Saussure's linguistic terms, concepts, and distinctions. Semioticians subscribe to Saussure's basic concept of the linguistic sign as containing a **signifier** (a linguistic "sound image" used to represent some more **abstract** concept) and **signified** (the abstract concept being represented). They have also found generally useful his notion that the relationship between signifiers and signified is arbitrary; that is, no intrinsic or natural relationship exists between them, and meanings we derive from signifiers are grounded in the differences *among* signifiers themselves. Particularly useful are Saussure's concept of the **phoneme** (the smallest basic speech sound or unit of pronunciation) and his idea that phonemes exist in two kinds of relationships: **diachronic** and *synchronic.*

A phoneme has a diachronic, or "horizontal," relationship with those other phonemes that precede and follow it (as the words appear, left to right, on this page) in a particular usage, utterance, or **narrative** — what Saussure called *parole* (French for "word"). A phoneme has a synchronic, or "vertical," relationship with the entire system of language within which individual usages, utterances, or narratives have meaning — what Saussure called *langue* (French for "tongue," as in "native tongue," meaning language). *Up* means what it means in English because those of us who speak the language are plugged into the same system (think of it as a computer network where different individuals access the same information in the same way at a given time). A principal tenet of semiotics is that signs, like words, are not significant in themselves, but instead have meaning only in relation to other signs and the entire system of signs, or *langue.* Meaning is not inherent in the signs themselves, but is derived from the differences among signs.

Given that semiotic theory underlies structuralism, it is not surprising that many semioticians have taken a broad, structuralist approach to signs, studying a variety of phenomena — ranging from rites of passage to methods of preparing and consuming food — in order to understand the cultural codes and conventions they reveal. Furthermore, because of the broad-based applicability of semiotics, structuralist anthropologists (such as Claude Lévi-Strauss), **psychoanalytic theorists** (such as Jacques

Lacan and Julia Kristeva), and literary critics (such as Roland Barthes, before his turn to **poststructuralism**) have made use of semiotic theories and practices. The affinity between semiotics and structuralist literary criticism derives from the emphasis placed on *langue*, or system. Structuralist critics were reacting against **formalists** and their method of focusing on individual words as if meanings did not depend on anything external to the **text**.

See also **structuralism, structuralist criticism.**

Senecan tragedy: A term used to refer both to (1) **tragedies** written by Seneca, a first-century A.D. Roman playwright (who modelled his own work on that of the fifth-century B.C. Greek playwright Euripides); and (2) **Renaissance** tragedies written during the **Elizabethan Age** and modelled on Seneca's **classical** tragedies.

Seneca composed tragedies in five **acts,** a structure used more or less consistently by playwrights until the nineteenth century. He frequently employed **bombast,** a **chorus,** and a ghost; his plays showcased drastically conflicting emotions, emphasized violence and revenge, and inevitably ended in **catastrophe.** Seneca's emphasis on presenting highly charged human emotion has been cited by many critics as crucial to the development of English drama, which had previously been used merely to portray events in an **allegorical** or **symbolic** manner.

Elizabethan playwrights **imitating** Seneca used these same basic elements but changed the character of Seneca's tragedies in two crucial ways, one intended and one unintended. First — and deliberately — Elizabethan playwrights such as Thomas Kyd (*Spanish Tragedy* [1586]) brought violence *on*stage; in Seneca's tragedies, **characters** merely reported violent acts, which occurred offstage. Second, ignorant of the fact that Seneca's tragedies were **closet dramas** (plays meant to be read or recited, not actually performed), they presented their plays using actors. Elizabethan playwrights also employed an even more **rhetorical** style than Seneca, who was himself noted for his bombastic language. Aside from bombast, Elizabethans favored such devices as **hyperbole,** intensely dramatic and drawn-out **soliloquies,** and *stichomythia* (a sort of repartee or verbal fencing in which two actors exchange barbed and pregnant one-liners). Thomas Sackville and Thomas Norton's *Gorboduc* (1562), commonly recognized as the first Elizabethan tragedy, was just such a Senecan tragedy.

As the Elizabethan Age progressed, two distinct forms of Senecan tragedy began to emerge. One form, exemplified by *Gorboduc,* closely parallels Seneca's tragedies and is learned, even pedantic, in spirit. The other form, pitched at a broad audience, including commoners, and noted for its extreme emotion, blood, and gore, has proved far more influential in the development of English literature and of English tragedy more specifically. This latter form, known as the **revenge tragedy** (or, in its most extreme manifestation, the *tragedy of blood*) mixed English **medieval** tragic tradition with classical Senecan tragedy. Such widely acclaimed plays as William Shakespeare's *Hamlet* (1602) have emerged as the result.

See also **revenge tragedy.**

sensibility: An emphasis on or susceptibility to emotions, feelings, and sentiments (rather than logic, reason, and thought). A whole **literature of sensibility,** including the **sentimental comedy** and the **sentimental novel,** developed and flourished during the eighteenth century, largely in reaction to seventeenth-century stoicism and in opposition to Thomas Hobbes's theory that humanity is inherently selfish. Sentimental comedies, novels, and poems exalted humanity's inherently benevolent nature, as demonstrated by the capacity for and expression of sympathy for the plights and joys of other human beings. Some critics confine the term *literature of sensibility* to sentimental works produced during the eighteenth century, but others use it to refer to any work following in that tradition. Today the term *sentimental* is often used to derogate these or more modern works containing what we would view as an overabundance of sensibility.

Sensibility has a second application in modern critical **discourse,** one referring to the inherent nature or quality of an individual's sensitivity (both intellectual and emotional) to **aesthetics** and sensory experience. Thus, one might speak of a writer — or, for that matter, of a friend — as having a romantic or poetic sensibility. T. S. Eliot used the phrase **dissociation of sensibility** to refer to authors whose works reveal a division between intellect and emotion. Eliot believed that these two faculties tended to be intertwined and to work together aesthetically in poems written in English by the so-called **metaphysical poets** and their great precursors.

EXAMPLES: Eighteenth-century examples include Laurence Sterne's *A Sentimental Journey* (1768) and Henry Mackenzie's *The Man of Feeling* (1771). A typical passage from the latter follows:

> Had you seen us, Mr. Harley, when we were turned out of South-hill, I am sure you would have wept at the sight. You remember old Trusty, my shag house-dog; I shall never forget it while I live; the poor creature was blind with age, and could scarce crawl after us to the door; he went however as far as the gooseberry-bush; which you may remember stood on the left side of the yard; he was wont to bask in the sun there; when he had reached that spot, he stopped; we went on: I called to him; he wagged his tail, but did not stir: I called again; he lay down: I whistled, and cried 'Trusty'; he gave a short howl, and died! I could have laid down and died too; but God gave me strength to live for my children.

Movies like *Old Yeller* (1957), *Terms of Endearment* (1983), and *My Girl* (1991) are more recent works following in the tradition of literature of sensibility; many would include *Ghost* (1990) in this category as well. Serious film critics tend to refer pejoratively to such films as "sentimental tearjerkers."

See also **Age of Johnson.**

sententia: See **aphorism**.

sentimental comedy (drama of sensibility): One of the literary manifestations of **sentimentalism** and the **literature of sensibility** in the eighteenth century, a type of **drama** that reacted against what was viewed as the excess, impropriety, and debauchery of **Restoration Age** drama. These plays, which flourished during the first half of the eighteenth century and were geared toward a growing middle class that prided itself on respectability, typically depict middle-class **characters** to engage the audience's sympathy and even tears. As such, these dramas inevitably present virtuous characters who, although nearly overpowered by evil or immorality, eventually triumph over these forces with their virtue intact. Characters in sentimental comedies tend to be **flatly** represented as either completely good or completely bad.

Due to the **caricatures** — and also the jarring **plot** twists — that tend to accompany works designed to teach moral lessons, sentimental comedies almost invariably strike modern audiences as unconvincing and unrealistic. The popularity of the **genre** began to decline in the latter half of the eighteenth century, although sentimental dramas continued to be written — and to be popular in some quarters — well into the nineteenth century.

EXAMPLES: Jeremy Collier's *Short View of the Immorality and Profaneness of the English Stage* (1698) inaugurated the genre, but Richard Steele is generally credited with establishing it. Steele's *The Conscious Lovers* (1722) and Richard Cumberland's *The West Indian* (1770) are typical dramas of sensibility.

sentimentalism: A term usually used pejoratively today to refer to works that play excessively and unconvincingly on the audience's emotions, particularly those of pity and sympathy. Authors are open to the charge of sentimentalism when, having failed to establish adequate **motivation** for the emotions they seek to elicit, they produce those emotions through fast-acting, artificial means (for example, scenes involving drawn-out, tearful goodbyes and the use of saccharine romantic music). Literature is also labeled *sentimental* when an author exploits and exaggerates **sensibility** (an emphasis on feeling rather than reason and the belief that humans are inherently benevolent rather than essentially selfish).

What is viewed as sentimental in one era may not seem so in another; furthermore, what strikes one person as unvarnished sentimentalism may seem compelling and moving to another. Although contemporary critics and readers find incredibly exaggerated and "hokey" the types of deathbed scenes common in eighteenth- and nineteenth-century **sentimental novels** and **comedies,** many critics and readers of those eras were impressed by the power of such works to express and evoke genuine emotion.

EXAMPLES: Harriet Beecher Stowe's *Uncle Tom's Cabin* (1852) is a nineteenth-century example of a work steeped in sentimentalism. Famous scenes include the one in which the slave Eliza crosses the Ohio

River by leaping from ice floe to ice floe while carrying her young child in a desperate attempt to escape the slave trader, and the deathbed scene of the young, angelic — and aptly named — Evangeline (Eva), the daughter of slaveholders. Shortly before Eva dies, she gives each of the slaves a lock of her hair, having preached to them the value of living a good Christian life:

> "I'm going to give all of you a curl of my hair; and, when you look at it, think that I loved you, and am gone to heaven, and that I want to see you all there."
>
> It is impossible to describe the scene, as, with tears and sobs, they gathered round the little creature, and took from her hands what seemed to them a last mark of her love. They fell on their knees; they sobbed, and prayed, and kissed the hem of her garment; and the elder ones poured forth words of endearment, mingled in prayers and blessings, after the manner of their susceptible race.

The play (and movie version of) *Annie* (1977, 1981) and the television series *Lassie* (1954–73) are seen by many modern audiences as extremely — and sometimes excessively — sentimental; critically acclaimed films noted for their sentimental power include *West Side Story* (1961), *Field of Dreams* (1989), and *Braveheart* (1995).

See also **sensibility** for additional examples of sentimental writing.

sentimental novel: One of the literary manifestations of **sentimentalism** and the **literature of sensibility** in the eighteenth century, a type of **novel** that typically appealed to the middle class in its emphasis on the importance of good conduct and rewards for adhering to moral standards. Sentimental novels also exalted emotion, portraying its expression as the mark of the virtuous. Tearfully lamenting someone's misfortune, for instance, revealed a kind and sympathetic heart. Even **villains** often broke down by the story's end in a flood of teary apologies and expressions of regret as they saw the error of their ways.

EXAMPLES: Samuel Richardson's *Pamela, or Virtue Rewarded* (1740). Harriet Jacobs drew on the techniques and **conventions** of the sentimental novel in her **slave narrative** *Incidents in the Life of a Slave Girl* (1861) in order to represent her vulnerability to the sexual advances of white men and thereby evoke readers' sympathy. Her target audience was largely made up of white women opposed to slavery who prized what were then viewed as the "feminine" values of chastity and piety, home and hearth.

septenary: A synonym for **heptameter,** a line of **verse** consisting of seven **metrical feet.** A **fourteener** is a type of septenary that has fourteen syllables per line, especially if the lines are written in **iambic** meter.

When used as an adjective, the term *septenary* simply refers to the number seven.

sestet (sextet): Broadly speaking, any six-line poem or **stanza.** *Sestet* is more frequently applied to the second part (the last six lines) of an **Italian sonnet,** however. The **rhyme scheme** of such a sestet is usually *cdecde,* although variations occur.

sestina: A tightly structured French **verse** form consisting of six **sestets** (six-line **stanzas**) and a three-line **envoy.** Widely acknowledged to be one of the most complicated of verse forms, the sestina originated in **medieval** Provence. The six terminal words of the first stanza (1-2-3-4-5-6) are repeated in a specific and complex pattern as the terminal words in each of the succeeding stanzas (6-1-5-2-4-3; 3-6-4-1-2-5; 5-3-2-6-1-4; 4-5-1-3-6-2; and 2-4-6-5-3-1). The envoy's terminal words follow the pattern 5-3-1 (and to make the form even more difficult, the other three terminal words from the preceding stanzas must appear in the middle of each of the three envoy lines in a 2-4-6 pattern). Despite the complexity of this form, poets representing diverse artistic movements and styles from different historical epochs have used it successfully. Practitioners include Sir Philip Sidney, Algernon Charles Swinburne, Rudyard Kipling, Ezra Pound, and W. H. Auden.

EXAMPLE: Auden's "Paysage Moralisé" (1933) is a sestina with an irregular, 3-1-4 envoy. Kathleen Craker Firestone's "Island Sestina" (1988) perfectly follows the sestina pattern:

> There's something magical about an island.
> No other meets the feeling, quite serene,
> of walking on a quiet beach of white sand
> and skipping stones across the liquid blue.
> The solitude is seen in wandering footprints
> and heard in whispering leaves of nearby trees.
>
> The kingbird and the bluebird perched in song trees
> bring music to the silence of the island,
> and chipmunks on the ground leave tiny footprints.
> The flight of gulls above is so serene.
> The flowers in the meadow, bells of soft blue,
> and daisies spring up sweetly from the sand.
>
> The dune is but a mountain made of beach sand.
> Its borders are made green with cedar trees.
> The green appears more bright against the sky's blue
> to compliment dune's bleakness on the island.
> The dune crest, place for resting, so serene,
> gives way in gentle servitude to footprints.
>
> A blowout in the dune is crossed by footprints.
> One dancing in delight across the sand
> falls silently to sand and rests serene
> beside decaying trunks of cedar trees
> and feels the peace of being on an island,
> while gazing up at skies of brilliant blue.

The dune slopes down to meet the water's blue.
The water fills small craters left by footprints.
Footprints trace the border of the island,
leaving peaceful stride marks in the sand;
and inland from the beach, the whispering trees
still sing a gentle melody, serene.

Is there a place on earth that's more serene?
A place where there's no cause for feeling blue?
If they could speak, these solid, stately trees,
of past explorers who have left their footprints,
what messages would they write in the sand,
of solitude discovered on an island?

The mood of peace serene is left by footprints.
The water, tranquil blue, caresses sand,
as songs from whispering trees praise such an island.

setting: That combination of place, historical time, and social milieu that provides the general background for the **characters** and **plot** of a literary work. The general setting of a work may differ from the specific setting of an individual scene or event; nonetheless, specific settings may be said to contribute to the overall setting. In drama, *setting* may refer to the physical backdrop of the play, that is, the scenery and sometimes even the props. Setting frequently plays a crucial role in determining the **atmosphere** of a work.

Seven Cardinal Virtues: The seven virtues identified by **medieval** Christian theologians as being of paramount importance. These virtues included charity (love), faith, hope, fortitude, justice, prudence, and temperance. Biblical teachings (especially the New Testamant) were the source of the first three virtues; as such, they have often been called the *theological virtues*. The latter four virtues, emphasized by ancient Greek philosophers, have been called the *natural virtues*.

Seven Deadly Sins: The seven capital or cardinal sins that the **medieval** Christian church believed entailed spiritual death. Once a deadly sin had been committed, eternal damnation could only be averted through absolute and complete penitence on the part of the sinner. The seven sins were divided into three categories: the sins of the Devil, which included pride, wrath (anger), and envy; the sins of the world, which included avarice (greed); and the sins of the flesh, which included lust, gluttony, and sloth (often defined as laziness, but in fact more similar to what we would today call depression). Of the deadly sins, pride was considered the worst, since it was seen as the cause of Satan's original fall from grace. The Seven Deadly Sins were common subject matter for medieval (including **Middle English**) and **Renaissance** literature, especially **allegories.**

EXAMPLES: In very different ways, Geoffrey Chaucer's "The Parson's Tale," one of the *Canterbury Tales* (c. 1387), and the fourth **canto** of the first book of Edmund Spenser's *The Faerie Queene* (1590, 1596) present and characterize each of the Seven Deadly Sins.

sextet: See **sestet.**

sexualities criticism: See **gay and lesbian criticism, queer theory.**

sexuality: A term referencing the perceived identities *heterosexual, homosexual, bisexual, transgendered, transsexual,* and so forth.

Queer theorists, as well as **gender critics** and some **gay and lesbian critics,** take a **constructionist** view of sexuality — that is, they contend that sexuality is socially constructed, the product of prevailing cultural **discourses,** mores, and institutions. Drawing on gender theory, which posits that the characteristics associated with the **gender** designations masculine / feminine are learned rather than innate, such critics argue that the various characteristics associated with homosexuality and heterosexuality are also culturally determined. Moreover, they tend to reject the simple **binary opposition** heterosexual / homosexual, instead viewing sexuality as a continuum encompassing degrees of sexual orientation as well as behaviors and practices ranging from fetishes to transvestism.

Other gender, gay, and lesbian critics take an **essentialist** view, maintaining that sexuality, like sex — the biological designation male / female — is innate (genetically determined). Such critics believe that homosexuals and heterosexuals are different by nature, just as a number of **feminist critics** believe men and women to be inherently different. They may also contend that there are distinct homosexual and heterosexual ways of reading and writing.

Whether critics have a constructionist or essentialist perspective, most agree that Western culture has **privileged** heterosexuality while devaluing and marginalizing all other forms of sexuality.

Shakespearean sonnet (English sonnet): A fourteen-line **sonnet** consisting of three **quatrains** with the **rhyme scheme** *abab cdcd efef,* followed by a **couplet** rhyming *gg.* The **Spenserian sonnet,** developed by English poet Edmund Spenser, follows the same basic **stanzaic** form — three quatrains followed by a couplet — but links the quatrains together by its rhyme scheme: *abab bcbc cdcd ee.*

EXAMPLE: In Sonnet 118 (1609), William Shakespeare approximates the standard rhyme scheme by using **eye-rhyme** and **half-rhyme:**

> Let me not to the marriage of true minds
> Admit impediments. Love is not love
> Which alters when it alteration finds,
> Or bends with the remover to remove:
> Oh, no! It is an ever-fixèd mark,
> That looks on tempests and is never shaken;
> It is the star to every wandering bark,
> Whose worth's unknown, although his height be taken.

Love's not Time's fool, though rosy lips and cheeks
Within his bending sickle's compass come;
Love alters not with his brief hours and weeks,
But bears it out even to the edge of doom.
If this be error and upon me proved,
I never writ, nor no man ever loved.

shaped verse: See **concrete poetry.**

short story: A brief **fictional prose narrative** that may range from about five hundred to two thousand words (the short short story) to twelve thousand to fifteen thousand words (the long short story, sometimes referred to as a **novella**). The short story may be distinguished from the even briefer prose narrative form we call the **anecdote** by its meticulous and deliberate craftsmanship, which may involve definite **plot** structure, complexity of **characterization,** and often a **point of view** from which the story is told. It may also be distinguished from the longer **novel** form by its relatively simple purpose, which is generally to reveal essential aspects of a **character** or characters, not to show character development over time. Unlike novels, short stories usually have a single focus and produce a specific dramatic revelation or effect (often the result of opposing motivations or forces) toward which the story builds and to which everything else in the story is subordinate. Short stories are like novels, however, insofar as they may be plausible or implausible, philosophic or romantic, and so forth; they are also like novels insofar as they have the chameleon capability of reflecting characteristics and elements of any number of other major **genres** (including **comedy, tragedy,** and **satire** — three of the six **classical** genres).

The short story has a long history. Short stories have been told in the form of **parables,** *fabliaux,* **fables, beast fables,** and **tales** (including fairy tales) in works as diverse as the Bible and **medieval romances.** The nineteenth century ushered in a revolution in short-story **narration,** as authors such as Edgar Allan Poe began to write **theoretically** about the genre. Other nineteenth-century writers who significantly developed the short story into an artistic narrative form include Nathaniel Hawthorne in the United States, Honoré de Balzac and Guy de Maupassant in France, E. T. A. Hoffmann in Germany, and Anton Chekhov in Russia. In the twentieth century, the short story emerged as a dominant literary genre through the work of writers such as Sherwood Anderson, Jorge Luis Borges, Willa Cather, F. Scott Fitzgerald, Ernest Hemingway, James Joyce, Franz Kafka, D. H. Lawrence, Katherine Mansfield, Flannery O'Connor, Katherine Anne Porter, Saki (H. H. Munro), Jean-Paul Sartre, and Eudora Welty. The presentation of action declined somewhat in the twentieth century as short-story writers chose to emphasize such things as the harsh realities of modern life or their characters' internal, psychological states.

FURTHER EXAMPLES: Guy de Maupassant's *"La parure"* ("The Necklace") (1884), Ambrose Bierce's "An Occurence at Owl Creek Bridge" (1898), Anton Chekhov's "The Bishop" (1902), O. Henry's "The Gift of the

Magi" (1906), Shirley Jackson's "The Lottery" (1948). Contemporary short-story writers include Raymond Carver, John Cheever, Nadine Gordimer, Ha Jin, Bernard Malamud, Alice Munro, Joyce Carol Oates, John Edgar Wideman, and Banana Yashimoto.

sibilance: A type of **alliteration** involving repetition of the consonant *s* to produce a soft or hissing sound.

EXAMPLES: The tongue twister "Sally sells sea shells by the seashore." The **narrator** of Thomas Hardy's *Tess of the d'Urbervilles* (1891) sibilantly comments that "the serpent hisses where the sweet bird sings." The Eagles' song "Hotel California" (1976) bristles with sibilance, juxtaposing words like "stab," "steely," "summer," "sweat," and "sweet" in evocative, almost **surrealistic** lyrics.

sign: Something that stands for something else. Different types of signs exist. Most theorists distinguish between the **icon** and the **index.** An icon signifies what it **represents** by its inherent similarity to that object, person, place, and so on. The famous cave paintings at Lascaux, France, for instance, are icons representing a variety of animals. An index has some natural cause-effect relationship to what it signifies. Clouds darkening the sky could thus be an index for an approaching thunderstorm, as smoke is for fire. American philosopher Charles Sanders Peirce contends that **symbols** are also signs; he calls the symbol a "sign proper." Peirce argues that symbols do not involve natural or inherent relationships between **signifier** and **signified,** but rather an arbitrary, socially and culturally determined relationship. For instance, when flown by ships, monochromatic flags of certain colors are internationally understood to represent specific conditions; red signifies danger or revolution, yellow signifies quarantine, black signifies death or protest, white signifies truce or surrender, green signifies proceed, and orange signifies distress.

Swiss linguist Ferdinand de Saussure defined the "linguistic sign" as composed of a signifier (a linguistic "sound-image" used to represent some more **abstract** concept) and a signified (the abstract concept being represented). He argued that the relationship between signifier and signified is completely arbitrary; that is, that no intrinsic or natural relationship exists between them. For instance, French speakers regard the signifier *pour* as meaning "for," whereas to English speakers the same signifier means "cause to flow in a continuous stream" or "rain heavily." Saussure further argued that the meaning of any given sign arises from the difference between it and other signs in the same linguistic system; as Saussure put it, a sign has no "positive qualities."

Differences in language make meanings recognizable; the word *pour* means what it does in English because it is distinct from other words (such as *four* and *shore* and *leave*) with which it can be compared and contrasted. Differences in meaning—including subtle differences between meanings that the same words have when embedded in different verbal contexts — are learned **conventions** that language users understand *as if* they were positive qualities, givens of Nature.

significance: A term used in **hermeneutics** to designate how readers relate the *verbal meaning* of a work to other elements in their lives, such as personal experiences, values, beliefs, and general cultural mores. Significance is typically distinguished from verbal meaning, which refers to the author's intended meaning. Hermeneutic theory, whose best-known proponent is E. D. Hirsch, postulates that verbal meaning can be determined but that significance cannot, since various readers bring different beliefs, values, and experiences to a **text.** Whereas verbal meaning can be construed as constant, significance changes from reader to reader; thus, no one significance is more right or wrong than any other. Hirsch has therefore argued that significance is not the proper subject of hermeneutic analyses.

signified: A term used by Swiss linguist Ferdinand de Saussure to refer to the comparatively **abstract** idea being represented by the **signifier.**
See **signifier.**

signifier: A term used by Swiss linguist Ferdinand de Saussure to refer to the **linguistic** "sound-image" used to represent some more **abstract** concept, called the **signified.** The signifier and signified are inseparable, even though the relationship between them is arbitrary. (There is no intrinsic reason why the idea of a tiger could not be called up by the sound-image, or signifier, "poof.") The signifier and signified together make up what Saussure called a **sign.** The study of signs, called **semiotics** or **semiology,** takes into account all signifying of semiotic systems, of which language is only one.
FURTHER EXAMPLES: The word *flag* is the sound-image, or signifier, for the abstract idea of a flag (the signified) that the word calls up in the mind of an English-speaking person. A flag itself is, in turn, a signifier of still more abstract signifieds, for instance, country or patriotism. **Poststructuralists** have pointed out that every signified is also a signifier in an endless chain of signification.

simile: A **figure of speech** (more specifically a **trope**) that compares two distinct things by using words such as *like* or *as* to link the **vehicle** and the **tenor.** Simile is distinguished from **metaphor,** another trope that associates two distinct things, but without the use of a connective word. To say "That child is like a cyclone" is to use a simile, whereas to say "That child is a cyclone" is to use a metaphor.
An **epic,** or **Homeric, simile** is an extended and elaborate simile in which the vehicle is described at such length that it nearly obscures the tenor.
EXAMPLES: Robert Burns used a simile in "A Red, Red Rose" (1796):

O My Luve's like a red, red rose.

Percy Bysshe Shelley's "Adonais" (1821) also contains a simile:

> Life, like a dome of many-coloured glass,
> Stains the white radiance of Eternity
> Until Death tramples it to fragments. . . .

Twentieth-century Indian sage Ramana Maharshi made use of a simile in imparting philosophical advice:

> Wanting to reform the world without discovering one's true self is like trying to cover the world with leather to avoid the pain of walking on stones and thorns. It is much simpler to wear shoes.

Thomas Keneally's novel *Schindler's List* (1982), made into an Academy Award–winning movie (1993), describes a Nazi official as follows: "He could sometimes be discovered wearing the smirk of his unexpected power like a childish jam stain in the corner of his mouth." Yiddish novelist Isaac Bashevis Singer once declared: "The short story is like a room to be furnished; the novel is like a warehouse." In the movie *Point Break* (1991), a baffled police officer says of a ring of armed robbers who have consistently eluded arrest: "They vanish like a virgin on prom night."

The following, highly **alliterative** passage from Jane Urquhart's *Away* (1993) concludes with a simile involving *as* rather than *like:*

> In this vibrant September he remembered the terror of late summer storms that had darkened noon and thundered at the door while lightning tore at the tops of thrashing pines, and because most of his previous life had been erased he played with these memories and even the fear connected to them as if they were bright new toys.

A more recent example of simile occurs in David Mamet's film *The Spanish Prisoner* (1997): "Worry is like interest paid in advance on a debt that never comes due."

Sins, Deadly: See **Seven Deadly Sins.**

site: A nongeographic "space," or place, where identity or meaning is formed or determined, largely by external forces such as those of history, language, or **ideology.** When a **text** is referred to as a site — an approach taken primarily by **poststructuralist** critics — the creative role of the author is diminished. Similarly, when the human subject, or self, is viewed as a site — whether influenced by what certain **psychoanalytic critics** term **the Other** or by the social and economic forces **privileged** by **Marxist critics** — the status of the individual is reduced from that traditionally accorded it in Western society.

situational irony: See **irony.**

situation comedy: See **comedy.**

slant rhyme: See **half-rhyme.**

slave narrative: A type of **narrative** written by a former African American slave that typically recounts that individual's life as a slave and how he or she managed to escape from what has euphemistically been referred to as the "peculiar institution." Although **autobiographical,** slave narratives were chiefly intended to convince the reader that slavery needed to be abolished because of its devastating impact on human lives and the human spirit. Given this overriding social and moral purpose, scholars have debated the extent to which these narratives were strictly autobiographical. Many have maintained that numerous **characters,** events, and **anecdotes,** though based in truth, were often **represented** in a manner designed to achieve the most persuasive impact on the reader. For instance, events could be relayed out of their proper chronological time, and some characters were composites or even based on stereotypes. The first slave narrative was published in 1760, but the **genre** was most prominent in the thirty years leading up to the Civil War (1861–65), after which slavery was abolished by the Thirteenth Amendment.

EXAMPLES: Frederick Douglass's *Narrative of the Life of Frederick Douglass* (1845) is the best-known American slave narrative. Other examples include Olaudah Equiano's *The Interesting Narrative of the Life of Olaudah Equiano* (1789) and Harriet Jacobs's *Incidents in the Life of a Slave Girl* (1861).

socialist realism: A term used to describe works that place a **Marxist** emphasis on **class** struggle as the catalyst for historical change and that employ the techniques of nineteenth-century **realism.** The term was used with reference to works in all of the arts, from literary works to sculptures to posters produced explicitly for propagandistic purposes. Artists were viewed as agents of the state whose principal role was to reinforce and advance doctrinally "correct" thinking. Socialist realism became the approved and official literary form of the former Soviet Union in 1934 during the First Congress of the Union of Soviet Writers; it subsequently became an important form in Eastern European countries under Soviet domination. The term was used not only to praise works that followed the official Communist line, accentuating the oppression of the proletariat under the capitalist bourgeoisie and lauding life under socialism in the USSR, but also to prescribe the content of those works.

sociohistorical criticism: See **new historicism, the.**

sociological novel: A **novel** detailing the political and economic conditions prevalent during the period in which the work is set. Sometimes called a *problem novel, social novel,* or *thesis novel,* a sociological novel usually implicitly or explicitly advocates some kind of social or political change.

EXAMPLES: Charles Dickens's *Hard Times* (1854), Upton Sinclair's *The Jungle* (1906), John Steinbeck's *The Grapes of Wrath* (1939). A more recent example is T. Coraghessan Boyle's *The Tortilla Curtain* (1995).

Socratic irony: See **irony.**

soliloquy: In a **play,** a **monologue** delivered by a **character** while alone on stage that reveals inner thought, emotions, or some other information that the audience needs to know.

EXAMPLES: William Shakespeare's *Hamlet* (1602) contains perhaps the most famous soliloquy in English literature, which begins "To be, or not to be." In the movie *The Candidate* (1972), Robert Redford plays the part of a once-idealistic young man who has been gradually corrupted by the process of campaigning for election; at one point, when he is alone, he delivers an anguished soliloquy in which he incredulously repeats a medley of the slick slogans and senseless blather that have boosted his standing in the polls to the point that, against all odds, victory is in sight.

In Peter Shaffer's 1973 play *Equus,* psychiatrist Martin Dysart muses about the "normalizing" goal of professional therapy; his speech is effectively a soliloquy since the only other character onstage is his deeply disturbed patient Alan Strang, whom he has hypnotized:

> The Normal is the good smile in a child's eyes — all right. It is also the dead stare in a million adults. It both sustains and kills — like a God. It is the Ordinary made beautiful; it is also the Average made lethal. The Normal is the indispensable, murderous God of Health, and I am his Priest. My tools are very delicate. My compassion is honest. I have honestly assisted children in this room. I have talked away terrors and relieved many agonies. But also — beyond question — I have cut from them parts of individuality repugnant to this God, in both his aspects. Parts sacred to rarer and more wonderful Gods. And at what length. . . . Sacrifices to Zeus took at the most, surely, sixty seconds each. Sacrifices to the Normal can take as long as sixty months.

sonnet: From the Italian word *sonnetto,* meaning "little song," a **lyric poem** that almost always consists of fourteen lines (usually printed as a single **stanza**) and that typically follows one of several **conventional rhyme schemes.** Sonnets may address a range of issues or **themes,** but love, the original subject of the sonnet, is perhaps still the most common.

Two major types of sonnets exist: the **Italian,** or *Petrarchan,* **sonnet** and the **Shakespearean,** or *English,* **sonnet.** The Italian sonnet has fourteen lines and consists of two parts: the **octave,** eight lines with the rhyme scheme *abbaabba,* and the **sestet,** six lines usually **rhyming** *cdecde* or *cdcdcd.* The Shakespearean sonnet, which also has fourteen lines, is divided into three **quatrains** and a **couplet,** rhyming *abab cdcd efef gg.* The **Spenserian sonnet,** which follows the same basic stanzaic form as the Shakespearean sonnet, consists of three quatrains rhyming *abab bcbc cdcd,* to link the quatrains together, and a couplet, rhyming *ee.*

Originally an Italian form practiced by poets such as Dante and Petrarch, the sonnet was introduced into English in the sixteenth century by Thomas Wyatt and the Earl of Surrey. (Sonnets written in English have usually employed **iambic pentameter.**) The form flourished during the **Re-**

naissance Period but declined during the **Neoclassical Period.** In the nineteenth century, the **romantic** poets revived the form, and it continues to be used today, though only occasionally.

FURTHER EXAMPLES: Joachim du Bellay is a famous French sonneteer. William Shakespeare is the best-known author of sonnets in English. Nineteenth-century sonneteers include John Keats, Dante Gabriel Rossetti, and Elizabeth Barrett Browning. Playwright, novelist, and poet Oscar Wilde included "Hélas," an Italian sonnet about his career as a writer, as an **epigraph** to his *Poems* (1881):

> To drift with every passion till my soul
> Is a stringed lute on which all winds can play,
> Is it for this that I have given away
> Mine ancient wisdom, and austere control? —
> Methinks my life is a twice-written scroll
> Scrawled over on some boyish holiday
> With idle songs for pipe and virelay°   *jingle*
> Which do but mar the secret of the whole.
> Surely there was a time I might have trod
> The sunlit heights, and from life's dissonance
> Struck one clear chord to reach the ears of God:
> Is that time dead? lo! With a little rod
> I did but touch the honey of romance —
> And must I lose a soul's inheritance?

In the twentieth century, poets as various as Ted Berrigan, Bernadette Mayer, Delmore Schwartz, and Allen Tate have written sonnets.

See **sonnet sequence** for further examples.

sonnet sequence (sonnet cycle): A series or group of **sonnets** interconnected by **theme** and written by one poet. The sonnet sequence typically explores the theme of love and the poet's fluctuating attitudes toward it, particularly with regard to a specific relationship and its progress (or lack thereof).

EXAMPLES: William Shakespeare's 154 sonnets constitute the most famous sonnet sequence in English; other well-known examples include Elizabeth Barrett Browning's *Sonnets from the Portuguese* (1850), George Meredith's *Modern Love* (1862), and Dante Gabriel Rossetti's *The House of Life* (1881). Not surprisingly, all of these sequences deal with the theme of love; they vary dramatically, however, in **tone** and range of attitude.

speech-act theory: A critical **theory** of language originally developed by philosopher John L. Austin. Austin vigorously opposed the tendency of most philosophers of language to presume that: (1) all possible sentences are either *kernel* (basic) sentences or variations of them; and (2) these kernel sentences declare something that can be determined to be either true or false. Austin also believed that the common practice of analyzing a sentence out of context was inappropriate and misleading.

In his most influential work, *How to Do Things with Words* (1962), Austin classified **locutions** (utterances) as **constatives** or **performatives.** Constative locutions, according to Austin, are sentences that state something that can be determined to be true or false. Performative locutions, by contrast, are sentences that actively "do" something, such as question, admonish, or plead. Some performatives, which Austin called "explicit performatives," actually create the result they intend when they are uttered. For instance, when a minister pronounces, "I baptize you in the name of the Father, the Son, and the Holy Ghost," you are baptized by virtue of that very utterance; when the dealer states, "Deuces are wild," in a card game, deuces become wild cards. Having made the distinction between constatives and performatives, however, Austin then demonstrated that the two categories are not mutually exclusive, which means that a sentence can involve both simultaneously. For instance, the sentence "You are in trouble" is a constative insofar as it asserts a state of affairs and a performative insofar as it makes a threat.

After Austin's death, "ordinary-language philosopher" John R. Searle expanded speech-act theory in his *Speech Acts: An Essay in the Philosophy of Language* (1969). Searle distinguished among four types of speech acts: **utterance acts, propositional acts, illocutionary acts,** and **perlocutionary acts.** An utterance act is a locution (simply saying something). As such, an utterance act may be a sentence, a phrase, or even one or more words that have no logical relation to one another. A propositional act has two components: referring to an object and predicating something upon that object; in short, a propositional act involves saying something about something else. The "referring expression," according to Searle, is "any expression which serves to identify any thing, process, event, action, or any other kind of 'individual' or 'particular'"; the object referred to in a locution may thus be the grammatical subject of that locution. For instance, in an example Searle provides, "Sam smokes habitually," Sam is the object of the locution. An illocutionary act involves uttering a statement that performs a particular function, such as asserting a fact, ordering, begging, promising, or threatening. A perlocutionary act occurs when an illocutionary act somehow affects the state of mind or the actions of the person to whom it has been directed. Searle maintained that speaking (or writing) always involves the first three speech acts, but he held that a perlocutionary act occurs only when an illocutionary act actually produces a change in the hearer's (or reader's) actions or state of mind. That is to say, when an illocutionary act is not only understood by the hearer but also has some type of effect on the hearer, it is also called a perlocutionary act. Furthermore, a perlocutionary act occurs whenever an illocutionary act affects the hearer, regardless of whether the speaker intended the statement to affect the hearer at all — and regardless of whether the statement had the effect the speaker intended it to have.

H. P. Grice, another "ordinary-language philosopher," has also made significant contributions to speech-act theory in essays such as "Logic and Conversation" (1975), where he developed his concept of the *communicative presumption,* a set of assumptions that he claims are shared by speakers of any given language.

Many of the tenets of speech-act theory have been incorporated into contemporary approaches to literary criticism, especially since 1970. Grice's concept of the communicative presumption, for instance, played a major role in the development of **discourse analysis.** Searle's speech acts have provided a conceptual model for critics from a variety of approaches for the systematic analysis of **discourse.** Certain speech-act theorists have revised **mimetic criticism,** arguing that literature — rather than offering a **representation** or **mimesis** of real places, things, people, and the things they say — is instead "mimetic discourse," language that represents the language through which we represent ourselves in the real world. Other critics using speech-act theory to revise traditional concepts of literature and, more specifically, prose **narratives** have proposed that readers and authors alike share the assumption that the overall fictional framework set up by the author in a work may violate ordinary standards of verisimilitude. However, *within* that framework, illocutionary statements made by characters must be taken at face value — that is, assumed to be reliable and to rest on a commitment to truth of assertion, just as if they were illocutionary statements made not in fiction but rather in our day-to-day world. **Deconstructors,** who view **texts** as **rhetoric** (rather than as a picture window through which a fixed and reliably correct meaning or truth may be glimpsed), have used speech-act theory to suggest that the performative nature of language leads readers to interpretive impasses, points at which they must choose between contradictory interpretive possibilities and accede to the **undecidability** of the text's meaning.

See **illocutionary act, perlocutionary act, propositional act,** and **utterance act** for examples of these types of speech acts.

Spenserian sonnet: A type of **sonnet** developed by sixteenth-century English poet Edmund Spenser that follows the same basic **stanzaic** form as the **Shakespearean sonnet** — three **quatrains** followed by a **couplet** — but whose **rhyme scheme** — *abab bcbc cdcd ee* — links the three quatrains together.

EXAMPLE: The seventy-fifth sonnet from Spenser's *Amoretti* (1595):

> One day I wrote her name upon the strand,
> But came the waves and washéd it away:
> Agayne I wrote it with a second hand,
> But came the tyde, and made my paynes his prey.
> "Vayne man," sayd she, "that doest in vaine assay,
> A mortall thing so to immortalize,
> For I my selve shall lyke to this decay,
> And eek my name bee wypéd out lykewize."

> "Not so," quod I, "let baser things devize
> To dy in dust, but you shall live by fame:
> My verse your vertues rare shall eternize,
> And in the heavens write your glorious name.
> Where whenas death shall all the world subdew,
> Our love shall live, and later life renew."

Spenserian stanza: A complex **stanzaic** form developed by sixteenth-century English poet Edmund Spenser for his long **narrative** poem, *The Faerie Queene* (1590, 1596). A Spenserian stanza is made up of nine lines with the **rhyme scheme** *ababbcbcc.* The first eight lines are written in **iambic pentameter,** and the final line is an **Alexandrine** (iambic **hexameter**).

EXAMPLES: The opening stanza of Spenser's *The Faerie Queene:*

> A gentle Knight was pricking on the plaine,
> Y-cladd in mightie armes and silver shielde,
> Wherein old dints of deepe woundes did remaine,
> The cruell markes of many a bloody fielde;
> Yet armes till that time did he never wield:
> His angry steede did chide his foming bitt,
> As much disdayning to the curbe to yield:
> Full jolly knight he seemed, and faire did sitt,
> As one for knightly giusts and fierce encounters fitt.

Other poets who have used this form include George Gordon, Lord Byron; John Keats; and Percy Bysshe Shelley. Byron modifies the **meter** of the Spenserian stanza in *Childe Harold's Pilgrimage* (1812–18):

> I have not loved the world, nor the world me —
> But let us part fair foes; I do believe,
> Though I have found them not, that there may be
> Words which are things, hopes which will not deceive,
> And virtues which are merciful nor weave
> Snares for the failing: I would also deem
> O'er others' griefs that some sincerely grieve;
> That two, or one, are almost what they seem —
> That goodness is no name, and happiness no dream.

Keats employed the Spenserian stanza form in "The Eve of St. Agnes" (1820):

> Anon his heart revives: Her vespers done,
> Of all its wreathéd pearls her hair she frees;
> Unclasps her warméd jewels one by one;
> Loosens her fragrant bodice; by degrees
> Her rich attire creeps rustling to her knees:
> Half-hidden, like a mermaid in sea-weed,
> Pensive awhile she dreams awake, and sees,
> In fancy, fair St. Agnes in her bed,
> But dares not look behind, or all the charm is fled.

spondee: A **metrical foot** in **poetry** that consists of two **stressed** syllables (´´). The use of the spondee as the base, or predominant, foot of a poem is rare.

EXAMPLES: *dáylíght, cárpóol, séa bréeze.* The first **stanza** of Dylan Thomas's poem "Do Not Go Gentle into That Good Night" (1952) is heavily spondaic:

> Dó nót gó géntle into that góod níght,
> Óld áge shóuld búrn and rave at close of day;
> Ráge, ráge against the dying of the light.

sprung rhythm: A type of **meter** in which the number of **stressed** syllables in a line is constant but the number of unstressed syllables varies. Each of the stressed syllables must occur as the first syllable of a **foot,** and each foot may contain between one and four syllables. Accordingly, a foot written in sprung rhythm may have from zero to three unstressed syllables. Four types of feet may thus be used—the *monosyllabic* (one stressed syllable), **trochee** (´ ˘), **dactyl** (´ ˘ ˘), and **paeon** (´ ˘ ˘ ˘). Sprung rhythm was developed by the nineteenth-century English poet Gerard Manley Hopkins, who considered himself to be its **theorist** rather than its inventor because he identified sprung rhythm as the **rhythm** of common English speech, reflected in works such as early English poems and even nursery rhymes. The irregular, punctuated rhythm produced by sprung rhythm may be the closest to natural patterns of speech and written prose.

EXAMPLE: Hopkins's "The Windhover" (1918) (the marks identifying stressed syllables are the poet's own):

> I caúght this mórning mórning's mínion, kíng-
> dom of dáylight's dáuphin, dapple-dáwn-drawn Fálcon, in his ríding
> Of the rólling level úndernéath him steady aír, and stríding. . . .

spy fiction, spy novel: See **mystery fiction.**

stanza: A grouped set of lines in a **poem,** usually physically set off from other such clusters by a blank line. Stanzas in a given poem need not have the same **rhyme scheme,** and, technically speaking, **rhyme** need not be present for a group of lines to be called a stanza. Nonetheless, the term usually refers to line clusters that have a regular, recurrent form—that is, a constant number of lines, a constant number of **feet** per line, the same **metrical** pattern, and the same rhyme scheme. Each stanza of a poem, for example, might contain four lines (a **quatrain**) with four feet per line (**tetrameter**), a meter consisting of alternating unstressed and **stressed** syllables (**iambic**), and a pattern in which the first and third lines as well as the second and fourth lines rhyme, respectively (rhyme scheme *abab*).

stichomythia: See **Senecan tragedy.**

stock character: A type of **character** who regularly appears in certain literary forms. The audience or reader ascribes specific characteristics to such a character by virtue of **convention** — perceptions held in common by a cultural community. Stock characters are often, but not always, stereotyped or **flat** types or **caricatures** drawn simply and defined by a single idea or quality.

EXAMPLES: In fairy tales, a wicked stepmother and her intended victim, a beautiful, innocent young girl, are stock characters. The **villain** with an oily-looking "handlebar" mustache was a stock character in **Victorian melodramas** and early movies, as was the strong, silent, gun-toting macho cowboy in American Westerns. Many contemporary Disney movies include wise-cracking sidekicks such as the crab, Sebastian, in *The Little Mermaid* (1989), the parrot, Iago, in *Aladdin* (1992), and the three gargoyles, Victor, Hugo, and LaVerne, in *The Hunchback of Notre Dame* (1996).

stock response: An uncritical, automatic, "knee-jerk" response to a given situation from the audience or reader; a response according to **convention** rather than true feeling or appropriate judgment.

EXAMPLES: The death of a child typically elicits sadness; soldiers going into battle carrying the flag evoke a feeling of patriotism.

Storm and Stress: See *Sturm und Drang.*

story: A **narrative** of events ordered chronologically.
See **plot** for the distinction between plot and story.

stream of consciousness and stream-of-consciousness narrative: *Stream of consciousness* is a literary technique that approximates the flow (or jumble) of thoughts and sensory impressions that pass through the mind each instant. Psychological association (rather than rules of **syntax** or logic) determines the presence or absence, as well as the order, of elements in the "stream." William James, in his *Principles of Psychology* (1890), gave currency to the term *stream of consciousness,* which he used to designate the flow and mixture of all past and present experience in the mind.

Works written by authors using this technique frequently appear to be choppy or fragmented — just as our thoughts, emotions, and sensory impressions often are. This lack of cohesion (or even coherence) in no way implies sloppiness, randomness, or purposelessness on the part of the author. Rather, the sudden countercurrents and unexpected branchings of **discourse** characteristic of *stream-of-consciousness narrative* are carefully designed to reveal specific characteristics of a fictional human mind.

In the *stream-of-consciousness novel,* the author typically presents the associative mental flow of one or more **characters,** often emphasizing the nonverbal level at which **images** express what words by themselves cannot. Great value is placed on the interior mental and emotional processes of individuals, rather than on the exterior world that their thinking reflects;

these processes, however, are acknowledged to be disjointed and the products of free association rather than of linear or logical thinking.

Although *stream of consciousness* and **interior monologue** are often used interchangeably, the former is the more general term. Interior monologue, strictly defined, is a type of stream of consciousness. As such, it presents a character's thoughts, emotions, and fleeting sensations to the reader. Unlike stream of consciousness more generally, however, the ebb and flow of the psyche revealed by interior monologue typically exists at a pre- or sublinguistic level, where images and the **connotations** they evoke supplant the literal **denotative** meanings of words.

EXAMPLES: Édouard Dujardin's *Les lauriers sont coupés (We'll to the Woods No More)* (1888), which is often said to be the first novel to use stream of consciousness. Later pioneers of stream of consciousness include Dorothy Richardson, Virginia Woolf, and James Joyce. Woolf's *To the Lighthouse* (1927) and William Faulkner's *The Sound and the Fury* (1929) make extensive use of stream of consciousness.

See also **interior monologue.**

stress: The emphasis placed on a syllable. The symbols ´ and ˇ are used for stressed and unstressed syllables, respectively, of a word. Many poets and critics use *stress* and *accent* interchangeably, but some differentiate between the two terms, reserving *stress* for metrical emphasis (the pattern of emphasized and nonemphasized syllables required by the prevailing **meter** of a poem) and *accent* for **word accent** (the emphasis used in everyday **discourse**).

See **accent.**

strophe: A term that may be used to refer to a poetic **stanza,** although some critics reserve the term *stanza* for the repeated, **rhymed** divisions of a poem while using *strophe* for irregular, unrhymed divisions. *Strophe* also has other, more specialized meanings dating back to the ancient Greeks, who used the word to refer to: (1) that part of the Greek choral **ode** chanted by the **chorus** as it danced in one direction before retracing its steps during the **antistrophe;** or (2) one of the three recurrent parts of the **Pindaric ode,** modelled on choral odes.

structural irony: See **irony.**

structuralism: A **theory** of humankind whose proponents attempted to show systematically, even scientifically, that all elements of human culture, including literature, may be understood as parts of a system of **signs.** Critic Robert Scholes has described structuralism as a reaction to "'modernist' alienation and despair." **Modernism,** a movement that encompassed all of the creative arts, arose in the wake of the physically devastating and psychologically disillusioning experience of World War I, and as such, modernist works expressed and reflected the pervasive sense of loss, decay, and disillusionment engendered by the Great War. Although the end of World War II, with its shocking experience of mass destruction and genocide, similarly evoked tremendous disillusionment in many Westerners, others in the West were eager to embrace systems of thought that emphasized comprehensibility and significance, rather than absurdity and meaninglessness. Structuralism, which arose in France in the 1950s, proved to be just such a system. Before being critiqued and, to a great extent, superseded by **poststructuralist** thought, it influenced a number of disciplines ranging from anthropology to literary criticism.

European structuralists such as Roman Jakobson, Claude Lévi-Strauss, and Roland Barthes (before his shift toward poststructuralism) attempted to develop a **semiology,** or **semiotics** (science of signs). For structuralists, anything that people do or use to communicate information (of any type) to others is a sign. Everything from road signs to Braille to handshakes to articles of clothing falls under the broad umbrella of structuralist concern. Barthes, among others, sought to recover literature and even language from the isolation in which they had been studied by showing that all social practices (such as those involving clothes and dressing, food and eating) involve systems of signification that function like a language and are, as such, interpretable by those familiar with their "grammar" and "syntax."

According to structuralists, the signs that govern all human communication are arbitrary. In other words, there is no inherent reason why a handshake should be used as a means of meeting or greeting, no inherent reason why a green light should mean "go." Furthermore, since these signs have no inherent or "natural" meaning, signification derives from the differences *among* signs. A green light means what it does both because a red light and a handshake mean something else. However arbitrary a sign may be, it does have a meaning that is understood by reference to a set of **conventions** and **codes.** Structuralists thus view signification as both "determinable" (capable of being determined) and "determinate" (fixed and reliably correct); they posit the possibility of approaching a **text** or other signifying system systematically, even scientifically, and of revealing the "grammar" behind its form and meaning.

Structuralism was heavily influenced by **linguistics,** especially by the pioneering work of linguist Ferdinand de Saussure. Particularly useful to structuralists were Saussure's concept of the **phoneme** (the smallest basic speech sound or unit of pronunciation) and his idea that phonemes exist in two kinds of relationships: **diachronic** and *synchronic.* A phoneme has a diachronic, or "horizontal," relationship with those phonemes that precede and follow it (as the words appear, left to right, on this page) in a particular usage, utterance, or **narrative** — what Saussure called *parole* (French for "word"). A phoneme has a synchronic, or "vertical," relationship with the entire system of language within which individual usages, utterances, or narratives have meaning — what Saussure called *langue* (French for "tongue," as in "native tongue," meaning language). *An* means what it means in English because those of us who speak the language are plugged into the same system (think of it as a computer network where different individuals can access the same information in the same way at a given time.)

Following Saussure, Lévi-Strauss, an anthropologist, studied hundreds of **myths,** breaking them into their smallest meaningful units, which he called "mythemes." Removing each from its diachronic relations with other mythemes in a single myth (such as the myth of Oedipus and his mother), he vertically aligned those mythemes that he found to be homologous (structurally correspondent). He then studied the relationships within as well as between vertically aligned columns, in an attempt to understand scientifically, through ratios and proportions, those thoughts and processes that humankind has shared, both at one particular time and across time. Whether Lévi-Strauss was studying the **structure** of myths or the structure of villages, he looked for recurring, common elements that transcended the differences within and among cultures.

Structuralists followed Saussure in preferring to think about the overriding *langue,* or language, of myth, in which each mytheme and mytheme-constituted myth fits meaningfully, rather than about isolated individual *paroles,* or narratives. Structuralists also followed Saussure's lead in believing that sign systems must be understood in terms of **binary oppositions** (a proposition later disputed by poststructuralist Jacques Derrida). In analyzing myths and texts to find basic structures, structuralists found that opposite terms modulate until they are finally resolved or reconciled by some intermediary third term. Thus, a structuralist reading of Milton's *Paradise Lost* (1667) might show that the war between God and the rebellious angels becomes a rift between God and sinful, fallen man, a rift that is healed by the Son of God, the mediating third term.

Although structuralism was largely a European phenomenon in its origin and development, it was influenced by American thinkers as well. Noam Chomsky, for instance, who powerfully influenced structuralism through works such as *Reflections on Language* (1975), identified and distinguished between "surface structures" and "deep structures." According to Chomsky, deep structure, the primary and elementary structure of language, controls the meaning of an utterance, whose surface structure is made up of some combination of words and sounds. The surface structure of an utterance may vary but still have the same essential meaning. For instance, the sentences "Harry kissed Sally" and "Sally was kissed by Harry" have different surface structures but the same deep structure. By contrast (to use Chomsky's example), the sentences "John is eager to please" and "John is easy to please" are similar in terms of surface structure but very different in terms of deep structure.

Beginning in the late 1960s, structuralism came under increasing attack, especially from poststructuralist critics. Opponents of structuralism reject its claim to **objective,** systematic, and even scientific, analysis. Poststructuralists in particular also reject the structuralist claim that meanings are not only determinable but also determinate by those who understand the rules that governed the text's production. They believe that signification is an intricate and interminable web of **connotations** and associations, continually deferring the determination of determinate meaning. Jacques Derrida has used the word **dissemination** — in which he **puns** on the Greek roots of the words *seed* (*seme*) and *sign* (*sem*) — to refer to the scattering of semantic possibilities that takes place as soon as any statement is made, the resulting multiplication of interpretive possibilities, and the subsequent impossibility of choosing one meaning (among myriad possible meanings) as the true or correct one.

See also **structuralist criticism.**

structuralist criticism: A type of literary **criticism** that derives from **structuralism,** a **theory** of humankind whose proponents believe that all elements of human culture, including literature, may be understood as parts of a system of **signs.** Structuralist criticism was at first mainly a French phenomenon, centered in Paris, but then spread throughout Europe and the United States in the 1960s.

Structuralist critics, using Swiss linguist Ferdinand de Saussure's **linguistic** theory as a model and employing **semiotic** theory (the general science of signs developed independently by American philosopher Charles Sanders Peirce and Saussure, who called his theory **semiology**), posit the possibility of approaching and analyzing a **text** systematically, even scientifically. Structuralists believe that signification is arbitrary rather than inherent or absolute, and that all signs derive their meaning based on their differences from one another. They generally follow Saussure's lead in believing that sign systems must be understood in terms of **binary oppositions.** In analyzing **myths** and texts to find basic **structures,** they tend to find that opposite terms modulate until they are finally reconciled by some intermediary third term. Structuralist critics also typically believe that meaning(s) in a text, as well as the overall meaning *of* a text, can be determined by uncovering the system of signification — the "grammar" that governed its production and that operates within it. Readers understand a text because they have mastered this grammar, this special set of literary **conventions** and **codes,** which it is the job of the structuralist critic to identify.

Insofar as structuralist literary critics eschew consideration of the author and other external references such as historical circumstance, structuralist criticism may be called a text-centered approach. Structuralist critics, however, may focus either on individual literary works or on literature in general. Those who follow the first path examine linguistic patterns in a specific work, arguing that some patterns serve a unifying purpose whereas other patterns serve to accentuate particular elements of the work. More often, however, structuralist critics take a broader perspective, drawing heavily on semiotic theory to examine literary conventions and devices generally — how they are organized and how they function to create meaning in any literary work.

Structuralist critics have challenged several traditional tenets of literary criticism. First, they have rejected the term *work* in favor of *text* to accentuate their point that all literature is subject to a set of codes. They have also rejected the idea that a text is a **representation** of reality; structuralists

spurn any notion of an inherent reality since they believe that all signification is arbitrary. Readers conceive of a text as **realistic,** they argue, only
because they have unconsciously internalized certain codes as norms.
Third, structuralist critics have drastically revised the traditional concept of
the author as a unique figure who produces a unique opus, arguing that the
author, too, has internalized a set of conventions and rules. Thus the
reader, rather than the author, becomes the chief object of critical analysis,
but readers are themselves denied the status of purposive individuals who
creatively interpret texts. Instead, structuralist critics speak of a process of
reading whereby conventions and rules govern understanding of the text.

Structuralist literary criticism was at its inception directed chiefly at the
examination of prose works, but soon spread to encompass poetic works
as well as the examination of **poetics** itself. Jonathan Culler, for instance,
developed a theory of structuralist poetics in which he concentrates on the
reader instead of the text. In *Structuralist Poetics: Structuralism, Linguistics and the Study of Literature* (1975), Culler argued that a critic should
illuminate the process by which readers interpret texts rather than the
process by which authors compose them. Interpretation, or "literary competence," according to Culler, is regulated by literary conventions that can
be identified, whereas one cannot identify the conventions followed by the
author in composing the text.

Structuralist criticism has also had an impact on **narratology,** whose
practitioners view literary works as formal and intentional constructs; narratologists analyze the structural components of a **narrative,** the way in
which those components interrelate, and the relationship between this
complex of elements and the narrative's basic story line. (For instance, a
narratologist would be interested in why an author quotes statements representing the views of some **characters** while merely summing up the views
of others.) In addition, structuralist critical practices continue to influence
the field of semiotics, which was revitalized by literary critics including
Roland Barthes, Michael Riffaterre, and Susan Sontag. Contemporary
semioticians view literature and other social "texts" in terms of the
"codes" and interpretive rules that cause a particular social group to view
those texts as meaningful. They are especially indebted to Barthes, who
pronounced the death of the author, emphasized the role of the reader (or,
more precisely, *lecture,* or reading), and differentiated the *lisible* (readerly)
text (one that would provide the reader with a world replete with fixed
meanings) from the more open, *scriptible* (writerly) text (one that invites
readers to create meaning or multiple meanings, using all the codes and
conventions at their disposal).

Structuralism and structuralist criticism began to wane in the late 1960s,
when they came under vigorous attack by **poststructuralists.** Poststructuralists rejected the structuralist claim to scientific analysis. More importantly, they argued that meaning could not be definitively determined since
all systems of signification endlessly defer meaning through a chain of **signifiers.** Each word, according to poststructuralists, evokes a number of

possible significations, which in turn evoke other significations in an interminable sequence so that no single meaning can ever be positively ascertained to be the correct meaning. In fact, some significations may even be contradictory, making an absolute determination of meaning impossible.

structure: When equated with **form,** a term that refers to the arrangement of material in a work, that is, the ordering of its component parts or the design devised by the author to convey content and meaning. In a poem, for instance, structure encompasses the division of the material into **stanzas.** Some critics extend the use of the term to include the arrangement of ideas or **images.** In a play, structure refers to the division of the material into **acts** and **scenes** as well as to the logical progression of the action. (**Freytag's pyramid** provides one model for analyzing the sequence of events in a **tragedy:** introduction, **rising action, climax, falling action, catastrophe.**) In discussing novels, critics typically use the term to refer to **plot** (the ordering of the events that make up the **story**).

Critics following **Chicago School** critic R. S. Crane distinguished between structure and form. Going back to Aristotle's concept of form (the "dynamis") from the *Poetics* (c. 330 B.C.), Crane argued that form is the emotional force behind a literary work, the "shaping principle" that gives rise to and governs the structure, or arrangement, of parts in a work.

The New Critics, notably John Crowe Ransom, used the term *structure* to refer to the general intellectual content of a poem, that is, whatever can be paraphrased. In contrast, they used the term **texture** to refer to the surface details of a work, such as **imagery, meter,** and **rhyme.** They believed that both structure and texture are essential to a poem and argued that these elements, taken in combination, yield the poem's ontology, its utterly unique quality of being.

***Sturm und Drang* (Storm and Stress):** A late-eighteenth-century German literary movement in which **drama** was the **genre** of choice and whose adherents emphasized inspiration, emotion, passion, and individualism. The term is taken from the title of Friedrick von Klinger's 1776 play *Der Wirwarr, oder Sturm und Drang* (*Confusion, or Storm and Stress*); thus, Anglo-American critics sometimes refer to the "Storm and Stress" movement in German Literature.

Johann Gottfried Herder is considered the founder of the movement, whose members and sometime-adherents included Johann Wolfgang von Goethe, Jakob Michael Reinhold (J. M. R.) Lenz, and Friedrich Schiller. *Sturm und Drang* writers rebelled against the strict tenets of French **neoclassicism** and the "reasonable" Enlightenment philosophies it sought to promote. They rejected the Graeco-Roman writers, to whom the classicists and Enlightenment thinkers turned for guidance, and followed instead the example of William Shakespeare, whom they considered liberated from the **conventions** of **classicism** and whose work had recently been translated into German. Furthermore, their writing tended to be extremely nationalistic, drawing heavily on **folk** traditions. Certain English novels, such as Emily Brontë's *Wuthering Heights* (1847), show the influence of the German Storm and Stress movement.

FURTHER EXAMPLES: Goethe's *Götz von Berlichingen* (1773) and Schiller's *Die Räuber* (*The Robbers*) (1781) are perhaps the most famous examples of the *Sturm und Drang* movement. Lenz's *Die Soldaten* (*The Soldiers*) (1775) and Heinrich Leopold Wagner's *Die Kindmörderin* (*The Childmurderess*) (1883) are also examples of the movement.

style: Used generally, the way in which a literary work is written, the devices the author uses to express his or her thoughts and convey the work's subject matter. The message or material that the author communicates to the reader, along with how the author chooses to present it, produce an author's individual style, which, given the quirks of human personality, necessarily varies from author to author. Style, however, is as elusive to define as it is to identify and analyze in a particular work or a group of works.

Style can be investigated from a number of vantage points. It may be viewed, for instance, in light of the means an author uses to create an effect; a critic may thus focus on such things as a work's **diction, imagery, and rhetorical** devices. Style may also be discussed with regard to a literary period, movement, or even author; in this case, a critic might identify and analyze only those aspects of a given work that reflect the general style in question. In either — but especially in the latter — case, the critic is likely to draw his or her vocabulary from a set of descriptive terms that have been developed over the years to characterize the styles of particular periods, movements, and authors (for example, ornate, **Augustan,** Wordsworthian, transparent, formal, high **Renaissance, alliterative,** Jamesian).

Traditional theories of **rhetoric** divide style into three major categories: the *high* (grand), the *middle* (mean), and the *low* (base, plain). Fairly recently, critic Northrop Frye invented a new stylistic distinction, one based on whether a work employs the expression and **rhythms** of ordinary speech or, instead, makes use of formal devices and elaborations in order to differentiate its language from the quotidian. Frye calls these styles the **demotic** and the **hieratic,** respectively; he does, however, identify a high, middle, and low level in each of these two classifications.

A style is said to be decorous when it conforms to its speakers, subject matter, and audience; in other words, decorous style is attained when the language of a work is appropriate to the **genre** in which it is written, the social **class** of those who speak in the work, the subject or contexts being represented, and the occasion of its production or reception. **Decorum** was an actual **convention** of writing in the eighteenth century, one that called for the style of a work to "match" or be consistent with all of its other aspects.

Discussions of style frequently consider whether the sentences of a work are predominantly periodic or loose (nonperiodic). A **periodic sentence,** unlike a **loose sentence,** is not grammatically complete until its very end. Typically, several dependent clauses and parallel constructions precede the final independent clause in a periodic sentence, so the meaning of the sentence cannot be ascertained until the entire sentence has been read. In contrast, a loose sentence typically contains a number of independent clauses joined only by coordinating conjunctions such as *and* or *but.* As such, it can usually be divided into multiple sentences, each of which has an independent — and thus readily apparent — meaning. Periodic sentences seem more formal or elevated than loose sentences, which tend to be informal or conversational.

Works predominantly featuring periodic or loose sentences can often be classified as having *hypotactic* or *paratactic* styles, respectively. Predominantly hypotactic works are made up of sentences containing subordinate clauses; these sentences are often logically linked together by a connective, whether temporal, causal, **syntactic,** or rhetorical (*therefore, consequently, moreover,* and *nevertheless).* Paratactic works, by contrast, exhibit sequences of sentences bearing a loose logical relation to one another; elements within those sentences tend to be joined by simple conjunctions (like *and*) that do little to show or explain causal or temporal relation. Although there is a high correlation between hypotactic style and periodic sentences on the one hand and between paratactic style and loose sentences on the other, the members of each pair of terms are not synonymous. The terms *periodic* and *loose* refer to sentences, for instance, whereas *hypotactic* and *paratactic* refer to the overall style of a work. Furthermore, even when *hypotactic* or *paratactic* is used more loosely to refer to the **structure** of a given sentence, it simply describes patterns typical of periodic or loose sentences, respectively. A periodic sentence with a hypotactic structure, for instance, contains hypotactic elements — multiple dependent clauses linked by connectives such as *therefore* (rather than simple conjunctions such as *and*) — but also exhibits an element that may — but need not — be present in a sentence featuring hypotactic structure: no periodic sentence is grammatically complete until its very end.

Whereas paratactic style is characteristic of many well-known **classic** works of literature (the Old Testament of the Bible, *Beowulf* [c. A.D. 700], and *La chanson de Roland* [c. 1100], for instance), hypotactic style is usually found in works that appeared at a later stage of language development. It should be noted, however, that certain modern authors whose works are by no means simple or simplistic (Ernest Hemingway, for instance) have reverted to loose sentence construction and a casual, paratactic style.

Those critics who analyze literary works on the basis of style are called stylisticians and are said to practice **stylistics.**

FURTHER EXAMPLES: The following passage from Robert Penn Warren's novel *All the King's Men* (1946) exhibits paratactic style:

And the bonds were issued and the schoolhouse built and more than a dozen years later the big black Cadillac with the Boss whipped past the schoolhouse, and Sugar-Boy really put his foot down on the gas and we headed out, still on the almost new slab of Number 58.

Hypotactic style is exemplified in the following passage from **Victorian** novelist George Meredith's *The Egoist* (1871):

> Nevertheless, she had been so good as to diminish his apprehension that the marriage of a lady in her thirtieth year with his cousin Vernon would be so much of a loss to him; hence, while parading the lawn, now and then casting an eye at the room where his Clara and Vernon were in council, the schemes he indulged for his prospective comfort and his feelings of the moment were in such stirring harmony as that to which we hear orchestral musicians bringing their instruments under the process called tuning.

stylistics: A critical method that analyzes literary works on the basis of **style.** Its practitioners focus on analyzing a writer's stylistic choices with regard to **diction, syntax, phonology, figurative language,** vocabulary, and even spatial and graphic characteristics. In analyzing literary works, stylisticians explore topics such as whether writers use everyday speech or elevated language, whether they use **periodic** or **loose sentences,** and whether they employ predominantly visual or auditory **images,** for example.

There are two major types of stylistics. Formal stylistics upholds the traditional definition of style, that is, how a writer writes (the devices authors use to express their thoughts and to convey the subject matter of a work), as opposed to *what* the writer writes (the content, which these critics refer to as "information" or "message"). Formal stylisticians understand style as the ways authors can present the content of a work, ways that invariably affect its **aesthetic** quality and the reader's emotional reaction. They claim that particular writers, works, **genres,** and even historical eras can be distinguished on the basis of their style, which is composed of a set of interactive stylistic elements. This claim, of course, necessitates that stylisticians be able to distinguish stylistic from other elements of the **text,** the feasibility of which many other critics dispute. Formal stylisticians have borrowed heavily from **linguistics** in identifying these "formal properties," which include such elements as auditory, **metrical,** or image patterns; diction; the use of **rhyme;** and sentence structure.

The second group of stylisticians has broadened the range of formal stylistics. These critics argue that stylistics encompasses the myriad ways in which language is used in literature. Although these stylisticians cross the traditional boundary of stylistics, especially by their interest in **rhetoric,** they maintain the emphasis on **objectivity** through their text-centered approach and by seeking to detect those rules that generate the various effects and significance of language in literary texts.

As a method of analysis, stylistics largely owes its origin to (and has been heavily influenced by) **Russian formalism** (particularly the writings of Roman Jakobson) and European **structuralism.** These two critical schools have provided stylisticians with models for analyzing literary texts.

Stylisticians claim to study works in an objective, or "scientific," manner. Many stylisticians thus perform quantitative analyses of literary works, calculating the frequency with which various stylistic and grammatical elements appear. (This kind of analysis could include, for example, the percentage of sentences beginning with introductory dependent clauses or the ratio of adjectives to nouns in a writer's work.) Some stylisticians use computer technology to produce frequency tables that they claim can distinguish one style from another in much the same way as a human fingerprint or DNA sample distinguishes one person from another. Certain stylisticians even verge on conducting psychological analysis, seeking to identify the author's characteristics or viewpoints based on the stylistic "profile" that has been developed. The stylistic claim to scientific accuracy has been much criticized, especially on the grounds that style cannot be divorced from content and that it cannot be objectively separated out from the web of language in which it is embedded. That is, an author's language in a work is greatly determined, on the one hand, by linguistic **conventions** and conditions prevailing at the time of writing and, on the other, by the subject matter of that particular work. Furthermore, the use of any one component, element, or feature (say, diction or **imagery**) in a given work both depends on and determines the use of others. Critics of stylistics would thus argue that style is too much the product of synergistic interactions external to any one text or even author to be identified as belonging uniquely *to* that author.

Other stylisticians reject quantitative analysis and instead borrow from other critical perspectives as different as **speech-act theory** and **transformational linguistics.**

subjectivity: A term sometimes used to refer to the evident presence, in a literary work, of the personal feelings and opinions of the author. Subjectivity is the opposite of **objectivity,** a term sometimes used to describe works from which the author's personal perspective is distant or even seems **absent.** Authors writing subjectively may comment on the actions of **characters** in a moralizing way, making judgments based on their own life experiences. Subjectivity can also refer to the thoughts and feelings of the characters themselves in a work. **Confessional poetry,** a contemporary poetic mode in which poets reflect on even the most painful matters in their private lives — such as abuse, alienation, madness, and suicide — epitomizes authorial subjectivity.

Psychoanalytic theorist Jacques Lacan has used the term *subjectivity* to refer to that which we would (but may be unable to) know, that which we do (or believe ourselves to) know, and individual or cultural ways of knowing — or of trying to know. (He thereby erases the boundary between the conscious human "subject" and "subjects" to be understood by human consciousness.

Lacan identifies three orders of subjectivity: **the Real,** the **Imaginary order,** and the **Symbolic order.** The Real is not what we typically perceive as reality; rather, it is that which straddles the lines between conscious and unconscious. We may partially, intuitively, sense its existence, but it defies interpretation, especially our attempts to name or **symbolize** it directly. The Imaginary order, linked to the five senses, produces a false but comforting sense of unity in the individual, who perceives himself or herself as one coherent whole distinct from other individuals. The individual, however, is internally divided between the conscious and unconscious, which renders the illusion of coherence just that — an illusion. The Symbolic order, a preestablished order of law and language in any given society, represents the cultural realm to which all individuals must submit.

See **Imaginary order; Real, the;** and **Symbolic order** for further discussion of these terms.

sublime, the: That quality in a literary work that elevates the reader to a higher plane. When an author achieves the transport of the reader, that author has attained the sublime. Most writers have sought to achieve sublimity through a grand **style** or nobility of sentiment or subject.

The term derives from a Greek treatise called *Peri Hypsous* (*On the Sublime*), once ascribed to the third-century A.D. scholar Cassius Longinus but now thought to be the work of an anonymous, first-century A.D. author, sometimes referred to as "pseudo-Longinus." The sublime is achieved, according to Longinus or pseudo-Longinus, when great thoughts, noble sentiments, elevated **figures of speech,** lofty **diction,** and **aesthetic** arrangement coincide.

Edmund Burke's 1757 treatise, *A Philosophical Inquiry into the Origin of our Ideas of the Sublime and the Beautiful,* is the preeminent treatment of the subject written since the **Renaissance Period.** In this treatise, Burke makes an important distinction between the sublime and the beautiful, arguing that the sublime, associated with the most powerful of emotions, is infinite, whereas the beautiful is finite. He also associates the sublime with terror.

Several decades after the publication of Burke's seminal treatise, German philosopher Immanuel Kant further developed the concept of the sublime in his *Critique of Judgment* (1790). Kant suggested that the sublime must be thought of *as if* it resonates with metaphysical design in the same way that living things must be thought of *as if* they have been authorized by something other than mechanical production (given that human beings cannot mechanically produce living things). Kant, however, stopped short of grounding sublimity in the work of some supernatural design, preferring instead to speak of it as something that, unlike the merely beautiful, is simultaneously awe-inspiring, unsettling, and even ethically motivating.

Sublimity in writing was especially sought after by eighteenth- and early-nineteenth-century writers, particularly those associated with the **romantic** movement.

EXAMPLES: Very few works have been said to achieve sublimity. Among them are Dante Alighieri's *The Divine Comedy* (1321), several of William

Shakespeare's plays (1590–1611), and Johann Wolfgang von Goethe's *Faust* (1808, 1832).

superego: See **id.**

superstructure: See **Marxist criticism.**

surrealism: A literary and artistic movement whose proponents sought to express the irrational, the unconscious (especially as manifested in dreams), and the creative products of their **imagination.** Guillaume Apollinaire, a French poet, invented the term *surrealism* (from *superrealism*), but André Breton, another French poet, is recognized as the movement's founder because he wrote the first surrealist manifesto, entitled *Manifeste du surréalisme (Manifesto of Surrealism)* in 1924. Influenced by Sigmund Freud's **psychoanalytic theory,** surrealism arose most immediately out of **Dadaism** in the 1920s and the 1930s; it was particularly strong in France, its country of origin. The movement did not really affect the American literary scene until after World War II.

Surrealists wished to transcend the reality to which we are accustomed — the world shaped and represented by rationality, **conventions,** and middle-class values — and to enter the realm of the "super-real," which includes unconscious components. Moreover, they believed that conventional reality distorts the realm of the super-real. They prized spontaneity and sincere expressions of emotion, two common qualities of **romanticism.** Automatic writing — writing given over to and guided by unconscious impulses — became a favored technique, one the surrealists believed helped them enter and represent the realm of dream and hallucination. Rejecting conventions, surrealists undertook literary experiments involving unusual **syntax,** achronological sequencing, free association, nightmarish or hallucinative **images,** and the juxtaposition of jarringly incongruous elements.

EXAMPLES: Writers associated with surrealism include French poet Paul Éluard, René Char, and Louis Aragon. The work of certain writers typically associated with several other **genres** markedly shows the influence of surrealism. **Absurdist** writers Eugène Ionesco and Samuel Beckett are indebted to the movement, as are **postmodernist** novelist William Burroughs and **magic realist** Gabriel García Márquez.

Surrealist painters include Salvador Dalí, Jean Arp, André Breton, René Magritte, Joan Miró, and Max Ernst. (Although many of his paintings are surrealistic in character, Pablo Picasso was never a member of the surrealist movement.) One of the best-known visual examples of surrealism is Dalí's *The Persistence of Memory* (1931) shown on page 469 — a dreamlike but precisely rendered painting that **alludes** to the nightmarish art of Hieronymus Bosch (1450?–1516) even as it conveys a modern sense of time, infinity, and paranoid unease. Surrealism has also had a strong im-

pact on film, where Louis Bunuel's *Un chien andalou* (1928) and, in collaboration with Dalí, *L'âge d'or* (1930), evidence its **influence.**

suspense fiction, suspense novel: See **mystery fiction.**

suspension of disbelief: A phrase used by Samuel Taylor Coleridge in his *Biographia Literaria* (1817) to point out that readers will, in the interest of what Coleridge called "poetic faith," forgo the temptation to doubt the veracity or likelihood of what is expressed in a literary work.

EXAMPLES: Readers of George Orwell's *Animal Farm* (1949) suspend disbelief in the idea of pigs occupying political positions in a social hierarchy. To read and enjoy Anne Rice's *Interview with the Vampire* (1976) or *The Witching Hour* (1990), readers must suspend disbelief in the existence of vampires and witches, respectively.

Sometimes artists exceed their audience's capacity to suspend disbelief, as is evident from Peter H. Lewis's reaction to the movie *Independence Day* (1996) in his "Personal Computers" column of the *New York Times:*

> The surprising part was not how easily the Mac OS operating system melded with the computer operating system and networking protocols used by the evil, tentacled creatures from the dying planet Zartron-9. . . . No, what made me spill my popcorn in disbelief was how easily the hero was able to find just the right cable to connect the Mac to the Zartronian computer. Let's see, do the Zartronians use ADB cables or SCSI? Serial or parallel?

Other viewers have had even more difficulty suspending disbelief in the idea that a United States president, aeronautical experience notwithstanding, would suit up and take to the skies in a fighter plane to personally do battle with an alien mother ship.

syllepsis: See **zeugma.**

symbol: Something that, although it is of interest in its own right, stands for or suggests something larger and more complex — often an idea or a range of interrelated ideas, attitudes, and practices.

Within a given culture, some things are understood to be symbols: the flag of the United States is an obvious example, as are the five intertwined Olympic rings. More subtle cultural symbols might be the river as a symbol of time and the journey as a symbol of life and its manifold experiences. Instead of appropriating symbols generally used and understood within their culture, writers often create their own symbols by setting up a complex but identifiable web of associations in their works. As a result, one object, **image,** person, place, or action suggests others, and may ultimately suggest a range of ideas.

A symbol may thus be defined as a **metaphor** in which the **vehicle** — the image, activity, or concept used to represent something else — represents many related things (or **tenors**) or is broadly suggestive. The urn in John Keats's "Ode on a Grecian Urn" (1820) suggests interrelated concepts, including art, truth, beauty, and timelessness. Certain poets and groups of poets have especially exploited the possibilities inherent in **symbolism;** these include the **French Symbolist** poets of the late nineteenth and early twentieth centuries, such as Charles Baudelaire, Stéphane Mallarmé, Arthur Rimbaud, Paul Valéry, and Paul Verlaine.

Symbols are distinguished from both **allegories** and **signs.** Like symbols, allegories present an **abstract** idea through more **concrete** means, but a symbol is an element of a work used to suggest something else (often of a higher or more abstract order), whereas an allegory is typically a **narrative** with two levels of meaning that is used to make a general statement or point about the real world. Symbols are typically distinguished from signs insofar as the latter are arbitrary constructions that, by virtue of cultural agreement, have one or more particular significations. Symbols are much more broadly suggestive than signs. As a sign, the word *water* has specific **denotative** meanings in the English language, but as a symbol, it may suggest concepts as varied or even divergent as peace or turmoil, the giver of life or the taker of it. Some theorists (such as Charles Sanders Peirce), however, have argued that symbols are in fact a type of sign, their meanings just as arbitrary and culturally determined as those of signs.

Symbols have been of particular interest to **formalists,** who study how meanings emerge from the complex, patterned relationships among images in a work, and **psychoanalytic critics,** who are interested in how individual authors and the larger culture both disguise and reveal unconscious fears and desires through symbols. Recently, French **feminist critics** have also focused on the symbolic. They have suggested that, as wide-ranging as it seems, symbolic language is ultimately rigid and restrictive. They favor **semiotic** language and writing — writing that neither opposes nor hierarchically ranks qualities or elements of reality nor symbolizes one thing but not another in terms of a third — contending that semiotic language is at once more fluid, **rhythmic,** unifying, and feminine.

EXAMPLES: In the following passage from *The Old Man and the Sea* (1952), Ernest Hemingway uses traditional literary and biblical symbols to speak suggestively about human mortality, faith that flies in the face of suffering and death, and the ultimate spiritual triumph over limitation and loss. These symbols include the quiet harbor, the sheltering rock, the struggle with a cross-like mast, and the great, slippery, luminous fish:

> When he sailed into the little harbour the lights of the Terrace were out and he knew everyone was in bed. The breeze had risen steadily and was blowing strongly now. It was quiet in the harbour though and he sailed up onto the little patch of shingle below the rocks. There was no one to help him so he pulled the boat up as far as he could. Then he stepped out and made her fast to a rock.
>
> He unstepped the mast and furled the sail and tied it. Then he shouldered the mast and started to climb. It was then he knew the depth of his tiredness. He stopped for a moment and looked back and saw in the reflection from the street light the great tail of the fish standing up well behind the skiff's stern.

William Golding's *Lord of the Flies* (1954) also contains numerous symbolic passages, such as the scene depicting Simon's death, inflicted by a mob-like group of young boys. The young but wise Simon is a Christ figure who dies unjustly; he is killed, in fact, by his peers (reminiscent of the judgment of Christ's peers condemning him to death) while trying desperately to help them by bringing knowledge that will change their lives. Even nature protests Simon's death with the opening of the clouds, torrential rain, and a great wind, just as God opened the heavens, darkened the sky, and let the rain pour down at the moment of Christ's death:

> The sticks fell and the mouth of the new circle crunched and screamed. The beast was on its knees in the center, its arms folded over its face. It was crying out against the abominable noise something about a body on the hill. The beast struggled forward, broke the ring and fell over the steep edge of the rock to the sand by the water. At once the crowd surged after it, poured down the rock, leapt on to the beast, screamed, struck, bit, tore. There were no words, and no movements but the tearing of teeth and claws.
>
> Then the clouds opened and let down the rain like a waterfall. The water bounded from the mountain-top, tore leaves and branches from the trees, poured like a cold shower over the struggling heap on the sand. Presently the heap broke up and figures staggered away. Only the beast lay still, a few yards from the sea. Even in the rain they could

see how small a beast it was; and already its blood was staining the sand.

Now a great wind blew the rain sideways, cascading the water from the forest trees. . . .

In the February 2001 episodes of the "reality-TV" series *Survivor II: The Australian Outback*, the recurring image of a spider served not only as a symbol of the predatory nature of certain characters but also of the "game" of survival more generally.

See **symbolism**.

Symbolic order: Along with the **Imaginary order** and **the Real,** one of the three orders of **subjectivity** according to the **psychoanalytic critic** and theorist Jacques Lacan. The Symbolic order is the realm of law, language, and society; it is the repository of generally held cultural beliefs. Its symbolic system is language, whose agent is the father or lawgiver, the one who has the power of naming. The human subject is forced into this preestablished order by language (a process that begins long before a child can actually speak) and must submit to its orders of communication (grammar, **syntax,** etc.). Entrance into the Symbolic order determines subjectivity according to a primary law of referentiality that takes the male **sign** (**phallus**) as its ordering principle. Lacan states that both sexes submit to the law of the phallus (the law of order, language, and differentiation), but their individual relation to the law determines whether they see themselves as — and are seen by others to be — either "masculine" or "feminine."

The Symbolic institutes repression (of the Imaginary), thus creating the unconscious, which itself is structured like the language of the Symbolic. The unconscious, a timeless realm, cannot be known directly, but it can be understood by a kind of translation that takes place in language — psychoanalysis is the "talking cure." The Symbolic is not a "stage" of development (as is Freud's "oedipal stage") nor is it set in place once and for all in human life. We constantly negotiate its threshold (in sleep, in drunkenness) and can "fall out" of it altogether in psychosis. Lacan's concept of the Symbolic — like his schema and terminology more generally — has proved useful to psychoanalytic critics analyzing the interplay among **texts,** language, and the unconscious.

See also **Imaginary order; Real, the.**

symbolism: From the Greek *symballein,* meaning "to throw together," the serious and relatively sustained use of **symbols** to **represent** or suggest other things or ideas. In addition to referring to an author's explicit use of a particular symbol in a literary work ("Joseph Conrad uses snake symbolism in *Heart of Darkness*" [1899]), the term *symbolism* sometimes refers to the presence, in a work or body of works, of suggestive associations giving rise to incremental, implied meaning ("I enjoyed the symbolism in George Lucas's *Star Wars* movies" [1977–]).

When spelled with a capital *S, Symbolism* refers to a literary movement that flourished in late-nineteenth-century France and whose adherents rebelled against literary **realism.** Symbolists (often referred to specifically by nationality as the *French Symbolists*) held that writers create and use **subjective,** or private (rather than **conventional,** or public), symbols in order to convey very personal and intense emotional experiences and reactions. They argued that networks of such symbols form the real essence of a literary work. Because of the subjective and individual character of their symbolic systems, the work of the French Symbolists is more suggestive than explicit in meaning. Charles Baudelaire, Stéphane Mallarmé, Arthur Rimbaud, Paul Valéry, and Paul Verlaine are probably the best known of the French Symbolists.

Many other writers could also be called symbolists because of the sustained use in their works of "private" symbol systems — even though they preceded, succeeded, or simply did not participate in the better known (and more organized) French movement. Such writers include William Blake, Edgar Allan Poe, Herman Melville, D. H. Lawrence, and William Butler Yeats. Poe's poetic practice and theory in particular had a considerable **influence** on the French Symbolists. Thus, although literary historians tend to limit the use of *Symbolism* to refer to a specific literary movement that developed in France, the movement in fact had its roots — and perhaps has had its greatest impact and influence — beyond French borders. Twentieth-century European and American writing owes a particular debt to Symbolism. Authors ranging from the German Rainer Maria Rilke to the English Arthur Symons to the Irish Yeats and James Joyce to Americans like Wallace Stevens and T. S. Eliot have drawn on but also extended the work of the French Symbolists.

See **symbol.**

Symbolism, Symbolist movement: See **symbolism.**

synaesthesia (synesthesia): Generally, a psychological process whereby one kind of sensory stimulus evokes the **subjective** experience of another. For instance, the sight of ants might make you feel itchy. When used with reference to literature specifically, *synaesthesia* refers to the practice of associating two or more different senses in the same **image.** It speaks of one sensation in terms of another. Writers have employed synaesthesia since the time of the ancient Greeks, but the **French Symbolists** used it with particular frequency in their poetry.

EXAMPLES: To speak of coal, for instance, as "red hot" associates color (sight) with heat (touch). The first line of this excerpt from Dame Edith Sitwell's "Trio for Two Cats and a Trombone" (1922) associates three senses. Sight ("light") is described in terms of touch ("hard") and sound ("braying"):

> The hard and braying light
> Is zebra'd black and white. . . .

The title of the Red Hot Chili Peppers' song "Taste the Pain" (1989) is an example of synaesthesia.

synecdoche: A **figure of speech** (more specifically a **trope**) in which a part of something is used to **represent** the whole or, occasionally, the whole is used to represent a part. In synecdoche, the **vehicle** (the **image** used to represent something else) of the figure of speech is part of the **tenor** (the thing being represented).

EXAMPLES: To refer to a boat as a "sail" is to use synecdoche, whereas to refer to a monarch as "the crown" is to use **metonymy.** Other examples of synecdoche include referring to a car as "wheels" and to the violins, violas, cellos, and basses in an orchestra as the "strings." In William Shakespeare's *Romeo and Juliet* (1596), Capulet uses the phrase "two more summers" to mean "two more years":

> My child is yet a stranger in the world,
> She hath not seen the change of fourteen years;
> Let two more summers wither in their pride
> Ere we may think her ripe to be a bride.

Sent from Birkenau to Auschwitz, fed little and worked nearly to death, Eliezer, the boy who narrates Elie Wiesel's short novel *Night* (1958), speaks of himself as "a body. Perhaps less than that even: a starved stomach."

synesthesia: See **synaesthesia.**

syntax: The arrangement — the ordering, grouping, and placement — of words within a sentence. Some critics would extend the meaning of the term to encompass such things as the degree of complexity or fragmentation within these arrangements. Syntax is a component of grammar, though it is often used — incorrectly — as a synonym for grammar.

Syntax has also been viewed as one of the two components of **diction** (the other being vocabulary), which may refer either to word choice or the general character of language used by a speaker or author. The sentences "I rode across the meadow" and "Across the meadow rode I" exhibit different syntax but identical vocabulary. To replace "meadow" with "sea of grass" is to alter the vocabulary but not the syntax. And to say "Rode I across the sea of grass" is to use diction very different from "I rode across the meadow." The combination of unusual syntax and vocabulary in the first sentence as opposed to the second is a feature that often differentiates **poetic diction** from that of prose.

syuzhet: See **fable, Russian formalism.**

T

---

tail-rhyme stanza: A **stanza** ending with a short line that **rhymes** with an earlier, similarly short line from which it is separated by several longer lines. The French term for tail-rhyme is *rime couée*.

Geoffrey Chaucer's "Rime of Sir Topas" (c. 1387) is written in tail-rhyme stanzas.

tale: A comparatively simple **narrative,** either fictitious or true, written or recounted orally in prose or verse. A tale often recounts a strange event, focusing on something or someone exotic, marvelous, or even supernatural. Tales may be attributable to a particular author, whether known or anonymous, or may simply be part of the lore of a given culture. Whatever their origin, tales tend to be relatively short narratives; nevertheless, the term is broad enough that both critics and authors have applied it to longer works ranging up to full-length novels.

Tale is sometimes used interchangeably with **short story,** or even as a general term encompassing the short story, among other literary forms, but modern critics typically distinguish between the two. The tale places more emphasis on actions and results than on **character,** which is the chief focus of the short story. Furthermore, tales are more casually constructed — and, consequently, far looser in terms of **plot** and **structure** — than short stories, which bear the mark of an author's careful and conscious fashioning.

EXAMPLES: Traditional "short" tales include *The Thousand and One Nights* (also called *The Arabian Nights*), an anonymous collection of Arabic tales from the **Middle Ages** such as the stories of Aladdin and Sinbad; *The Canterbury Tales* of Geoffrey Chaucer (c. 1387), including "The Miller's Tale" and "The Wife of Bath's Tale"; Jonathan Swift's *A Tale of a Tub* (1704); and a variety of **folk tales,** fairy tales, and tall tales. Famous folk tales include the story of Chicken Little, who repeatedly exclaimed "The sky is falling!" Fairy tales include such well-known tales as those of Rapunzel, Cinderella, and Hansel and Gretel. Noted tall tales include Pecos Bill and his bouncing bride and Mark Twain's "The Celebrated Jumping Frog of Calaveras County" (1867). A modern example of a relatively short tale is Nobel Prize–winning author José Saramago's *O conto da ilha desconhecida* (*The Tale of the Unknown Island*) (1998).

Examples of broader use of the term *tale* to encompass longer works include Lady Shikibu Murasaki's *The Tale of Genji* (c. 1001–15), Charles Dickens's novel *A Tale of Two Cities* (1859), and Margaret Atwood's more recent novel *The Handmaid's Tale* (1985). The term has even been used in reference to musical works, such as Jacques Offenbach's opera *Tales of Hoffman* (1880).

tenor: The subject of any **figure of speech;** the thing being represented by the **vehicle** of such a figure. Every figure of speech includes a vehicle and tenor; the vehicle is the **image,** activity, or concept used to illustrate or **represent** the tenor.

The terms *tenor* and *vehicle* were first used by critic I. A. Richards, who introduced them in reference to **metaphor,** one of many figures of speech, in a book entitled *The Philosophy of Rhetoric* (1936). (Today the terms are used with reference to any figure of speech.) According to Richards, both tenor and vehicle typically undergo change in the metaphorical process, hence Richards's notable definition of metaphor as "a transaction between contexts." Unlike his predecessors, Richards viewed tenor and vehicle as the two equivalent parts of a metaphor. (Prior to Richards — and thus prior to his use of *tenor* and *vehicle* — critics commonly viewed what we now call the vehicle as mere ornament, less important then what we now call the tenor, the idea or subject of the figure.)

EXAMPLES: In describing a kind and patient friend, you say, "Ann is an angel." Here *Ann* is the tenor — the subject of the figure of speech illustrated by the vehicle *angel.* Instead of saying, "Last night I read a book," you might say "Last night I plowed through a book." *Plowed through* (or the activity of plowing) is the vehicle of the metaphor; *read* (or the act of reading) is the tenor, the thing being figured. In the moment in which reading and plowing are metaphorically associated, intellectual activity is suddenly placed in an agricultural context (and vice versa), thereby altering slightly the significance of each of the metaphor's two terms.

tension: As used by **New Critic** Allen Tate in "Tension in Poetry" (1938), the totality of, or interrelation between, what he defines as the two types of meaning in a poem: "extension" (**concrete, denotative** meaning) and "intension" (**abstract, metaphorical** meaning).

In a distinct but related usage, other New Critics drew on Tate's use of *tension* to refer to "conflict structures," that is, the **binary oppositions** of various ideas and qualities (such as general / particular, **structure / texture,** abstract / concrete, and **tragic / comic**). These critics evaluated poems in part based on how well their authors organized these oppositions (that is, established these tensions), particularly as they involved **irony** and **paradox.** Some critics maintained that the tension itself gives a work its **form** and even its cohesiveness.

Tension is typically used today either to signify oppositions that give a poem stability or wholeness or to refer to poems that have densely interrelated components.

tercet: Broadly speaking, a group of three lines of **verse.** *Tercet* is often used synonymously with **triplet,** a term referring to a group of three lines with the same **rhyme** (*aaa*). *Tercet* may also mean any three-line group of poetry, regardless of **rhyme scheme.** In this sense, a triplet is a type of tercet. The term is commonly applied to a *terza rima* stanza or to either of the two three-line components of a **sestet** in the **Italian sonnet.** A tercet may thus be a **stanza** in itself or part of a larger stanza.

EXAMPLE: The following three-line stanza, one of six in Trumbull Stickney's "Mnemosyne" (1902), qualifies as a tercet within the term's broadest meaning but not as a triplet since it rhymes *aba* rather than *aaa*.

> I had a sister lovely in my sight:
> Her hair was dark, her eyes were very sombre;
> We sang together in the woods at night.

terza rima: **Verse** composed of three-line (**tercet**) **stanzas** with an interlocking **rhyme scheme.** The final word of the second line of each tercet rhymes with the final words of the first and third lines of the succeeding tercet, hence the rhyme scheme *aba bcb cdc ded* etc. Dante Alighieri is famous for his *terza rima* compositions, but the form has not been very popular in English due to the difficulty of composing such repeated rhyme.

EXAMPLE: Percy Bysshe Shelley's "Ode to the West Wind" (1820) is probably the most famous English example. The first three stanzas follow:

> O wild West Wind, thou breath of Autumn's being,
> Thou, from whose unseen presence the leaves dead
> Are driven, like ghosts from an enchanter fleeing,
>
> Yellow, and black, and pale, and hectic red,
> Pestilence-stricken multitudes: O thou,
> Who chariotest to their dark wintry bed
>
> The wingèd seeds, where they lie cold and low,
> Each like a corpse within its grave, until
> Thine azure sister of the Spring shall blow. . . .

Twentieth-century poets who used or adapted this form include Archibald MacLeish (in "Conquistador" [1932]) and W. H. Auden (in *The Sea and the Mirror* [1944]).

tetrameter: A line of **verse** consisting of four **metrical feet.**
EXAMPLE: In Thomas Hardy's "Channel Firing" (1914), written in **iambic** tetrameter, skeletons resting in a churchyard are momentarily disturbed by the noise of gunnery practice on the English Channel:

> That night | your great | guns, un|awares,
> Shook all | our cof|fins as | we lay,
> And broke | the chan|cel win|dow-squares,
> We thought | it was | the Judg|ment-day
>
> And sat | upright. | While drear|isome
> Arose | the howl | of wa|kened hounds:
> The mouse | let fall | the al|tar-crumb,
> The worms | drew back | into | the mounds. . . .

text: From the Latin *texere,* meaning "to weave," a term that may be defined in a number of ways. Some critics restrict its use to the written word, although they may apply the term to objects ranging from a poem to the words in a book to a book itself to a biblical passage used in a sermon to a written transcript of an oral statement or interview. Other critics include nonwritten material in the designation *text,* as long as that material has been isolated for analysis.

French **structuralist critics** took issue with the traditional view of literary compositions as "works" with a **form** intentionally imposed by the author and a meaning identifiable through analysis of the author's use of language. These critics argued that literary compositions are texts rather than works, texts being the product of a social institution they called *écriture* (writing). By identifying compositions as texts rather than works, structuralists denied them the personalized character attributed to works wrought by a particular, unique author. Structuralists believed not only that a text was essentially impersonal, the confluence of certain preexisting attributes of the social institution of writing, but that any interpretation of the text should result from an impersonal *lecture* (reading). This *lecture* included reading with an active awareness of how the **linguistic** system functions. Some structuralist critics felt that they were not bound in their readings by the **conventions** that governed the production of the text; most, however, maintained that interpretation involves being guided by such conventions, **codes,** and combinations thereof.

The French writer and theorist Roland Barthes, a structuralist who later turned toward **poststructuralism,** distinguished *text* from *work* in a different way, characterizing a text as open and a work as closed. According to Barthes, works are bounded entities, conventionally classified in the **canon,** whereas texts engage readers in an ongoing relationship of interpretation and reinterpretation. Regardless of this distinction, however, he argued that any particular composition may be viewed as text or work. In *S/Z* (1974), Barthes further divided texts into two categories: *lisible* (readerly) and *scriptible* (writerly). Texts that are *lisible* depend more heavily on convention, making their interpretation easier and more predictable. Texts that are *scriptible* are generally experimental, flouting or seriously modifying traditional rules. Such texts cannot be interpreted according to standard conventions; in fact, Barthes argued that their very rejection of conventions makes them essentially *illisible,* or unreaderly. Ultimately, texts that are *lisible* restrict participation more than those that are *scriptible,* which encourage or even demand cocreative involvement and effort by the reader.

textual criticism: A form of **criticism** involving the scholarly attempt to establish the authoritative version of a **text.** Textual critics try to discover the original version or manuscript of a particular literary work. If that is unavailable, lost, or destroyed, they collect all available printed versions of the text, plus any manuscripts or parts thereof (such as rough drafts) that have survived. They then compare these versions to examine the evolution of the work, to find and rectify any publishing errors, and ultimately to produce an edited version of the text that is as close as possible to what appears to be the **intention** of the author.

texture: A term referring to the surface details or elements of a work (especially a poem) apart from its basic **structure,** argument, or meaning. Textual details therefore include **imagery, meter,** and **rhyme,** the sensuous and **concrete** aspects of a poem as opposed to its intellectual content. The **connotations** of words may also be viewed as part of a work's texture; the **denotative** meanings of those same words may not. **New Critics,** such as John Crowe Ransom, used *texture* in opposition to *structure* in analyzing a poem; they further noted that the two components together yield the poem's ontology, that is, its utterly unique quality of being.

theater of the absurd: See **Absurd, the.**

theme: Not simply the subject of a literary work, but rather a statement that the **text** seems to be making about that subject. The statement can be (and often was, in older literature) moral, or even *a* moral or lesson; in more modern works, the theme may emanate from an unmoralized, or less obviously moral, perspective.

Theme is distinguished from **motif,** a term that usually refers to a unifying element in an artistic work, especially any recurrent **image, symbol, character** type, subject, or **narrative** detail. In a broader sense, *motif* can even refer to any recurrent theme that helps to unify a given work of literature.

EXAMPLE: The subject of a work might be suffering. The theme, depending on the view of the individual author, might be that suffering is in God's plan and should therefore simply be accepted — or that it is a drain on an individual's spirit or mind and should therefore be avoided at all costs.

theoretical criticism: A type of **criticism** that emphasizes the formulation of general principles for all **texts** rather than **explicating** individual works, as in **practical criticism.** Theoretical critics postulate a set of **aesthetic** principles that can be applied to literary works in general, both to analyze as well as to evaluate them. Aristotle's *Poetics* (written during the fourth century B.C.) is perhaps the best-known example of theoretical criticism, but many twentieth-century examples exist (for example, I. A. Richards's *Principles of Literary Criticism* [1924]).

American critics by and large wrote practical rather than theoretical criticism during the first half of the twentieth century. With the advent of the **Chicago School** around 1950, however, theoretical criticism came into vogue in American literary critical circles. Since that time, theoretical criticism has been written by **formalists, Marxists, structuralists, poststructuralists, feminist** and **gender critics, new historicists, cultural critics,** and others.

See also **practical criticism.**

theory: A set of principles and assumptions used in certain situations to explain or make predictions about a particular phenomenon. The term *theory* may also be used, especially in opposition to the term *practice*, to refer more generally to **abstract** reasoning or hypothesizing. In this sense, one might speak of the district attorney's theory of what happened the night Nicole Brown Simpson and Ronald Goldman were murdered or of a sociologist's theory of the utility of human love. In scientific circles, however, *theory* is distinguished from *hypothesis,* the latter being an educated guess subject to verification through experimentation, the former being a hypothesis that has so far withstood the test of time and experimentation and, consequently, is viewed as a given or a fact. Scientists hypothesize without data, but never theorize without it; as writer Sir Arthur Conan Doyle had detective Sherlock Holmes assert in "A Scandal in Bohemia," a short story published in *The Strand Magazine* in 1891, "It is a capital mistake to theorize before one has data." Nevertheless, as British philosopher A. J. Ayer noted in *Philosophy in the Twentieth Century* (1982), "There never comes a point where a theory can be said to be true. The most that one can claim for any theory is that it has shared the successes of all its rivals and that it has passed at least one test which they have failed." Hence one may speak of the theory of evolution or Einstein's theory of relativity, but conducting an experiment involves seeking to prove or disprove a particular hypothesis — for instance, the statement "Flatworms can survive in acidic environments" — rather than a theory.

In literary criticism, *theory* has traditionally referred to a set of general principles that can be used to classify or otherwise analyze literary works, and in some cases to interpret or even evaluate them. A given critical reading may not explicitly ground itself in a particular theory of literary interpretation, but some general theory or set of assumptions about literature is implicit in most such interpretations or analyses. Theory — even of the most general and implicit kind — provides justification or, at least, explanation for the questions raised and conclusions reached by the critic. Critics who do not work within a theoretical framework are vulnerable to the charge of making arbitrary, idiosyncratic, or utterly **impressionistic** judgments. They are also susceptible to the claim that they fail to justify their judgments of the **aesthetic** qualities, critical arguments, or interpretive theories they examine.

Numerous types of literary criticism, generally grounded in theories of literary criticism, have arisen over the centuries. In the twentieth century alone, one may speak of theories ranging from **Russian formalism** to **discourse analysis** to **reception theory** to **feminist criticism.** Within each of these theories are narrower critical principles, which have also been called theories. Hence *écriture féminine* — the idea, advocated by a group of critics working within feminist theory, that there is such a thing as feminine or women's writing — may itself be called a theory.

Although theory has always been important in literary criticism, it has become even more prominent since the rise of **poststructuralism,** an approach to language and literature that might itself be called a theory, or perhaps an assemblage of theories. Poststructuralists have radically revised the traditional concept of theory even as they have elevated its importance. In the view of poststructuralists, theory has more than literature to account for, since everything from the unconscious to social and cultural practices is seen as functioning like a language; thus, the goal of poststructuralist theorists is to understand what controls interpretation and meaning in all possible systems of signification. Not surprisingly, this novel and far-ranging concept has facilitated the development of theories that challenge the very underpinnings of traditional thought. The poststructuralist concept of theory, however, has been challenged by a number of influential critics, including Steven Knapp, Walter Benn Michaels, Stanley Fish, and Jean-François Lyotard. Nonetheless, theorizing one's critical practices remains imperative for poststructuralists, who also expect other types of critics to theorize their positions and criticize those who do not.

thesis: A term with several distinct meanings but perhaps most commonly used in universities to refer to one of two things: a paper or monograph written by a degree-seeking candidate in fulfillment of academic requirements; and the position taken by someone expostulating on a particular topic with the intent of proving that position plausible or correct. Some people also use the term as equivalent to **theme** (the dominant or controlling idea advanced by an author in a **text**). Finally, in **prosody** (the study of **versification**), *thesis* is used by those who follow the original Greek usage to refer to a **stressed** syllable in a **foot** of verse (as opposed to the **arsis,** or unstressed syllable). In the later Latin usage — in which the terms became reversed — *thesis* refers to an unstressed syllable (and *arsis* refers to a stressed syllable). According to Greek usage, the thesis of the word *thesis* falls on the first (the stressed) syllable, whereas under the Latin usage, the thesis of the word *thesis* falls on the second (the unstressed) syllable.

EXAMPLE: Film critic Terence Rafferty used the word *thesis* to mean both argumentative position and artistic theme in stating that Edward Burns's films *The Brothers McMullen* (1995) and *She's the One* (1996) are **romantic comedies** "designed to illustrate the thesis that young Irish American guys are utterly confounded by the opposite sex."

See also **accent.**

thick descriptions: A term used by Clifford Geertz, an anthropologist whose work has greatly influenced contemporary literary criticism, to refer to contextual **close readings** of cultural products or events. The goal of thick description is to reveal the interlocking **conventions** or **discourses** that cause a production (like William Shakespeare's *Hamlet* [1602]) or event (such as the coronation of Queen Elizabeth I) to have a particular meaning or meanings for people within a given culture (such as that of **Renaissance** England). Thick description has become a favorite tool of **new historicist critics,** who in describing and analyzing literary works try not to wall them off from history and politics. In providing a thick description, such critics relate **representational** devices within the **text** to historical, economic, and **symbolic** (and often non**linguistic**) structures operative outside it in the culture at large.

third-person point of view: See **point of view.**

three unities: See **unities.**

threnody: In the original Greek usage, a **choral dirge,** a song lamenting someone's death. *Threnody* is now used essentially interchangeably with any type of dirge.

EXAMPLES: Ralph Waldo Emerson's "Threnody" (1846), written on the death of his young son. Depeche Mode's song "Blasphemous Rumours" (1987) is a more recent example of threnody. Samuel Barber's *Adagio for Strings* (1936), often referred to as a musical threnody, was performed by a number of symphony orchestras throughout the United States during the weekend following September 11, 2001.

thriller: See **mystery fiction.**

tone: The attitude of the author toward the reader or the subject matter of a literary work. An author's tone may be serious, playful, mocking, angry, commanding, apologetic, and so forth. The term is now often used to mean "tone of voice," a difficult-to-determine characteristic of **discourse** through which writers (and each of us in our daily conversations) reveal a range of attitudes toward everything from the subject at hand to those whom we are addressing. Some critics simply equate *tone* with *voice,* a term referring to the authorial **presence** that pervades a literary work, lying behind or beyond such things as **imagery, character, plot,** or even **theme.**

Although the terms *tone* and **atmosphere** may both be equated with **mood,** *tone* and *atmosphere* are distinguished. Unlike *tone,* which refers to the author's attitude, *atmosphere* refers to the general feeling created in the reader or audience by a work at a given point.

tone color: A phrase invented by poet Sidney Lanier in *The Science of English Verse* (1880) to compare the musicality of the sounds of words to timbre in music.

trace: A term used by French theorist Jacques Derrida to refer to the myriad possible meanings that differ from the one a spoken or written utterance is deemed to have, that is, the "definitive" meaning established and constituted by its very difference from innumerable, nonpresent meanings. These nonpresent meanings, which Derrida views as features of any utterance, are neither fully **present** nor wholly **absent.** Such meanings are not exactly present, for they differ from what the utterance is deemed to signify, yet they are not entirely absent, for they remind us of and lend import to the meaning we assign to that utterance by virtue of their difference. The significance of any utterance thus depends just as surely on those potential meanings that are rejected (the trace) as on the single meaning that is ultimately accepted. Derrida further argues that the whole concept of determinate meaning — the general sense that a given word in a given context has a single meaning — is illusory. Trace itself makes the definitive determination of meaning for any utterance impossible, for it points up the maddening, capricious, and ultimately uncertain *jeu* (play) of language.

tragedy: A serious and often somber **drama,** written in prose or verse, that typically ends in disaster and that focuses on a **character** who undergoes unexpected personal reversals. From the Greek *tragoidia* (for "goat song"), tragedy is thought by many scholars to have originally referred to an ancient Greek ritual, accompanied by a choral **hymn,** in which a goat was sacrificed to Dionysus, the god of wine and fertility. The Greek tragedian Thespis is usually credited with transforming these choral hymns honoring Dionysus into songs that told a story about a famous **hero** or god. Many scholars also believe that Thespis was the first Greek dramatist to have used an actor, rather than merely a **chorus,** to recount and advance the action.

Competitions in tragedy writing took place at an annual festival held to honor Dionysus, and from these events the great traditions of Greek tragedy developed; competitors typically entered a tetralogy of plays in which three tragedies were followed by one *satyr play,* a lighter piece in which a hero (often of one of the preceding tragedies) appears in the company of satyrs, half-human creatures whose raunchiness provided comic relief from the unrelenting seriousness of the preceding, tragic trilogy. (Some literary historians take Gerald Else's view that tragedy got its name because a goat was awarded to the winner of this dramatic festival, not because it originally involved the ritualistic killing of a goat.) The principal ancient Greek tragedians were Aeschylus, Euripides, and Sophocles. Although all three wrote prolifically, only a handful of their works survive; these include *Prometheus Bound* (c. 465 B.C.), *Medea* (c. 413 B.C.), and *Antigone* (c. 441 B.C.), respectively.

In the *Poetics* (c. 330 B.C.), Aristotle defined tragedy as a dramatic **imitation** of a serious, complete action of some magnitude that evokes both fear and pity in the audience and thereby allows **catharsis** — which in Greek means "purgation" or "purification" — to occur. The typical **classical** tragic hero was an individual of considerable social standing whose character was neither unusually good nor bad. In fact, Aristotle viewed both stature and a mixed or balanced character as necessary to arouse both pity and fear in the audience. For the hero's fall from good fortune to seem significant, it must occur from a tremendous height, Aristotle reasoned. Furthermore, if the hero is completely virtuous or completely villainous, the audience is unlikely to identify with that hero and thus unlikely to see that their pride or jealousy or even foolhardy bravado could be the source of their own downfall. As Aristotle said, "Pity is aroused by unmerited misfortune, fear by the misfortune of a man like ourselves." Although Aristotle maintained that tragedy can involve a propitious turn of events and end happily so long as the overall **tone** of the play remains serious, all the dramas that we would today view as tragic involve some worsening situation that leads to sorrow and loss. Thus, tragedies often begin happily, but that initial happiness is abruptly shattered by some unexpected occurrence; **catastrophic** consequences for the **protagonist** (and often for other individuals in tragic works) result from some error in judgment (**hamartia**) made by the protagonist.

Hamartia is often used synonymously with **tragic flaw,** but this usage is not strictly accurate. A tragic flaw is inherent in the protagonist; tragic flaws are often, though not necessarily, character flaws. They range from moral flaws such as jealousy and overweening pride (**hubris**) to traits normally considered virtues, such as courage. Hamartia, on the other hand, may result from a character's tragic flaw but is not, technically speaking, the flaw itself; it is, rather, the misstep or mistake that leads the protagonist to his downfall and may thus include errors in judgment based on something as simple as lack of knowledge regarding a given situation. In most ancient (classical) tragedies, the hamartia causes the protagonist to break a divine or moral law, with disaster and misery as the consequence. Despite the cataclysmic events that befall tragic protagonists, tragedy often ultimately celebrates the dignity of the human spirit in confronting such overwhelming misfortune and in accepting the consequences of actions.

In Sophocles' *Oedipus Rex* (c. 430 B.C.), one of the most famous ancient tragedies, King Oedipus' tragic flaw — hubris — leads him to the hamartia of trying to avoid the prophecy that he will kill his father and marry his mother, an error he compounds by his insistence on finding and banishing the murderer of his royal predecessor, Laius. What he learns, in the course of the play's action, is that an old man he killed long ago was Laius, that Laius was his father, and that the woman he is now married to is his mother. Horrified, Oedipus blinds himself in an act of self-inflicted punishment.

In the **Middle Ages,** when the plays of the ancient Greek tragedians were essentially unknown, tragedy encompassed any **narrative** work in which a well-positioned individual falls from high standing into disgrace or poverty due to some unexpected reversal in fortune. **Medieval** tragedy, influenced heavily by **miracle plays** and **morality plays,** is less complex than classical tragedy in that the importance of the hamartia is minimized. As in classical tragedies, the conduct of protagonists may or may not merit the consequences that befall them, but in medieval, unlike classical, tragedies, little stress is placed on errors in judgment and actions that lead to the protagonist's downfall. "The Monk's Tale," one of Geoffrey Chaucer's *Canterbury Tales* (c. 1387), is perhaps the most famous example of medieval tragedy.

During the **Renaissance,** classical tragedies were rediscovered and exerted a strong **influence** on the development of the **genre.** In England, tragedy had its heyday during the **Elizabethan Age,** when English dramatists wrote tragedies influenced by Seneca, an ancient Roman playwright known for relatively intellectual tragedies meant to be recited, not performed. Elizabethan **Senecan tragedies** fall into two major groups. One consists of plays that are rather academic in spirit, given that they closely **imitated** Seneca's **forms** and **conventions.** The other, more important, group of Senecan tragedies is composed of works geared toward a popular audience. These tragedies resemble Seneca's insofar as they involve considerable violence and an occasional ghost. There, however, all similarities end. In Seneca's tragedies horrifying events take place offstage (and are only reported by the actors); in Elizabethan Senecan tragedies, pitched at a popular audience, events are brought onstage for the audience to see and experience. This form of Senecan tragedy, commonly called the **revenge tragedy** (or, in its most extreme manifestations, the *tragedy of blood*), proved far more important to the history of English theater — and to literature in general — than did the more academic form of Elizabethan Senecan tragedy. Revenge tragedy merges classical **themes** with English tradition; William Shakespeare's *Hamlet* (1602) is the most famous example of this mixed tradition.

Elizabethan tragedians were responsible for a number of other innovations. They modified the classical tragic protagonist; unlike Aristotelian tragic heroes, who could not be characterized as being unusually good or bad, Elizabethan protagonists were often predominantly ruthless people. The protagonists were still, however, generally individuals of high standing. Elizabethan tragedies also differ from their ancient counterparts insofar as they tend to present, in order, the events leading up to the tragedy instead of beginning *in medias res* and relying on **flashbacks** to explain how the disaster came to pass. In addition, Elizabethan tragedians introduced the element of humor into their works; William Shakespeare's gravediggers in *Hamlet,* for instance, provide a level of **comic relief** that is usually absent from classical tragedies. Elizabethan dramatists were also responsible for the development of **tragicomedy,** a new genre that blended the essential elements of tragedy and **comedy.** During the **Restoration Age** (late seventeenth century), another blended genre called the *heroic tragedy,* or *heroic drama,* developed.

Classical tragedy exerted a particularly strong influence in seventeenth-century France, where dramatists such as Jean Racine and Pierre Corneille systematically studied and imitated classical tragedians, frequently even taking ancient classical heroes and heroines as their subjects. Corneille wrote his own *Médée* (1635), although he also immortalized heroes from other national traditions, such as the Spaniard El Cid in his play, *Le Cid* (1636). Racine, too, drew on Greek lore in *Andromaque* (1667) and *Phèdre* (1677), but, like Corneille, also wrote about nonclassical heroines, such as *Esther* (1689) and *Athalie* (1691). So strong was the classical influence that both playwrights, like their contemporaries, also tried to follow the so-called classical **unities** (unity of action, time, and place); deviation from these rules risked critical condemnation. The seventeenth-century adulation of classical tragedy was not limited to France, however. Play-wrights in Spain and Germany, in particular, relied heavily on the classical tragic tradition. German poet and playwright Andreas Gryphius, for instance, modelled his dramas on Senecan tragedy.

During the eighteenth century, several writers of tragedy broke with tradition, replacing noble protagonists with middle-class characters as the tragic heroes of so-called *domestic* (or *bourgeois*) *tragedies*. Prose also became the dominant mode of expression for tragedy. Verse never recovered its prominence, although it remained a vehicle for tragic expression throughout the nineteenth and twentieth centuries.

In the nineteenth century, the **novel** in particular became the main tragic form. In his influential critical study entitled *Mimesis: The Representation of Reality in Western Literature* (1946), Erich Auerbach posits that the **realistic novel** is the culmination of Western literary expression because it treats ordinary characters in a serious and tragic way. Drama, however, did not disappear. In fact, Scandinavian playwrights Henrik Ibsen and August Strindberg expanded the boundaries of what was previously considered tragedy by introducing disease, psychological imbalance, and personal quirkiness as tragic subjects. In Ibsen's play *A Doll's House* (1879), the protagonist, Nora, becomes increasingly dissatisfied with the traditional female role of wife and mother. Strindberg's works include *Dance of Death* (1901), which portrays an even more horribly destructive marriage.

Few modern works may be called tragedies, at least if we use the term as it has been developed to describe and define classical, medieval, or even Elizabethan versions of the genre. Today's "tragic" heroes are apt to be thoroughly ordinary, middle-class or proletarian, even down-and-out individuals. Such heroes are often called **antiheroes** to emphasize their difference from the noble and dignified tragic protagonists of centuries past; their downfall is likely to be attributable to society or to some psychological abnormality, rather than to fate or a moral flaw. Arthur Miller's pathetic salesman, Willy Loman, in *Death of a Salesman* (1949), is just one example of the twentieth-century tragic hero, as is Tennessee Williams's unstable Southern belle, Blanche, from *A Streetcar Named Desire* (1947).

Some modern playwrights have stretched the boundaries of the tragic genre by incorporating **the Absurd** and **black humor** into their works. Others have imported classical elements (such as the chorus) into their works; still others have injected **psychoanalytic theory** and analysis into "ancient" stories. Despite these variations, a number of plays are generally said to be tragedies; among them are Eugene O'Neill's *Mourning Becomes Electra* (1931), Federico García Lorca's *Blood Wedding* (1935), Arthur Miller's *A View from the Bridge* (1955), Jean Anouilh's *Becket* (1960), and David Henry Hwang's *M. Butterfly* (1988).

tragedy of blood: See **revenge tragedy.**

tragic flaw: A character trait in a **tragic hero** or **heroine** that brings about his or her downfall. Traits like arrogance or **hubris** (excessive pride) are common tragic flaws, but a **protagonist's** tragic flaw is not necessarily a "bad" character trait; rather, it is simply the characteristic from which the reversal of the tragic hero's fortune ensues. Courage or jealousy may equally be the trait whose expression leads to the direst of consequences.

The term *tragic flaw* is often used as a synonym for **hamartia,** but this usage is not strictly correct. *Hamartia* is the more general of the two terms, applicable to any error in judgment that brings about the protagonist's downfall; *tragic flaw* refers specifically to an inherent character trait. Hamartia may result from a **character's** tragic flaw but is not, technically speaking, the flaw itself. Rather, hamartia is the misstep or mistake that engenders the protagonist's downfall and may thus include errors in judgment based on incomplete information regarding a situation as well as those based on character traits such as trepidation or envy.

See also **hamartia.**

tragic irony: See **irony.**

tragicomedy (tragi-comedy): A **play** that encompasses elements from both **tragedy** and **comedy.** The **plot** typically begins with tragic implications that are happily avoided at the drama's end. The expected **catastrophe** does not come to pass as the **protagonist,** once threatened with disaster, experiences a surprising (and usually somewhat improbable) reversal of fortune. Tragicomedies often involve subjects (such as love) and **characters** that cut across the social **classes.**

Early-seventeenth-century collaborative dramatists Francis Beaumont and John Fletcher are often credited with inaugurating this hybrid **genre** in English. They wrote highly **melodramatic** plays dealing with love, jealousy, and intrigue that appeared to be snowballing toward disaster — only to end happily in a reversal of fortune for protagonists who once seemed doomed. Whether or not Beaumont and Fletcher originated the genre, Fletcher first defined it: "a tragie-comedie is not so called in respect of mirth and killing, but in respect it wants deaths, which is inough to make it no tragedie, yet brings some neere it, which is inough to make it no comedie."

EXAMPLES: Beaumont and Fletcher's *The Faithful Shepherdess* (1608), William Shakespeare's *Cymbeline* (1610).

transcendentalism: A movement that originated in Europe but flourished particularly in the United States in the middle of the nineteenth century. At first a religious philosophy emphasizing intuition and individual conscience, transcendentalism was translated into literary terms by the so-called American transcendentalists, a loosely formed group of New England writers and intellectuals that included Bronson Alcott, Ralph Waldo Emerson, Margaret Fuller, and Henry David Thoreau. Influences on transcendentalist thought include **Neoplatonism,** German Idealism (as influenced by the philosopher Immanuel Kant), the **mystical** philosophy of Emanuel Swedenborg, and the work of individual authors as various as Johann Wolfgang von Goethe, Samuel Taylor Coleridge, and Thomas Carlyle.

Although transcendentalists were united more in their opposition to John Locke's empiricism and rigid Calvinist (Christian) doctrines than by points of agreement among themselves, they did hold certain general beliefs in common. Foremost among these was the conviction that each human being is innately divine, that God's essence lies within all individuals. Transcendentalists expanded on Kant's idea that there are transcendental categories of knowledge (that is, *a priori* categories that govern our experience and understanding, such as time and causality) by adding other categories of knowledge (such as moral truth) and by contending that individuals have the ability to discover higher truths intuitively or mystically, without recourse to the senses or logic. Indeed, transcendentalists suggested that reliance on sensory experience and rational thought may actually impede the acquisition of transcendent truths. People can discover moral truths in nature, the transcendentalists argued, with the guidance of their own conscience rather than dogmatic religious doctrine.

Transcendentalists kicked off the movement in 1836 by forming the Transcendental Club to discuss this "new thought," which extolled individual rather than ritualistic spiritual living, the virtues of nature and manual labor, and the need for intellectual stimulation. They encouraged self-reliance and self-trust, instigating two major projects in the 1840s — a literary magazine called *The Dial* (1840–44) and Brook Farm, a **utopian** experiment in communal living. Furthermore, the transcendentalists were reformers optimistic about human potential, allying themselves with such causes as women's suffrage and abolitionism.

EXAMPLES: Thoreau's *Walden* (1854) is perhaps the most famous **text** associated with transcendentalism. The following lines from Emerson's poem "Mottoes" (1844) capture something of the spirit and the ideas of the movement:

> The rounded world is fair to see,
> Nine times folded in mystery:
> Though baffled seers cannot impart
> The secret of its laboring heart,
> Throb thine with Nature's throbbing breast,
> And all is clear from east to west.
> Spirit that lurks each form within
> Beckons to spirit of its kin;
> Self-kindled every atom glows
> And hints the future which it owes.

transformational linguistics: One of the two components of Noam Chomsky's **theory** of **linguistics,** which he postulated in *Syntactic Structures* (1951). Chomsky's theory is termed *transformational* in its belief that a certain set of transformative rules produces numerous variations on "kernel sentences" (basic sentences) in the "deep structure" of any given language. In English, such a kernel sentence might be "Tom chased Jerry." Various transformative rules in English allow us to take this basic sentence and modify it. For example, we might use a passive construction ("Jerry was chased by Tom") or a question ("Was Tom chasing Jerry?" or "Was Jerry being chased by Tom?") or an imperative form ("Tom, chase Jerry!"), and so forth.

See also **generative linguistics.**

travesty: A type of low **burlesque** that treats a dignified subject in an especially, often **grotesquely,** undignified way. Travesty ridicules a subject, literary **convention,** or specific work by employing a grossly low **style.**

EXAMPLES: William Shakespeare provides a travesty of heroic speech in lines spoken by Ancient Pistol, a **character** in *Henry V* (c. 1599). The TV sitcom *Married... With Children* (1987–97) is a show that, according to *Newsweek* critic Rick Marin, makes "nuclear waste of the nuclear family" through scenes that less amused commentators have found base, lewd, and even obscene. Playwright Tom Stoppard, author of *Rosencranz and Guildenstern Are Dead* (1967), has written *a metatravesty* — a travesty of travesties — appropriately entitled *Travesties* (1974).

See also **burlesque.**

trimeter: A line of **verse** consisting of three **metrical feet.**

EXAMPLE: These well-known lines from Robert Browning's "Home Thoughts, from Abroad" (1845) are written in **trochaic** trimeter:

> Oh to | be in | England
> Now that | April's | there. . . .

triolet: A **medieval** French **verse** form consisting of eight lines involving only two **rhymes,** with the **rhyme scheme** *abaaabab.* The first two lines are repeated verbatim in the last two lines, and the fourth line is the same as the first line.

EXAMPLES: Robert Bridges, like many authors of triolets, takes up the subject of love in his poem "Triolet" (1873):

> When first we met we did not guess
> That Love would prove so hard a master;
> Of more than common friendliness
> When first we met we did not guess.
> Who could foretell this sore distress,
> This irretrievable disaster
> When first we met? — We did not guess
> That Love would prove so hard a master.

Less typical is Thomas Hardy's triolet "The Puzzled Game-Birds" (1901):

> They are not those who used to feed us
> When we were young — they cannot be —
> These shapes that now bereave and bleed us?
> They are not those who used to feed us,
> For did we then cry, they would heed us.
> — If hearts can house such treachery

> They are not those who used to feed us
> When we were young — they cannot be!

triple rhyme: See **feminine rhyme, rhyme.**

triplet: A **tercet** (a group of three lines of **verse**) in which all three lines rhyme (*aaa*).

EXAMPLE: Alfred, Lord Tennyson's "The Eagle: A Fragment" (1851) is composed of two triplets:

> He clasps the crag with crooked hands;
> Close to the sun in lonely lands,
> Ringed with the azure world, he stands.
>
> The wrinkled sea beneath him crawls:
> He watches from his mountain walls,
> And like a thunderbolt he falls.

trochee: A **metrical foot** in **poetry** that consists of one **stressed** syllable followed by one unstressed syllable (´˘).

EXAMPLES: party, trochee, tercet, bummer, little. The speaker in Robert Browning's "Soliloquy of the Spanish Cloister" (1842) uses trochaic **tetrameter** when he says "Twenty-nine distinct damnations. . . ."

trope: One of the two major divisions of **figures of speech** (the other being **rhetorical figures**). *Trope* comes from a word that literally means "turning"; to trope (with figures of speech) is, figuratively speaking, to turn or twist some word or phrase to make it mean something else. **Metaphor, metonymy, personification, simile,** and **synecdoche** are sometimes referred to as the principal tropes.

troubadour: A **lyric** poet, associated with the Provence region of southern France, who composed verse in *provençal* (known as the *langue d'oc*). Troubadours, active between the late eleventh and early fourteenth centuries, created many new verse forms and were instrumental in the development of the ideal of **courtly love.**

EXAMPLES: Guillaume d'Aquitaine (1071–1127), Arnaut Daniel (fl. 1180–1200).

true rhyme: See **perfect rhyme.**

truncation: See **catalexis.**

turning point: See **crisis.**

U

***ubi sunt* (theme):** From the Latin for "where are," a common literary **motif** that laments the passage of time by asking what has happened to beloved people, things, or ideas of the past. This motif is often repeated throughout a work, particularly one written in verse, as a **refrain**.

EXAMPLE: In a **ballad** entitled "Ballade des dames du temps jadis" (1489) by the fifteenth-century French poet François Villon, the *ubi sunt* theme appears in the refrain, "Mais où sont les neiges d'antan?" This ballad has been translated into English by Dante Gabriel Rossetti as "The Ballad of Dead Ladies" (1870); its corresponding refrain is "But where are the snows of yester-year?"

A more recent example is "Where Have All the Flowers Gone?," a **folk song** written by Pete Seeger in the mid-1950s but popularized during the Vietnam War era in versions recorded in 1962 by The Kingston Trio and Peter, Paul, and Mary.

undecidability: See **deconstruction**.

understatement: See **meiosis**. See also **litotes**.

unintrusive narrator: An **omniscient, third-person narrator** who relates a **story** without (or with a minimum of) personal commentary or observation. Also called an *objective* or *impersonal narrator*, an unintrusive narrator "states the facts" and, as far as possible, leaves matters of judgment up to the reader. The most drastic examples of unintrusive narrators are those who do not even relate the **characters'** feelings, motives, or states of mind. Many contemporary critics doubt whether there is such a thing as an objective, impersonal, or unintrusive narrator; they argue that a self-effacing **voice** does not and probably cannot exist.

EXAMPLES: The following **realistic** works feature unintrusive narrators: Stendhal's *The Red and the Black* (1830), Leo Tolstoi's *War and Peace* (1864–66), and the novels in Anthony Trollope's Barsetshire series (1855–67) and Palliser series (1864–80).

unities: The concept that a drama should follow three rules: (1) unity of action (all the action of the work must occur within one continuous **plot** without extraneous subplots); (2) unity of time (all the action of the work must occur within twenty-four hours, or one whole day); and (3) unity of place (all the action of the work must occur in one place or city). Aristotle discusses unity of action in his *Poetics* (c. 330 B.C.) and suggests the need for some sort of unity of time but never mentions unity of place as a dramatic principle. For Aristotle, unity of action means action from which no part can be taken without interrupting the overall causal and explanatory pattern. The three unities were intended as devices to assure verisimilitude (believability); critics claimed that a play performed of necessity in one place over a few hours could not seem realistic if its action took place in a number of **settings** over long periods of time.

During the sixteenth and seventeenth centuries, the unities became important dramatic rules to which Italian and French critics, in particular, demanded adherence. Unity of place was invented by the Italians and the French; sixteenth-century Italian critics after Ludovico Castlevetro were responsible for strictly limiting unity of time to a twenty-four hour period and for establishing it as an important doctrine. A dramatist failing to adhere to the unities of action, time, and place risked the condemnation of literary critics — and perhaps even the banishment of the "offending" play from the stage. So seriously was the requirement of adherence to the unities taken that when rival playwrights accused French playwright Pierre Corneille of violating these rules in *Le Cid* (1636), Cardinal Richelieu ordered the Académie Française (the French Academy of Letters) to settle the bitter (and very public) quarrel (known as "La querelle du *Cid*") by passing judgment on the merits of the accusations. After a period of prolonged deliberation, the Académie concluded that Corneille had in fact violated the putatively **classical** rules, although it conceded that the passion, force, and charm of the play garnered for it both public adulation and a considerable place in French theater.

On the other side of the English Channel, a few seventeenth-century dramatists (such as Francis Beaumont and John Fletcher) attempted to adopt or, at least, adapt the unities, but, unlike the French and the Italians, the English generally ignored them. Except for unity of action, the unities were largely abandoned with the waning of **neoclassicism** and the rise of **romanticism.**

unreliable narrator: A **narrator** who, for some reason, cannot or does not fully comprehend the world about him or her and whose conclusions and judgments the reader thus mistrusts. An author who uses an unreliable narrator generally provides clues indicating the narrator's fallibility and expects the reader to be wary of anything that narrator reports. Some authors, however, may purposely fail to provide the reader with the means to correct the narrator's false perceptions; others even intentionally fail to give the reader adequate clues to determine whether a narrator is unreliable in the first place.

EXAMPLES: Charlie Marlow in Joseph Conrad's *Heart of Darkness* (1899) and *Lord Jim* (1900); Nick Carraway in F. Scott Fitzgerald's *The Great Gatsby* (1925). John Dowell in Ford Madox Ford's *The Good Soldier* (1927) is an example of an unreliable narrator whose fallibility is not revealed to the reader until late in the novel.

Leonard, the **character** played by Guy Pearce in the movie *Memento* (2001) is an unreliable narrator due to brain damage he suffered while trying to thwart an attack on his wife: Leonard's inability to form new memories precludes him from remembering anything that happened more than a few minutes before.

urban legend (urban myth): See **myth.**

utopia: An ideal place that does not exist in reality. The word *utopia,* which comes from the Greek for *outopia,* meaning "no place," and *eutopia,* meaning "good place," is itself a **pun** referring to a nonexistent good place.

Utopian literature describes, but does not necessarily promote, an author's vision of the ideal place. In 1516, Thomas More wrote one of the most famous pieces of utopian literature. More called his ideal place "Utopia" and also entitled his book *Utopia,* hence the use of the term today to refer not only to an imaginary, perfect place but also to a work describing such a place. The utopian **genre** reached its height much later, flourishing in nineteenth-century Anglo-American literature.

Utopias are frequently depicted as places that have been lost, forgotten, or unknown to the society of the author or to any other society. They are generally "rediscovered" by some fictitious, adventurous traveller who somehow ends up in a very distant and delightful land and then returns to tell stories about this fantastic place. Some utopian **texts** subtly **satirize** the specific utopia described; others satirize humanity's dreams about and longings for utopia in general. **Dystopias** are the opposite of utopias; they are horrific places, usually characterized by degenerate or oppressive societies.

EXAMPLES: Plato's *The Republic* (c. 360 B.C.), Francis Bacon's *The New Atlantis* (1627), Samuel Butler's *Erewhon* (1872), Edward Bellamy's *Looking Backward: 2000–1887* (1881), William Morris's *News from Nowhere* (1888), H. G. Wells's *A Modern Utopia* (1900).

See also **dystopia.**

utterance act: A term used in John R. Searle's expansion of John Austin's **speech-act theory** to refer to a **locution,** that is, simply saying something. An utterance act occurs whenever someone says something, regardless of whether or not it makes sense.

The utterance act is one of four types of **speech acts;** the other three are: the **propositional act,** referring to an object upon which something is predicated (saying something about something else); the **illocutionary act,** the utterance of a statement that performs a particular function (such as ordering, promising, etc.); and the **perlocutionary act,** an illocutionary act that affects the state of mind and/or the actions of the person to whom it has been directed. Some speech-act theorists refer to the *utterance act* as the *locutionary act.*

V

Varronian satire: See **Menippean satire.**

vehicle: The **image,** activity, or concept used to illustrate or represent the **tenor,** or subject, of any **figure of speech.**

See **tenor** for further discussion of the relationship between tenor and vehicle and the critical origins of these terms.

verbal irony: See **irony.**

verbal meaning: See **significance.**

vers de société: A subclass of **light verse** that simultaneously reflects and (gently) critiques polite society and its concerns. *Vers de société* frequently makes use of elaborate French forms such as the **rondeau** and the **villanelle.** Though it is characterized by **wit** or mild **satire,** *vers de société* is always polished, elegant, and graceful.

EXAMPLES: Walter Learned's "Time's Revenge" (1889):

> When I was ten and she fifteen —
>   Ah me, how fair I thought her!
> She treated with disdainful mien
>   The homage that I brought her,
> And, in a patronizing way
> Would of my shy advances say:
>   "It's really quite absurd, you see;
>   He's very much too young for me."
>
> I'm twenty now; she, twenty-five —
>   Well, well, how old she's growing!
> I fancy that my suit might thrive
>   If pressed again; but, owing
> To great discrepancy in age,
> Her marked attentions don't engage
>   My young affections, for, you see,
>   She's really quite too old for me.

Elizabeth Barrett Browning's "A Man's Requirements" (1846) ends with the following biting **stanza:**

> Thus, if thou wilt prove me, dear,
>   Woman's love no fable,
> I will love *thee* — half a year —
>   As a man is able.

verse: When used in its broadest sense, a term referring either to **poetry** or to an individual **poem,** that is, any **metrical** composition. (Although no one would refer to William Wordsworth's "I Wandered Lonely as a Cloud" (1807) as *a* verse, the poem can properly be referred to *as* verse.) In the narrow (and perhaps most correct) sense of the word, a verse is an individual line of poetry. A technically incorrect, although common, use of *verse* is to refer to a **stanza** of a poem or song. Some critics make a distinction between poetry and verse, noting that all poetry is verse, but that not all verse is poetry. Many of those who make this distinction give it a valuative spin, arguing that verse is a lower form of expression than poetry; verse, they suggest, is notable mainly for its **rhythmic** and metrical form, whereas poetry is characterized by **imagination,** a less obvious (and more intricate) **structure,** and a lofty purpose. Other scholars distinguish between verse and poetry in a less loaded manner, simply stating that verse is the more inclusive term, covering **forms** (such as **light verse**) that are typically not classified as poetry. Of course, even this distinction implies a certain hierarchy in which poetry is valued more highly than "mere" verse.

versification: A term referring to: (1) the art of composing **verse;** (2) the **form** of verse used in a particular poem. *Versification* is also used as a synonym for **prosody,** the study of **rhythm, rhyme, meter,** and **stanzaic** form.

vers libre: The French term for **free verse.**
See **free verse.**

Victorian Period (in English literature): An era in English literary history extending from 1837, the year in which Queen Victoria was crowned, to 1901, the year of her death. This period is often divided into two parts, the early Victorian Period (ending around 1870) and the late Victorian Period (commencing thereafter). Major literary movements during the Victorian Period include **realism, Pre-Raphaelitism,** and **Aestheticism.**

The Victorian Period witnessed rapid technological, political, and socioeconomic change due to the Industrial Revolution; it was also an epoch in which science advanced and long-standing religious ideas and institutions were challenged and even attacked. Not surprisingly, much of the writing of the period addressed the pressing issues of the day, and many of the greatest literary achievements were by nonfiction prose writers such as Thomas Carlyle, John Stuart Mill, John Henry (Cardinal) Newman, and John Ruskin.

Extraordinary works of prose fiction were also produced during the Victorian Period; these included novels by writers such as Charlotte Brontë, Charles Dickens, George Eliot, Thomas Hardy, William Makepeace Thackeray, and Anthony Trollope. Major poets of the Victorian Period include Matthew Arnold, Robert Browning, Dante Gabriel Rossetti, and Alfred, Lord Tennyson, whose **elegy** for Arthur Henry Hallam, entitled "In Memoriam A. H. H." (1850), is sometimes singled out as the quintessential Victorian poem, perhaps because the **theme** most common in Victorian poetry is that of loss with its attendant uncertainty. This is not to say that Victorian poets never celebrated life or the present; Robert Browning's

"Rabbi Ben Ezra" (1864) contains the famous lines "Grow old along with me! / The best is yet to be, / The last of life, for which the first was made." But Matthew Arnold's characterization, in "Stanzas from the Grande Chartreuse" (1867), of a generation "Wandering between two worlds, one dead, / The other powerless to be born" better conveys the generally wistful, elegiac **mood** of Victorian poetry.

The common conception we now have of the Victorians as prudish, hypocritical, stuffy, narrow-minded, and complacent is not entirely accurate, although it is true that: (1) segments of English society, particularly the growing middle class, did espouse many of the priggish attitudes and values that led to this conception; and (2) a number of Victorian writers euphemistically dance around certain subjects (notably sex) that are dealt with more directly in the literatures of previous as well as subsequent periods. Still, the stereotype of Victorianism — bound up as it is with the identity of a pious, proper, and beloved queen who reputedly advised her daughter to "Lie back and think of England" on her wedding night — fails to take into account the richness of the period, which produced a number of outlandishly comic writers (such as two writers of **nonsense verse,** Lewis Carroll and Edward Lear, and W. S. Gilbert, the whimsical humorist, poet, and playwright best known for the comic operas he wrote with Sir Arthur Sullivan).

Thus the Victorians were much more diverse and lively than we typically acknowledge, just as many of us are less shallow and materialistic than the stereotype that has been created about our age would suggest. The unattractive characteristics of Victorian thinking, behavior, and character were recognized and condemned by Victorians themselves, many of whom rebelled against the "spirit" of the era and others of whom were prone to critical self-examination. The literature of the period comes in virtually all **forms** and **genres** and was written in **styles** and combinations of styles that included the **romantic,** the realistic, the **satirical,** and the **decadent.**

villain: See **antagonist.**

villanelle: A French **verse** form consisting of nineteen lines in five **tercets** followed by a **quatrain** with the **rhyme scheme** (based on two **rhymes**) *aba aba aba aba aba abaa.* The first line of the first tercet is repeated as the last line of the second and fourth tercets while the third line of the first tercet is repeated as the last line of the third and fifth tercets. Finally, these two lines are repeated as a **couplet** in the last two lines of the quatrain.

EXAMPLES: W. E. Henley's "Villanelle" (1888) and Dylan Thomas's "Do Not Go Gentle into That Good Night" (1952). Edwin Arlington Robinson wrote a villanelle called "The House on the Hill" (1896):

> They are all gone away,
> The House is shut and still,
> There is nothing more to say.

Through broken walls and gray
   The winds blow bleak and shrill.
They are all gone away.

Nor is there one to-day
   To speak them good or ill:
There is nothing more to say.

Why is it then we stray
   Around the sunken sill?
They are all gone away,

And our poor fancy-play
   For them is wasted skill:
There is nothing more to say.

There is ruin and decay
   In the House on the Hill:
They are all gone away,
There is nothing more to say.

Martha Collins's "The Story We Know" (1980) is a villanelle that employs **incremental repetition**:

The way to begin is always the same. Hello,
Hello. Your hand, your name. So glad, Just fine,
and Good-bye at the end. That's every story we know,

and why pretend? But lunch tomorrow? No?
Yes? An omelette, salad, chilled white wine?
The way to begin is simple, sane, Hello,

and then it's Sunday, coffee, the *Times*, a slow
day by the fire, dinner at eight or nine
and Good-bye. In the end, this is a story we know

so well we don't turn the page, or look below
the picture, or follow the words to the next line:
The way to begin is always the same Hello.

But one night, through the latticed window, snow
begins to whiten the air, and the tall white pine.
Good-bye is the end of every story we know

that night, and when we close the curtains, oh,
we hold each other against that cold white sign
of the way we all begin and end. *Hello,*
Good-bye is the only story. We know, we know.

voice: See **tone.**

weak ending: The final syllable of a line of **verse** that is **stressed** to conform to the **meter** but would be unstressed in ordinary speech. A line containing — but not necessarily ending with — such a syllable is said to have a **wrenched accent;** thus a weak ending can be defined as a wrenched accent that occurs at the end of a line of verse.

EXAMPLE: The last line of this **stanza** from Samuel Taylor Coleridge's "The Rime of the Ancient Mariner" (1798) has a wrenched accent that is also a weak ending:

> Oh! dream of joy! is this indeed
> The lighthouse top I see?
> Is this the hill? is this the kirk?
> Ĭs thís mĭne ówn cŏuntrée?

whodunit: See **detective fiction.** See also **mystery fiction.**

wit: Derived from the **Old English** *witan,* meaning "to know," a term whose meaning has changed several times over the centuries. In the late **Middle Ages,** *wit* referred to intellect and intelligence as opposed to knowledge. During the **Renaissance,** it came to signify wisdom. In the seventeenth century, when it began to suggest creativity or **fancy,** the term was frequently associated with a group we now call the **metaphysical poets,** writers prized for the originality and agility of their poetic expressions. In the eighteenth century, the **Neoclassical Period,** a reaction against this definition set in, and wit came to be associated not with ingenious twists and turns of fancy but rather with judgment, reason, and the ability to articulate commonly held truths in an original and persuasive manner. Joseph Addison distinguished between true and false wit according to its focus; true wit, he claimed, revealed similarities between apparently unlike ideas, whereas false wit associated unlike words through ornamental devices such as **puns.**

Today, the meaning of *wit* is closest to the seventeenth-century definition, although we are likely to associate the term with **comedy** and laughter in addition to creativity. Wit is now most commonly thought of as clever expression — whether aggressive or harmless, that is, with or without derogatory intent toward someone or something in particular. We also tend to think of wit as being characterized by a mocking or **paradoxical** quality, evoking laughter through apt phrasing (**epigrammatic** writings are common vehicles for wit, for instance). Even today, however, wit retains the **medieval** sense of intelligence, insofar as it is viewed as an intellectual form of humor.

EXAMPLES: Writers often cited for their wit include Aphra Behn, John Donne, Alexander Pope, Jane Austen, Oscar Wilde, George Bernard Shaw, and Dorothy Parker. Virginia Woolf's description of James Joyce's novel *Ulysses* (1922) as "The work of a queasy undergraduate scratching his pimples" is witty, as is Nancy, Lady Astor's famous statement: "I married beneath me. All women do." The French novelist Colette wittily remarked that "Among all the forms of absurd courage, the courage of girls is outstanding. Otherwise there would be fewer marriages." Flannery O'Connor, best known for her short stories, once said: "Everywhere I go I'm asked if I think the university stifles writers. My opinion is that they don't stifle enough of them. There's many a bestseller that could have been prevented by a good teacher."

word accent: See **accent.**

wrenched accent: In a line of **verse,** the **stress** placed on a syllable that would be unstressed in everyday speech but that is "forced" to conform to the **meter.** When a wrenched accent occurs at the end of a line of verse, that line is said to have a **weak ending.**

EXAMPLES: "Morning" in this **stanza** from Christopher Marlowe's "The Passionate Shepherd to His Love" (1599) exhibits wrenched accent (as well as being a weak ending); the **accent** would normally fall on the first syllable but due to the meter falls on the second instead:

> The shepherd swains shall dance and sing
> For thy delight each May morning:
> If these delights thy mind may move,
> Then live with me and be my love.

Samuel Taylor Coleridge's "The Rime of the Ancient Mariner" (1798) includes several examples of wrenched accent. In one such example, which occurs in the middle of the following line, the accent would normally fall on the first syllable of "uproar" but instead falls on the second syllable to meet the requirements of the meter:

> What loud uproar bursts from that door!

Y

Yale Poets: See **Revolutionary Period (in American literature)**.

Z

zeugma: From the Greek for "yoking," a **rhetorical figure** that generally refers to a grammatical **structure** in which some word or phrase governs or is otherwise related to two or more different words or phrases, but in a strikingly or suggestively different way. (In the sentence "He leaned on his lectern and his stale jokes," a single verb — *leaned* — suggests a likeness between two different kinds of props upon which second-rate lecturers are overdependent.) Zeugma usually involves several nouns that govern or are the objects of a single verb. Sometimes, however, the same adjective may be used to modify two different nouns, or two nouns may be the objects of the same preposition. Authors have sometimes used zeugma to suggest subtle but significant parallels between things commonly differentiated or subtle but significant differences between things commonly equated. Alternatively, zeugma may be employed to produce the comic effect that results from using the same word in very different senses (for example, "They made cookies, plans, and love that night").

Some scholars reserve this term for constructions that involve or imply some sort of grammatical error. (The sentence "The car was stolen, the bicycles left untouched" involves zeugma in this strict sense, insofar as the subjects *car* and *bicycles* are yoked to the same predicate (*was*); although the independent clause "The car was stolen" is grammatically correct, the implied independent clause "The bicycles was left untouched" is not. Scholars using zeugma in this way refer to grammatically correct yokings with the term *syllepsis*.

EXAMPLE: The line in which the **narrator** of Alexander Pope's poem "The Rape of the Lock" (1712) expresses fear that the **heroine,** Belinda, may "lose her heart, or necklace, at a ball." In this case, zeugma is used to show how "society types" often equate the significant and insignificant, valuing material goods (jewelry) as highly as spiritual good (love).

More contemporary examples of zeugma can be found in Gore Vidal's **historical novel** *1876* (1976), in which the **protagonist** Charles Schuyler reports that his daughter Emma has given newspaperman Jamie Bennett "her Medusa gaze, causing him to turn if not to stone to me"; in Amy Tan's novel *The Hundred Secret Senses* (1995), in which protagonist Olivia Laguni, who is sitting in a half-empty restaurant with her husband Simon, muses "We were partners, not soul mates, two separate people who happened to be sharing a menu and a life"; and in Alanis Morissette's song "Head over Feet" (1995), which refers to a man holding his breath — and the door — for her.

Acknowledgments

W. H. Auden. "Heavy Date" (4 lines), "Postscript" (8 lines) to "Prologue: The Birth of Architecture," "The Cave of Nakedness" (3 line epigram) from *W. H. Auden: The Collected Poems* by W. H. Auden. Copyright © 1976 by Edward Mendelson, William Meredith and Monroe K. Spears, executors of the estate of W. H. Auden. Used by permission of Random House, Inc., and Faber and Faber Ltd.

Imamu Amiri Baraka. "An Agony, As Now" (6 lines) from *The Dead Lecturer* by Imamu Amari Baraka. Copyright © 1964 by Amiri Baraka. Reprinted by permission of Sterling Lord Literistic, Inc.

John Berryman. Dream Song #23 "The Lay of Ike" from *The Dream Songs* by John Berryman. Copyright © 1969 by John Berryman. Copyright renewed 1997 by Kate Donahue Berryman. Reprinted by permission of Farrar, Straus & Giroux, LLC, and Faber & Faber Ltd.

Elizabeth Bishop. "The Fish" (9 lines) from *The Complete Poems 1927–1979* by Elizabeth Bishop. Copyright © 1979, 1983 by Alice Helen Methfessel. Reprinted by permission of Farrar, Straus & Giroux, LLC.

Robert Bridges. "Triolet" from *Poetical Works of Robert Bridges* by Robert Bridges. Copyright © 1913 by Oxford University Press. Reprinted by permission of Oxford University Press.

Gwendolyn Brooks. "Mentors" (excerpt) from *A Street in Bronzeville* by Gwendolyn Brooks. Copyright © 1945 by Gwendolyn Brooks. Reprinted by permission of the estate of Gwendolyn Brooks.

Martha Collins. "The Story We Know." From *The Catastrophe of Rainbows,* Cleveland State University Press, 1985. First appeared in *Poetry,* December 1980. Copyright © 1980 by The Modern Poetry Association. Reprinted by permission of the author and by the editor of *Poetry.*

e. e. Cummings. "1(a" from *Complete Poems: 1904–1962* by e. e. Cummings, edited by George J. Firmage. Copyright © 1958, 1986, 1991 by the Trustees for the e. e. Cummings Trust. Reprinted by permission of Liveright Publishing Corporation.

Emily Dickinson. "Faith is a fine invention," "I taste a liquor never brewed," and "In Winter in my Room." Copyright © 1951, 1955, 1979, 1983 by the President and Fellows of Harvard College. Reprinted by permission of the publishers and Trustees of Amherst College, The Belknap Press of Harvard University Press. Also from *Complete Poems of Emily Dickinson,* edited by Thomas H. Johnson. Copyright © 1929 by Martha Dickinson Bianchi. Copyright © renewed 1957 by Mary L. Hampson. By permission of Little, Brown and Company.

George Dillon. "The World Goes Turning" (5 lines) from *Boy in the Wind* by George Dillon. Copyright © 1927 by Viking Press. Copyright renewed 1955 by George Dillon. Reprinted by permission of Nan Sherman Sussman.

H. D. "Oread" (6 lines) and "The Helmsman" (12 lines) from *Collected Poems 1912-1944* by H. D. Copyright © 1982 by the estate of Hilda

Doolittle. Reprinted by permission of New Directions Publishing Corporation and Carcanet Press Limited.

T. S. Eliot. "The Dry Salvages" (9 lines) from *Four Quartets* by T. S. Eliot. Copyright © 1941 by T. S. Eliot and 1969 by Esme Valerie Eliot. "The Hollow Men" (7 lines) from *Collected Poems 1909-1962* by T. S. Eliot. Copyright © 1936 by Harcourt Brace & Company. Copyright © 1964, 1963 by T. S. Eliot. Reprinted by permission of Harcourt Brace & Company and Faber & Faber Ltd. "The Waste Land" (2 lines) from *Collected Poems 1909-1962* by T. S. Eliot. Reprinted by permission of Faber & Faber Ltd.

Kathleen Craker Firestone. "Island Sestina." From *The Fox Islands, North and South* by Kathleen Craker Firestone. Copyright © 1996 by Kathleen Craker Firestone. Reprinted by permission of the author.

Allen Ginsberg. First 3 lines from "Howl" from *Collected Poems 1947–1980* by Allen Ginsberg. Copyright © 1955 by Allen Ginsberg. Reprinted by permission of HarperCollins Publishers Inc. and The Wylie Agency (UK).

Thom Gunn. "Considering the Snail" (8 lines). From *My Sad Captains* by Thom Gunn. Copyright © 1994 by Thom Gunn. Reprinted by permission of Farrar, Straus & Giroux, LLC, and Faber & Faber Ltd.

Langston Hughes. "Dream Deferred ("Harlem")" from *Collected Poems* by Langston Hughes. Copyright © 1994 by the estate of Langston Hughes. Reprinted by permission of Alfred A. Knopf, a division of Random House, Inc., and Harold Ober Associates, Inc.

Jane Kenyon. "Having It Out with Melancholy" (first stanza) from *Constance* by Jane Kenyon. Copyright © 1993 by Jane Kenyon. Reprinted with the permission of Greywolf Press, Saint Paul, Minnesota.

Philip Larkin. "Toads" (4 lines) from *The Less Deceived* by Philip Larkin. Copyright © 1955 by The Marvell Press. Reprinted by permission of The Marvell Press, England and Australia.

D. H. Lawrence. "Fish" (4 lines) Eds. De Sola Pinto & Roberts, "Love on the Farm" and "Poetry of the Present" (1 paragraph) from *The Complete Poems of D. H. Lawrence,* edited by V. de Sola Pinto & F. W. Roberts. Copyright © 1964, 1971 by Angelo Ravagli and C. M. Weekley, executors of the estate of Frieda Lawrence Ravagli. Used by permission of Viking Penguin, a division of Penguin Putnam, Inc., and Pollinger Limited, and the estate of Frieda Lawrence Ravagli.

Robert Lowell. "Waking Early Sunday Morning" (stanza) from *Selected Poems* by Robert Lowell. Copyright © 1976 by Robert Lowell. Reprinted by permission of Farrar, Straus & Giroux, LLC.

Archibald MacLeish. "Speech to Those Who Say Comrade" (1 line) from *Collected Poems 1917–1982* by Archibald MacLeish. Copyright © 1985 by the estate of Archibald MacLeish. Reprinted by permission of Houghton Mifflin Company. All rights reserved.

Michael McClintock. Haiku "a broken window . . ." from *Maya: Poems 1968–1975* by Michael McClintock, Los Angeles: Seer Ox Press.

1950 by Edith Sitwell. Reprinted by permission of David Higham Associates Limited.

Stevie Smith. "Our Bog is Dood" (stanza) from *Collected Poems of Stevie Smith.* Copyright © 1972 by Stevie Smith. Reprinted by permission of New Directions Publishing Corp. and Hamish MacGibbon, James & James (Publishers) Ltd.

Wallace Stevens. "Study of Two Pears" (2 lines) and "Sunday Morning" (7 lines) from *The Collected Poems of Wallace Stevens* by Wallace Stevens. Copyright © 1954 by Wallace Stevens and renewed 1982 by Holly Stevens. "Of Mere Being" (3 lines) from *Opus Posthumous* by Wallace Stevens, edited by Samuel French Morse. Copyright © 1957 by Elsie Stevens and Holly Stevens. Used by permission of Alfred A. Knopf, a division of Random House, Inc., and Faber & Faber Ltd.

Rabindranth Tagore. "Poem 35" (9 lines) as published in *Gitanjali* by Rabindranth Tagore. Copyright © 1956 by Rabindranth Tagore. Published by Macmillan and Co. Ltd. Reprinted by permission.

Don Taylor. Excerpt from translation of *Iphigenia at Aulis* by Euripides from *Euripides: The War Plays,* Metheun Drama Series, 1990. Copyright © 1990 by Don Taylor. Reprinted by permission of Random House, UK.

Dylan Thomas. "A Refusal to Mourn the Death, by Fire, of a Child in London" (6 lines) and "Do Not Go Gentle Into That Good Night" (3 lines and first stanza) from *The Poems of Dylan Thomas* by Dylan Thomas. Copyright © 1952 by Dylan Thomas. Reprinted by permission of New Directions Publishing Corp. and David Higham Associates.

Makoto Ueda. "Beyond the Clouds . . ." Translation of Matsuo Basho haiku from *Matsuo Basho* by Makoto Ueda. Twayne Publishers, 1970. Copyright © 1970 by Makoro Ueda. Reprinted by permission of Makoto Ueda.

Derek Walcott. "A Far Cry from Africa" (stanza) from *Collected Poems 1948-1984* by Derek Walcott. Copyright © 1986 by Derek Walcott. Reprinted by permission of Farrar, Straus and Giroux LLC, and Faber & Faber Ltd.

Jerry W. Ward. "Jazz to Jackson to John" (13 opening lines, plus 7 other lines). Copyright © 1988 by Jerry W. Ward, Jr. Reprinted by permission of the author.

C. Webster Wheelock. "Monocle-bonocle" and "Arrogant paragon" (2 double dactyls) from *History Gistory* (unpublished). Reprinted by permission of the author.

William Carlos Williams. "The Red Wheelbarrow" and "Poem (As the Cat)" from *Collected Poems: 1909-1939,* Volume 1. Copyright © 1938 by New Directions Publishing Corp. Reprinted by permission of New Directions Publishing Corp. and Carcanet Press.

Elinor Wylie. "Fair Annet's Song" (first stanza) from *Collected Poems* by Elinor Wylie. © 1932 by Alfred A. Knopf, Inc., and renewed 1960 by Edwina C. Rubenstein. Reprinted by permission of Alfred A. Knopf, a division of Random House, Inc.

W. B. Yeats. "The Second Coming" (4 lines) from *The Collected Works of W. B. Yeats: Volume 1: The Poems, Revised,* by Richard J. Finneran. Copyright © 1924 by The Macmillan Company. Copyright renewed 1952 by Bertha Georgie Yeats and A. P. Watt Ltd. on behalf of Michael B. Yeats.

Art

Sarah Boxer. Cartoon from *In the Floyd Archives* by Sarah Boxer. Copyright © 2001 by Sarah Boxer. Used by permission of Pantheon Books, a division of Random House, Inc., and IMG Literary Agency.

Raul Colon. Cover art by Raul Colon. Originally published in THE NEW YORKER, January 8, 2001. © 2001 Conde Nast Publications, Inc. Reprinted by permission of Conde Nast and Raul Colon/Morgan Gaynin, Inc. All rights reserved.

Salvador Dali. *The Persistence of Memory,* 1931. Oil on Canvas. Digital Image © The Museum of Modern Art/Licensed by SCALA/Art Resource, NY.

Matt Groening. "Mistakes Were Made" cartoon from *The Big Book of Hell* © 1990 by Matt Groening. All Rights Reserved. Reprinted by permission of Pantheon Books, a division of Random House, Inc., NY.

Gary Larson. "Pregnant Witch" (Release date 8/1/90) and "Werewolf Mystery" (Release date 5/18/94). *The Far Side* ® by Gary Larson. © 1990, 1994 FarWorks, Inc. All Rights Reserved. Used with permission.

The Onion (2 drawings) from *Dispatches from the Tenth Circle* by The Onion. Copyright © 2001 by The Onion, Inc. Used by permission of Three Rivers Press, a division of Random House, Inc.

Gary Trudeau. (2) *Doonesbury* cartoons © 1997 by Gary Trudeau. Reprinted by permission of Universal Press Syndicate.

Index of Authors
and Titles

About the Authors

Ross Murfin, professor of English and provost of Southern Methodist University, has also taught at the University of Virginia, Yale University, and the University of Miami, where he was the dean of the College of Arts and Sciences until 1996. He is the author of *Swinburne, Lawrence, Hardy, and the Burden of Belief* (1978); *The Poetry of D. H. Lawrence: Texts and Contexts* (1983); *Sons and Lovers: A Novel of Division and Desire* (1987); and *Lord Jim: After the Truth* (1992); and the editor of *Conrad Revisited: Essays for the Eighties* (1983). The series editor of Bedford /St. Martin's popular Case Studies in Contemporary Criticism, he has also edited two volumes in the series, Joseph Conrad's *Heart of Darkness* (second edition 1996) and Nathaniel Hawthorne's *The Scarlet Letter* (1991). In 2001–2002 he served as the chair of the Publications Committee of the Modern Language Association of America.

Supryia M. Ray is an attorney in Seattle. While studying for her Bachelor of Arts at the University of Miami, she assisted Ross Murfin in the research and preparation of more than a dozen volumes in the Case Studies in Contemporary Criticism series. In 1995, she graduated summa cum laude from the University, achieving recognition as the outstanding student in the honors program and the College of Arts and Sciences. She graduated magna cum laude from Harvard Law School in 1998, served as a law clerk on the U.S. District Court and the U.S. Court of Appeals, and then entered private practice. As an active member of Literacy AmeriCorps, she coordinates a speakers' bureau of adult learners and teaches English as a Second Language as well as reading, writing, and math skills.